PRINCIPLES OF
EUROPEAN CONTRACT LAW

PARTS I AND II

Combined and Revised

Prepared by
The Commission of European Contract Law
Chairman: Professor Ole Lando

Edited by

OLE LANDO AND HUGH BEALE

KLUWER LAW INTERNATIONAL
THE HAGUE / LONDON / BOSTON

Library of Congress Cataloging-in-Publication Data

QM LIBRARY
(MILE END)

ISBN 90-411-1305-3

Published by Kluwer Law International,
P.O. Box 85889, 2508 CN The Hague, The Netherlands.

Sold and distributed in North, Central and South America
by Kluwer Law International,
675 Massachusetts Avenue, Cambridge, MA 02139, U.S.A.

In all other countries, sold and distributed
by Kluwer Law International, Distribution Centre,
P.O. Box 322, 3300 AH Dordrecht, The Netherlands.

Printed on acid-free paper

All Rights Reserved
© 2000 The Commission on European Contract Law
Kluwer Law International incorporates the publishing programmes of
Graham & Trotman Ltd, Kluwer Law and Taxation Publishers,
and Martinus Nijhoff Publishers.

No part of the material protected by this copyright notice may be reproduced or
utilized in any form or by any means, electronic or mechanical,
including photocopying, recording or by any information storage and
retrieval system, without written permission from the copyright owner.

Permission is given by the copyrightowner
for unlimited reproduction for non-commercial
purposes only of the pages containing the
texts of the articles.

Printed in the Netherlands.

PRINCIPLES OF EUROPEAN CONTRACT LAW

Full text of Parts I & II combined

Table of Contents

CHAPTER 1 : GENERAL PROVISIONS

CHAPTER 5 : INTERPRETATION

CHAPTER 6 : CONTENTS AND EFFECTS

CHAPTER 7 : PERFORMANCE

CHAPTER 8 : NON-PERFORMANCE AND REMEDIES IN GENERAL

CHAPTER 9 : PARTICULAR REMEDIES FOR NON-PERFORMANCE

Preface

How it started

In 1974 a symposium was held at the Copenhagen Business School. The subject was the EEC Draft Convention on the Law Applicable to Contractual and Noncontractual Obligations. At a dinner in Tivoli Gardens after the symposium I sat next to Dr Winfried Hauschild who was Head of Division in the Directorate General for the Internal Market of the Commission of the European Communities, and who assisted the working group of experts which prepared the Draft Convention. We agreed that the proposed choice of law rules would be insufficient. They would never establish the legal uniformity necessary for an integrated European market. Uniform substantive law rules were needed. Dr Hauschild said: "We need a European Code of Obligations".

In 1976 another symposium was held in the newly established European University Institute near Florence. Its subject was New Perspectives of a Common Law of Europe. I was asked to present a paper and found here an opportunity to argue for what I then called a European Uniform Commercial Code.

In the years that followed efforts were made to find qualified people from all the EC Member States who were interested in preparing what now became the Principles of European Contract Law and to get the necessary funds. This took some time.

Members and meetings

First Commission

With the help of Dr Hauschild and his Directorate General, meetings were held in Brussels in December 1980 and November 1981 with lawyers from the EC Member States most of whom were later to become Members of the Commission on European Contract Law. The purpose of the first meetings was to prepare the future work. We were short of funds, and if it had not been for the Legal Services of the Commission of the European Communities and its Director General, Dr Claus Ehlermann, we would not have been able to continue. We got the funds necessary to

xi

cover the travel expenses of the Members, and the discussions of the principles started at the third meeting which was held in Hamburg in November 1982. At this and at the following five meetings (Paris, June 1983; Rome, November 1983; Thessaloniki, May 1984; Brussels, February 1985; and Copenhagen, October 1985) the participating Members of the Commission were:

Professor Brigitte Berlioz-Houin, Université de Paris IX,

Professor Massimo Bianca, Università degli Studi di Roma,

Professor M.J. Bonell, Università Cattolica del Sacro Cuore, Milano; later Universita degli Studi di Roma,

Professor Ulrich Drobnig, Director at the Max Planck Institut für ausländisches und internationales Privatrecht, Hamburg,

Maître André Elvinger, Luxembourg,

Professor Dimitri Evrigenis, Centre of International and European Economic Law, Thessaloniki,

Professor Roy M. Goode, Queen Mary College, University of London; later, St John's College, Oxford University,

Professor Guy Horsmans, Université Catholique de Louvain, Louvain-la-Neuve,

Professor Roger Houin, Paris,

Professor Ole Lando, Copenhagen Business School,

Professor Bryan McMahon, University College, Cork,

Professor Denis Tallon, Université de Paris II, Director of Institut de Droit Comparé de Paris,

Deputy Director J.A. Wade, T.M.C. Asser Institute, The Hague,

Dr Frans J.A. van der Velden, University of Utrecht, and

Professor William A. Wilson, University of Edinburgh.

By January 1, 1986, Spain and Portugal had become Members of the European Communities. From the ninth meeting in London in October 1986 Professor de Magelães Collaço, University of Lisbon and Professor Alberto Bercovitz, Autonomous University of Madrid participated as members of the Commission.

We had the misfortune of losing Professor Roger Houin and Professor Dimitri Evrigenis who both died in 1986. Due to pressing work at her University, Professor Brigitte Berlioz-Houin was unable to participate in further meetings.

From the tenth meeting in Luxembourg in March 1987 and through the succeeding meetings (Madrid, November 1987; Lisbon, May 1988; Utrecht, December 1988; and Oxford, December 1990) the following new Members participated:

Professor Hugh Beale, University of Bristol, later University of Warwick,

Professor K. Kerameus, University of Athens,

Professor Georges Rouhette, Université d'Auvergne, Clermont Ferrand.

Second Commission, 1992-1996

In September 1992 the Second Commission on European Contract Law began its work. At its first six meetings (Ghent September 1992; Brussels, January 1993; Barcelona, July 1993; Osnabrück, December 1993; Utrecht, May 1994; and Palermo, December 1994) the participating Members were:

Professor Christian von Bar, University of Osnabrück,
Professor Hugh Beale, University of Warwick,
Professor Michael Joachim Bonell, University of Rome (La Sapienza),
Professor Michael Bridge, University of Nottingham,
Professor Carlo Castronovo, Università Cattolica del Sacra Cuore, Milan
Professor Isabel de Magelhães Collaço, University of Lisbon,
Professor Ulrich Drobnig, Director of the Max Planck Institut für ausländisches und
internationales Privatrecht in Hamburg,
Maître Marc Elvinger, Luxembourg,
Professor Arthur Hartkamp, Advocate-General of the Hoge Raad der Nederlanden,
Professor Ewoud Hondius, University of Utrecht,
Professor Guy Horsmans, University of Louvain la Neuve,
Professer Konstantinos Kerameus, University of Athens,
Professor Ole Lando, Copenhagen Business School,
Professor Bryan McMahon, University of Galway,
Professor Georges Rouhette, University of the Auvergne,
Professor Pablo Salvador Coderch, Universitat Pompeu Fabra, Barcelona,
Professor Matthias E. Storme, University of Leuven, and
Professor Denis Tallon, Université de Paris II, Director of the Institut de Droit
Comparé de Paris

In January 1995 Austria, Finland and Sweden became Members of the European
Union. At the seventh meeting in September 1995 in Galway and at the eighth and
last meeting in Stockholm in May 1996 Professor Willibald Posch, University of
Graz, Professor Jan Ramberg, University of Stockholm and Professor Thomas
Wilhelmsson, University of Helsinki joined as Members of the Commission, as did
Professor Hector MacQueen, University of Edinburgh.

As it appears, most of the Members of the two Commissions have been academics. However, several of them are also practising lawyers.

Secretaries to the Commission

Dr Oliver Remien of the Max Planck Institut für ausländisches und internationales
Privatrecht in Hamburg served as secretary of the First Commission from the third
through the seventh meeting. Henning Klinkenberg of the Max Planck Institute served
at the eigth meeting, and Dr Remien at the following six meetings. Professor Matthias
E. Storme served as secretary of the Second Commission. The Commission is indebted to the secretaries for their valuable work. Their main task was to prepare the min-
utes of the meetings, a task which was performed with great competence and care.

For Part 1 Dr Michael Peglow and for the present edition Ms Bettina Picone-
Maxion and Mr. Dirk Maxion produced the list of abbreviations, the bibliographies
and the table of cases.

Parts 1 and 2 of the Principles

Part 1

Believing that, within the law of contracts, the rules on due performance and the remedies for non-performance were of paramount importance, the first Commission chose these subjects for the first phase of its work. *The Principles of European Contract Law, Part 1, Performance, Non Performance and Remedies, Prepared by the Commission on European Contract law* and edited by Hugh Beale and Ole Lando was published by Martinus Nijhoff Publishers, Dordrecht, in 1995. By 1997 it was sold out. A French edition of Part 1, *Les principes du droit europèen du contrat, L' exécution, l'inexécution et ses suites. Version francaise,* translated and edited by *Isabelle de Lamberterie, Georges Rouhette and Denis Tallon,* was published by *La documentation Francaise,* Paris, in 1997. As of March 1998 this version was still available. A German version of the articles of Part 1 has been published in *Zeitschrift für europäisches Privatrecht,* 1995, p. 864.

The Present Second Part and future work

This Volume contains new principles and rules on formation of contracts, authority of agents to bind their principal, the validity of contracts, interpretation and contents and effects. Futhermore, it contains a revised edition of the general provisions and the rules on performance, non-performance and remedies for non-performance which were provided in Part 1.

Even this volume does not provide a complete statement of the general principles of contract law. The Commission is continuing its work. Additional chapters will deal with the effects of illegality and immorality, compound interest, conditions, extinctive prescription of claims and with topics which cover both contractual and non-contractual obligations such as assignment of claims, assumption of debts, plurality of debtors and creditors, and set-off.

How we worked

The drafting of the articles, comments and notes was the task of a Reporter. The Reporters of the First Commission were:
Professor Hugh Beale (from 1987)
Professor Ulrich Drobnig
Professor Roy Goode,
Professor Ole Lando, and
Professor Denis Tallon.

In the second Commission the task was divided between:
Professor Hugh Beale,
Professor Ulrich Drobnig,
Professor Ewoud Hondius,

Professor Ole Lando, and
Professor Denis Tallon

Each Reporter presented his draft with comments to the other Reporters in a Drafting Group, which met to prepare the texts to be submitted to the Commission. At its meetings the Commission approved the texts, changed them or sent them back for further consideration by the Reporter and the Drafting Group.

An Editing Group worked to improve the terminology and the presentation of the texts.

In the First Commission the Members of this group were:
Professor Bryan McMahon,
Professor de Magelhães Collaço,
Professor Georges Rouhette, who acted as chairman, and
Professor William Wilson.

In the Second Commission the Members were:
Professor Michael Bridge
Professor Hector Mac Queen
Professor Georges Rouhette, who acted as chairman, and
Professor Carlo Castronovo.

At its last meeting in 1990 the First Commission adopted the Articles of Part 1, and at its last meeting in 1996 the Second Commission approved the Articles of Part 2 and the amendments of Part 1, each time leaving it to the Drafting Group and the Editing Group to finalize the Comments.

The notes to the Articles, which bring a survey of the relevant law of the Member States, have been written by the Reporters on the basis of information received by the Members of the Commissions. Additional information on Irish law has been provided by Mr Eoin O'Dell, Trinity College, Dublin and Ms Nicola Murphy of University College, Galway; and on Spanish law by Professor Fernando Martinez Sanz, Universidad Jaime I, Castellon. The final editing of the notes was done by Professors Hugh Beale and Ole Lando.

THE SPONSORS

Until the end of 1994 the Commission of the European Community, and notably its Legal Service, provided most of the funds necessary for carrying out our work. Before and after that time contributions have been received from the *Stiftverband der deutschen Wissenschaft*; ARAG Insurance Co, Germany; Baker & McKenzie, Solicitors, London; Edge & Ellison, Solicitors, Birmingham; The Lord Chancellor's Department, London; *Foreningen til unge Handelsmænds Uddannelse,* Copenhagen; *Haniel Stiftung*, Germany; Masons, Solicitors, London; the *Max Planck Institut für ausländisches und internationales Privatrecht,* Hamburg; the French *Centre National de le Recherche Scientifique (Institut de Recherche Comparée sur les Institutions et le Droit)*; the Law Department of the Copenhagen Business School; the University of Warwick; St John's College, Oxford; and Queen Mary and Westfield College, London.

The *Università degli Studi di Roma*, the Centre of International and Economic Law, Thessaloniki, the Belgian *Centre Interuniversitaire de Droit Comparé*, the University of Utrecht together with the Netherlands Ministry of Justice, the German Leibnitz Foundation through a grant administered by Professor von Bar, the Government of Catalonia, the University of Palermo, and the University of Stockholm paid a substantial part of the expenses of the meetings in Rome, Thessaloniki, Brussels, Utrecht, Osnabrück, Barcelona, Palermo and Stockholm respectively. In almost every place we met, the local universities made meeting rooms, photocopying machines and secretarial assistance available to us without charge.

We are most grateful to all these sponsors for their generous contributions. However, the most important support was provided by my colleagues, the members of the two Commissions, who without being paid for it gave their time and efforts for the cause.

Holte, February 1999
Ole Lando

Members of the Commissions of European Contract Law

First Commission:
Professor Hugh Beale (from 1987)
Professor Alberto Bercovitz (from 1986)
Professor Brigitte Berlioz-Houin (until 1986)
Professor Massimo Bianca
Professor Michael Joachim Bonell
Professor I. de Magelhães Collaço (from 1986)
Professor Ulrich Drobnig
Maître André Elvinger
Professor Dimitri Evrigenis (until 1986)
Professor Roy M. Goode
Professor Guy Horsmans
Professor Roger Houin (until 1986)
Professor Konstantinos Kerameus (from 1987)
Professor Ole Lando
Professor Bryan McMahon
Professor Georges Rouhette (from 1987)
Professor Denis Tallon
Dr. J.A. Wade
Dr. Frans J.A. van der Velden
Professor William Wilson

Second Commission:
Professor Christian von Bar,,
Professor Hugh Beale,
Professor Michael Joachim Bonell
Professor Michael Bridge
Professor Isabel de Magelhães Collaco
Professor Ulrich Drobnig
Maître Marc Elvinger, Luxembourg

Professor Arthur Hartkamp
Professor Ewoud Hondius
Professor Guy Horsmans
Professor Konstantinos Kerameus
Professor Ole Lando
Professor Hector MacQueen
Professor Bryan McMahon
Professor Willibald Posch
Professor Jan Ramberg
Professor Georges Rouhette
Professor Pablo Salvador Coderch
Professor Matthias E. Storme
Professor Denis Tallon
Professor Thomas Wilhelmsson.

CHAIRMAN OF THE COMMISSIONS:

Ole Lando

MEMBERS OF THE DRAFTING GROUPS:

First Commission:
Hugh Beale (from 1987)
Ulrich Drobnig
Roy M. Goode
Ole Lando
Denis Tallon

Second Commission:
Hugh Beale
Ulrich Drobnig
Ewoud Hondius
Ole Lando
Denis Tallon

MEMBERS OF THE EDITING GROUPS:

First Commission:
I. de Magelhães Collaço
Bryan McMahon
Georges Rouhette (Chairman)
William Wilson

Second Commission:
Michael Bridge
Carlo Castronovo
Hector MacQueen
Georges Rouhette (Chairman)

SECRATARIES TO THE COMMISSIONS:

Oliver Remien (First Commission)
Matthias E. Storme (Second Commission)

Introduction

1. The Need for Uniform Rules

The Principles of European Contract are the product of work carried out by the Commission on European Contract Law, a body of lawyers drawn from all the member States of the European Union, under the chairmanship of Professor Ole Lando. They are a response to a need for a Union-wide infrastructure of contract law to consolidate the rapidly expanding volume of Community law regulating specific types of contract. There are many benefits to be derived from a formulation of principles of contract law within Europe.

A) *The Facilitation of Cross-Border Trade Within Europe*

Both within and outside Europe there is a growing recognition of the need for measures of harmonisation to eliminate those differences in national laws which are inimical to the efficient conduct of cross-border business within Europe. Such harmonisation measures confer particular benefits on contracting parties carrying on business in different States, enabling them to contract with reference to a set of rules which apply uniformly over the territories of the various States, which are detached from any particular legal system, which are available in languages of which at least one is likely to be known to the parties, and which over time will become much more familiar to those who use them than the individual national laws of the various foreign countries in which they transact business.

B) *The Strengthening of the Single European Market*

The harmonisation of principles of contract law is of especial importance to the proper functioning of the Single European Market, the very essence of which is a broadly unitary approach to law and regulation that surmounts the obstacles to trade and the distortions of the market resulting from differences in the national laws of Member States affecting trade within Europe.

C) *The Creation of an Infrastructure for Community Laws Governing Contracts*

The lawmakers of the European Community are increasingly active in the field of contracts. Directives have been issued affecting contracts relating to insurance, employment, commercial agency, consumer credit, consumer safety, doorstep sales and unfair terms in consumer contracts, to mention but a few, and the list is steadily growing. Yet there is no general contract law infrastructure to support these specific Community measures. There are at present considerable disparities between the laws of the Member States governing contracts, including such major matters as formation, formal and essential validity, substantive effects, remedies for non-performance and the conditions under which performance is excused. There is not even a common terminology. Hence the Principles are designed not merely to reduce the adverse effects of differences in national laws within the Single European Market but also to provide a foundation of contract law within the Community upon which more specific harmonisation measures can be constructed. Without such a body of Community-wide principles of contract law the effect of many of the measures being taken towards European legal integration in relation to consumer and commercial transactions is likely to be weakened significantly.

D) *The Provision of Guidelines for National Courts and Legislatures*

The Principles are intended to reflect the common core of solutions to problems of contract law. Some of these have proved increasingly troublesome for national courts and legislators. The Principles are also intended to be progressive. On many issues covered by national law they may be found to offer a more satisfactory answer than that which is reached by traditional legal thinking. For example, their provisions relating to the assurance of performance and to the grant of relief where a change of circumstances renders performance of the contract excessively onerous deal in a balanced way with recurrent difficulties on which most national laws are silent. The Principles are thus available for the assistance of European courts and legislatures concerned to ensure the fruitful development of contract law on a Union-wide basis. Even beyond the borders of the European Union, the Principles may serve as an inspiration for the Central and Eastern European legislators who are in the course of reforming their laws of contract to meet the needs of a market economy.

E) *The Construction of a Bridge between the Civil Law and the Common Law*

One of the most intractable problems of European legal integration is the reconciliation of the civil law and the common law families. It is, of course, true that there are significant differences even between one civil law system and another; it is also true that in many cases common problems will be solved in much the same way by the various legal systems, to whichever legal family they may belong. But there remain major differences between civil law and common law systems in relation to legal structure and reasoning, terminology, fundamental concepts and classifications and legal policy. Two examples from the field covered by the Principles suffice to make the point. The first is that in civil law systems there is a general and pervasive principle of good faith; in the European common law systems there is no such general principle. They have a requirement of good faith only in limited situations and have a series of specific rules achieving some of the same results as might be required by good faith but without referring to that concept. The second is that the civil law considers it legitimate for a contract to contain penalty clauses designed to deter a party from breaking the contract; the common law regards the imposition of penalties (as opposed to liquidated damages by way of compensation for anticipated loss) as improper and unenforceable. Differences of these kinds are inimical to the efficient functioning of the Single European Market. One of the major benefits offered by the Principles is to provide a bridge between the civil law and the common law by providing rules designed to reconcile their differing legal philosophies.

2. THE PURPOSES FOR WHICH THE PRINCIPLES ARE DESIGNED

It will be apparent from the foregoing that the Principles of European Contract Law are intended to be of service in a number of ways to a wide range on institutions, enterprises and individuals.

A) *A Foundation for European Legislation*

The Principles provide a necessary legal foundation for measures taken and to be taken in the future by the organs of the European Union. The Principles will assist both the organs of the Community in drafting measures and courts, arbitrators and legal advisers in applying Community measures.

In 1989 the European Parliament passed a Resolution requesting that a start be made on the preparatory work for drawing up a European Code of Private Law. The preamble to the Resolution states that

"...unification can be carried out in branches of private law which are highly important for the development of a Single Market, such as contract law..." (Resolution of 26 May 1989, OJEC No. C 158/401 of 26 June 1989.

This request was repeated in 1994 (Resolution of 6 May 1994, OJEC No. C 205 (519) of 25 July 1994.)

One objective of the Principles of European Contract Law is to serve as a basis for any future European Code of Contracts. They could form the first step in the work.

B) *Express Adoption by the Parties*

The Principles will be useful for parties who are living or carrying on business in different States and who wish their contractual relations to be governed by a set of neutral rules not based on any one national legal system but drawing on the best solutions offered by the laws of jurisdictions within (and sometimes outside) Europe.

They can declare that the contract is to be governed by the Principles of European Contract Law.

C) *A Modern Formulation of a Lex Mercatoria*

Parties to international contracts who want their agreement to be governed by internationally accepted principles, or who are unable to agree on a reference to a national legal system, have the option to adopt the *lex mercatoria* to govern their contract. It not infrequently happens that they opt for arbitration according to, if not the *lex mercatoria* by name, "general principles of law", "internationally accepted principles" or some other such phrase. Where is the arbitrator who has to deal with such a contract to find those principles? He may feel that he knows what is customarily accepted, or he may feel able to make a common sense judgment, but neither is a reliable way of deciding the case. If there is a statement of internationally accepted principles, the arbitrator's life will be much easier and the uncertainty engendered by adopting such a phrase will be reduced. One of the immediate aims of the Principles is to provide such a statement that is acceptable within Europe and which can be applied directly by arbitrators in the type of case envisaged - in effect a modern European *lex mercatoria*.

D) *A Model for Judicial and Legislative Development of Contract Law*

The Principles offer help to courts and arbitrators called upon to decide issues which are not adequately governed by the national law or other system of rules applicable. The court or arbitrator may adopt the solution provided by the Principles knowing that it represents the common core of the European systems, or a progressive development from that common core. Equally the solutions of the Principles may be adopted by legislators reforming their contract law. The Commission hopes in particular that the Principles will be of service to those charged with reform of contract law in the newly-emerged democracies of Central Europe.

E) *A Basis for Harmonisation*

Ultimately the Member States of the European Union may wish to harmonise their contract law. The Principles can serve as a model on which harmonisation work may be based.

Thus the Principles have both immediate and longer-term objectives. They are available for immediate use by parties making contracts, by courts and arbitrators in deciding contract disputes and by legislators in drafting contract rules whether at the European or the national level. Their longer-term objective is to help bring about the harmonisation of general contract law within the European Union.

3. THE SUBJECTS COVERED

The law of contract is considered to be the part of the general law for which the international business community most urgently needs harmonisation. Those attempting to unify European contract law, particularly within the Community, need above all uniform principles and a uniform terminology.

The Principles are confined to the general law of contractual obligations. They do not deal with any specific types of contract, nor do they make special provision for consumer contracts, which raise policy issues more appropriately determined by Community law and national legislation. On the other hand, the Principles are not confined to commercial relationships but are intended to apply to contracts generally, including contracts between merchants and consumers.

The Commission has not hesitated to borrow from legislation and Conventions dealing with specific types of contract through provisions which are suitable for general application. Thus the United Nations Convention on Contracts for the International Sale of Goods of 1980 (CISG) has been a particularly fruitful source of ideas for the Principles. But while the Principles will be found particularly useful in international trade transactions within Europe, they are not confined to such transactions and may be applied equally to purely domestic contracts.

The Commission has taken a functional approach in deciding which topics to be included in the Principles. The Principles embrace rules which in some legal systems are considered to form part of the law of torts or the law of restitution when the rules in question are closely linked to issues in contract covered by the Principles. Thus, chapter 2 on the formation of contracts includes liability for negotiations (*culpa in contrahendo* etc.), although in some legal systems this liability is considered to form part of the law of torts. The Principles govern the restitutionary effects of the avoidance for invalidity of contracts; in chapter 4 on validity it is provided that on avoidance either party may claim restitution of whatever it has supplied under the contract provided it makes concurrent restitution of whatever it has received. If restitution cannot be made in kind for any reason, a reasonable sum must be paid for what has been received. In Chapter 9 Section 3 on Termination of the Contract for Non-performance, the Principles provide for the recovery of money paid or property transferred by a party for a performance which it did not receive, and recovery of a reasonable sum for a performance which was received and cannot be returned.

4. SOURCES

The Principles are designed primarily for use in the Member States of the European Union. They have regard to the economic and social conditions prevailing in the Member States. The Commission on European Contract Law has therefore drawn in some measure on the legal systems of every Member State. This does not, of course, imply that every legal system has had equal influence on every issue considered. In fact no single legal system has been made the starting point from which the Principles and the terminology which they employ are derived. Nor have the draftsmen of the Principles seen it as their task to make interpolations or compromises between the existing national laws, except as is necessary in order to weld the Principles into a workable system.

The Commission has not confined its sources to the national laws of Member States. It has drawn on a wide range of legal materials from both within and outside Europe, including the American *Uniform Commercial Code* and *Restatements* of contract and of restitution. Some of the provisions in the Principles reflect suggestions and ideas which have not yet materialised in the law of any State.

5. STRUCTURE AND METHOD

The Principles contained in this volume consist of a set of principles and rules embodied in 131 Articles divided into nine chapters, namely

Chapter 1   General Provisions
Chapter 2   Formation
Chapter 3   Authority of Agents
Chapter 4   Validity
Chapter 5   Interpretation
Chapter 6   Contents and Effects
Chapter 7   Performance
Chapter 8   Non- performance and Remedies in General
Chapter 9   Particular Remedies for Non-performance

Each chapter consists of a series of Articles; in some of the chapters (1, 2, 3 and 9) the Articles are for convenience grouped into sections.

Each Article is followed by a Comment stating the reasons for the rule, and its purpose, operation and relationship to other rules. The operation of the rule is further explained by the use of Illustrations. A concluding Note to the rule identifies the principal sources utilised and describes briefly the manner in which the issue is dealt with in the various legal systems of the Member States of the European Union.

The method adopted may be compared with the American *Restatement of the Law of Contract*, the second edition of which was published in 1981. However, the task is different. The Restatement is broadly intended as a formulation of existing law, since in almost all States the law of contract is based on the common law. In the Union, which is characterised by the existence of a number of divergent legal systems, general principles applicable across the Union as a whole must be established by a more creative process whose purpose is to identify, so far as possible, the common core of the contract law of all the Member States of the Union and on the basis of this common core to create a workable system.

Every effort has been made to draft short and general rules which will be easily understood not only by lawyers but also by their clients. With a view to ensuring that the rules are readily comprehensible and are responsive to the needs of prospective users, earlier drafts of the Principles have been discussed with practising lawyers in six of the Member States (Belgium, France, Germany, Portugal, Spain and the United Kingdom) and appropriate additions and modifications made.

6. THE ACCOMMODATION OF FUTURE DEVELOPMENTS

The Principles of European Contract Law are a set of general rules which are designed to provide maximum flexibility and thus to accommodate future developments in legal thinking in the field of contract law. The Commission has therefore resisted the temptation to seek to cover every particular eventuality, which would lead to excessive detail and specificity and inhibit the future development of European contract law. Thus Article 1:106, which provides that the Principles are to be interpreted in accordance with their purposes and that issues not expressly settled by them are so far as possible to be settled in accordance with the ideas underlying them, is of fundamental importance to the creative function of the Principles.

Survey of Chapters 1-9

CHAPTER 1: GENERAL PROVISSIONS

(a) *Application.* The Principles are intended primarily to be applied within the European Union. They may be applied by the courts of the European Community to disputes which are not governed by any national law, and may be relied on in the drafting of Community legislation affecting contracts. Further, they may be adopted expressly by the parties, either by incorporation into their contract or to govern it. When the parties have not expressly incorporated the Principles, they may be applied by arbitrators or courts in the circumstances set out in Article 1:101(3) and (4). Parties to a contract which is not governed by the law of a Member State are also free to adopt the Principles so far as permitted by the applicable law. If the Principles purport to have been adopted by the parties, the Principles may (subject to one exception, see Article 1:104) be used to determine questions of the existence and validity of the parties' consent.

Adoption of the Principles to govern a contract will not, however, exclude the "super-mandatory" rules of the national law which would otherwise apply, see Article 1:103(2).

(b) *Non-mandatory nature of the Principles.* For the most part the Principles provide rules which the parties are free to vary or exclude, see Article 1:102. But certain provisions are considered to be of such fundamental importance as to be mandatory in character. Such provisions are contained in:

Article 1:201   The duty of good faith and fair dealing;
Article 2:105(2), (3) Merger clauses not individually negotiated;
Article 6:105   Unilateral determination of terms by one party;
Article 4:118   Remedies for fraud, threat, excessive benefit or unfair advantage-taking and for unfair terms not individually negotiated. Remedies in respect of mistake and incorrect information can only be excluded or restricted if the exclusion or restriction is not contrary to good faith and fair dealing;

Article 8:109   Remedies in respect of non-performance can only be excluded or restricted if the exclusion or restriction is not contrary
to good faith and fair dealing;

Article 9:509(2)   Judicial discretion to reduce grossly excessive sums payable
on non-performance.

(c) *Usages and practices.* Parties frequently do not express their agreement fully.
Article 1:105 provides that, within certain limits, usages and practices established
either between the parties or generally in their situation will form part of the contract. Further provisions on the terms of the contract when nothing has been agreed
expressly and there are no relevant usages will be found in Chapter 6.

(d) *Interpretation and supplementation.* Various rules governing interpretation and
development of the Principles are stated in Article 1:106. These rules are designed
to promote good faith and fair dealing, predictability and uniformity.

Various terms used in the Principles are defined in Article 1:301, while Articles
1:302 to 1:305 show how certain key concepts featuring in subsequent Chapters are
to be interpreted and applied. These are the provisions covering Reasonableness
(Article 1:302: see (e) below), Notice (Article 1:303), Computation of Time (Article
1:304) and Imputed Knowledge and Intention (Article 1:305).

(e) *Basic duties*
The remainder of Chapter 1 is concerned with general duties which apply under the
Principles. Article 1:201 sets out the duty of good faith and fair dealing (which as
already mentioned, cannot be excluded); Article 1:202 states the duty to co-operate.
Many Articles of the Principles also express the duty to act reasonably or fix standards
by what is reasonable. As just mentioned, reasonableness is defined by Article 1:302.

CHAPTER 2: FORMATION

(a) *Basic requirements of contract.* Section 1 of Chapter 2 sets out the basic requirements of contract under the Principles. These are merely an intention to be bound
and agreement which is sufficiently definite that the agreement can be enforced or
determined under the Principles (see Articles 2:101 and 2:103). A promise intended
to be binding without acceptance is binding even without the promisee's agreement,
Article 2:107. The rules of contract apply to such promises by analogy, Article 1:107.
It should be noted that under the Principles there is no requirement of cause or consideration; and a contract may exist even though performance was impossible at the
time the contract was made (Article 4:102), though the contract may well be avoidable on the ground of mistake (see Article 4:103, described further below).

A party's intention to be bound is to be determined objectively, in that it is to be
determined from what the party said as it was reasonably understood by the other
party (Article 2:102).

(b) *Terms of the contract.* Terms which were not individually negotiated will not be binding on a party which did not know of them unless reasonable notice of them had been given (Article 2:104). A merger clause in a written contract will not create more than a presumption that the parties intended the writing to be a complete statement of the terms, and will not prevent use of prior statements to interpret the contract, unless in either case the clause was individually negotiated (Article 2:105). A clause requiring modifications to the contract to be in writing will only create a presumption that a modification which was not written was not meant to be binding (Article 2:106).

(c) *Offer and acceptance.* Section 2 of Chapter 2 lays down general principles for determining whether there has been an offer (see in particular Article 2:201) and whether there has been acceptance. An offer may be revoked before the offeree has dispatched an acceptance, unless the offer was irrevocable either because its terms so stated or because it stated a fixed time for acceptance (Article 2:202). The contract will become binding once the acceptance (with certain exceptions based on the terms of the offer, practice or usage) has become known to the offeror (Articles 2:204 and 2:205), provided the acceptance is in time (Article 2:207).

Unless it provides otherwise, the offer may be accepted by a purported acceptance which does not quite match it, provided the differences are not material and are not objected to (Article 2:208); where each party uses general conditions, a contract may be formed despite material conflicts between the general conditions. The contract will contain the conditions only to the extent that they are not in substantial conflict (Article 2:209). Between professionals, if a contract has been agreed, a confirmation note may be taken to state the terms of the contract unless it materially alters what was agreed or it is objected to (Article 2:210).

(d) *Liability for negotiations.* There will be liability for continuing to negotiate, and for breaking of negotiations, if the party concerned does not act in good faith (Article 2:301). There will also be liability for disclosing confidential information obtained during negotiations (Article 2:302).

CHAPTER 3: AUTHORITY OF AGENTS

(a) *Scope of the Chapter.* Chapter three deals with the "external" aspects of consensual agency, that is, the relations between the principal and the third party and, exceptionally, between the agent and the third party, but not the "internal" relationship between principal and agent (Article 3:101). It covers both cases of "direct representation" in which the agent acts on behalf of a principal and those of "indirect representation" in which the agent appears to act in his own name (commission agents and undisclosed principal: see Article 3:102).

(b) *Direct representation.* Where the agent has express or implied authority, or the principal has led the third party to believe that the agent is authorised, the acts of the agent bind the principal and third party. The agent will normally be personally liable to the third party only when he purported to act with authority which he did not have and the supposed principal does not ratify what the agent has done (see Articles 3:101 – 3:204 and 3:207). If the third party is in doubt as to the agent's authority, it may seek confirmation from the principal (Article 3:208). The agent continues to have power to bind the principal and third party until the latter knows or should know that the agent's authority has come to an end, and even then the agent may remain authorised for a short time in order to perform acts necessary for the protection of the principal or its successors (Article 3:209).

(c) *Conflicts of interest.* The principal may avoid a contract concluded by an agent if it involved the agent in a conflict of interests of which the third party knew or could not have been unaware (Article 3:205).

(d) *Sub-agents.* An agent may normally appoint a sub-agent, whose authorised acts will have the same effect as if done by the agent (Article 3:206).

(e) *Indirect representation.* Where a person (the intermediary) appears to act in his own name, though on the instructions of a principal (e.g. a commission agent) or though in fact acting on behalf of a principal (undisclosed principal), the normal effect will be that the third party and the intermediary are bound to each other. The principal may only intervene to exercise any rights against the third party, and the third party intervene against the principal, if the agent has become insolvent or committed a fundamental non-performance of his obligations towards the party seeking to intervene (Articles 3:301 – 3:303). The party seeking to intervene must first give notice to both the intermediary and the other party, after which the other party is no longer entitled to perform to the intermediary (Article 3:304)

CHAPTER 4: VALIDITY

(a) *Scope and approach of the Chapter.* Chapter 4 deals with mistake (including initial impossibility), fraud, incorrect information, threats, excessive or unfair advantage-taking and unfair terms which have not been negotiated. It does not deal with the effects of illegality or immorality (these may be covered in a further chapter yet to be drafted), nor with incapacity, see Article 4:101.

The principle of freedom of contract suggests that a party should be bound only when its consent to the contract was informed and free from constraint by the other party. While freedom of contract is an important value, it must be balanced against the need for security of transactions. The other party should in general terms be able to rely on the existence of the contract unless it

    (a)   has not acted in good faith; or

    (b)   has taken deliberate advantage of the first party in circumstances in which standards of fair dealing would not permit this or

    (c)   has behaved carelessly or in some other way which was unreasonable.

Another way of putting the point is in terms of risk. When making a contract, each party undertakes certain risks. For example the buyer may take the risk that the goods or service it is contracting for will not be as useful to it as it anticipates. However there are certain risks that it should not be required to bear; these include the risk of bad faith, certain types of advantage-taking and of misapprehensions which would have been avoided had there not been careless or unreasonable behaviour by the other party.

Thus the Principles normally permit a party which has been subjected to fraud or threats to avoid a contract; avoidance on the ground of mistake or excessive benefit or advantage-taking is permitted but under more limited conditions. Particular terms may be avoided if they were not individually negotiated and, contrary to the requirements of good faith, create a significant imbalance in the rights and obligations of the parties to the detriment of the party seeking to avoid the term.

(b) *Avoidance for mistake.* A party which has entered a contract under a mistake as to the facts or law may avoid the contract, but only if it is shown (in the light of a correct interpretation of the contract under the rules of Chapter 5) that the mistake was very serious; and that the mistake was caused by information given by the other party, or that the other party knew or ought to have known of the mistake and it was contrary to good faith and fair dealing to leave the mistaken party in error, or the other party made the same mistake. Avoidance is not permitted if the mistake was inexcusable or if the mistaken party had assumed the relevant risk (Article 4:103).

Mistakes and misunderstandings over the terms of the contract due to errors in communication should also first be approached under the rules of interpretation contained in Chapter 5 (see below). These may lead to one party's version of the terms being accepted as correct. If these rules do not resolve the matter, a mistaken party may avoid the contract subject to the same conditions as for mistakes as to fact or law (Article 4:104)

The contract may not be avoided if the other party is prepared to perform it in the way the first party understood it or, in cases of shared mistake, if the court can adapt it to bring it into line with what had been understood (Article 4:105).

(c) *Fraud.* A party which has been induced to enter a contract by the other party's fraud may avoid the contract (Article 4:107) and claim damages (Article 4:117). Fraud may include both positive misrepresentation and failures to disclose what should have been disclosed according to standards of good faith and fair dealing.

(d) *Inaccurate information.* Where a party has been induced to enter a contract by inaccurate information but there was no fraud, but the person who gave the information had no reasonable grounds for believing that it was true, the first party may recover damages (Article 4:106). If the incorrect information resulted in a fundamental mistake, the first party may avoid the contract under Article 4:103.

(e) *Threats.* A party which has entered a contract as the result of an illegitimate threat by the other party may also avoid it (Article 4:108) and claim damages (Article 4:117).

(f) *Excessive or unfair advantage-taking.* Article 4:109 allows for avoidance or the adaptation of a contract where one party has taken advantage of the other's needs or situation to take an excessive benefit or unfair advantage. Damages may be recovered under Article 4:117.

(g) *Unfair terms which have not been individually negotiated.* Article 4:110 applies the approach of the EC Directive on Unfair terms in Consumer Contracts to terms in contract between parties of any kind where the term has not been individually negotiated: the term may be avoided if, contrary to the requirements of good faith, it creates a significant imbalance in the parties' rights and obligations. Terms setting the price or defining the main subject matter of the contract are not covered but might be challenged under Article 4:109, above.

(h) *Third persons.* In accordance with the approach set out in (a) above, behaviour such as fraud by a third person only gives a party a remedy if the other party was responsible for the third person (see Article 1:305) or knew or ought to have known of the third person's behaviour (Article 4:111)

(i) *Ancillary provisions on avoidance.* Articles 4:112 – 4:116 govern the means of avoidance, the ways in which the right to avoid may be limited or lost – for example, by failure to give notice within a reasonable time – and the effects of avoidance and partial avoidance.

(j) *Alternative remedies.* The same set of facts may give rise to remedies under both this chapter and the chapters on non-performance. In such a case the aggrieved party may pursue either remedy (Article 4:119).

(k) *Exclusion of remedies.* As noted earlier, under Article 4:118 remedies for fraud, threat and excessive benefit or unfair advantage-taking cannot be excluded or restricted. Remedies in respect of mistake and incorrect information cannot be excluded or restricted if the exclusion or restriction is contrary to good faith and fair dealing.

CHAPTER 5: INTERPRETATION

(a) *General.* As do the majority of laws of Member States of the EU, the Principles contain rules on the interpretation of contracts. Taking into account the noticeable divergences between some of these laws, it has been thought useful to provide contracting parties, judges and arbitrators with a sort of uniform guide. The rules which it contains are designed to be applied to any sort of contract, including those made on general conditions.

(b) *Guidelines rather than rigid rules.* The rules are supple, leaving judges considerable latitude. Moreover, the rules may point in opposite directions. It will then be for the judge to choose which is most appropriate in the circumstances of the case and which to disregard.

(c) *The place of rules of interpretation.* Problems of interpretation may arise at different stages in the life of a contract: formation, performance, non-performance. It is often at the point at which one party complains of defective performance that it becomes necessary to determine exactly to what the parties were bound.

The question of interpretation is prior to and logically distinct from the question of validity or that of remedies. It is necessary to determine the precise meaning of the contract before one can tell whether there has been a mistake or a non-performance which will give rise to a remedy. Indeed, it may be necessary to interpret the parties' statements in order to determine whether a contract has been made.

(d) *Common intention and objective interpretation.* The first question is to determine what was the common intention of the parties. Thus if it can be shown that they shared a common intention, or that one party's intention was or must have been known to the other party, the contract will be interpreted accordingly even if that is not the literal meaning of the word used (Article 5:101 (1) and (2)).

If it is not possible to establish a common intention, the contract is to be interpreted objectively, according to the meaning that reasonable persons of the same kind (condition) as the parties would give to it in the same circumstances (Article 5:101 (3)).

(e) *Contract to be interpreted in the light of the circumstances.* Consistently with the objective approach, the contract should be interpreted in the light of the circumstances. Article 5:102 lists the most important of these.

(f) *Rules where contract ambiguous, vague or self-contradictory.* The Articles 5:103 – 5:106 provide a number of rules, mostly widely known and accepted, to deal with cases where the contract is ambiguous, vague or self-contradictory: the *Contra Proferentem* rule, the rule giving preference to individually negotiated terms, the rule requiring the contract to be read as a whole and the rule of full effect. Article 5:107 adds a rule particularly appropriate to international contracts: where a contract is drawn up in two or more language versions none of which is stated to be authoritative, and there is a discrepancy between the versions, preference should be given to the version in which the contract was originally drawn up.

CHAPTERS 6 & 7: CONTENTS AND EFFECTS; PERFORMANCE

(a) *What are the terms of the contract?* It is frequently difficult to determine what the terms of a contract were intended to be, either because it is not clear whether certain statements made prior to the conclusion of the contract were intended to form part of it, or because nothing at all was agreed on a particular point (on the latter, see (c) below).

Leaving aside pure sales talk which does not give rise to any legal liability (puffs, *dolus bonus*), the Principles recognise that statements made before the conclusion of the contract may fall into two categories. They may be contractual undertakings, so that if the party does not do what it has said it would, or if the statement is incorrect, there will be a non-performance of the contract. Alternatively, the statement may not amount to a term of the contract but, if it is incorrect, may give rise to a right to avoid the contract or to claim damages under the provisions of Chapter 4, Validity (see above). Article 6:101 sets out criteria by which it may be determined whether or not a particular statement should be treated as a contractual undertaking.

(b) *Simulation.* It sometimes happens that parties deliberately draw up their contract so that they appear to agree one thing when in fact their agreement is different. As between the parties, the true agreement should prevail (Article 6:103). The Principles do not deal with the position of third persons who may have relied on the apparent agreement, except in the case of the undisclosed principal (*prête-nom*), see Chapter 3 above.

(c) *Terms omitted.* Parties frequently fail to make express provision for certain aspects of performance which need to be determined in order to operate the contract. Sometimes, as already mentioned, usages can supply the missing terms, but this is not always the case. Most legal systems have some "gap-filling" rules to make the contract effective and to prevent it being rendered void for uncertainty, though the extent to which systems do this varies considerably. Chapters 6 and 7 contain various rules as to the obligations of the parties and the way in which they must or may perform where the contract makes no provision.

First, Article 6:102 sets out general criteria by which it may be determined what terms should be implied into a contract. There follow a number of more particular rules. These include:

Failure to fix a price (Article 6:104)

Absence or disappearance of a factor of reference (Article 6:107)

Quality of performance (Articles 6:108)

Reference should also be made to Chapter 7 on Performance (see below) which contains rules on the place and time of performance (Articles 7:101 and 7:102).

(d) *Determination of term by one party or by a third person.* It is not uncommon for parties to leave the price, or some other term, to be determined either by a third party or even by one of the parties. The Principles recognise the validity of such clauses but provide that if the third person or the party fixes a price or other term which is grossly unreasonable, the parties should not be bound by it: a reasonable price or other term is to be substituted (Articles 6:106(2) and 6:105). If the third person is unable or unwilling to act, the parties are assumed to have empowered the court to act for them (Article 6:106(1)).

(e) *Contracts in favour of a third party.* In some legal systems there is a general principle that only the parties to a contract can take rights under it or be subjected to obligations by it. However many systems permit a third party to enforce a contract made for its benefit provided that the parties intended that the third party should have the right to do so. Article 6:110 adopts this approach.

(f) *Change of circumstances.* One of the most vexed questions of modern contract law is the effect on the parties' obligations to perform if, after the contract has been concluded, there is a change of circumstances for which neither party is responsible. Contract law has to resolve a tension between two conflicting principles, *pacta sunt servanda* (agreements must be observed) and *rebus sic stantibus* (undertakings are based on the premise that circumstances remain as they are).

Article 6:111 stresses that normally *pacta sunt servanda* is the paramount principle; but that in certain extreme circumstances it would be considered inequitable for one party to insist on strict performance when that would be excessively overous for the other. The Article imposes a duty to negotiate with a view to adapting or terminating the contract; in default of agreement the arbitrator or court is given wide powers to adapt or terminate the contract and to impose damages for loss caused by a party's refusal or failure to negotiate in good faith.

The case where the circumstances were always very different to those which the parties had assumed falls to be dealt with under Article 4:103, Mistake as to Facts or Law (see above).

(g) *Rules on performance.* Chapter 7 contains various rules setting out the obligations of the parties in relation to performance when the contract contains no provision to the contrary. The provisions on the place and time of performance (Articles 7:101 and 7:102) were referred to earlier. Further provisions include:

Early performance (Article 7:103)
Order of performance (Article 7:104)
Alternative performances (Article 7:105)
Performance by a third party (Article 7:106)
The form and currency of payment (Articles 7:107 and 7:108)
Appropriation of performance (Article 7:109)
Failure of a party to accept property or money to which it is entitled (Articles 7:110 and 7:111)
Costs of performance (Article 7:112)

CHAPTERS 8 & 9: NON-PERFORMANCE AND REMEDIES IN GENERAL;
PARTICULAR REMEDIES

It is convenient first to give an account of these two Chapters together, as to explain the general approach of the Principles to remedies involves referring to the particular remedies which the Principles provide. A more detailed overview of the contents of each Chapter will be found below.

Whenever one party fails to meet its obligations under the contract, whether it performs defectively, performs late, does not perform at all or defaults in some other way, the issue of remedies becomes important. The first thing that the aggrieved party will want to know is what can be done about the non-performance.

(a) *Remedies for all forms of non-performance.* The Principles do not distinguish between the various possible forms that non-performance may take. For example the same basic rules apply to defective performance, late performance and a total failure to do anything. All these situations are simply termed "non-performance". Preventing the other party from performing itself may also be a non-performance (see Article 8:101.)

Naturally the way the rules actually apply will vary from situation to situation, and in some situations not every remedy will be available; but each type of non-performance is governed by the same general rules so that it is unnecessary to distinguish between them. There are some additional rules (on notice) which apply to late performance. These are aimed at reducing the uncertainty which often arises when one party is late in performing (see further below, Article 8:106).

(b) *Anticipated non-performance.* Remedies may be available under the Principles even though the time for the other party to perform has not yet arrived, if it appears clear, or the first party reasonably believes, that the other party will default when the time comes (see Articles 8:103(c) and 9:304).

(c) *Excused and non-excused non-performance.* The Principles do provide different remedies according to why the non-performance has occurred, in that some non-performances are treated as excusable. In the paradigm case in which there is no excuse for the non-performance, the aggrieved party may exercise one or more of the following remedies:

Compel the other party to perform (see Chapter 9, Section 1);

Withhold its own performance until the other party does perform (see Chapter 9, Section 2);

Escape from the contract by terminating it because of the non-performance, and possibly recover money paid or the value of other benefits transferred to the non-performing party (see Chapter 9, section 3);

Reduce the price payable to the non-performing party for any part of the contract which it has performed, by the amount by which the non-performance has made it less valuable (see Chapter 9, Section 4); and

Claim damages for the loss caused by the non-performance (see Chapter 9, Section 5).

Liability under the Principles is "strict" and it is not necessary to prove fault in order to prove non-performance. However, where the contract is such that the party has only undertaken to use reasonable care and skill, or to use its best endeavours, there will of course only be a non-performance if it is shown that the reasonable skill or care, or best endeavours, have not been employed.

However, even in cases of "strict" liability, the Principles recognise that sometimes a party's performance will be prevented by events which are outside its control and which could not have been foreseen. In such a situation the non-performance may be excused (see Article 8:108) and the aggrieved party's remedies will be more limited. It will still be able to withhold performance and terminate, and to reduce the price, but it will neither be able to compel performance of the contract nor to claim damages (see Article 8:101).

(d) *Performance or a substitute*. In principle, the Civil Law systems consider the normal remedy for non-performance to be a claim for performance *in natura* (broadly speaking, specific performance or the recovery of money due). However, other remedies such as termination and damages are available at the option of the aggrieved party or when performance *in natura* cannot be obtained. The Common Law considers damages and termination as the normal remedies and specific performance as exceptional. The Principles take the approach that, unless non-performance is excused, compelling the non-performing party to perform should not be an exceptional remedy; but that the availability of performance *in natura* should be excluded in certain cases. Thus an aggrieved party will not be able to compel performance if it could reasonably be expected to make a substitute transaction (see Articles 9:101 and 9:102).

(e) *Remedies limited by good faith and fair dealing*. Several of the remedies are limited by commercial convenience and reasonableness. The right to withhold performance is limited to withholding as much as may be reasonable in the circumstances (see Article 9:201); the right to terminate does not arise in every case of non-performance, only when the non-performance is fundamental (see Article 9:301); and even the right to damages is limited to the recovery of losses that the aggrieved party could not have avoided by taking reasonable steps to look after its own interests (see Article 9:505). The scheme of remedies laid down by the Principles is a flexible one to suit the realities of the diverse situations in which the rules may apply.

(f) *Providing remedies which can be exercised easily*. Remedies such as withholding performance and termination give the obligor a strong incentive to perform. Thus, if the contract is terminated the obligor may lose all that it has invested in preparing to perform. The more easily the remedy can be operated by the obligee, the more effective it is likely to be to induce the obligor to perform. Remedies that the aggrieved party can exercise without having to obtain a court or arbitrator's order are thus particularly effective, and the Principles endeavour to encourage such "self-help" by minimising the need for formal steps. Thus whether the aggrieved party has the right to terminate depends only on whether the non-performance is fundamental and whether notice is given to the non-performing party; it is not necessary to obtain a court order.

(g) *Freedom to choose remedies*. When there has been a non-performance, the aggrieved party should be given the greatest possible freedom to choose its remedy to fit its needs, subject only to the requirements of good faith and fair dealing already mentioned. Under the Principles the aggrieved party may choose any of the remedies applicable in its case and attempting to use one remedy does not prevent simultaneous or subsequent recourse to another. There is no rule against cumulation of remedies (see Articles 8:102 and 9:103. In addition, as stated above, the aggrieved party may sometimes have a choice between remedies for non-performance and under Chapter 4.).

Thus the aggrieved party may seek an order for performance, or may terminate the contract, and still claim damages. The only limitations are the ones applicable to each remedy (see (b), above) and that a remedy cannot be used if on the facts it is not compatible with what the aggrieved party has done earlier. Thus if the aggrieved party has already terminated the contract it is too late to seek an order for performance. But it would be perfectly permissible to seek an order for performance first and then, if there seems little prospect of the order being obeyed, to terminate the contract.

(h) *The parties' freedom to provide their own remedies and to limit remedies.* Under the Principles the parties remain free, within very broad limits, to fashion their own remedies as they wish. Thus an express provision permitting termination in certain circumstances will be enforced. Similarly, the parties may agree on the damages or penalty to be paid in case of a non-performance, subject only to the court's power to reduce a penalty which is grossly excessive (Article 9:509).Equally the parties may agree to limit or even exclude the normal remedies by use of a limitation of liability or exclusion clause. Such a clause will be enforced unless to invoke it would be contrary to good faith and fair dealing (Article 8:109).

CHAPTER 8: NON-PERFORMANCE AND REMEDIES IN GENERAL

To give a little more detail of the contents of Chapter 8, the Chapter starts by setting out the basic rules governing remedies mentioned earlier. Thus Article 8:101 states which remedies are available in a case of non-excused non-performance and which are available when the non-performance is excused; Article 8:108 defines excused non-performance, which may occur when a party is prevented from performing by an impediment beyond its control and which it could not reasonably be expected to take into account at the time of conclusion of the contract. Where there is a total and permanent impediment to performance, the contract will terminate automatically, see Article 9:303(3); the remedies available in other cases of excused non-performance were described in *(c)* above. Article 8:102 states that there is no rule against cumulation of remedies. More specific provisions follow.

(a) *Defining fundamental non-performance.* As mentioned earlier, a party aggrieved by a non-performance by the other should only have a right to termination if the non-performance is fundamental. This is defined in Article 8:103.

(b) *Time when an aggrieved party may terminate.* It is important to establish when a party aggrieved by a non-performance may terminate the contract. Article 8:104 sets out when a defaulting party may cure a performance which does not conform to the contract, and Article 8:106 provides for the fixing of an additional time for performance by the service of a notice by the aggrieved party. Article 8:105 provides that a party which reasonably believes that there may be a non-performance in the future may demand an assurance of performance.

(c) *Performance entrusted to another.* It is common for a party to delegate performance of its obligation to another, e.g. an employee or a sub-contractor. This is normally permitted under the Principles if the contract does not require personal performance (see Article 7:106) but Article 8:107 confirms that the party which delegates remains responsible for proper performance of the obligation.

CHAPTER 9: PARTICULAR REMEDIES FOR NON-PERFORMANCE

This Chapter is sub-divided into sections, one for each remedy.

(a) *Compelling performance.* Section 1 states when an aggrieved party may compel the other to perform, dealing first with the recovery of money (Article 9:101) and then with specific performance of other obligations (Article 9:102). Article 9:103 reiterates the principle that remedies are cumulative: compelling performance does not preclude a claim for damages.

(b) *Withholding performance.* The right of a party to withhold its performance, or such part of it as may be reasonable, until the other party has performed is set out in Section 2 (Article 9:201).

(c) *Termination.* Section 3 states the circumstances in which a party may terminate a contract or a separate part of it (Articles 9:301 and 9:302). It provides that termination is effected by notice to the non-performing party and states when notice of termination can be given (Article 9:303).

   If it is clear that there will be a fundamental non-performance in the future, it is pointless to make the aggrieved party wait to terminate until the date for performance has passed. Therefore Article 9:304 allows immediate termination in this situation.

   The remainder of the Section deals with the effects of termination on the contract (Article 9:305) and the restitutionary remedies which are available after termination (Articles 9:306 – 9:309).

(d) *Price reduction.* A party which has not received the full performance it contracted to receive should be able to reduce the price it has to pay proportionately; this is particularly important where the non-performance was excused and therefore the aggrieved party cannot claim damages for the deficit. Section 4 provides for price reduction (Article 9:401).

(e) *Damages.* Section 5 lays down the principles by which damages are to be assessed. It states the general principle that the aggrieved party is entitled to be put into the same position as if the contract had been performed, which may include compensating it for non-pecuniary loss or future loss (Articles 9:501 and 9:502).

   The general principle is qualified by three other rules: the aggrieved party should not normally be compensated for losses which the non-performing party could not reasonably have anticipated (Article 9:503), which were due to its own unreasonable actions (Article 9:504) or which the aggrieved party would not have incurred had it taken reasonable steps to avoid the losses (Article 9:505).

The methods by which damages will normally be calculated when a contract has been terminated for non-performance are set out in Articles 9:506 (where the aggrieved party has made a cover transaction) and 9:507 (where it has not done so). The currency by which the damages should be measured is dealt with by Article 9:510.

If money is paid late, the creditor normally suffers a loss. Some legal systems do not allow the recovery of interest or damages in lieu of interest on late payments. The Principles state that the aggrieved party is entitled to both interest and damages for any further loss suffered (Article 9:508).

(f) *Agreed payment for non-performance.* As stated earlier, the parties are free to agree the amounts which should be paid by a party which has failed to perform its obligations. However the Principles provide that, despite any agreement to the contrary, if the sum agreed is grossly excessive it may be reduced to a reasonable amount (Article 9:509).

Abbreviations

ABGB	Allgemeines Bürgerliches Gesetzbuch (Austrian Civil Code)
A.C.	Appeal Cases (1891–) Law Reports
ADC	Annuario de Derecho Civil
AGBG	German Unfair Contract Terms Act
A.L.J.R.	Australian Law Journal Reports (1958–)
All E.R.	All England Law Reports (1936–)
Alm. Del.	Almindelig Del
Annal.dr.	Annales de droit (1965–)
A.P.	Areios Pagos (Greek Supreme Court in Civil Matters)
App.Cas.	Appeal Cases (1875-1890) Law Reports
Ar.	See RAJ, below
Arch.civ.	Archivio civile
Arch.N.	Archeio Nomologias
Arr.Cass.	Arresten van het Hof van cassatie/Arrêts de Cassation
art(s).	article(s)
B. [Bull.]	Bulletin officiel des arrêts de la Cour de cassation
B. & Ald	Barnewalk & Alderson's King's Bench Reports (1817-1822).
Bull. civ.	Bulletin des arrêts de la Chambre Civile de la Cour de Cassation (1792–)
B.& S.	Best & Smith's Queen's Bench Reports (1861-1865)
BB	Betriebs-Berater
Beav.	Beavan's Rolls Court Reports (1838-66)
Betr.	Der Betrieb
BGB	Bürgerliches Gesetzbuch (German Civil Code)
BGBl	Bundesgesetzblatt (Ger.) Federal Law Gazette
BGH	Bundesgerichtshof (German Supreme Court)
BGHZ	Entscheidungen des Bundesgerichtshofs in Zivilsachen
B.I.B.D.C.	Bulletin Institut Belge Droit Comparé
BMJ	Boletim do Ministerio da Justica (Portugal)
Building L.R.	Building Law Reports (U.K.)

BVerfG	Bundesverfassungsgericht (German Federal Constitutional Court.
BW	Burgerlijk Wetboek
C.A.	Court of Appeal
Camb.L.J.	Cambridge Law Journal (1921–)
Camp.	Campbell's Nisi Prius Reports (1808-1816)
Cass.	Cour de cassation (Belgium, France, Italy, Luxembourg)
Cass.civ.1	Cour de cassation (1st civil chamber)
Cass.civ.2	Cour de cassation (2nd civil chamber)
Cass.civ.3	Cour de cassation (3rd civil chamber)
Cass.com.	Cour de cassation (Chambre commerciale et financière)
Cass.req.	Cour de cassation (Chambre des requêtes)
Cass.soc.	Cour de cassation (Chambre sociale)
CBns	Common Bench (new series)
CC	Civil Code (Belgium, France, Greece, Italy, Luxembourg, Portugal, Spain, Switzerland)
C.C.Proc.	Code of Civil Procedure (Belgium, France, Germany, Greece, Portugal)
CDC	Cuaternos de Derecho y Comercio
cf.	confer
Chap.	Chapter
Ch.App.	Chancery Appeal Reports
Ch.D.	Chancery Division (1875-1890) Law Reports
Ch.	Chancery Division (1891–) Law Reports
CISG	United Nations Convention on Contracts for the International Sale of Goods
Civ.	See Cass.Civ.
CJ	Colectanea de jurisprudência (Portugal)
Cm	Command Papers 6th series (1987-)
Cmnd.	Command Papers 5th series (1957-86)
C.L.R.	Commonwealth Law Reports (Australia)
Co.	Company
Com.	See Cass.com.
Comm.C.	Commercial Code (Belgium, France, Spain, Portugal))
Corp.	Corporation
C&P	Carrington & Payne's Nisi Prius Reports (1823-1841)
C.P.D	Law Reports, Common Pleas Division (1875-1880)
D.	Recueil Dalloz
D.H.	Recueil hebdomadaire Dalloz (1924-1940)
diss.	Dissertation
D.Jur.	Répertoire Dalloz de juriprudence générale
D.L.R.	Dominion Law Reports (Canada)
D.P.	Dalloz périodique
Dr. & Sm.	Drewry & Smale's Vice-Chancellor's Reports (1860-1865)
E. & B.	Ellis & Blackburn's Queen's Bench Reports (1852-58)
ECJ	European Court of Justice

ECR	European Court Reports
ed.	edition
E&E	Ellis & Ellis' Queens Bench Reports (1858-61)
e.g.	exempli gratia
EEN	Ephimeris Hellinon Nomikon (Journal of Greek Jurists)
EKG	Einheitliches Kaufgesetz (Uniform Law of Sales)
Enc.giur.	Enciclopedia giuridica
Enc.dir.	Enciclopedia del diritto
END	Epitheonissi Nautiliakon Dikaion (Review of Maritime Law)
E.R.	English Reports
Erm.AK	Commentary to the Greek Civil Code
Eur. T.S.	European Treaty Series
EvBl	Evidenz blatt der Rechtsmittelentscheidungen (pair of Osterreichisehe Juristenzeitung)
EVHGB	Verordnung zur Einführung handelsrechtlicher Vorschriften im Lande Österreich (Implementation of German Commercial Code in Austria in 1938, published RGBL 1938 I 1999)
Ex.	Exchequer Reports
Exch.	Exchequer Reports
Ex.D.	Exchequer Division (Law Reports, 1875-80)
F.	Fraser, Session Cases, 5th series (1898-1906)
Fasc.	Fascicule
ff.	following
Foro It.	Il Foro Italiano
F.Supp.	Federal Supplement (United States, 1932–)
Gaz.Pal.	Gazette du Palais
Giust.civ.	Giustizia civile
GmbH	Gesellschaft mit beschränkter Haftung
Harm.	Harmenopoulos
HD	Højesteretsdomme (Danish Supreme Court)
H.L.	House of Lords
Hell.Dni.	Helliniki Dikaiosyni
HGB	Handelsgesetzbuch (Austrian and German Commercial Codes)
ibid.	ibidem
IECL	International Encyclopedia of Comparative Law
I.H.	Inner House of Court of Session
I.L.R.M.	Irish Law Reports Monthly (1981–)
I.L.T.R.	Irish Law Times Reports (1867–)
I.R.	Irish Reports (1894–)
Ir.Jur.Rep.	Irish Jurist Reports (1935–)
I.R.L:R.	Industrial Relations Law Reports (1972–)
J.	Mr.Justice (Judge of English High Court)
JBl	Juristiche Blätten (Austria)
J.C.B./B.R.H.	Jurisprudence Commerciale de Bruxelles/ Belgische Rechtsraak in Handelzaken

J.Cl.	Jurisclasseur
J.Cl.civ.	Jurisclasseur civil (civil cases)
J.C.P.	Jurisclasseur périodique – Semaine juridique
J.L.	Jurisprudence de la Cour d'Appel de Liège
J.T.	Journal des Tribunaux
J.Cl.Resp.Civ	Jurisclasseur Responsabilité Civile
J.P.A R.M.A.	[Belgian court report?] Jurisprudence du Port d'Anvers/recht-spraak van de Haven van Antwerpen
K.B.	King's Bench Division (1891–) Law Reports
KKO	Korkein oikens (Finland)
KSchG	Austrian Consumer Protection Act of 8 March 1979
Law Q.R.	Law Quarterly Review (1885–)
lit.	litera
L.J.	Lord Justice (Judge of English Court of Appeal)
L.J.Ch.	Law Journal Reports, Chancery Division (1883-1949)
L.J.K.B.	Law Journal Reports, King's Bench Division (1883-1949)
Lloyd's Rep.	Lloyd's List Reports (1951–)
LM	Lindenmaier-Möhring Nachschlagewerk des Bundesgerichtshofes (German Supreme Court)
loc.cit.	loco citato
L.R.	Law Reports (1865–)
Ltd.	Limited
Mass.Foro It	Massimario de Foro Italiano
Mer.	Merivale (1815-1817)
Mich.L.Rev.	Michigan Law Review (1902–)
Modern L.R.	Modern Law Review (1937–)
NBW	Nieuw Nederlands Burgerlijk Wetboek
N.C.P.C.	Nouveau Code de Procedure Civile
ND	Neon Dikaion (New Law)
n.	note
Ned.Jur.	Nederlandse Juresprudentie
NJA	Nytt Juridiskt Arkiv (Swedish Supreme Court Annual, 1874–)
NJW	Neue Juristische Wochenschrift
no.	number
NoB	Nomiko Vima
NV	Naamloze vennootschap
ÖBA	Österreichisches Bankar
obs.	observation
OGH	Oberster Gerichtshof (Austrian Supreme Court)
O.H.	Outer House of Court of Session
O.J.E.C.	Official Journal of the European Communities
OLG	Oberlandesgericht (German Court of Appeal)
OLGE	Entscheidungen der Oberlandesgerichte
op.cit.	opus ciratum
Ord.	Ordonnance

P.	Pacific Reporter
p.	page(s)
Pa.	Pennsylvania
para.	paragraph
Pas.	Pasicrisie (Belgium, Luxembourg)
P.D.	Probate Division (1875-1890) Law Reports
Principles	The Principles of European Contract Law
Q.B.	Queen's Bench Division (1891–) Law Reports
Q.B.D.	Queen's Bench Division (1875-1890) Law Reports
R	Rettie's Session Cases (Scotland, 1873-98)
RabelZ	Rabels Zeitschrift für ausländisches und internationales Privatrecht
RAJ	Reperteri Aranzadi de Jurisprudencia (Spanish Supreme Court)
R.C.J.B.	Revue Critiques de Jurisprudence Belge
RDC/TBH	Revue de droit commercial/Tijdschrift voor Belgisch Handelsrecht
RDIDC	Revue de droit international et du droit comparé
ref(s).	reference(s)
Rel.	Tribunal da Relaçã (Portugese Court of Appeal)
Rep.Droit civ.	Répertoire Dalloz de droit civil
Resp.civ.prev.	Responsabilità civile a prevdenza
Rev.	Revue
Rev.crt.d.i.p.	Revue critique de droit international privé
Rev.trim.dr.civ.	Revue trimestrielle de droit civil
RG	Reichsgericht (German Supreme Court 1871-1945)
RGDC/TBBR	Revue générale de droit civil/Tijdschrift voor Belgisch Burgerlijk Recht
RGRK	Reichsgerichtsräte-Kommentar zum Bürgerlichen Gesetzbuch
RGZ	Entscheidungen des Reichsgerichts in Zivilsachen
Riv.Cir.Tra.	Rivista Circulazione e Trasporti
Riv.dir.comm.	Rivista del diritto commerciale 1903-
Rn.	Randnummer
ROHG	Reichsoberhandelsgericht (German Commercial Supreme Court (–1871)
ROHGE	Entscheidungen des Reichsoberhandelsgerichts
Rob.	Robinson's Scottish Appeal Cases (1840-41)
RPD	Revista de Derecho Privado
RPfleger	Der Rechtspfleger
R.W.	Rechtskundig Weekblad
RZ	Österreichische Richterzeitung
Rz	Randzeichen
S.	Recueil Sirey
S.	Shaw's cases (Scotland).
s.	section(s)
SA	Société Anonyme

S.C.	Session Cases
Sch.	Schedule(s)
SCLR	Scottish Civil Law Reports
sent.	sentence(s)
seq.	sequentia
Sh.Ct.	Sheriff Court
SGA	Sale of Goods Act
SI	Statutory Instrument (U.K.)
SLT	Scots Law Times
Som.	Sommaire
StGB	Strafgesetzbuch (Austrian and German Criminal Codes)
STJ	Supremo Tribunal de Justiça (Portugese Supreme Court)
SZ	Sammlung der Entscheidungen des Östereichischen Obersten Gerichtshofes in Zivil- und Justizverwaltungssachen
TBH/RDC	Tijdschrift voor Belgisch Handelsrecht/Revue de droit commerciale
TBBR/RGDC	Tijdschrift voor Belgisch Burgerlijk Recht/Revue générale de droit civil
Th.	Thesis
T.L.R.	Times Law Reports
TPR	Tijdschrift voor Privaatrecht
T.S.	Tribunale Supremo
Trib.	Tribunal
Trib. comm.	Tribunal de commerce
UCC	Uniform Commercial Code (United States)
U.f.R.	Ugeskrift for Retsvæsen (Denmark)
ULIS	Uniform Law on the International Sale of Goods
Unidroit	Unidroit Principles of International Commercial Contracts
Univ.	University
unrep.	unreported
v.	versus
VersR	Versicherungsrecht
Vol.	Volume
WBl	Wirtschaftsrechtliche Blätter (Austria)
W.L.R.	Weekly Law Reports
W.M.	Wertpapier-Mitteilungen
Yale L.J.	Yale Law Journal (1891–)
Y.C.A.	Yearbook of Commercial Arbitration
ZPO	Zivilprozeßordnung (Austria and Germany)

PRINCIPLES OF EUROPEAN CONTRACT LAW

TEXT OF ARTICLES IN ENGLISH AND FRENCH

CHAPTER 1

General Provisions

Section 1: Scope of the Principles

ARTICLE 1:101: APPLICATION OF THE PRINCIPLES

(1) These Principles are intended to be applied as general rules of contract law in the European Union.
(2) These Principles will apply when the parties have agreed to incorporate them into their contract or that their contract is to be governed by them.
(3) These Principles may be applied when the parties:
    (a) have agreed that their contract is to be governed by "general principles of law", the "lex mercatoria" or the like; or
    (b) have not chosen any system or rules of law to govern their contract.
(4) These Principles may provide a solution to the issue raised where the system or rules of law applicable do not do so.

ARTICLE 1:102: FREEDOM OF CONTRACT

(1) Parties are free to enter into a contract and to determine its contents, subject to the requirements of good faith and fair dealing, and the mandatory rules established by these Principles.
(2) The parties may exclude the application of any of the Principles or derogate from or vary their effects, except as otherwise provided by these Principles.

ARTICLE 1:103: MANDATORY LAW

(1) Where the law otherwise applicable so allows, the parties may choose to have their contract governed by the Principles, with the effect that national mandatory rules are not applicable.
(2) Effect should nevertheless be given to those mandatory rules of national, supranational and international law which, according to the relevant rules of private international law, are applicable irrespective of the law governing the contract.

CHAPITRE 1

Dispositions générales

Section 1: Objet des Principes

ARTICLE 1:101: APPLICATIONS DES PRINCIPES

(1) Les présents Principes sont destinés à s'appliquer en tant que règles générales du droit des contrats dans le'Union européenne.
(2) Ils s'appliquent lorsque les parties sont convenues de les incorporer à leur contrat ou d'y soumettre celui-ci.
(3) Ils peuvent recevoir application lorsque les parties
   (a) sont convenues que leur contrat serait régi par "les principes généraux du droit", la *"lex mercatoria"* ou une expression similaire,
   (b) ou n'ont pas choisi de système ou de règles de droit devant régir leur contrat.
(4) Ils peuvent, en cas d'insuffisance du système ou des règles de droit applicables, procurer la solution de la question posée.

ARTICLE 1:102: LIBERTÉ CONTRACTUELLE

(1) Les parties sont libres de conclure un contrat et d'en déterminer le contenu, sous réserve des exigences de la bonne foi et des règles impératives posées par les présents Principes.
(2) Les parties peuvent exclure l'application d'un quelconque des présents Principes ou y déroger ou en modifier les effets, à moins que les Principes n'en disposent autrement.

ARTICLE 1:103: RÈGLES IMPÉRATIVES

(1) Lorsque le droit applicable le permet, les parties peuvent choisir de soumettre leur contrat aux Principes de telle sorte que les règles impératives nationales ne s'appliquent pas.
(2) Elles doivent toutefois respecter les règles impératives du droit national, supra-national ou international qui, selon les règles pertinentes du droit international privé, s'appliquent indépendamment du droit qui régit le contrat.

ARTICLE 1:104: APPLICATION TO QUESTIONS OF CONSENT

(1) The existence and validity of the agreement of the parties to adopt or incorporate these Principles shall be determined by these Principles.

(2) Nevertheless, a party may rely upon the law of the country in which it has its habitual residence to establish that it did not consent if it appears from the circumstances that it would not be reasonable to determine the effect of the party's conduct in accordance with these Principles.

ARTICLE 1:105: USAGES AND PRACTICES

(1) The parties are bound by any usage to which they have agreed and by any practice they have established between themselves.

(2) The parties are bound by a usage which would be considered generally applicable by persons in the same situation as the parties, except where the application of such usage would be unreasonable.

ARTICLE 1:106: INTERPRETATION AND SUPPLEMENTATION

(1) These Principles should be interpreted and developed in accordance with their purposes. In particular, regard should be had to the need to promote good faith and fair dealing, certainty in contractual relationships and uniformity of application.

(2) Issues within the scope of these Principles but not expressly settled by them are so far as possible to be settled in accordance with the ideas underlying the Principles. Failing this, the legal system applicable by virtue of the rules of private international law is to be applied.

ARTICLE 1:107: APPLICATION OF THE PRINCIPLES BY WAY OF ANALOGY

These Principles apply with appropriate modifications to agreements to modify or end a contract, to unilateral promises and to other statements and conduct indicating intention.

ARTICLE 1:104: APPLICATION AUX QUESTIONS DE CONSENTEMENT

(1) L'existence et la validité de l'accord par lequel les parties adoptent ou incorporent les présents Principes sont régies par ceux-ci .

(2) Néanmoins, une partie peut se fonder sur le droit du pays où elle a sa résidence habituelle afin d'établir qu'elle n'a pas consenti s'il résulte des circonstances qu'il ne serait pas raisonnable d'apprécier les conséquences de son comportement conformément aux présents Principes.

ARTICLE 1:105: USAGES ET PRATIQUES

(1) Les parties sont liées par les usages auxquels elles ont consenti et par les pratiques qu'elles ont établies entre elles.

(2) Elles sont liées par tout usage que des personnes placées dans la même situation qu'elles tiendraient pour généralement applicable, à moins que son application ne soit déraisonnable.

ARTICLE 1:106: INTERPRÉTATION ET COMBLEMENT DES LACUNES

(1) Les présents Principes devront être interprétés et développés conformément à leurs objectifs. On aura égard en particulier à la nécessité de promouvoir la bonne foi, la sécurité des relations contractuelles et l'uniformité d'application.

(2) Les questions qui entrent dans le champ d'application des présents Principes mais que ceux-ci ne tranchent pas expressément seront, dans la mesure du possible, réglées conformément aux idées dont ils s'inspirent. A défaut, on appliquera le système de droit que désignent les règles du droit international privé.

ARTICLE 1:107: APPLICATION DES PRINCIPES PAR ANALOGIE

Les présents Principes s'appliquent avec les modifications appropriées aux accords qui tendent à modifier ou résilier un contrat, aux promesses unilatérales ainsi qu'aux autres déclarations ou comportements indiquant une intention.

Section 2: General Duties

ARTICLE 1:201: GOOD FAITH AND FAIR DEALING

(1) Each party must act in accordance with good faith and fair dealing.
(2) The parties may not exclude or limit this duty.

ARTICLE 1:202: DUTY TO CO-OPERATE

Each party owes to the other a duty to co-operate in order to give full effect to the contract.

Section 2: Devoirs généraux

ARTICLE 1:201: BONNE FOI

(1) Chaque partie est tenue d'agir conformément aux exigences de la bonne foi.
(2) Les parties ne peuvent exclure ce devoir ni le limiter.

ARTICLE 1:202: DEVOIR DE COLLABORATION

Chaque partie doit à l'autre une collaboration qui permette au contrat de produire son plein effet.

Section 3: Terminology and Other Provisions

ARTICLE 1:301: MEANING OF TERMS

In these Principles, except where the context otherwise requires:
(1) 'act' includes omission;
(2) 'court' includes arbitral tribunal;
(3) an 'intentional' act includes an act done recklessly;
(4) 'non-performance' denotes any failure to perform an obligation under the contract, whether or not excused, and includes delayed performance, defective performance and failure to co-operate in order to give full effect to the contract;
(5) a matter is 'material' if it is one which a reasonable person in the same situation as one party ought to have known would influence the other party in its decision whether to contract on the proposed terms or to contract at all;
(6) 'written' statements include communications made by telegram, telex, telefax and electronic mail and other means of communication capable of providing a readable record of the statement on both sides

ARTICLE 1:302: REASONABLENESS

Under these Principles reasonableness is to be judged by what persons acting in good faith and in the same situation as the parties would consider to be reasonable. In particular, in assessing what is reasonable the nature and purpose of the contract, the circumstances of the case and the usages and practices of the trades or professions involved should be taken into account.

Section 3: Terminologie et autres dispositions

ARTICLE 1:301: DÉFINITIONS

Dans les présents Principes :
(1) le terme "acte" s'applique aussi à une omission,
(2) le terme "tribunal" s'applique aussi au tribunal arbitral,
(3) le terme "intentionnel" s'applique aussi à une action inexcusable,
(4) le terme "inexécution" dénote le fait de manquer à exécuter une obligation issue du contrat, qu'il bénéficie ou non d'une exonération, et s'applique aussi à une exécution tardive ou défectueuse et au refus d'une collaboration qui permette au contrat de produire son plein effet,
(5) un point "substantiel" est celui dont une personne raisonnable, placée dans la même situation qu'une partie, aurait dû savoir qu'il influencerait le cocontractant quant à sa décision de contracter aux conditions proposées ou de conclure le contrat;
(6) les déclarations par "écrit" incluent les communications faites par télégramme, télex, télécopie et courrier électronique, et les autres modes de communication qui sont de nature à procurer de part et d'autre un enregistrement pouvant être lu,
à moins que le contexte n'impose une interprétation différente.

ARTICLE 1:302: CARACTÈRE RAISONNABLE

Doit être tenu pour raisonnable aux termes des présents Principes ce que des personnes de bonne foi placées dans la même situation que les parties regarderaient comme tel. On a égard en particulier à la nature et au but du contrat, aux circonstances de l'espèce et aux usages et pratiques des professions ou branches d'activité concernées.

ARTICLE 1:303: NOTICE

(1) Any notice may be given by any means, whether in writing or otherwise, appropriate to the circumstances.

(2) Subject to paragraphs (4) and (5), any notice becomes effective when it reaches the addressee.

(3) A notice reaches the addressee when it is delivered to it or to its place of business or mailing address, or, if it does not have a place of business or mailing address, to its habitual residence.

(4) If one party gives notice to the other because of the other's non-performance or because such non-performance is reasonably anticipated by the first party, and the notice is properly dispatched or given, a delay or inaccuracy in the transmission of the notice or its failure to arrive does not prevent it from having effect. The notice shall have effect from the time at which it would have arrived in normal circumstances.

(5) A notice has no effect if a withdrawal of it reaches the addressee before or at the same time as the notice.

(6) In this Article, 'notice' includes the communication of a promise, statement, offer, acceptance, demand, request or other declaration.

ARTICLE 1:304: COMPUTATION OF TIME

(1) A period of time set by a party in a written document for the addressee to reply or take other action begins to run from the date stated as the date of the document. If no date is shown, the period begins to run from the moment the document reaches the addressee.

(2) Official holidays and official non-working days occurring during the period are included in calculating the period. However, if the last day of the period is an official holiday or official non-working day at the address of the addressee, or at the place where a prescribed act is to be performed, the period is extended until the first following working day in that place.

(3) Periods of time expressed in days, weeks, months or years shall begin at 00.00 on the next day and shall end at 24.00 on the last day of the period; but any reply that has to reach the party which set the period must arrive, or any other act which is to be done must be completed, by the normal close of business in the relevant place on the last day of the period.

ARTICLE 1:303: NOTIFICATIONS

(1) Une notification peut être faite par tout moyen approprié aux circonstances, que ce soit par écrit ou d'une autre façon.

(2) Sous réserve des dispositions des alinéas (4) et (5), une notification produit effet lorsqu'elle atteint son destinataire.

(3) Une notification atteint son destinataire lorsqu'elle lui est remise, ou est remise à son établissement ou son adresse postale, ou, si elle n'a pas d'établissement ou d'adresse postale, à sa résidence habituelle.

(4) Si une partie fait une notification à l'autre en conséquence de l'inexécution de cette dernière ou parce qu'il est raisonnable de prévoir l'inexécution, et que la notification est dûment faite ou expédiée, un retard ou une inexactitude dans sa transmission, ou le fait qu'elle ne parvienne pas à destination, ne l'empêche pas de produire effet. La notification produit effet au moment où, dans les conditions normales, elle serait parvenue à destination.

(5) Une notification ne produit aucun effet si sa révocation atteint son destinataire avant elle, ou au même moment.

(6) Dans le présent article, le terme "notification" s'applique aussi à la communication d'une promesse, une déclaration, une offre, une acceptation, une demande, une requête ou toute autre énonciation.

ARTICLE 1:304: COMPUTATION DES DÉLAIS

(1) Le délai qu'une partie fixe dans un document écrit à son destinataire pour qu'il réponde ou accomplisse un autre acte a pour origine la date indiquée comme étant celle du document. En l'absence de date, le délai a pour origine le moment où le document atteint son destinataire.

(2) Les jours fériés ou chômés sont comptés dans le délai. Toutefois, le délai qui expirerait un jour qui est férié ou chômé à l'adresse du destinataire ou au lieu où un acte imposé doit être exécuté, est prorogé jusqu'au premier jour ouvrable suivant en ce lieu.

(3) Lorsqu'un délai est exprimé en jours, en semaines, en mois ou en années, il a pour origine le jour suivant la date qui le fait courir, à zéro heure, et expire le dernier jour à vingt-quatre heures; mais la réponse qui doit parvenir à la partie qui a fixé le délai doit atteindre celle-ci, ou l'acte imposé doit être accompli, le dernier jour du délai, avant l'heure normale de cessation des affaires au lieu approprié.

ARTICLE 1:305: IMPUTED KNOWLEDGE AND INTENTION

If any person who with a party's assent was involved in making a contract, or who was entrusted with performance by a party or performed with its assent:

(a) knew or foresaw a fact, or ought to have known or foreseen it; or

(b) acted intentionally or with gross negligence, or not in accordance with good faith and fair dealing,

this knowledge, foresight or behaviour is imputed to the party itself.

ARTICLE 1:305: IMPUTATION DE CONNAISSANCE ET D'INTENTION

Si un tiers qui est intervenu dans la conclusion d'un contrat avec l'accord d'une partie, ou à qui celle-ci a confié l'exécution ou qui a exécuté avec son accord,
(a) a connu ou prévu un fait, ou aurait dû le connaître ou le prévoir,
(b) ou a accompli un acte intentionnel ou constitutif d'une faute lourde, ou non con-
    forme aux exigences de la bonne foi,
la connaissance, la prévision ou la conduite est imputée à la partie elle-même.

CHAPTER 2

Formation

Section 1 : General Provisions

ARTICLE 2:101: CONDITIONS FOR THE CONCLUSION OF A CONTRACT

(1) A contract is concluded if:
    (a) the parties intend to be legally bound, and
    (b) they reach a sufficient agreement
    without any further requirement.
(2) A contract need not be concluded or evidenced in writing nor is it subject to any other requirement as to form. The contract may be proved by any means, including witnesses.

ARTICLE 2:102: INTENTION

The intention of a party to be legally bound by contract is to be determined from the party's statements or conduct as they were reasonably understood by the other party.

ARTICLE 2:103: SUFFICIENT AGREEMENT

(1) There is sufficient agreement if the terms:
    (a) have been sufficiently defined by the parties so that the contract can be enforced, or
    (b) can be determined under these Principles.
(2) However, if one of the parties refuses to conclude a contract unless the parties have agreed on some specific matter, there is no contract unless agreement on that matter has been reached.

CHAPITRE 2

Formation

Section 1: Dispositions générales

ARTICLE 2:101: CONDITIONS POUR LA CONCLUSION D'UN CONTRAT

(1) Un contrat est conclu dès lors que
   (a) les parties entendaient être liées juridiquement,
   (b) et sont parvenues à un accord suffisant,
   sans qu'aucune autre condition soit requise.
(2) Le contrat n'a pas à être conclu ni constaté par écrit et n'est soumis à aucune autre exigence de forme. Il peut être prouvé par tous moyens, y compris par témoins.

ARTICLE 2:102: INTENTION

L'intention d'une partie d'être liée juridiquement par contrat résulte de ses déclarations ou de son comportement, tels que le cocontractant pouvait raisonnablement les entendre.

ARTICLE 2:103: ACCORD SUFFISANT

(1) Un accord est suffisant si ses termes
   (a) ont été définis par les parties de telle sorte que le contrat puisse être exécuté,
   (b) ou peuvent être déterminés en vertu des présents Principes.
(2) Si toutefois une des parties refuse de conclure un contrat faute d'accord sur un point particulier, il n'y a point de contrat si l'accord sur ce point ne s'est pas réalisé.

ARTICLE 2:104: TERMS NOT INDIVIDUALLY NEGOTIATED

(1) Contract terms which have not been individually negotiated may be invoked against a party which did not know of them only if the party invoking them took reasonable steps to bring them to the other party's attention before or when the contract was concluded.
(2) Terms are not brought appropriately to a party's attention by a mere reference to them in a contract document, even if that party signs the document.

ARTICLE 2:105: MERGER CLAUSE

(1) If a written contract contains an individually negotiated clause stating that the writing embodies all the terms of the contract (a merger clause), any prior statements, undertakings or agreements which are not embodied in the writing do not form part of the contract.
(2) If the merger clause is not individually negotiated it will only establish a presumption that the parties intended that their prior statements, undertakings or agreements were not to form part of the contract. This rule may not be excluded or restricted.
(3) The parties' prior statements may be used to interpret the contract. This rule may not be excluded or restricted except by an individually negotiated clause.
(4) A party may by its statements or conduct be precluded from asserting a merger clause to the extent that the other party has reasonably relied on them.

ARTICLE 2:106: WRITTEN MODIFICATION ONLY

(1) A clause in a written contract requiring any modification or ending by agreement to be made in writing establishes only a presumption that an agreement to modify or end the contract is not intended to be legally binding unless it is in writing.
(2) A party may by its statements or conduct be precluded from asserting such a clause to the extent that the other party has reasonably relied on them.

ARTICLE 2:107: PROMISES BINDING WITHOUT ACCEPTANCE

A promise which is intended to be legally binding without acceptance is binding.

ARTICLE 2:104: CLAUSES N'AYANT PAS ÉTÉ L'OBJET D'UNE NÉGOCIATION INDIVIDUELLE

(1) Les clauses d'un contrat qui n'ont pas été l'objet d'une négociation individuelle ne peuvent être invoquées à l'encontre d'une partie qui ne les connaissait pas que si la partie qui les invoque a pris des mesures raisonnables pour attirer sur elles l'attention de l'autre avant la conclusion du contrat ou lors de cette conclusion.
(2) La simple référence faite à une clause par un document contractuel, n'attire pas sur elle de façon satisfaisante l'attention du cocontractant, alors même que ce dernier signe le document.

ARTICLE 2:105: CLAUSE D'INTÉGRALITÉ

(1) Si un contrat écrit contient une clause qui a été l'objet d'une négociation individuelle aux termes de laquelle l'écrit renferme toutes les conditions convenues (clause d'intégralité), les déclarations, engagements ou accords antérieurs que ne renferme pas l'écrit ne s'intègrent pas au contrat.
(2) La clause d'intégralité qui n'a pas été l'objet d'une négociation individuelle fait seulement présumer que les parties entendaient que leurs déclarations, engagements ou accords antérieurs ne s'intègrent pas au contenu du contrat. La présente règle ne peut être exclue ou restreinte.
(3) Les déclarations antérieures des parties peuvent servir à l'interprétation du contrat. La présente règle ne peut être exclue ou restreinte que par une clause objet d'une négociation individuelle.
(4) Les déclarations ou le comportement de l'une des parties peuvent l'empêcher de se prévaloir d'une clause d'intégralité si l'autre partie s'est fondée raisonnablement sur eux.

ARTICLE 2:106: MODIFICATION PAR ÉCRIT

(1) La clause d'un contrat écrit qui stipule que toute modification ou résiliation amiable sera faite par écrit fait seulement présumer que l'accord tendant à modifier ou résilier le contrat n'est juridiquement obligatoire que s'il est fait par écrit.
(2) Les déclarations ou le comportement de l'une des parties peuvent l'empêcher de se prévaloir de cette clause si l'autre partie s'est fondée raisonnablement sur eux.

ARTICLE 2:107: PROMESSES OBLIGATOIRES SANS ACCEPTATION

La promesse qui tend à être juridiquement obligatoire sans acceptation lie son auteur.

Section 2: Offer and Acceptance

ARTICLE 2:201: OFFER

(1) A proposal amounts to an offer if:
    (a) it is intended to result in a contract if the other party accepts it, and
    (b) it contains sufficiently definite terms to form a contract.
(2) An offer may be made to one or more specific persons or to the public.
(3) A proposal to supply goods or services at stated prices made by a professional supplier in a public advertisement or a catalogue, or by a display of goods, is presumed to be an offer to sell or supply at that price until the stock of goods, or the supplier's capacity to supply the service, is exhausted.

ARTICLE 2:202: REVOCATION OF AN OFFER

(1) An offer may be revoked if the revocation reaches the offeree before it has dispatched its acceptance or, in cases of acceptance by conduct, before the contract has been concluded under Article 2:205(2) or (3).
(2) An offer made to the public can be revoked by the same means as were used to make the offer.
(3) However, a revocation of an offer is ineffective if:
    (a) the offer indicates that it is irrevocable; or
    (b) it states a fixed time for its acceptance; or
    (c) it was reasonable for the offeree to rely on the offer as being irrevocable and the offeree has acted in reliance on the offer.

ARTICLE 2:203: REJECTION

When a rejection of an offer reaches the offeror, the offer lapses.

Section 2: Offre et acceptation

ARTICLE 2:201: OFFRE

(1) Une proposition constitue une offre lorsque
    (a) elle indique la volonté d'aboutir à un contrat en cas d'acceptation
    (b) et renferme des conditions suffisamment précises pour qu'un contrat soit formé.
(2) L'offre peut être faite à une ou plusieurs personnes déterminées ou au public.
(3) La proposition, faite par un fournisseur professionnel, dans une publicité ou un catalogue ou du fait de l'exposition de marchandises, de procurer des biens ou services à un prix fixé, est censée constituer une offre de vendre ou de procurer les services à ce prix jusqu'à épuisement du stock de marchandises ou des possibilités de rendre le service.

ARTICLE 2:202: RÉVOCATION DE L'OFFRE

(1) L'offre peut être révoquée si la révocation parvient à son destinataire avant que celui-ci n'ait expédié son acceptation ou, en cas d'acceptation du fait du comportement, avant que le contrat n'ait été conclu en vertu des alinéas (2) ou (3) de l'article 2:205.
(2) L'offre faite au public peut être révoquée de la même façon qu'elle avait été faite.
(3) La révocation est cependant sans effet
    (a) si l'offre indique qu'elle est irrévocable,
    (b) ou fixe un délai déterminé pour son acceptation,
    (c) ou si son destinataire était raisonnablement fondé à la croire irrévocable et s'il a agi sur la foi de l'offre.

ARTICLE 2:203: REJET DE L'OFFRE

L'offre prend fin lorsque son rejet parvient à l'offrant.

ARTICLE 2:204: ACCEPTANCE

(1) Any form of statement or conduct by the offeree is an acceptance if it indicates assent to the offer.
(2) Silence or inactivity does not in itself amount to acceptance.

ARTICLE 2:205: TIME OF CONCLUSION OF THE CONTRACT

(1) If an acceptance has been dispatched by the offeree the contract is concluded when the acceptance reaches the offeror.
(2) In the case of acceptance by conduct, the contract is concluded when notice of the conduct reaches the offeror.
(3) If by virtue of the offer, of practices which the parties have established between themselves, or of a usage, the offeree may accept the offer by performing an act without notice to the offeror, the contract is concluded when the performance of the act begins.

ARTICLE 2:206: TIME LIMIT FOR ACCEPTANCE

(1) In order to be effective, acceptance of an offer must reach the offeror within the time fixed by it.
(2) If no time has been fixed by the offeror acceptance must reach it within a reasonable time.
(3) In the case of an acceptance by an act of performance under Article 2:205(3), that act must be performed within the time for acceptance fixed by the offeror or, if no such time is fixed, within a reasonable time.

ARTICLE 2:207: LATE ACCEPTANCE

(1) A late acceptance is nonetheless effective as an acceptance if without delay the offeror informs the offeree that he treats it as such.
(2) If a letter or other writing containing a late acceptance shows that it has been sent in such circumstances that if its transmission had been normal it would have reached the offeror in due time, the late acceptance is effective as an acceptance unless, without delay, the offeror informs the offeree that it considers its offer as having lapsed.

ARTICLE 2:204: ACCEPTATION

(1) Constitue une acceptation toute déclaration ou comportement du destinataire indiquant qu'il acquiesce à l'offre.
(2) Le silence ou l'inaction ne peuvent à eux seuls valoir acceptation.

ARTICLE 2:205.: MOMENT DE CONCLUSION DU CONTRAT

(1) Si le destinataire de l'offre expédie son acceptation, le contrat est conclu lorsque celle-ci parvient à l'offrant.
(2) Si l'acceptation résulte d'un comportement, le contrat est conclu lorsque ce comportement parvient à la connaissance de l'offrant.
(3) Si, en vertu de l'offre, des pratiques établies entre les parties ou d'un usage, le destinataire peut accepter l'offre en accomplissant un acte sans notification à l'offrant, le contrat est conclu lorsque débute l'accomplissement de l'acte.

ARTICLE 2:206: DÉLAI D'ACCEPTATION

(1) L'acceptation d'une offre doit, pour produire effet, parvenir à l'offrant dans le délai qu'il a imparti.
(2) Si aucun délai n'a été fixé par l'offrant, l'acceptation doit lui parvenir dans un délai raisonnable.
(3) Si l'acceptation s'effectue par l'accomplissement d'un acte, conformément à l'alinéa (3) de l'article 2:205, cet accomplissement doit débuter dans le délai fixé par l'offrant ou, à défaut, dans un délai raisonnable.

ARTICLE 2:207: ACCEPTATION TARDIVE

(1) Une acceptation tardive n'en produit pas moins effet en tant qu'acceptation si l'offrant fait savoir sans retard au destinataire qu'il la tient pour telle.
(2) Si une lettre ou un écrit autre renfermant une acceptation tardive a été expédiée dans des circonstances telles que, si sa transmission avait été normale, elle serait parvenue à temps à l'offrant, l'acceptation tardive produit effet en tant qu'acceptation à moins que, sans retard, l'offrant n'informe le destinataire qu'il considère que son offre a pris fin.

ARTICLE 2:208: MODIFIED ACCEPTANCE

(1) A reply by the offeree which states or implies additional or different terms which would materially alter the terms of the offer is a rejection and a new offer.

(2) A reply which gives a definite assent to an offer operates as an acceptance even if it states or implies additional or different terms, provided these do not materially alter the terms of the offer. The additional or different terms then become part of the contract.

(3) However, such a reply will be treated as a rejection of the offer if:
  (a) the offer expressly limits acceptance to the terms of the offer; or
  (b) the offeror objects to the additional or different terms without delay; or
  (c) the offeree makes its acceptance conditional upon the offeror's assent to the additional or different terms, and the assent does not reach the offeree within a reasonable time.

ARTICLE 2:209: CONFLICTING GENERAL CONDITIONS

(1) If the parties have reached agreement except that the offer and acceptance refer to conflicting general conditions of contract, a contract is nonetheless formed. The general conditions form part of the contract to the extent that they are common in substance.

(2) However, no contract is formed if one party:
  (a) has indicated in advance, explicitly, and not by way of general conditions, that it does not intend to be bound by a contract on the basis of paragraph (1); or
  (b) without delay, informs the other party that it does not intend to be bound by such contract.

(3) General conditions of contract are terms which have been formulated in advance for an indefinite number of contracts of a certain nature, and which have not been individually negotiated between the parties.

ARTICLE 2:210: PROFESSIONAL'S WRITTEN CONFIRMATION

If professionals have concluded a contract but have not embodied it in a final document, and one without delay sends the other a writing which purports to be a confirmation of the contract but which contains additional or different terms, such terms will become part of the contract unless:
(a) the terms materially alter the terms of the contract, or
(b) the addressee objects to them without delay.

ARTICLE 2:208: MODIFICATION DE L'ACCEPTATION

(1) La réponse du destinataire qui énonce ou implique des adjonctions ou des modifications qui altéreraient substantiellement les termes de l'offre constitue un rejet de l'offre et une offre nouvelle.

(2) La réponse dont il est certain qu'elle acquiesce à l'offre mais qui énonce ou implique des adjonction ou modifications à celle-ci n'en constitue pas moins une acceptation si ces adjonctions ou modifications n'altèrent pas substantiellement les termes de l'offre. Les adjonctions ou modifications s'intègrent alors au contrat.

(3) La réponse sera cependant traitée comme un rejet de l'offre si
    (a) l'offre restreint expressément l'acceptation à ses termes mêmes,
    (b) l'offrant s'oppose sans retard à ces adjonctions ou modifications ,
    (c) ou le destinataire subordonne son acceptation à l'agrément donné par l'offrant aux adjonctions ou modifications et cet agrément ne lui parvient pas dans un délai raisonnable.

ARTICLE 2:209: INCOMPATIBILITÉ ENTRE CONDITIONS GÉNÉRALES

(1) Lorsque les parties sont parvenues à un accord mais que l'offre et l'acceptation renvoient à des conditions générales incompatibles, le contrat est néanmoins conclu. Les conditions générales s'intègrent au contrat pour autant qu'elles sont pour l'essentiel communes aux parties.

(2) Le contrat, cependant, n'est pas formé si une partie
    (a) a indiqué à l'avance, explicitement et non dans ses conditions générales, qu'elle ne veut pas être liée par contrat en vertu de l'alinéa premier,
    (b) ou informe ultérieurement et sans retard l'autre partie qu'elle n'entend pas être liée par le contrat.

(3) Les conditions générales du contrat sont les clauses qui ont été établies à l'avance par une partie pour un nombre indéfini de contrats d'une certaine nature et qui n'ont pas été l'objet d'une négociation individuelle entre les parties.

ARTICLE 2:210: CONFIRMATION ÉCRITE D'UN PROFESSIONNEL

Si des professionnels ont conclu un contrat mais ne l'ont pas renfermé dans un document définitif, et que sans retard l'un d'eux envoie à l'autre un écrit qui se veut la confirmation du contrat mais contient des adjonctions ou modifications, celles-ci s'intègrent au contrat à moins que
(a) elles n'en substantiellement les termes,
(b) ou que le destinataire ne s'y oppose sans retard.

ARTICLE 2:211: CONTRACTS NOT CONCLUDED THROUGH OFFER AND ACCEPTANCE

The rules in this Section apply with appropriate adaptations even though the process of conclusion of a contract cannot be analysed into offer and acceptance.

ARTICLE 2:211: CONTRATS NON CONCLUS PAR UNE OFFRE ET UNE ACCEPTATION

Quand bien même le processus de conclusion d'un contrat ne pourrait s'analyser en une offre et une acceptation, les règles de la présentes section s'appliquent, avec les adaptations appropriées.

Section 3: Liability for negotiations

ARTICLE 2:301: NEGOTIATIONS CONTRARY TO GOOD FAITH

(1) A party is free to negotiate and is not liable for failure to reach an agreement.
(2) However, a party which has negotiated or broken off negotiations contrary to good faith and fair dealing is liable for the losses caused to the other party.
(3) It is contrary to good faith and fair dealing, in particular, for a party to enter into or continue negotiations with no real intention of reaching an agreement with the other party.

ARTICLE 2:302: BREACH OF CONFIDENTIALITY

If confidential information is given by one party in the course of negotiations, the other party is under a duty not to disclose that information or use it for its own purposes whether or not a contract is subsequently concluded. The remedy for breach of this duty may include compensation for loss suffered and restitution of the benefit received by the other party.

Section 3: Responsabilité à l'occasion des négociations

ARTICLE 2:301: NÉGOCIATIONS CONTRAIRES À LA BONNE FOI

(1) Les parties sont libres de négocier et ne peuvent encourir de responsabilité pour ne pas être parvenues à un accord.

(2) Toutefois, la partie qui conduit ou rompt des négociations contrairement aux exigences de la bonne foi est responsable du préjudice qu'elle cause à l'autre partie.

(3) Il est contraire aux exigences de la bonne foi, notamment, pour une partie d'entamer ou de poursuivre des négociations sans avoir de véritable intention de parvenir à un accord avec l'autre.

ARTICLE 2:302: MANQUEMENT À LA CONFIDENTIALITÉ

Lorsqu'une information confidentielle est donnée par une partie au cours des négociations, l'autre est tenue de ne pas la divulguer ni l'utiliser à ses propres fins, qu'il y ait ou non conclusion du contrat. Le manquement à ce devoir peut ouvrir droit à la réparation du préjudice souffert et à la restitution du profit qu'en aurait retiré l'autre partie.

CHAPTER 3

Authority of Agents

Section 1 : General Provisions

ARTICLE 3:101 : SCOPE OF THE CHAPTER

(1) This Chapter governs the authority of an agent or other intermediary to bind its principal in relation to a contract with a third party.
(2) This Chapter does not govern an agent's authority bestowed by law or the authority of an agent appointed by a public or judicial authority.
(3) This Chapter does not govern the internal relationship between the agent or intermediary and its principal.

ARTICLE 3:102: CATEGORIES OF REPRESENTATION

(1) Where an agent acts in the name of a principal, the rules on direct representation apply (Section 2). It is irrelevant whether the principal's identity is revealed at the time the agent acts or is to be revealed later.
(2) Where an intermediary acts on instructions and on behalf of, but not in the name of, a principal, or where the third party neither knows nor has reason to know that the intermediary acts as an agent, the rules on indirect representation apply (Section 3).

CHAPITRE 3

Pouvoir de représentation

Section 1: Dispositions générales

ARTICLE 3:101: OBJET DU CHAPITRE

(1) Le présent chapitre régit le pouvoir d'un représentant ou d'un autre intermédiaire d'obliger le représenté en vertu d'un contrat avec un tiers.

(2) Le présent chapitre ne régit pas le pouvoir conféré par la loi à un représentant, ni celui d'un représentant nommé par une autorité publique ou judiciaire.

(3) Le présent chapitre ne régit pas les rapports entre le représentant ou intermédiaire et le représenté.

ARTICLE 3:102: ESPÈCES DE REPRÉSENTATION

(1) Lorsqu'un représentant agit au nom d'un représenté, les règles sur la représentation directe, qui font la matière de la section 2, reçoivent application. Il importe peu que l'identité du représenté soit révélée lorsque le représentant agit ou qu'elle doive être révélée ultérieurement.

(2) Lorsqu'un intermédiaire agit sur les instructions et pour le compte, mais non point au nom d'un représenté, ou lorsque le tiers ignore et n'a pas de raisons de savoir que l'intermédiaire agit en tant que représentant, les règles sur la représentation indirecte, qui font la matière de la section 3, reçoivent application.

Section 2: Direct Representation

ARTICLE 3:201: EXPRESS, IMPLIED AND APPARENT AUTHORITY

(1) The principal's grant of authority to an agent to act in its name may be express or may be implied from the circumstances.
(2) The agent has authority to perform all acts necessary in the circumstances to achieve the purposes for which the authority was granted.
(3) A person is to be treated as having granted authority to an apparent agent if the person's statements or conduct induce the third party reasonably and in good faith to believe that the apparent agent has been granted authority for the act performed by it.

ARTICLE 3:202: AGENT ACTING IN EXERCISE OF ITS AUTHORITY

Where an agent is acting within its authority as defined by Article 3:201, its acts bind the principal and the third party directly to each other. The agent itself is not bound to the third party.

ARTICLE 3:203: UNIDENTIFIED PRINCIPAL

If an agent enters into a contract in the name of a principal whose identity is to be revealed later, but fails to reveal that identity within a reasonable time after a request by the third party, the agent itself is bound by the contract.

Section 2: Représentation directe

ARTICLE 3:201: POUVOIR EXPRÈS, IMPLICITE ET APPARENT

(1) L'attribution au représentant, par le représenté, du pouvoir d'agir en son nom peut être exprès ou implicite, découlant des circonstances.
(2) Le représentant a le pouvoir d'accomplir tous les actes nécessaires à l'exécution de sa mission, compte tenu des circonstances.
(3) Celui dont les déclarations ou le comportement ont incité le tiers à croire de façon raisonnable et de bonne foi que le représentant apparent avait reçu pouvoir pour l'acte qu'il a accompli, est tenu pour avoir conféré le pouvoir.

ARTICLE 3:202: ACTION DU REPRÉSENTANT EN VERTU DE SES POUVOIRS

Lorsque le représentant agit dans la limite de ses pouvoirs tels qu'ils sont définis par l'article 3:201, ses actes lient directement le représenté et le tiers. Le représentant n'est pas engagé envers le tiers.

ARTICLE 3:203: REPRÉSENTÉ NON IDENTIFIÉ

Le représentant qui conclut un contrat au nom d'un représenté dont l'identité doit être révélée ultérieurement mais manque à révéler cette identité dans un délai raisonnable après que le tiers en ait fait la demande, est personnellement engagé par le contrat.

ARTICLE 3:204: AGENT ACTING WITHOUT OR OUTSIDE ITS AUTHORITY

(1) Where a person acting as an agent acts without authority or outside the scope of its authority, its acts are not binding upon the principal and the third party.

(2) Failing ratification by the principal according to Article 3:207, the agent is liable to pay the third party such damages as will place the third party in the same position as if the agent had acted with authority. This does not apply if the third party knew or could not have been unaware of the agent's lack of authority.

ARTICLE 3:205: CONFLICT OF INTEREST

(1) If a contract concluded by an agent involves the agent in a conflict of interest of which the third party knew or could not have been unaware, the principal may avoid the contract according to the provisions of Articles 4:112 to 4:116.

(2) There is presumed to be a conflict of interest where:
    (a) the agent also acted as agent for the third party; or
    (b) the contract was with itself in its personal capacity.

(3) However, the principal may not avoid the contract:
    (a) if it had consented to, or could not have been unaware of, the agent's so acting; or
    (b) if the agent had disclosed the conflict of interest to it and it had not objected within a reasonable time.

ARTICLE 3:206: SUBAGENCY

An agent has implied authority to appoint a subagent to carry out tasks which are not of a personal character and which it is not reasonable to expect the agent to carry out itself. The rules of this Section apply to the subagency; acts of the subagent which are within its and the agent's authority bind the principal and the third party directly to each other.

ARTICLE 3:207: RATIFICATION BY PRINCIPAL

(1) Where a person acting as an agent acts without authority or outside its authority, the principal may ratify the agent's acts.

(2) Upon ratification, the agent's acts are considered as having been authorised, without prejudice to the rights of other persons.

ARTICLE 3:204: ACTION DU REPRÉSENTANT SANS POUVOIR OU AU-DELÀ DE SON
POUVOIR;

(1) Lorsqu'une personne agit en qualité de représentant mais sans pouvoir ou au-delà de ses pouvoirs, ses actes ne lient pas le représenté et le tiers.

(2) En l'absence de ratification par le représenté conformément à l'article 3:207, le représentant est tenu de payer au tiers les dommages et intérêts qui rétabliront ce dernier dans la situation où il se serait trouvé si le représentant avait agi en vertu d'un pouvoir. Cette règle ne reçoit point application si le tiers avait ou aurait dû avoir connaissance du défaut de pouvoir.

ART. 3:205: CONFLIT D'INTÉRÊTS

(1) Si le contrat conclu par un représentant implique celui-ci dans un conflit d'intérêts que le tiers connaissait ou ne pouvait ignorer, le représenté peut annuler le contrat conformément aux dispositions des articles 4:112 à 4:116.

(2) Il y a présomption de conflit d'intérêts lorsque le représentant
    (a) a agi également en tant que représentant du tiers,
    (b) ou a contracté avec lui-même pour son propre compte.

(3) Le représenté ne peut cependant annuler le contrat
    (a) s'il a consenti à l'acte du représentant ou ne pouvait l'ignorer,
    (b) ou si le représentant lui a révélé le conflit et s'il n'a pas soulevé d'objection dans un délai raisonnable.

ART. 3:206: SUBSTITUTION DE REPRÉSENTANT

Le représentant a le pouvoir implicite de désigner un représentant substitué pour accomplir les tâches qui n'ont pas un caractère personnel et dont il n'est pas raisonnable de penser qu'il les accomplira personnellement. Les règles de la présente section s'appliquent à la représentation par substitution; les actes du représentant substitué qui entrent dans ses pouvoirs et dans ceux du représentant engagent directement le représenté et le tiers.

ARTICLE 3:207: RATIFICATION PAR LE REPRÉSENTÉ

(1) Les actes accomplis par un représentant sans pouvoir ou au-delà de son pouvoir peuvent être ratifiés par le représenté.

(2) Une fois ratifiés, les actes du représentant sont censés avoir été autorisés, sans préjudice du droit des autres intéressés.

Article 3:208: Third Party's Right with Respect to Confirmation of Authority

Where the statements or conduct of the principal gave the third party reason to believe that an act performed by the agent was authorised, but the third party is in doubt about the authorisation, it may send a written confirmation to the principal or request ratification from it. If the principal does not object or answer the request without delay, the agent's act is treated as having been authorised.

Article 3:209: Duration of Authority

(1) An agent's authority continues until the third party knows or ought to know that:
   (a) the agent's authority has been brought to an end by the principal, the agent, or both; or
   (b) the acts for which the authority had been granted have been completed, or the time for which it had been granted has expired; or
   (c) the agent has become insolvent or, where a natural person, has died or become incapacitated; or
   (d) the principal has become insolvent.
(2) The third party is considered to know that the agent's authority has been brought to an end under paragraph (1)(a) above if this has been communicated or publicised in the same manner in which the authority was originally communicated or publicised.
(3) However, the agent remains authorised for a reasonable time to perform those acts which are necessary to protect the interests of the principal or its successors.

ARTICLE 3:208: DROITS DU TIERS À L'ÉGARD DE LA CONFIRMATION DU POUVOIR

Lorsque les déclarations ou le comportement du représenté ont donné au tiers raison de croire que le représentant avait pouvoir d'accomplir un acte, mais que le tiers a des doutes sur l'existence de ce pouvoir, il peut envoyer une confirmation écrite au représenté ou requérir de lui une ratification. Si le représenté ne s'oppose pas à la confirmation ou fait droit sans retard à la requête, l'acte du représentant est censé avoir été autorisé.

ARTICLE 3:209: DURÉE DU POUVOIR

(1) Le pouvoir d'un représentant subsiste jusqu'à ce que le tiers sache ou doive savoir que
   (a) ce pouvoir s'est éteint du fait du représentant, du représenté ou des deux,
   (b) les actes pour lesquels le pouvoir avait été conféré ont reçu complète exécution, ou la durée pour laquelle il avait été conféré est expirée,
   (c) le représentant devient insolvable ou, si c'est une personne physique, décède ou devient incapable,
   (d) ou le représenté devient insolvable.
(2) Le tiers est censé savoir que le pouvoir du représentant s'est éteint en vertu de l'alinéa premier, lettre (a), si la cause en a été communiquée ou rendue publique comme l'avait été l'attribution du pouvoir.
(3) Le représentant conserve toutefois, pendant une durée raisonnable, le pouvoir d'accomplir les actes nécessaires à la protection des intérêts du représentant ou de ses ayants-droit.

Section 3: Indirect Representation

ARTICLE 3:301: INTERMEDIARIES NOT ACTING IN THE NAME OF A PRINCIPAL

(1) Where an intermediary acts:
   (a) on instructions and on behalf, but not in the name, of a principal, or
   (b) on instructions from a principal but the third party does not know and has no reason to know this,
   the intermediary and the third party are bound to each other.
(2) The principal and the third party are bound to each other only under the conditions set out in Articles 3:302 to 3:304.

ARTICLE 3:302: INTERMEDIARY'S INSOLVENCY OR FUNDAMENTAL NON-PERFORMANCE TO PRINCIPAL

If the intermediary becomes insolvent, or if it commits a fundamental non-performance towards the principal, or if prior to the time for performance it is clear that there will be a fundamental non-performance:
(a) on the principal's demand, the intermediary shall communicate the name and address of the third party to the principal; and
(b) the principal may exercise against the third party the rights acquired on the principal's behalf by the intermediary, subject to any defences which the third party may set up against the intermediary.

Section 3: Représentation indirecte

ARTICLE 3:301: INTERMÉDIAIRES N'AGISSANT PAS AU NOM D'UN REPRÉSENTÉ

(1) Lorsqu'un intermédiaire agit
   (a) sur les instructions et pour le compte, mais non point au nom, d'un représenté,
   (b) ou sur les instructions d'un représenté, sans que le tiers le sache ni ait de raisons de le savoir,
   l'intermédiaire et le tiers sont engagés l'un envers l'autre.
(2) Le représenté et le tiers ne sont engagés l'un envers l'autre que dans les conditions prévues aux articles 3:202 à 3:204

ARTICLE 3:302: INSOLVABILITÉ DE L'INTERMÉDIAIRE OU INEXÉCUTION ESSENTIELLE À L'ÉGARD DU REPRÉSENTÉ

Si l'intermédiaire devient insolvable ou commet une inexécution essentielle à l'égard du représenté ou si, dès avant la date à laquelle il doit exécuter, il est manifeste qu'il y aura une inexécution essentielle,
(a) il doit communiquer le nom et l'adresse du tiers au représenté, sur la demande de celui-ci,
(b) et le représenté peut exercer à l'encontre du tiers les droits que l'intermédiaire a acquis pour son compte, sous réserve des exceptions que le tiers peut opposer à l'intermédiaire.

Article 3:303: Intermediary's Insolvency or Fundamental Non-performance to Third Party

If the intermediary becomes insolvent, or if it commits a fundamental non-performance towards the third party, or if prior to the time for performance it is clear that there will be a fundamental non-performance:

(a) on the third party's demand, the intermediary shall communicate the name and address of the principal to the third party; and

(b) the third party may exercise against the principal the rights which the third party has against the intermediary, subject to any defences which the intermediary may set up against the third party and those which the principal may set up against the intermediary.

Article 3:304: Requirement of Notice

The rights under Articles 3:302 and 3:303 may be exercised only if notice of intention to exercise them is given to the intermediary and to the third party or principal, respectively. Upon receipt of the notice, the third party or the principal is no longer entitled to render performance to the intermediary.

ARTICLE 3:303: INSOLVABILITÉ DE L'INTERMÉDIAIRE OU INEXÉCUTION ESSENTIELLE À L'ÉGARD DU TIERS

Si l'intermédiaire devient insolvable ou commet une inexécution essentielle à l'égard du tiers ou si, dès avant la date à laquelle il doit exécuter, il est manifeste qu'il y aura une inexécution essentielle,

(a) il doit communiquer le nom et l'adresse du représenté au tiers, sur la demande de celui-ci,

(b) et le tiers peut exercer à l'encontre du représenté les droits qu'il possède à l'encontre de l'intermédiaire, sous réserve des exceptions que l'intermédiaire peut lui opposer et de celles que le représenté peut opposer à l'intermédiaire.

ARTICLE 3:304: EXIGENCE DE NOTIFICATION

Les droits conférés par les articles 3:302 et 3:303 ne peuvent être exercés que si notification de l'intention de les exercer est faite à l'intermédiaire ainsi qu'au tiers ou au représenté, selon le cas. À compter de la réception de la notification, le tiers ou le représenté n'est plus en droit d'exécuter entre les mains de l'intermédiaire.

CHAPTER 4

Validity

ARTICLE 4:101: MATTERS NOT COVERED

This chapter does not deal with invalidity arising from illegality, immorality or lack of capacity.

ARTICLE 4:102: INITIAL IMPOSSIBILITY

A contract is not invalid merely because at the time it was concluded performance of the obligation assumed was impossible, or because a party was not entitled to dispose of the assets to which the contract relates.

ARTICLE 4:103: FUNDAMENTAL MISTAKE AS TO FACTS OR LAW

(1) A party may avoid a contract for mistake of fact or law existing when the contract was concluded if:
   (a) (i) the mistake was caused by information given by the other party; or
       (ii) the other party knew or ought to have known of the mistake and it was contrary to good faith and fair dealing to leave the mistaken party in error; or
       (iii) the other party made the same mistake,
       and
   (b) the other party knew or ought to have known that the mistaken party, had it known the truth, would not have entered the contract or would have done so only on fundamentally different terms.
(2) However a party may not avoid the contract if:
   (a) in the circumstances its mistake was inexcusable, or
   (b) the risk of the mistake was assumed, or in the circumstances should be borne, by it.

CHAPITRE 4

Validité

ARTICLE 4:101: QUESTIONS NON TRAITÉES

Le présent chapitre ne traite pas de l'invalidité découlant de l'illicéité ou de l'immoralité du contrat, ni de l'incapacité des parties.

ARTICLE 4:102: IMPOSSIBILITÉ INITIALE

Un contrat n'est pas invalide du seul fait que, lors de sa conclusion, l'exécution de l'obligation était impossible ou que l'une des parties n'était pas en droit de disposer des biens qui en forment l'objet.

ARTICLE 4:103: ERREUR ESSENTIELLE DE FAIT OU DE DROIT

(1) La nullité du contrat pour une erreur de fait ou de droit qui existait lors de la conclusion du contrat ne peut être provoquée par une partie que si
  (a) (i) l'erreur a été causée par une information donnée par l'autre partie,
      (ii) l'autre partie connaissait ou aurait dû avoir connaissance de l'erreur et il était contraire aux exigences de la bonne foi de laisser la victime dans l'erreur,
      (iii) ou l'autre partie a commis la même erreur,
  (b) et l'autre partie savait ou aurait dû savoir que la victime, si elle avait connu la vérité, ne se serait pas engagée ou ne l'aurait fait qu'à des conditions essentiellement différentes.
(2) La nullité ne peut cependant être invoquée lorsque
  (a) l'erreur de la partie était inexcusable étant données les circonstances,
  (b) ou que le risque d'erreur était ou, eu égard aux circonstances, aurait dû être assumé par elle.

ARTICLE 4:104: INACCURACY IN COMMUNICATION

An inaccuracy in the expression or transmission of a statement is to be treated as a mistake of the person which made or sent the statement and Article 4:103 applies.

ARTICLE 4:105: ADAPTATION OF CONTRACT

(1) If a party is entitled to avoid the contract for mistake but the other party indicates that it is willing to perform, or actually does perform, the contract as it was understood by the party entitled to avoid it, the contract is to be treated as if it had been concluded as the that party understood it. The other party must indicate its willingness to perform, or render such performance, promptly after being informed of the manner in which the party entitled to avoid it understood the contract and before that party acts in reliance on any notice of avoidance.

(2) After such indication or performance the right to avoid is lost and any earlier notice of avoidance is ineffective.

(3) Where both parties have made the same mistake, the court may at the request of either party bring the contract into accordance with what might reasonably have been agreed had the mistake not occurred.

ARTICLE 4:106: INCORRECT INFORMATION

A party which has concluded a contract relying on incorrect information given it by the other party may recover damages in accordance with Article 4:117(2) and (3) even if the information does not give rise to a fundamental mistake under Article 4:103, unless the party which gave the information had reason to believe that the information was correct.

ARTICLE 4:104: INEXACTITUDE DANS LES COMMUNICATIONS

L'inexactitude commise dans l'expression ou la transmission d'une déclaration est censée être une erreur de l'auteur ou l'expéditeur de la déclaration, et l'article 4:103 reçoit application.

ARTICLE 4:105: ADAPTATION DU CONTRAT

(1) Lorsqu'une partie est fondée à annuler le contrat pour erreur mais que l'autre indique qu'elle désire l'exécuter ou l'exécute effectivement, ainsi que la victime l'entendait, le contrat est censé avoir été conclu dans les termes envisagés par la victime. L'autre partie doit indiquer son intention d'exécuter ou procéder à l'exécution promptement après avoir été informée du sens donné au contrat par la victime et avant que celle-ci n'ait notifié l'annulation et agi sur la foi de cette notification.

(2) L'indication ou l'exécution fait perdre le droit d'annuler et toute notification antérieure d'annulation est dépourvue d'effet.

(3) Lorsque les deux parties ont commis la même erreur, le tribunal peut, à la requête de l'une d'elles, mettre le contrat en accord avec ce qui aurait pu raisonnablement être convenu s'il n'y avait point eu d'erreur.

ARTICLE 4:106: INFORMATION INEXACTE

La partie qui s'est engagée sur le fondement d'une information inexacte donnée par l'autre partie peut obtenir des dommages et intérêts conformément aux alinéas (2) et (3) de l'article 4:117 alors même que l'information n'a pas occasionné une erreur essentielle au sens de l'article 4:103, à moins que la partie qui a donné l'information n'ait eu des raisons de croire que l'information était exacte.

ARTICLE 4:107: FRAUD

(1) A party may avoid a contract when it has been led to conclude it by the other party's fraudulent representation, whether by words or conduct, or fraudulent non-disclosure of any information which in accordance with good faith and fair dealing it should have disclosed.

(2) A party's representation or non-disclosure is fraudulent if it was intended to deceive.

(3) In determining whether good faith and fair dealing required that a party disclose particular information, regard should be had to all the circumstances, including:

   (a) whether the party had special expertise;

   (b) the cost to it of acquiring the relevant information;

   (c) whether the other party could reasonably acquire the information for itself; and

   (d) the apparent importance of the information to the other party.

ARTICLE 4:108: THREATS

A party may avoid a contract when it has been led to conclude it by the other party's imminent and serious threat of an act:

(a) which is wrongful in itself, or

(b) which it is wrongful to use as a means to obtain the conclusion of the contract, unless in the circumstances the first party had a reasonable alternative.

ARTICLE 4:109: EXCESSIVE BENEFIT OR UNFAIR ADVANTAGE

(1) A party may avoid a contract if, at the time of the conclusion of the contract:

   (a) it was dependent on or had a relationship of trust with the other party, was in economic distress or had urgent needs, was improvident, ignorant, inexperienced or lacking in bargaining skill, and

   (b) the other party knew or ought to have known of this and, given the circumstances and purpose of the contract, took advantage of the first party's situation in a way which was grossly unfair or took an excessive benefit.

(2) Upon the request of the party entitled to avoidance, a court may if it is appropriate adapt the contract in order to bring it into accordance with what might have been agreed had the requirements of good faith and fair dealing been followed.

(3) A court may similarly adapt the contract upon the request of a party receiving notice of avoidance for excessive benefit or unfair advantage, provided that this party informs the party which gave the notice promptly after receiving it and before that party has acted in reliance on it.

ARTICLE 4:107: DOL

(1) Une partie peut provoquer la nullité du contrat lorsque l'autre, par ses manoeuvres dolosives, en paroles ou en actes, a déterminé la conclusion du contrat ou a omis dolosivement de révéler une information que la bonne foi lui commandait de révéler.

(2) Des manoeuvres ou une non-révélation sont dolosives lorsqu'elles sont destinées à tromper.

(3) Pour établir si la bonne foi commandait à une partie de révéler une information particulière, on a égard à toutes les circonstances, notamment

    (a) le point de savoir si la partie a des connaissances techniques spéciales,

    (b) ce qu'il lui en a coûté pour se procurer l'information en cause,

    (c) le point de savoir si l'autre partie aurait pu raisonnablement se procurer l'information pour son compte,

    (d) ainsi que l'importance que présentait apparemment l'information pour l'autre partie.

ARTICLE 4:108: CONTRAINTE

Une partie peut provoquer la nullité du contrat lorsque l'autre a déterminé la conclusion du contrat par la menace imminente et grave d'un acte

(a) qui en soi est illégitime

(b) ou qu'il est illégitime d'employer pour obtenir la conclusion du contrat,

à moins que, eu égard aux circonstances, la partie n'ait eu une autre solution raisonnable.

ARTICLE 4:109: PROFIT EXCESSIF OU AVANTAGE DÉLOYAL

(1) Une partie peut provoquer la nullité du contrat si, lors de la conclusion du contrat,

    (a) elle était dans un état de dépendance à l'égard de l'autre partie ou une relation de confiance avec elle, en état de détresse économique ou de besoins urgents, ou était imprévoyante, ignorante, inexpérimentée ou inapte à la négociation,

    (b) alors que l'autre partie en avait ou aurait dû en avoir connaissance et que, étant donnés les circonstances et le but du contrat, elle a pris avantage de la situation de la première avec une déloyauté évidente ou en a retiré un profit excessif.

(2) À la requête de la partie lésée, le tribunal peut, s'il le juge approprié, adapter le contrat de façon à le mettre en accord avec ce qui aurait pu être convenu conformément aux exigences de la bonne foi.

(3) Le tribunal peut également, à la requête de la partie qui a reçu une notification d'annulation pour profit excessif ou avantage déloyal, adapter le contrat, pourvu que cette partie, dès qu'elle a reçu la notification, en informe l'expéditeur avant que celui-ci n'ait agi sur la foi de celle-ci.

ARTICLE 4:110: UNFAIR TERMS NOT INDIVIDUALLY NEGOTIATED

(1) A party may avoid a term which has not been individually negotiated if, contrary to the requirements of good faith and fair dealing, it causes a significant imbalance in the parties' rights and obligations arising under the contract to the detriment of that party, taking into account the nature of the performance to be rendered under the contract, all the other terms of the contract and the circumstances at the time the contract was concluded.

(2) This Article does not apply to:

(a) a term which defines the main subject matter of the contract, provided the term is in plain and intelligible language; or to

(b) the adequacy in value of one party's obligations compared to the value of the obligations of the other party.

ARTICLE 4:111: THIRD PERSONS

(1) Where a third person for whose acts a party is responsible, or who with a party's assent is involved in the making of a contract:

(a) causes a mistake by giving information, or knows of or ought to have known of a mistake,

(b) gives incorrect information,

(c) commits fraud,

(d) makes a threat, or

(e) takes excessive benefit or unfair advantage,

remedies under this Chapter will be available under the same conditions as if the behaviour or knowledge had been that of the party itself.

(2) Where any other third person:

(a) gives incorrect information,

(b) commits fraud,

(c) makes a threat, or

(d) takes excessive benefit or unfair advantage,

remedies under this Chapter will be available if the party knew or ought to have known of the relevant facts, or at the time of avoidance it has not acted in reliance on the contract.

ARTICLE 4:112: NOTICE OF AVOIDANCE

Avoidance must be by notice to the other party.

ARTICLE 4:110: CLAUSES ABUSIVES QUI N'ONT PAS ÉTÉ L'OBJET D'UNE NÉGOCIATION
INDIVIDUELLE

(1) Une clause qui n'a pas été l'objet d'une négociation individuelle peut être annulée par une partie si, contrairement aux exigences de la bonne foi, elle crée à son détriment un déséquilibre significatif entre les droits et obligations des parties découlant du contrat, eu égard à la nature de la prestation à procurer, de toutes les autres clauses du contrat et des circonstances qui ont entouré sa conclusion.

(2) Le présent article ne s'applique pas
    (a) à une clause qui définit l'objet principal du contrat, pour autant que la clause est rédigée de façon claire et compréhensible,
    (b) ni à l'adéquation entre la valeur respective des prestations à fournir par les parties.

ARTICLE 4:111: TIERS

(1) Lorsqu'un tiers dont une partie doit répondre ou qui participe à la conclusion du contrat avec l'accord de cette partie
    (a) provoque une erreur en donnant une information, ou connaissait ou aurait dû avoir connaissance d'une erreur,
    (b)   donne une information inexacte,
    (c) commet un dol,
    (d) est l'auteur de menaces
    (e) ou retire du contrat un profit excessif ou un avantage déloyal,
les moyens offerts par le présent chapitre peuvent être employés dans les mêmes conditions que si le comportement ou la connaissance avaient été ceux de la partie elle-même.

(2) Lorsqu'une autre personne
    (a) donne une information inexacte,
    (b) commet un dol,
    (c) est l'auteur de menaces
    (d) ou retire du contrat un profit excessif ou un avantage déloyal,
les moyens offerts par le présent chapitre peuvent être employés si la partie avait ou aurait dû avoir connaissance des faits pertinents ou si, au moment de l'annulation, elle n'a pas agi sur la foi du contrat.

ART. 4:112: ANNULATION PAR NOTIFICATION

L'annulation a lieu par voie de notification au cocontractant.

ARTICLE 4:113: TIME LIMITS

(1) Notice of avoidance must be given within a reasonable time, with due regard to the circumstances, after the avoiding party knew or ought to have known of the relevant facts or became capable of acting freely.
(2) However, a party may avoid an individual term under Article 4:110 if it gives notice of avoidance within a reasonable time after the other party has invoked the term.

ARTICLE 4:114: CONFIRMATION

If the party who is entitled to avoid a contract confirms it, expressly or impliedly, after it knows of the ground for avoidance, or becomes capable of acting freely, avoidance of the contract is excluded.

ARTICLE 4:115: EFFECT OF AVOIDANCE

On avoidance either party may claim restitution of whatever it has supplied under the contract, provided it makes concurrent restitution of whatever it has received. If restitution cannot be made in kind for any reason, a reasonable sum must be paid for what has been received.

ARTICLE 4:116: PARTIAL AVOIDANCE

If a ground of avoidance affects only particular terms of a contract, the effect of an avoidance is limited to those terms unless, giving due consideration to all the circumstances of the case, it is unreasonable to uphold the remaining contract.

ART. 4:113: DÉLAIS

(1) L'annulation doit être notifiée dans un délai raisonnable, eu égard aux circonstances, à partir du moment où la partie qui annule a connu ou aurait dû connaître les faits pertinents, ou a pu agir librement.
(2) Une partie peut toutefois annuler une clause particulière en vertu de l'article 4:110 en notifiant l'annulation dans un délai raisonnable après que l'autre partie se soit prévalue de la clause.

ARTICLE 4:114: CONFIRMATION

Le contrat ne peut être annulé lorsque la partie en droit de le faire l'a confirmé de façon expresse ou implicite, après avoir eu connaissance de la cause d'annulation ou pu agir librement.

ARTICLE 4:115: EFFETS DE L'ANNULATION

En conséquence de l'annulation, chaque partie est en droit de demander la restitution de ce qu'elle a fourni en exécution du contrat, pourvu qu'elle restitue simultanément ce qu'elle a reçu. Si la restitution en nature est impossible, elle s'effectue par le paiement d'une somme raisonnable.

ARTICLE 4:116: ANNULATION PARTIELLE

Lorsqu'une cause d'annulation n'affecte que certaines clauses du contrat, l'annulation se limite à ces clauses à moins qu'eu égard aux circonstances de la cause il ne soit déraisonnable de maintenir les autres dispositions du contrat.

ARTICLE 4:117: DAMAGES

(1) A party who avoids a contract under this Chapter may recover from the other party damages so as to put the avoiding party as nearly as possible into the same position as if it had not concluded the contract, provided that the other party knew or ought to have known of the mistake, fraud, threat or taking of excessive benefit or unfair advantage.

(2) If a party has the right to avoid a contract under this Chapter, but does not exercise its right or has lost its right under the provisions of Articles 4:113 or 4:114, it may recover, subject to paragraph (1), damages limited to the loss caused to it by the mistake, fraud, threat or taking of excessive benefit or unfair advantage. The same measure of damages shall apply when the party was misled by incorrect information in the sense of Article 4:106.

(3) In other respects, the damages shall be in accordance with the relevant provisions of Chapter 9, Section 5, with appropriate adaptations.

ARTICLE 4:118: EXCLUSION OR RESTRICTION OF REMEDIES

(1) Remedies for fraud, threats and excessive benefit or unfair advantage-taking, and the right to avoid an unfair term which has not been individually negotiated, cannot be excluded or restricted.

(2) Remedies for mistake and incorrect information may be excluded or restricted unless the exclusion or restriction is contrary to good faith and fair dealing.

ARTICLE 4:119: REMEDIES FOR NON-PERFORMANCE

A party which is entitled to a remedy under this Chapter in circumstances which afford that party a remedy for non-performance may pursue either remedy.

ARTICLE 4:117: Dommages et intérêts

(1) La partie qui annule un contrat en vertu du présent chapitre peut obtenir de son cocontractant des dommages et intérêts qui permettent de la placer autant que possible dans la situation où elle se serait trouvée si le contrat n'avait pas été conclu, dès lors que l'autre partie avait, ou aurait dû avoir, connaissance de l'erreur, du dol, de la contrainte ou du fait qu'elle retirait du contrat un profit excessif ou un avantage déloyal.

(2) Lorsqu'une partie est en droit d'annuler un contrat en vertu du présent chapitre mais n'exerce pas ce droit, ou l'a perdu en application des dispositions des articles 4:113 ou 4:114, elle peut, sous réserve de l'alinéa premier, obtenir des dommages et intérêts limités au préjudice que lui a fait subir l'erreur, le dol, la contrainte ou la prise d'un profit excessif ou d'un avantage déloyal. Le montant des dommages et intérêts est pareillement évalué lorsque la partie a été trompée par une information inexacte au sens de l'article 4:106.

(3) Les dispositions pertinentes de la section 5 du chapitre 9 s'appliquent pour le surplus, avec les adaptations appropriées.

ARTICLE 4:118: Exclusion ou restriction des moyens

(1) Les parties ne peuvent exclure ni restreindre les moyens qui sanctionnent le dol, la contrainte et la prise d'un profit excessif ou d'un avantage déloyal, non plus que le droit d'invoquer la nullité d'une clause abusive qui n'a pas été l'objet d'une négociation individuelle.

(2) Les parties peuvent, à moins que ce ne soit contraire aux exigences de la bonne foi, exclure ou restreindre les moyens qui sanctionnent l'erreur et l'information inexacte.

ARTICLE 4:119: Moyens ouverts en cas d'inexécution

La partie qui, dans des circonstances qui donneraient ouverture à un moyen fondé sur l'inexécution, est en droit de recourir à l'un des moyens que lui ouvre le présent chapitre, peut recourir au moyen de son choix.

CHAPTER 5

Interpretation

ARTICLE 5:101: GENERAL RULES OF INTERPRETATION

(1) A contract is to be interpreted according to the common intention of the parties even if this differs from the literal meaning of the words.
(2) If it is established that one party intended the contract to have a particular meaning, and at the time of the conclusion of the contract the other party could not have been unaware of the first party's intention, the contract is to be interpreted in the way intended by the first party.
(3) If an intention cannot be established according to (1) or (2), the contract is to be interpreted according to the meaning that reasonable persons of the same kind as the parties would give to it in the same circumstances.

ARTICLE 5:102: RELEVANT CIRCUMSTANCES

In interpreting the contract, regard shall be had, in particular, to:
(a) the circumstances in which it was concluded, including the preliminary negotiations;
(b) the conduct of the parties, even subsequent to the conclusion of the contract;
(c) the nature and purpose of the contract;
(d) the interpretation which has already been given to similar clauses by the parties and the practices they have established between themselves;
(e) the meaning commonly given to terms and expressions in the branch of activity concerned and the interpretation similar clauses may already have received;
(f) usages; and
(g) good faith and fair dealing.

ARTICLE 5:103: CONTRA PROFERENTEM RULE

Where there is doubt about the meaning of a contract term not individually negotiated, an interpretation of the term against the party which supplied it is to be preferred.

CHAPITRE 5

Interprétation

ARTICLE 5:101: RÈGLES GÉNÉRALES D'INTERPRÉTATION

(1) Le contrat s'interprète selon la commune intention des parties, même si cette interprétation s'écarte de sa lettre.

(2) S'il est prouvé qu'une partie entendait le contrat en un sens particulier et que lors de la conclusion du contrat l'autre ne pouvait ignorer son intention, on doit interpréter le contrat tel que la première l'entendait.

(3) Faute de pouvoir déceler l'intention conformément aux alinéas (1) et (2), on donne au contrat le sens que des personnes raisonnables de même qualité que les parties lui donneraient dans les mêmes circonstances.

ARTICLE 5:102: CIRCONSTANCES PERTINENTES

Pour interpréter le contrat on a égard en particulier

(a) aux circonstances de sa conclusion, y compris les négociations préliminaires,

(b) au comportement des parties, même postérieur à la conclusion du contrat,

(c) à la nature et au but du contrat,

(d) à l'interprétation que les parties ont déjà donnée à des clauses semblables et aux pratiques qu'elles ont établies entre elles,

(e) au sens qui est communément attribué aux termes et expressions dans le secteur d'activité concerné et à l'interprétation que des clauses semblables peuvent avoir déjà reçue,

(f) aux usages

(g) et aux exigences de la bonne foi.

ARTICLE 5:103: RÈGLE *contra proferentem*

Dans le doute, les clauses du contrat qui n'ont pas été l'objet d'une négociation individuelle s'interprètent de préférence contre celui qui les a proposées.

ARTICLE 5:104: PREFERENCE TO NEGOTIATED TERMS

Terms which have been individually negotiated take preference over those which have not.

ARTICLE 5:105: REFERENCE TO CONTRACT AS A WHOLE

Terms are to be interpreted in the light of the whole contract in which they appear.

ARTICLE 5:106: TERMS TO BE GIVEN EFFECT

An interpretation which renders the terms of the contract lawful, or effective, is to be preferred to one which would not.

ARTICLE 5:107: LINGUISTIC DISCREPANCIES

Where a contract is drawn up in two or more language versions none of which is stated to be authoritative, there is, in case of discrepancy between the versions, a preference for the interpretation according to the version in which the contract was originally drawn up.

ARTICLE 5:104: Préférence aux clauses négociées

Les clauses qui ont été l'objet d'une négociation individuelle sont préférées à celles qui ne l'ont pas été.

ARTICLE 5:105: Référence au contrat dans son entier

Les clauses du contrat s'interprètent en donnant à chacune le sens qui résulte du contrat entier.

ARTICLE 5:106: Interprétation utile

On doit préférer l'interprétation qui rendrait les clauses du contrat licites et de quelque effet, plutôt que celle qui les rendrait illicites ou de nul effet.

ARTICLE 5:107: Divergences linguistiques

En cas de divergences entre les différentes versions linguistiques d'un contrat dont aucune n'est déclarée faire foi, préférence est donnée à l'interprétation fondée sur la version qui a été rédigée en premier.

CHAPTER 6

Contents and Effects

ARTICLE 6:101: STATEMENTS GIVING RISE TO CONTRACTUAL OBLIGATIONS

(1) A statement made by one party before or when the contract is concluded is to be treated as giving rise to a contractual obligation if that is how the other party reasonably understood it in the circumstances, taking into account:
    (a) the apparent importance of the statement to the other party;
    (b) whether the party was making the statement in the course of business; and
    (c) the relative expertise of the parties.
(2) If one of the parties is a professional supplier which gives information about the quality or use of services or goods or other property when marketing or advertising them or otherwise before the contract for them is concluded, the statement is to be treated as giving rise to a contractual obligation unless it is shown that the other party knew or could not have been unaware that the statement was incorrect.
(3) Such information and other undertakings given by a person advertising or marketing services, goods or other property for the professional supplier, or by a person in earlier links of the business chain, are to be treated as giving rise to a contractual obligation on the part of the professional supplier unless it did not know and had no reason to know of the information or undertaking.

ARTICLE 6:102: IMPLIED TERMS

In addition to the express terms, a contract may contain implied terms which stem from
(a) the intention of the parties,
(b) the nature and purpose of the contract, and
(c) good faith and fair dealing.

CHAPITRE 6

Contenu et effets

ARTICLE 6:101: DÉCLARATIONS DONNANT NAISSANCE À DES OBLIGATIONS
CONTRACTUELLES

(1) La déclaration faite par une partie avant ou lors de la conclusion du contrat est censée avoir donné naissance à une obligation contractuelle si c'est ainsi que l'autre partie l'a entendue eu égard aux circonstances et notamment
   (a) l'importance apparente de la déclaration pour l'autre partie,
   (b) le point de savoir si la déclaration a été faite dans les conditions normales du commerce,
   (c) et les connaissances techniques respectives des parties.
(2) Si l'une des parties est un fournisseur professionnel qui, avant la conclusion du contrat, donne des informations sur la qualité ou l'usage de services, marchandises ou autre biens par publicité, mise sur le marché ou de toute autre façon, ses déclarations sont censées donner naissance à une obligation contractuelle à moins qu'il ne soit établi que l'autre partie savait ou aurait dû savoir qu'elles étaient inexactes.
(3) Les mêmes informations et autres engagements d'une personne par publicité ou mise sur le marché de services, marchandises ou autres biens pour le compte d'un fournisseur professionnel, ou d'une personne située plus en amont de la chaîne de commercialisation, sont censés donner naissance à des obligations contractuelles du fournisseur, à moins que celui-ci n'ait pas eu et n'ait pas eu raisons d'avoir connaissance de ces informations ou engagements.

ARTICLE 6:102: OBLIGATIONS IMPLICITES

En plus de clauses expresses, un contrat peut contenir des clauses implicites qui découlent
(a) de l'intention des parties,
(b) de la nature et du but du contrat,
(c) et de la bonne foi.

ARTICLE 6:103: SIMULATION

When the parties have concluded an apparent contract which was not intended to reflect their true agreement, as between the parties the true agreement prevails.

ARTICLE 6:104: DETERMINATION OF PRICE

Where the contract does not fix the price or the method of determining it, the parties are to be treated as having agreed on a reasonable price.

ARTICLE 6:105: UNILATERAL DETERMINATION BY A PARTY

Where the price or any other contractual term is to be determined by one party and that party's determination is grossly unreasonable, then notwithstanding any provision to the contrary, a reasonable price or other term shall be substituted.

ARTICLE 6:106: DETERMINATION BY A THIRD PERSON

(1) Where the price or any other contractual term is to be determined by a third person, and it cannot or will not do so, the parties are presumed to have empowered the court to appoint another person to determine it.
(2) If a price or other term fixed by a third person is grossly unreasonable, a reasonable price or term shall be substituted.

ARTICLE 6:107: REFERENCE TO A NON-EXISTENT FACTOR

Where the price or any other contractual term is to be determined by reference to a factor which does not exist or has ceased to exist or to be accessible, the nearest equivalent factor shall be substituted.

ARTICLE 6:108: QUALITY OF PERFORMANCE

If the contract does not specify the quality, a party must tender performance of at least average quality.

ARTICLE 6:103: SIMULATION

Lorsque les parties ont conclu un contrat apparent qui dissimule leur véritable accord, c'est l'accord caché qui prévaut entre elles.

ARTICLE 6:104: DÉTERMINATION DU PRIX

Lorsque le contrat ne fixe pas le prix ou la façon de le déterminer, les parties sont censées être convenues d'un prix raisonnable.

ARTICLE 6:105: DÉTERMINATION UNILATÉRALE PAR UNE PARTIE

Lorsque le prix ou tout autre élément du contrat doit être déterminé unilatéralement par l'une des parties et que la détermination de celle-ci est manifestement déraisonnable, un prix ou un autre élément raisonnable lui est substitué, nonobstant toute stipulation contraire.

ARTICLE 6:106: DÉTERMINATION PAR UN TIERS

(1) Lorsque le prix ou tout autre élément du contrat doit être déterminé par un tiers et que celui-ci ne peut ou ne veut le faire, les parties sont présumées avoir donné au tribunal pouvoir de lui désigner un remplaçant qui procèdera à cette détermination.
(2) Si le prix ou un autre élément déterminé par le tiers est manifestement déraisonnable, un prix ou un autre élément raisonnable lui est substitué.

ARTICLE 6:107: INEXISTENCE DU FACTEUR DE RÉFÉRENCE

Lorsque le prix ou tout autre élément du contrat doit être déterminé par référence à un facteur qui n'existe pas ou a cessé d'exister ou d'être accessible, celui-ci est remplacé par le facteur qui s'en rapproche le plus.

ARTICLE 6:108: QUALITÉ DE L'EXÉCUTION

A défaut de stipulation sur la qualité, le débiteur doit offrir une exécution qui soit au moins de qualité moyenne.

ARTICLE 6:109: CONTRACT FOR AN INDEFINITE PERIOD

A contract for an indefinite period may be ended by either party by giving notice of reasonable length.

ARTICLE 6:110: STIPULATION IN FAVOUR OF A THIRD PARTY

(1) A third party may require performance of a contractual obligation when its right to do so has been expressly agreed upon between the promisor and the promisee, or when such agreement is to be inferred from the purpose of the contract or the circumstances of the case. The third party need not be identified at the time the agreement is concluded.

(2) If the third party renounces the right to performance the right is treated as never having accrued to it.

(3) The promisee may by notice to the promisor deprive the third party of the right to performance unless:
   (a) the third party has received notice from the promisee that the right has been made irrevocable, or
   (b) the promisor or the promisee has received notice from the third party that the latter accepts the right.

ARTICLE 6:111: CHANGE OF CIRCUMSTANCES

(1) A party is bound to fulfil its obligations even if performance has become more onerous, whether because the cost of performance has increased or because the value of the performance it receives has diminished.

(2) If, however, performance of the contract becomes excessively onerous because of a change of circumstances, the parties are bound to enter into negotiations with a view to adapting the contract or ending it, provided that:
   (a) the change of circumstances occurred after the time of conclusion of the contract,
   (b) the possibility of a change of circumstances was not one which could reasonably have been taken into account at the time of conclusion of the contract, and
   (c) the risk of the change of circumstances is not one which, according to the contract, the party affected should be required to bear.

(3) If the parties fail to reach agreement within a reasonable period, the court may:
   (a) end the contract at a date and on terms to be determined by the court; or
   (b) adapt the contract in order to distribute between the parties in a just and equitable manner the losses and gains resulting from the change of circumstances.

In either case, the court may award damages for the loss suffered through a party refusing to negotiate or breaking off negotiations contrary to good faith and fair dealing.

ARTICLE 6:109: CONTRAT À DURÉE INDÉTERMINÉE

Chacune des parties peut résilier un contrat à durée indéterminée en notifiant un préavis d'une durée raisonnable.

ARTICLE 6:110: STIPULATION POUR AUTRUI

(1) Un tiers est fondé à exiger l'exécution d'une obligation contractuelle lorsque les parties sont expressément convenues de lui conférer ce droit ou que cette stipulation s'induit du but du contrat ou des circonstances de l'espèce. Il n'est pas nécessaire que le tiers soit identifié au moment de la stipulation.
(2) Si le tiers renonce au droit à l'exécution, il est censé ne l'avoir jamais acquis.
(3) Le stipulant peut priver le tiers du droit à l'exécution par une notification faite au promettant, sauf si
    (a) le tiers a reçu du stipulant une notification l'informant que son droit était irrévocable,
    (b) ou le promettant ou le stipulant a reçu du tiers une notification l'informant que ce dernier voulait profiter de son droit.

ARTICLE 6:111: CHANGEMENT DE CIRCONSTANCES

(1) Une partie est tenue de remplir ses obligations, quand bien même l'exécution en serait devenue plus onéreuse, soit que le coût de l'exécution ait augmenté, soit que la valeur de la contre-prestation ait diminué.
(2) Cependant, les parties ont l'obligation d'engager des négociations en vue d'adapter leur contrat ou d'y mettre fin si cette exécution devient onéreuse à l'excès pour l'une d'elles en raison d'un changement de circonstances
    (a) qui est survenu après la conclusion du contrat,
    (b) qui ne pouvait être raisonnablement pris en considération au moment de la conclusion du contrat,
    (c) et dont la partie lésée n'a pas à supporter le risque en vertu du contrat.
(3) Faute d'accord des parties dans un délai raisonnable, le tribunal peut
    (a) mettre fin au contrat à la date et aux conditions qu'il fixe,
    (b) ou l'adapter de façon à distribuer équitablement entre les parties les pertes et profits qui résultent du changement de circonstances.
Dans l'un et l'autre cas, il peut ordonner la réparation du préjudice que cause à l'une des parties le refus par l'autre de négocier ou sa rupture de mauvaise foi des négociations.

CHAPTER 7

Performance

ARTICLE 7:101: PLACE OF PERFORMANCE

(1) If the place of performance of a contractual obligation is not fixed by or determinable from the contract it shall be:
   (a) in the case of an obligation to pay money, the creditor's place of business at the time of the conclusion of the contract;
   (b) in the case of an obligation other than to pay money, the debtor's place of business at the time of conclusion of the contract.
(2) If a party has more than one place of business, the place of business for the purpose of the preceding paragraph is that which has the closest relationship to the contract, having regard to the circumstances known to or contemplated by the parties at the time of conclusion of the contract.
(3) If a party does not have a place of business its habitual residence is to be treated as its place of business.

ARTICLE 7:102: TIME OF PERFORMANCE

A party has to effect its performance:
(a) if a time is fixed by or determinable from the contract, at that time;
(b) if a period of time is fixed by or determinable from the contract, at any time within that period unless the circumstances of the case indicate that the other party is to choose the time;
(c) in any other case, within a reasonable time after the conclusion of the contract.

ARTICLE 7:103: EARLY PERFORMANCE

(1) A party may decline a tender of performance made before it is due except where acceptance of the tender would not unreasonably prejudice its interests.
(2) A party's acceptance of early performance does not affect the time fixed for the performance of its own obligation.

CHAPITRE 7

Exécution

ARTICLE 7:101: LIEU D'EXÉCUTION

(1) Lorsque le lieu d'exécution d'une obligation contractuelle n'est pas fixé par le contrat ou déterminable d'après le contrat, l'exécution a lieu
  (a) pour les obligations de somme d'argent là où le créancier a son établissement au moment de la conclusion du contrat ;
  (b) pour les obligations autres que de somme d'argent, là où le débiteur a son établissement au moment de la conclusion du contrat.
(2) Si une partie a plusieurs établissements, l'établissement au sens de l'alinéa (1) est celui qui a le lien le plus étroit avec le contrat, compte tenu des circonstances connues des parties ou envisagées par elles lors de la conclusion du contrat.
(3) Si une partie n'a pas d'établissement, sa résidence habituelle en tient lieu.

ARTICLE 7:102: DATE D'EXÉCUTION

Une partie doit exécuter
(a) si une date est fixée par le contrat ou déterminable d'après le contrat, à cette date ;
(b) si une période de temps est fixée par le contrat ou déterminable d'après le contrat, à un moment quelconque au cours de cette période, à moins qu'il ne résulte des circonstances de l'espèce que c'est à l'autre partie de choisir le moment ;
(c) dans tous les autres cas, dans un délai raisonnable à partir de la conclusion du contrat.

ARTICLE 7:103: EXÉCUTION ANTICIPÉE

(1) Une partie peut refuser une offre d'exécution faite avant l'échéance, excepté lorsque l'acceptation de cette offre n'affecterait pas ses intérêts de façon déraisonnable.
(2) L'acceptation par une partie d'une exécution anticipée n'a aucun effet sur la date à laquelle elle doit exécuter sa propre obligation.

ARTICLE 7:104: ORDER OF PERFORMANCE

To the extent that the performances of the parties can be rendered simultaneously, the parties are bound to render them simultaneously unless the circumstances indicate otherwise.

ARTICLE 7:105: ALTERNATIVE PERFORMANCE

(1) Where an obligation may be discharged by one of alternative performances, the choice belongs to the party which is to perform, unless the circumstances indicate otherwise.
(2) If the party which is to make the choice fails to do so by the time required by the contract, then:
    (a) if the delay in choosing is fundamental, the right to choose passes to the other party;
    (b) if the delay is not fundamental, the other party may give a notice fixing an additional period of reasonable length in which the party to choose must do so. If the latter fails to do so, the right to choose passes to the other party.

ARTICLE 7:106: PERFORMANCE BY A THIRD PERSON

(1) Except where the contract requires personal performance the creditor cannot refuse performance by a third person if:
    (a) the third person acts with the assent of the debtor; or
    (b) the third person has a legitimate interest in performance and the debtor has failed to perform or it is clear that it will not perform at the time performance is due.
(2) Performance by the third person in accordance with paragraph (1) discharges the debtor.

ARTICLE 7:107: FORM OF PAYMENT

(1) Payment of money due may be made in any form used in the ordinary course of business.
(2) A creditor which, pursuant to the contract or voluntarily, accepts a cheque or other order to pay or a promise to pay is presumed to do so only on condition that it will be honoured. The creditor may not enforce the original obligation to pay unless the order or promise is not honoured.

ARTICLE 7:104: ORDRE DES PRESTATIONS

Dans la mesure où les prestations des parties peuvent être exécutées simultanément, les parties sont tenues de les exécuter de la sorte, à moins que les circonstances n'indiquent le contraire.

ARTICLE 7:105: OBLIGATION ALTERNATIVE

(1) Lorsque le débiteur peut se libérer par l'une de plusieurs prestations alternatives, le choix lui appartient, à moins que les circonstances n'indiquent le contraire.
(2) Si la partie à qui revient le choix ne l'a pas arrêté dans le délai fixé par le contrat,
    (a) si le délai est essentiel, le droit de choisir passe à l'autre partie,
    (b) si le délai n'est pas essentiel, l'autre partie peut procéder à une notification qui impartit un délai supplémentaire de durée raisonnable au cours duquel la partie doit arrêter son choix. Si elle ne le fait, le droit de choisir passe à l'autre.

ARTICLE 7:106: EXÉCUTION PAR UN TIERS

(1) Excepté lorsque le contrat requiert une exécution personnelle, le créancier ne peut refuser l'exécution par un tiers lorsque celui-ci
    (a) agit avec l'accord du débiteur,
    (b) ou a un intérêt légitime à l'exécution et que le débiteur n'a pas exécuté ou qu'il est manifeste qu'il n'exécutera pas à l'échéance.
(2) L'exécution par le tiers conformément à l'alinéa précédent libère le débiteur.

ARTICLE 7:107: MODE DE PAIEMENT

(1) Une dette de somme d'argent peut être payée par tout moyen en usage dans les conditions normales du commerce.
(2) Le créancier qui, en vertu du contrat ou volontairement, accepte un chèque ou un autre ordre de paiement, ou un engagement de payer, n'est présumé le faire que sous la condition qu'il sera honoré. Il ne peut poursuivre le paiement de la dette originelle que si l'ordre ou l'engagement n'est pas honoré.

ARTICLE 7:108: CURRENCY OF PAYMENT

(1) The parties may agree that payment shall be made only in a specified currency.

(2) In the absence of such agreement, a sum of money expressed in a currency other than that of the place where payment is due may be paid in the currency of that place according to the rate of exchange prevailing there at the time when payment is due.

(3) If, in a case falling within the preceding paragraph, the debtor has not paid at the time when payment is due, the creditor may require payment in the currency of the place where payment is due according to the rate of exchange prevailing there either at the time when payment is due or at the time of actual payment.

ARTICLE 7:109: APPROPRIATION OF PERFORMANCE

(1) Where a party has to perform several obligations of the same nature and the performance tendered does not suffice to discharge all of the obligations, then subject to paragraph (4) the party may at the time of its performance declare to which obligation the performance is to be appropriated.

(2) If the performing party does not make such a declaration, the other party may within a reasonable time appropriate the performance to such obligation as it chooses. It shall inform the performing party of the choice. However, any such appropriation to an obligation which:
(a)   is not yet due, or
(b)   is illegal, or
(c)   is disputed,
is invalid.

(3) In the absence of an appropriation by either party, and subject to paragraph (4), the performance is appropriated to that obligation which satisfies one of the following criteria in the sequence indicated:
(a)   the obligation which is due or is the first to fall due;
(b)   the obligation for which the creditor has the least security;
(c)   the obligation which is the most burdensome for the debtor;
(d)   the obligation which has arisen first.
If none of the preceding criteria applies, the performance is appropriated proportionately to all obligations.

(4) In the case of a monetary obligation, a payment by the debtor is to be appropriated, first, to expenses, secondly, to interest, and thirdly, to principal, unless the creditor makes a different appropriation.

ARTICLE 7:108: Monnaie de paiement

(1) Les parties peuvent convenir que le paiement ne pourra être fait qu'en une monnaie déterminée.

(2) S'il n'en a été ainsi convenu, une somme libellée en une monnaie autre que celle du lieu où doit être effectué le paiement peut être payée dans la monnaie de ce lieu selon le taux de change qui y est en vigueur à l'échéance.

(3) Lorsque, dans le cas prévu à l'alinéa précédent, le débiteur n'a pas payé à l'échéance, le créancier peut exiger le paiement dans la monnaie du lieu où doit être effectué le paiement selon le taux de change qui est en vigueur en ce lieu soit à l'échéance, soit au moment du paiement.

ARTICLE 7:109: Imputation des paiements

(1) Lorsqu'une partie est tenue de plusieurs dettes de même nature et que l'exécution qu'elle offre ne suffit pas à les éteindre toutes, elle peut, sous réserve des dispositions de l'alinéa (4), déclarer au moment de l'exécution sur quelle dette elle impute le paiement.

(2) A défaut de déclaration du débiteur, le créancier peut, dans un délai raisonnable, imputer le paiement sur la dette de son choix. Il doit informer le débiteur de son choix. Néanmoins est de nul effet, l'imputation sur une dette qui
    (a) n'est pas échue,
    (b) est illicite,
    (c) ou est litigieuse.

(3) A défaut d'imputation par l'une ou l'autre partie, et sous réserve des dispositions de l'alinéa (4), le paiement est imputé sur la dette qui satisfait à l'un des critères suivants dans l'ordre fixé :
    (a) la dette échue ou à échoir en premier lieu ;
    (b) la dette pour laquelle le créancier a la garantie la plus faible ;
    (c) la dette la plus onéreuse pour le débiteur ;
    (d) la dette la plus ancienne.
    Si aucun des précédents critères ne peut recevoir application, l'imputation se fait proportionnellement sur toutes les dettes.

(4) Lorsque la dette est de somme d'argent, le paiement est imputé d'abord sur les frais, puis sur les intérêts, enfin sur le capital, s'il n'y a imputation contraire de la part du créancier.

ARTICLE 7:110: PROPERTY NOT ACCEPTED

(1) A party which is left in possession of tangible property other than money because of the other party's failure to accept or retake the property must take reasonable steps to protect and preserve the property.

(2) The party left in possession may discharge its duty to deliver or return:
    (a) by depositing the property on reasonable terms with a third person to be held to the order of the other party, and notifying the other party of this; or
    (b) by selling the property on reasonable terms after notice to the other party, and paying the net proceeds to that party.

(3) Where, however, the property is liable to rapid deterioration or its preservation is unreasonably expensive, the party must take reasonable steps to dispose of it. It may discharge its duty to deliver or return by paying the net proceeds to the other party.

(4) The party left in possession is entitled to be reimbursed or to retain out of the proceeds of sale any expenses reasonably incurred.

ARTICLE 7:111: MONEY NOT ACCEPTED

Where a party fails to accept money properly tendered by the other party, that party may after notice to the first party discharge its obligation to pay by depositing the money to the order of the first party in accordance with the law of the place where payment is due.

ARTICLE 7:112: COSTS OF PERFORMANCE

Each party shall bear the costs of performance of its obligations.

ARTICLE 7:110: REFUS DE RECEVOIR UN BIEN

(1) La partie qui a été laissée en possession d'un meuble corporel autre qu'une somme d'argent parce que le cocontractant a refusé de prendre livraison du bien ou de le reprendre, doit raisonnablement s'employer à en assurer la protection et la conservation.

(2) Elle peut se libérer de son obligation de livrer ou restituer

    (a) en déposant le bien chez un tiers qui le gardera à des conditions raisonnables pour le compte de l'autre partie, et en en faisant notification à celle-ci ;

    (b) en vendant la chose à des conditions raisonnables après notification faite à l'autre partie, et en versant à celle-ci les profits nets de la vente.

(3) Toutefois, si le bien est sujet à détérioration rapide ou que sa conservation est d'un coût déraisonnable, elle doit raisonnablement s'employer à le vendre. Elle peut se libérer de son obligation de livrer ou restituer en versant à l'autre partie les profits nets de la vente.

(4) La partie laissée en possession est en droit d'obtenir le remboursement de tous frais raisonnablement engagés ou d'en retenir le montant sur le produit de la vente.

ARTICLE 7:111: REFUS DE RECEVOIR UNE SOMME D'ARGENT

Lorsque le créancier refuse de recevoir une somme d'argent dûment offerte par le débiteur, celui-ci, après notification, peut se libérer en consignant l'argent pour le compte du créancier selon le droit du lieu où doit s'effectuer le paiement.

ARTICLE 7:112: COÛT DE L'EXÉCUTION

Chaque partie supporte les frais de l'exécution de ses obligations.

CHAPTER 8

Non-Performance and Remedies in General

ARTICLE 8:101: REMEDIES AVAILABLE

(1) Whenever a party does not perform an obligation under the contract and the non-performance is not excused under Article 8:108, the aggrieved party may resort to any of the remedies set out in Chapter 9.
(2) Where a party's non-performance is excused under Article 8:108, the aggrieved party may resort to any of the remedies set out in Chapter 9 except claiming performance and damages.
(3) A party may not resort to any of the remedies set out in Chapter 9 to the extent that its own act caused the other party's non-performance.

ARTICLE 8:102: CUMULATION OF REMEDIES

Remedies which are not incompatible may be cumulated. In particular, a party is not deprived of its right to damages by exercising its right to any other remedy.

ARTICLE 8:103: FUNDAMENTAL NON-PERFORMANCE

A non-performance of an obligation is fundamental to the contract if:
(a) strict compliance with the obligation is of the essence of the contract; or
(b) the non-performance substantially deprives the aggrieved party of what it was entitled to expect under the contract, unless the other party did not foresee and could not reasonably have foreseen that result; or
(c) the non-performance is intentional and gives the aggrieved party reason to believe that it cannot rely on the other party's future performance.

CHAPITRE 8

Inexécution et moyens en général

ARTICLE 8:101: MOYENS DONT DISPOSE LE CRÉANCIER

(1) Toutes les fois qu'une partie n'exécute pas une obligation résultant du contrat et qu'elle ne bénéficie pas de l'exonération prévue à l'article 8:108, le créancier est fondé à recourir à l'un quelconque des moyens prévus au chapitre 9.

(2) Lorsque le débiteur bénéficie de l'exonération prévue à l'article 8:108, le créancier est fondé à recourir à l'un quelconque des moyens prévus au chapitre 9 excepté les demandes d'exécution en nature et de dommages et intérêts.

(3) Une partie ne peut recourir à aucun des moyens prévus au chapitre 9 dans la mesure où l'inexécution de l'autre partie est imputable à un acte de sa part.

ARTICLE 8:102: CUMUL DES MOYENS

Les moyens qui ne sont pas incompatibles peuvent être cumulés. En particulier, une partie ne perd pas le droit de demander des dommages et intérêts en exerçant son droit de recourir à tout autre moyen.

ARTICLE 8:103: INEXÉCUTION ESSENTIELLE

L'inexécution d'une obligation est essentielle lorsque
(a) la stricte observation de l'obligation est de l'essence du contrat ;
(b) l'inexécution prive substantiellement le créancier de ce qu'il était en droit d'attendre du contrat, à moins que le débiteur n'ait pas prévu ou n'ait pas pu raisonnablement prévoir ce résultat ;
(c) ou l'inexécution est intentionnelle et donne à croire au créancier qu'il ne peut pas compter dans l'avenir sur une exécution par l'autre partie.

ARTICLE 8:104: CURE BY NON-PERFORMING PARTY

A party whose tender of performance is not accepted by the other party because it does not conform to the contract may make a new and conforming tender where the time for performance has not yet arrived or the delay would not be such as to constitute a fundamental non-performance.

ARTICLE 8:105: ASSURANCE OF PERFORMANCE

(1) A party which reasonably believes that there will be a fundamental non-performance by the other party may demand adequate assurance of due performance and meanwhile may withhold performance of its own obligations so long as such reasonable belief continues.

(2) Where this assurance is not provided within a reasonable time, the party demanding it may terminate the contract if it still reasonably believes that there will be a fundamental non-performance by the other party and gives notice of termination without delay.

ARTICLE 8:106: NOTICE FIXING ADDITIONAL PERIOD FOR PERFORMANCE

(1) In any case of non-performance the aggrieved party may by notice to the other party allow an additional period of time for performance.

(2) During the additional period the aggrieved party may withhold performance of its own reciprocal obligations and may claim damages, but it may not resort to any other remedy. If it receives notice from the other party that the latter will not perform within that period, or if upon expiry of that period due performance has not been made, the aggrieved party may resort to any of the remedies that may be available under chapter 9.

(3) If in a case of delay in performance which is not fundamental the aggrieved party has given a notice fixing an additional period of time of reasonable length, it may terminate the contract at the end of the period of notice. The aggrieved party may in its notice provide that if the other party does not perform within the period fixed by the notice the contract shall terminate automatically. If the period stated is too short, the aggrieved party may terminate, or, as the case may be, the contract shall terminate automatically, only after a reasonable period from the time of the notice.

ARTICLE 8:107 PERFORMANCE ENTRUSTED TO ANOTHER

A party which entrusts performance of the contract to another person remains responsible for performance.

ARTICLE 8:104: CORRECTION PAR LE DÉBITEUR

La partie dont l'offre d'exécution n'est pas acceptée par le cocontractant pour défaut de conformité au contrat peut faire une offre nouvelle et conforme si la date de l'exécution n'est pas arrivée ou si le retard n'est pas tel qu'il constituerait une inexécution essentielle.

ARTICLE 8:105: ASSURANCES RELATIVES À L'EXÉCUTION

(1) La partie qui croit raisonnablement qu'il y aura inexécution essentielle de la part du cocontractant peut exiger de lui des assurances suffisantes d'exécution correcte et dans l'intervalle suspendre l'exécution de ses propres obligations aussi longtemps qu'elle peut raisonnablement persister dans sa croyance.

(2) Lorsque ces assurances ne sont pas fournies dans un délai raisonnable, la partie qui les a exigées est fondée à résoudre le contrat si elle peut toujours croire raisonnablement qu'il y aura inexécution essentielle du cocontractant, à condition de notifier sans délai la résolution.

ARTICLE 8:106: NOTIFICATION D'UN DÉLAI SUPPLÉMENTAIRE POUR L'EXÉCUTION

(1) Dans tous les cas d'inexécution, le créancier peut notifier au débiteur qu'il lui impartit un délai supplémentaire pour l'exécution.

(2) Avant l'expiration de ce délai, le créancier peut suspendre l'exécution de ses obligations corrélatives et demander des dommages et intérêts, mais il ne peut se prévaloir d'aucun autre moyen. S'il reçoit du cocontractant une notification l'informant que celui-ci n'exécutera pas pendant le délai, ou si à l'expiration du délai supplémentaire l'exécution correcte n'est pas intervenue, il peut se prévaloir de l'un quelconque des moyens prévus au chapitre 9.

(3) Lorsque le retard dans l'exécution ne constitue pas une inexécution essentielle et que le créancier a dans sa notification imparti un délai supplémentaire de durée raisonnable, il est fondé à résoudre le contrat à l'expiration dudit délai si le débiteur n'a pas exécuté. Le créancier peut stipuler dans sa notification que l'inexécution dans le délai imparti emportera de plein droit résolution du contrat. Si le délai fixé est trop court, la résolution peut intervenir, à l'initiative du créancier ou s'il y a lieu de plein droit, au terme d'une durée raisonnable à compter de la notification.

ARTICLE 8:107: EXÉCUTION CONFIÉE À UN TIERS

Celui qui confie l'exécution du contrat à un tiers n'en demeure pas moins tenu de l'exécution.

ARTICLE 8:108: EXCUSE DUE TO AN IMPEDIMENT

(1) A party's non-performance is excused if it proves that it is due to an impediment beyond its control and that it could not reasonably have been expected to take the impediment into account at the time of the conclusion of the contract, or to have avoided or overcome the impediment or its consequences.

(2) Where the impediment is only temporary the excuse provided by this Article has effect for the period during which the impediment exists. However, if the delay amounts to a fundamental non-performance, the creditor may treat it as such.

(3) The non-performing party must ensure that notice of the impediment and of its effect on its ability to perform is received by the other party within a reasonable time after the non-performing party knew or ought to have known of these circumstances. The other party is entitled to damages for any loss resulting from the non-receipt of such notice.

ARTICLE 8:109: CLAUSE EXCLUDING OR RESTRICTING REMEDIES

Remedies for non-performance may be excluded or restricted unless it would be contrary to good faith and fair dealing to invoke the exclusion or restriction.

ARTICLE 8:108: EXONÉRATION RÉSULTANT D'UN EMPÊCHEMENT

(1) Est exonéré des conséquences de son inexécution le débiteur qui établit que cette inexécution est due à un empêchement qui lui échappe et que l'on ne pouvait raisonnablement attendre de lui qu'il le prenne en considération au moment de la conclusion du contrat, qu'il le prévienne ou le surmonte ou qu'il en prévienne ou surmonte les conséquences.

(2) Lorsque l'empêchement n'est que temporaire, l'exonération prévue par le présent article produit son effet pendant la durée de l'empêchement. Cependant, si le retard équivaut à une inexécution essentielle, le créancier peut le traiter comme tel.

(3) Le débiteur doit faire en sorte que le créancier reçoive notification de l'existence de l'empêchement et de ses conséquences sur son aptitude à exécuter dans un délai raisonnable à partir du moment où il en a eu, ou aurait dû en avoir, connaissance. Le créancier a droit à des dommages et intérêts pour le préjudice qui pourrait résulter du défaut de réception de cette notification.

ARTICLE 8:109: CLAUSE EXCLUANT OU LIMITANT LES MOYENS

Les moyens accordés en cas d'inexécution peuvent être exclus ou limités à moins qu'il ne soit contraire aux exigences de la bonne foi d'invoquer l'exclusion on la restriction.

CHAPTER 9

Particular Remedies for Non-Performance

Section 1 : Right to Performance

ARTICLE 9:101: MONETARY OBLIGATIONS

(1) The creditor is entitled to recover money which is due.
(2) Where the creditor has not yet performed its obligation and it is clear that the debtor will be unwilling to receive performance, the creditor may nonetheless proceed with its performance and may recover any sum due under the contract unless:
    (a) it could have made a reasonable substitute transaction without significant effort or expense; or
    (b) performance would be unreasonable in the circumstances.

ARTICLE 9:102: NON-MONETARY OBLIGATIONS

(1) The aggrieved party is entitled to specific performance of an obligation other than one to pay money, including the remedying of a defective performance.
(2) Specific performance cannot, however, be obtained where:
    (a) performance would be unlawful or impossible; or
    (b) performance would cause the debtor unreasonable effort or expense; or
    (c) the performance consists in the provision of services or work of a personal character or depends upon a personal relationship, or
    (d) the aggrieved party may reasonably obtain performance from another source.
(3) The aggrieved party will lose the right to specific performance if it fails to seek it within a reasonable time after it has or ought to have become aware of the non-performance.

ARTICLE 9:103: DAMAGES NOT PRECLUDED

The fact that a right to performance is excluded under this Section does not preclude a claim for damages.

CHAPITRE 9

Les divers moyens en cas d'inexécution

Section 1: Droit à l'exécution

ARTICLE 9:101: DETTES DE SOMME D'ARGENT

(1) Le créancier a droit d'obtenir paiement d'une dette de somme d'argent exigible.

(2) Lorsque le créancier n'a pas encore exécuté sa propre obligation et qu'il est manifeste que le débiteur n'acceptera pas de recevoir l'exécution, le créancier peut néanmoins passer à l'exécution et obtenir paiement de toute somme exigible en vertu du contrat à moins

    (a) qu'il n'ait eu la possibilité d'effectuer une opération de remplacement raisonnable sans efforts ni frais appréciables,

    (b) ou que l'exécution de son obligation n'apparaisse déraisonnable eu égard aux circonstances.

ARTICLE 9:102: OBLIGATIONS AUTRES QUE DE SOMME D'ARGENT

(1) Le créancier d'une obligation autre que de somme d'argent a droit d'exiger l'exécution en nature, y compris la correction d'une exécution défectueuse.

(2) Toutefois, l'exécution en nature ne peut être obtenue lorsque

    (a) l'exécution serait impossible ou illicite;

    (b) elle comporterait pour le débiteur des efforts ou dépenses déraisonnables;

    (c) elle consiste à fournir des services ou réaliser un ouvrage présentant un caractère personnel ou dépend de relations personnelles;

    (d) ou le créancier peut raisonnablement obtenir l'exécution par un autre moyen.

(3) Le créancier est déchu du droit à l'exécution en nature s'il manque à la demander dans un délai raisonnable à partir du moment où il a eu, ou aurait dû avoir, connaissance de l'inexécution.

ARTICLE 9:103: CONSERVATION DU DROIT D'OBTENIR DES DOMMAGES ET INTÉRÊTS

Les dispositions précédentes en vertu desquelles l'exécution en nature n'est pas admise ne font point obstacle à une demande de dommages et intérêts.

Section 2: Withholding Performance

ARTICLE 9:201: RIGHT TO WITHHOLD PERFORMANCE

(1) A party which is to perform simultaneously with or after the other party may withhold performance until the other has tendered performance or has performed. The first party may withhold the whole of its performance or a part of it as may be reasonable in the circumstances.
(2) A party may similarly withhold performance for as long as it is clear that there will be a non-performance by the other party when the other party's performance becomes due.

Section 2: Exception d'inexécution

ARTICLE 9:201: DROIT DE SUSPENDRE L'EXÉCUTION

(1) Une partie tenue d'exécuter dans le même temps que l'autre ou après elle peut, tant que le cocontractant n'a pas exécuté ou offert d'exécuter, suspendre l'exécution de sa prestation en tout ou en partie, ainsi qu'il est raisonnable eu égard aux circonstances.

(2) Une partie peut de même suspendre l'exécution de sa prestation dès lors qu'il est manifeste qu'il y aura inexécution de la part du cocontractant à l'échéance.

Section 3: Termination of the Contract

ARTICLE 9:301: RIGHT TO TERMINATE THE CONTRACT

(1) A party may terminate the contract if the other party's non-performance is fundamental.
(2) In the case of delay the aggrieved party may also terminate the contract under Article 8:106(3).

ARTICLE 9:302: CONTRACT TO BE PERFORMED IN PARTS

If the contract is to be performed in separate parts and in relation to a part to which a counter-performance can be apportioned, there is a fundamental non-performance, the aggrieved party may exercise its right to terminate under this Section in relation to the part concerned. It may terminate the contract as a whole only if the non-performance is fundamental to the contract as a whole.

Section 3: Résolution du contrat

ARTICLE 9:301: DROIT DE RÉSOUDRE LE CONTRAT

(1) Une partie peut résoudre le contrat s'il y a inexécution essentielle de la part du cocontractant.
(2) En cas de retard, le créancier peut également résoudre le contrat en vertu de l'article 8:106, alinéa (3).

ARTICLE 9:302: CONTRATS À EXÉCUTION FRACTIONNÉE

Lorsque le contrat doit être exécuté par tranches et que, relativement à une tranche à laquelle peut être assignée une fraction de la contre-prestation, il y a inexécution essentielle, le créancier est fondé à exercer le droit de résolution que lui confère la présente Section quant à la tranche du contrat en cause. Il ne peut résoudre le contrat en son entier que si l'inexécution est essentielle pour le contrat en son entier.

ARTICLE 9:303: NOTICE OF TERMINATION

(1) A party's right to terminate the contract is to be exercised by notice to the other party.

(2) The aggrieved party loses its right to terminate the contract unless it gives notice within a reasonable time after it has or ought to have become aware of the non-performance.

(3) (a) When performance has not been tendered by the time it was due, the aggrieved party need not give notice of termination before a tender has been made. If a tender is later made it loses its right to terminate if it does not give such notice within a reasonable time after it has or ought to have become aware of the tender.

   (b) If, however, the aggrieved party knows or has reason to know that the other party still intends to tender within a reasonable time, and the aggrieved party unreasonably fails to notify the other party that it will not accept performance, it loses its right to terminate if the other party in fact tenders within a reasonable time.

(4) If a party is excused under Article 8:108 through an impediment which is total and permanent, the contract is terminated automatically and without notice at the time the impediment arises.

ARTICLE 9:304: ANTICIPATORY NON-PERFORMANCE

Where prior to the time for performance by a party it is clear that there will be a fundamental non-performance by it, the other party may terminate the contract.

ARTICLE 9:305: EFFECTS OF TERMINATION IN GENERAL

(1) Termination of the contract releases both parties from their obligation to effect and to receive future performance, but, subject to Articles 9:306 to 9:308, does not affect the rights and liabilities that have accrued up to the time of termination.

(2) Termination does not affect any provision of the contract for the settlement of disputes or any other provision which is to operate even after termination.

ARTICLE 9:306: PROPERTY REDUCED IN VALUE

A party which terminates the contract may reject property previously received from the other party if its value to the first party has been fundamentally reduced as a result of the other party's non-performance.

ARTICLE 9:303: NOTIFICATION DE LA RÉSOLUTION

(1) La résolution du contrat s'opère par notification au débiteur.

(2) Le créancier est déchu du droit de résoudre le contrat s'il n'adresse pas notification dans un délai raisonnable à partir du moment où il a eu, ou aurait dû avoir, connaissance de l'inexécution.

(3) (a) Lorsque l'exécution n'est pas offerte à l'échéance, le créancier n'a pas à adresser notification avant qu'une offre ne soit faite. En cas d'offre d'exécution tardive, il est déchu du droit de résoudre le contrat s'il n'adresse pas notification dans un délai raisonnable à partir du moment où il a eu, ou aurait dû avoir, connaissance de l'offre d'exécution.

(b) Si toutefois le créancier sait ou a justes raisons de savoir que le débiteur entend toujours offrir l'exécution dans un délai raisonnable, et si, de façon déraisonnable, il manque à lui notifier qu'il n'acceptera pas l'exécution, il est déchu du droit de résoudre le contrat dans le cas où le débiteur offre effectivement l'exécution dans un délai raisonnable.

(4) Lorsqu'une partie est exonérée en vertu de l'article 8:108, en raison d'un empêchement absolu et permanent, le contrat est résolu à compter de la survenance de l'empêchement, de plein droit et sans qu'il soit besoin d'aucune notification.

ARTICLE 9:304: INEXÉCUTION PAR ANTICIPATION

Lorsque, dès avant la date à laquelle une partie doit exécuter, il est manifeste qu'il y aura inexécution essentielle de sa part, le cocontractant est fondé à résoudre le contrat.

ARTICLE 9:305: EFFETS DE LA RÉSOLUTION EN GÉNÉRAL

(1) La résolution du contrat libère les deux parties de leur obligation d'effectuer la prestation ou de la recevoir dans le futur ; mais, sous réserve des articles 9:306 à 9:308, elle est sans effet sur les droits et obligations qui avaient pris naissance au moment où elle est intervenue.

(2) La résolution n'a point d'effet sur les stipulations du contrat relatives au règlement des différends, non plus que sur toutes autres clauses appelées à produire effet même en cas de résolution.

ARTICLE 9:306: RÉDUCTION DE VALEUR D'UN BIEN

La partie qui résout le contrat peut refuser de conserver un bien antérieurement reçu du cocontractant si la valeur qu'il représente pour elle a subi une réduction substantielle en conséquence de l'inexécution du cocontractant.

ARTICLE 9:307: RECOVERY OF MONEY PAID

On termination of the contract a party may recover money paid for a performance which it did not receive or which it properly rejected.

ARTICLE 9:308: RECOVERY OF PROPERTY

On termination of the contract a party which has supplied property which can be returned and for which it has not received payment or other counter-performance may recover the property.

ARTICLE 9:309: RECOVERY FOR PERFORMANCE THAT CANNOT BE RETURNED

On termination of the contract a party which has rendered a performance which cannot be returned and for which it has not received payment or other counter-performance may recover a reasonable amount for the value of the performance to the other party.

ARTICLE 9:307: RECOUVREMENT DE SOMMES D'ARGENT

Après résolution du contrat, une partie peut recouvrer des sommes payées pour une prestation qu'elle n'a pas reçue ou a légitimement refusée.

ARTICLE 9:308: RECOUVREMENT DE BIENS

Après résolution du contrat, la partie qui a fourni des biens qu'il est possible de restituer et pour lesquels elle n'a pas reçu paiement ou une autre contre-partie, peut en obtenir la restitution.

ARTICLE 9:309: RECOUVREMENT POUR UNE PRESTATION INSUSCEPTIBLE DE RESTITUTION

Après résolution du contrat, la partie qui a effectué une prestation insusceptible de restitution, et pour laquelle elle n'a pas reçu paiement ou une autre contre-partie, peut obtenir une somme raisonnable correspondant à la valeur qu'a eue la prestation pour le cocontractant.

Section 4: Price Reduction

ARTICLE 9:401: RIGHT TO REDUCE PRICE

(1) A party which accepts a tender of performance not conforming to the contract may reduce the price. This reduction shall be proportionate to the decrease in the value of the performance at the time this was tendered compared to the value which a conforming tender would have had at that time.

(2) A party which is entitled to reduce the price under the preceding paragraph and which has already paid a sum exceeding the reduced price may recover the excess from the other party.

(3) A party which reduces the price cannot also recover damages for reduction in the value of the performance but remains entitled to damages for any further loss it has suffered so far as these are recoverable under Section 5 of this Chapter.

Section 4: Réduction du prix

ARTICLE 9:401: DROIT DE RÉDUIRE LE PRIX

(1) La partie qui accepte une offre d'exécution non conforme au contrat peut réduire le prix. La réduction est proportionnelle à la différence entre la valeur de la prestation au moment où elle a été offerte et celle qu'une offre d'exécution conforme aurait eue à ce moment.

(2) La partie qui est en droit de réduire le prix en vertu de l'alinéa précédent et qui a déjà payé une somme qui excède le prix réduit, peut obtenir du cocontractant le remboursement du surplus.

(3) La partie qui réduit le prix ne peut de surcroît obtenir des dommages et intérêts pour diminution de valeur de la prestation ; mais elle conserve son droit à dommages et intérêts pour tout autre préjudice qu'elle a souffert, pour autant que ces dommages et intérêts seraient dus en vertu de la section 5 du présent Chapitre.

Section 5: Damages and Interest

ARTICLE 9:501: RIGHT TO DAMAGES

(1) The aggrieved party is entitled to damages for loss caused by the other party's non-performance which is not excused under Article 8:108.
(2) The loss for which damages are recoverable includes:
    (a) non-pecuniary loss ; and
    (b) future loss which is reasonably likely to occur.

ARTICLE 9:502: GENERAL MEASURE OF DAMAGES

The general measure of damages is such sum as will put the aggrieved party as nearly as possible into the position in which it would have been if the contract had been duly performed. Such damages cover the loss which the aggrieved party has suffered and the gain of which it has been deprived.

ARTICLE 9:503: FORESEEABILITY

The non-performing party is liable only for loss which it foresaw or could reasonably have foreseen at the time of conclusion of the contract as a likely result of its non-performance, unless the non-performance was intentional or grossly negligent.

ARTICLE 9:504: LOSS ATTRIBUTABLE TO AGGRIEVED PARTY

The non-performing party is not liable for loss suffered by the aggrieved party to the extent that the aggrieved party contributed to the non-performance or its effects.

Section 5: Dommages et intérêts

ARTICLE 9:501: DROIT À DOMMAGES ET INTÉRÊTS

(1) Le créancier a droit à dommages et intérêts pour le préjudice que lui cause l'inexécution lorsque le débiteur ne bénéficie pas de l'exonération prévue à l'article 8:108.
(2) Le préjudice réparable inclut :
   (a) le préjudice non pécuniaire,
   (b) le préjudice futur dont la réalisation peut raisonnablement être tenue pour vraisemblable.

ARTICLE 9:502: MESURE DES DOMMAGES ET INTÉRÊTS EN GÉNÉRAL

Les dommages et intérêts sont en règle générale d'un montant qui permette de placer, autant que possible, le créancier dans la situation où il se serait trouvé si le contrat avait été dûment exécuté. Ils tiennent compte tant de la perte qu'il a subie que du gain dont il a été privé.

ARTICLE 9:503: PRÉVISIBILITÉ DU DOMMAGE

Le débiteur n'est tenu que du préjudice qu'il a prévu ou aurait dû raisonnablement prévoir au moment de la conclusion du contrat comme étant une conséquence vraisemblable de l'inexécution, lorsque ce n'est point intentionnellement ou par sa faute lourde que l'obligation n'est pas exécutée.

ARTICLE 9:504: PRÉJUDICE IMPUTABLE AU CRÉANCIER

Le débiteur n'est point tenu du préjudice souffert par le créancier pour autant que ce dernier a contribué à l'inexécution ou aux conséquences de celle-ci.

ARTICLE 9:505: REDUCTION OF LOSS

(1) The non-performing party is not liable for loss suffered by the aggrieved party to the extent that the aggrieved party could have reduced the loss by taking reasonable steps.
(2) The aggrieved party is entitled to recover any expenses reasonably incurred in attempting to reduce the loss.

ARTICLE 9:506: SUBSTITUTE TRANSACTION

Where the aggrieved party has terminated the contract and has made a substitute transaction within a reasonable time and in a reasonable manner, it may recover the difference between the contract price and the price of the substitute transaction as well as damages for any further loss so far as these are recoverable under this Section.

ARTICLE 9:507: CURRENT PRICE

Where the aggrieved party has terminated the contract and has not made a substitute transaction but there is a current price for the performance contracted for, it may recover the difference between the contract price and the price current at the time the contract is terminated as well as damages for any further loss so far as these are recoverable under this Section.

ARTICLE 9:508: DELAY IN PAYMENT OF MONEY

(1) If payment of a sum of money is delayed, the aggrieved party is entitled to interest on that sum from the time when payment is due to the time of payment at the average commercial bank short-term lending rate to prime borrowers prevailing for the contractual currency of payment at the place where payment is due.
(2) The aggrieved party may in addition recover damages for any further loss so far as these are recoverable under this Section.

ARTICLE 9:505: RÉDUCTION DU PRÉJUDICE

(1) Le débiteur n'est point tenu du préjudice souffert par le créancier pour autant que ce dernier aurait pu réduire son préjudice en prenant des mesures raisonnables.

(2) Le créancier a droit au remboursement de tous frais qu'il a raisonnablement engagés en tentant de réduire le préjudice.

ARTICLE 9:506: CONTRAT DE REMPLACEMENT

Le créancier qui a résolu le contrat et passé un contrat de remplacement dans un délai et d'une manière raisonnables, est fondé à obtenir la différence entre le prix du contrat originel et celui du contrat de remplacement, ainsi que des dommages et intérêts pour tout autre préjudice, pour autant que ces dommages et intérêts seraient dus en vertu de la présente section.

ARTICLE 9:507: PRIX COURANT

Le créancier qui a résolu le contrat sans passer de contrat de remplacement alors que la prestation promise a un prix courant, est fondé à obtenir la différence entre le prix du contrat originel et le prix courant au moment de la résolution, ainsi que des dommages et intérêts pour tout autre préjudice, pour autant que ces dommages et intérêts seraient dus en vertu de la présente section.

ARTICLE 9:508: RETARD DANS LE PAIEMENT D'UNE SOMME D'ARGENT

(1) En cas de retard dans le paiement d'une somme d'argent, le créancier a droit aux intérêts de cette somme entre l'échéance et la date du paiement, au taux bancaire de base à court terme moyen pratiqué pour la monnaie de paiement du contrat au lieu où le paiement doit être effectué.

(2) Le créancier peut en outre obtenir des dommages et intérêts pour tout autre préjudice, pour autant que ces dommages et intérêts seraient dus en vertu de la présente section.

ARTICLE 9:509: AGREED PAYMENT FOR NON-PERFORMANCE

(1) Where the contract provides that a party which fails to perform is to pay a spec-ified sum to the aggrieved party for such non-performance, the aggrieved party shall be awarded that sum irrespective of its actual loss.

(2) However, despite any agreement to the contrary the specified sum may be reduced to a reasonable amount where it is grossly excessive in relation to the loss resulting from the non-performance and the other circumstances.

ARTICLE 9:510: CURRENCY BY WHICH DAMAGES TO BE MEASURED

Damages are to be measured by the currency which most appropriately reflects the aggrieved party's loss.

ARTICLE 9:509: CLAUSES RELATIVES AUX CONSÉQUENCES PÉCUNIAIRES DE
L'INEXÉCUTION

(1) Lorsque le contrat porte que celui qui manquera de l'exécuter paiera une certaine somme à raison de l'inexécution, cette somme sera allouée au créancier indépendamment de son préjudice effectif.

(2) Cependant, nonobstant toute stipulation contraire, la somme peut être réduite à un montant raisonnable si elle est manifestement excessive par rapport au préjudice résultant de l'inexécution et aux autres circonstances.

ARTICLE 9:510: MONNAIE D'ÉVALUATION DU DOMMAGE

Les dommages et intérêts sont évalués dans la monnaie qui exprime de la façon la plus adéquate le préjudice du créancier.

CONCORDANCE

Destination of Articles published in Part I (1995) under new arrangement of Parts I
& II combined. Please note that the numbering system 0.00 refers to the old
arrangement, 0:00 to the new.

1.101	...1:101	3.104	...8:104
1.102 (pt)	...1:102	3.105	...8:105
1.103	...1:105	3.106	...8:106
1.104	...1:106	3.107	...8:107
1.105	...1:301	3.108	...8:108
1.106	...1:201	3.109	...8:109
1.107	...1:202	4.101	...9:101
1.108	...1:302	4.102	...9:102
1.109	...1:305	4.103	...9:103
1.110	...1:304	4.201	...9:201
2.101	...6:104	4.301	...9:301
2.102	...6:105	4.302	...9:302
2.103	...6:106	4.303	...9:303
2.104	...6:107	4.304	...9:304
2.105	...6:108	4.305	...9:305
2.106	...7:101	4.306	...9:306
2.107	...7:102	4.307	...9:307
2.108	...7:103	4.308	...9:308
2.109	...6:109	4.309	...9:309
2.110	...7:107	4.401	...9:401
2.111	...7:108	4.501	...9:501
2.112	...7:109	4.502	...9:502
2.113	...7:110	4.503	...9:503
2.114	...7:111	4.504	...9:504/5
2.115	...6:110	4.505	...9:506
2.116	...7:106	4.506	...9:507
2.117	...6:111	4.507	...9:508
3.101	...8:101	4.508	...9:509
3.102	...8:102	4.509	...9:510
3.103	...8:103		

CHAPTER 1

General Provisions

Section 1: Scope of the Principles

Article 1:101: Application of the Principles

(1) These Principles are intended to be applied as general rules of contract law in the European Union.

(2) These Principles will apply when the parties have agreed to incorporate them into their contract or that their contract is to be governed by them.

(3) These Principles may be applied when the parties:

  (a) have agreed that their contract is to be governed by 'general principles of law', the 'lex mercatoria' or the like; or

  (b) have not chosen any system or rules of law to govern their contract.

(4) These Principles may provide a solution to the issue raised where the system or rules of law applicable do not do so.

COMMENT

A. *General Remarks*

The Principles as such do not have the authority of national, supranational or international law. Consequently, it is impossible to define their scope of application in the same way as has become usual for formal instruments creating uniform law.

Instead, this Article invites all those concerned with the drafting of contracts, the application of legal rules on contracts or the preparation of legislation on contract law to use these Principles, whether for international or domestic contracts, wherever this seems appropriate. Six situations are envisaged.

B. *European contract law*

Paragraph (1) states the primary purpose of the Principles, namely to provide a general system of rules of contract law in the European Union based on the national laws of the 15 member states. Wherever in intra-Common Market dealings the general rules of contract law of the Member States are relevant for individuals, organisations, the organs of the Union or the European Court of Justice, these Principles offer a carefully worked out system of rules based on comparative research.

C. *Parties' choice of the Principles*

Paragraph (2) invites contracting parties to submit their contract to the Principles, particularly when parties to an international contract face difficulties in agreeing on a national system of law to govern their relationship.

As the text indicates, a choice of the Principles can be made in two different forms which have differing effects.

The first type of clause may be drafted upon the following lines:

'This contract incorporates the Principles of European Contract Law'.

Such a clause merely incorporates the Principles into the body of the specific contract. The contract remains subject to that national legal system which is applicable according to the forum state's conflict of law rules, including its mandatory provisions.

Alternatively, the parties may agree upon a clause drafted along the following lines:

'This contract is subject to the Principles of European Contract Law.'

Such a contractual clause would not necessarily give the contract the character of a 'supranational' or 'anational' contract. Since the Principles have a limited scope, aspects of contract law not covered by the Principles may still have to be determined by the applicable national law. As in contractual choice of law, a choice of the Principles need not necessarily be by express clause; a choice can also be implied from the terms of the contract.

Whether a choice of the Principles is valid and effective will depend upon the relevant rules (including the conflict of law rules) of the forum state. Moreover, by choosing these Principles the parties may not always be in a position to avoid the application of certain national rules of a mandatory character. Which law or which mandatory rules are applicable, will depend upon the relevant conflict of law rules.

D. *Application though not chosen by the Parties*

Paragraph (3) deals with two situations in which the Principles may be applicable even though the parties have not chosen them.

Subparagraph (a) envisages contractual clauses by which the parties submit their contract to 'general principles of (contract) law' or to the '*lex mercatoria*', or use clauses of similar meaning. The common feature of clauses of this type is that the precise contents of those general principles is rather vague and therefore a great deal of effort is required to determine appropriate solutions. The parties, courts or arbitrators are therefore invited to regard such clauses as referring to these Principles because they contain well considered and specific formulations of general principles of contract law based upon extensive comparative research. By mentioning the '*lex mercatoria*' the Principles do not and need not take a position as to the nature of those rules.

Subparagraph (b) addresses the different situation where the parties have not made any choice as to the applicable law, even impliedly. Ordinarily in this case the proper law of a contract is determined according to the rules of the conflict of laws relating to contracts by using the so-called objective connecting factors (e.g. the criteria of the closest connection, the characteristic performance, etc.).

However, some international courts (including the European Court of Justice) and arbitral tribunals do not have any specific rules on the conflict of laws (even though according to EEC Treaty Article 215 (1) the contractual liability of the Community is governed by the 'law applicable to the contract'). Subparagraph (b) invites these courts and arbitral tribunals to apply the Principles although the parties have not chosen them. The justification for such application is the comparative preparation and international discussion which is reflected by the Principles. For the adjudication of an international contract the Principles may furnish a more appropriate basis than any specific system of national contract law.

Subparagraph (b) may also apply if the parties have made an express or implied choice of law only for part of a contract.

E. *Application to claims arising out of the contract*
The Principles may be applied to claims which arise out of the contract, even if under some national systems the claim might be qualified as delictual rather than contractual, for example a claim for misrepresentation. See further above, Introduction, p. xxv, and below, Comment F to Article 2:301 and Comment G to Article 4:106.

F. *The filling of Gaps*
Even if the contract is subject to a specific national legal system, because of the parties' choice of law or by virtue of the objective connecting factors of the conflict of laws, the Principles may perform a function. Paragraph (4) envisages the case where a national legal system does not contain a rule for the solution of a specific issue. In such a case the court or arbitral tribunal is invited to use the Principles as a source of law from which to fill the gap. Such recourse to the Principles is in line with the practice of many courts to use foreign decisions or legal writings if confronted with a novel problem. A set of rules elaborated on the basis of a careful and comprehensive comparative study of the legal systems of all the Member States may carry at least the same persuasive authority as cases or writings from an individual country.

G. *Application to contracts of Public Authorities*
Public authorities (such as the European Union, a state, an administrative subdivision of a state or a commune) often conclude contracts with a private person (an enterprise or an individual) for the delivery of goods or the performance of services or work.

Insofar as such contracts are, according to the law of the respective public authority, subject to private law, these Principles may apply to them under the conditions set out in Article 1:101.

However, insofar as rules of public law intervene, these have, of course, precedence. This exception applies, in particular, where a public authority submits such contracts to an autonomous regime especially designed for 'public contracts' (*marchés publics*).

NOTES

1. *Harmonization of the law of contracts by the Institutions of the European Union other than the ECJ*
    In the last decades there have been important developments of what may be called the Community contract law. The Community Directive of 18 December 1986 on the Self-employed Agent contains mandatory rules most of which protect the agent. More important perhaps is the Directive on Unfair Terms in Consumer Contracts, 93/13 of 5 April 1993, OJEC No L 95/29, see notes to Article 4:110 below. In addition, the Communities have issued several other Directives providing protection for the consumer as a contracting party, see for instance Directives on Doorstep Sales (20 December 1985, No. 85/577), Consumer Credit (22 December 1986, No. 87/102), Package Tours (13 June 1990, No. 90/314), Time Share Agreements (26 October 1994, No. 94/47) and Distance Selling (20 May 1997 No. 97/7). Some of the Directives on labour relations provide rules for the protection of the employee. Futhermore, the Communities have established a law of competition which provides restrictions of the parties' contractual freedom by laying down which contract terms are permissible and which are not.
    The Community legislation mentioned above has provided some Europeanization of contract law. However, it is only a fragmentary harmonisation. It is not well co-ordinated, and, since the national laws of contract are different, it causes problems when it is to be adjusted to the various national laws, see *Zimmermann:* Civil Code and Civil Law, 73 and *Kötz,* Rechtsvereinheitlichung. There is no uniform European law of contract to support these specific measures.

2. *Harmonization of the law of obligations by the ECJ*
    The Court of Justice of the European Communities has taken a few steps towards a harmonisation of the European law of obligations. In the cases 284/82 *Bussoni,* ECJ 1984 557 and 209/83 *Valsabbia* ECR 1984 3089 it has, for instance, established rules on *force majeure,* see also the Communication by the Commission in OJEC 1988 No. C 259/10.
    Art. 215 (2) of the Treaty of Rome provides that in case of non-contractual liability, the Community shall, in accordance with the general principles common to the laws of the Member States, make good any damage caused by its institutions or by its servants in the performance of their duties. As such general principles existed only to a limited extent the Court has had to establish them. Its case law relating to issues in damages, such as the concept of damage (see for instance 13-24/ 1966, *Kampffmeyer I,* ECR 1967 351), remoteness (see 6-60/74 *Kampffmeyer II,* ECR 1976 711, and 210/86 *Mulder,* ECR 1988 3244) and loss attributable to the plaintiff (see 169/73 *Compagnie Continentale Française,* ECR 1975 119) comes close to the Principles of European Contract Law on damages for non-performance of contracts, and could have bearing also upon the contractual liability of the Community.

3. *On 'general principles of law' and 'the lex mercatoria'*
    It has been debated whether parties to an international contract should be permitted to submit the contract to general principles of law such as international customs and usages, the Principles of European Contract Law, and other common rules of law (the *lex mercatoria).*
    (a)   May arbitrators apply the Principles?
    The laws of several of the Member States now recognize that arbitrators may apply such rules of law.
    Art. 28 (1) of the *United Nations (UNCITRAL) Model Law on International Commercial Arbitration 1985* (see *Sanders & van den Berg)* provides:
    'The arbitral tribunal shall decide the dispute in accordance with *the rules of law* as are chosen by the parties' (emphasis added).
    The term 'rules of law' implies that the parties may choose the *lex mercatoria* to govern their contract. The model law has been adopted by SCOTLAND, and outside the Union by Canada, Australia, Hong Kong, Bermuda, Bulgaria, Cyprus, Egypt, Mexico, Nigeria, The Russian Federation, Peru, Tunisia and Ukraine, and by eight of the United States, namely California, Connecticut, Florida, Georgia, North Carolina, Ohio, Oregon and Texas, see *Sanders.*
    The BELGIAN, ITALIAN, FRENCH, and DUTCH codes of civil procedure have similar provisions. They even allow the arbitrators to apply the *lex mercatoria* when the parties have not chosen it, see art. 1700 of the Belgian Judiciary Code, art. 1496 of the French Code of Civil Procedure, art. 1054 of the Dutch Code of Civil Procedure, and art. 834 of the Italian Code of Civil Procedure. A similar attitude was taken by the AUSTRIAN Supreme Court in its decision of 18 November 1982 in the case of *Pabalk v. Norsolor,* see Y.C.A. ix (1984), 194.
    Section 46 (1) (b) of the ENGLISH Arbitration Act 1996 provides that
    'if the parties so agree the arbitral tribunal shall decide the dispute in accordance with such other considerations [than the law] as are agreed between them or determined by the tribunal'.

In the explanatory notes to the Bill of July 1995 issued by a Departmental Advisory Committee on Arbitration (see *Department of Trade and Industry*, Consultative paper, Section 1, and Section 2: Draft Clauses of an Aribitration Bill, p.38), it was said that the section corresponds to art. 28 of the Model Law.

(b)   *May state courts apply the Principles?*
The EC Convention on the Law Applicable to Contractual Obligations of 19 June 1980 (O.J.E.C. No. 266/1 of 9 October 1980), which is in force in the 15 Member States, governs the choice of law by the courts. The prevailing view seems to have been that under the Rome Convention a contract will always be governed by a national legal system. Before courts the parties cannot therefore agree to have the Principles of European Contract Law govern as a legal system. Several authors, however, have argued that a choice of law of the Principles is possible, see *Boele Woelki* 666; *Hartkamp*, Unidroit, 256; and *Lando*, Applicable Law 60.

Even when the contract is governed by a national legal system, the state courts of the Member States will not prevent the parties from incorporating the Principles of European Contract Law as the rules governing their contract. The Principles will then be applied to the extent they do not violate any mandatory provision of the law applicable to the contract, see on this concept note 1 to Article 1:103 below, and on incorporation, *Lando*, IECL s. 25.

Article 1:102: Freedom of Contract

(1)   Parties are free to enter into a contract and to determine its contents, subject to the requirements of good faith and fair dealing, and the mandatory rules established by these Principles.

(2)   The parties may exclude the application of any of the Principles or derogate from or vary their effects, except as otherwise provided by these Principles.

COMMENT

Like the national legal systems of the European Union, the Principles acknowledge the right of the citizens and their enterprises to decide with whom they will make their contracts and to determine the contents of these contracts.

This rule is, however, subject to important restrictions:

First, the parties' freedom to decide the terms of their contract is subject to the principles of good faith and fair dealing. A party cannot enforce an agreed contract or contract term which is unconscionable towards the other party. See also Article 1:201.

Second, the freedom is restricted by the mandatory rules of these Principles: see for instance Articles 4:118, 6:105 and 8:109.

Third, both the freedom to lay down the terms of the contract and the freedom to decide with whom to contract may be limited by the mandatory rules of national law which are applicable to the contract, see Article 1:103.

NOTES

The freedom of the parties to make the contract and provide the contract terms they wish, is recognized in all the Member States. It is provided in art. 2(1) of the GERMAN Consitution and art. 5 (1) of the GREEK Constitution and in art 3 of the Greek CC; in the old DANISH code 'Danske Lov' of 1683 art 5.1.1; in FRENCH, BELGIAN and LUXEMBOURG CCs arts. 1134(l); ITALIAN CC art 1322, NETHERLANDS BW art. 6:248, PORTUGUESE CC art. 405; and SPANISH CC arts. 6 and 1255. Under AUSTRIAN law freedom of contract is derived from § 859 of the ABGB. In the

Member States where no statutory provision can be invoked, freedom of contract is a basic principle. However, freedom of contract exists only within the limits set by the mandatory rules. In modern law considerations of policy, notably the need to protect the weaker party to a contract, have led to a restriction of contractual freedom by statute, see notes to Article 1:103.

Article 1:103: Mandatory Law

(1) Where the law otherwise applicable so allows, the parties may choose to have their contract governed by the Principles, with the effect that national mandatory rules are not applicable.

(2) Effect should nevertheless be given to those mandatory rules of national, supranational and international law which, according to the relevant rules of private international law, are applicable irrespective of the law governing the contract.

COMMENT

If allowed by the law applicable, as determined by the choice of law rules of the forum before which the substance of a dispute between the parties is brought, or which tries the validity of an arbitration clause, the validity of an arbitral award or the enforcement of a foreign arbitral award under the New York Convention of 15 June 1958 on the Recognition and Enforcement of Foreign Arbitral Awards, the parties may choose to have their dispute governed by the Principles as if they were a legal system. This has the effect that, subject to paragraph (2), the mandatory and non-mandatory rules of the Principles govern those issues which they cover, or which are within the scope of the Principles, see Article 1:106(2).

> *Illustration 1*: A Swedish seller S and a French buyer B have made an contract in France for the sale of an aeroplane. The seller is an aircraft manufacturer, the buyer a professional which will use the aeroplane in its business but which has no expert knowledge of aircraft. They have agreed that their contract should be subject to the Principles; it would otherwise be subject to French law. They have also agreed that the seller shall not be liable for hidden defects, a clause which in French law would be invalid under the mandatory French rules on the seller's liability for *vices cachées*. Under Article 8:109 of the Principles it would not be contrary to good faith and fair dealing for the seller to invoke this clause. The case is brought before an arbitrator sitting in France.
> As the doctrine on *vices cachées* does not fall under the category of rules in French law which are mandatory irrespective of the law governing the contract, and since under French law the parties may choose the Principles to govern the contract, the arbitrator should uphold the clause.

Issues which are not covered by the Principles will be governed by the law applicable to the contract.

Furthermore, under paragraph (2) a court or an arbitrator must give effect to national rules which are mandatory irrespective of which law governs the contract, the so-called directly applicable rules *(règles d'application immédiate)*, see article 7 (1) and (2) of the Rome Convention on the Law Applicable to Contractual Obligations (hereinafter the Rome Convention). These are rules which are expressive of a fundamental public policy of the enacting country and to which effect should be given when the contract has a close connection to this country.

Illustration 2: Under the rules of country X on restrictive trade practices, the agreement between supplier S of country Y and distributor D, which prohibits D from selling to co-operative supermarkets in X, is illegal and subject to penal sanctions. In spite of the fact that the parties have agreed that the distributorship contract is to be governed by the Principles, which in Article 1:102 provide for freedom of contract, the Courts of X will and, it is submitted, the courts in other Union Countries and arbitrators, wherever they sit in the Union, should give effect to the said rule in X, which is directly applicable.

NOTES

1. *Mandatory rules*
    The parties' freedom of contract is curtailed by the so-called mandatory rules. A rule is mandatory when the parties cannot deviate from it when they make their contract. It is non-mandatory when they may deviate from it. The distinction between mandatory and non-mandatory rules, from which the parties may deviate when they make their contract, is well know in the CIVIL LAW. In French law mandatory rules are called *lois de police* or *règles d'ordre public* or, depending upon their effects, *régles de droit impératives*; non-mandatory rules are called *régles de droit supplétives*. In DUTCH, mandatory rules are called, depending on the effect of the rule, *'regels van openbare orde'* or *'dwingende rechtsregels'*, and non-mandatory rules *'aanvullende rechtsregels'* or *'regelend recht'*. In GERMAN, mandatory rules are called *'zwingende Rechtsvorschriften'*, non-mandatory rules *'abdingbare'* or *'dispositive Rechtsvorschriften'*. In ITALIAN, non-mandatory rules are *'norme dispositive'* and mandatory rules are *'norme imperative'*; in SPANISH, *'normas cogentes'* and *'normas dispositivas'* are used similarly, see CC art. 1255.
    The distinction between the two sets of rules was formerly unknown – or nameless – in the COMMON LAW. It is now becoming known, see e.g. the ENGLISH and SCOTTISH Unfair Contract Terms Act 1977 and Sale of Goods Act 1979, the IRISH Sale of Goods and Supply of Services Act 1980. It has also been named, see the Rome Convention on the Law Applicable to Contractual Obligations of 19 June 1980 (UK Contracts (Applicable Law) Act 1990, Irish Contracts (Applicable Law) Act 1991 Schedule 1, Article 3 (3), where the term mandatory is used
    If the question whether a statutory provision is mandatory or non-mandatory is not laid down in the statute, it is for the court to decide the issue.
2. *The Principles and mandatory rules*
    (a) *Parties have agreed that the arbitrator shall apply the Principles*
        Where the parties have submitted their dispute to arbitration, it is widely held that they may also agree to let the Principles govern their dispute. This means that no national legal system will be applicable to the contract and that national mandatory provisions which are not directly applicable rules or rules of public policy (see note 3 below) will not apply. It is expressly provided in the UNCITRAL Model Law art. 28(1) that the arbitrator shall decide the dispute in accordance with such rules of law which are chosen by the parties as applicable to the substance of the dispute. Such rules of law include non-national principles as those of the Principles of European Contract Law. The Principles will then govern the existence and validity of the contract as well as its effects and interpretation.
        Provisions similar to art. 28(1) the are found in s.46(1) of the ENGLISH Arbitration Act 1996 (see Note to Article 1:101 above), art. 1496 of the FRENCH Code of Civil Procedure, art. 1054 of the DUTCH Code of Civil Procedure, art. 1700 of the BELGIAN Judiciary Code and art. 834(1) of the ITALIAN Code of Civil Procedure. There is reason to believe that the

courts of the other Member Countries will give effect to arbitral awards in international commercial disputes where the arbitrators, following an agreement by the parties, have applied the Principles. Art. 33 of the PORTUGUESE law on voluntary arbitration of 29 August 1986 provides that in an international dispute the parties may choose the *'direito'* applicable to the contract, which permits them to choose the *lex mercatoria* and therefore also the Principles, see *Collaço* 61 and *dos Santos* 48. This also seems to be the view in DENMARK and SWEDEN, see *Lando,* Lex mercatoria 567.

(b)   *Parties have not agreed which rules of law the arbitrator shall apply*

Where the parties have not chosen the rules of law applicable to the merits of the dispute, some laws will permit the arbitrators to apply the rules of law which they deem appropriate. This is true of FRENCH, ITALIAN, BELGIAN and DUTCH law, see the provisions cited above. The arbitrators may then choose to apply the *lex mercatoria* and may let the Principles govern the existence and validity of the contract as well as its effects and interpretation.

In ENGLAND, however, it is the prevailing view that the arbitrators must in such circumstances choose a law of a state, see section 46(2) of the Arbitration Act 1996. This also seems to be the attitude of the UNCITRAL Model Law art 28(2) which has been adopted by SCOTLAND.

(c)   *Can the mandatory provisions of Principles be avoided?*

The mandatory provisions of the Principles cannot be excluded by parties who have chosen to have their contract governed by them. This is in harmony with FRENCH law where it has been held that parties who have agreed to have their contract governed by a treaty which is not *ipso iure* applicable to the contract may not exclude the mandatory provisions of the treaty, see Cass. Com. 4 February 1992, *Revue critique de droit international privé* 1992 495 with the note by *Paul Lagarde.*

If the parties choose to incorporate the Principles in a contract which is governed by a national law, the mandatory rules of that law will govern the contract. Whether in such a case the parties may exclude the mandatory provisions of the Principles will depend on the circumstances. Such a manoeuvre may be an evasion (*fraude à la loi*) which is contrary to the *ordre public* of the forum country.

See notes to Article 1:201 on the good faith principle

3.   *'Ordinary' mandatory rules and mandatory rules carried by a strong public policy*

In spite of the fact that the Rome Convention does not bind arbitrators, some of the principles on the application of mandatory provisions embodied in the Rome Convention will probably be applied by arbitrators.

The Convention impliedly makes a distinction between 'ordinary' mandatory rules, see arts. 3(3), 5(2) and 6 (1), the so-called 'directly applicable rules', which are applicable irrespective of which law governs the contract, see art. 7, and the rules of 'international public policy', see art. 16. The rules of the second and third category express a strong public policy of the enacting state.

If the parties' or the arbitrators' choice of the Principles is a choice of law, an arbitrator need not apply national mandatory rules of law of the first category. He or she must, however, apply the mandatory rules of the Principles. If this choice is only an incorporation, see note 2(b) to Article 1:101, he or she must apply the mandatory rules of the national law applicable to the contract. The same holds true of a court which applies the Principles by virtue of an incorporation, see note 2 supra.

The laws of most Member States will probably allow the parties, if they so wish, to make their choice of the Principles a choice of law. However, it is the prevailing view in GREECE that where the merit of the dispute is to be governed by Greek law, the parties' choice of the Principles or other non-national source of law will only operate as an incorporation of the relevant rules, see Greek CC Proc. art. 890(1).

However, a State court and an arbitrator in the Union will always give effect to the directly applicable rules and the public policy of the forum country, see arts. 7(2) and 16 of the Rome Convention.

When applying the law of a country, a state court may also give effect to the directly applicable rules of another country with which the situation has a close connection, see art. 7(1) of the Rome Convention. A court sitting in Belgium and applying Dutch law may, for instance, give effect to a directly applicable rule in French law with which the situation has a close connection. Five Member States, GERMANY, IRELAND, LUXEMBOURG, PORTUGAL and the U.K., have used an option in the Convention not to apply art. 7(1). However, the law applicable to the contract may direct the court in these countries to give effect to a directly applicable rule in another country. If, for instance, a court finds that English law is applicable to the contract, it will, under certain circumstances, give effect to a statutory prohibition of the law of the foreign place of performance, see

Dicey & Morris 1243ff. When applying German law to a contract, German courts may give effect to a foreign statutory prohibition, *see Kropholler* § 52, IX.

Whether he or she is sitting in one of the five countries or not, an arbitrator who applies the Principles may choose to give effect to a directly applicable rule or a rule of public policy of a country to which the situation has a close connection also when the law of this country would not have been the law applicable to the contract. Since he must see to it that the award is made enforceable the arbitrator will probably give effect to a directly applicable rule of law in the country where the award is to be enforced. If he or she does not do so, the award may be refused enforcement by a court in that country.

Article 1:104: Application to Questions of Consent

(1) The existence and validity of the agreement of the parties to adopt or incorporate these Principles shall be determined by these Principles.

(2) Nevertheless, a party may rely upon the law of the country in which it has its habitual residence to establish that it did not consent if it appears from the circumstances that it would not be reasonable to determine the effect of the party's conduct in accordance with these Principles.

COMMENT

As it is generally accepted that the existence and validity of the parties' choice of a national law are governed by the chosen law, see articles 3(4) and 8(1) of the Rome Convention, it is also provided in Article 1:104 that the existence and validity of the parties' consent to the application of these Principles is to be governed by them, notably the rules on Formation, see chapter 2, on interpretation, chapter 5 and on validity, chapter 4.

Illustration: A Dutch lessor sends an offer to lease a container to the German lessee on a standard form contract providing for arbitration and for the application of the Principles. The lessee accepts and refers to its standard form conditions which provides that disputes are to be settled by arbitration but which also contains a clause under which German law is to govern the contract.

After the parties have performed the contract a dispute arises relating to the quality of the container. The lessor claims that the Principles must govern, the lessee that German law must govern. Applying Article 2:209 of the Principles, the arbitrator will come to the conclusion that the two choice of law clauses 'neutralise' each other, that the Rome Convention, in force in Germany and Holland, will apply to decide which law governs in the absence of an effective choice of law by the parties, and that the law of the lessor, Dutch law, will govern the contract, see article 4(2) of the Convention.

The application of the Principles to the question of consent may, however, sometimes cause hardship. Article 1:104(2) is designed to prevent a party being taken by surprise. If, for example, under the law of the country in which a party has its usual residence, the effect which Article 2:210 of the Principles gives to a professional's confirmation is unknown, and therefore when the party receives such a confirmation he does not respond to it although he does not agree to the additional or different terms stated in it, it might be unreasonable to treat him as having agreed to the terms set out in the confirmation in accordance with Article 2:210. The rules of the law of the place of the party's residence should govern the question of consent.

NOTE

As is mentioned in the Comment, the rules laid down in Article 1:104 are in accordance with the rules provided in arts. 3 (4) and 8 of the Rome Convention on the Law Applicable to Contractual Obligations, to which all the Member States are parties.

Article 1:105: Usages and Practices

(1) The parties are bound by any usage to which they have agreed and by any practice they have established between themselves.

(2) The parties are bound by a usage which would be considered generally applicable by persons in the same situation as the parties, except where the application of such usage would be unreasonable.

COMMENT

A. *Scope*

Article 1:105 deals with usages and with practices which the parties have established between themselves. Under Article 1:105(1) a usage applies if the parties have expressly or tacitly agreed that it should. Under Article 1:105(2) a usage which would be considered applicable by persons in the same situation as the parties will bind them even without their agreement, provided the usage is not unreasonable and is consistent with the express terms of the agreement.

A usage may be described as a course of dealing or line of conduct which is and for a certain period of time has been generally adopted by those engaged in trade or in a particular trade.

A practice which the parties have established between themselves may arise as a result of a sequence of previous conduct to a particular transaction or a particular kind of transaction between the parties. It is established when their conduct may fairly be regarded as a common understanding. The conduct may not only lend a special meaning to words and expressions which they use between themselves but may also create rights and duties.

B. *Priority of usages and practices over the rules of law*

Both usages and practices will, when applicable to the contract, set aside the rules of law – including those of the present Principles – which would otherwise apply. However, although not stated, it is implicit in Article 1:105 that usages and practices are only valid in so far as they do not violate mandatory rules of the law applicable to the contract or to the particular issue in question, see comment H to Article 1:201.

C. *Parties Refer to a Usage*

Sometimes the parties may refer to a usage which otherwise would not operate between them under Article 1:105(2). Such a usage then becomes binding under Article 1:105(1).

> *Illustration 1*: A who operates in Copenhagen and who has bought a commodity in Hamburg resells it to B, his fellow townsman. In their contract the parties agree to have the local usages of the Hamburg Commodity Exchange apply which will then bind both of them.

D. *A practice between the parties*

A practice established between the parties may vary their initial agreement, and it may create other mutual rights and obligations between them.

> *Illustration 2*: Having been called a couple of times to fill A's oil tank, B, on the basis of information which it receives regarding A's consumption, has done so for more than 5 years without having been called. B has seen to it that A whose factory is dependant on the oil never runs out of oil. A has always paid B close to but not later than 90 days after receipt of the oil.
>
> The initial agreement between the parties that B should only fill the tank when called upon has been changed by their practice; a duty on B to see to it that the tank never runs out of oil has been created. Also, although never expressly agreed upon, a practice between the parties extending to a credit of not more than 90 days after receipt has been established between them.

It goes without saying that the parties may later agree to vary a practice which they have established between them.

In case of a conflict between a practice between the parties (Article 1:105(1)) and a usage not agreed upon by the parties (Article 1:105(2)), the former will take precedence over the latter.

The principle stated in (2), according to which an unreasonable usage will not operate, applies also to usages chosen by the parties.

E. *Usages not agreed upon*

A usage may operate without having been agreed upon by the parties. For such a usage to be binding, Article 1:105(2) requires that it is one which would be considered applicable by persons in the same situation as the parties, and which is not unreasonable.

(1) Persons in the same situation

The usage must be so well established and have such general application among those engaged in the trade that persons in the same situation as the parties would consider it applicable. Parties may thus be bound by usages which have application to all or several trades and by usages which apply in a particular trade only.

Article 1:105 applies to local, national and international usages. A usage may be international either in the sense that it operates in the world trade, or in the sense that in a contract between parties which have their place of business in two different states, it operates in both states.

A local or national usage which operates at the place of business of one of the parties but not at that of the other party can only bind the latter if it would be reasonable to bind him. If a party comes into a market of the other party it will often be bound by the local usages.

> *Illustration 3*: A in Brussels sends an order to B, a broker in Paris, to be executed on the Paris Stock Exchange. A is ignorant of stock exchange transactions and has no knowledge of the usages of the Paris exchange. She can, therefore, have no intention to submit to these usages. Nevertheless the order is to be executed in accordance with the reasonable usages of the Paris Stock Exchange.

> *Illustration 4*: A, a merchant from Milan, goes to London and there negotiates and concludes a contract to deliver to B in London 'ground walnuts'. These words mean a finer grinding in London than the corresponding expression does in Milan. Unless otherwise agreed the contract is taken to refer to the London usage.

(2) Not unreasonable

The application of a usage must not be unreasonable, see Comment D, last paragraph. A usage can never set aside a mandatory rule of law (see comment B), but if the law merely supplies a term in the absence of contrary agreement, the usage may reverse what would otherwise be the normal rule applied by the Principles, provided its application is not unreasonable, see Article 1:201. Commercial acceptance by regular observance by business people is *prima facie* evidence that the usage is reasonable but even a usage which is regularly observed may be disregarded by the court if it finds the application of the usage unreasonable.

(3) Proof of the Usage

The way in which the usages are ascertained – through expert witnesses, by opinions submitted by the national or local Chamber of Commerce etc. – is decided by the applicable national law.

NOTES

1. *Definition of Usage*
    Statutes, courts and authors have offered various definitions of usages:
    (a)   Some have required that if a trade practice is to be classified as a usage, it must be accepted as binding by those engaged in that line of business, see *Schmitthoff* 14, and the GERMAN RG 10 January 1925, RGZ 110, 47 (48). This test has not been adopted by the Commission, see Comment A.
    (b)   The UNITED STATES UCC § 1.205 defines a usage as 'any practice or method of dealing having such regularity of observance in a place, vocation or trade as to justify an expectation that it will be observed with respect to the transaction in question'. This definition does not take into consideration the possibility that a usage may bind the parties even though, at the time of the conclusion of the contract, none of them were aware of the usage, see the ENGLISH House of Lords decision in *Comptoir d'Achat et de Vente Belge SA v. Luis de Ridder Limitada* [1949] A.C. 293.

(c)   The definition adopted by the Commission agrees with the one provided in *Halsbury* 12, 445: a usage is 'a particular course of dealing or line of conduct generally adopted by persons engaged in a particular department of business life'.

2.   *Proof of a usage*

The way in which a usage is proved differs from country to country, see on the laws *Schmitthoff* 20ff.

3.   *Parties' choice of usage and practice*

Article 1:105(1) is drafted in the same way as CISG art. 9(1) which is now in force in AUSTRIA, BELGIUM, DENMARK, FINLAND, FRANCE, GERMANY, ITALY, THE NETHERLANDS, SPAIN and SWEDEN. See also ULIS art. 9(1).

(a)   The first branch of the rule, providing that the parties are bound by any usage they have agreed upon, seems to be generally accepted by the legal systems, see *Dölle (-Junge)* Art. 9 no. 8.

(b)   The second branch of Article 1:105(1), which provides that practices established between the parties will bind them, is applied in several legal systems. In case of a conflict between a practice established between the parties and a usage not expressly agreed upon, see Article 1:105(2), the former takes priority, see FRENCH Cass. Com. 14 June 1977, Bulletin IV No. 172, p. 148.

The rule in Article 1:105(1) has also been adopted in NORDIC, DUTCH, SCOTTISH and SPANISH law: see Nordic Contracts Acts § 1 and Spanish CC art. 1282 as interpreted by the courts; see also PORTUGUESE CC art. 405(1).

Under Portuguese law practices established between the parties are only considered to be a guide for the interpretation and supplementation of the contract.

4.   *Usages not expressly chosen by the parties*

(a)   *Implied intention*

Some legal systems refer to the implied intention of the parties. For the position in ENGLAND, see *Treitel*, Contract 194-195; see also the ENGLISH law on incorporation of terms through a course of dealings, e.g. *Henry Kendall & Sons* v. *Lillico & Sons Ltd* [1969] 2 A.C. 31 (H.L.). On FRENCH law see the current interpretation of CC art. 1135 (*Ghestin, Goubeaux & Fabre-Magnan* Nos. 522ff.); on AUSTRIAN law, see ABGB §§ 863(2), 914; and BELGIAN law, Cass. 29 May 1947, Pas. I 217. These laws consider the will of the parties as the legal basis for the application of usages. CISG art. 9(2) provides that the parties are considered impliedly to have made certain usages applicable to the contract. In contrast, Article 1:105(2) treats usages as legal norms applicable independant of the volition of the parties (cf., in Greece, Athens 7388/1991, EEN 58 (1991) 336, 337-338); usages may bind parties who were unaware of them when they made the contract. On NORDIC law see *Ramberg*, Köplagen 160.

(b)   *Imputed knowledge*

CISG art. 9(2) relies on the knowledge or the imputed knowledge of the parties in question. This test leaves doubt as to whether newcomers in the trade or outsiders are bound by a usage of which they cannot reasonably have any knowledge. It has not been included in Article 1:105(2). A usage conceived as a legal norm will apply to everybody within its scope and will bind even the newcomer to the market.

(c)   *Unreasonable usage*

In several legal systems unreasonable usages will not bind the parties. This holds true of AUSTRIA, see ABGB § 863(2); DENMARK, see *Lynge Andersen & Nørgaard*, 28; ENGLAND, see the discussion in *Treitel*, Contracts 194-195; GREECE, see Athens 2449/1960, EEN 28 (1961) 225-226, note *Pothos*; GERMANY, see *Baumbach-Duden-Hopt* § 346 No. 11; NETHERLANDS, see BW art. 6:248(2); PORTUGAL see CC art. 3(1); SPAIN, see CC art 3.1 and *Vicent Chuliá* I, 1, 44; SWEDEN, see *Ramberg*, Köplagen 161; SCOTLAND, see '*Strathlorne*' *S.S. Co* v. *Baird & Sons* 1916 S.C. (H.L.) 134 ; and probably for FRANCE, see the discussion in *Marty & Raynaud*, Introduction No. 114. In ITALY *Disposizioni sulla legge in generale*, art. 8 seems to exclude any usage which is contrary to statutory law.

CISG does not expressly require the usage to be reasonable, as does Article 1:105(2). Writers on CISG, however, regard this requirement to be implied. Under CISG, which does not treat questions of the validity of the contract, the recognition of usages is left to national law see *v. Caemmerer & Schlechtriem* Art. 9 No. 5.

(d)   *International, national and local usages*

Unlike CISG art. 9(2), which applies only to usages in international trade, Article 1:105(2) applies also to national and local usages, see Comment E, (1).

Article 1:106: Interpretation and Supplementation

(1) These Principles should be interpreted and developed in accordance with their purposes. In particular, regard should be had to the need to promote good faith and fair dealing, certainty in contractual relationships and uniformity of application.

(2) Issues within the scope of these Principles but not expressly settled by them are so far as possible to be settled in accordance with the ideas underlying the Principles. Failing this, the legal system applicable by virtue of the rules of private international law is to be applied.

COMMENT

A. *The Aim of Article 1:106*
The aim of the Article is to lay down guidelines for the interpretation and supplementation of the Principles. Interpretation is the ascertainment of the meaning of the Article in question when it is applied to an issue covered by the Principles. Supplementation is needed when an issue to be decided is not covered by the language of the Principles but is within their scope, see paragraph 2.

B. *The purposes of the Principles*
Article 1:106(1) lays down that the interpretation and the development of the Principles are to be guided by their purposes. These purposes are derived from the Articles and the comments to the Articles. One of the aims of paragraph (1) is to avoid a strict and narrow interpretation.

C. *Development of the Principles*
The 'liberal' interpretation has a static and a dynamic aspect. The first envisages situations which may occur today but which have been overlooked or omitted, the second situations which we cannot imagine today, as the authors of the French civil code could not imagine an industrialized society. In both kinds of situations the Principles should be applied in accordance with their purposes. See also paragraph (2) on supplementation.

D. *Good faith and fair dealing*
Article 1:201 imposes upon each party a duty of good faith and fair dealing in exercising its rights and performing its duties under the contract. Good faith and fair dealing also operates as a rule of interpretation of each Article, see as an example Comment F to Article 9:102.

E. *Certainty in contractual relationships*
The text of each Article should be interpreted so as to promote certainty, which is very important in contractual relations.

F. *Uniformity of application*
It is one of the main purposes of rules provided for international application that they should be given a uniform interpretation. This aim has been expressed in several uniform laws and reflects the purpose of establishing these Principles, see the Preface and Article 1:101. In case of doubt an interpretation which is in accordance with the general ideas on which these Principles are based should be preferred to one which would be in harmony with the national law otherwise applicable, see paragraph (2) on supplementation.

G. *Supplementation*
Issues which fall within the scope of these Principles but which are not expressly settled by them are, as far as possible, to be settled in accordance with the ideas underlying the Principles, see Comment C.

If this way of solving a problem is not possible because it is one to which the ideas underlying the Principles cannot be applied, the legal system applicable under the conflict of law rules of the forum is to be applied. Such rules are found in the Rome Convention on the Law Applicable to Contractual Obligations of 19 June 1980 (O.J.E.C. No L 266/1 of 9 October 1980). An arbitrator may hold other choice of law rules applicable, see UNCITRAL MODEL LAW ON INTERNATIONAL ARBITRATION of 21 June 1985, Article 33(1).

It follows from Article 1:105 that a usage which is applicable to the contract will supplement the Principles.

NOTES

1. *Interpretation and Supplementation in Civil and Common Law*
   The methods of interpretation to be followed under Article 1:106 are similar to those expressed in CISG art. 7. In several aspects the Article corresponds with the maxims of interpretation adopted by the CIVIL LAW countries, see *Zweigert & Kötz* 265ff.; AUSTRIAN ABGB § § 6,7; ITALIAN *Disposizioni sulla legge in generale* art. 12; SPANISH CC arts. 3, 1258 and 1281ff. and SWISS CC art. 1.

   (a) It is in harmony with the canons of interpretation in the CIVIL LAW countries that statutory provisions are interpreted in accordance with the purposes of the statute and the general principles underlying it. In the civil law countries the courts often extract general principles of law from statutes.

   This idea was alien to the ENGLISH tradition which was to interpret the statutes narrowly and to find the general principles in the unwritten common law, though now the English courts regularly interpret legislation in the light of its purpose: see *Zweigert & Kötz, loc.cit.*

   In the UNITED STATES, however, the civil law approach is adopted under the UCC, see § 1.102(1): 'This Act should be liberally construed and applied to promote its underlying purposes and policies'.

   (b) Likewise the idea of supplementation is accepted in the CIVIL LAW countries where the general principles laid down in the statutes may be applied to situations not covered by the language of the statutory provisions. This, however, is not in accordance with the ENGLISH, IRISH and SCOTTISH tradition. English, Irish and Scottish courts will generally not extend statutory provisions by analogy to deal with situations not covered by the words of the statute, see *Zweigert & Kötz , loc. cit.*

2. *Good faith and fair dealing*
   More controversial, even in the CIVIL LAW countries, is the question whether the statute should be interpreted in accordance with good faith and fair dealing. A similar provision is found in CISG art. 7 (1) and in the U.C.C. § 1.203, see also Article 1:201 of the present Principles. Several authors in

the Civil Law countries have maintained that judges should, and in fact do, interpret statutes in accordance with good faith, see *Zweigert & Kötz, loc. cit.*. See also the DUTCH BW art 6:2(2), which reads:

> 'A rule binding upon [the creditor and debtor] by virtue of law, usage or a juridical act does not apply to the extent that, given the circumstances, this would be unacceptable according to criteria of reasonableness and equity'.

3. *Certainty and uniformity*
Certainty in contractual relationships and uniformity of application mentioned in Article 1:106(1) express the same idea which, as far as the uniformity of application is concerned, is found in CISG art. 7(1) and in UCC § 1.102(2)(c).

4. *National law as source of supplementation*
For the cases where the ideas underlying the Principles do not give any guideline for the supplementation of the Principles, national law must be applied. This is in accordance with CISG art. 7(2).

Article 1:107 : Application of the Principles by Way of Analogy

These Principles apply with appropriate modifications to agreements to modify or end a contract, to unilateral promises and to other statements and conduct indicating intention.

COMMENTS

A. *General*

The Principles have been developed to govern contracts, that is to say, agreements intended to create obligations. They also apply to agreements which are intended to alter or to put an end to obligations. Many of the rules may also apply to declarations of will by one party alone, whether these are promises which are binding without acceptance, see Article 2:107, or other forms of voluntary declaration or communications which have legal consequences, such as offers or acceptances; appropriation of payments; the various notices which may be given in case of change of circumstance; notices of termination of a contract; renunciations of rights; and so on.

The rules concerned are many: for example, on intention to be bound and the sufficiency of the terms (Articles 2:101 and 2:102); the various rules on consent and the vitiating factors (mistake, threat, fraud; see Chapter 4); those concerning performance (a party make seek specific performance of a unilateral promise of a reward, which may be governed by the Principles); non-performance; and also interpretation. Certainly many of the rules will need to be adapted to the circumstances, to take account of the fact that these may not involve any assumption that the parties have a common intention (though this will not always matter: for example, a unilateral promise may have been made as the result of fraud).

Thus, in questions of interpretation, it may be necessary to consider just the intention of the party which made the declaration. On the other hand, it will be necessary to consider how the recipient of the declaration understood, or should have understood, it. This will be the case with an offer or a promise of a reward. The guidance given on interpretation by Article 5:103, letters (d), (e) and (f) will be very useful here.

B. *Validity*

Under Article 2:107 a unilateral promise which is intended to be binding without acceptance is treated as a contract. Such a promise may be given as the result of fraud or any of the other grounds of invalidity set out in Chapter 4 (except, perhaps, excessive disparity, since there is no exchange involved). The rules of Chapter 4 therefore apply *mutatis mutandis*.

> *Illustration 1*: A contract of sale requires the buyer to have an irrevocable letter or credit opened in favour of the seller. The confirming bank is not quite sure of the seller's address and attempts to contact it. By mistake it in fact contacts a company with a similar name. The director of this company fraudulently states that his company is indeed the seller and the bank notifies it that a credit has been opened in its favour. The bank may avoid the credit.

The same is true for other unilateral declarations which have effect on the contract.

> *Illustration 2*: A has agreed to perform a service for B by a fixed date. A is late, which amounts to a fundamental non-performance. A does not want to have to perform and tricks B into giving notice of termination by telling B that he can easily find someone else to perform the service in A's place. A knows very well that this is untrue. B may avoid the effect of his declaration of termination and enforce the contract against A.

> *Illustration 3*: Under an f.o.b. contract B is to nominate a ship which can load the goods during the contract period. The parties have discussed which ships might be available; they agree informally that either the *Georgios C* or the *Evita* would be suitable. B intends to nominate the *Georgios C* but its declaration refers by mistake to the *Georgios D* which S knows to be a slip, as both know that this ship cannot reach the loading port in time. S cannot treat this declaration as one of the *Georgios D*.

Application of the rules of Chapter 4 to unilateral declarations. Will not always result in the unilateral declaration being avoidable, however, as this may be inconsistent with the implicit allocation of risk under Article 4:103(2).

> *Illustration 4*: A seller is contacted by a confirming bank notifying the seller of the opening of a irrevocable credit in its favour. The seller knows that the bank assumes that the buyer and its bank are both solvent and also that in fact both are on the verge of failure. The bank cannot avoid the credit on the ground of mistake.

NOTES

1.   *A generally accepted rule*

It appears to be part of the common core of the legal systems that the rules on formation, validity, authority of agents, interpretation and contents of contracts also apply with appropriate modifications to agreements to modify or end the obligations arising out of a contract, to promises which do not require acceptance (see notes to Article 2:107) and other statements and conduct indicating an intention to establish, modify or extinguish legal relationships.

In AUSTRIA this result follows from the general principle of analogous application of the Civil Code, see ABGB § 7.

The COMMON LAW is thought to be broadly the same in so far as it recognises unilateral legal acts as affecting contactual rights; thus a notice of withdrawal of a ship under a charterparty was treated as analogous to acceptance of an offer in *Brinkibon Ltd* v. *Stahag Stahl und Stahlwarenhandelsgesellschaft mbH (The Brimnes)* [1983] 2 A.C. 34, H.L.

2.   *Agreements to modify or end the contract*

Some systems treat the agreements to modify or end a contract as *conventions* not contracts, see on FRENCH law *Ghestin,* Formation p. 1ff .The same holds true of BELGIAN and PORTUGUESE law. Other systems consider these agreements, unilateral promises and other statements and conduct indicating an intention to establish, modify or extinguish legal relationships.as 'legal acts', e.g. GERMAN BGB §§ 116-144 and see *Larenz/Wolff,* AT §22; DANISH *retshandel,* and SWEDISH and FINNISH, *rättshandling,* Nordic Act on Contracts and other Legal Acts; and for GREECE, CC art 127f. Also DUTCH law uses the term *rechtshandeling,* BW art. 3:32ff, and provides in BW art. 6:126 that the rules on contracts apply to agreements other than contracts. For unilateral acts the same rules is adopted in the legal writing, see *Asser-Hartkamp*, Algemene leer nr 83ff).

3.   *Unilateral promises*

FRENCH and BELGIAN law apply the rules on contracts by way of an analogy to statements and conduct indicating an intention to establish legal relationships. See also PORTUGESE CC art. 295.

Section 2: General Duties

Article 1:201: Good Faith and Fair Dealing

(1) Each party must act in accordance with good faith and fair dealing.
(2) The parties may not exclude or limit this duty.

COMMENT

A. *Good Faith and Fair Dealing*

This Article sets forth a basic principle running through the Principles. Good faith and fair dealing are required in the formation, performance and enforcement of the parties' duties under a contract, and equally in the exercise of a party's rights under the contract. Particular applications of this rule appear in specific provisions of the present Principles such as the duty of a party not to negotiate a contract with no real intention of reaching an agreement with the other party (Article 2:301), not to disclose confidential information given by the other party in the course of negotiations (Article 2:302), and not to take unfair advantage of the other party's dependence, economic distress or other weakness (Article 4:109). Good faith and fair dealing are an important factor when implied terms of a contract are to be determined (Article 6:102); and they give an debtor a right to cure a defective performance before the time for performance (Article 8:104) and to refuse to make specific performance of a contractual obligation if this would cause the debtor unreasonable effort and expense (Article 9:102).

B. *Not Confined to Specific Rules*

The concept is, however, broader than any of these specific applications. It applies generally as a companion to Article 1:104 on Usages. Its purpose is to enforce community standards of decency, fairness and reasonableness in commercial transactions, see Article 1:108 on Reasonableness. It supplements the provisions of the Principles, and it may take precedence over other provisions of these Principles when a strict adherence to them would lead to a manifestly unjust result. Thus, even if the non-performance of an obligation is fundamental because strict compliance with the obligation is of the essence of the contract under Article 8:103, a party would not be permitted to terminate because of a trivial breach of the obligation.

The principle of good faith and fair dealing also covers situations where a party without any good reason stands on ceremony.

> *Illustration 1*: In its offer to B, A specifies that in order for B's acceptance to be effective B must send it directly to A's business headquarters where it must be received within 8 days. An employee of B overlooks this statement and sends the acceptance to A's local agent who immediately transmits it to A's headquarters where it is received 4 days later. A cannot avoid the contract.

The principle covers a party's dishonest behaviour.

> *Illustration 2*: The contract between A and B provides that A must bring suit against B within two years from the final performance by B if A wants to make B liable for defects in B's performance. Some time before the expiration of this time limit A discovers a serious defect in B's performance and notifies B that it intends to claim damages. B uses dilatory tactics to put A off. On several occasions it assures A that A has no reason for concern. B undertakes to look into the matter, but insists that it will have to investigate it carefully.
>
> When after the expiration of the two years's time limit, A loses patience and sues B, B invokes the time limit. Not having acted in good faith, B is estopped from relying on the time limit.

In relationships which last over a period of time (*Dauerschuldverhältnisse*) such as tenancies, insurance contracts, agency and distributorship agreements, partnerships and employment relationships, the concept of good faith has particular significance as a guideline for the parties' behaviour.

> *Illustration 3*: In 1945 A, a car manufacturer in country Y, appoints B its sole distributor of automobiles for country X. The contract takes effect on January 1, 1946, and runs for one year. It provides that A, though not obliged to do so, may give B a one month notice if A does not wish to renew the contract. On this condition one year contracts are issued by A and signed by B during the following years. A does not wish to renew the contract for 1999 and so informs B on November 30, 1998. Considering that a contractual relationship between the parties has lasted for 51 years, B, despite the provision on notice in the contract, is entitled to damages because in the circumstances the notice is too short.

C. *Inconsistent Behaviour*

A particular application of the principle of good faith and fair dealing is to prevent a party, on whose statement or conduct the other party has reasonably acted in reliance, from adopting an inconsistent position. This translates directly into a number of provisions of the Principles, e.g. Article 2:202(3), which provides that a revocation of an offer is ineffective if it was reasonable for the offeree to rely on the offer as being irrevocable, and the offeree has acted in reliance of the offer, and Articles 2:105(3) and 2:106(2), under which a party by its statement or conduct may be precluded from asserting a merger clause or a no-oral-modification clause to the extent that the other party has reasonably relied on them. See also Article 3:201(3), which lays down that an apparent authority of an agent that has been established by a principal's statements or conduct will bind the principal to the acts of the agent, and compare Article 5:101(3), which provides that if a common intention of the parties as to the interpretation of a contract cannot be established, the contract is to be understood according to the meaning that reasonable persons of the same kind as the parties would give to it in the same circumstances.

The rule is, however, broader than any of these specific provisions. It is a general principle that a person should not be allowed to set up the invalidity of an act or another reason for its not being binding upon him when he has induced another person to alter his position on the faith of the act.

Illustration 4: An importer asked its bank to collect on a negotiable instrument. The bank mistakenly reported to the customer that the money had been paid and paid the customer its value. When it was discovered that the amount had not been paid, the importer had irrevocably credited the amount to its foreign business partner. The bank is estopped from reclaiming the payment.

D. *Mutual Consideration*

Article 1:201 imposes upon each party a duty to observe reasonable standards of fair dealing and to show due regard for the interests of the other party. This applies, *inter alia*, to their handling of contingencies which were not contemplated in their agreement or in the rules of law governing the contract.

Illustration 5: Constructor C, whose employees have fallen ill in great numbers, has asked Owner O for the time agreed for C's completion of O's liquor store to be extended by one month. O has refused to grant the extension. After that a licence to sell liquor which O expected to get as a routine matter is held up due to a long lasting strike among civil servants which means that O will not be able to use the building until three months after the agreed completion time. Good faith requires that O notify C that it will not need to have the building completed on time. See also Article 1:202.

Good faith and fair dealing is required of the party which is to perform its obligations under a contract and of a party which wishes to have the contract enforced when the other party has failed to perform. Good faith and fair dealing require, for instance, the aggrieved party to limit as far as possible the loss which it will suffer as a result of a breach by the other party, thereby reducing the amount of damages, see Article 9:505.

E. *Good faith and fair dealing distinguished*

'Good faith' means honesty and fairness in mind, which are subjective concepts. A person should, for instance, not be entitled to exercise a remedy if doing so is of no benefit to him and his only purpose is to harm the other party. 'Fair dealing' means observance of fairness in fact which is an objective test, see as an example illustration 3. In the French language both these concepts are covered by the expression *'bonne foi'* and in German by *'Treu und Glauben'*.

The notion of good faith (*bonne foi*) as set out in Article 1:201 is different from the 'good faith' of a purchaser who acquires goods or documents of title without notice of third-party claims in the goods or documents. Article 1:201 does not deal with *bona fide* acquisitions. The notion of good faith in this Article is also different from that used in Article 3:201(3) under which a principal is treated as having granted authority to an agent when its conduct induces the third party in good faith to believe that the agent has authority.

F. *Good faith presumed*
Good faith is to be presumed. The party which alleges that the other party has failed to observe good faith and fair dealing has to prove it.

G. *Limitations of Article 1:201*
Sometimes there is a conflict between a legal rule and justice. The law or an otherwise valid contract term may under the circumstances lead to a manifestly unjust result. Whether in such cases the court should let justice prevail will depend, *inter alia*, upon to what extent certainty and predictability in contractual relationships would suffer by letting justice get the upper hand.

H. *Article 1:201 is mandatory*
Paragraph (2) provides that the parties cannot by their agreement exclude the duty of good faith and fair dealing as provided in paragraph (1). Nor can they vary its effects.

What is good faith will, however, to some extent depend upon what was agreed upon by the parties in their contract. Thus, parties may agree that even a technical breach may entitle the aggrieved party to refuse performance, when, for instance, its agents can ascertain a technical breach but not whether it is a trifle or not.

However, a party should not have a right to take advantage of a term in the contract or of one of these Principles in a way that, given the circumstances, would be unacceptable according to the standards of good faith and fair dealing. Contract language which gives a party such a right should not be enforced.

NOTES

1.   *Survey of the Laws*
   The principle of good faith and fair dealing is recognised, or at least appears to be acted on as a guideline for contractual behaviour, in all Member States. There is, however, a considerable difference between the legal systems as to how extensive and how powerful the penetration of the principle has been. At the one end of the spectrum figures a system where the principle has revolutionized the contract law (and other parts of the law as well) and added a special feature to the style of that system (GERMANY). At the other end we find systems which do not recognize a general obligation of the parties to conform to good faith, but which in many cases by specific rules reach the results which the other systems have reached by the principle of good faith (ENGLAND and IRELAND).

The other systems in the European Union range between these two opposites. They recognize a principle of good faith and fair dealing as a general provision, but have not given it the same degree of penetration into their law of contract as has German law.

2. *Germany*

   (a) *In general*

     In GERMANY § 242 BGB has been used to make possible what has been called a 'moralization' of contractual relationships. § 242 states in general terms that everyone must perform his contract in the manner required by good faith and fair dealing (*Treu und Glauben*) taking into consideration the general practice in commerce.

     The provision has been used to qualify a rigorous individualism of the original contract law of the BGB. It has operated as a 'superprovision' which may modify the effect of other statutory provisions. Based on BGB § 242, German courts have developed new institutions (see (b) below), and have created a number of obligations to ensure a loyal performance of a contract such as a duty of the parties to co-operate, to protect each others' interests, to give information and to submit accounts.

     There is, however, one important limit to the operation of the good faith principle. It does not permit the courts to establish a general principle of fairness and equity. A court may not replace the effects of a contract or of a statutory provision by an outcome which it believes to be more fair and equitable (see *Staudinger* § 242 No.4).

   (b) *The Institutions*

     Among the institutions created by the courts relying on the good faith principle the following should be mentioned:

- a change of circumstances (*Wegfall der Geschäftsgrundlage*) which makes the performance of the contract extremely onerous for one party may lead to the modification or termination of his contractual obligation. See also Article 6:111 of these Principles;
- a party's right may be limited or lost if enforcing it would amount to an abuse of right. Abuse of right is found in the following typical cases: (1) A party cannot acquire a right through dishonest behaviour (*exceptio doli specialis*); this rule bears some resemblance with the concept of 'unclean hands' in English equity (see *Palandt(-Heinrichs)* § 242 No. 4 B.a.). (2) A party will lose a right by breach of his own duty (*Verwirkung* – equitable estoppel). (3) A party cannot claim a performance which he will soon have to give back to the debtor (*dolo facit, qui petit, quid statim redditurus est*). (4) A party may not pursue an interest which is not worth protecting. (5) A party may not rely on a behaviour which is inconsistent with his earlier conduct (*venire contra factum proprium*);
- ending of contractual obligations which extend over a period of time. These obligations may be ended for compelling reasons (*wichtiger Grund*) even though this is not supported by a statutory or contractual provision. The right to end these obligations may be limited by the contract, but it may not be completely excluded (BGH 4 April 1973, BB 1973, 819). See also Article 6:109 of these Principles.

3. *England and Ireland*

   As was mentioned above, note 1, the common law of ENGLAND and IRELAND does not recognize any general obligation to conform to good faith and fair dealing. However, many of the results which in other legal systems are achieved by requiring good faith have been reached in English and Irish law by more specific rules: see the judgment of Bingham L.J. in *Interfoto Picture Library Ltd. v. Stilletto Visual Programmes Ltd.* [1989] Q.B. 433 (C.A.); but contrast *Walford* v. *Miles* [1992] 2 A.C. 208 (H.L.). For example, the courts have on occasion limited the right of a party who is the victim of a slight breach of contract to terminate the contract on that ground when the real motive appears to be to escape a bad bargain: see *Hoenig* v. *Isaacs* [1952] 2 All E.R. 176 (C.A.), and *Hong Kong Fir Shipping Co Ltd.* v. *Kawasaki Kisen Kaisha Ltd.* [1962] 2 Q.B. 26 (C.A.). Conversely, the victim of a wrongful repudiation is not permitted to ignore the repudiation, complete his own performance and claim the contract price from the repudiating party, unless the victim has a legitimate interest in doing so: see *Attica Sea Carriers Corp.* v. *Ferrostaal Poseidon Bulk Reederei Gmbh* [1976] 1 Lloyd's Rep. 250 (C.A.). There are many examples of the courts interpreting the terms of a contract in such a way as to prevent one party using a clause in circumstances in which it was probably not intended to apply. The clearest examples of this occur in relation to clauses excluding or limiting liability (*Treitel*, Contract 201-222 and *Coote* [1970] Cambridge LJ 221) but other terms have been construed similarly: see for example *Carr* v. *JA Berriman Pty Ltd.* (1953) 27 A.L.J.R. 273 (High Court of Australia), where it was held that an architect under a construction contract could not exercise a power to order work to be omitted simply in order to give the same work to another contractor who was prepared to do it for less. Thus to some extent Article 1:201 merely articulates trends already present in English law. But the English approach based on construction of the agreement is a weak one as it cannot prevail against clear contrary provisions in the agreement (see *Photo Production Ltd. v. Securicor Transport Ltd.* [1980] A.C. 827 (H.L.), clauses excluding or limiting liability) or even clear implication from the circumstances (*Bunge Corporation v. Tradax SA* [1981] 1 W.L.R. 711 (H.L.): right to terminate for breach which might not have any serious consequences). Thus Article 1:201 represents an advance on English and Irish law.

4.   *The Other EU Systems*

(a)   *Sources*

Provisions laying down a principle of good faith in the performance of the contract are found in BELGIUM, FRANCE and LUXEMBOURG, see CC arts. 1134(3); GREECE: CC art. 288; ITALY: CC art. 1375, and see also art. 1175; THE NETHERLANDS: BW arts. 6:2 and 248; PORTUGAL: CC art. 762(2); and SPAIN: CC arts. 7 and 1258 and Commercial Code art. 57.

In the NORDIC countries the principle is recognized by the courts and the legal writers. Although it has not been expressed in the statutes in the same general terms as it has in the countries mentioned above, several statutory provisions presuppose its existence, see for instance Contract Acts § 33 (on validity) and § 36 (see also *Ussing*, Alm. Del. 23; *Telaranta* 344; *Ramberg*, Avtalsrätt 239). In AUSTRIA the good faith principle is a generally acknowledged ethical rule (*cf* OGH 29 April 1965, SZ 38/72), which is derived from the Imperial Decree of 1 June 1811, introducing the General Civil Code, where 'the general principles of justice' are recognized as basis of civil law (*cf* OGH 7 October 1974, SZ 47/104) and expressly mentioned as 'fair dealing' in the Code: see ABGB §§ 863, 914. Therefrom it is clear that performance of contractual obligations are subject to 'good faith' see *Mayrhofer*, 20). However, the 'good faith requirement' is not as extensively construed as *'Treu und Glauben'* in BGB § 242.

As has recently been recognised by the House of Lords in *Smith v. Bank of Scotland* 1997 S.L.T. 1061, there is also an underlying principle of good faith in the SCOTTISH law of contract although it is difficult to find a clear and comprehensive statement of it in modern law. Many particular examples of reference to *bona fides* can be found apart from the class of contracts *uberrimae fidei* (see *Scottish Law Commission*, Defective Consent para. 3.68).

(b)   *Degree of Penetration*

It is not easy to measure and compare how deeply into the contract law the good faith principle has been integrated in the various legal systems.

The DUTCH BW art. 6:2 uses strong language. Good faith will not only supplement obligations arising from contract but may also modify and extinguish them. Under art. 6:2(2) a rule which binds the parties by virtue of law, usage or legal act does not apply to the extent that under the circumstances this would be unacceptable under the standards of reasonableness and equity, see also art. 6:248 (see *Hartkamp*, Civil Code XXI). In some ways the BW goes further than German law: under exceptional circumstances arts. 6:2 and 6:248(2) allow the court to replace the effects of a contract or of a statutory provision by an outcome which it believes to be more fair and equitable.

Extensive application of the good faith principle is also found in PORTUGUESE and GREEK law. In Portugal the principle is expressed not only generally in the CC art. 762(2), but also in special provisions such as art. 227 on *culpa in contrahendo*, art. 239 on omitted terms, art. 334 on abuse of rights and art. 437 on change of circumstances. In Greece the courts have given the principle as laid down in CC arts. 200, 281, 288 and 388 a broad application, see Full Bench of AP 927/1982, NoB 31 (1983) 214 and AP 1537/1991, Hell, Dni 34 (1993) 318 on the courts' power to change the terms of the contract, and AP 433/1953, NoB 1 (1953) 747-748, note *Sakketas*, on adaptation of money obligations.

Several provisions of the ITALIAN CC refer to good faith and fair dealing, see on good faith arts. 1337 (negotiation of contracts), 1366 (interpretation) and 1375 (performance). Art. 1175 dealing with obligations in general provides that the debtor and creditor shall behave in accordance with the rules of fair dealing (*correttezza*). The writers point out that good faith and fair dealing are objective concepts which refer to the behaviour of the honest businessman (*Betti* 65ff.). They operate as a limitation on a party's exercise of his rights and protect the other party's interests in matters other than the main performance: *Castronovo*, *Protezione* passim.

Arts. 1134 of the FRENCH, BELGIAN and LUXEMBOURG CC provide that contracts must be performed in good faith, and the principle has been extended to the formation and the interpretation of contracts. The French courts have not given the rule the same importance as have the courts of Germany and other countries mentioned above in the determination of the parties' obligations. However, similar results have often been obtained without reference to good faith, for instance by using the well-established theory of abuse of rights (see *Malaurie & Aynès,* Obligations 50ff.) and *apparence.* In the last two decades the courts have frequently and openly used the good faith principle in the determination of the parties' obligations. The writers invoke the principle in order to impose upon the parties a duty of mutual loyalty, of information and co-operation and to restrict the operation of clauses exempting a party from liability for breach of contract, etc., see *Malaurie & Aynès,* Obligations No. 622; *Marty & Raynaud,* Obligations I No. 246; and Cass.com. 22 October 1996, D. 1997 121 (*SA Banchereaus v. Sté Chronopost*). In BELGIUM the courts have used good faith extensively to supplement contractual obligations but have used it to limit obligations only in cases of disproportion and abuse of rights (e.g. Cass. 17 Sept. 1983, R.W. 1983-84, 1482, R.C.J.B. 1986, 282). The principle is also applied to contract formation (Cass. 7 February 1994, JTT (1994) 208, RW (1994-95) 121). Some of the German ideas described earlier have been accepted. See *van Ommeslaghe,* TBBR/RGDC 1987, 101; *Fagnart,* R.C.J.B. 1986, 285; *Dirix* TBH/RDC 1988, 660; *M.E.Storme,* Invloed; *van Gerven & Dewaele* 103. The same is true of SPANISH law. Art 7 of the CC imposes a duty to act in good faith when exercising one's rights. Futhermore, as the FRENCH, BELGIAN and LUXEMBOURG CCs art. 1135, art. 1258 of the SPANISH CC provides that once a contract has come into existence the obligations of the contract extends not only to what is expressly stipulated but also to everything that by the nature of things, good faith, usage and law is considered as incidental to the particular contract or necessary to carry it into effect. The Spanish Commercial Code art. 57 requires the parties to execute commercial contracts in accorance with the standards of good faith (see *Lacruz (-Rams),* II, 11, §69, 534).

5. *Mandatory*
In GERMANY and in the systems mentioned in note 4 above the good faith rule is mandatory.

Illustration 4 is based on *Deutsche Bank v. Beriro* (1895) 73 I.T 669, cited in *Zweigert & Kötz* 586.

Article 1:202: Duty to Co-operate

Each party owes to the other a duty to co-operate in order to give full effect to the contract.

COMMENT

A. *The Duty to Co-operate*
Each party has a duty to co-operate with the other to secure full performance of the contract. This includes a duty to allow the other party to perform its obligations and thereby earn the fruits of performance stipulated in the contract.

Illustration 1: S in Hamburg agrees to sell goods to B in London at a stated price f.o.b. Hamburg. B fails to nominate a vessel to carry the goods. Such failure constitutes non-performance of B's obligations under the sales contract and also infringes this Article by preventing S from performing its own obligation to ship the goods and thereby earn the contract price. S is excused from performance under Article 8:101(3) and can terminate the contract and recover damages.

Illustration 2: B contracts to erect an office building for O. As the result of O's failure to apply for a building licence, which would have been granted, B is unable to proceed with the building works. O thereby infringes the requirements of this Article, whether or not its contract with B imposed on it an express obligation to apply for the licence. O has no remedy against B for failing to build and is itself liable to B for breach of contract.

A party has to inform the other party if the other party in performing the contract may not know that there is a risk of harm to persons or property.

> *Illustration 3*: Subcontractor S of country A is about to send some of its staff to perform its duty to Contractor C, also from A, to assist in building a dam in country Y. C learns that the government of Y intends to detain any citizens from A who are found in Y as hostages, in order to exert pressure on the government of A to release some of Y's citizens who have been detained in A charged with terrorism. C has a duty to inform S of the risks involved in sending its staff to Y.

B. *Non-performance of a Collateral Duty*

Obstruction of performance may result either from non-performance of a correlative obligation imposed on a party by the contract or from some other act which, though not in itself constituting a failure to perform, has the effect of preventing or inhibiting performance by the other party. For example a party's failure to accept a tender of performance constitutes a breach of the duty to co-operate where the other party has an interest in having such tender accepted.

> *Illustration 4*: S contracts to sell goods to B and tenders delivery in conformity with the contract. B refuses to accept delivery. This constitutes non-performance by B, whether or not it has paid for the goods, for S is entitled to have them taken off its hands by B, thereby avoiding the expense and inconvenience of disposing of them elsewhere.

Under these Principles failure to co-operate is a breach of a contractual duty, see Article 1:301(4), and attracts the various remedies prescribed for non-performance of contract. The debtor also enjoys the rights and immunities conferred by Articles 7:110 and 7:111.

C. *Duty to Co-operate Limited to Acts in the Performance of which the Other Party has an Interest*

The duty to co-operate is imposed only for the purpose of giving full effect to the contract. Accordingly a party does not infringe the duty to co-operate by failing to perform an act which it has not undertaken to perform and is of no interest to the other party, for example, a failure to accept a tender of performance by the other party where that failure is of no consequence to it.

> *Illustration 5*: B buys a theatre ticket from the S Theatre and pays for it in advance by credit card. He does not collect the ticket or attend the performance. This does not constitute a failure to co-operate or any other non-performance of the contract, for S Theatre, having been paid for the ticket, has no interest in its collection.

D. *Right to Withhold Co-operation*

By Article 9:201(1) a party may refuse to co-operate where its co-operation is dependent on an unfulfilled obligation by the other party, or in cases within Article 9:201(2) (anticipated non-performance by the other party).

Illustration 6: The facts are as in Illustration 1 except that S is given the right to ship the goods at any time during July or August. B is under no duty to nominate a vessel until it has received notification from S of the time at which S intends to ship the goods.

NOTES

1. Civil law countries

In the CIVIL LAW systems the duty to co-operate is derived from the principle of good faith and fair dealing, see Article 1:201.

Thus under the GERMAN BGB § 242 the debtor and the creditor have a duty to co-operate in the performance of the contract. For instance, they must both help to obtain a permission from a third party or a government authority, where this is required (see *Palandt (-Heinrichs)* § 242 No. 3 B b). The duty to co-operate may also oblige a party to support the other party to a contract when a third party may threaten his rights, but § 242 BGB does probably not entail a duty to safeguard the other party's interests in general, see *Staudinger (- J Schmidt)* § 242, No. 754 with references. Under AUSTRIAN law, it follows from the requirement of fair dealing (ABGB § 1914) that the partners to a contract are subject to a collateral contractual duty to take the necessary efforts to make sure that the contract is correctly performed.

A similar duty to assist the other party in the performance of the contract, and derived from the goodfaith principle, is to be found in GREECE, AP 179/1956, NoB 4 (1956) 707, see *Tsirintanis* II/1 art. 288 No. 6 (1949); ITALY, CC art 1175, (see *Breccia* 413, with references) and *Bianca*, Il contratto 471 - 493; THE NETHERLANDS, BW arts. 6:2, 6:248, see also 6:58 on *mora creditoris*; PORTUGAL, *Varela* II 13, *Costa*, Obrigações 872, see also CC arts. 762(2) and 813; and SPAIN, *Diez-Picazo* I 733; *Lacruz(-Rams)*, II, 1 Obligaciones, §69, No. 320, 534).

In FRANCE the duty to co-operate has recently been accepted as flowing from the principle of good faith. The courts have applied it to contracts for the supply of sophisticated products such as computer software, see *Picod* JCP 1988 I 3318. In BELGIUM also good faith has been used as the basis for a duty to co-operate: see references in note to Article 1:201 above, para. 4(b).

NORDIC statutes do not provide a general duty to co-operate in the performance of the contract, but this duty pervades the provisions of the Sale of Goods Acts (DENMARK, 1906; FINLAND and SWEDEN 1987-1990) which in many respects are considered to provide general principles of contract law. See also the emphasis on the duty to co-operate in authors such as *Taxell*, Avtalsrättens normer II and *Wilhelmsson*, Perspectives 21.

2. The United Kingdom

ENGLISH law will impose an implied duty to co-operate where this is necessary in order to give business efficacy to the agreement: see *The Moorcock* (1889) 14 P.D. 64 (C.A.). Beyond this the attitude of the English courts has not been very consistent. See *Burrows* (1968) 31 Modern L.R. 390. The strongest recognition has perhaps been in relation to contracts of employment: see *Secretary of State for Employment* v. *ASLEF (No.2)* [1972] 2 Q.B. 455 (C.A.).

In SCOTS law a duty to co-operate may be found in the implied terms of the contract, see *Mackay* v. *Dick & Stevenson* (1881) 6 App. Cas. 251 (H.L.), per Lord Blackburn .

Section 3: Terminology and Other Provisions

Article 1:301: Meaning of Terms

In these Principles, except where the context otherwise requires:
(1) 'act' includes omission;
(2) 'court' includes arbitral tribunal;
(3) an 'intentional' act includes an act done recklessly;
(4) 'non-performance' denotes any failure to perform an obligation under the contract, whether or not excused, and includes delayed performance, defective performance and failure to co-operate in order to give full effect to the contract;
(5) a matter is 'material' if it is one which a reasonable person in the same situation as one party ought to have known would influence the other party in its decision whether to contract on the proposed terms or to contract at all;
(6) 'written' statements include communications made by telegram, telex, telefax and electronic mail and other means of communication capable of providing a readable record of the statement on both sides.

COMMENT

A. *Act*

As in most legal systems, this includes an omission. The definition is relevant, for example, for the purposes of Articles 1:201(1) and 8:101(3).

B. *Court*

Since these Principles are designed for use by arbitrators as well as by courts, the term 'court' is defined to include an arbitral tribunal. The definition is relevant for the purposes of Articles 4:105(3), 4:109(2) and (3), 6:106(1) and 6:111.

C. *Intentional*

The definition of 'intention' is relevant for the purposes of Articles 1:305(2), 4:107, 8:103(c) and 9:503. A person's act is intentional when he does it deliberately, with the purpose of producing the consequences of the act, or recklessly, that is, when aware of the possible consequences but regardless whether or not they will ensue.

By contrast, one who merely acts carelessly, without considering the consequences that may flow from his act, is not treated as acting intentionally.

The Principles therefore distinguish between intention and mere negligence. So the third category of fundamental non-performance set out in Article 8:103 applies only to intentional non-performance, not to negligent non-performance. This is normally so whether the negligence is gross, that is, serious, or slight, e.g. a momentary oversight.

> *Illustration 1*: A, an architect, is engaged by O to prepare the drawings and specifications for a new factory building. A has recently attended a conference at which he learns that concrete made from a very quick-drying cement he has been specifying for many years has been found to lose its strength to a substantial degree in certain conditions, resulting in the total or partial collapse of the structure in which it used.

Nevertheless A, who has been promised an additional fee if the factory building is completed ahead of the normal schedule, decides to take a chance and specify the use of the cement. Some years after completion of the building part of it collapses as the result of loss of strength of the concrete. O sues A for breach of the contractual duty to exercise reasonable care and skill. Some of the losses suffered by O were not forseeable at the time the contract was made. Since A acted recklessly in specifying the use of the cement when aware of the risks this entailed, his non-performance is intentional within the definition in Article 1:301(3), so that under Article 9:503 he is liable for all losses unavoidably caused by the non-performance, even if these were not foreseeable at the time the contract was made.

> *Illustration 2*: C agrees to paint a house for B. The painting is being done in a very slipshod fashion and is likely to continue to be unsatisfactory even though C is doing his best. The non-performance is not intentional and therefore cannot be treated as fundamental under Article 8:103(3) even if it is grossly negligent.

D. *Non-performance*

The word 'non-performance' is used as a general term covering any failure to perform, for whatever cause. Even a failure in performance which is excused under Article 8:108 falls within the definition of non-performance, for such an excuse deprives the aggrieved party only of the remedies of specific performance and damages, not other remedies set out in Chapter 9 (see Article 8:101(2)). The definition embraces all forms of failure in performance, whether the failure consists of total inactivity (i.e. no step towards performance) or of conduct in or towards performance which in some way fails to conform to the contract, e.g. because it is late, incomplete or otherwise defective. Non-performance also includes failure to fulfil the duty imposed by Article 1:202 to co-operate in order to give full effect to the contract. See Comment and Illustrations to that Article.

A non-conforming tender of performance which is properly rejected results in non-performance but the non-performing party may still have time to make a fresh and conforming tender (Article 8:104).

In general the Principles do not distinguish one type of non-performance from another. However, certain Articles are directed to particular kinds of non-performance, in particular:

failure to accept, take or retake property (Article 7:110)
failure to accept money (Article 7:111)
non-conforming tender of performance (Articles 8:104, 9:401)
delay in payment of money (Article 9:508)

Non-performance of a contract is to be distinguished from breach of contract in the common law sense. By a breach of contract is meant a non-performance which is not excused, e.g. under the rules as to frustration. By contrast, the Principles are framed on the basis that any failure in performance, whether or not excused, produces legal effects, so that the term 'non-performance' includes a failure in performance which is excused under Article 8:108, though the remedies of the other will typically be more restricted in the case of excused non-performance.

> *Illustration 3*: As the result of an embargo S is unable to perform a contract to ship goods to B. The embargo is likely to continue indefinitely and the circumstances are such that S's failure to perform is excused under Article 8:108. S is not liable for damages for breach of contract but under Article 8:108(2) B may treat the non-performance as fundamental and terminate the contract under Article 9:301(1).

E. *Material*

Under the Principles it is sometimes necessary to decide whether a matter is material. Thus under Article 2.208: Modified Acceptance, a reply which gives a definite assent to an offer will not amount to an acceptance if it contains additional or different terms which materially alter the offer; and under Article 2.210: Professional's written Confirmation, additional or different terms contained in a confirmation of the contract will not become part of it if they would alter it materially.

The test is whether the party proposing the additional or different terms should expect them to have any influence on the other's decision. If a reasonable person in his position would not expect this the matters are not material.

Under the Principles, 'material' is different to 'fundamental', which is the standard used to determine whether a non-performance justifies termination (see Article 9:301 and associated Articles) and is also referred to in determining whether a mistake as to facts or law is sufficiently serious to justify avoidance (see Article 4:103). A matter which is fundamental is more important than one which is only material.

It should be noted that the French version of the Principles uses the word *'substantielle'* in place of the English 'material'. This is because *'materiel'* has a different meaning to the English 'material'; conversely, the English word 'substantial' carries overtones of seriousness or significant importance which the word 'material,' at least as defined in Article 1:301(f), does not have.

F. *Writing*

For some purposes under these Principles contracts and statements must be in writing, see Article 2:106(1) and 2:210.

In cases of telecommunications other than telegram, telex and telefax the statement is only in writing if it is possible to provide a readable record of the message as transferred on both sides. A readable record produced by a telephone receiver which is capable of converting sound into writing is not a written statement under Article 1:301(6).

Written statements are opposed to oral statements which cover statements made both in the presence and in the absence of the other party. Oral statements may be made by the use of telephone or other electronic means (e.g. radio).

NOTES

1. *Act*
   In all European legal systems, the term 'act' generally includes an omission (e.g. AUSTRIA, ABGB § 861 sent.1; GERMANY, BGB § 241 sent. 2; GREECE, *Simantiras* No. 555). However, in Germany the statutory provisions which have been drafted for acts are not automatically applicable to omissions (e.g RG 31 March 1909, RGZ 70, 234 (241)).

2. *Court*
   In private disputes several European legal systems regard an 'arbitral tribunal' as in many respects equivalent to a court (e.g. AUSTRIA, ZPO §§ 577ff.; ENGLAND: e.g. Misrepresentation Act 1967, s.2(2); GERMANY: ZPO §§1027a, 1040; GREECE: Drafts and Reports for a New Code of Civil Procedure, 1957, Vol.V, 286 under VI, 520); NETHERLANDS BW art. 3:305. The same also holds true for PORTUGAL. See also CISG art.45.

3. *Intentional*
   In several European legal systems, in the absence of any specific differentiation by the law, the notion 'intentional act' includes an act done recklessly. The latter is sometimes referred to as '*dolus eventualis*'. See for DENMARK: *Vinding Kruse* 52; ENGLAND: *Derry* v. *Peek* (1889) 14 App. Cas. 337; FRANCE, where *faute lourde* is treated as *dol, Viney*, Conditions nos. 605-608; GERMANY: BGH 18 October 1952, BGHZ 7, 311 (313); GREECE: *Stathopoulos*, Contract 156; NETHERLANDS, e.g. BW art. 6:170(3); PORTUGAL: *Telles* 342f. The Principles treat gross negligence as equivalent to intentional or reckless behaviour, as in the maxim *culpa lata dolo aequiparatur* which is adhered to, e.g., by the AUSTRIAN law of contractual (and delictual) liability: *cf.* ABGB § 1331.

4. *Non-Performance*
   See Notes to Article 8:101 below.

5. *Material*
   The meaning of 'material' adopted in the Principles, and the distinction between 'material' and 'fundamental', is derived from the COMMON LAW. Thus in the law of misrepresentation, and of non-disclosure in relation to insurance contracts, a matter is material if it would affect the judgment of a reasonable person in deciding whether, or on what terms to enter a contract (*Treitel*, Contract 312; *Chitty* § 6-022; Marine Insurance Act 1906, s. 20(2), which is said to represent the general law, *Lockyer & Woolf Ltd v. W Australian Insurance Co. Ltd* [1936] 1 K.B. 408; *Pan Atlantic Insurance Co. Ltd v. Pine Top Insurance Co. Ltd* [1995] 1 A.C. 501). In contrast, a term is fundamental if it 'goes to the root of the contract' (see the judgment of Lord Upjohn in *Suisse Atlantique Société d'Armement Maritime SA v. Rotterdamsche Kolen Centrale NV* [1967] 1 A.C. 361, 422).
   CISG appears to adopt a similar distinction. Under art. 19, a purported acceptance which states terms which do not materially alter the terms of the offer constitutes an acceptance; whereas under art. 49 the buyer may declare the contract avoided only if the seller's failure to perform is fundamental. Although art. 19(3) gives examples of what *will* be material, neither 'material' nor 'fundamental' is defined in CISG. *Bianca & Bonell (-Farnsworth)* §2.8 gives examples of 'material' discrepancies, some of which seem quite minor; the importance of the distinction is noted at § 3.1 but no criterion is suggested. Honnold § 169 states merely that 'material' covers 'most aspects of contract', which does not suggest that a mtter must be fundamental in order to be material.

Other systems adopt a criterion similar to this definition of 'material' in the contexts in which the Principles use it. For example, GREEK CC art. 196 states that, by way of exception to the requirement of agreement, if the parties consider that they have concluded a contract even though they are disagreed on a particular point, they will be bound if it appears that the agreement would have been concluded without any consensus on that point. Both doctrine and case law refer to such a matter as 'immaterial'.

In contrast, some systems tend to use 'material' in the sense of 'substantial' (e.g. SCOTTISH law) or do not distinguish the two concepts (e.g. DANISH statutes and writers).

6. *Written*

The definition of 'written' statements in Article 1:301(6) is in line with instances of modern legislation in EU Member States. For example, PORTUGUESE Law 31/86 of 29 August 1986, which requires a written form for contracts for arbitration, accepts telegrams, telex and 'other means of communication of which there may be written proof' (art. 2); similarly GERMAN ZPO § 1031(1) as revised by Law of 22 December 1997. Both provisions seem to be based on the UNCITRAL Model Law on Arbitration art. 7(2).

Other international provisions are narrower. Thus CISG art.13 refers simply to telegrams and telexes. It is thought that this might be applied to a telefax or even an email which has been printed out, but not to one which at the relevant time had only appeared on a screen, *von Caemmerere & Schlechtriem* 126; *Honnold* No.130.

National statutes frequently require a document with a signature, either simply because they were passed before the electronic age or because the requirement of writing is thought to have a protective function, e.g GERMAN BGB § 126; ENGLISH Consumer Credit Act 1974, s.60; Law of Property (Miscellaneous Provisions) Act 1989, s.2(3). For an analysis of which English statutes that require writing, or similar formalities, may be satisfied by electronic messages, see *Reed*. Even if this is not expressly provided, the statutes may be interpreted in that way if that seems appropriate (e.g. in DENMARK, see *Gomard,* Kontraktsret 171).

Article 1:302: Reasonableness

Under these Principles reasonableness is to be judged by what persons acting in good faith and in the same situation as the parties would consider to be reasonable. In particular, in assessing what is reasonable the nature and purpose of the contract, the circumstances of the case and the usages and practices of the trades or professions involved should be taken into account.

COMMENT

A. *The terms 'reasonable' and 'unreasonable' in the Principles*
(i) *'Reasonable'*
In these Principles the term reasonable is used to express various requirements for example:
–   What may one expect a party to know or to take into account? Articles 1:303(4), 2:102, 2:202(3), 3:201(3), 3:206, 3:209(3), 5:101(3), 6:111(2)(a), 8:103(2), 8: 108(1) and 9:503.
–   How long may a party wait to act? Articles 2:206(2) and (3), 3:203, 7:109(2), 7:102(3), 8:106(3), 8:105(2), 8:108(3), 9:303(2) and (3) and 9:506.
–   How long may the parties take to reach agreement? Article 6:111(3).
–   How long should the notice be? Articles 4:113(1) and (2), 6:109 and 8:104(3).
–   Is a price or a term equitable? Articles 4:105(3), 4:115, 6:104, 6:105, 6:106(2), 7:110(2)(a) and (b), 9:101(2)(a), 9:506 and 9:509(2).

- Which efforts can one expect a party to make? Articles 7:110(1), 9:102(2)(d) and 9:505(1).
- Is there a proportionate relationship between value and effort? Article 7:110(3).
- Is there a proportionate relationship between the seriousness of the non-performance and the remedy exercised? Article 9:201(1).
- How great is the likelihood of a future contingency? Article 1:303(2), 8:105(1) and 9:501(2)(b).

See also Article 6:108.

(ii) *'Unreasonable'*
The term unreasonable is used:
- To explain how great a nuisance a party must suffer from the other party's behaviour: Article 7:103.
- What constitutes an unconscionable usage or an unreasonable term: Articles 1:105(2), 6:105, and 6:106(2).
- Whether there is a proportionate relationship between value and cost (unreasonably expensive): Article 7:110(1).
- What constitutes an unreasonable omission? Article 9:303(3)(b).
- What makes the burden upon the party too great: Article 9:101(2)(b) and 9:102(2)(b).

B. *Standards to measure reasonableness*
Reasonableness in the contexts of the Articles mentioned in Comment A is to be judged by what parties acting in good faith and the same situation as the parties would consider to be reasonable.

In deciding what is reasonable all relevant factors should be taken into consideration. Account should be taken of the nature and purpose of the contract. Thus the period of time within which a notice of termination under Article 9:303 must be given will depend upon whether the contract requires quick action by the aggrieved party. This may be the case if by deferring the notice it may take advantage of price fluctuations which are frequent in the trade.

The circumstances of the case will have to be considered. Thus the notice to end a distributorship contract made to last for an indefinite period of time, see Article 6:109, is longer when the contract has lasted for a long period, or when the distributor has made considerable investments in the performance of the contract, and shorter if the contract has not lasted for a long period or if the distributor has made few or no investments.

Furthermore, the usages and practices of the trade or profession should be taken into account. These generally reflect the behaviour of reasonable parties. Thus, in determining whether a price or another contractual term is reasonable for the purpose of Articles 6:104, 6:105 or 6:106(2) comparable contracts made in analogous situations should be considered. Also here the nature and the purpose of the contract, the status of the parties, and the practices and usages in the trade or profession concerned should be taken into account.

NOTE

Article 1:302 expresses what seems to be the common core of the legal systems. There is, as far as is known, no statutory provision of this kind in any of the Member States. Some provisions of the UNITED KINGDOM Unfair Contract Terms Act 1977 refer to 'the requirements of reasonableness', and to what is 'fair and reasonable', to describe under which circumstances a contract term excluding or limiting liability may be enforced. Schedule 2 of the Act gives 'guidelines' for the application of this reasonableness test. However, these guidelines are linked to the special problems relating to clauses excluding or limiting liability. For the interpretation of Article 8:109 on terms limiting or excluding liability, see the Comment to that provision. On the Unfair Contract Terms Act and Schedule 2, see *Cheshire, Fifoot & Furmston* 193-196 and *Chitty* I §§ 14-045 ff and 14-068 ff. Similar but less extensive statutory provisions on 'reasonableness' exist in IRELAND, Sale of Goods and Supply of Services Act 1980, see *Clark* 172; and some of the criteria referred to in Article 1:302 will be found in the general fairness rule of Contract Acts § 36 in FINLAND and SWEDEN.

DUTCH BW art. 3:12 states that: 'In determining what reasonableness and equity require, reference must be made to generally accepted principles of law, to current juridical views in the Netherlands and to the particular societal and private interests involved.' This appears to have a broader application than Article 1:302.

Article 1:303: Notice

(1) Any notice may be given by any means, whether in writing or otherwise, appropriate to the circumstances.

(2) Subject to paragraphs (4) and (5), any notice becomes effective when it reaches the addressee.

(3) A notice reaches the addressee when it is delivered to it or to its place of business or mailing address, or, if it does not have a place of business or mailing address, to its habitual residence.

(4) If one party gives notice to the other because of the other's non-performance or because such non-performance is reasonably anticipated by the first party, and the notice is properly dispatched or given, a delay or inaccuracy in the transmission of the notice or its failure to arrive does not prevent it from having effect. The notice shall have effect from the time at which it would have arrived in normal circumstances.

(5) A notice has no effect if a withdrawal of it reaches the addressee before or at the same time as the notice.

(6) In this Article, 'notice' includes the communication of a promise, statement, offer, acceptance, demand, request or other declaration.

COMMENT

A. *Notices Broadly Defined*
The rules in this Article apply to the whole range of notices, declarations and other communications: see (6).

B. *The Form of Notices*
Under the Principles notices may be made in any form – orally, in writing, by telex, by fax or by electronic mail, for example – provided that the form of notice used is

appropriate to the circumstances. It would not be consistent with good faith and fair dealing (see Article 1:201) for a party to rely on, for instance, a purely casual remark made to the other party. For notices of major importance written form may be appropriate. (See further comment D) below.)

C. *The Receipt Principle*

The general rule adopted by these Principles is that a party cannot rely on a notice sent to the other party unless and until the notice reaches that party. It is not necessary that the notice should actually have come to the addressee's attention provided that it has been delivered to him in the normal way, e.g. a letter placed in his letter box or a message sent to his telex or fax machine. Similarly the risk of errors in the notice is normally placed upon the sender (see Article 4:104). The principle of good faith and fair dealing (Article 1:201) means that a party cannot complain that it has not received a notice, or has not received it in time, if it has deliberately evaded receiving it.

> *Illustration*: A notice to extend a charterparty must be given to the owner's office, which is open round the clock, by 17.00 on April 1. The charterer telephones at 16.59. The owners are expecting the call but do not want the charter to be extended. Therefore they deliberately let the phone ring until after 17.00 has passed; they then answer it and say that the notice is too late. The notice is treated as having been given in time.

Sometimes, as the result of practices or usages, an acceptance may be effective without communication: see Article 2:205: Time of Conclusion of the Contract.

D. *The Dispatch Principle for Cases of Default*

However, many of the situations in which these Principles envisage one party giving a notice to the other are situations in which the party to be notified is in default, or it appears that a default is likely. Here it seems appropriate to put the risk of loss, mistake or delay in the transmission of the message on the defaulting party rather than on the aggrieved party. The dispatch principle thus applies to notices given under the following articles:

7:109   Property not accepted
7:110   Money not accepted
8:105   Assurance of performance
8:106   Notice fixing additional time for performance
9:102(3) Non-monetary obligation (loss of right to specific performance)
9:301   Right to terminate the contract
9:303   Notice of termination
9:304   Anticipatory non-performance

The dispatch rule does not apply to a notice which is to be given by the defaulting party, e.g. under Article 8:108(3), or by a party which wishes to invoke hardship, see Article 6:111, or to an assurance of performance under 8:105(2).

E. *Means of Notice Given on Default Must Be Appropriate*
The dispatch principle will not apply if the means of notice was not appropriate in the circumstances. For instance, for the dispatch principle to apply, the means chosen must be fast enough. If great speed is needed a letter sent by air mail may not be appropriate and the sender may not rely on the fact that it was dispatched. It will be able to rely on it only if and when it arrives.

F. *Time at which Notice Takes Effect*
A notice subject to the general 'receipt' principle takes effect when it is received. A notice subject to the dispatch principle may be effective even though it never arrives or is delayed, but it is not effective the moment it is dispatched. It would not be fair that even a non-performing party should be affected by a notice as from a time at which it could not have known about it. Accordingly the notice takes effect only from the time at which it would normally have been received.

G. *Simultaneous Withdrawal*
A notice is not effective if at the same time, or earlier, the recipient gets a withdrawal or countermand of the notice, Article 1:303(5).

NOTES

1. *The general 'receipt' principle*
   Although some systems, particularly the COMMON LAW, recognise special rules in relation to the postal acceptance of an offer (see *Zweigert & Kötz* 358-359), under most systems notices in general must arrive if they are to be effective; and this applies even to notices given because of the other's default. Several systems assume that the basic principle is that actual knowledge is required, e.g. SPANISH CC art. 1262 and ITALIAN CC art. 1335, which states circumstances in which the recipient is deemed to have knowledge; COMMON LAW, see the case of *Car & Universal Finance Co Ltd v. Caldwell* [1965] 1 Q.B. 525, C.A. (rescission for fraud); SCOTTISH law, see *MacLeod v. Kerr* 1965 S.C. 253.

   In FRENCH law discussion of the topic is restricted to formation of contracts. It appears that the matter is within the *appréciation souveraine* of the judge (Cass.soc. 21 Nov. 1966, JCP 67 II 15012; Cass.com. 6 March 1961, B.III No.123, p.109), but *la jurisprudence* shows a marked preference for the dispatch principle, notably Cass.com 7 January 1981, B.IV No.14, which adopts it explicitly, see *Terré, Simler & Lequette*, Introduction No.521). In LUXEMBOURG, in contrast, the receipt principle is favoured: Cour 16 July 1896, Pas.4, 209; Cour 27 March 1903, Pas.6, 248.

   In SPANISH law the receipt principle applies generally (CC art 1262) but the dispatch principle is applied to commercial contracts (Comm C. art. 54).

   Under CISG art.24 the receipt principle governs offers, acceptances and most other statements covered by Part II on formation of contracts.

   In NORDIC law the receipt principle generally applies. However the dispatch principle governs certain notices given in order to prevent a contract arising, such as notices given under Contract Acts § 4(2), see note 2 to Article 2:207, and § 6(2), see note 3 to Article 2:208.

2. *Actual knowledge not required*
   Many systems, though adopting the receipt principle, explicitly recognise that actual communication to the recipient is not necessary provided that the notice has been properly delivered to the recipient's address: eg COMMON LAW (dicta in *Holwell Securities Ltd v. Hughes* [1974] 1 W.L.R. 155, C.A.); BELGIAN law (Cass. 25 May 1990, Arr. Cass. No.561, R.W. 1990-91, 149; AUSTRIAN ABGB § 862; GREEK law (AP 482/1956, NoB 5 (1957) 94; Athens 3347/1973, NoB 21 (1973) 1474-1475); SCOTTISH law (*Burnley v. Alford* 1919 S.L.T. 123). In NORDIC law a notice countermanding an earlier offer or acceptance is effective if it reaches the recipient before or at the same time as the offer or acceptance comes to his attention, see Nordic Contracts Acts § 7).

ITALIAN CC art. 1335 provides that a notice will still not be effective if the addressee shows that it was not possible for him to learn of the notice and that he himself was not in default. Other systems which use the receipt principle also adopt the rule that the addressee cannot rely on non-receipt if it was his own fault (DUTCH BW art 3:37(3); PORTUGUESE CC art. 224) or if he had deliberately prevented communication (COMMON LAW: *Car & Universal Finance Co Ltd* v. *Caldwell* [1965] 1 Q.B. 525, C.A.). In SCOTLAND, however, notice of rescission of a contract must reach the party at fault: *Macleod v. Kerr* 1965 S.C. 253.

It should be noted, however, that many systems draw a distinction between a notice which will be binding on the recipient and a declaration such as a promise or offer which will bind the sender. Such a declaration will be binding on the sender only when the recipient has actual knowledge of it (e.g. NORDIC law, Contracts Acts § 7); COMMON LAW, *R.* v. *Clarke* (1927) 40 C.L.R. 227 (High Court of Australia).

3. *Dispatch principle when notice because of a default*
DANISH Sale of Goods Act § 61 explicitly provides that as long as the notice is properly dispatched, it does not cause a loss for the sender that the notice is delayed or does not reach the person to whom it is given. The new Sale of Goods Acts adopted in FINLAND and SWEDEN provide that certain notices, in particular notices sent to a party who is in breach of contract, will be effective even though they do not reach the recipient, § 82. See also Nordic Sale of Goods Acts § 40 concerning notices to be given by a party who wishes to avoid a contract; reasonable means of communication must be used. In AUSTRIAN and GERMAN law a number of rules of consumer protection and commercial law – especially HGB § 377(4) – provide that timely sending of certain notices is sufficient. However, these rules do not relieve the sender from the risk of loss, only from the risk of delay (BGH 13 May 1987, BGHZ 101, 49 (53)).

ULIS art.39(3) applies the dispatch principle to notices of non-conformity and CISG art.27, in contrast to its provisions on most other statements (see note 1 above), applies the dispatch principle to notices which the aggrieved party gives to the other under Part III relating to non-performance: see *Honnold* §§162 and 189-190.

The illustration is based on *Nissho Iwai Petroleum Co Inc.* v. *Cargill International SA* [1973] 1 Lloyd's Rep. 80.

Article 1:304: Computation of Time

(1) A period of time set by a party in a written document for the addressee to reply or take other action begins to run from the date stated as the date of the document. If no date is shown, the period begins to run from the moment the document reaches the addressee.

(2) Official holidays and official non-working days occurring during the period are included in calculating the period. However, if the last day of the period is an official holiday or official non-working day at the address of the addressee, or at the place where a prescribed act is to be performed, the period is extended until the first following working day in that place.

(3) Periods of time expressed in days, weeks, months or years shall begin at 00.00 on the next day and shall end at 24.00 on the last day of the period; but any reply that has to reach the party which set the period must arrive, or any other act which is to be done must be completed, by the normal close of business in the relevant place on the last day of the period.

COMMENT

A. *Importance of Certainty for Both Parties*
It is important to have clear rules governing the computation of time so a party which has been told by the other that it must reply or do some other act by or within a certain time may know how long it has, but also so that the party which set the time may know whether or not the other has replied or acted within the time set.

B. *Oral Communications*
If a party sets a period of time in an oral communication, whether face to face or by phone, and does not state from when it is to run, the natural assumption is that it runs from the moment of communication. (This would apply even to a message left on a telephone answering machine: the period will start from the moment the message is recorded.) No special rule is needed for this case. Problems arise only with communications in writing (which as defined in Article 1.301 include email and similar electronic forms of communication if they are capable of leaving a written record).

C. *Express Starting Time Prevails*
If the party setting the time has stated how it is to be computed, that should govern. In some situations the Principles require that it set a reasonable time. For example under Article 8:106, Notice fixing additional time for performance, para. (3), the notice must set a reasonable period of time for performance. Choosing an inappropriate method of computation might mean that the notice given is not adequate and the period will have to be extended.

D. *Starting Time Not Expressly Stated*
In default of a stated method of computation, there might be uncertainty whether the period should start from the time the communication was prepared, the time it was sent or the time it was received.

It is well known that delays occur not only in the actual transmission of communications such as telegrams or letters but also in the sending out of all types of communication. For example a fax may be signed on one day but the sender's office may not dispatch it until the next. This will not necessarily be apparent to the sender, who may simply be given back the original; nor to the person in the recipient's office who is charged with responding. Although fax machines record the time the message was received at the top or bottom of the page, this is very easily lost when the document is photocopied again. For this reason the Principles adopt the rule that the date shown as the date of the letter or other document should normally be treated as the starting date by whatever method the document was transmitted.

E. *No Date Shown*
With non-instantaneous communications like letters or telegrams, if the letter or telegram itself is undated, time should run from the date at which it was received, which will be all that is clear to the recipient. (With instantaneous written communications like a fax, there is little difficulty because the sending and receipt are simultaneous.)

F. *Non-working Days Count unless the Last Day of the Period*

The Principles follow European convention (see the 1972 Convention on the Calculation of Time-Limits, Article 5) in including official non-working days (e.g. Saturday and Sunday) and official holidays in the period, except that if the last day of a period is an official non-working day or official holiday in the relevant place (i.e. where the message is to be delivered or the action performed) the period is extended to include the next working day. If in the relevant trade there is a usage of working on what is officially a holiday, or if there is a local usage of working or not working on the relevant day, the usage will prevail, see Article 1:105.

G. *Time runs from Midnight to Midnight*

Also in accordance with the European Convention, the Principles provide that time runs from midnight to midnight.

> *Illustration 1*: An offer dated Monday 1 April says that the offeree must let the offeror know within seven days if he wishes to accept. The seven day period starts from midnight on April 1 and ends at midnight on April 8.

However, the party which has set the period should not have to wait for a reply or other action beyond the normal working day in its business in the country. Moreover, the relevant close of business should be the one where the party is, since the person who has been told to reply within a certain time should not be entitled to assume that this means the period calculated by his own time.

> *Illustration 2*: As in Illustration 1 but the offeror is in Paris and the offeree is in London, which is one hour behind the time in Paris. The offeree must get his reply to the offeror by the close of business in Paris, not the later close of business in London.

NOTES

1. *Period runs from date of document or, if no date stated, of receipt*
   Some legal systems calculate time periods set in a document from the date stated in the document, rather than, for example, the date the document was received by the party who is to respond within the time stated: NORDIC Contracts Act § 2(2) (offers). In most countries the question is one of interpretation and the period may run from the date of receipt if this is what is stated or seems appropriate in the circumstances (cf. the ENGLISH case of *Dodds* v. *Walker* [1981] 1 W.L.R. 1207, H.L. (by statute, tenant could apply for renewal of tenancy within 'four months of the giving of the landlord's notice' to quit: time started on receipt of notice and expired on corresponding day of fourth month after)). In GERMAN law the question is also left to general rules on interpretation, see *Larenz/Wolf* § 28 No. 99, 101, § 52 No.1.

2. *Official holidays and non-working days*
   Many systems also presume that official holidays and non-working days are included in the period of time: ENGLAND, see *Chitty* §21-019, *Halsbury* vol.45, para. 1140; GERMANY, *Larenz/Wolf* § 52 No. 10.
      The rule that if the last day of the period is a holiday or non-working day, the time is extended to the next working day is also found widely: e.g. AUSTRIAN ABGB § 903; BELGIAN Judicial Code art. 53; FRENCH NCPC art. 642; GERMAN BGB § 193; NORDIC Instruments of Debt Act

§5 (2); PORTUGUESE CC art. 279(e), which also refers to judicial holidays. In England, however, the rule applies only to acts to be done by a court or in court; in other cases, the general rule is that the fact that the last day is a Sunday or a holiday does not extend the time, *Halsbury* vol. 45, para. 1138.

Article 1:304(2), first sentence, corresponds to the European Convention on Time-Limits of 16 May 1972 (Eur. T.S. No. 76), art.5.

3. *Time runs from start of next day to midnight of last day*
    This rule is very common: e.g. AUSTRIAN ABGB § 902; BELGIAN Judical Code art. 52(1); ENGLAND, presumption to this effect, see *Chitty* § 21-020 and *Halsbury*, vol. 45, paras. 1134-1135; FINLAND, specific rule in Insurance Contracts Act of 1994, § 11 (5); FRENCH NCPC arts. 641-642; GERMAN BGB §§ 187(1) and 188(1); GREEK CC art. 241, Code of Civil Procedure art. 144(1); PORTUGUESE CC art. 279 (c). Article 1:304(3), first sentence, corresponds to the European Convention on Time-limits, art.3(1).

4. *Time ends at close of business on last day*
    This rule is found in some systems: e.g. BELGIAN Judicial Code art. 52(2); ENGLAND, presumption to this effect, see *Chitty* § 21-019. In GERMAN commercial law, performance must be effected by the close of business on the last day, HGB § 358. In other systems the rule would probably follow from the good faith principle, e.g. in PORTUGAL. Article 1:304(3), second sentence, corresponds to the European Convention on Time-limits, art.3(2).

Article 1:305: Imputed Knowledge and Intention

If any person who with a party's assent was involved in making a contract, or who was entrusted with performance by a party or performed with its assent:
(a) knew or foresaw a fact, or ought to have known or foreseen it; or
(b) acted intentionally or with gross negligence, or not in accordance with good faith and fair dealing,
this knowledge, foresight or behaviour is imputed to the party itself.

COMMENT

A. *Purpose*

It is the common purpose of both rules to neutralize the legal risks that inhere in the modern division of labour in trade and industry. This is achieved by imputing actual or constructive knowledge or a legally relevant state of mind, such as intention, negligence or bad faith, of a person assisting in the making or performance of the contract to the contracting party to whom that assistance is rendered.

B. *Scope*

Under modern conditions, most contracts are not made or performed by the contracting parties personally. Rather, the parties make contracts through the agency of employees or other persons and entrust performance of their contracts to employees, agents, subcontractors and other third persons. Article 8:107, Performance Entrusted to Another, provides that a party cannot escape its obligation of performance by delegating it to another; if the obligation is not performed, the party will remain responsible. The present Article is complementary to Article 8:107. It deals with two other aspects of this modern division of labour, namely the imputation of actual or constructive knowledge of persons assisting in the making or performance of a contract to the contracting party itself (subparagraph (a)); and with the imputation of intention or gross negligence with respect to non-performance (subparagraph (b)).

C. *Imputed Knowledge and Foresight*
Several provisions use the criteria of knowledge, awareness, foreseeability, contemplation (see Articles 1:301(5), 2:104, 3:102(2), 3:204(2), 3:205(1) and (3), 3:208, 3:209(1), 3:301(1), 4:103(1), 4:109(1), 4:111(2), 4:113(1), 4:114, 4:117(1), 6:101 (2) and (3), 6:110(3), 6:111(2), 7:101(2), 8:103 subparagraph (b), 8:108(3), 9:102 (3), 9:303(2) and (3), 9:503). A party which should have known or foreseen a fact is usually treated as if it had the knowledge or foresight.

When the contract is being made, a party is normally only fixed with the knowledge imputed to his employees or agents involved in making the contract. Under some Articles (e.g. Article 9:303), knowledge or foreseeability at the time of non-performance is relevant. In this case, for the purposes of Article 1:305 knowledge or intention even of any subcontractor or other person to whom it has entrusted performance may be imputed to the party.

However, there is one limitation. The employee or other person must have been someone who was, or who appeared to be, involved in the negotiation or performance of the contract. If a person not so related to the contract knows a relevant fact he may not be able to appreciate its relevance to the contract and thus might not report it. The burden of proving that the person for whom the contracting party is held responsible was not and did not reasonably appear to the other party to be involved in the making or performance of the contract rests on the first party.

D. *Imputed Intention, Negligence and Bad Faith*
According to subparagraph (b), certain states of mind or behaviour of the person acting are also imputed to the contracting party for whom a contract has been concluded or an act of performance is rendered.

Under several rules intentional or grossly negligent behaviour or bad faith by a party creates or increases his liability (see Articles 2:301(2), 4:107(2), 8:103 subparagraph (c), 9:503; cf. also Article 1:201(1)).

Even if the contracting party has not entrusted performance to a third person, a third person may nevertheless under certain conditions be entitled to perform the contract, see Article 7:106. If the third person acted with the contracting party's assent (Article 7:106(1) (a)) that is equivalent to an entrustment and therefore falls under Article 1:305. In contrast, if the third person has acted by virtue of a legitimate interest in the performance under Article 7:106(1) (b), that falls outside the scope of Article 1:305. It should be noted that under these Principles liability is not generally based on the notion of fault. Only intentional or grossly negligent non-performance are therefore mentioned as attracting greater liability.

The intentional or grossly negligent behaviour of a party or of a person whose state of mind is imputed to a party only refers to the act or omission which constitutes the non-performance. It is not necessary that the intention or gross negligence also extend to the consequences that may follow from the non-performance.

NOTES

The issues covered by Article 1:305 are not always clearly regulated in the existing national laws.

1.   Imputation of knowledge

Imputation of knowledge (Article 1:305 lit. (a)) is dealt with in rules on agency in BELGIUM (*De Page & Dekkers* I No. 52), GERMANY (BGB § 166), ITALY (CC art. 1391) and PORTUGAL (CC art. 259(1)). In Germany it is held that the rule of BGB § 166 on agency expresses a general principle: a person who entrusts another with executing certain affairs on his own responsibility will have imputed to him knowledge which the other has acquired in that context (BGH 25 March 1982, BGHZ 83, 293 (296)); this principle corresponds to the idea underlying Article 1:305 lit. (a). Although there is no explicit rule in the AUSTRIAN Code, the OGH reaches the same result by reference to ABGB § 1017 (OGH 13 February 1963, SZ 36/25; see *Schwimann (-Apathy)* ABGB § 1017 N 12). In ENGLISH and SCOTTISH law the question is also treated as one of agency (cf. *Chitty* §§ 6-031 and 6-037; *Treitel*, Contract 319 with references). In the NORDIC countries the agent's knowledge is imputed to the principal, *Kaisto* s. 265.

In BELGIUM a similar rule is justified by analogy to the rule on performance entrusted to another (see Article 8:107 below). In FRANCE, a corresponding rule has apparently not yet been formulated; but it may be compatible with the solutions to be found in case law, especially in determining foreseeability of damage (cf. *Viney*, Effets No. 325).

In Germany (BGB § 166(1), Greece (CC art. 214), Italy (CC art. 1391(1)) and Portugal (CC art. 259(1)), only the agent's state of mind is, as a rule, considered. If, however, the agent has acted according to instructions, also the principal's state of mind is considered in Germany (BGB § 166(2)) and Greece (CC art. 215); by contrast, in Italy (cf. supra) and Portugal (CC art. 259 (2)) only the principal is then considered. A very flexible rule has been enacted in THE NETHERLANDS: either the agent or the principal or both are taken into account, depending on the extent to which each of them took part in concluding the contract or in determining its contents (BW art. 3:66(2)).

2.   Imputation of intention

In some national laws, the imputation of intention, negligence and bad faith (Article 1:305 lit. (b)) is very important in the framework of fault principle for liability. According to several provisions, a non-performing party is responsible for the culpable behaviour of persons whom he has charged with performing his obligations (AUSTRIAN ABGB § 1313a; BELGIUM: Cass. 24 January 1974, Pas.I 553 and Cass. 21 June 1979, Pas. I 1226; DENMARK: Danske Lov 1683 art. 3-19-2; GERMANY: BGB § 278 sent. 1; GREECE: CC arts. 330 and 334; ITALY: CC art. 1228; NETHERLANDS: BW art. 6:76; PORTUGAL: CC art. 800(1)). FRENCH law reaches the same result for exclusion clauses (*Malaurie & Aynès*, Obligations No. 861).

In SPANISH law, there is no corresponding general rule for contractual liability, but legal writers and case law acknowledge contractual liability for acts of persons for whom the non-performing party is responsible (*Diez-Picaso* I paras. 724-726; *Jordano Frago* 561 ff.; STS 22 June 1989 (Ar. 4776); STS 1 March 1990 (Ar. 1656)), although intention probably cannot be imputed. In ENGLISH law, the question does not arise because the fact that a breach is deliberate usually does not affect a party's liability.

Some of the aforementioned modern codes in Civil Law countries also deal with good and bad faith. Italy and Portugal start out from the general principle set out *supra* (sub 1). If, however, the principal is in bad faith, he cannot invoke the agent's ignorance or good faith (Italian CC art. 1391(2) and Portuguese CC art. 259(2)).

See generally *Treitel*, Remedies § 15 and literature cited there.

CHAPTER 2

Formation of Contracts

Section 1 : General Provisions

Article 2:101: Conditions for the Conclusion of a Contract

(1) A contract is concluded if:
(a) the parties intend to be legally bound, and
(b) they reach a sufficient agreement
without any further requirement.
(2) A contract need not be concluded or evidenced in writing nor is it subject to any other requirement as to form. The contract may be proved by any means, including witnesses.

COMMENTS

A. *Contract*
In these Principles the notion contract covers:
- agreements under which two or more parties have undertaken an obligation to make a performance,
- agreements where the offeree accepts the offer by doing the act or suffering the forbearance which the offeror asks of it,
- agreements where only one party has obligations and where its promise needs acceptance by the offeree,
- promises to which one party is bound without acceptance by the other, as provided in Article 2:107 below.

The rules on contract also govern agreements to modify or end existing contracts, see Article 1:107.

B. *Intention*
In order to be bound by a contract a party must have an intention to be legally bound. Whether in fact it has such intention is immaterial if the other party has reason to infer from the first party's statement or other conduct that it intends to be bound, see Article 2:102.

C. *Agreement*

Where more than one party is to be bound the parties must agree. Their agreement may be reached by one party's acceptance of the other's offer, see Section 2, by agreeing to a contract which has been drafted by a third party, or in other ways. What constitutes sufficient agreement is spelled out in Article 2:103.

In some cases where only one party is to be bound an expression of agreement by the other party is not needed. Promises which are intended to become binding without acceptance are to be treated as contracts, see Article 2:107.

D. *No Further Requirement*

Whether or not agreement is needed there are no further requirements. No form is required, see Comment F. Nor is it necessary that a promisee undertakes to furnish or furnishes something of value in exchange for the promise (consideration). Even an undertaking to lend money and a promise to receive a deposit are effective before they have been performed. A contract is not invalid because at the time of its conclusion it was impossible to perform the obligation assumed, see Article 4:102.

E. *Binding Character of a "Gratuitous" Promise*

Some legal systems do not enforce a party's "gratuitous" promise. Some do so but only if it is couched in a solemn form or is found to serve a socially desirable purpose which cannot be achieved by other means.

The fear that the enforcement of such "gratuitous" promises, even though no formality has been observed, will lead to socially undesirable results is not well founded. In fact many of these promises serve legitimate commercial purposes.

Nor is it necessary to inquire into the social desirability of the promise if it is sincerely made. Experience shows that the legal systems which enforce gratuitous promises do not encounter problems. "Crazy" promises made by persons of a sound mind are so rare that they may be disregarded, while even the presence of a formality or of an exchange does not guarantee that the contract is a sensible one. On the other hand, those legal systems which do not enforce "gratuitous" promises have faced problems when such promises sincerely made have since been revoked. These problems do not only arise when the promisee has acted in reliance on the promise, and injustice can be avoided only be enforcing the promise, but also in other situations. For this reason these promises should be enforced.

F. *No Formal Requirement*

Article 2:101(2) lays down the principle that, unless the parties otherwise agree, the conclusion as well as the modification and the termination by agreement of a contract are valid without any form, be it writing, sealing, authentication by a notary, filing in a public registry etc. This principle is widely accepted among the legal systems at least as far as commercial contracts are concerned. For international contracts it is particularly important since many such contracts have to be concluded or modified without the delays which the observance of formalities will cause.

This provision also applies to unilateral promises, see Article 2:107.

NOTES

1. *Introduction. National Laws*

   In BELGIUM, FRANCE and LUXEMBOURG the rules on formation are laid down in the decided cases which are inspired by the 18th century writer *Pothier, Obligations.* Art. 1108 of the *Code civil* of BELGIUM, FRANCE and LUXEMBOURG is the only provision of the codes dealing with the formation of contracts. It provides that the necessary conditions for the validity of a contract are consent of the party which assumes an obligation, capacity to contract, a certain object which forms the matter of the agreement and a lawful *cause.* The SPANISH CC. has similar rules in arts. 1261 and 1262. It mentions that the agreeement of the parties mainfests itself by the offer and acceptance.

   In ENGLAND, IRELAND and SCOTLAND the rules on the formation of contracts are based on case law. In the other Member States rules on the conclusion of contracts are provided in codes and statutes.

2. *Art 2:101(1) "A contract is concluded when..."*

   The concept of contract as adopted in the Principles is an agreement which creates legal obligations. It generally involves two or more parties whose obligations are reciprocal. However, contract also covers promises to perform, for instance to pay a sum of money, if the other party performs an act, and it covers obligations assumed only by one party, such as a promise for a gift, and promises which are binding without acceptance, see Article 2:107.

   In this and other respects there are differences between the legal systems, mostly of a terminological character. FRENCH, BELGIAN and LUXEMBOURG CCs art. 1101 define contract as an agreement by which one party binds himself to another to give, to do or not to do something. The Codes distinguishe between *contrats synallagmatiques* and *contrats unilatéraux*, see CCs arts. 1103 and 1104. The former create reciprocally binding obligations for the parties; the seller, for instance, must deliver the goods and the buyer in return pay the purchase money. *Les contrats unilatéraux* only create obligations for one party and rights for the other. They need acceptance by the offeree in order to be concluded.

   Promises which are not accepted by the promisee are generally not binding as contracts. However, certain unilateral engagements, for example a promise to fulfil a "natural obligation", may under certain conditions bind the promisor without acceptance, see *Terré, Simler & Lequette, Obligations* nos. 47 ff.

   In ENGLAND *Treitel* describes a contract as an agreement giving rise to obligations which are enforced or recognized by law, see *Treitel,* Contracts 1 The common law makes a distinction between *bilateral* and *unilateral* contracts. A bilateral contract is a synallagmatic contract. A unilateral contract is one under which a counter promise of the offeree is not required. His acceptance consists in *doing the act or suffering the forbearance* which is asked of him. Under the doctrine of consideration, see note 3(a) below, the act or forbearance is the counter-performance which makes the promise of the offeror binding. An offer for a reward made to the public is accepted when a person being aware of the offer does the act which is asked for. Gift promises are not enforceable unless made in the form of a deed which is not considered to be a contract. Unilateral promises which are binding without acceptance are very seldom recognized in English law, see notes to Article 2:107.

   In GERMAN and AUSTRIAN law a contract is one of several *juristic acts.* A *juristic act (Rechtsgeschäft)* is an act by one or more persons the purpose of which is bring about legal effects. Every *juristic act* must consist of at least one declaration (or conduct) which expresses a person's intention to be legally bound by the effect which the declaration purports to bring about, also called a *declaration of will (Willenserklärung),* and to which the law gives that effect because it is intended. A promise is a *Willenserklärung* which binds the promisor, and it may bind him without acceptance. Some promises, such as a promise of a reward made to the public *(Auslobung),* are binding on the promisor even though they do not reach the promisee. Others are only binding when they reach the offeree, such as an act whereby a person confers upon another person the power to act for him *(Auftrag).* The rules on *"Willenserklärungen"* are to be found in title 2 of book 1 part 3, of the BGB.

   A contract *(Vertrag)* is a legal transaction which consists of at least two declarations of will which express agreement. It may be unilaterally binding or bilaterally binding. A unilaterally binding contract, such as a promise to make a gift or to stand surety for another person, only creates duties in one person. In principle it needs acceptance by the other party. However, acceptance of a promise to make a gift is presumed when the other party remains silent, see BGB § 516(2). A bilaterally binding contract is one which creates reciprocal duties on both parties, such as a sale and a lease. It presupposes the parties' concordant intention to be legally bound, see *Larenz/Wolf,* AT §§ 22 and 23, *RGRK-Piper* § 145, Rz. 42/43, *Erman (-Hefermehl),* Vor § 145, Rz. 1. The formation of a contract *(Vertrag)* is treated in title 3 of book 1 part 3 of the BGB.

DUTCH and PORTUGUESE law also treat juristic acts and contracts separately in their Codes. In Portuguese law a unilateral promise, which only binds the promisor, and which requires a acceptance, is a juristic act not a contract.

3.   *"without any further requirement"*

Article 2:101 also provides that a contract is concluded if the parties intended to be legally bound and they reach a sufficient agreement, "without any further requirement". On the intention to be bound, see notes to Article 2:102 and on sufficient agreement, notes to Article 2:103.

As was mentioned in the Comment, the words "without any further requirement" implies that the Principles do not require consideration or *cause*, nor do the Principles require that to create certain contracts, property must be handed over to the party who is to receive it (real contracts).

(a)   Consideration

In ENGLAND and IRELAND a promise by one party which is not supported by consideration is generally not binding. The doctrine of consideration is complex and unclear, but its essence seems to be that a promise, even if seriously meant and accepted by the promisee, will not be binding unless the promisee gives or does something ("unilateral" contract), or promises to give or do something ("bilateral" contract), in exchange for the promise. Thus a "gratuitous promise" for which there was no exchange is not binding, see e.g. *Re Hudson* (1885) 54 LJ Ch 811. Equally, a promise made in respect of an act which has already been performed (e.g. a promise to reward someone who has just rescued the promisor) is not binding, since the rescue was not exchanged for the promise, cf *Re McArdle* [1951] Ch 669, C.A.; "past consideration is no consideration".

It is not necessary that the action taken or promised is of direct benefit to the promisor. What is important is that the promisee has in some sense acted to his detriment in exchange for the promise. Thus a promise to a bank to guarantee a loan made to a third party is made for good consideration though the guarantor may obtain no benefit; the bank incurs a detriment by advancing the money to the debtor. But if the money has been advanced already, and the bank does not give the debtor any concession as a result of the guarantee, e.g. extra time to pay, the guarantee will be without consideration, see *Treitel*, Contract 75; compare *Alliance Bank* v. *Broom* (1864) 2 Dr & Sm 289 (actual forbearance by creditor, therefore consideration).

Certain actions, or promises of actions, are treated as not being good consideration because they involve the promisee in no detriment. For example, a promise to pay someone to perform an act he is already obliged to do under the general law is usually treated as being for no consideration: *Glasbrook Bros.* v. *Glamorgan CC* [1925] A.C. 270, H.L.

However, consideration is not required if the promise is made by a deed. This is a document which is expressed to be a deed and which must be witnessed. It no longer has to be sealed, see Law of Property (Miscellaneous Provisions) Act 1989, s. 1. Further, the doctrine does not often prevent enforcement of a promise which the courts wish to enforce. There are a number of points:

(i)   The consideration need not be "adequate", i.e. of equivalent value, so that a small or even a purely nominal payment is good consideration, e.g. *Thomas* v. *Thomas* (1842) 2 QB 851.

(ii)   The courts seem to "invent" consideration by fixing on some action, or the possibility of some action, by the promisee and treating it as exchanged for the promise: e.g. *de la Bere* v. *Pearson* [1908] 1 KB 280. In that case a newspaper's promise to give readers financial advice was held to be contractual, because the newspaper had the right to publish the readers' letters if it so wished. See generally *Treitel*, Contract 67-68. *Atiyah* argues that this means that the doctrine is incoherent and means no more than "a good reason to enforce the promise": *Essays* 241.

(iii) In cases of promises to convey property, if the promisee has acted on the promise to his detriment, it may be enforceable even without consideration on the basis of "proprietary estoppel": e.g. *Crabb* v. *Arun DC* [1976] Ch. 179, C.A.

However, ENGLISH law has not yet followed American law in treating a gratuitous promise on which the promisee has reasonably relied as binding (cf Restatement, 2d. Contracts, § 90). In ENGLAND the doctrine of promissory estoppel applies only to promises not to enforce existing rights, *Combe* v. *Combe* [1951] 2 K.B. 215, C.A. In IRELAND, however, the Supreme Court in *Webb* v. *Ireland* [1958] I.L.R.M. 565 held that a promise by the Director of the National Museum to a finder of historic aretfacts that he would be honourable treated, would be enforced against the State, see *McMahon & Binchy* 155 ff. with references.

In relation to agreements to alter the terms of existing contracts, there were formerly in ENGLISH law considerable difficulties when the terms were varied in a way that benefited only one of the parties; e.g. one party promised to release the other from part of his obligation (*Foakes* v. *Beer* (1884) 9 App. Cas. 605, H.L.) or to increase the price payable to the other (*Stilk* v. *Myrick* (1809) 2 Camp. 317). More recently, the courts have prevented the promisor from going back on his word (unless it was unfairly extorted from him) via, in the first situation, the doctrine of promissory estoppel (see *WJ Alan & Co Ltd* v. *El Nasr Export & Import Co* [1972] 2 Q.B. 189, C.A.) or, in the second, by treating the promise as being for good consideration if the promisor got a "practical benefit", even though the promisee was doing no more than it was previously bound to do (*Williams* v. *Roffey Bros & Nicholls (Contractors) Ltd* [1991] 1 Q.B. 1, C.A.).

SCOTLAND and the CIVIL LAW COUNTRIES do not require consideration.

(b)   Cause, causa

The Principles do not expressly provide for a requirement of *cause* or *causa*. *Causa* is, however, mentioned as a requirement for the formation of a contract in AUSTRIAN law, in FRENCH, BELGIAN and LUXEMBOURG CCs arts. 1108 and 1131-1133, ITALIAN CC arts. 1325 and 1343-45 and SPANISH CC art. 1261.

In AUSTRIAN law the *causa* signifies the economic purpose of the contract, which has to be transparent from the contract itself or the circumstances. A promise which has no apparent purpose is not binding.

It is not possible to give a definition of *cause* in FRENCH law which will be accepted universally. However, many authors distinguish the "objective and abstract *cause*" that would apply to all parties to a contract of a particular type (e.g., in a contract of sale, to obtain the property or the money) and the "subjective and concrete *cause*" or motive (e.g. the seller sells the property to raise money to pay his other debts, or the buyer buys property in order to smuggle it out of the country): see, e.g., *Terré, Simler & Lequette* Nos. 312 ff.. A contract will not be valid unless it has an objective and abstract cause; the mere intention to incur an obligation is not sufficient. If for example the cause is erroneous, the contract will not be valid. Thus a person who has promised to pay a debt, but who had forgotten that he had already paid it, is not obliged to do so, because his obligation had a false *cause,* see notes to Article 4:103 on Mistake as to Facts or Law. Under the second aspect the *cause* must be legal. Therefore, the sale of an object intended to be used for committing a crime is void. On French law, see *Malaurie & Aynès,* Obligations no. 492 ff., and on BELGIAN law, *t'Kint* 138. On illegality, see Article 4:101.

Some DUTCH authors argue that *causa,* although no longer mentioned in the DUTCH BW., does remain a requirement for the validity of a contract – see *van Schaick* (with summaries in English, French and German) and *Smits* (with a summary in English). Other authors consider *causa* as "the content of the contract as a whole", see on these theories *Becker* 237. If used in this sense the *causa* is hardly a requirement other than that the contract must contain legal obligations for the debtor.

The GREEK and PORTUGUESE civil codes do not require cause as a condition for the formation of the contract, but articles 174-178 of the Greek CC provide that contracts the contents of which is unlawful are invalid and arts. 904-913 that payments made without a cause or without a lawful cause may be recovered. On this basis, some Greek writers infer that cause is an essential element for the validity and enforceability of contracts *(Kerameus-Kozyris* 65f). The same is the predominant view in Portugal, see *Fernandes* s. 287.

Causa has no role in the formation and validity of contracts in the COMMON LAW. Nor is the concept used in GERMANY, see *Zweigert & Kötz* 381, the NORDIC COUNTRIES, see for DENMARK, *Ussing.* Aftaler 113, or SCOTLAND, see *Smith*, Short Commentary 742 f.

(c)   Real contracts

In FRANCE, BELGIUM and LUXEMBOURG it has been held that the so-called "real contract" (*contrat réel)* was not validly concluded until the property to which it relates had been handed over to the creditor or some other person authorized to receive it. This applied to donations, loans of money and other property, bailment *(dépôt)* and pledge. However, the writers do not like the idea that these contracts are not enforceable. Today these agreements are often interpreted as a promise to make a contract to lend, deposit, pledge, etc. which is enforceable (see on the formal requirments note 4 below), and when performed these contracts are governed by the same rules as the other contracts (see for France *Ghestin*, Formation nr 447ff and for Belgium *de Page, Traité II* nr 505). Under the PORTUGUESE CC the rules on real contracts are applied to loans, bailment and pledge. However under the influence of *C. Mota Pinto's Cessào da posicao contractual,* 11ff, it has been held that the mere agreement between the parties makes these contracts enforceable.

In SPAIN, AUSTRIA and the NETHERLANDS the concept of the "real contract" still exists: in Spain for loans, including gratituous loans, bailment *(deposito)*, and pledge, see *Diez-Picazo* p 139; and in Austria for bailments, loans for use, loans of money and "orders to sell" *(Kaufaufträge)*, scc ABGB § 1086 and *Rummel* § 86, Rz 9. In the Netherlands the rules only apply to loans.

"Real contracts" are not known in the other countries. It is not necessary as a condition for the coming into existence of a contract that the goods or money contracted for should be handed over to the creditor. However, in the common law a unilateral contract requires an act or the commencement of an act by the offeree for completion, see note 1(b) above.

The handing over may, however, be a condition for the perfection of a security interest in relation to third parties.

Some laws also require the existence of an *objet*. On this see the notes to Article 4:102.

4.   *Formal requirements*

(a)   *No formal requirement for contracts in general*

In the majority of countries of the European Union, writing or other formalities are not required for the validity of contracts in general. This holds true of DENMARK, see Danske Lov art. 5.1.1, SWEDEN, see *Adlercreutz* I 147; FINLAND, see *Hoppu*, 36; GREECE, CC art. 158; GERMANY, BGB § 125 (impliedly); AUSTRIA, AGBG § 883; PORTUGAL, CC 219ff.; and of the UK. The DUTCH BW art. 3:37 lays down that unless otherwise provided declarations, including communications, may be made in any form. The same rule applies in SPAIN, see CC art. 1258, Commercial Code art. 51 and art. 11 of the Retail Trading Act (1996). The GREEK CC provides that contracts and other juridical acts have to be made in a certain form when the law so provides (CC art. 158) or the parties have agreed on it (art. 159 (1)) and this holds true of the other laws which do not require form. On merger- and no oral modification clauses, see notes to Articles 2:105 and 2:106 below.

CISG art. 11 provides that a contract for the sale of goods need not be concluded in writing and is not subject to any other requirement as to form. It may be proved by any means, including witnesses. Under art. 29(1) a contract may be modified or terminated by the mere agreement of the parties. A State which is party to the Convention may, however, make a declaration to the effect that articles 11 and 29 do not apply where any party has his place of business in that State. None of the Members of the European Union has made such a declaration.

Art. 1.2 of the UNIDROIT Principles provides that nothing in the Principles requires a contract to be concluded in any form. It may be proved by any means, including witnesses.

(b)   *Writing required*

Unless the defendant is a merchant, the FRENCH courts will not admit proof of contracts for the value of FF 5000 or more unless it is in writing, see CC art. 1341. But the requirements of writing are not great. A *"commencement de preuve par écrit"* (a first step towards evidence in writing) is sufficient, see CC art. 1347, and in special cases where it was not possible for a party to provide a written document, oral testimony is allowed, see art. 1348. Under art. 109 of the Commercial Code, oral testimony of contracts made between merchants is allowed. BELGIUM and LUXEMBOURG have similar rules. In BELGIUM writing is needed for contracts for a value of 15000 francs or more.

In ITALY proof will not be allowed for contracts above the value of 5000 lire unless they are in writing, see CC art. 2721 (1), but there are a number of exceptions from this rule. Thus art. 2721 (2) provides that the court can admit proof by witness even beyond that limit, taking into account the character of the parties, the nature of the contract and any other circumstances.

In FRANCE, BELGIUM, LUXEMBOURG and ITALY, where CISG is in force, an international contract of sale which is governed by the Convention is not subject to any requirement as to form, see CISG art. 11.

(c)   *Specific contracts*

In all the countries, specific contracts need to be in writing or in a notarial document in order to be valid.

(aa)   Formal requirements for special agreements are found in some conventions. For arbitration clauses, the New York Convention on the Recognition and Enforcement of Foreign Arbitral Awards of 1958, art. II requires writing. Art. 17 of the Brussels Convention on Jurisdiction and Enforcement of Judgments in Civil and Commercial Matters puts formal requirements on a jurisdiction clause. See also arts. 12 and 96 of CISG.

(bb) In IRISH law informality is the rule but a considerable number of contracts must be evidenced in writing: contracts of guarantee, contracts for which the consideration is marriage, contracts for the sale of land or an interest therein, contracts that will not be performed within one year (see Statute of Frauds (Ireland) 1964, s. 2), contracts for the sale of goods in excess of £10 (Sale of Goods Act 1893, s. 4) and hire purchase contracts (Consumer Credit Act, 1995, s. 30)

In ITALY writing is required for the sale of land, see CC art. 1350, which includes a number of other contracts regarding land. In GERMANY, BGB § 313 requires a notarial document, as do PORTUGUESE CC art. 875 and SPAINISH CC art. 1280. In the U.K., contracts for the sale of land must be in writing and signed by both parties (not by deed – that is required for the conveyance), see Requirements of Writing (SCOTLAND) Act 1995 s.1 and ENGLISH Law of Property (Miscellaneous Provisions) Act 1989, s. 2. (replacing the earlier requirement that the contract be evidenced in writing; the Statute of Frauds 1664 still requires that guarantees be evidenced in writing). In SWEDEN writing and in FINLAND writing and the signature of an official sales witness are required, see SWEDISH Land Code ch 4, 1§ and FINNISH Land Code ch. 2, 1§.

In several systems a contract for the sale of land will not transfer the property to the buyer; further formalities are necessary to achieve this.

(cc) Also a promise for a gift, but not a perfected gift, requires form in a number of countries. In FRANCE, BELGIUM and LUXEMBOURG it must be made before a notary, see CCs art. 931; for ITALY, see CC art. 782; for the NETHERLANDS, see BW art. 7A:1719; for GERMANY, see BGB § 518, for AUSTRIA, see the Law on Compulsory Notarial Acts of 1871; for SPAIN see CC arts. 632 and 633; and for PORTUGAL see CC art. 947. In the COMMON LAW gratuitous promises are enforceable only if made in the form of a deed or for a nominal consideration.

In SCOTLAND gratuitous promises not undertaken in the course of business must be in writing, see s. 1 of the Requirements of Writing Act 1995. In the NETHERLANDS a draft for a title on gifts in the BW purports to strike out the present requirement of the old code for a notarial document for a promise to make a gift. Writing will then suffice. In FINLAND and SWEDEN a promise for a gift must be made in writing or made public, for instance in the press, see Finnish Act on Gift Promises § 1 and Swedish Act on Gifts § 1. DENMARK is, as far as is known, the only Union country where a promise to make a gift is valid without any formality.

This enumeration is not exhaustive. In some legal systems mandatory rules require form for some specific contracts such as consumer contracts, for the establishment of companies, loans, guarantees, sales of motor vehicles, employment contracts and tenancies.

Article 2:102: Intention

The intention of a party to be legally bound by contract is to be determined from the party's statements or conduct as they were reasonably understood by the other party.

COMMENTS

A. *Intention*

As provided in Article 2:101(1)(a) a contract is only concluded if the parties to it indicate an intention to be legally bound. Parties often make preliminary statements which precede the conclusion of a contract but which do not indicate any intention to be morally or legally bound at that stage.

Sometimes the person who makes a statement intends only to be morally but not legally bound. Depending on the words used and the circumstances, letters of intent and letters of comfort may be regarded as statements which are morally binding only.

Illustration 1: When subsidiary company asked the plaintiff bank to grant it a loan of 8 million Euros, the plaintiff asked the defendant parent company to guarantee the loan. The defendant refused, but gave a letter of comfort instead. This read: "It is our policy to ensure that the business of (the subsidiary) is at all times in a position to meet its liabilities to you under the loan facility arrangement". The letter also stated that the defendant would not reduce their financial interests in the subsidiary company until the loan had been repaid. When during the negotiations the plaintiff learned that a letter of comfort would be issued rather than a guarantee, its response was that it would probably have to charge a higher rate of interest. When later the subsidiary company went into liquidation without having paid, the plaintiff brought an action against the defendant to recover the amount owing. The action failed since the defendant had not made a legally binding promise to pay the subsidiary's debt.

However under certain circumstances the person may incur liability when it has acted contrary to good faith, see Article 2:301.
    Letters of intent and letters of comfort may also be couched in terms which show an intention to be legally bound.

Illustration 2: Parent company M declares to a bank which lends money to its subsidiary company D that M is aware of D's engagement towards the bank, that by all appropriate means it will see to it that D is able to meet its obligations towards the bank, and that it will give notice to the bank if it wishes to change this policy. Before M has given such notice to the bank D goes bankrupt.
    M's letter of comfort is to be considered as a guarantee which obliges M to pay D's debt.

See also Illustration 2 of Comments to Article 2:107.
    A party's statement is sometimes an invitation to one or more other parties to make an offer. Such an invitation is not meant to bind the party which makes it. It may, however, produce effects later if it has provoked an offer and acceptance which refer to the terms and conditions stated in the invitation. See also Article 6:101.

B. *The Appearance of Intention*

Article 2:102 lays down a general principle on the effects of a party's statement or other conduct. They are to be determined as they reasonably appear to the other party. If the party's true intention is actually understood by the other party, the former is bound. The way in which it expressed its intention does not matter. This is in accordance with the rule of interpretation provided in Article 5:101(1) that the common intention of the parties prevails even if this departs from the literal meaning of the words used. In other cases the contract is to be interpreted according to the meaning that reasonable persons of the same kind as the parties would give to it in the circumstances, see Article 5:101(2).
    Other rules of interpretation such as arts. 5:102, 5:103(a) and (c-f) and 5:104 may also be applied to determine the offer.

C. *Silence or Inactivity*

Silence or inactivity will generally not bind a person, see Article 2:204(2). However, exceptions from this rule are provided in several articles of these principles, see for example articles 2:209, 2:210 and 3:208.

Silence and inactivity may also cause a party to lose a right, see for example Articles 4:113, 8:102(3) and 8:303.

NOTES

1.   *Social engagements, engagements involving patrimonial imterests, moral engagements*

In all the legal systems, a party's intention to be legally bound is a condition of the formation of a contract. Promises given as a joke do not bind. A party is not bound if the other party to whom it makes a statement knows or ought to know that the first party does not intend to be bound.

In all the systems an intention to be legally bound is presumed when the transaction involves a patrimonial interest for the parties, but not when it is only a social engagement, such as a dinner appointment. Friends and family members often offer to help each other, and such offers are not legally enforceable, the help given is not to be paid for, see *Kötz*, European Contract 118 who cites the ENGLISH case *Balfour* v. *Balfour* [1919] 2 KB 571, C.A., FRENCH Cass. 19 March 1974 Bull. Cass. I no. 117, and the GERMAN BGH 22 June 1956 BGHZ 21, 102. See also for DENMARK *Gomard, Kontraktsret* 30 and for IRELAND, *Friel* 78.

Even in business relations, parties make undertakings which only oblige them morally, not legally. It may follow from the language of an undertaking or be implied from the circumstamces that the promisor, or the parties, assumed only a moral obligation, for example if the agreement provides, "this agreement shall be binding in honour only", as in the English case of *Rose & Frank.* v. *JR Crompton & Bros Ltd.* [1925] AC 445, H.L.), see further *Cheshire, Fifoot & Furmston* 111 f and 116 f. and, for Ireland, *Cadbury Ireland Ltd* v. *Kerry Co-operative Creameries Ltd* [1982] ILRM 77, HC. See also notes to Article 2:107 below.

In ENGLAND collective labour agreements are p.resumed not to be intended to create legal relations: *Ford Motor Co Ltd* v. *AUEFW* [1969] 2 Q.B. 303, Q.B. In IRELAND statements made *obiter* in several cases suggest that they are, see *Goulding Chemicals Ltd* v. *Bolger* [1977] IR 211, SC and *Ardmore Studios* v. *Lynch* [1965] IR 1, HC.

2.   *Real or apparent intention?*

(a)   *Party bound by apparent intention*

Even if in his inmost mind a party had no intention to be legally bound, most of the laws will hold that he is bound if the other party to whom the statement or other conduct was addressed had reason to assume that the first party intended to be bound. Whether this is the case is to be decided under the rules of interpretation, see notes to chapter 5.

The rule is provided in the DUTCH BW art 3:35: a person's absence of intention cannot be invoked against another person to whom his declaration or conduct was addressed and who gave it a meaning which was reasonable in the circumstances. In AUSTRIA, a similar rule is inferred from ABGB §§ 861 and 863, see *Schwimann (-Apathy) § 863* comments 1-4 and § 863 comments 1-2, where the author uses the term *"normativer Konsens"*. In NORDIC LAW, the rule is based on an interpretation *e contrario* of the Contracts Acts § 32, according to which an error in expression does not bind the promisor if the promisee knew or should have known of the mistake, see for DENMARK *Dahl (-Møgelvang)* 231 and *Gomard,* Kontraktsret 56; for SWEDEN, *Ramberg,* Avtalsrätt 34. In GREECE the rule is based on CC art. 200, which provides that contracts are to be interpreted in accordance with good faith, see AP 1340/1977, NoB 1978.1053; see also for GERMANY *Larenz/Wolf* § 28 Rdnr. 16 ff. In ITALY and PORTUGAL the rules on interpretation apply to ascertain the intention of the parties; good faith and reasonableness play an important part, see on Italy: *Bianca,* Il contratto 397-402 and on Portugal *Almeida,* Negocio juridico 719ff. However, the statement is not binding if the party who made it was convinced that the other party would realize that his statement was not serious or where he was not consious of having made a statement, see CC arts. 245 and 246.

The same rule applies in the COMMON LAW law. ENGLISH contract law is concerned with objective appearance rather than with the actual fact of agreement.The classic statement of the principle is that of Blackburn J. in *Smith* v. *Hughes* (1871) L.R. 6 Q.B. 597, 607:

"If, whatever, a man's real intention may be, he so conducts himself that a reasonable man would believe that he was assenting to the terms proposed by the other party, and that the other party upon that belief enters into the contract with him, the man thus conducting himself would be equally bound as if he had intended to agree to the other party's terms."

See also *The Hannah Blumental*, [1983] 1 A.C. 854 (H.L.) and *Treitel*, Contract 1; for IRISH law, see *Friel* 78ff. In SCOTLAND the majority view is to the same effect. In *Muirhead & Turnbull* v. *Dickson* [1905] 7 S.C. 686, 694, Lord Dunedin said:

".. commercial contracts cannot be be arranged by what people think in their inmost minds. Commercial contracts are made by what people say."

See also *McBryde*, Contract 51-54 and 1992 Juridical Review 274; cf *Stewart*, 1991 Juridical Review 216 and 1993 Juridical Review 83.

(b)   *Subjective intention governs*

In contrast to most other laws, FRENCH law will only hold a person bound in contract if it is his real intention to be bound, see *Malaurie & Aynès*, Obligations nos. 347 ff. However, a party alleging that, contrary to his statement, he had no intention to be bound must make this allegation plausible. If he succeeds he is not contractually bound, but may be held liable in damages in tort if he has acted negligently, see *Terré, Simler et Lequette, Obligations* no. 87, no. 131. The same rules apply in LUXEMBOURG. PORTUGUESE CC arts. 245 and 246 impose liability on a person who acted negligently when makinge a statement which he did not mean seriously or when making a statement unconsciously, see (a) above.

(c)   *Divided opinion*

In BELGIUM there is one school which sticks to the traditional FRENCH "doctrine of the intention", see e.g. *Verougstraete* 1195-96, and another school which will apply the same rule as the one in Article 2:102, see *van Ommeslaghe*, R.D.I.D.C. 1983 144 and *M.E. Storme, Tijdschrift voor belgisch burgerlijk recht* 1993, 336. The rule in Article 2:102 has been applied by the *Cour de Cassation* in a decision of 20 June 1988, Pas. 1988 I 1256, where it was held that a principal was bound by an act done by the agent when the third party had reason to rely on the agent's apparent authority; see also Court of Appeal of Brussels 26 May 1996, *Tijdschrift voor belgisch burgerlijk recht* 1996, 333 where the rule was also applied.

Article 2:103: Sufficient Agreement

(1) There is sufficient agreement if the terms:

   (a)   have been sufficiently defined by the parties so that the contract can be enforced, or

   (b)   can be determined under these Principles.

(2) However, if one of the parties refuses to conclude a contract unless the parties have agreed on some specific matter, there is no contract unless agreement on that matter has been reached.

COMMENTS

A. *Agreement on the Terms*

Where two or more parties conclude a contract agreement must be reached on the terms which are necessary for determining their mutual rights and obligations and which are decisive for each of them.

Thus, sufficient agreement covers two requirements:

−   terms which are determinable, and

−   consensus on disputed terms.

B. *Terms which are Determinable*

The parties must have made an agreement the terms of which are so definite that it can be enforced.

Most contracts belong to the usual types of contract (sale of goods, supply of services, employment, insurance, etc.). For these contracts the parties' agreement on the type of contract (e.g. sale) and a few crucial terms (type of goods and quantity) will suffice. If the parties are silent on other issues (e.g. price and quality) these issues will be decided by the rules of Chapter 6, notably Articles 6:104 - 6:108 of these Principles. These issues may also be determined by other means such as usages and practices between the parties, see Article 1:105, or by supplying an omitted term, see Article 6:102.

If it is not apparent what type of agreement is being made, the agreement cannot be enforced unless the parties' essential rights and duties have been agreed upon.

Illustration 1: Two enterprises have entered into negotiations about their "future co-operation in the market". There will be no contract between them until they have agreed upon the essential features of their co-operation, viz. the main rights and duties of both parties.

See also on offers Article 2:201.

C. *Terms Made Essentiel*

An agreement to negotiate a contract (a contract to contract) is in itself a binding contract which entails a duty on both parties to make serious attempts to conclude the planned contract, see also comment A to Article 2:102 on letters of intent. However the parties are not obliged to reach agreement, see Article 2:301(1).

A party may consider a term to be so essential for it that it will make its assent to the contract dependent upon agreement on that point. For example, if the parties bargain over the price of the goods to be sold, they show that the price is a decisive term. Even points which are normally not considered essential points can be made so by one party.

However a party which has made one or more points essential to its assent to the contract may nevertheless accept performance of the envisaged contract by the other party. In that case the contract is to be considered concluded by the conduct of the parties, and the Principles and other factors, see comment B, will supply the disputed terms.

Although two parties have not agreed on all terms they may agree to commence performance of the contract. In that event, the factors mentioned in comment A will supply the missing terms.

Illustration 2: A has negotiated with B to maintain B's computers. Although they have not agreed on A's fee they have decided that A shall begin. After one month they realize that they cannot reach agreement and B asks A to stop. B will have to respect the agreed notice of termination and to pay A a reasonable fee, see Article 6:104.

NOTES

1. *Terms determinable*

Under all the systems, there is only a contract when the terms of the parties' agreement can be determined. The question may arise when the parties have left terms open, see notes to Article 6:104-6:107, when they have agreed that they will later make a contract, and when they have made a framework agreement (*contrat cadre*).

(a) *Object required*

The *Romanistic* systems require that a contract has an *objet*. Art. 1108 of the FRENCH, BELGIAN and LUXEMBOURG CCs makes it a condition for the validity of a contract that the contract has an object which constitutes the subject matter of the agreement; see also the rules in arts. 1126-1130. This object must be legal and determined or determinable. Similar provisions are found in ITALIAN CC art. 1325(3) and arts. 1346-1349, in SPANISH CC arts. 1261 and 1271-1273 and in PORTUGUESE CC art. 280(1).

The purpose of the *object* is also to prevent agreements where one of the parties arbitrarily fixes the contents of his or the other party's obligation, and the other party is left at his mercy. On recent developments in FRENCH law concerning the price, see notes to Article 6:104 and *Ghestin, Formation* 516 f.

(b) *No requirement of object*

Objet is not mentioned as a requirement in the other legal systems. However, as provided in the NETHERLANDS BW art 6:227, it is everywhere a condition for the formation of a contract that "the obligations which the parties assume are determinable". The parties' agreement must make it possible for a court which is asked to enforce it (either specifically or by awarding damages) to do so, with the help of the terms of the contract and the rules of law, see the UNITED STATES Restatement 2d, § 33, and for AUSTRIA *Schwimann (-Apathy)* § 869 no 3 ff.; for DENMARK, *Ussing, Aftaler* 33; for FINLAND, *Kivimäki & Ylöstalo*, 167 f.; for GERMANY, *RKGK-Piper*; Introduction before § 145 Rn. 3; and for GREECE, Full Bench of Areios Pagos 1381/1983, NoB 1984.1193-1194 and Athens 1027/1971, NoB 1971 1277-1278.

The common law of ENGLAND also requires that the parties' agreement is sufficiently definite to be enforced. There is no fixed minimum content ; but if a critical term of the contract is left open or vague, and the court has no way of determining what was intended, the contract will fail, e.g. *Scammell & Nephew Ltd* v. *Ouston* [1941] A.C. 251, H.L., where an agreement to *"sell"* a truck "on hire purchase terms" was held to be too imprecise, since the precise terms of the hire purchase were not settled and at that date such contracts took a variety of forms. The rule is the same in IRELAND, see *Central Meat Products* v. *Corney* (1944) 10 Ir.Jur.Rep. 34. Also under SCOTS law the contract must be sufficiently clear to be enforceable, see *Mc Bryde*, Contracts 44-51.

2. *Terms left open*

Agreement between the parties to a contract is a condition for its formation. This is expressed in several laws, for instance FRENCH, BELGIAN and LUXEMBOURG CCs art. 1108, ITALIAN CC arts. 1321 and 1325(1) and SPANISH CC arts. 1258 and 1261.

However, the agreement of the parties need not always be perfect. After having ended their negotiations the parties may not have reached agreement on a term. Some point brought up by them or one of them has not been settled. Several of the laws seem to agree on the following rules: If the unsettled point is one which is generally regarded as material, there is no contract until agreement on that point is reached. If the term is generally considered to be immaterial the contract is considered to have been concluded, and the rules of law – or a later agreement – will settle the matter.

Parties may, however, have agreed expressly or by implication that their failure to settle a point which is normally material, such as the price, shall not prevent the contract from coming into existence. In these cases the rules of law will supply the term which the parties have not agreed. Conversely, one part may state or let the other party understand that he considers a term, which is normally held to be immaterial, to be material, and the parties' failure to reach agreeement on that term will then prevent the conclusion of a contract, see for AUSTRIA, *Rummel*, § 869 no 10; FRANCE, *Ghestin, Formation* no. 319 ff.; BELGIUM, *Kruithof & Bocken* 313f.; DENMARK, *Lynge Andersen* 66ff.; FINLAND, *Kivimäki & Ylöstalo*, 188 f. and SGA § 45; SPAIN, *Durany.* 1059ff; and SWEDEN, *Adlercreutuz* I 62.

The DUTCH BW art. 6:225 provides that where a reply which was intended to accept an offer only deviates from the offer on points of minor importance, the reply is considered to be an acceptance and the contract is formed according to the terms of the reply, unless the offeror objects to the difference without delay, see also notes to Article 2:208. This principle also covers terms which have been left open without there having been an offer and a reply. In that case the rules of law will decide the issue.

PORTUGUESE law makes no distinction beween material and non-material terms. Every term is material if one of the parties connsider it necessary for the agreement, see CC art. 232 and *Vaz Serra* 130ff.

In the COMMON LAW the parties must have reached agreement, and if some matter is left "to be agreed" there will be no concluded contract (*May & Butcher Ltd* v. *R* [1934] 2 KB 17n, H.L.) unless there are clear indications that the parties intended to be bound nonetheless (e.g. the matter was minor and they have commenced performance: *Foley* v. *Classique Couches* [1934] 2 KB 1, C.A.). In SCOTLAND there are essentials in law for particular contracts on which the parties must have agreed before there is a contract, see also *Rt. J Dempster* v. *Motherwell Bridge & Engineering Co* 1964 SC 308; *Avintair* v. *Ryder Air* 1994 SLT 613.

The GERMAN BGB provides in § 154 that in case of doubt a contract is not concluded until the parties have agreed on all the points on which they or one of them require agreement. § 155 BGB lays down that if the parties regard a contract to have been concluded, without realizing that in fact agreement has not been reached on some term, then what has been agreed upon is binding if it is shown that the contract would have been concluded even without agreement on that term, see *Münchener Kommentar* (- *Kramer*) §§ 154, 155; *Staudinger* (- *Dilcher*, §§ 154, 155. GREEK CC arts. 195 and 196 has similar provisions as the BGB, see on their application, AP 69/1966, NoB 1966,800; 827/1986, EEN 1987 265, 266 I; Athens 1010/1976, NoB 1976.737, 738 I.

A different question is where the parties have put forward differing proposals and neither has agreed to the other's proposal. On this see the notes to Articles 2:208: Modified acceptance, 2:209: Conflicting general conditions and 2:210: Professional's written confirmation.

Article 2:104: Terms Not Individually Negotiated

(1) Contract terms which have not been individually negotiated may be invoked against a party which did not know of them only if the party invoking them took reasonable steps to bring them to the other party's attention before or when the contract was concluded.

(2) Terms are not brought appropriately to a party's attention by a mere reference to them in a contract document, even if that party signs the document.

COMMENTS

A. *Acceptance required*
Under Articles 2:101 and 2:103 a contract is only concluded if the parties have agreed on its express terms. This rule must also apply when a party invokes standard terms or other not individually negotiated terms as part of the contract. The other party can only be held to terms which the first party took appropriate steps to bring to the other's knowledge before or when the latter accepted the contract.

This requirement will be fulfilled when the standard terms form part of the contract document which the other party has signed. It is also fulfilled when the terms are printed on the back side of the letter containing the offer or on a separate enclosure when reference has been made to the standard terms in the offer.

However, terms are not brought appropriately to a party's attention by a mere reference to them in the contract document, even if signed on behalf of that party, unless it knew of them beforehand – for instance, because in earlier similar contracts

between the parties the other party has brought the terms to the first party's attention; then a reference to them may suffice. If the first party does not know of the
terms referred to, they must be included in the document or other steps taken to
inform the party of them. It is not sufficient, for instance, to send the terms with the
letter which contains the offer without making a reference to them in the letter.

B. *Before or at the Time of Conclusion*
General conditions must be brought to the attention of the party when the contract is
made or before. Standard terms sent with a supplier's acceptance of the customer's
offer may be treated as a modified acceptance, see Article 2:208. Terms which the
seller sends with the goods which the buyer has ordered may be considered as
accepted by the buyer when it accepts the goods. However, terms sent with a supplier's bill which the customer receives after it has received the performance will not
bind the customer.

C. *Waiver*
A party cannot unilaterally discharge the duty to bring its general conditions to the
attention of its contracting partner by a term in its offer or at a notice board in its
premises. However, before or after the conclusion of the contract, the other party may
waive its right to be informed of the terms, and such a waiver can be implied when
under the circumstances it would not be reasonable to require such information.

> *Illustration*: On Friday A sends an advertisement to B, a newspaper, asking B to
> publish it on Sunday. B receives A's letter on Saturday. It cannot be required to
> inform A about its general conditions regarding advertising before it publishes
> the advertisement in the paper.

D. *Usage*
It may follow from a usage that not individually negotiated terms may be binding upon
a party who did not know of them. Thus in a particular trade, terms which have been
published by the association of suppliers as the terms which its members will apply, may
be binding upon customers without further steps by suppliers who are members of the
association. Such usages may even bind foreign customers, see on usages Article 1:105.

E. *Effects*
Terms which have been duly brought to the attention of a party will become part of
the contract. If a party has not taken appropriate steps to bring the terms to the other
party's attention the contract is treated as having been made without the terms.

NOTES

1.   *In general*
     The mere reference in the contract document to terms which were not included in the document and
     which the stipulator had not brought to the notice of the adhering party will generally bind the lat-
     ter if it knew of them.

In ENGLAND, if a party has signed a contract document, all the terms in the document, or referred to in it, form part of the contract (*L'Estrange* v. *F Graucob Ltd* [1934] 2 K.B. 394, C.A.) However, the degree of notice given will be highly relevant to whether the terms are unfair under the Unfair Terms in Consumer Contract Regulations 1994 or unreasonable under Unfair Contract Terms Act 1977. If the terms were not in a signed document, they will not form part of the contract at all unless either reasonable notice was given of them when or before the contract was made (*Parker* v. *South Eastern Railway Co* (1877) 2 C.P.D. 416) or they are incorporated by a course of previous dealing (*Hollier* v. *Rambler Motors AMC Ltd.* [1972] 2 Q.B. 71, C.A.) or trade understanding (*British Crane Hire Corp. Ltd* v. *Ipswich Plant Hire Ltd* [1975] Q.B. 303, C.A.) See also on the "Red Hand Rule" below.

Some laws like the ITALIAN CC art. 1341(1) provide that general conditions of contract prepared by one party are binding upon the other party if at the time of the conclusion of the contract the latter knew them or, using ordinary diligence, should have known them.

Other countries have general rules which protect both businessmen and consumers. Under AUSTRIAN AGBG § 864a, enacted in 1979, unusual terms in general conditions and standard form contracts which a party uses do not become part of the contract if, considering the circumstances and the appearance of the contract document, they are disadvantageous and surprising for the other party, unless the stipulator has explicitly referred to them. Art 1135-1 of the LUXEMBOURG CC, as amended in 1987, provides that general contract conditions which have been established in advance by one of the parties, are not binding upon the other party unless the latter has had the opportunity of acquainting himself with them when he signed the contract, or if under the circumstances he must be considered to have accepted them.

DUTCH BW art. 6:233(b) lays down that general conditions of contract are voidable if the stipulator has not offered the other a reasonable opportunity to take notice of the general conditions. Art 6:234 enumerates the ways in which the stipulator gives the other party a reasonable opportunity. One way is to give the other party a copy of the conditions before or at the time of the conclusion of the contract. These provisions protect consumers and smaller enterprises.

Under the PORTUGUESE Decree Law 446 / 85 of October 25 1985, art. 5 the stipulator shall communicate the general contract terms in their entirety to the adhering party, and the communication shall be made in an adequate manner and at such an early stage that, taking into consideration the importance, the length and complexity of the clauses, it is possible for a person using ordinary care to acquire complete and effective knowledge of them. Under art. 6 the stipulator must also where appropriate supply all the explanations necesaary of for their clarification.

ITALIAN CC art. 1341(2) provides that in order to be valid, certain contract terms which have been drafted in advance by one of the parties must be specifically approved in writing by the other party. This applies, *inter alia*, to exemption clauses, cut-off clauses, and jurisdiction and arbitration clauses.

2. *The "red hand rule"*

In GERMANY and the NORDIC COUNTRIES, the stipulator must give the other party a particularly clear and perceptible notice of unusually burdensome terms. In GERMANY, General Conditions of Business Act of 1976, § 3 protects both consumers *and* businessmen. In the Nordic countries the rule is based on case law, see for DENMARK, *Lynge Andersen* 78 ff., for FINLAND, *Wilhelmsson*, Standardavtal 87 and for SWEDEN, *Grönfors*, Avtalslagen 40f.

This rule, which is called the "red hand rule", applies also in ENGLAND, see *Interfoto Picture Library Ltd* v. *Stiletto Visual Productions* Ltd [1989] Q.B. 433, C.A., and probably also in SCOTLAND. However, unless the contract is a consumer contract governed by the 1994 Unfair Terms in Consumer Contracts Regulations, which implements the EEC Directive, the "red hand rule" does not apply if the party against whom the clause is invoked has signed the contract document.

3. *Rules covering consumers only*

The "Indicative and illustrative list of terms which may be regarded as unfair" which is annexed to the EEC Council Directive on Unfair Terms in Consumer Constracts of 3 April 1993, and which have been inserted in the Comments to Article 4:110, includes in para. 1(i) a term which has the object or effect of "irrevocably binding the consumer to terms with which he had no real opportunity of becoming acquainted before the conclusion of the contract". This provision seems to presuppose that in the absence of a clause as the one mentioned in 1(i), such inaccessible terms will not be binding upon the adhering party in any of the Member States of the European Union. On the Council Directive on Unfair Terms in Consumer Contracts and the Indicative and illustrative list of terms mentioned above, see notes to Article 4:110.

§ 2 of The GERMAN General Conditions of Business Act of 1976 requires that the stipulator makes express reference to his general conditions of business, and that the other party agrees to them, an agreement which does not need to be express and may be implied from the circumstances, see *Münchener Kommentar (- Kötz)* I 1816. This provision protects only consumers, see § 24 of the Act.

§ 6 of the AUSTRIAN Consumer Protection Act of 1979 contains a provision similar to § 864a of the AGBG dealt with at no 2 *supra*.

Under art. 30 of the BELGIAN Act of 14 July 1991 on Commercial Practices and Information and Protection of Consumers, the supplier, acting in accordance with the requirements of good faith, shall provide the consumer with correct and useful information on the characteristics of the goods or services supplied and the *conditions of supply,* having regard to the information needs expressed by the consumer and the use which he has indicated to make of the good and services or which were foreseeable for the supplier (italics added).

The SPANISH Act of 19 July 1984 on Consumers and Users art. 10(1)(a) requires the clauses, terms or stipulations generally applied by the suppliers to be written in a specific, clear and simple language which may be easily understood without resort to texts or documents not provided prior to or at the time of conclusion of the contract, and to which in all events an express reference shall be made in the contractual document.

The GREEK Law 2251/994 on Consumer Protection requires that the the stipulator brings the standard terms to the consumer's attention so that the consumer is able to learn their contents.

Article 2:105: Merger Clause

(1) If a written contract contains an individually negotiated clause stating that the writing embodies all the terms of the contract (a merger clause), any prior statements, undertakings or agreements which are not embodied in the writing do not form part of the contract.

(2) If the merger clause is not individually negotiated it will only establish a presumption that the parties intended that their prior statements, undertakings or agreements were not to form part of the contract. This rule may not be excluded or restricted.

(3) The parties' prior statements may be used to interpret the contract. This rule may not be excluded or restricted except by an individually negotiated clause.

(4) A party may by its statements or conduct be precluded from asserting a merger clause to the extent that the other party has reasonably relied on them.

COMMENTS

Merger Clauses

When concluding a written contract the parties sometimes agree that the writing contains their entire agreement, and that earlier statements and agreements shall not be considered. Such a merger clause may be useful when during the negotiations the parties made promises and statements based on assumptions which were later abandoned. A merger clause which has been individually negotiated, i.e. inserted in the contract as a result of a mutual discussion between the parties, will prevent a party from invoking prior statements and agreements not embodied in the writing. This follows from the principle of freedom of contract embodied in Article 1:102.

The merger clause will not apply to prior agreements or statements which, though made when the contract was negotiated, are distinct and separate from the contract.

If, on the other hand, the prior agreement is one which has such a connection with the contract that it would be natural to include it in the written contract, the merger clause will apply.

Illustration: During the negotiations for the sale of a property the parties orally agree that the seller shall remove an unsightly ice house from a nearby tract. This agreement was not mentioned in the written contract which contained an individually negotiated merger clause. The buyer cannot require the ice house to be removed.

If, however, the merger clause has not been individually negotiated it will only establish a rebuttable presumption that the parties intended that their prior statements should not form part of the contract, see Article 2:105(2). Experience shows that in such cases a party should be allowed to prove that the merger clause was not intended to cover a particular undertaking by the other party which was made orally or in another document. It often happens that parties use standard form contracts containing a merger clause to which they pay no attention. A rule under which such a clause would always prevent a party from invoking prior statements or undertakings would be too rigid and often lead to results which were contrary to good faith.

A merger clause will not prevent the parties' prior statements from being used to interpret the contract. This rule in Article 2:105(3) applies also to individually negotiated merger clauses, but in an individually negotiated clause the parties may agree otherwise.

On a party's reliance on the other party's later conduct, see Comment B to Article 2:106, below.

NOTES

1. Merger Clauses in General

(a)   Clauses upheld

A provision similar to Article 2:105(1) is to be found in UNIDROIT art. 2.17. Article 2:105 is also in accordance with PORTUGUESE law where it follows from the good faith principle that a person shall not be allowed go back on an agreement earlier made (*venire contra factum proprium*). Merger clauses are most often enforced in the U.S.A., see *Farnsworth* II § 7, 3 ff.

(b)   Merger clause probably not conclusive

This is so in ENGLAND. At one time it appears that English law prohibited the bringing of "parol evidence" (that is, evidence of terms which were not contained in the document) to add to, vary or contradict a written contract. However, when faced with clear evidence that the parties had in fact agreed on some term which was not in the document, the courts evaded the rule by the simple expedient of saying that the contract was not wholly in writing, so that the rule did not apply, see for example *J. Evans & Son (Portmouth) Ltd* v. *Andrea Merzario Ltd* [1976] 1 W.L.R. 1078, C.A. As the Law Commission points out, this renders the rule meaningless, and it is now agreed that there is at most a presumption that the written documents contains all the terms of the contract (*Treitel*, p 178). It is generally thought that a merger clause will do no more than add weight to this presumption (*Law Commission*, Report on Parol Evidence Rule) and it will not be conclusive; see *Thomas Witter Ltd* v. *TBP Industries Ltd* [1976] 2 All E.R. 573, noted at (1995) 111 LQR 385). The Contract (Scotland) Act 1977 has abrogated the parol evidence rule for SCOTLAND. In IRELAND the rule, if it still exists, has been greatly modified, see *Friel*, 153-154.

Under DUTCH law, evidence of oral agreements may always be brought: there is no such thing as a parol evidence rule. The landmark case is HR 13 March 1981, Nederlandse Jurisprudentie 1981, 635 *(Haviltex)*. It has been argued that clauses which purport to import the parol evidence rule into the Netherlands are invalid, at least when they are to be found in general conditions of contract: *Hondius*, Entire Agreement Clauses 24-34.

In FRANCE, LUXEMBOURG and SPAIN merger clauses are reported to be rare, and there does not seem to be literature about them. In Luxembourg the rule on evidence in CC art 1341. quoted in note 4(b) to Article 2:101 (2) above might indicate that merger clauses will be enforced. They would probably be covered by the rules on proof of judicial acts which in France are treated in *Ghestin, Goubeaux & Fabre-Magnan* nos. 627 ff. In Spain the rules on intepretation may also be applied, see *Diez-Picazo* 259-261. There is no clear rule in BELGIAN law on the validity of merger clauses. The authors tend to give the clauses a restrictive interpretation, see *Storme*, Invloed no. 183.

Rules as those provided in Article 2:105 (1) and (2) are not to be found in the ITALIAN CC and the issues have not been dealt with in the legal writing or in reported cases. On the one hand a rule on evidence in CC article 2711 provides that "proof of witnesses is not permitted to establish clauses which have been added or are contrary to the contents of a document, and which are claimed to have been made prior to or at the same time as the document". This rule may be relevant for merger clauses. On the other hand CC art. 1362 (2) on interpretation of contracts provides that "in order to ascertain the common intention of the parties, their common behaviour, also after the conclusion of the contract, shall be taken into account." The mandatory character of this rule is confirmed by the writers, see *Bianca*, Il contratto I 399 and *Carresi* II 86, and by the courts, see for instance the Court of Cassation 2 March 1971 no. 528. This would exclude merger and no-oral modification clauses.

Merger clauses are not dealt with in the GREEK CC, nor in the reported cases. Whether they will be enforced will probably be viewed upon as a question of interpretation and of CC art. 200, which provides that "contracts are to be interpreted in accordance with good faith having regard to business practices". This provision is mandatory in the sense that parties are not allowed to contract out of it, see *Balis* para 53, *Papantoniou* para. 64 1, p 347-349; cf. AP 908/1978, NoB 1979,758.

(c)   Merger clauses disregarded

In the other countries of the Union a merger clause has the effect that the written contract is presumed to contain a complete record of the contract terms, but the courts will admit evidence of an oral agreement whereby the parties expressly or impliedly decide to disregard a merger clause. If the court is convinced, the merger clause will be disregarded, and an oral agreement which adds to it or varies it will be enforced. This holds true of the law in GERMANY, *Larenz/Wolf*, § 27 V p 528 and *Boergen;* Die Effektivität von Schriftformklauseln, *BB* 1971, 202; see also BGH WM 1966, 1335; BGHZ 66, 378; for AUSTRIA see the presumption is provided in ABGB § 884. For DENMARK see, *Lynge Andersen* 87. In FINLAND, a negotiated term, even if made orally, takes priority over written standard form terms. Parties may orally agree to disregard a merger clause, see *Telaranta* 191; *Wilhelmsson*, Standardavtal 86.

2.   Not-individually negotiated merger clauses

With the possible exception of THE NETHERLANDS, few of the countries seem to make any distinction between individually and not individually negotiated merger clauses. However, the *Indicative and illustrative list of tems which may be regarded as unfair,* annexed to the EEC Council Directive on Unfair Terms in Consumer Contracts of 5 April 1993 includes in para. 1(n) a term which has the object or effect of limiting the seller's or the supplier's obligation to respect commitments undertaken by his agent or making his commitments subject to the compliance with a particular formality. Under this rule a merger clause will (semble) not be upheld. § 10(3) of the AUSTRIAN Consumer Protection Act invalidates clauses like the one mentioned in para.1(n) of the EEC list of terms.

As under the PORTUGUESE Decree Law 446 / 85 of October 25 1985, art. 7 individually negotiated terms take priority over terms in a standard form contract, a merger clause in such a contract cannot set aside a prior or simultanerous individual agreement.

3.   Extrinsic evidence on interpretation of the contract

In the systems which enforce merger clauses, it is generally held that the parties' prior statements may be used to interpret the contract, see UNIDROIT Principles art. 2.17, second sentence, and notes to Articles 5:101 and 5:102 below.

On *reliance* on merger clauses, see note 4 to Article 2:106, below.

Article 2:106: Written Modification Only

(1)   A clause in a written contract requiring any modification or ending by agreement to be made in writing establishes only a presumption that an agreement to modify or end the contract is not intended to be legally binding unless it is in writing.

(2) A party may by its statements or conduct be precluded from asserting such a clause to the extent that the other party has reasonably relied on them.

COMMENTS

A. *"No oral modifications" Clauses in General*

Clauses in written contracts which provide that modification or termination (ending) by agreement must be in writing often occur, especially in long-term contracts. Under Article 2:106(1) such clauses will only establish a rebuttable presumption that later oral agreements or agreements made by conduct to end or to modify the written contract were not intended to be legally binding. It would be contrary to good faith to let the parties' agreement to use writing bind them to that form when later they have clearly made up their minds to use another form. If, therefore, it can be shown that both parties agreed to modify or end the contract, but did not use writing, effect must be given to their agreement. This applies even if in an individually negotiated clause in their contract they provided that they would not give effect to an oral agreement to disregard the "non oral modification" clause.

B. *Reliance in spite of a Merger or "No oral modification" Clause*

If the parties by their conduct – for instance by oral agreement – have agreed to modify a contract containing a merger clause or a "no oral modification" clause and one party has reasonably acted in reliance on this conduct, the other party will be precluded from invoking the clause.

Illustration: A construction contract contains a clause providing that "this contract may only be modified in writing signed by both parties". Subsequently the parties orally agree to some changes in favour of the owner which are performed. When later the contractor invokes another oral modification made in its favour the owner invokes the "no oral modification" clause.

The contractor may invoke the performance of the first oral agreement to show that the second oral agreement, in favour of the contractor, is binding on the owner. The contractor has in fact relied on the abrogation of the "no oral modification" clause.

NOTES

1. *Evidential value only*

   The rule in Article 2:106(1) which only gives evidential weight to the written modifications clause is in accordance with the laws of most of the countries of the Union as far as contracts in general are concerned.

   Thus in DANISH and SWEDISH law, even if the parties have agreed that any modification of their contract is without effect unless made in writing, they may nevertheless later orally agree to disregard their previous no oral modification agreement. However, a party invoking such a later oral agreement has to prove it, see *Ramberg*, Köplagen 1995, 108 and *Gomard & Rechnagel* 94.

   The same appears to be the case in GERMAN law see *v. Caemmerer & Schlechtriem* art. 29 Footnote 19. Parties who "seriously and definitely" wish to make an informal modification of a contract which contains a no-oral modification clause may do so. Such an informal agreement may, however, be difficult to prove, see *Dölle (- Reinhardt)* art. 15 no. 68.

The Supreme Court of GREECE has held that even if the parties have agreed to conclude their contract in writing, they may later orally agree to modify it (AP 1054/1976, NoB 1977, 508). Even contracts for which the law requires form for their modification may be ended by oral agreement (AP 1376/ 1982, EEN 1983, 600).

Article 2:106(1) also appears to be in accordance with the law of ENGLAND and IRELAND, although there is no authority on this exact point. There are cases holding that a contractor cannot recover extra payment when under the terms of a building contract he should have secured a written instruction for a variation of the contract, see *Hudson* §§ 7-058-060.

ITALIAN CC art. 1352 provides: "If the parties have agreed in writing to adopt a specified form for their future contract, it is presumed that such a form was intended as a requirement for the validity of the contract". However, the writers and the courts are hostile to the adoption of a special form for agreements to modify or determine the contract, see *Scognamiglio* 461 and the Court of Cassation 9 January 1996 no. 100. On the other hand, special formalities may be agreed for acts which enforce already existing rights and duties such as acts of communication or performance, see *Bianca*, Il contratto I 307.

2.   *A mixed approach, or the law is unsettled*
In those countries which refuse to admit proof of the existence of civil contracts not made in writing, modifications must also be in writing, see FRENCH, BELGIAN and LUXEMBOURG CCs art. 1341. Under art. 1793, in a contract providing a fixed price for the work as a whole, architects and contractors may only demand an increase in the price for extra work if this extra work and its price have been agreed in writing.

However, BELGIAN courts have admitted evidence of behaviour, often performance of the modification, which showed that the party invoking art. 1341 had admitted the modification, see e.g. Cass. 28 February 1980, Arr.Cass No. 410. Likewise in SPAIN both CC art. 1593 and the Supreme Court admit oral and tacit agreements on payment for extra work in building contracts once the work has been carried out.

In FRANCE and LUXEMBOURG the question whether in commercial contracts which need not be made in writing, no-oral modification clauses are valid, has not arisen. The rule is that agreements on evidence, be it agreements on whether evidence is to be admitted or on the effects of such evidence are enforced, see for France *Ghestin, Goubeaux & Fabre-Magnan* no. 631. In BELGIUM, however, the courts have admitted evidence by other means than writing of agreements on extra work in building contracts, once the extra work has been performed, see Cass. 22 March 1957, Pas. I, 887.

As any evidence is admitted for the existence of a commercial contract covered by art. 109 of the FRENCH and art. 25 of the BELGIAN Commercial Codes, the parties may orally agree to disregard a previous no-oral modification clause (*Dölle (-Reinhard)* 105, who for FRANCE quotes *Schlessinger* (-*Bonassies*) II 165).

SPANISH law is reported to be unsettled.

No-oral modification clauses are generally not enforced in USA, see *Farnsworth* II 228 ff. However the UCC § 2-209(2) enforces such clauses in sales contracts, but, except as between merchants, such a requirement on a form supplied by a merchant must be separately signed by the other party if the other is not also a merchant.

3.   *No oral modification clauses enforced*
CISG gives effect to no oral modification clauses. Art. 29(2), first sentence, provides that a contract in writing which contains a provision requiring any modification or termination by agreement to be in writing may not be otherwise modified or terminated by agreement, see also UNIDROIT art. 2.18. The AUSTRIAN law is reported to give effect to no oral modification clauses except in consumer contracts, see notes to Article 2:105(2) above.

4.   *Reliance despite merger clauses and no oral modification clause*
Articles 2:105 (4) and 2:106 (2) provide that a party by his word or conduct may be precluded from invoking a merger or no oral modification clause if the other party has acted in reliance of the word or conduct. Similar rules are provided for the no oral modification clause in US UCC arts. 2.209 (4) and (5), CISG art. 29 (2) second sentence, and UNIDROIT art. 2.18. The same rules on reliance apply in AUSTRIAN law, see *Schwimann (- Apathy)* § 884 no 3.

Even though they give effect to merger and "no oral modification" clauses, in those countries which allow the good faith and fair dealing principle to operate generally, a reliance rule will probably apply, see notes to Article 1:201. In GREEK law the principle of *venire contra factum proprium* would apply. On ITALIAN CC arts. 1175, 1337 and 1375 see *Bianca*, Il contratto I 171 and Court of Cassation 13 January 1993, no. 343.

In ENGLAND reliance may be invoked based on the doctrine of estoppel. If in a binding contract the court finds that the employer allowed extra work to be done, the contractor may recover payment for this work although the employer did not confirm its consent in writing, see *Hudson* §§ 7-077-078.

Article 2:107: Promises Binding without Acceptance

A promise which is intended to be legally binding without acceptance is binding.

COMMENTS

A. *Unilateral Promise*

An offer is a promise which requires acceptance. An offeror is not bound by its promise unless it is accepted. Other promises are binding without acceptance and they are nevertheless to be treated as contracts albeit with some modifications. Whether there is such a promise depends on the language of the promise or other circumstances. The promise must of course be communicated to the promisee or to the public.

> *Illustration 1*: When the Gulf War started in 1990 the enterprise X in country Y published a statement in several newspapers in Y promising to establish a fund of 1 million Euros to support the widows and dependent children of soldiers of country Y who were killed in the war. After the war X tried to avoid payment invoking big losses recently made. X will be bound by its promise.

Some promises made in the course of business are binding without acceptance. An irrevocable documentary credit issued by a bank (the issuing bank) on the instructions of a buyer binds the issuing bank; a confirmation of such a credit by an advising bank binds the bank as soon as it is delivered to the seller. Some guarantees and some promises in favour of third parties also fall under this category, see Article 6:110.

> *Illustration 2*: C sends a letter to the creditors of its subsidiary company D, which is in financial difficulties, promising that C will ensure that D will meet its existing debts. The promise is made in order to save the reputation of the group of companies to which C and D belong. It is binding upon C without acceptance since it is to be assumed that C intends to be bound without the acceptance of each creditor.

Under some legal systems a promisor may issue an instrument of debt containing a promise which is binding *per se*, i.e. without regard to any underlying relationship. These "abstract" promises which often require a form are not covered by Article 1:207.

Even though a promise does not require acceptance it may be rejected by the promisee. A rejection will destroy the promise, see Article 2:203.

B. *Application of the Principles to Promises which Do Not Need Acceptance*

The Principles, including several rules of this section, apply to promises which do not need acceptance, see Article 1:107. This holds true of Article 2:102 and 2:103.

The rules on notice in Article 1:303 also apply to such promises, and they are binding as contracts under the rules in chapters 5 and 6. Some of the remedies provided in chapters 8 and 9 apply in case of non-performance, notably damages and specific performance. As they are binding without acceptance they are generally irrevocable. See however Article 6:110 on stipulations in favour of third parties.

NOTES

1. *Promises binding*
    Under some of the legal systems of the Union, promises may be binding without acceptance when this is stated in the promise or follows from the nature of the promise. This applies to GERMAN and AUSTRIAN law where, for instance, promises of rewards *(Auslobung)* are binding without acceptance, see note 3(b)(dd) to Article 2:201.
    A promise is also binding on the promisor without acceptance in FINNISH and SWEDISH law. These impose formal requirements for a promise to make a gift, but do not require acceptance by the promisee, see for Finland, *Timonen* 280. The promise is also binding without acceptance in DANISH law, which does not require formalities for gift promises.
    In THE NETHERLANDS such promises may be binding, see BW art 6:219 and 6:220, and the same holds true of BELGIAN law, see Arr.Cass 1979-80 1132 and 1139; Cass. 3 Sept 1981, *Tijdschrift Aannemingsrecht- L'entreprise et droit*, 1982, 131; *van Ommeslaghe*, J.T. 1982, 144. However, for special contracts subject to formal requirements, such as gifts, Belgian law explicitly requires acceptance, see CC art. 932.
    In SCOTS law there are "unilateral" promises for which no consideration is required and which are binding without acceptance, see *McBryde, Contract*, 13-27 and Requirement of Writing (Scotland) Act 1995, s 1.
2. *Acceptance required*
    The COMMON LAW differs from the Principles in two respects. First, promises generally need acceptance. The only clear cases of a binding promise which do not require acceptance are (i) the deed – the beneficiary need not know of it – but this is seen as kind of property transfer, and not as a contract, and (ii) the irrevocable letter of credit. The latter is considered binding as soon as the confirming bank notifies the seller that the credit has been openened, see *Atiyah*, Sale of Goods 422; *Treitel*, Contract 140-141; *Goode*, Abstract payment undertakings. In the common law a party can accept a promise by performing an act, see note 2 to Article 2:101 above. Second, the common law requires promises to be supported by consideration, see note 2(a) to Article 2:101 above.
    FRENCH, LUXEMBOURG and PORTUGUESE law require acceptance of promises, including when (as in France and Luxembourg) the contract is *a contrat unilatéral*, and (in Portugal) where it is a unilateral act where only the promisor is obliged, see note 2 to Article 2:101 above. *In* SPANISH law promises are not binding unless accepted which may take place by performing the act required, see SPANISH Supreme Court 17 Oct 1975, RAJ (1975) 3675 and 6 March 1976 RAJ (1976) 1175 and *Sancho*, Elementos 173-181.
    Equally acceptance is generally required under GREEK law; a mere promise is not enough. However, CC art. 193 provides that under special circumstances the acceptance as such may suffice, regardless of whether it has been dispatched or arrives at the offeror's place, see *Erm AK (- Simantiras)* 193 no 11.
    ITALIAN CC art. 1987 provides that a unilateral promise of a performance, i.e. an undertaking which does not require acceptance, is not binding except in specific cases provided by law, such as an offer to the public for a reward.
3. *Application of rules of Contract*
    On the application of the rules of Contract to promises binding without acceptance see notes to Article 1:107.

Section 2 : Offer and Acceptance

Article 2:201: Offer

(1) A proposal amounts to an offer if:
(a)   it is intended to result in a contract if the other party accepts it, and
(b)   it contains sufficiently definite terms to form a contract.
(2) An offer may be made to one or more specific persons or to the public.
(3) A proposal to supply goods or services at stated prices made by a professional supplier in a public advertisement or a catalogue, or by a display of goods, is presumed to be an offer to sell or supply at that price until the stock of goods, or the supplier's capacity to supply the service, is exhausted.

COMMENTS

A. *The "Offer and Acceptance Model"*
This section deals with contracts concluded by an offer followed by an acceptance, which is the usual model for the conclusion of contracts.

However, there are other models for the conclusion of a contract. Agreements are often made under circumstances where it is not possible to analyse the process of conclusion into an offer and an acceptance. The rules of this section may sometimes apply to these cases, see Article 2:211 below.

B. *Requirements for an Offer to Become Effective*
An offer is a proposal to make a contract. If it is accepted it becomes a contract provided that the conditions in Article 2:201 are met.

For a proposal to become effective it must
(a)   be communicated to one or more specific persons or to the public;
(b)   show an intention to be bound, see Article 2:102 and chapter 5 on Interpretation; and
(c)   contain terms which are sufficiently definite, see Article 2:103.

C. *Proposals to the Public*

Proposals which are not made to one or more specific persons (proposals to the public) may take many shapes advertisements, posters, circulars, window displays, invitations of tenders, auctions etc. These proposals are generally to be treated as offers if they show an intention to be legally bound. However, proposals made "with an eye to the person" are generally presumed to be invitations to make offers only. This applies to an advertisement of a house for rent at a certain price. Further, an advertisement for a job-opening for persons who meet certain requirements does not oblige the advertiser to employ the one offerring his or her services and meeting the requirements. Construction contracts are often made on the basis of public bidding. Owners generally only invite tenders, which are the offers.

Other considerations may also lead to the assumption that, unless otherwise indicated, a proposal is only an invitation to make an offer.

Putting up of an item for auction is generally only an invitation to bid. The auctioneer need not accept a bid and may withdraw the goods, even when the bid is the highest made, if it is too low. The bid is the offer which is accepted by the fall of the hammer. A clear indication that the goods are sold "without reserve" or the like may, however, turn putting them up for auction into an offer.

On the other hand, in order for a proposal to have effect it may be necessary for the proposer to make an offer which may bind it if accepted. This applies for example to an offer of a commission if an agent effects a sale of the proposer's property. Furthermore, persons who make advertisements etc. may wish prospective suppliers or purchasers to know that they will be able to deliver or acquire the goods or services by accepting the proposal, and that they do not risk refusal of their "acceptance" and the consequent waste of their efforts and reliance costs. Therefore, proposals which are sufficiently definite and which can be accepted by anybody without respect of person are to be treated as offers. This consideration has led to the provision in paragraph (3) and will also result in a proposal being an offer in other cases.

> *Illustration 1*: Merchant A advertises in a trade paper that he will buy "all fresh eggs delivered to him before 22 February" and pay a certain price. A's advertisement is to be considered an offer which may be accepted by bringing the eggs to his premises.

> *Illustration 2*: In the local paper Bell advertises a plot of land for sale to the first purchaser to tender 25,000 Euros in cash. This constitutes an offer and when Mart tenders 25,000 Euros there is a contract.

D. *Goods and Services Offered at Stated Prices*

Article 2:201(3) provides that a proposal to supply goods and services at stated prices made by a professional supplier in a public advertisement or a catalogue or by display of goods is presumed to be an offer to sell or supply at that price until the stock of goods, or the supplier's capacity to supply the service, is exhausted.

The professional supplier which advertises goods in the way described is, unless it indicates otherwise, taken to have a reasonable stock of goods and a reasonable capacity to provide services.

The rule states a presumption. A different intention may appear from the advertisement, etc. and may follow from the circumstances. Thus, if the goods or services are offered on credit terms the supplier may refuse to deal with persons of poor credit-worthiness.

NOTES

1. *The "offer and acceptance" model in the laws*
   The "offer and acceptance" model, by which one person makes an offer to another person which the latter accepts, has been the prototype for the conclusion of contracts in all the legal systems of the Union, see GERMAN BGB §§ 145-150, AUSTRIAN AGBG §§ 861- 864a, NORDIC Contract Acts §§ 1-9, GREEK CC arts. 185-192, ITALIAN CC arts. 1326-1329, and DUTCH BW art. 6:217- 6:225. It is also the main model used in CISG part II, arts. 14-24, and in chapter 2 of the UNIDROIT Principles. In all the countries of the Union, including those which do not have any statutory provisions on the conclusion of contracts in general, writers treat the offer and acceptance as the principal model. On situations in which the model is not easy to apply see the notes to Article 2:211.
2. *What is required for an offer to be binding?*
   All the laws of the UNION require that the offer must show an intention to be bound, and that it must be sufficiently definite to establish an enforceable contract, see notes to Articles 2:101-2:103. Thus the AUSTRIAN ABGB § 869 provides that "the acceptance of an offer as well as the offer itself must be declared freely, seriously, precisely and intelligibly." SPANISH law also requires seriousness of intention, definitiveness and completeness, see Supreme Court decisions of 28 May 1945 RAJ (1945) 692 and 10 October 1980, RAJ (1980) 3623. Under ENGLISH and IRISH law a proposal does not amount to an offer if it expresses some reservation on the part of the maker or if the terms proposed are not sufficiently specific. On both points see, e.g., the English case of *Gibson v. Manchester City Council* [1979] 1 W.L.R. 294, H.L.
3. *Proposals to the public*
   All the legal systems accept that in some situations proposals to the public may amount to an offer. However, in a number of situations the laws reach different results on the question whether a proposal is an offer. Most of them have general principles, and provide special rules applicable to special situations.
   (a) *In general*
       (aa) *Statutory provisions*
           The ITALIAN CC art. 1336(1) provides that a proposal to the public which contains the main elements of the contract towards whose formation the proposal is directed is effective as an offer unless it appears otherwise from the proposal or from usages, see *Bianca*, II contratto II 251, who stresses the necessity of a clear undertaking.
           For the international sale of goods, CISG art. 14(2) provides that a proposal other than one addressed to one or more specific persons is to be considered merely an invitation to make offers unless the contrary is clearly indicated by the person making the proposal.
           Art 2.201(2) differs from the ITALIAN rule and CISG in that it does not establish a presumption one way or the other, but leaves the issue to be decided by the rules of interpretation. This also appears to the attitude taken by the UNIDROIT Principles which do not provide rules on offers to the public, see Comment 2 to art. 2.2.
       (bb) *Case law*
           Apart from these rules there are no general statutory provisions on the subject in the European Union. Its regulation is left to the courts. Whether a proposal to the public is an offer or only an invitation to make an offer has been a question of interpretation of the proposal. However, the rules of interpretation which the courts have established differ.
           In FRANCE the courts have shown an inclination to treat proposals to the public as offers, see *Ghestin*, Formation no. 297. However, in some contracts the offeror wants to know with whom he is dealing. Therefore in France, as in BELGIUM and LUXEMBOURG, the proposal is probably only an offer if the proponent will be ready to con-

clude a contract without further investigations once the proposal has been accepted, see for Belgium *Cornelis*, TBH 1983, 39.

In the COMMON LAW and in SCOTLAND proposals to the public are in general treated as invitations to make an offer, see below at (b), but they may amount to an offer, see *Carlill* v. *Carbolic Smoke Ball Co.* [1893] 1 Q.B. 256. C.A.; *Treitel*, Contract 13; and the IRISH case of *Billings* v. *Arnott* (1945) 80 ILTR 50, H.C. In SCOTLAND they may also amount to a unilateral promise, see note 1 to Article 2:107 above. In AUSTRIAN law the proposal to the public does not, as a rule, qualify as an offer since it is not sufficiently definite and therefore does not show any intention of the offeror to be bound, see OGH 3 October 1972, SZ 45/102. It is treated as a mere invitation to anybody who might be interested to negotiate.

In THE NETHERLANDS there is no general rule. An offer in an advertisement to sell real property will generally be an invitation to submit an offer, even if the person who is the first to respond agrees to pay the full price charged. But a department store which offers a free teddy bear to every purchaser who buys goods for over 100 Hfl will generally be bound.

(b)   Specific issues

(aa) *Proposals to supply goods and services at stated prices*

The presumption established in Article 2:201(3) applies in several countries to proposals made in advertisements in the press and in the television, and to advertising material and price lists communicated to a large number of addressees: for DENMARK, see *Lynge Andersen* 52ff.; for GERMANY, see *Münchener Kommentar (-Kramer)* § 145 Rz 8; and for ITALY, see *Bianca*, Il contratto II 256.

In FRANCE and LUXEMBOURG it has been held that such proposals constitute offers "which bind the offeror to the first acceptor" unless the contrary follows from the proposal or from the circumstances, see French Cass.civ. 28 November 1968, Bull.civ. III 389. A proposal for an employment, a lease, the granting of loan or other contracts where the proponent may want to know with whom he is dealing are only invitations to make an offer, see *Ghestin*, Formation no. 297. BELGIAN law does not generally regard proposals made in advertisments in papers as offers, see *Cornelis*, Tidschridt voor Belgisch Handelsrecht 1983, 39.

In the COMMON LAW public advertisements of goods are generally invitations to make offers, see *Grainger & Son* v. *Gough* [1896] A.C. 325, H.L.) and *Treitel*, Contract 13. SCOTS law is to the same effect, see *Hunter* v. *General Accident Corporation* 1909 SC 344, aff'd. 1909 SC (HL) 30. The AUSTRIAN courts also generally do not treat such proposal as offers.

In SWEDEN advertisements are invitations to make offers and it is uncertain whether the special rule in the Contracts Act § 9 on the effects of silence by the offeree applies, see *Ramberg*, Avtalsrätt 49 and 113, *Adlercreutz* I 52, and on § 9 note 2(b) to Article 2:204, below. This is also the prevailing view in FINLAND, see *Hemmo, Sopimusoikeus* I 1997, 78, and in PORTUGAL, unless the offer contains all the elements required for an offer including the price see *Almeida*, Negocio juridico *804* and *Hörster 457*.

In SPAIN there is reported to be no case law.

(bb) *Display of priced goods*

In FRANCE, LUXEMBOURG and BELGIUM, displays of priced goods in windows and self-service stores are held to be offers, see *Ghestin*, Formation no. 297 and *Dekkers*, *Handboek van Burgerlijk Recht II nr 92*. The same applies in SPAIN, see Retail Trading Act (1996), art. 9, where special rules apply to consumer contracts. In ITALY too a priced display is considered an offer to the public, see note (a) (aa) above. *Bianca*, Il contratto II 256 maintains that in the retail business such proposals remain offers as long as there is stock at hand, see on the cases, the Court of Cassation 4 February 1986, no. 708 and 10 January 1986, no. 63.This is also true of PORTUGAL, see *Almeida*, Negocio juridico *804* and *Hörster 457*. In DENMARK a shopkeeper is taken to have made an offer of the displayed goods, but not of all goods which are in stock, see *Lynge Andersen 52.*

Displays of priced goods in shops and markets are treated as invitations to make an offer in the COMMON LAW and in SCOTS law, see for ENGLAND, *Fisher* v. *Bell* [1961] 1 Q.B. 394 (display of goods in shop window) and *Pharmaceutical Society of GB* v. *Boots Cash Chemists (Southern) Ltd* [1953] 1 Q.B. 401, C.A. (display of goods marked with prices on self-service shop shelves) and, for IRELAND, *Minister for Industry and Commerce* v. *Pim* [1966] I.R. 156. The same holds true of GERMANY, see BGH in NJW

1980, 1388; AUSTRIA, see *Rummel* § 831 Rz 7; SWEDEN, see *Grönfors,* Avtalslagen 28; and in FINLAND, see *Hemmo, Sopimusoikeus* I 1997, 78.

(cc) *Auctions*

Applying the offer-acceptance model, some laws consider the putting up of property for an auction as an invitation, and each bid as an offer which lapses when a higher bid is made; the final bid is then accepted if and when the auctioneer lets the hammer fall. This rule, which means that either party may withdraw his offer before the hammer falls, is applied in GERMANY, BGB § 156, see *Münchener Kommentar I (- Kramer)* 1316; GREECE, see CC art.199; PORTUGAL, see *Almeida,* Negocio juridico 804 and *Hörster* 457; BELGIUM, see *Kruithof & Bocken* 307, the NETHERLANDS; DENMARK, see *Lynge Andersen* 53; SWEDEN, see *Grönfors,* Avtalslagen 37; and FINLAND, see Finnish Contract Act § 9. The same rule applies in ENGLAND, SCOTLAND and IRE-LAND, see the English Sale of Goods Act 1979, s.57, and *Treitel* Contract 11.

However, in ENGLAND, SCOTLAND and IRELAND, if the sale has been an advertised as being "without reserve", the highest bidder will have a remedy. However, this will be not aganist the seller but against the auctioneer who allows the goods to be withdrawn, see the English case of *Warlow* v. *Harrison* (1859) 1 E&E 309 and the Irish case of *Tully* v. *Irish Land Commission* (1961) 97 ILTR 174, H.C. For Scotland see *Gloag,* Contract, 22-3.

In contrast, in FRANCE, LUXEMBOURG, ITALY and SPAIN the proposal to the public to bid is the offer, and the highest and last bid is the acceptance, see for France, *Malaurie & Aynès,* Obligations no 334; Spanish Retail Trading Act 1996 art. 56 and *Diez-Picazo* 300f.; and for Italy, *Bianca,* Il contratto 234f.

(dd) *Rewards*

It appears that in most, if not all the systems, an offer for a reward is held to have been accepted by performing the act for which the award is offered. This rule is expressly provided in the DUTCH BW art. 6:120, and is adopted in DENMARK, see *Ussing, Aftaler* 51 and in SPAIN, see Supreme Court 17 October 1975, RAJ (1975) 3675 and 6 March 1976, RAJ (1976)1175. In GERMANY, GREECE, and ITALY the offeror must pay the reward to the person who performs the rewarded act even though that person did not act in response to the award, in most cases because he did not know of it, see the GERMAN BGB § 657, GREEK CC art. 709ff. and ITALIAN CC 1989. This is also the unanimous opinion of AUSTRIAN writers, see e.g. *Korio/Welser,* Grunriss des bürgerlichen Rechts 10th ed (1995) 203.

In ENGLAND an advertisement of a reward is an offer but he who acts must have been conscious of the offer. A person cannot claim a reward for information given if when he gave the information he did not know of or had forgotten the offer. His act is then not an acceptance of the offer: see *R.* v. *Clarke* (1927) 40 C.L.R. 227, H.Ct of Australia, and *Treitel,* Contract 13 and (on unilateral contracts in the English sense of the word) 36 ff. In SCOTLAND advertisements of rewards are offers, see *Hunter* v. *General Accident Corporation,* 1909 SC (HL) 30 or promises, see *Petrie* v. *Earl of Airlie* (1834) 13 S. 68.

In FRANCE and LUXEMBOURG the issue is not settled by statute or precedent. The French authors are divided. Some regard the promise of a reward as an offer: thus an offer of a reward to the one who returns a lost dog will only bind the offeror to pay the person who returns the dog, if that person in awareness of the offer has accepted it (*Nicolas* 39). Others regard it as an *engagement unilatéral,* see *Malaurie & Aynès,* Obligations no 345. In BELGIUM it is held to be a promise which does not need acceptance, see De *Page, Traité* II nos 528-530.

In FINLAND and SWEDEN the law on this point is unsettled.

Article 2:202: Revocation of an Offer

(1) An offer may be revoked if the revocation reaches the offeree before it has dispatched its acceptance or, in cases of acceptance by conduct, before the contract has been concluded under Article 2:205(2) or (3).

(2) An offer made to the public can be revoked by the same means as were used to make the offer.

(3) However, a revocation of an offer is ineffective if:

  (a) the offer indicates that it is irrevocable; or

  (b) it states a fixed time for its acceptance; or

  (c) it was reasonable for the offeree to rely on the offer as being irrevocable and the offeree has acted in reliance on the offer.

COMMENTS

A. *Revocation and Withdrawal Distinguished*

An offer becomes effective when it reaches the offeree, see Article 1:303(2) and (6). However, before it reaches the offeree the offer may be countermanded or withdrawn, and it will not become effective, see Article 1:303(5). It cannot then be accepted by the offeree. However, an offer may be revoked before the offeree has dispatched its acceptance; the offer which is revoked has become effective, and might have been accepted, but if the acceptance has not been dispatched, and if the contract has not been concluded by an act of performance or other act by the offeree, see Article 2:205 (2) and (3), the offer is revoked when the revocation reaches the offeree.

B. *Acceptance by Conduct*

In case of acceptance by conduct the contract is concluded when the offeror learns of it, see Article 2:205(2). In this case the revocation is effective if it reaches the offeree before the offeror has learned of the conduct, see Article 2:202(1). In the cases envisaged in Article 2:205(3), where the offeree can accept by performing an act without notice to the offeror, the revocation must reach the offeree before the latter begins to perform.

C. *Offers to the Public*

Revocation of offers to the public which are not irrevocable under Article 2:202(2) can be made by the same means as the offer. The revocation must then be as conspicuous as the offer. If the offer appeared as an advertisement in a newspaper the revocation must appear at least as visibly in the paper as the advertisement.

The revocation of an offer made in an advertisement which was mailed to the offeree must reach it before it dispatches its acceptance. If the offer has been published in a newspaper the paper bringing the revocation must be in the offeree's mailbox or available in the news-stands before the offeree dispatches its acceptance.

D. *Irrevocable Offer*
Under paragraph 2 there are three exceptions to the general rule in paragraph 1:
  (a) if the offer indicates that it is irrevocable;
  (b) if it states a fixed time for its acceptance;
  (c) if the offeree had reason to rely on the offer as being irrevocable,
       and has acted in reliance on the offer.

In these cases the offer if accepted becomes binding even though it was purportedly revoked before it was accepted. If the offeror does not perform the contract it may become liable for non-performance, and will have to pay damages under the rules of chapter 9, section 5.

E. *Irrevocability Stated*
The indication that the offer is irrevocable must be clear. It may be made by declaring that the offer is a "firm offer" or by other similar expressions. It may also be inferred from the conduct of the offeror.

F. *Fixed Time for Acceptance*
Another way of making the offer irrevocable is to state a fixed time for its acceptance. This statement must also be clear. If the offeror states that its offer "is good till January 1" the offer is irrevocable. The same applies if it states that the offer "lapses on September 1". If on the other hand the offeror only advises the offeree to accept quickly, its offer will be revocable.

G. *Reliance*
The third exception to the rule in paragraph 1 concerns cases where "it was reasonable for the offeree to rely on the offer as being irrevocable" and the "offeree has acted in reliance on the offer". Reliance may have been induced by the behaviour of the offeror. It may also be induced by the nature of the offer.

> *Illustration 1*: Contractor A solicits an offer from sub-contractor B to form part of A's bid on a construction to be assigned within a stated time. B submits its offer and A relies on it when calculating the bid. Before the expiry of the date of award, but after A has made its bid, B revokes its offer. B is bound by its offer until the date of assignment.

An offer of a reward may be irrevocable with regard to persons who have acted in reliance of the offer.

> *Illustration 2*: In an advertisement A promises a "reward" of £1,000 in addition to damages to purchasers of its "high pressure" cooker, which will be on the market the following day, if the cooker explodes. A month later it revokes the promise in another advertisement. Customers who before the offer was revoked have bought a cooker which eventually explodes can claim the "reward".
> See also comment C to Article 1:201.

H. *Incompatible Contracts*

It may happen that an offeree accepts an offer knowing that it is incompatible with another contract which the offeror has made. A collector accepts the offer of an art dealer to sell a picture knowing that the dealer has already sold the same picture to another collector. A theatre manager accepts the offer of an actor to perform at her theatre for a period during which the actor has engaged himself to perform at another theatre. Knowing that both contracts cannot be performed the offeree may still accept the offer: the contract is not invalid. However, these Principles do not deal with the question which of the collectors or which of the theatres may claim performance. Nor do they deal with the question whether the offeree may incur liability towards the first buyer or towards the owner of the other theatre.

As provided in Article 4:102, neither the fact that at the time of the conclusion of the contract the performance of the obligation was impossible, nor the fact that at that time the party was not entitled to dispose of the assets to which the contract relates, will prevent the contract from coming into existence.

I. *Supervening Events*

A contract which is made through acceptance of an offer which is irrevocable under Article 2:202(3) may nevertheless be terminated if supervening events covered by the rules on excuse due to an impediment make performance of the offer impossible (see Article 8:108), or have to be re-negotiated if changed circumstances make it excessively onerous (see Article 6:111).

Promises which do not need acceptance are irrevocable. However, they are also governed by the rules on change of circumstances in Article 6:111 and on excuse due to an impediment in Article 8:108.

NOTES

1.   *Are offers revocable? Effects of wrongful revocation.*
     In this matter the laws of the Union differ on various questions. Is an offer revocable or irrevocable before it has been accepted? If it is revocable, can an offeror make its offer irrevocable? What are the effects of an improper revocation?
2.   *Offers are revocable but may be made irrevocable*
     Like Article 2:202, some laws provide that an offer is revocable, but that it may follow from the offer or from the circumstances that it is irrevocable. If in spite of its revocation the offeree accepts an irrevocable offer in due time, there is a contract.
          Art.1328 of the ITALIAN CC provides that the offeror may revoke the offer until he learns of the offeree's acceptance. However, the offeror's revocation is without effect if he has made the offer irrevocable or has undertaken to keep the promise open for a certain time, see CC art. 1329. If the offer is accepted within the time originally envisaged by the offer, there is a contract in spite of the revocation. And if the offeree has acted in reliance on the offer in good faith the offer may be revoked but the offeree may claim damages under the rules on precontractual liability, see notes to Article 2:301 and *Bianca*, Il contratto I 236; Cass. 8 March 1972, no. 664 and 19 July 1972 no. 193. The rules in the DUTCH BW art. 2:119 come close to those of the Italian CC with the exception that an offer can be revoked until the offeree has dispatched his acceptance. In SCOTLAND the offer is generally revocable unless the offeror states otherwise. A firm offer is treated as promise not to revoke the offer for whatever is the stated period, see *McBryde*, Contract 68-71. In SPANISH case law offers are generally revocable, see Supreme Court 23 March 1988, RAJ (1988) 3623 and 3 Nov 1993, RAJ (1993) 8963, but an option given by a seller to a prospective buyer is irrevocable. See Supreme Court 4 February 1994 RAJ (1994) 910 and 14 February 1995, RAJ (1995) 837.

CISG art. 16, and art. 2.4 of the UNIDROIT Principles provide:

(1) Until a contract is concluded an offer may be revoked if the revocation reaches the offeree before he has dispatched an acceptance.

(2) However, an offer cannot be revoked

(a) if it indicates whether by stating a fixed time for acceptance or otherwise that it is irrevocable; or

(b) if it was reasonable for the offeree to rely on the offer as being irrevocable, and the offeree has acted in reliance of the offer.

The wording of art. 16 para para 2 (a) reflects a disagreement among the delegates of the Diplomatic Conference which in 1980 adopted CISG. The common lawyers wished the offeror's fixing of a period for acceptance to be a time limit after which the offer could no longer be accepted but before which it could still be revoked. The civil lawyers saw the fixing of a time limit for acceptance as a promise by the offeror not to revoke the offer within that time limit (see also ULFIS art. 5 (2)).The wording of art. 2(a) was a compromise. The offer can be made irrevocable, but the provision has not cleared the controversy as to whether the mere fixing of a time for acceptance makes the offer irrevocable. Common lawyers believe that it does not *per se* make the offer irrevocable, there must be additional grounds for assuming that, see v. *Caemmerer & Schlechtriem* art. 16 note 10 and *Honnold* no 141 ff. The question is to be solved by the rules in CISG art. 8 on interpretation of statements.

Article 2:202 of the Principles obviates this doubt. The fixing of a time for acceptance will make the offer irrevocable for that period.

3. *Tort liability for improper revocation*

The FRENCH courts have held that the offeror can revoke his offer until it has been accepted. The offeror may, however, expressly or by implication, for instance by fixing a time limit for acceptance, promise not to revoke his offer; and even if no such promise is made it may follow from the circumstances of the case or from usage that the offeror cannot revoke it without incurring liability. If the offeror nevertheless revokes his offer there will generally be no contract but the offeror will incur liability in damages if he revokes the offer before a reasonable time has lapsed, see notes to Article 2:301. The amount for which the offeror will be held liable in damages is to be finally settled by the *"juges au fond"*, see *Ghestin,* Formation no. 301. The rules are reported to be the same in LUXEMBOURG.

4. *Even offer stated to be irrevocable may be revoked*

In the COMMON LAW the offer is revocable even if it is stated to be irrevocable. By giving a notice to the offeree the offeror may revoke his offer before acceptance.The offeree can make the offer irrevocable with the offeror's consent by furnishing a consideration for holding the offer open, for instance by paying the offeror £1, or by using a deed. Apart from this the offeror cannot by his own act make the offer irrevocable, see *Treitel* 40ff.

5. *Offers are generally irrevocable*

Under some laws the offer is binding and remains so until it lapses, either because it has not been accepted within the time limit set for its acceptance, which is either the time fixed by the offeror or a reasonable time, or because it has been rejected. An acceptance of the offer in due time makes it into a contract even though it has been revoked. The offeror may, however, in his offer state that it is revocable.

These rules apply in GERMANY, see BGB § 145, AUSTRIA, see ABGB § 862, GREECE see CC art. 185, PORTUGAL see CC art. 230, BELGIUM, see *Dirix & van Oevelen, "Kroniek verbintenissensrecht 1985-1992" Rechtskundig Weekblad* 1992-93, 1210 and in the NORDIC LAW, see Contracts Act §§ 1, 3, 7, and 9. § 9 of the DANISH and SWEDISH Contract Acts provide that where a person has stated in his proposal that it is made "without obligation", or has used similar expressions, his statement shall be regarded as an invitation to make an offer. In FINLAND, which has not adopted § 9, the same rule applies.

6. *Revocation of offers to the public*

The general rule seems to be that a proposal to the public which is an offer to make a contract can be revoked by taking reasonable steps to revoke it, see *Schlesinger* I 113. Thus the ITALIAN CC art. 1336(2) provides that a revocation of an offer to the public, if made in the same form or in equivalent form as the offer, is effective even towards persons who have no notice of it (on rewards see below). A similar rule is found in PORTUGAL, see CC art. 230(3); BELGIUM; DENMARK, see *Ussing, Aftaler* 51; AUSTRIA; ENGLAND, see *Treitel,* Contract 41; and IRELAND. In SCOTLAND a proposal which is a promise cannot be revoked but will lapse after a reasonable time. If the proposal is an offer it is on principle revocable by whatever means the proposal itself was made.

In FRANCE and LUXEMBOURG some offers to the public are not revocable for a certain period, see *Ghestin,* Formation no. 315. In GREECE, authors consider proposals to the public as invitations to make an offer and they will therefore never become binding, see *Georgiadis/ Stathopoulos* CC 199 no. 2, p. 322. In SPAIN the issue is reported not to be regulated.

7.   *Offers of rewards*

Under GERMAN and AUSTRIAN law, an offer for a reward is not revocable if its revocation was renounced when it was published, either expressly or impliedly by fixing a time limit for the act to be accomplished, see BGB § 658 (2) and ABGB § 860a. The same rule is adopted in SPAIN, see *Diez-Picazo* 288f.

In THE NETHERLANDS and ITALY an offer of a reward may only be revoked or modified for important reasons, see BW art. 6:220 and ITALIAN CC art. 1990. The BW art. 6.220 provides that even in the event of a valid revocation the court may grant equitable compensation to a person who has prepared the requested performance on the basis of the offer.

Article 2:203: Rejection

When a rejection of an offer reaches the offeror, the offer lapses.

COMMENTS

When a rejection of an offer reaches the offeror, the offer lapses, even if the offer is irrevocable under Article 2:202(3) and even if the time for acceptance has not yet run out.

The rejection need not be express but may be implied by the offeree's conduct, for instance if the offeree makes a counter-offer or states that it would consider a lower bid or a smaller consignment than the one offered.

An acceptance which contains a modification of the offer may be, but is not always, a rejection, see Article 2:208.

A rejection may be withdrawn provided that the withdrawal – whether accompanied by an acceptance or not – reaches the offeror before or at the same time as the rejection, see Article 1:303.

A promise which need not be accepted may be rejected, see Comment B to Article 2:107.

An offer will normally also lapse if, when the time for acceptance provided in Article 2:206 has run out, the offer has not been accepted.

NOTE

In most if not all the countries of the Union, an offer lapses if it is rejected, see for instance, the NORDIC Contracts Act § 5; the GERMAN BGB § 146; GREEK CC art. 187; for PORTUGAL, *Cordeiro* 1, 606; and see also CISG art. 17 and the UNIDROIT Principles art. 2.5.

The rejection takes effect when it reaches the offeror so that, as stated in art. 235(2) of the PORTUGUESE CC, the offer will be regarded as accepted if an acceptance which is dispatched later than the rejection reaches the offeror before or at the same time as the rejection.

Similar rules apply in countries where there is no statutory provision on rejection, see on SCOTLAND *Mc Bryde*, Contract 64 f. In ENGLAND it is probable that the offer lapses if the rejection reaches the offeror before an acceptance sent earlier by the offeree reaches him, even if the acceptance was posted, and therefore would have concluded the contract, before the rejection reached the offeror, see *Treitel*, Contract 41. There is no case authority for this rule. In IRELAND there is, see *Kelly v. Cruise Catering* [1994] 2 ILRM 394.

Article 2:204: Acceptance

(1) Any form of statement or conduct by the offeree is an acceptance if it indicates assent to the offer.

(2) Silence or inactivity does not in itself amount to acceptance.

COMMENTS

A. *Acceptance*

Like other declarations of intention a party's acceptance of an offer can be made by a statement and by conduct, e.g. by performing an act, see Article 2:205.

Whether the offeree's statement or conduct is an assent to the offer is to be decided by the rules on interpretation. See the comments to Article 2:102 on the intention to be legally bound, and chapter 5.

The acceptance must be unconditional. It may not be made subject to final approval by the offeree, or its board of directors, or by a third party, unless the offeror knew or ought to know that the approval of a third party (e.g. government authorities) was required. A modified acceptance may, as provided in Article 2:208(2), be an acceptance. On an acceptance which contains modifications, see also Article 2:209.

On promises which need no acceptance, see Article 2:107.

B. *Silence or Inactivity*

Silence and inactivity will generally not amount to acceptance, see Article 2:204(2). There are, however, exceptions, see Article 2:207 (2) on late acceptance.

Nor is acceptance required when it follows from an earlier statement by the offeree, e.g. an invitation to make an offer, or from usage or practices between the parties, that silence will bind the offeror.

Illustration 1: O asks P for a bid to paint the railing surrounding O's factory telling P that it can start painting a week after it has sent its bid unless before that time O has rejected the offer. Having sent the bid and heard nothing from O, P starts painting. O is bound by the contract.

Further, it may follow from a framework agreement between the parties that a party's silence to an offer by the other party will amount to acceptance.

Under the usages of some trades, an order to provide goods or services from one professional to the other will be considered as accepted unless it is rejected by the offeree without delay. It may also follow from practices between the parties that silence will be considered as acceptance.

Illustration 2: Between A who runs a maintenance service and B which owns a factory, a practice has developed according to which A sends B a note telling B the day A intends to service B's machinery. If B does not want A's services, it informs A immediately. If B keeps silent, A will come. A's note will oblige A to come at the date fixed by it. B is obliged to receive A if B does not cancel A's visit immediately upon receipt of the note.

NOTES

1. *What is Acceptance?*
   Under all the legal systems of the Union, and as provided in Article 2:204(1), acceptance is any statement or conduct by the offeree which manifests assent. In general no form is required, see *Rodière, Formation* 135. On rejections which reach the offer or before and after the acceptance, see the note to Article 2:203.

2. *Silence*
   There is also general agreement that silence in itself does not amount to acceptance, see on BELGIUM, *Kruithof & Bocken* 265; NORDIC Contracts Act § 8 and on DENMARK, *Ussing, Aftaler* 393 and on SWEDEN, *Ramberg*, Avtalsrätt 122-124; FRANCE, *Ghestin*, Formation nos. 402 ff.; LUXEMBOURG; GERMANY, *Münchener Kommentar (- Kramer)* before § 116, Rz 23 and *Medicus*, § 25 IV, 116; AUSTRIA, *Rummel* § 863 Rz 15 and OGH 18 December 1991 SZ 64/ 185; GREECE, *Simantiras*, no. 653; ITALY, *Bianca*, Il contratto 214 ff.; PORTUGAL, CC art. 218; SPAIN, Supreme Court decisions of 2 February 1990 and 19 December 1990, RAJ (1990) 10287; and for ENGLAND, *Treitel*, Contract 30 ff. The same rule applies in IRELAND, see *Friel* 50ff., and is provided in CISG art. 18(1) second sentence and in the UNIDROIT Principles art. 2.6, second sentence.
   Silence may, however, amount to acceptance if before the offer was made the offeree had indicated to the offeror or let him believe that the offeree's silence would mean acceptance. Thus the offeree will generally be bound by his silence if the offer followed an invitation to deal by the offeree. § 9 of the NORDIC Contract Acts, which deals with an invitation to make an offer, provides that if an offer arrives within reasonable time from anyone invited, and the person who made the invitation must realize that the offer was caused by it, he is bound by the offer unless he rejects it by sending a notice to the offeror without delay. See on this provision note 1(d) to Article 2:202, above. In Finland, which has not adopted § 9, a similar rule is applied. In the AMERICAN Restatement 2d § 69 it is provided generally that the offeree will be bound by his silence if the offer followed an invitation to deal by the offeree.
   ENGLISH authors support the proposition that if an offeror has indicated to the offeree that the offeree need not communicate his acceptance, and the offeree, although willing to accept, remains silent, the principle of estoppel will prevent the offeror from arguing that the offer had never been accepted, see *Beale, Bishop and Furmston* 201 and *Miller, Felthouse* v. *Bentley Revisited* [1972] M.L.R. 489. However, the only decided case on the issue seems to be against the rule, see Kerr in *Fairline Shipping Corpn* v. *Adamson* [1975] Q.B.180.
   Further, silence will be considered an acceptance if the parties have established a practice between themselves to this effect, or if it follows from usage, see on BELGIUM, *van Gerven* 300; on the NORDIC COUNTRIES, see for DENMARK, *Ussing*, Aftaler 393, and for SWEDEN *Ramberg*, Avtalsrätt 122-124. This holds true also of FRANCE, *Ghestin*, Formation no. 404, LUXEMBOURG, see Cour 26 June 1914, Pasicrisie 11, 89; SCOTLAND, *McBryde*, Contract 74-77; GERMANY, *Münchener Kommentar (- Kramer)* § 151 Rz 4a; AUSTRIA, see e.g. OGH 18 October 1968, NZ 1969, 157 and 26 June 1991, WBI 1992, 23; ITALY, *Bianca*, Il contratto 214 f., PORTUGAL CC art. 218; and SPAIN, Supreme Court decisions of 18 October 1982 and 3 December 1993 RAJ (1993), 9494. The same rule is applied in IRELAND, see *Friel* 51. In ENGLAND this view is maintained by *Treitel*, Contract 31 ff., but there is no case authority.
   Some laws have provided further exceptions to the main rule, see the NORDIC Law on Commission Agents § 5, art. 22 (2) of the PORTUGUESE decree no. 177/86 on commercial agents, and the SPANISH Retail Trading Act (1996), art. 41).
   § 362 of the GERMAN and AUSTRIAN Commercial Codes provides that if a merchant is asked to act for another merchant with whom he has business connections or for whom he has offered to act, he is obliged to answer without delay; his silence is then considered as an acceptance.
   See also notes to Articles 2:209 and 2:210 and generally, *Schlesinger* I, 134 and *Kötz*, European Contract 41.

Article 2:205: Time of Conclusion of the Contract

(1) If an acceptance has been dispatched by the offeree the contract is concluded when the acceptance reaches the offeror.

(2) In the case of acceptance by conduct, the contract is concluded when notice of the conduct reaches the offeror.

(3) If by virtue of the offer, of practices which the parties have established between themselves, or of a usage, the offeree may accept the offer by performing an act without notice to the offeror, the contract is concluded when the performance of the act begins.

COMMENTS

A. *Significance of the Time of Conclusion under Article 2:205*

Article 2:205 lays down when the contract is considered to have been concluded. From this moment each party is bound to the other and cannot revoke or withdraw its consent. It may also have effects in other respects, see e.g. Articles 7:101(1) and (2), 7:102(c).

B. *Moment of Acceptance; Notice.*

This article deals with the moment when the acceptance becomes effective and the offer cannot any longer be revoked or withdrawn. Article 2:206 deals with the period of time with which an acceptance in order to become effective must have reached the offeror or have been effected by an act of performance.

The general rule is that once the acceptance has been dispatched the offeror can no longer revoke the offer. However, the acceptance becomes binding on the offeree when it reaches the offeror. The offeree cannot then revoke the acceptance, and the contract is concluded.

The statement or conduct must show an intention to be bound, see Article 2:102. The acceptance need not be made by the same means as the offer. An offer sent by letter may be accepted by telefax or even orally by telephone.

C. *Conduct*

In case of acceptance by conduct the contract is concluded when the offeror learns of it. An offeree may accept by delivering goods ordered by the offeror, by accepting unsolicited goods sent by the offeror, by opening a credit in the offeror's favour, by starting a production of goods ordered etc. Whether a conduct amounts to acceptance will depend upon the circumstances.

Illustration 1: Having learned from a colleague that B may be interested in buying and reselling A's goods, A sends unsolicited goods to B. B accepts by advertising the goods for sale in a trade paper which A reads. A learns of the acceptance when she reads the advertisement.

In case of a more complicated offer, especially if it is one for a contract of duration, a conduct which shows a positive attitude to the offer may not amount to an acceptance of the offer.

> *Illustration 2*: Having learned from a colleague that B may be interested in selling A's goods, A sends B goods with a draft distributorship contract by which B is to become A's sole distributor in B's country. B's advertisement of the goods in a trade paper, which A reads, without mention of any distributorship agreement does not amount to an acceptance of the latter.
>
> If, however, the relationship develops, and both parties observe the terms of the draft contract, B's behaviour will be considered an acceptance of the offer though it never signs the draft contract.

When notice of conduct, such as the production of goods ordered or other preparations by the offeree, will not reach the offeror within the time set for acceptance, an express assent by the offeree will be needed. If the offeree starts performance it does so at its own risk.

> *Illustration 3*: Opera Manager M offers soprano S the part of Susanna in *The Marriage of Figaro*, which will start in two months time. S immediately starts rehearsing the part, but does not send M any answer. M engages another soprano. S claims to play the part. M is not bound by any contract to S.

D. *Acceptance without Notice*

However, if it follows from the offer or from practices between the parties or from usage that the offeree may indicate assent by performing an act without notice to the offeror, the acceptance is effective at the moment performance of the act begins, see paragraph 3. In these cases the start of production or other preparations makes the acceptance effective even though the offeror does not get notice of these acts.

> *Illustration 4*: The facts are the same as in Illustration 3 except that M in his offer to S advises her to start rehearsing at once and by herself, because the rest of the company will tour the province during the next two weeks and cannot be reached. S starts immediately rehearsing. M and S have concluded a contract when S starts rehearsing.

A similar acceptance which is effective from the moment a performance begins may also follow from practice between the parties, see Article 1:104.

In cases covered by paragraph (3) the acceptance is effective when the act is performed even if the offeror learns of it after the time for acceptance.

The performance which will bind both parties under paragraph (3) is one which the offeree itself cannot revoke. It only applies to acts which are real performances not to acts which prepare a performance. If in view of the offer the offeree addresses its bank to obtain a cash credit in order to increase its available funds this act in itself will not constitute a beginning of a performance covered by paragraph (3).

NOTES

1. *Significance of the time of conclusion*

Among the various effects of the time of conclusion of the contract, the one which is considered here is the time when the parties are bound to the contract and none of them can withdraw from it. Like the Principles, the laws attach various other effects to the time of conclusion, see, for instance, CISG art. 35(2)(b) and (3), 42(1), 55, 66, 74, 79(1) and 100(2), and, generally, *Rodière, Formation* 136 f.

2. *Time of conclusion when acceptance is communicated by language*

In determining the moment when a contract is concluded through communication of an acceptance, the laws are divided.

Some laws consider the contract to be concluded when the acceptance reaches the offeror. This is the rule of CISG art. 23 and the UNIDROIT Principles 2.6(2), and the main rule in GERMANY, see *Larenz* § 27 II; AUSTRIA, see § 862a ABGB; GREECE see CC art. 192; THE NETHERLANDS, see BW art. 3: 37 (3); PORTUGAL, see CC art. 224; the NORDIC countries, see Contract Acts §§ 2 and 3. On the "receipt" principle see note 1 to Article 1:303.

The receipt rule is also the main rule in ENGLAND, but there are important exceptions. The most important is the "postal rule" whereby an acceptance sent by post or telegram takes effect when the letter of acceptance is dispatched (put in the mailbox) or the telegram is communicated to a person authorized to receive it for transmission to the addressee. From that moment a withdrawal of the offer, even if it has been posted previously, has no effect, see *Henthorn v. Fraser* [1892] 2 Ch. 27, C.A. The acceptance has effect even though the letter or telegram never reaches the offeror, and the contract is considered concluded, *Household Fire and Carriage Accident Insurance Co Ltd v. Grant* (1879) 4 Ex D. 216, unless perhaps the loss or delay was the fault of the offeree, cf. *Adams v. Lindsell* (1818) 1 B&Ald 681. But the offeree may prevent conclusion by sending an "overtaking" withdrawal of his acceptance, see *Treitel*, Contract 27-28. The "postal rule" only applies when it was reasonable to use the post, and it does not apply if the offeror has stipulated that the acceptance must be communicated to him, see *Holwell Securities Ltd v. Hughes* [1974] 1 W.L.R. 155, C.A.. For an acceptance made by instantaneous means of communication, such as email, telefax and telephone, the main rule applies, and so does an acceptance sent through a messenger, see *Treitel*, Contract 21 ff. The IRISH law is basically the same as the English. However, in *Kelly v. Cruise Catering Ltd* [1994] 2 ILRM 394 the Irish Supreme Court suggested obiter that the mailbox rule would not apply if the letter of acceptance was lost in the post.

SCOTS law is to the same effect as English law, but there is an official proposal to abolish the postal acceptance rule (*Scottish Law Commission*, Report No. 144, 1993) which in July 1998 had still not been enacted.

Other laws consider the offeror's knowledge of the acceptance as decisive, however, with the proviso that the offeror is considered or presumed to have the knowledge when the acceptance reaches him. This rule applies in BELGIUM, see Cass. 25 May 1990, Arr. Cass. 1990-91 1218, and in ITALY CC arts. 1326(1) and 1335, which provides as a general rule that a person is presumed to have knowledge of a message at the moment it reaches his address. On these laws and on NORDIC law see note 2 to Article 1:303.

In PORTUGUESE law the contract is also concluded when the offeror gets effective knowledge of the acceptance or if by his fault he has prevented it from reaching him. On the other hand, the contract is not concluded if without his own fault the offeror was prevented in from getting knowledge of it, see CC art. 224.

The same rule applies in SPAIN, see CC art. 1262(2); however, the courts will consider a contract concluded when the acceptance reaches the offeror. see Supreme Court decisions of 29 September 1960, 22 October 1974, RAJ (1974) 3971, 28 May 1976, RAJ (1976) 2366, 29 September 1981, RAJ (1981) 3247, 10 December 1982, RAJ (1982) 7474 and 22 December 1992, RAJ (1992) 10642 and 24 April 1995, RAJ (1995) 3546. For commercial contracts concluded inter absentes, art. 54 of the Commercial Code provides that the contract is concluded when the offeree has expressed his assent, which the courts interpret to mean when the offeree has dispatched his acceptance.

In FRANCE and LUXEMBOURG the question appears to be unsettled. The French *Cour de Cassation* has considered it a question of fact left to the sovereign appreciation of the lower courts. However, in a case where the acceptance had to be given before a certain date the Court has stated that the acceptance had to be dispatched before that date, see Cass. 7 January 1981, Bull. civ. IV no. 14. This may be considerered a general decision on when a contract by correspondence is concluded, see *Ghestin, Formation* no. 360.

3.   *Acceptance by conduct*
The systems agree that an offer may be accepted by conduct. Under most systems the contract is concluded when a notice of the conduct reaches the offeror, see on ENGLISH law, *Treitel,* Contract 17 and 21; on the DUTCH BW art; 3:38 (1); for GERMANY, *Erman- Hefermehl,* § 147, Rz 2; for GREECE, *Simantiras* in *ErmAK* 189 nos. 2-5.; see also CISG art. 18(2), UNIDROIT art. 2.6 (2). The same rule applies in IRISH law, see *Package Investments* v. *Shandon Park Mills,* unreported High Court decision of 2 May 1991, *Friel* 52.
        However, in SCOTLAND the offeror must know of and consent to the acceptance by conduct, see *Mc Bryde,* Contract 75-77.
        In FRANCE the courts oscillate beteen the moment the act is performed and the moment notice of the performance reaches the offeror, see *Terré, Simler & Lequette* no 117. The laws of SPAIN, BELGIUM and LUXEMBOURG also seem to be unsettled on that point.

4.   *Performance of an act without notice*
Article 2:205(3) is similar to CISG art. 18(3) and UNIDROIT Principles art. 2.6(3). In all the systems the offeror may stipulate the way by which the offer is to be accepted – except by silence – and practices between the parties and usages may also regulate the mode of acceptance.
        The GERMAN BGB § 151 provides that the contract is concluded without a declaration of acceptance by the offeree to the offeror being required, if it follows from general commercial practices that such a declaration is not to be expected or the offeror has renounced it. It seems to be the prevailing view that the act which shows acceptance must be one which manifests itself to the outer world. The mere fact that the offeree has made up his mind that he will accept is not enough, see on the German BGB § 151 *Münchener Kommentar I (- Kramer)* § 151 note 49.
        Similar solutions are to be found in or follow from AUSTRIAN ABGB § 864; SCOTS law, *McBryde,* Contract 74f.; FRENCH law, *Terré, Simler & Lequette* no. 117; NORDIC Contracts Act § 1 (2); GREEK CC art. 193 (1); ITALIAN CC art. 1327(1); PORTUGUESE law, see *Cordeiro* 1, 616, *P.M. Pinto,* Declaracào tacita 620 and *Almeida,* Negocio juridico 794; and ENGLISH law, see *Weatherby* v. *Banham* (1832) 5 C&P 228 and *Treitel,* Contract 23f. and 36f.

Article 2:206: Time Limit for Acceptance

(1) In order to be effective, acceptance of an offer must reach the offeror within the time fixed by it.

(2) If no time has been fixed by the offeror acceptance must reach it within a reasonable time.

(3) In the case of an acceptance by an act of performance under Article 2:205(3), that act must be performed within the time for acceptance fixed by the offeror or, if no such time is fixed, within a reasonable time.

COMMENTS

A. *Time for Acceptance*
This Article provides for the period of time within which the offeree's acceptance must reach the offeror in order to be effective.

B. *Time Fixed*
Acceptance of offers must reach the offeror within the time fixed by it. Acceptance may be made by an express statement or by conduct, see Article 2:205(1) and (2).

C. *Reasonable Time*
If the time for performance has not been fixed by the offeror the offeree's acceptance must reach it within a reasonable time. Due account has to be taken of the circum-

stances of the transaction. One factor is the rapidity of the means of communication used by the offeror.

Another factor is the type of the contract. Offers relating to the trade of commodities or other items sold in a fluctuating market will have to be accepted within a short time. Offers relating to the construction of a building may need longer time for reflection.

In the cases covered by paragraphs (1) and (2), the acceptance must reach the offeror in time. The offeree will generally be expected to use the same means of communication as the offeror. However, the time for acceptance is to be counted as an entirety. An offeree which receives an offer by mail may, if it has used too much time for reflection, catch up by accepting in a telegram.

See on delays in transmission Article 2:207.

In case of acceptance by conduct as provided in Article 2:205(2), notice of the conduct must reach the offeror within the time for acceptance.

D. *Acceptance by Performance (Article 2:205(3))*

In the situations described in Article 2:205(3), where an act of performance by the offeree will constitute acceptance even before the offeror gets notice of it, the performance must be commenced within the time fixed by the offeror or, if no such time is fixed, within a reasonable time, but it is not required that the offeror learns of it before that time.

NOTE

The rules in Article 2:206(1) and (2) are similar to CISG art. 18(2), and (3), UNIDROIT art. 2.6 and 2.7, NORDIC Contracts Act §§ 2 and 3, GERMAN BGB §§ 147(2) and 148, AUSTRIAN ABGB § 862, GREEK CC art. 189, DUTCH BW art. 6: 221(1) and BELGIAN law. The ITALIAN CC art. 1326(2) provides that the acceptance must reach the offeror within the time set by him, or within the time which is ordinarily required according to the nature of the transaction or usage. Art. 228(1) of the PORTUGUESE CC provides that the acceptance must reach the offeror within the time set by him or within 5 days after the time which is reasonable according to the nature of the transaction.

The rules in Article 2:206(1) and (2) also apply in ENGLISH, SCOTS and IRISH law. In English law it is not clear whether, if the offeror has set a time limit for acceptance, it suffices that the acceptance is dispatched within the period or whether it must reach the offeror within the period, cf. *Holwell Securities Ltd v. Hughes* [1974] 1 W.L.R. 155, C.A. However, in Scotland and Ireland an acceptance by post or telegraph is timely, if dispatched before the time set for acceptance, see on Scotland, *Jacobsen v. Underwood* (1894) 21 R 654.

Under FRENCH law the acceptance by correspondence is made in time if dispatched before the time set by the offeror, Cass. 7 January 1981, see note 2 to Article 2:205, above. Unless the offeror has set a time limit, the acceptance must be dispatched within a reasonable time, see *Terré, Simler & Lequette*, no. 164. The latter rule has also been adopted in SPAIN, see Supreme Court decision of 23 March 1988, RAJ (1988) 2422.

On Article 2: 206(3) on acceptance by performance of an act without notice, see Article 2:205, note 4.

Article 2:207: Late Acceptance

(1) A late acceptance is nonetheless effective as an acceptance if without delay the offeror informs the offeree that he treats it as such.

(2) If a letter or other writing containing a late acceptance shows that it has been sent in such circumstances that if its transmission had been normal it would have reached the offeror in due time, the late acceptance is effective as an acceptance unless, without delay, the offeror informs the offeree that it considers its offer as having lapsed.

COMMENTS

A. *Late Acceptance Ineffective*
It is laid down in Article 2:206(1) and (2) that in order for an acceptance to be effective it must reach the offeror within the time for acceptance. Any acceptance which reaches the offeror after that time may be disregarded by the offeror. Normally it does not even have to reject the acceptance.

B. *Assent to a Late Acceptance*
Article 2:207(1) states, however, that notwithstanding the rule in Article 2:206 the offeror may render the late acceptance effective by accepting it. It must then without delay inform the offeree. If it does so the contract become effective from the moment the late acceptance reached the offeror, and the offeree is then bound by the acceptance.

The notice need not be an express statement of acceptance. A telegraphic transfer of the purchase money, which will reach the offeree as quickly as a notice may suffice to make the contract effective.

Illustration 1: A has indicated 31 July as the last day for an acceptance of its offer. B's acceptance reaches A on 2 August. A immediately orders a transfer of the purchase money demanded by B. Notwithstanding that the payment does not come to B's notice until 4 August the contract is concluded on 2 August. Even if B now regrets its acceptance it cannot invoke its late acceptance to avoid the contract.

C. *Late Acceptance Caused By Delay In Transmission*
If the acceptance is late because the offeree did not send it in time, it is ineffective unless the offeror immediately indicates its assent to the contract. If, however, the offeree has sent its acceptance in time, but the acceptance reaches the offeror after the time set for acceptance because of a delay in transmission, the offeree should be notified if the offeror does not want to assent to the contract. The late acceptance should be considered effective unless the offeror without delay informs the offeree that it considers its offer as having lapsed or gives notice to that effect. The offeror, however, only has this duty if the acceptance shows that it was sent in time and that it arrived late due to an unexpected delay in transmission.

Illustration 2: A has indicated 31 July as the last day for an acceptance of its offer. B, knowing that the normal time of transmission of letters is two days, sends its letter of acceptance on 25 July. Owing to a sudden strike of the postal service in A's country the letter, which shows the date 25 July on the envelope, arrives on August 2. B's acceptance is effective unless A objects without undue delay.

D. *Late Acceptance as a New Offer*

Some legal systems treat a late acceptance as a new offer which the offeror may accept within the time set for acceptance which is often longer than the time provided for in paragraph 1. The Principles do not contain such a rule.

NOTES

1. *Late acceptance*
   Article 2:207(1) is in accordance with CISG, art. 21(1) and UNIDROIT Principles art. 2.9(1), and is similar to the DUTCH BW art. 6:223(1), PORTUGUESE CC art. 229, and ITALIAN CC art. 1326(3).
   Under some systems the late acceptance operates as a new offer which requires acceptance by the offeror, see NORDIC Contracts Act § 4(1), GERMAN BGB § 150, AUSTRIAN law, see *Rummel,* § 862 Rz 4 and OGH 24 November 1976 SZ 49/142, and GREEK CC art. 191. In FRANCE, LUXEMBOURG and BELGIUM it is the general opinion that this is the rule (see, however, Trib.de Grande Instance de Paris 12 February 1980, D. 1980, I.R. 261 note *Ghestin*), but there are no recent cases of authority. SPANISH law has no provision similar to Article 2:207(1). In ENGLAND, SCOTLAND and IRELAND there is no authority on the point.
2. *Delay in transmission*
   Article 2:207(2) is identical to CISG art. 21 (2), see note 1 above, and UNIDROIT art. 2.9 (2) and is similar to the NORDIC Contracts Acts § 4(2), GERMAN BGB § 149, AUSTRIAN law, see *Rummel* § 862a Rz 6, GREEK CC art. 190 and NETHERLANDS BW 6:223 (2). In BELGIAN law the offeror's obligation to inform the offeree would follow from the principle of good faith and fair dealing.
   In the UK, where the acceptance has effect when posted or sent by telegram, the offeror will carry the risk of a delay in transmission unless it is due to the fault of the offeree who, for instance, misunderstood or misspelt the address, see on ENGLISH law *Treitel*, Contracts 26 and on SCOTS law *Jacobsen v. Underwood* (1894) 21 R 654. On IRISH law see note 2 to Article 2:205 above.
   FRENCH, LUXEMBOURG, ITALIAN, PORTUGUESE and SPANISH law have no rule similar to Article 2:207(2).

Article 2:208: Modified Acceptance

(1) A reply by the offeree which states or implies additional or different terms which would materially alter the terms of the offer is a rejection and a new offer.

(2) A reply which gives a definite assent to an offer operates as an acceptance even if it states or implies additional or different terms, provided these do not materially alter the terms of the offer. The additional or different terms then become part of the contract.

(3) However, such a reply will be treated as a rejection of the offer if:

   (a) the offer expressly limits acceptance to the terms of the offer; or

   (b) the offeror objects to the additional or different terms without delay; or

   (c) the offeree makes its acceptance conditional upon the offeror's assent to the additional or different terms, and the assent does not reach the offeree within a reasonable time.

COMMENT

A. *The Main Principles*

Article 2:208 contains the following rules.

- *(1)* A contract is concluded if the reply expresses a definite assent to the offer.
- *(2)* A reply containing terms which materially alter the terms of the offer is a rejection and a new offer.
- *(3)* Additional and different terms which do not materially alter the terms of the offer become part of the contract.
- *(4)* If in the case mentioned in (3) the offeror has limited the acceptance to the terms of the offer, or if without delay it objects to the different or additional terms, the offer is considered to have been rejected by the different or additional terms. The same applies if the offeree makes acceptance conditional upon the offeror's assent to the additional or different terms, and the offeror does not give assent within a reasonable time.

B. *Considerations Underlying the Main Principles*

- *(1)* *Non-material Terms*

  The notion that non-material additions or modifications become part of the contract has been widely accepted. Such additions and modifications are frequently attempts to clarify and interpret the contract, or to supply terms which would otherwise be considered "omitted terms". The offeror should object to them if it finds it worthwhile to express its disagreement.

- *(2)* *Material Terms*

  The rule that the contract comes into existence in spite of additions or modifications which materially alter the terms of the contract is, as far as is known, provided in certain national laws. It has not been accepted in these Principles. An answer which contains additions or modifications which materially alter the terms of the contract are to be considered as a counter-offer which the offeror may accept either by its express assent or by conduct, for instance by performance of the contract. On the "battle of forms" (conflicting general conditions), see Article 2:209, below.

C. *What are Material Terms?*

A term is material if the offeree knew or as a reasonable person in the same position as the offeree should have known that the offeror would be influenced in its decision as to whether to contract or as to the terms on which to contract, see Article 1:301(5).

Consideration was given to providing, as does CISG art. 19(3), a list of additional and different terms which are to be considered material such as terms relating, among other things, to the price, payment, quality and quantity of the goods, place and time of delivery, extent of one party's liability to the other, or the settlement of disputes.

This list was not provided in Article 2:208. It could only have been illustrative. For example, though a clause relating to settlement of disputes is often material, if among merchants in the trade it is usual, though not customary, to refer disputes to settlement by arbitration, an arbitration clause in the offeree's answer will not materially alter the terms of the contract. Equally, the list could not have been exhaustive.

In determining whether a term materially alters the terms of the contract one cannot take into account whether the discrepancy is one relating to the existing dispute between the parties.

D. *Modification by Conduct*
An acceptance by conduct may contain additional or different terms. These terms may be material, for instance, if the offeree dispatches a much smaller quantity of a commodity than that which was ordered by the offeror, or immaterial if only a very small quantity is missing.

E. *Acceptance of Modification by Conduct*
A modification is an "acceptance" which makes the answer a rejection and a new offer. It may be accepted by the offeror's conduct. After having received the modified acceptance the offeror may perform the contract or accept the offeree's performance and this will amount to an acceptance of the new offer.

> *Illustration*: S offers B a contract under which B is to buy 350 tonnes of coal at a certain price to be delivered in instalments. The contract also contains a jurisdiction clause. B returns the contract in which it has struck out the jurisdiction clause and inserted instead an arbitration clause. The contract is then put into S's manager's desk by one of S's employees. S subsequently delivers the first instalment which B accepts. Before the second instalment is to be delivered there is a sharp rise in the market price of coal, and S then tries to avoid the contract invoking B's modified acceptance to which, it says, it never has agreed. However, S is to be considered as having accepted the contract by delivery of the first instalment.

F. *Modified Acceptance and Conflicting General Conditions*
A reference in a typed or hand-written reply to the offeree's general conditions which contains terms which materially alter the terms of the contract is covered by Article 2:208 when the offeror has not made any reference to general conditions. If it has, the case is covered by Article 2:209 on conflicting general conditions (the battle of forms) even though the reference is made in a hand-written or typed letter.

NOTES

1. Modified acceptance as rejection and a new offer
The rule in Article 2:208(1) is almost identical with CISG art. 19(1) and UNIDROIT art. 2.11(1). It is in accordance with AUSTRIAN law, the NORDIC Contracts Acts § 6(1), GERMAN BGB § 150(1), GREEK CC art. 191, PORTUGUESE CC art. 213, ITALIAN CC art. 1326(5), DUTCH BW art. 2:226 (1) and the laws of BELGIUM, see *Kruithof & Bocken*, TPR 1994 no. 97, ENGLAND, see *Treitel*, Contracts 18, SCOTLAND, see *Rutterford v. Allied Breweries*, 1990 SLT 249, and IRELAND.
2. Contract upheld in spite of non-material modifications
With slight modifications the rules in Article 2:208(2) and (3) are the same as in CISG art. 19(2)

and UNIDROIT art. 2.11(2). They were first introduced in the UCC § 2.207, see also ULFIS art. 7(2) and the DUTCH BW art. 6:225(2).

Several other systems also accept that in case of non-material modifications, the contract is concluded on the terms of the offeree, see on FRENCH law, *Ghestin, Formation no. 319* and further, note 2 to Article 2:210 below; on SPANISH law, Supreme Court decisions of 26 March 1993 and 26 February 1994, RAJ (1994) 1198. In LUXEMBOURG and SCOTLAND there is no authority to this effect but the Scottish jurists have advocated the same approach, see for instance *Mc Bryde*, Contract 79-80.

In BELGIAN law the prevailing view is that the law or usages will determine the terms on which there is disagreement even when the terms differ materially but not when the difference is substantial, *Kruithof & Bocken*, TPR 1994 no 97, contra *Cornelis*, TBH 1983, 37

3.   *Complete agreement required: the "mirror image rule"*

Most of the systems do not have rules corresponding to Article 2:208(2) and (3). Several of them seem to require complete agreement between the parties so that even non-material modifications in the offeree's reply prevent the contract from coming into existence – with the proviso that mere trifles are to be disregarded. This seems to be the position in GERMAN law, see *Soergel- Wolf* § 15o Rz 8-18; AUSTRIAN law, see OGH 31 May 1988 SZ 61/ 136; PORTUGUESE law, see CC art. 232 and *Vaz Serra* 130ff.; ITALIAN law, Cass. 9 Jan. 1993 n.77 in *Mass. Foro italiano* 1993 and 4 May 1994, no 4 in *Repertorio del Foro Italiano*, 1994 727 n.272; and in ENGLAND, see *Treitel*, Contract 18, and IRELAND. The same rule applies in the NORDIC countries, see Contracts Acts § 6 (1) and for DENMARK, *Lynge Andersen* 66, for FINLAND, *Telaranta* 147. However, under § 6 (2) of the Contracts Acts the "mirror image rule" does not apply where (1) the offeree considered his reply to be in conformity with the offer, and (2) the offeror must have realized this. If in that case the offeror does not wish to be bound by the terms of the reply, he must give notice without unreasonable delay. Otherwise he is bound to the contract as contained in the reply. The "double awareness test" of (1) and (2) does not leave much room for application of the rule in practice, see *Ramberg*, Avtalsrätt 119.

4.   *Modification accepted by conduct*

When because the acceptance was not in the same terms as the offer a contract has not come into existence, it may nevertheless be "healed" by the subsequent conduct of the parties, e.g. by performance by one party and acceptance of performance by the other party. It seems that several of the legal systems accept this solution. The ENGLISH case *Trentham Ltd* v. *Archital Luxfer Ltd* [1993] 1 Lloyd's Rep 25, 27 supports the view that it will be easier for the courts to infer that the outstanding point of disagreement is inessential and that therefore there is a contract if the parties have begun performance. In SCOTLAND also there may be acceptance by conduct in this situation, see *Uniroyal* v. *Miller* 1985 SLT 101. But if negotiations are still pending an English case has held that there was no contract and that any performance made would have to be paid for on a restitutionary basis, see *British Steel Corpn.* v. *Cleveland Bridge Engineering Co Ltd* [1994] 1 All E.R. 94, Q.B.

It is often held that by his counter-offer, the offeree becomes the offeror and that the offeror becomes the offeree who by his conduct accepts the counter-offer, see on CISG, *Bianca-Bonell (- Farnsworth)* 179 and *Honnold* no. 170 ff and on FRENCH law, *Ghestin, Formation no. 327*. On the battle of forms see notes to Article 2:209.

DANISH cases and writers support the rule that performance may heal a contract. An offeror who has received an acceptance with modifications but who acts as if the contract is concluded must be considered to have accepted the modifications of the offeree, see UfR 1990 295 H. In other cases of performance where there is no basis for giving preference to one party's conditions, the conflicting conditions may be disregarded, and the rules of law will apply, see *Gomard*, Kontraktsrek 104 f. and *Lynge Andersen* 73f. See also on SWEDISH law, *Adlercreutz* I 62 and *Ramberg*, Avtalsrätt 142-144.

Article 2:209: Conflicting General Conditions

(1)   If the parties have reached agreement except that the offer and acceptance refer to conflicting general conditions of contract, a contract is nonetheless formed. The general conditions form part of the contract to the extent that they are common in substance.

(2)   However, no contract is formed if one party:

(a) has indicated in advance, explicitly, and not by way of general conditions, that it does not intend to be bound by a contract on the basis of paragraph (1); or

(b) without delay, informs the other party that it does not intend to be bound by such contract.

(3) General conditions of contract are terms which have been formulated in advance for an indefinite number of contracts of a certain nature, and which have not been individually negotiated between the parties.

COMMENT

A. *The Commercial Background. The Battle of Forms*
Today's standardized production of goods and services has been accompanied by the standardized conclusion of contracts through the use of pre-printed supply- and purchase orders.The form has blank spaces meant for the description of the performance, the quantity, price and time of delivery. All other terms are printed in advance. Each party tends to use conditions which are favourable to it. Those prepared by the supplier, or by a trade organization representing suppliers, may, for example, contain limitations of liability in case of difficulties in production and supply or of defective performance, and provide that customers must give notice of any claim within short time limits. The forms prepared by the customer or its trade association, in contrast, hold the supplier liable for these contingencies, and give the customer ample time for complaints.

A special rule for this battle of forms is called for because it often happens that the parties purport to conclude the contract each using its own form although the two forms contain conflicting provisions. There is an element of inconsistency in the parties' behaviour. By referring to their own general conditions, neither wishes to accept the general conditions of the other party, yet both wish to have a contract. A party will only be tempted to deny the existence of the contract if the contract later proves to be disadvantageous for that party.The purpose of the rule is to uphold the contract and to provide an appropriate solution to the battle of forms.

B. *Scope of the rule*
The rule of Article 2:209 is not needed in every situation in which the parties each has a set of general conditions and these are not in identical terms.

First, the parties may have agreed that one or other set should apply. This may happen because they have agreed explicitly that one set should govern their contract, for example when a party has signed a document which is to be treated as the contract, although in previous correspondence that party has referred to its conditions of contract. It may also happen because one party fails to bring its general conditions to the other party's attention as required by Article 2:104.

Secondly, the question as to which terms govern only arises when the general conditions are in real conflict. This is not always the case. It may be that one party's general conditions contain terms which are implied in any contract of that kind, or that they merely list technical specifications of the goods or services to be supplied or performed by A. Such clauses are often not at variance with the general conditions of B, which do not contain any clauses on these points.

There is, however, a battle of forms even if only one party's conditions contain provisions on an issue, when its conditions deviate from the general rules of law, and it is to be understood that the other party meant the rules of law to cover the issue. Thus Article 2:209 will govern the situation where in its offer the supplier's general conditions contain a price escalation clause and the buyer in its acceptance uses a form which says nothing about later changes in the price.

C. The solutions.

1. Is there a Contract?
Article 2:209 provides that there may be a contract even though the general conditions exchanged by the parties are in conflict. This is an exception to the general rule in Article 2:208 on modified acceptance. Under Article 2:208, an acceptance which is different to the offer will be effective only if the differences are not material. Otherwise, the "acceptance" would be (i) a rejection of the offer and (ii) a new offer. It is true that, if the party who receives the new offer does not object to it and performs the contract, it will be deemed to have accepted that there is a contract, see Article 2:204. The difference made by Article 2:209, is that the contract may be formed by the exchange of general conditions, rather than only if and when the performance takes place.

Under Article 2:209, a party who does not wish to be bound by the contract may indicate so either in advance, or later.

If done in advance, this must be indicated explicitly and not by way of general conditions of contract. Experience has shown that a party which in its general conditions has provided that it does not intend to be bound unless its conditions prevail (such a clause is often called a "clause paramount") often remains silent to the other party's conflicting conditions, and acts as if a contract had come into existence. The provison is often contradicted by the party's own behaviour. To uphold it would erode the rule.

A party, however, may avoid the contract if after the exchange of the documents which purport to conclude the contract, it informs the other without delay that it does not wish to be bound by the contract.

2. Which Terms Govern?
If despite a conflict between the two sets of conditions, a contract does come into existence, the question is: which conditions will apply? Until recently many legal systems would answer the question as follows: By performing without raising objections to the new offer, the recipient must be considered to have accepted the general conditions contained in the new offer (the "last shot" theory). Under another theory it is argued that a party which states that it accepts the offer should not be allowed to change its terms. Under this theory (the so-called "first shot" theory) the conditions of the first offeror prevail.

Under Article 2:209 the general conditions form part of the contract only to the extent that they are common in substance. The conflicting conditions "knock out" each other. As neither party wishes to accept the general conditions of the other party, neither set of conditions should prevail over the other. To let the party which fired the first or the last shot win the battle would make the outcome depend upon a factor which is often coincidental.

It is then for the court to fill the gap left by the terms which knock each other out. The court may apply the Principles to decide the issue on which the conditions are in conflict. Usages in the relevant trade and practices between the parties (see Article 1:105) may be particularly important here, for example if there is a usage of employing conditions which have been made under the auspices of official bodies such as the General Conditions of the Economic Commission of Europe or standard forms promoted by some other neutral organisation. If the issue is not explicitly covered either by the Principles or by usages or practices, the court or the arbitrator may consider the nature and purpose of the contract and apply the standards of good faith and fair dealing to fill the gap, see Article 6:102.

> *Illustration 1*: A orders some goods from B. A's order form says that the seller must accept responsibility for delays in delivery even if these were caused by force majeure. The seller's sales form not only excludes the seller's liability for damages caused by late delivery where there was force majeure, but also states that the buyer shall not have any right to terminate the contract unless the delay is over six months. The delivery is delayed by force majeure for a period of three months and the buyer, which because of the delay no longer has any use for the goods, wishes to terminate the contract. The two clauses knock each other out and the general rule of the Principles will apply: thus, under Article 8:101(2) the seller is not liable in damages but under Article 8:108(2) the buyer may terminate if the delay was fundamental.

The term "common in substance" conveys that it is the identity in result not in formulation that counts. However, what is "common in substance", will not always be easy to decide.

> *Illustration 2*: A sends B an order, which has on the back general conditions providing, among other things, that any dispute between the parties will be submitted to arbitration in London. B sends A an acknowledgement accepting the offer. On the back of the acknowledgement is a clause submitting all disputes to arbitration in Stockholm. Although offer and acceptance have in common that they both refer to arbitration, the clauses are not "common in substance" and accordingly neither of the places of arbitration are agreed upon. But did the parties agree on arbitration? A court siezed with a dispute may conclude that the parties preferred arbitration to litigation in any case. Applying the principle laid down in art. 2 of the Brussels Convention on Jurisdiction and Enforcement of Judgments in Civil and Commercial Matters, the court may then decide that the place of arbitration is the defendant's place of business.
>
> If, however, the court finds that the parties or one of them would only have agreed to arbitration if it was to be held at a certain place the arbitration clause may be disregarded and the court may then admit the action.

NOTES

1. *Is there a contract?*

    In most of those countries where the courts have addressed the battle of forms it seems to be held that a contract has come into existence by the offer and its purported acceptance unless the offeror objects to the purported acceptance without undue delay. Thus the contract is held to exist even before the parties have acknowleged it in any other way, for instance by tendering performance, see references under note 2. This is also the position of some of the writers in the countries where there is no case law on the subject, see note 2c.

    In countries where the classical rules on offer and acceptance govern the battle of forms, a contract only comes into existence when these rules so provide. Under the classical rules on the conclusion of contracts the contract may also come into existence when the parties treat it as concluded expressly or by conduct, for instance by performing the contract. This is the position in COMMON LAW, see *Souter Automation Ltd* v. *Goodman (Mechanical Services) Ltd* (1986) 34 Building L.R. 81. See on PORTUGAL, *Almeida,* Negocio juridico 886 and on SPAIN, *Diez-Picaso* 211. In FRENCH law the contract is not formed unless both parties consider the conflicting terms as unessential,see *von Mehren* s. 164.

    In sales governed by CISG part II, where the terms of the purported acceptance do not materially alter the terms of the offer, the acceptance will conclude the contract unless the offeror objects without undue delay, see art. 19(2). If the terms of the purported acceptance materially alter the terms of the offer, there is a counter-offer, and therefore no contract until the offeror has shown that he accepts the counter-offer by his statements or conduct, for instance by performing the contract, see arts. 19(1) and 18(1), and *Farnsworth* in *Bianca & Bonell* art. 19, ss 2.3-2.6.

2. *Which terms govern?*

    a. *The "knock out" rule*

        Article 2:209 is in accordance with the UNIDROIT Principles art. 2.22, see *Bonell,* International Restatement 124ff. The GERMAN courts have adopted a similar "knock out" principle. In most of the cases they have solved the conflict by applying the rules of law (*das dispositive Recht)* governing the issue, see BGH 20 March 1985, NJW 1985, 1838, and BGH 23 January 1991, NJW 1991 1606, and *Kötz* in *Münchener Kommentar* Vol. 1, AGBG § 2 No 31 and *Larenz/ Wolf,* AT § 43 Rn 32. Basically the same position has been taken by the AUSTRIAN courts, see OGH 22 September 1982, Sz 55/135 and OGH 7 June 1990, JBL 1991, 120; see also *Rummel,* ABGB 2ed § 864a No 3.

        In FRENCH and BELGIAN Law the contract is concluded provided the conflicting conditions do not cover an essential element, *"cause determinante*" of the contract, see note 1 above. It is held that in such cases no conditions have been agreed upon, and the rules of law will fill the gap, see *de Ly & Burggraaf* 47 and *Mahé.*

    b. *The last shot theory*

        The last shot theory seems to be the prevailing view in ENGLAND, see *B.R.S.* v. *Arthur Crutchley* [1967] 2 All E.R. 285, 287, although the outcome will depend on the exact facts, see *Butler Machine Tool Co* v. *Ex-Cell-O Corporation(England) Ltd* [1979] 1 W.L.R. 811, 817, C.A. and *Treitel,* Contract 19f. It is also the prevailing view in SCOTLAND, see *Stair,* vol. 15, § 636. CISG arts. 19 and 18 seem to lead to the same outcome, both in cases where the conflicting terms of the acceptance materially alter the terms of the offer, see arts. 19(1) and 18(3), and when they do not, see art. 19(2), see v. *Caemmerer & Schlechtriem* art. 19 section IV, Rn 19-20, who are "afraid that this is the solution", and Farnsworth in *Bianca & Bonell* art. 19, ss. 2.3-2.6.

    c. *The first shot rule*

        The DUTCH BW art. 6:225 (3) provides that if offer and acceptance refer to different general conditions, the second reference is without effect, unless it explicitly rejects the applicability of the general conditions contained in the first reference. It appears that the explicit rejection must be one which the offeree communicates for the occasion and not one which only appears in his general conditions.

        In the USA § 2-207 of the UCC provides a general rule on additional terms in acceptance or confirmation. It is the prevailing view that the result is similar to that of the Dutch BW. However, if the additional terms do not materially alter the terms of the offer, these additional terms will become part of the contract, unless the offer expressly limits acceptance to the terms of the offer or notification of objection has already been given or is given within a reasonable time after notice of them is received. Several authors have criticised the rules in § 2-207, see *von Mehren,* ss. 157-180.

d. *The law is unsettled*
In the law of several countries, statutory provisons on the conclusion of contracts do not address the issue or do not provide what the authors consider to be clear and satisfactory answers. There is no case law and the authors are sometimes divided.

There is no general rule in SPAIN, where the authors tend to favour the classical rules on offer and acceptance and on interpretation of contracts. This is also the position of the POR-TUGUESE authors. In cases where the offeror accepts the contract by conduct the last shot theory would therefore be adopted.

Many authors assert that there can be no hard and fast rule which solves the conflict. The cases are to be decided individually. This is the attitude of the SWEDISH authors, see *Ramberg*, Avtalsrätt 143; *Göransson,* passim, who seems to favour the first shot theory; *Adlercreutz*, Avtalsrätt II 73; and *Hellner,* Kommersiell avtalsrätt 50, who is not even sure what is the right approach, and who shows some sympathy for the last shot rule, a sympathy which *Ramberg*, Avtalsrätt seems to share; see also *Bernitz* 40.

The question is treated by the FINNISH author *Wilhelmsson*, Standardavtal 1995, who seems to prefer the knock out principle, see p. 79f. Among DANISH authors, *Lando,* Kampen, favours the knock out principle; *Gomard, Kontraktsret* argues for the last shot rule where the offeror treats the contract as concluded without objecting to the additional or different terms in the acceptance, while in other cases the rules of the law should apply, see p.105; *Lynge Andersen* 74 seems to prefer the last shot rule.

Article 2:210: Professional's Written Confirmation

If professionals have concluded a contract but have not embodied it in a final document, and one without delay sends the other a writing which purports to be a confirmation of the contract but which contains additional or different terms, such terms will become part of the contract unless:

(a) the terms materially alter the terms of the contract, or

(b) the addressee objects to them without delay.

COMMENTS

A. *Background*

Between professionals, i.e. persons engaged in business transactions, who have made a contract, it may not be entirely clear on what terms their contract has been concluded. A party may then send the other party a written confirmation containing the terms which it believes were agreed upon, and the terms which it believes to be implied. It needs to send this confirmation in order to be sure of the terms of the contract before it starts performance. In most cases the recipient will assent to the written confirmation by its silence. It will have no reason to reconfirm what has already been agreed upon and confirmed by the other party. Its silence will, therefore, be considered as assent. If it disagrees with the terms, it must object without delay.

In many cases the additional terms provided in the confirmation will take the shape of an interpretation of the contract.

Illustration 1: Upon the termination of a distributorship contract between the supplier S and the distributor D, D requests, and it is agreed orally, that S shall take over D's stock of machinery "at the usual trade discount". These words usually mean the discount applied in sales from S to D (30%). However, in a letter of confirmation sent to S immediately after the oral agreement D points out that it means the discount which it applies to its customers (28%). Since S does not object to D's letter, D's interpretation will prevail.

B. *Conditions*

In order for the professional's confirmation to become binding upon the recipient, the following requirements must be met:

(1) The rule only operates between professionals, i.e. persons operating in their business capacity, as distinguished from relationships between professionals and consumers or between private individuals.

(2) The confirmation must be in writing, see Article 1:301 (6).

(3) The contract was incomplete in the sense that it did not materialise into a document which was a record of all the contract terms.

(4) The confirmation must reach the recipient without delay after the negotiations and it must refer to them.

(5) If the recipient does not object without delay to the terms additional to or different from the terms agreed upon in the preceding negotiations, they become part of the contract unless they materially alter the terms agreed upon. On the concept of "materially alter" see Article 2:208, Comments D(2) and E.

Illustration 2: Upon the oral conclusion of a sales contract S sends B a letter of confirmation in which, inter alia, it is provided that B has to make an advance payment of half of the purchase price three months before delivery of the goods. S cannot prove that this was agreed when the contract was concluded; the clause is unusual in the trade, and would materially alter the terms of the contract. B is not bound by the clause on prepayment. S, on the other hand, must perform the contract without getting the advanced payment.

NOTES

1. *Unidroit, German and Nordic law*
    The rule laid down in art. 2:210 is provided in UNIDROIT, art. 2.12. The same rule probably also applies in SWEDEN in contracts between professionals, see *Adlercreutz* II 75 ff. The same rule applies in DENMARK, FINLAND and GERMANY, see references below.
        In these three countries a professional's written confirmation may also create a contract even though it was not clear that one existed already. The letter of confirmation will bind the addressee to a contract even if he did not believe this, if the sender of the confirmation had reason to believe that the negotiations between the parties had led to a contract, see on DANISH law, *Lynge Andersen* 94 and the Supreme Court's decision in UfR 1974 119 H; on FINNISH law, *Telaranta* 172; and on GERMAN law, *Baumbach-Duden-Hopt* § 346. However, in these case the recipient will not be bound, if the letter contains surprising terms, or the recipient objects to the writing without delay.

2. *The other CIVIL LAW systems*
    In most other CIVIL LAW countries, a party's silence to a letter of confirmation or other communication purporting to change the terms of the contract will only amount to acceptance if this follows from usages and a practice between the parties, or when under the principle of good faith and fair dealing silence must be interpreted as acceptance. See for instance the LUXEMBOURG Cass. 26

June 1914, Pasicrisie 11, 89, where it was stated that under the circumstances "the confirmation of a purchase is implied by the silence of the buyer to the letter of confirmation of the seller." In AUSTRIAN law a professional's silence to another professional's written confirmation which adds to or deviates from the agreement made is not regarded as an acceptance of the written confirmation, see *Rummel* § 861 Rz 13, and OGH 7 July 1982 SZ 55/106, 28 April 1993 JBl 1993, 782.

In FRANCE, LUXEMBOURG, BELGIUM, ITALY and THE NETHERLANDS there seems to exist a general usage under which the recipient of an invoice is taken to have accepted the terms in the invoice unless he objects to them. A party's acceptance of a performance without objecting to the terms communicated by the performing party before or with the performance, or other similar circumstances may also be interpreted as acceptance of these terms, if good faith and fair dealing so require: see on Belgian law, *Rodière, Formation* 53 and *Storme* in TBH 1991, 467 ff.; on French law, *Ghestin,* Formation nos. 400 and 429 (and cf. Note 2 to Article 2:208, above); on Italian law, *Bonell,* Enciclopedia guiridica Treccani and Cass. 14 March 1983 n.1888 in *Massimario del Foro italiano,* 1983, 393, *Schlesinger (-Gorla)* 1176; and on Dutch law, *Rodière, Formation* 100. See also SPANISH CC art. 1.224.

3.   *The Common Law*
It is argued that also under the COMMON LAW, usages and practices between the parties may mean that if a party receives a letter of confirmation or similar document modifying the terms of the contract, and does not object, he may nevertheless be bound. Although the principles of good faith and fair dealing are not generally adopted in ENGLISH law, some cases seem to show that even when there are no usages and practices between the parties, silence to such a communication may be regarded as acceptance when it would be unreasonable to hold otherwise, such as when the recipient had initiated the negotiations, see *Schlesinger (-Leyser)* 116 ff, *Treitel,* Contract 33 and *Rust* v. *Abbey Life Ins. Co.* [1979] 2 Lloyd's Rep 355. Although there is little authority in IRELAND to support this view, it appears to be in line with the spirit of the law. The same may be true in SCOTLAND.

Article 2:211: Contracts not Concluded through Offer and Acceptance

The rules in this Section apply with appropriate adaptations even though the process of conclusion of a contract cannot be analysed into offer and acceptance.

COMMENTS

A. *Other Models than the Offer and Acceptance Model*
The conclusion of a contract may not always be separated into an offer and an acceptance. The parties may start with a letter of intent or a draft agreement made by one party or a third party. Then follow negotiations either in each other's presence or in an exchange of letters. Or they start by sitting down together to negotiate, sometimes with rather vague ideas of where they will end. It is not easy to tell where in this process the parties reach an agreement which amounts to a binding contract, see Comments to Article 2:201. The same may be true of the many contracts that are made by conduct alone, as when a motorist parks his car in a car park and gets a ticket from a machine or a traveller takes out travel insurance by putting money into a slot machine and receiving the policy from the machine.

B. *Application of Section 2*
The rules in section 2 cannot always be applied to such other models. Sometimes, however, they may apply:

Illustration 1: Two parties meet to draft a written contract. When they have made the draft they agree that each party shall have two weeks to decide whether it will accept it. The draft is treated as an "offer". If after the two weeks each of them has not received the other party's acceptance there is no contract. The same applies if before that time a party receives the other's rejection. If during the respite a party makes proposals for additions which materially alter the terms of the draft, this is to be treated as a rejection and a "new offer".

Illustration 2: After conclusion of an oral agreement the counsel for two professional parties is asked to submit a written contract. She then sends both parties a draft accompanied by a letter saying that she considers this to be their agreement unless she does not hear from any of them. The draft contains the terms which the parties had agreed upon and some additional terms which reflect usual commercial practices in the trade. The rule in Article 2:210 applies so that the parties will be bound by their silence.

NOTE

The conclusion of a contract by way of an offer and acceptance is, as was mentioned in the notes to Article 2:201, the principal model in all the legal systems. Other models are only sparsely regulated in the statutes, and several of the problems are not solved in the case law, see for ENGLAND *Treitel*, Contract 45-47.

It seems, however, to be universally agreed that the rules on the principal model apply by way of analogy to the other models, in so far as this is possible and reasonable. In the civil law countries this follows from the general principle of analogous application of the laws. The authors are in agreement on this; see for GERMANY, impliedly *Larenz/Wolf* 8 ed. 574f and 592f.; for DENMARK, *Lynge Andersen* 85 ff.; and for SWEDEN, *Grönfors*, Avtalslagen 35f. This also appears to be the position in ENGLAND, see *Treitel*, Contract 45-47.

See generally *Schlesinger* II, 1583-1620.

Section 3: Liability for negotiations

Article 2:301: Negotiations Contrary to Good Faith

(1) A party is free to negotiate and is not liable for failure to reach an agreement.

(2) However, a party which has negotiated or broken off negotiations contrary to good faith and fair dealing is liable for the losses caused to the other party.

(3) It is contrary to good faith and fair dealing, in particular, for a party to enter into or continue negotiations with no real intention of reaching an agreement with the other party.

COMMENTS

A. *The Subject Matter*

In trying to obtain a contract a party may commit fraud, make misrepresentations or threats. For such behaviour it may become liable in damages whether there is a valid contract or not, see chapter 4 on validity.

Article 2:301 deals with a party's liability for the harm it has caused the other party by entering into or continuing negotiations with the intention not to make a contract or by breaking off negotiations contrary to good faith and fair dealing. Article 2:301 deals with a behaviour which aimed at capsizing the contract whereas chapter 4 deals with a party's use of improper means to obtain a contract.

B. *Freedom to Negotiate and to Break Off*

Apart from cases where the law imposes a duty on a party to make certain contracts, a party is free to decide whether it will conclude a contract. It may enter into negotiations even though it feels uncertain as to whether it will eventually make a contract. It may break off the negotiations, and does not have to disclose why it broke off. Shopkeepers and other sellers will generally have to accept that people inspect their goods and ask for prices and other terms without buying. The same applies to lessors and sellers of apartments and houses who invite inspection of the premises.

C. *Entering into Negotiations Contrary to Good Faith*

However, a party, and especially a professional party, who enters into negotiations knowing that it will never conclude a contract may be held liable to the other party if the other, in negotiating in vain, incurred not insignificant costs.

> *Illustration 1*: A intends to enter the trade as a competitor of B. He enters into negotiations with B claiming to be interested in becoming B's sales manager. B pays A's travel expenses and the cost of a short training programme for A, which A had wished to join, before signing the contract. When A has got the information about B's sales and production methods, which he can use as a future competitor of B's, he breaks off the negotiations and starts his own enterprise. A is liable to B for the costs B incurred in paying A's travel and tuition.

D. *Continuing Negotiations Contrary to Good Faith*

It may also be contrary to good faith to continue negotiations after one has decided not to conclude the contract.

> *Illustration 2*: The facts are the same as in illustration 1 except that when starting the negotiations A did intend to become B's sales manager. The decision to become B's competitor was made after his travels but before he joined the training programme. He then made his first preparations to start by himself, but continued the negotiations and joined the programme in order to learn more about the trade and B's business. A is liable to B for the costs incurred by B after A made his decision.

E. *Breaking off Negotiations Contrary to Good Faith*

A party may incur liability for breaking off negotiations.

> *Illustration 3*: B has offered to write a software programme for A's production. During the negotiations B incurs considerable expenses in supplying A with drafts, calculations and other written documentation. Shortly before the conclusion of the contract is expected to take place, A invites C, who can use the information supplied by B, to make a bid for the programme, and C makes a lower bid than the one made by B. A then breaks off the negotiations with B and concludes a contract with C. A is liable to B for his expenses in preparing the documentation.

F. *Basis of Liability*

Liability may be based on misrepresentation: see illustration 1 and 2 where A led B to believe that it intended to conclude a contract. In several of the Member countries such misrepresentation is an actionable tort, but if the claim arises out of the contract the Principles should apply, see Comment E to Article 1:101 above. Liability may also be imposed because a party gave promises during the negotiations.

> *Illustration 4*: A assures B that B will obtain a franchise to operate a grocery store as one of A's franchisees. The conditions are that B invest 18,000 Euro and

acquire some experience. In order to prepare herself for the franchise B sells her bakery store, moves to another town, and buys a lot. The negotiations, which last over two years, finally collapse when A charges a substantially larger financial contribution than the one originally contemplated, and B finds herself unable to make this contribution. Although there is no evidence that the promises originally made by A were made contrary to good faith, A's breach of these promises is contrary to good faith, and A will be held liable to B for the losses B suffered in preparing for the franchise.

G. *Heads of Damages*

The losses for which the person who acted contrary to good faith is liable include expenses incurred (illustration 1), work done (illustration 3) and loss on transactions made in reliance of the expected contract (illustration 4). In some cases loss of opportunities may also be compensated. However, the aggrieved party cannot claim to be put into the position in which it would have been if the contract had been duly performed. Article 9:502 does not apply.

Illustration 5: Weare, a clothing manufacturer, is about to order material of a registered design from Cloth, the copyright owner. Scham falsely claims that it owns the copyright and offers Weare to supply the material a lower price than Cloth has offered. By the time Weare discovers that Scham does not own the copyright and cannot sell the material, Weare has lost the chance to sell the dresses it intended to make from the material. Weare, which has not made any contract with Scham, may claim damages for lost opportunity and wasted expenses from Scham, but not the amount Weare would have saved by paying the lower price which Scham had offered.

NOTES

1. *Liability for negotiation contrary to good faith*
    Under the laws of the Union, a party is free to start negotiations even though he does not know whether he will conclude any contract. He may also break off negotiations, and, in general, he will not have to account for his reasons for doing so. For example, where the contracts are prepared by the parties' lawyers, there is in general no deal and no duty to make a deal until the contract documents are signed and delivered, see *von Mehren* no. 38.
    However, several systems have rules similar to Artcile 2:301, imposing liability on a party who, when negotiating a contract, acts contrary to good faith and fair dealing and thereby causes loss to the other party.
    In the 19th century the German writer *von Jhering* established a doctrine on *culpa in contrahendo*. Under this doctrine, entering into contractual negotiations creates a special legal relationship *(Rechtsverhältnis der Vertragsverhandlung)* which imposes on each party a duty of care *(Schutzpflicht)*. A violation of this duty of care constitutes *culpa in contrahendo*, which entails liability. The courts in GERMANY and AUSTRIA have adopted this doctrine, and so has the GREEK CC, see arts. 197 and 198, and art. 227 of the PORTUGUESE CC. Also the ITALIAN CC art. 1337 imposes upon the parties a duty to act in accordance with good faith when conducting negotiations and concluding contracts. The ITALIAN CC art. 1328 provides that if the offeree acting in good faith has commenced performance of the contract before knowing of the revocation of the offer, the offeror is liable for the expenses and losses incurred by the offeree. In SPAIN, liability is based on the good faith principle laid down in CC art. 7(1), see *Diez-Picaso* 274-76. The courts oscillate

between contractual liability (CC art. 1101, see Supreme Court decisions of 2 December 1976, RAJ (1976) 5246 and 30 October 1988 (labour court), RAJ (1988) 8183, and tort liability under art. 1902 of the CC, see Supreme Court decision of 16 May 1988, RAJ(1988) 4308.

FRENCH and probably LUXEMBOURG law also employ delictual liability under CC art. 1382 in case of a *"fautive"* breaking off of negotiations. One example is when a firm offer is wrongfully revoked, see on France, *Terré, Simler & Lequette* no.113 and supra note 3 to Article 2:202. (However, in exceptional cases the court might hold that a contract has been concluded in spite of the recovation.) The principle is used more widely, however. BELGIAN law tends in addition to impose tort liability under CC art. 1382 to apply the good faith principle, see *van Ommeslaghe,* T.B.B.R/R.G.D.C 1987, 101 ff.

In a few cases the NORDIC courts have imposed liability for *culpa in contrahendo* in the circumstances described in Article 2:301. See on DANISH law *Lynge Andersen* 104 and *Hondius,* Precontractual Liability (- *Lando*) 113 ff.; on SWEDISH law, *Adlercreutz* I 103 ff.

In contrast to the civil law systems, ENGLISH law does not impose any specific duty on the parties to enter into or continue negotiations in good faith, see *Walford* v. *Miles* [1992] A.C. 128, H.L.. Even an express agreement to negotiate cannot be enforced, see *Courtney & Fairbairn Ltd* v.*Tolaini Bros (Hotels) Ltd* [1975] 1 W.L.R. 297. Either party has a right to break off negotiations at any stage before the final conclusion of the contract. Liability for pre-contractual behaviour is only imposed under limited circumstances, see below.

2.   *Examples of a behaviour which entails liability*

 (a) In several of the systems a person who enters into or continues negotiations without any intention of concluding a contract may be held liable in damages. A party will have to inform the other party when he knows that he is not willing or able to conclude the contract. This view is supported by courts and writers in ITALY, see *Hondius,* Pre-contractual Liability *(- Alpa)* 200; DENMARK, *idem (-Lando)* 117; SWEDEN, see *Ramberg,* Avtalsrätt 101 and NJA 1990, 745, *(obiter dictum)*; AUSTRIA, see *Hondius,* Pre-contractual Liability *(-Posch)* 44; and GERMANY, see *idem (-Lorenz)* 165; see also UNIDROIT art. 2.15. There is also support for this view in the laws of ISRAEL, SWITZERLAND AND THE UNITED STATES, see *Hondius,* Pre-contractual Liability (*-Hondius*) 16.

 (b) Some CIVIL LAW countries will hold a party liable who has made the other party believe that he is prepared to conclude a contract, and then without good cause breaks off the negotiations. The GERMAN Supreme Court has held a person liable if, without good reason, he refuses to continue negotiations after having conducted himself in such a way that the other party had reason to expect a contract to come into existence with the content which had been negotiated, see BGH 6 February 1969. *Lindenmaier- Möhring,* § 276 no 28 and *Hondius,* Pre-contractual Liability *(-Lorenz)* 166. The same rule applies in AUSTRIA, see *idem (-Posch)* 44 and OGH 30 May 1979 SZ 52/90; BELGIUM, see *van Ommeslaghe* T.B.B.R./R.G.D.C. 1987, 101 ff.; DENMARK, *Hondius,* Pre-contractual Liability *(-Lando)* 117; FRANCE, see *Terré, Simler & Lequette* no. 113, THE NETHERLANDS, *Hondius,* Pre-contractual Liability HR.18 June 1982, NJ 1983, 723 *(-Dunné)* 228 and (*Plas* v. *Valburg)*; PORTUGAL, SJT 4 July 1991 and 3 October 1991, see BMJ 409, 743 and 410, 754 and *Prata* s. 16 p 135; ITALY *Hondius,* Pre-contractual Liability *(-Alpa)* 201 and *Castronovo,* in *Contract and Tort* 273ff.; and probably also in FINLAND, see *von Hertzen* 239.

  In ENGLAND a party will generally not be held liable for breaking off negotiations in such a situation. However, there may be liability if the innocent party has relied on a negligent misstatement by the other party who led him to believe that a contract would be concluded, whereby the innocent party suffered loss, and on the facts there was a special relationship between the parties, see *Hedley Byrne & Co. Ltd.* v. *Heller & Partners Ltd* [1964] A.C. 465, H.L. and *Box* v. *Midland Bank* [1979] Lloyds Rep 391. In IRELAND a "contract to enter into a contract" was held to be binding in *Guardians of Kelly Union* v. *Smith* (1917) 52 ILTR 65 H.C.

 (c) Generally a party will have to bear his own expenses for negotiating a contract. If, however, in the *bona fide* belief that a contract will be concluded, a party incurs expenses or does work which exceeds that which one can normally expect from an offeror, and he does so at the other party's request or with his consent, the other party will have to pay these expenses or compensate for the work done if the other party breaks off the negotiations without good reasons. This rule is applied in some countries sometimes on the basis of an alleged pre-contract, see on DENMARK *Hondius,* Pre-contractual Liability *(-Lando)* 121; the NETHERLANDS (semble) *idem (-van Dunné)* 227; and SPAIN, see *Diez-Picazo* 276-278. In ENGLAND compensation has been awarded on a *quantum meruit* basis, see *William Lacey Ltd* v. *Davies* [1967] 1 W.L.R. 932.

(d) Contracts for building and engineering works are often preceded by an invitation to make tenders for which the law provides certain rules of procedure. If, in violation of these rules, the employer does not award the contract to the plaintiff tenderer, the latter has sometimes been awarded damages, see e.g. the GERMAN Supreme Court decision of 25 Nov 1992 (BHZ 120, 281), the ENGLISH case of *Blackpool & Fylde Aero Club Ltd* v. *Blackpool Bororough Council* [1990] 1 W.L.R. 1195 C.A. (where however the facts were slightly different), and the DANISH SupremeCourt decision of 30 April 1985 (UfR 1985 550).

(e) The preceding situations have been illustrations. The laws include other situations as well. One is where a person misrepresents that he acts as an agent of another, see notes to Article 3:204 on an agent acting outside his authority. For other examples see *Hondius*, Pre-contractual Liability *(-Alpa)* 201.

3. *Remedy*
    (a) In most countries the remedy in such cases is damages, though in ENGLAND sometimes restitution is awarded and not damages. In DENMARK, GERMANY, AUSTRIA, FINLAND, and SWEDEN compensation will be made for expenses incurred in reliance of a contract but damages will generally not cover the expectation interest, see for Sweden NJA 1963 105.

    The ITALIAN Court of Cassation imposes liability in tort, see e.g. Cass.11 May 1990, Foro it. 1991 I 184. However, under the influence of *Mengoni*, Pre-contractual responsibility the lower courts tend to regard the liablity as contractual. In SPAIN damages are limited to the reliance interest, and do not cover lost opportunities. In exceptional circumstances, however, the damages awarded have gone beyond the reliance interest. This has happened in the tender cases mentioned *supra* in 1 (d). In PORTUGAL the opinions are divided between those who will only give compensation for expenses incurred in reliance on a contract and those who will cover any loss which is adequately caused by the loss of the contract, including lost profit; see on the one hand *Costa*, Responsibilidade s. 3712, p. 206ff., and on the other, *Lima/Varela* I 216 and *Prata* s.17 p 98ff. In THE NETHERLANDS the courts most often only award the reliance interest, which may include loss of other opportunities. However, in case of a breaking-off of negotiations they may also award expectation interest, see *Hartkamp*, Interplay.

    In FRANCE, which does not, and BELGIUM, which rarely makes, any distinction between reliance and expectation interest, damages may include, besides expenses incurred, the loss of another contract which the aggrieved party would have made, or another loss of a chance.

    In ENGLAND the party who has indicated that he would grant an interest in land to the plaintiff and who stood by while the plaintiff acted to his detriment on the assumption that he would get the interest, may be liable on the principle of proprietary estoppel, and the court may even order specific performance, see *Crabb* v. *Arun District Council* [1976] Ch. 179, C.A.

    See also notes to Article 3:204 on the damages to be paid by an unauthorized agent.
    (b) In FRANCE, in cases of wrongful axocation at least the remedy may be an order for specific performance, which means that the contract is considered to have been concluded, see *Malaurie & Aynès,* Obligations no. 385. In the NETHERLANDS the court may order the party who broke off the negotiations to resume them, see BW art. 3:296 and the case law of the *Hoge Raad* and other courts.

    See generally *Hondius*, Precontractual Liability.

Article 2:302: Breach of Confidentiality

If confidential information is given by one party in the course of negotiations, the other party is under a duty not to disclose that information or use it for its own purposes whether or not a contract is subsequently concluded. The remedy for breach of this duty may include compensation for loss suffered and restitution of the benefit received by the other party.

COMMENTS

A. *No General Duty of Confidentiality*

Parties who negotiate a contract have in general no obligation to treat the information they have received during the negotiations as confidential. Should there be no contract, the recipient may disclose the information it has received to others, and it may use it for his own purposes.

B. *Confidential Information*

A party, however, may be interested in confidentiality. It may expressly declare that information given is to be kept secret, and may not be used by the other party. Further, when no such declaration is made, the receiving party may be under an implied obligation to treat certain information as confidential. This implied duty may arise from the special character of the information, and from the parties' professional status. The other party knows or ought to know that this information is confidential. It will be contrary to good faith and fair dealing to disclose it or to use it for the recipient's own purpose in case no contract is concluded.

> *Illustration*: A has offered to acquire B's know-how for the use of special plastic bags in the dyeing industry. During negotiations B must give A some information about the essential features of the know-how in order to enable A to assess its value. Although B has not expressly requested A to treat the information given as confidential, he has sent the written documentation to A at A's personal address and by registered mail, and B has only talked to A about it when they were alone.
>
> A has a duty to treat the information given as confidential. He may not disclose it to others and, should there be no contract, he may not use it for his own purposes.

C. *Remedies*

Breach of a duty of confidentiality makes the person committing the breach liable in damages. The injured party may also be entitled to recover the benefit which the person in breach has received by disclosing the information or by using it for its own purposes even if that party has not suffered any loss.

Other remedies include injunctions.

NOTES

1. *Duty of confidentiality*

   The duty of confidentiality imposed by Article 2:302 seems to be accepted in most of the countries of the Union. The writers often treat it as an instance of the parties' duty to observe good faith in contract negotiations, see on DANISH, ITALIAN and DUTCH law, *Hondius*, Pre-contractual Liability *(-Lando)*. 201, *(-Alpa,* and 228 *(-van Dunné)* 120; on GREEK law CC art. 197; and on BELGIAN law, *Marchandise*. In FRANCE and LUXEMBOURG breach of confidentiality is a delict, a violation of a duty to act in good faith, see *Viney,* Conditions no. 474.

In GERMANY, AUSTRIA and PORTUGAL the duty of confidentiality follows from the duty of care in contractual negotiations, see for Germany, *Larenz/Wolf* 609 and for Portugal *Prata* s. 16, 116ff and 131 ff. In ENGLAND the courts have established "the broad principle of equity that he who received information in confidence shall not take unfair advantage of it", *see Seager* v. *Copydex Ltd* [1967] 1 W.L.R. 923, C.A., and *Hondius*, Pre-contractual Liability *(- Allen)* 137. SCOTLAND also recognizes a duty of confidentiality, see *MacQueen* in Stair, vol. 18, 1451-1492.

In FINLAND the duty of confidentiality seems to be limited to information on technical matters, see Act on Unfair Business Practices § 4; a party who wishes to obtain further protection must guard himself by a confidentiality clause.

SPAIN is reported not to have a rule similar to the one in Article 2:302.

2. *What is compensated?*

In AUSTRIA, BELGIUM, DENMARK, FRANCE and LUXEMBOURG the aggrieved party's loss is compensated, see for Belgium, *Marchandise* and for Denmark, *Vinding Kruse* 267 ff.

ITALIAN and PORTUGUESE law will compensate the aggrieved party for his loss, and will also let him get the benefit received by the party who misused the information even when the aggrieved party suffered no loss, see for Portugal *Prata* s. 16, 116ff and 131 ff. Under DUTCH law also the court may measure the damages by the profit received by the person liable, see BW art. 6:104.

In ENGLAND damages for a deliberate misuse of information given may include the defendant's profits, see *Peter Pan Manufacturing Corp* v. *Corsets Silhouette Ltd* [1964] 1 W.L.R. 96. If the defendant was merely negligent, the damages may be based on the market value of the information, see *Seager* v. *Copydex Ltd* [1967]1 W.L.R. 923, C.A.

In SCOTLAND the remedies include loss and enrichment, see *MacQueen* in Stair, vol.18, 1488-1491.

CHAPTER 3

Authority of Agents

Section 1: General Provisions

Article 3:101: Scope of the Chapter

(1) This Chapter governs the authority of an agent or other intermediary to bind its principal in relation to a contract with a third party.

(2) This Chapter does not govern an agent's authority bestowed by law or the authority of an agent appointed by a public or judicial authority.

(3) This Chapter does not govern the internal relationship between the agent or intermediary and its principal.

COMMENT

This provision sets out the scope of chapter 3.

A. *Agency in Contracts*
The chapter covers only agents who can bind their principal. It does not apply to agents who are allowed to negotiate the terms of a contract but have no power to conclude it and thereby to bind their principal.

Article 3:101(1) specifies that this chapter applies only within the framework of contractual relationships. However, conduct of an agent that affects the contract is covered by this chapter, even if under the applicable national law that conduct is qualified as being tortious.

> *Illustration*: Agent A fraudulently oversteps the limits of his authority and concludes a contract with a third party T. The consequences of this act are governed by these Principles even if they constitute also a tort under the applicable national law.

B. *Agency Based Upon Contract*
Article 3:101(2) expresses another limitation of the chapter. An agent's authority which is conferred by law or the authority of an agent appointed by a public or judicial authority is outside the terms of the chapter. For instance, the powers of representation which by statute are conferred upon the directors of a company are not cov-

ered. But if a company grants authority to act for it to one of its employees other than a director, the Principles do apply.

C. *External and Internal Relations Distinguished*
The title of the chapter and Article 3:101(1) make it clear that the chapter deals only with an agent's authority to bind his principal in relation to the third party.

The chapter governs only the external relationship created by an agent, i.e. the relationship between the principal and the third party; it does not govern the internal relationship, i.e. the relation between the principal and the agent.

However, that separation cannot completely be preserved. The internal relationship may well affect the external relationship. In particular, some of the grounds for termination of the agent's authority are rooted in that internal relationship (cf. Article 3:209). Termination of the agent's authority is an essential aspect and must therefore be regulated.

D. *Subsidiary Application of General Contract Rules*
A major consequence of the fact that this chapter mainly covers the authority of agents that is granted by agreement between the principal and the agent is that the general rules on contracts, including the general provisions laid down in Chapter 1, also apply. For the authority of commercial agents, usages are of particular importance (cf. Article 1:103). The authority of all agents is, of course, subject to the all-pervading imperative of observing good faith and fair dealing (cf. Article 1:201). The rules on formation and interpretation in Chapters 2 and 5 apply to the granting of an agent's authority. The Chapter on validity (Chapter 4) may also be relevant. The general rules of contract law are also relevant for other phases of an agent's authority, especially for its exercise and termination.

E. *Excluded Subject-Matters*
The internal relationship between the agent and his principal is not covered by this chapter, except insofar as it has an incidence upon the agent's authority, cf. e.g., Articles 3:205 and 3:209 and the illustration above.

Aspects of capacity (of the agent or the principal) are only dealt with insofar as they have a direct bearing on the external relationship (cf. Article 3:209(1) (c)).

NOTES

1. *Internal and external relations not clearly distinguished*
   Following the Roman tradition of mandate, the older European codifications (FRANCE, BEL-GIUM, and LUXEMBOURG: CCs art. 1984-2010; SPAIN: CC arts. 1709-1739; AUSTRIA: ABGB §§ 1002-1034) do not distinguish between the internal relationship between agent and principal on the one hand and the external relationship between principal and third party on the other hand. This separation has, however, been developed in these countries by legal writers.
   Under the COMMON LAW, the law of agency covers the relations both between principal and third party as well as between principal and agent.
2. *Internal and external relations distinguished*
   By contrast, several Civil Codes or special legislation enacted in the 20th century do make a distinction between the external and the internal relationship. The rules on representation govern the

relationship between principal and third party whereas the internal relationship between principal and agent is regulated by contract law in general. ITALY, for example, distinguishes expressly between mandate as a type of specific contract (CC arts. 1703-1730) and representation as a category of the general law of obligations (CC arts. 1387-1400). Similar distinctions are made by other Codes (GERMANY: BGB §§ 164-181 [representation], 662-676 [mandate]; GREECE: CC arts. 211-235 [representation], 713-729 [mandate] ; THE NETHERLANDS: BW arts. 3:60-3:67 [representation], 7:400-7:427 [mandate]; PORTUGAL: CC arts. 258-269 [representation], 1157-1184 [mandate]). The NORDIC Contract Acts of Denmark, Finland and Sweden of 1915-1917 deal in their chapters 2 only with the external relation between principal and third party. Italy (CC art. 1704) and even more explicitly Portugal (CC arts. 1178, 1180) distinguish between the mandates with and without power of representation. Most other countries also regard direct representation as a general category of private law or at least of patrimonial law.

3.   *Agents with limited authority*
     An agent normally has the power to bind the principal to a contract with the third party, but there are also classes of agents whose authority is often more limited. For example *Handelsvertreter* often have authority only to solicit offers, and not to sell.

4.   *Convention on Agency in International Sale of Goods*
     The scope of the Unidroit Convention on Agency in the International Sale of Goods, concluded in Geneva on 17 February 1983 (cited here: Geneva Convention on Agency), is confined to the external relationship between the principal and the agent on the one hand and the third party on the other (art. 1(3). The Convention has, however, not (yet) entered into force; it has been signed and ratified by three Member States of the European Union (France, Italy, and the Netherlands).

5.   *Authority based on contract and based on law*
     In some jurisdictions the agency rules only apply to the agent's authority based upon contract (DENMARK, FINLAND and SWEDEN: Contracts Act §§ 10-27). Similarly the Geneva Convention on Agency is not applicable in a number of cases where the agency arises from statutory or judicial authorization (art. 3(1), art. 4). In other jurisdictions a statutory power of representation is governed by the same rules as the authority of an agent conferred by contract (e.g. GERMANY: BGB § 164; GREECE: CC art. 211; ITALY: CC art. 1387; cf. also DUTCH BW arts. 3:78-3:79).

Article 3:102: Categories of Representation

(1)   Where an agent acts in the name of a principal, the rules on direct representation apply (Section 2). It is irrelevant whether the principal's identity is revealed at the time the agent acts or is to be revealed later.

(2)   Where an intermediary acts on instructions and on behalf of, but not in the name of, a principal, or where the third party neither knows nor has reason to know that the intermediary acts as an agent, the rules on indirect representation apply (Section 3).

COMMENTS

A. *Direct Representation*

Following a more or less explicit division recognized by all European countries, these Principles distinguish between two categories of representation, direct and indirect. The decisive criterion is whether or not an agent acts in the name of a principal and the third party knows or ought to know this. In this case, the rules on direct representation apply (cf. Section 2). This is the normal situation.

Direct representation also covers the case where an agent acts in the name of "a" principal but does not, at first, disclose that principal's name. The agent may not even have a principal at the time of the conclusion of the contract. The agent is, however, bound to reveal the name if the third party so requests; cf. for details Article 3:203.

By virtue of direct representation an agent establishes a direct relationship between his principal and the third person, cf. Article 3:202.

B. *Indirect Representation*

By contrast, where an intermediary acts in his own name but on behalf of a principal, there is indirect representation. That is so, even if the intermediary discloses that he acts on behalf (but not in the name) of a principal. The most typical commercial example is a so-called commission agent in the Continental countries.

There is indirect representation also if the intermediary acts in his own name and does not even disclose that he acts on behalf of a principal. This description covers the undisclosed agency of the English common law and the so-called strawman (*prête-nom*) in the Continental countries.

The rules on indirect representation are to be found in Section 3. Subject to exceptions, and in contrast to direct representation, no direct relationship between the principal and the third person comes into being. Rather, two separate relationships exist side by side: one between the principal and the intermediary and another between the intermediary and the third party.

NOTES

1. *Direct and indirect representation not distinguished*
   The Geneva Convention on Agency makes no distinction between direct and indirect representation. Under the Convention the same rules apply irrespective of whether the agent acts in his own name or in that of the principal (art. 1(4)). There are, however, special rules for the case where the third party does not know that the agent was acting as an agent.
2. *Direct representation only regulated*
   The Continental Civil Codes generally only regulate direct representation where the agent acts in the name of the principal (FRANCE, BELGIUM, and LUXEMBOURG: CCs art. 1984(1); AUSTRIA: ABGB § 1002; GERMANY: BGB § 164; GREECE: CC art. 211; ITALY: CC art. 1388; DENMARK, FINLAND and SWEDEN: Contracts Act § 10(1); THE NETHERLANDS: BW art. 3:60 (1); PORTUGAL: CC art. 258, see also art. 1178). Therefore in some countries the term "representation" is confined to what the Principles call direct representation. Whatever the terminology, in substance the distinction between direct and indirect representation can be found in most European countries.
3. *Direct representation where principal not identitifed*
   As in the Principles, many Member States apply the rules on direct representation even if the agent does not disclose the principal's identity (e.g. GERMANY: RG 2 March 1933, RGZ 140, 335; AUSTRIA: OGH 17 May 1950, SZ 23 no. 163; FRANCE, LUXEMBOURG: *Malaurie & Aynès*, Special Contracts no. 535 (*déclaration de command*); BELGIUM: *van Gerven* 481; THE NETHERLANDS: BW art. 3:67; GREECE: AP 58/1975, NoB 1975.879 (880 I); ENGLAND: *Bowstead & Reynolds* § 73). On the other hand, ITALIAN and PORTUGUESE law provide a set of special rules governing the "contract for a person to be nominated" (ITALY: CC arts. 1401-1405; PORTUGAL: CC arts. 452-456, CCom art. 465) who, upon nomination, must ratify the contract, unless he had already granted an authority (ITALY: CC art. 1402(2); PORTUGAL: CC art. 453(2).
4. *Special provisions on indirect representation*
   The SPANISH, ITALIAN and PORTUGUESE Civil Codes contain a general rule on indirect representation (Spain: CC art. 1717; Portugal: CC arts. 1180-1184; Italy: CC art. 1705). In several Continental European countries there are special provisions on the commission agent as a specific and important type of indirect representative (e.g. FRANCE and LUXEMBOURG: CComs art. 91; BELGIUM: CCom First book title VII (as amended by Law of 5 May 1872) art. 13; GERMANY and AUSTRIA: HGB § 383; Italy: CC arts. 1731-1736; NETHERLANDS: BW art. 7:425-7.427; PORTUGAL: CCom arts. 266-277; SWEDEN and DENMARK: Statute on Commission Agents).

5. *Disclosed and undisclosed agency*

The distinction between direct and indirect representation is not known in the COMMON LAW. English and Irish common law instead distinguish between disclosed and undisclosed agency. The principal may be bound by the acts of the agent whether or not the third party knows of the representation (*Freeman & Lockyer* v. *Buckhurst Properties (Mangal) Ltd.* [1964] 2 Q.B. 480, 502 (per Diplock L.J.). If the agent appears to be acting purely on behalf of himself, according to the Common Law the agency is undisclosed (*Bowstead & Reynolds*, § 1-007).) The same distinction is made by SCOTS law.

Section 2. Direct Representation

Article 3:201: Express, Implied and Apparent Authority

(1) The principal's grant of authority to an agent to act in its name may be express or may be implied from the circumstances.

(2) The agent has authority to perform all acts necessary in the circumstances to achieve the purposes for which the authority was granted.

(3) A person is to be treated as having granted authority to an apparent agent if the person's statements or conduct induce the third party reasonably and in good faith to believe that the apparent agent has been granted authority for the act performed by it.

COMMENT

A. *Methods of Granting Authority*

Article 3:201 enumerates the ways in which an agent's authority may be granted by the principal or in which the principal may be treated as having granted it. It also indicates the scope of the authority granted to the agent, unless this has been specified by the principal.

B. *Express and Implied Grant of Authority*

Paragraph 1 spells out that an agent's authority may be granted both expressly and impliedly. In giving express authority to the agent, no particular form needs to be observed since these Principles generally do not require formalities.

Frequently, but not necessarily, the authorization of the agent will be communicated by the principal to one or more third person(s).

Authority implied from the circumstances plays a very important role in practice.

Illustration 1: A store which employs a sales person in its sales department impliedly authorises him or her to transact any business relating to the merchandise offered for sale and to bind the shop by any such transaction.

An implied authority may supplement an express authority, especially its scope.

Illustration 2: The employee in the shop (cf. Illustration 1) will impliedly have authority to exchange defective goods bought in the shop.

An implied authority may well be subject to express limitations by the principal; such express limitations may even indicate the authority which is otherwise implied. On the other hand, an implied authority may be supplemented by a broader apparent authority (cf. D, below).

C. *Scope of Authority*
The scope of an agent's express or implied authority depends upon the purpose(s) for which it is granted by the principal. These Principles cannot give more than a general formula, cf. paragraph (2). In a more complex situation, the principal will be well advised to specify the scope of the authority in a written document.

D. *Apparent Authority*
An agent's authority is not necessarily based on statements or acts by which the principal intended to grant authority. Even without the principal's express or implied intention, an agent's authority may come into being if the principal has induced in a third party the good faith belief that the "agent" has been granted authority to represent the principal.

An agent who has apparent authority will have power to bind the principal as much as if the agent had express authority. This rule is provided in order to protect the third party, provided it has relied, and was entitled to rely, upon the impression that the principal had in fact granted authority.

On the other hand, the possibly countervailing interest of the principal not to be bound by the agent's act also deserves to be taken into account. Paragraph 3 balances these two interests by laying down three conditions for a justified reliance by the third party:

(a) there must be statements or conduct by the principal;
(b) this must have induced a reasonable and good faith belief in the third party; and
(c) the third party must have believed that the principal had granted authority for the specific act or acts performed by the agent that are in issue.

Illustration 3: A jeweller's shop has instructed its employee not to accept personal cheques from a customer. The employee disregards this instruction. The jewellers is bound by virtue of the employee's apparent authority to accept cheques since payment by personal cheque in jewellers' shops is general practice.

A specific situation in which an apparent authority may arise is the case where an authority is terminated, cf. Article 3:209(2).

NOTES

1. *Express and implied authority*
    In most European Member States, the agent's authority generally may be granted not only express-
    ly but also impliedly (SPAIN: CC art. 1710(1); PORTUGAL: STJ 8 February 1979, Revista de leg-
    islação e jurisprudencia 112, p. 219; THE NETHERLANDS: BW art. 3:61(1); GERMANY: *Palandt
    (-Heinrichs)* § 167 no. 1; AUSTRIA: *Rummel (-Strasser)* § 1002 no. 44 ss., see also ABGB § 863;
    ENGLAND: *Bowstead & Reynolds*, no. 3-003). The same is true under the Geneva Convention on
    Agency (art. 9(1).
        The Romanist countries, however, distinguish between "acts of administration" and "acts of
    disposition": a general authority empowers only to make the former but not the latter acts
    (FRANCE, BELGIUM and LUXEMBOURG: CCs art. 1988; SPAIN: CC art. 1713; ITALY: CC art.
    1708(2); cf. also NETHERLANDS: BW art. 3:62). In Belgium this distinction has, however, been
    overruled by the courts (cf. Cass. 3 May 1955, Pas. 1955 I 961, 962; Cass. 13 April 1984,
    Rechtskundig Weekblad 1984/85, 1495, 1497).
        However, formal requirements may limit the implied granting of authority. In some countries
    the granting of authority must fulfil the formal requirements prescribed for the authorized act (ITALY:
    CC art. 1392; GREECE: CC art. 217(2); IRELAND: *Athy Guardians* v. *Murphy* [1896] 1 I.R. 65, 75
    (V.C.); PORTUGAL: CC art. 262(2); the same is true if a writing is required for the underlying act
    ad probationem (FRANCE, BELGIUM and LUXEMBOURG: CCs arts. 1985(1), 1341). Under the
    Geneva Convention on Agency art. 10, as well as in GERMANY and the NORDIC countries, no form
    is required for the grant of authority (Germany: BGB § 167(2); Nordic Contract Acts § 10(2).
2. *What authority is implied*
    The general formula of Article 3:201(2) on the scope of an agent's authority corresponds almost lit-
    erally to Geneva Convention on Agency art. 9(2). Similar provisions can be found in ITALY (CC art.
    1708) and PORTUGAL (CC art. 1159(2), CCom. arts. 233, 249).
3. *Interpretation of principal's statement*
    As a general rule, the scope of an agent's authority is defined by the principal's statement and its
    interpretation. Some countries distinguish between general and specific authority (FRANCE, BEL-
    GIUM and LUXEMBOURG: CCs art. 1987; ITALY: CC art. 1708; SPAIN: CC art. 1712; THE
    NETHERLANDS: BW art. 3:62).
4. *Authority defined by legislation*
    There are also certain types of authority whose scope is defined by statute. The GERMAN, AUS-
    TRIAN, DANISH, FINNISH and ITALIAN commercial authority (*Prokura*) authorizes all transac-
    tions required in a commercial undertaking, except the selling of real estate (Austria and Germany:
    HGB §§ 48-53; Danish Act on Public Companies, §§ 60-62; Finnish Act on *procura* no. 130/1979;
    Italy: CC arts. 2203-2204). Germany, Austria and Italy also provide for another commercial author-
    ity with a somewhat narrower statutory scope, i.e. limited to ordinary commercial transactions
    (Germany and Austria: HGB § 54 (*Handlungsvollmacht*); Italy: CC arts. 2210-2213 (*commessi*)).
    Contractual limitations upon these types of authority agreed between principal and agent have no
    effect toward third parties.
5. *Apparent authority*
    The idea of apparent authority is almost nowhere laid down in legislation except in the Geneva
    Convention on Agency art. 14(2) and in the DUTCH BW art. 3:61(2) (cf. for PORTUGAL the spe-
    cial provision of Decree-Law no. 278/86 on commercial agents art. 23; cf. *P.M. Pinto*, Aparencia).
    The idea is very well known in the COMMON LAW: see *Bowstead & Reynolds* §§ 8-013-8-050. It
    is also accepted by BELGIAN and ITALIAN courts (Belgium: Cass. 20 June 1988, R.W. 1989/90
    p. 1425, 1426; Italy: Cass. 19 January 1987, no. 423, Nuova Giurisprudenza Civile Commentata
    1987 I 486, 487 with note Ceccherini); and see the FRENCH theory of *mandat apparent*, *Terré,
    Simler & Leguette* no. 169. Its essential elements are defined as being a declaration or conduct of
    the "principal" which induces a reasonable inference in the third person that a sufficient authority
    has been granted (for IRELAND: *Barrett* v. *Irvine* [1907] 2 I.R. 462 (K.B.) and *Allied
    Pharmaceutical Distributors Ltd.* v. *John F. Walsh* [1991] 2 I.R. 8 at 15 and 17 (H.Ct.)). GERMAN
    law distinguishes between two types of apparent authority: Authority by knowingly tolerating the
    agent's conduct (*Duldungsvollmacht*), cf. BGH 22 October 1996, NJW 1997, 312, 314) and author-
    ity by causing a misconception about the agent's authorization (*Anscheinsvollmacht*) (*Palandt (-
    Heinrichs)* § 173 no. 9 ss.). This distinction has been adopted by some writers in AUSTRIA
    (*Koziol/Welser*, Grundriss des bürgerlichen Rechts I, ed. 10 1996, p. 169 s.) and SWEDEN
    (*Grönfors*, Ställningsfullmakt 79-102, 164-194; *Ramberg* , Avtalsrätt 84. In Sweden it is controver-
    sial whether a principal can be bound contractually due to conduct of the second kind.)

In several countries specific situations are circumscribed by statute in which an authority is deemed to be present. Regardless of the principal's true intentions it then may be bound by the agent's acts. Under the NORDIC Contracts Act (§ 10(2)) everyone in the typical position of an agent is supposed to be authorized. The clerk in a shop or an open warehouse may be treated as being authorized to make ordinary sales and receive payments (Austria and Germany: HGB § 56. Austrian ABGB §§ 1027-1031 gives supplementary detailed rules). In the Common Law, the appointment of a person to a particular position normally gives rise to apparent authority to do what a person in that position would normally be empowered to do, e.g. *Waugh* v. *HB Clifford & Sons Ltd* [1982] Ch. 374, C.A., unless the third party knows that the person does not have the usual authority.

Article 3:202: Agent acting in Exercise of its Authority

Where an agent is acting within its authority as defined by Article 3:201, its acts bind the principal and the third party directly to each other. The agent itself is not bound to the third party.

COMMENTS

A. *Basic Effect of Representation*
Article 3:202 establishes the basic effect of any disclosed agency where the agent has acted within his authority: the agent creates, modifies or terminates a legal relationship between his principal and the third party.

B. *Third Party's Knowledge Necessary*
It is implicit in Article 3:202(1) that the third party knows or ought to know that the agent is acting in the name of a principal, see Article 3:102(2). If this is not the case, the rules on indirect representation apply.

C. *The Agent's Position*
The second sentence spells out the normal effect if an agent acts within his authority. He himself is not bound to the third party. Of course, the agent and the third party or the principal and the agent may by agreement depart from this rule and impose personal liability upon the agent. He may become a co-debtor or a guarantor of the principal's obligations. Article 3:203 establishes another exception.

NOTES

1. *Authorised act binds principal and third party*
   The general principle laid down in Article 3:202 is to be found in many European codifications (GERMANY: BGB § 164(1); FRANCE, BELGIUM and LUXEMBOURG: CCs art. 1998; ITALY: CC art. 1388; PORTUGAL: CC art. 258; THE NETHERLANDS: BW art. 3:66(1); AUSTRIA: ABGB § 1017; NORDIC Contracts Act § 10(1); for ENGLAND, see *Bowstead & Reynolds* art. 73).
   Since the Geneva Convention on Agency applies to indirect as well as to direct representation, there is an additional prerequisite. Under the Convention the principal and the third party are bound to each other only if the third party knew or ought to have known that the agent was acting as an agent, unless it follows from the circumstances that the agent is willing to bind himself only (art. 12).
2. *Exceptional circumstances when principal not bound*
   As an exception to the aforementioned general rule the agent cannot bind the principal – even though he acts within his authority – if he cooperates with the third party in order to harm the principal (col-

lusion) (GERMANY: BGH 17 May 1988, NJW 1989, 26; AUSTRIA: cf. OGH 13 February 1991, SZ 64 no. 13; GREECE: Thessaloniki 1010/1993, Harm. 1994.1019, 1020-1021).

A related idea which probably leads to the same results is expressed by Greek law under the heading "abuse of right" (CC art. 281): if the third party knows or should know that the agent acts against the principal's interest or against the purpose of such authority and the principal never would have concluded the contract if acting itself, such an act is not binding upon the principal and the third party (AP: 213/1965, EEN 1966.36; 466/1977, NoB 1978.47, 48 I). A similar rule prevails in POR-TUGAL: the agent's acts are treated as being unauthorized if the third party knew or should have known about an abuse of the agent's authority (CC art. 269).

Compare also Notes on Article 3:205, below.

Article 3:203: Unidentified Principal

If an agent enters into a contract in the name of a principal whose identity is to be revealed later, but fails to reveal that identity within a reasonable time after a request by the third party, the agent itself is bound by the contract.

COMMENT

A. *Unidentified Principal*
The rules on direct representation apply even if an agent, although acting in the name of "a" principal, does not at first reveal his identity (cf. Article 3:102(1), second sentence). But such secrecy cannot be continued *ad infinitum* if the third party demands to be told the principal's identity.

B. *Agent Failing to Identify Principal*
If the third party has asked for identification of the principal and the agent fails or refuses to reveal that identity (possibly on the principal's instruction), the agent becomes personally bound to the third party. This is justified because he assumed that risk by refusing to reveal the principal's identity.

To bind the agent to the contract is also justified by the fact that the agent usually will be able to transfer to his principal the assets received from the third party, and conversely the principal will usually reimburse the agent for the charges incurred vis-à-vis the third party. This distinguishes the cases covered by Article 3:203 from those in which the agent acts without or outside his authority where by virtue of his warranty of authority he is merely obliged to pay damages to the third party (Article 3:204(2)).

NOTES

1. *Rules on unidentified principal*
    Some recently enacted Civil Codes have rules which correspond to Article 3:203 (ITALY: CC art. 1405; THE NETHERLANDS: BW art. 3:67(2)). In other countries, the rule is recognized without statutory authority (FRANCE, BELGIUM and LUXEMBOURG [*déclaration de command*]: *Malaurie & Aynès*, Special Contracts no. 535).
2. *"Contracts for a person to be nominated": Italy and Portugal*
    As mentioned before, in ITALY and PORTUGAL the case of an unidentified principal is not governed by the rules on representation (*supra* Article 3:102(3)). The special rules of both countries on

the "contract for a person to be nominated" practically lead to the same result as Article 3:203, provided the third person is duly nominated: then the third person acquires the rights and assumes the obligations of the original party who has nominated him (Italy: CC art. 1404; Portugal: CC art. 455(1)). However, this nomination is subject to several requirements: it must be communicated to the other party within three or five days, unless another term has been agreed; and, to be effective, this communication must be accompanied by the third person's acceptance or of a power of attorney issued before the conclusion of the contract (Italy: CC art. 1402; Portugal: CC art. 453). If the third person is not validly nominated, the original parties to the contract remain bound by it (Italy: CC art. 1405; Portugal: CC art. 455(2)).

3. *Principal must be identified*

In GERMANY, GREECE, AUSTRIA and the NORDIC countries the agent who fails to disclose the principal's identity is not necessarily bound himself. Under German law the agent is treated as if he was acting without authority (BGH 20 March 1995, NJW 1995, 1739, 1742). Therefore he is, at the choice of the third party, liable either to perform the contractual duties or to pay damages (details in German BGB § 179). The same rule applies in Greece (CC art. 231(1)), in Austria for commercial transactions (4.EVHGB, art. 8 no. 11) and in the Nordic countries (Nordic Contracts Acts § 25 on the duty of the *falsus procurator* to compensate expectation interests). By contrast, in Austria in civil transactions the agent may only be liable for reliance damages provided he can be charged with negligence or intention. If the agent is sued for such damages he may still avoid this liablity for damages by identifying the principal until the opening of trial at first instance.

4. *Common Law*

Under ENGLISH common law the agent may incur personal liability under a contract where the principal is not named (*Bowstead & Reynolds*, § 9-042; *The Virgo* [1976] 2 Lloyd's Rep. 135, C.A.). On the other hand, the agent will not be personally liable if the third person does not prove a contractual intention that the agent should incur personal liability (*The Santa Carina* [1977] 1 Lloyd's Rep. 478, C.A.).

Article 3:204: Agent acting without or outside its Authority

(1) Where a person acting as an agent acts without authority or outside the scope of its authority, its acts are not binding upon the principal and the third party.

(2) Failing ratification by the principal according to Article 3:207, the agent is liable to pay the third party such damages as will place the third party in the same position as if the agent had acted with authority. This does not apply if the third party knew or could not have been unaware of the agent's lack of authority.

COMMENT

A. *Consequence of Lack of Authority*

Article 3:204 expressly states the consequence that results if the major condition of Article 3:202 is not fulfilled: the agent has acted without any or without sufficient authority, be it express, implied or apparent. Paragraph 2 and Articles 3:207 and 3:208 draw specific consequences from this rule.

B. *Partial Lack of Authority*

Where an existing authority of an agent covers an act done by him in part only, the effect of such partial lack of authority depends upon whether the contract involved is divisible or indivisible. In the latter case, the principal is not bound at all. If the contract is divisible, the authorised part of the act will bind the principal and the third party but not the unauthorised part.

Illustration: If an agent has power to overdraw her principal's account to an amount of £10,000 and he overdraws £11,000, the principal is bound to repay £10,000 only.

C. *Consequences of Breach of Warranty*

By acting in the principal's name, the agent warrants to the third party that he has the authority to bind the principal. If he does not in fact have this authority, this does not mean that the agent is bound by the contract; he is only obliged to pay damages to the third party according to paragraph 2. The compensation must put the third party into the same position as if the agent had acted with the principal's authority and within the scope of such authority. If the agent proves that the principal could not have performed the contract, nor have paid compensation (for instance because the principal is insolvent) the agent need not even pay damages.

D. *Effect of Third Party's Knowledge*

Of course, there is neither a warranty of authority nor, therefore, a breach of such a warranty if the third party knows or could not be unaware of the agent's lack of authority. This is spelt out by the last sentence of Article 3:204(2).

NOTES

1. *Principal not bound by unauthorised acts*

    The Geneva Convention on Agency (art. 14(1) and many European codifications provide for a rule comparable to the one contained in Article 3:204(1) (GERMANY: BGB § 177(1); AUSTRIA: ABGB § 1016; GREECE: CC art. 229; FRANCE, BELGIUM and LUXEMBOURG: CCs art. 1998 (2); SPAIN: CC art. 1259; THE NETHERLANDS: BW art. 3:66(1); PORTUGAL: CC art. 268 (1). The same rule is implied in ITALY (CC art. 1398) and in the NORDIC Contract Acts (§§ 10, 11 etc.) and is adopted by the COMMON LAW as well (*Xenos* v. *Wickham* (1866), L.R. 2 H.L. 296; *British Bank of the Middle East* v. *Sun Life Assurance Co* [1983] 2 Lloyd's Rep. 9, H.L.).

    In case of a partial lack of authority, the contract may be completely or partially invalid depending on whether it would have been entered into without the unauthorized part (Germany: BGB § 139; Greece: CC art. 181).

2. *Unauthorised agent liable to third party*

    The unauthorized agent's liability for damages as a consequence of acting without authority is, in principle, recognized by all Member States. However, the details of this liability vary to some degree. In the COMMON LAW, as under Article 3:204(2) and under the very similar Geneva Convention on Agency art. 16(1), the agent is liable even if he did not know that he lacked authority, since the agent's liability is strict and not based upon fault. The agent's ignorance of his lack of authority is irrelevant also under the NORDIC Contracts Acts of Denmark, Sweden and Finland (§ 25(1)) and in THE NETHERLANDS (BW art. 3:70). The Dutch Supreme Court has confirmed that the agent is liable for the full damage suffered by the third party (including the expectation interest) (H.R. 28 March 1997, N.J. 1997 no. 454).

    In GERMAN and GREEK law, if the agent was aware of his lack of authority, the third party may claim performance of the contract or damages, see BGB § 179(1) and CC art. 231(1) respectively. If the agent did not know of his lack of authority, the agent's liability is limited to reliance damages, BGB § 179(2), CC art. 231(2). The same is true in AUSTRIA with regard to commercial transactions (4.EVHGB, art. 8 no. 11(2)). In Austria in civil matters the damages are limited to the reliance interest, and in ITALY and PORTUGAL the agent is held liable for violation of his pre-contractual obligations so that the third party can only recover its reliance damages (Austria: OGH 19 November 1975, JBl. 1978, 32, 35, *Rummel (-Strasser)* §§ 1016, 1017 no. 18; Italy: Cass. 20 February 1987, no. 1817, Massimario Foro Italiano 1987, 304 and *Galgano-Visintini* 323 f.; Portugal: *C.M. Pinto*, General Theory 545). The aforementioned limitation also prevails in

FRANCE, BELGIUM and LUXEMBOURG, where the agent is liable in tort (France: *Malaurie & Aynès*, Special Contracts no. 575; Luxembourg: Supreme Court 7 January 1975, Pas. 23, 68), and as well in SPAIN.

However, in France, Belgium and Luxembourg the agent is liable for the third party's full damage if he had expressly or impliedly guaranteed his authority (*porte-fort*), see CC art. 1997 last clause. The same solution has been proposed in Portugal if the agent knew of the lack of his authority (*C.M. Pinto*, General Theory 545).

3. *Third party knew of lack of authority*
All countries agree on the exception contained in the last sentence of Article 3:204. The same solution is to be found in the Geneva Convention on Agency art. 16(2). Nowhere is the agent liable if the third party knew or should have known of the agent's lack of authority (GERMANY: BGB § 179(3); GREECE: CC art. 231(3); THE NETHERLANDS: BW art. 3:70; ITALY: CC art. 1398; NORDIC Contracts Acts § 25(2); FRANCE: Cass.civ. 16 June 1954, Bull. civ. 1954 I no. 200; ENGLAND: *Beattie* v. *Ebury* (1872) L.R. 7 Ch.App. 777, 800; *Bowstead & Reynolds*, no. 9-064). In France, BELGIUM and LUXEMBOURG, CCs art. 1997 is based upon the same principle.

Article 3:205: Conflict of Interest

(1) If a contract concluded by an agent involves the agent in a conflict of interest of which the third party knew or could not have been unaware, the principal may avoid the contract according to the provisions of Articles 4:112 to 4:116.

(2) There is presumed to be a conflict of interest where:

   (a) the agent also acted as agent for the third party; or

   (b) the contract was with itself in its personal capacity.

(3) However, the principal may not avoid the contract:

   (a) if it had consented to, or could not have been unaware of, the agent's so acting; or

   (b) if the agent had disclosed the conflict of interest to it and it had not objected within a reasonable time.

COMMENT

A. *The Basic Issue*
In the triangular situation in which an agent finds himself between principal and third party, the agent is exposed to the usually diverging interests of three persons. While being obliged to promote and preserve the principal's interests, the agent may be approached by the third party who is seeking to pursue its own interests. In addition, the agent will often be tempted to pursue his own interests at the expense of the principal.

B. *Relevant Conflict of Interests*
Sanctions affecting the contract concluded by the agent can only be imposed if this is equitable vis-à-vis the parties to the contract.

The principal's interests in this respect are protected by allowing it to decide whether or not it wants to avoid the contract.

The third party's interest in preserving the contract is protected by the condition that the third party must have known of the conflict of interests or must not have been unaware of it.

C. *Consequences of a Relevant Conflict of Interests*

According to 3:205(1), the principal may avoid the contract if the agent had concluded it in spite of a relevant conflict of interests. The procedure for avoidance is that provided in Articles 4:112 to 4:116.

D. *Special Cases*

Article 3:205(2) deals with two specific instances of a potential conflict of interests. A conflict may arise if the agent for principal A acts at the same time as agent for principal B and as such a dual agent concludes a transaction. Since in this situation the agent must take care of the potentially opposite interests of two persons, a risk of neglecting the interests of one of the two principals is often present.

The same duality and therefore potential conflict of interests exists if the agent acts with himself in his personal capacity, i.e. if he is also the third party vis-à-vis his own principal.

In these two situations, a material conflict of interests is presumed to exist. This presumption of a conflict of interests is, however, rebuttable.

> *Illustration*: Agent A is instructed by her principal to buy 50 shares of X Corp. at the current market price. Since A wishes to dispose of her own holding of shares in X Corp., she sells these shares to her principal for the current market price. The latter fact neutralises the conflict of interests.

E. *Consequences of a Conflict of Interests*

Where an agent in concluding a transaction acts for both contracting parties or with himself, the resulting contract can be avoided by the principal (Article 3:205(1)), unless one of the justifications enumerated in paragraph (3) applies. In the case dealt with in litt. (a) of paragraph (2), where the agent also acts as agent for the third party, each of the two principals is entitled to avoid the contract.

F. *Exceptions*

Customs and national legislation may give (commission) agents the option of dealing with themselves under certain conditions (*Selbsteintritt*).

G. *Avoidance of Contract Excluded*

The third paragraph lays down two instances in which avoidance of the contract is excluded. The first, consent of the principal or its constructive knowledge, is self-evident. The second, disclosure of the conflict of interests by the agent, requires a brief explanation. Disclosure must occur in advance of the agent's act so that the principal is in a position to prevent the agent from acting. Disclosure suffices to bar avoidance, unless the principal (or one of the two principals) objects within reasonable time. Once disclosure has been made, the principal must act; if it does not do that, it is regarded as having consented.

In the situation covered by paragraph (2) (a), disclosure must be made to both principals.

In addition to the two instances regulated in paragraph (3), avoidance is also excluded if the principal (or both principals, where applicable) have confirmed the agent's authority according to Article 4:114. By contrast, ratification according to Article 3:207 does not apply here.

NOTES

1. *Contract voidable or ineffective where conflict of interest*
   A few systems provide that where there is a conflict of interest, the contract may be avoided by the principal (ITALIAN CC art. 1394, and see also art.1395, contract with agent himself; POR-TUGUESE CC art 261, contract with agent himself) or is ineffective (DUTCH BW art. 3:68).
2. *No rule that contract affected by conflict*
   No conflict-of-interest rule is contained in the Geneva Convention on Agency.
   The COMMON LAW does not seem to know a rule comparable to Article 3:205(1). The contract concluded in a conflict of interests situation of which the third party knew is therefore not voidable. There is, however, English authority allowing the avoidance of the contract in the more extreme case where the third party bribes the agent (*Panama & South Pacific Telegraph Co. v. India Rubber Co.* (1875) L.R. 10 Ch.App. 515).
3. *Partial recognition of rule*
   In some Continental European countries, the invalidity (GERMANY: BGB § 181; GREECE: CC art. 235; THE NETHERLANDS: BW art. 3:68) or voidability (ITALY: CC art. 1395; PORTUGAL: CC art. 261(1) of an agent's transactions with himself is prescribed. The FRENCH (BELGIAN, LUX-EMBOURG) Civil Codes merely regulate the special case of a sale by public auction (CCs art. 1596), but this provision is considered to express a general principle (France: *Malaurie & Aynès*, Special Contracts no. 566; Belgium: Cass. 7 December 1978, Pas. 1979 I 408, 410); violation of the prohibition entails voidability of the contract (France: Cass. 29 November 1988, Bull.civ. 1988 I no. 341; Belgium: Cass. 7 December 1978, supra).
4. *In fact no conflict*
   In legal systems predicated on prohibiting conflicts of interests, an agent's transaction with himself is valid if in fact there can be no conflict of interests (ITALY: CC art. 1394, 1395; The NETHERLANDS: BW art. 3:68; PORTUGAL: CC art. 261(1); for AUSTRIA cf. *Koziol/Welser* I 177).
   By contrast, under GERMAN BGB § 181 contracts which the agent makes with himself or as agent for the third party are ineffective whether there is a conflict of interests or not. For this reason BGB § 181 provides that there may be conflicts of interests which do not preclude the agent from representing his principal; on the other hand, in some cases the agent cannot bind the principal even though a conflict of interests is impossible (BGH 24 January 1991, NJW 1991, 982, 983).
5. *Principal's consent*
   The principal's consent, of course, validates the contract. A specific provision comparable to Article 3:205(3) seems to exist only in PORTUGAL (CC art. 261(1)).

Article 3:206: Subagency

An agent has implied authority to appoint a subagent to carry out tasks which are not of a personal character and which it is not reasonable to expect the agent to carry out itself. The rules of this Section apply to the subagency; acts of the subagent which are within its and the agent's authority bind the principal and the third party directly to each other.

COMMENT

A. *General Framework*

Frequently, an agent cannot perform the acts or all the acts with which he is charged and it is necessary to involve other persons. This may occur, in particular, because of distance from the place where the necessary acts have to be performed or because of the agent's lack of specific competence. In these cases, it may be necessary to delegate some or all of the authority which the agent has received.

B. *Authority to Appoint a Subagent*

The agent may effectively appoint a subagent, if he has authority to do so. Whether such authority exists must be determined under the rules of this Chapter of the Principles.

The agent's authority may be express, implied or apparent (cf. Article 3:201). It is to be recommended that the principal clarify expressly whether or not the agent is so authorized. In order to clarify a situation where the principal has failed to do so, the first sentence establishes a rule which expresses the principal's presumed intention.

> *Illustration*: An old lady P living in Brighton has given a general power to her agent A living in the same place. She directs A to invest a substantial sum of money by acquiring an apartment house in New York. A has an implied power to appoint a qualified person in New York as subagent.

C. *Effects*

In case of delegation of authority to a subagent, the latter becomes a second agent, side by side with the first agent. The subagent acts in the name (or, as the case may be, on behalf) of the principal. All the provisions of this chapter apply to the subagent as if she were the main agent. This rule is laid down by the first part of the second sentence.

The subagent's authority is derived directly from the main agent and only indirectly from the principal. In order for the subagent to effect the same consequences that are achieved by the acts of the main agent, it is desirable to clarify the two conditions that must be satisfied: the acts of the subagent must be within both her own authority and that of the main agent. These two conditions are spelt out by the second part of the last sentence.

Under these conditions the acts of the subagent have the same effects as if these acts had been done by the main agent. They bind the principal and the third party directly, while the subagent is not bound, cf. Article 3:202.

D. *Substitution of Agent*

The appointment of a subagent must be distinguished from the substitution of the original agent by a new agent. The new agent assumes (usually) the same position as her predecessor. Her acts are fully subject to the rules of this chapter; no special rule is required to express this idea.

NOTES

1.   General rule against delegation
   Some European countries have statutory provisions on subagency (SPAIN: CC arts. 1721 ff.; THE NETHERLANDS: BW art. 3:64; AUSTRIA: ABGB § 1010; FRANCE, BELGIUM and LUXEMBOURG: CCs art. 1994; ITALY: CC art. 1717; GREECE: CC arts. 715-716; PORTUGAL: CC art.

264). As a general rule, subagency regularly is not allowed (*delegatus delegare non potest*). On the other hand, in SPAIN the agent is allowed to appoint a subagent, unless prohibited by the principal (CC art. 1721).

2. *Delegation permitted in certain situations*

Even though delegation of authority to a subagent is not allowed in general, certain exceptions from this principle are frequently admitted.

In the first place, the principal may expressly allow substitution (AUSTRIA: ABGB § 1010; PORTUGAL: CC art. 264(1); cf. implicitly FRANCE, BELGIUM and LUXEMBOURG: CCs art. 1994(1); ITALY: CC art. 1717(1)-(2); GREECE: Art. 715; and THE NETHERLANDS: BW art. 3:64). An implied permission may result from an interpretation of the principal's grant of authority.

Moreover, certain statutory authorizations may also be found in some countries. Thus the agent may delegate his authority to a subagent if he is unable or not authorized by law to perform certain necessary acts himself and subageny therefore is unavoidable (Austria: ABGB § 1010; The Netherlands: BW art. 3:64 lit. b; Greece: CC art. 715 and Athens 612/1974, NoB 1974.1077 I; ENGLAND: *Bowstead & Reynolds*, § 5-001 lit. b) or if the principal has no interest in the transaction in question being carried out by the agent personally (GERMANY: OLG Frankfurt 28 November 1974, VersR 1974, 173; OLG München 30 March 1984, WM 1984, 834; England: *Bowstead & Reynolds*, § 5-003). The Netherlands also allow appointment of a subagent if the agency relates to goods located outside the agent's country of residence (BW art. 3:64 lit. c).

3. *Usage*

The appointment of a subagent may as well be justified by usage (ENGLAND: *De Bussche* v. *Alt* (1878) 8 Ch.D. 286, 310-311; SCOTLAND: *Stair* 1, paras. 611, 633; THE NETHERLANDS: BW art. 3:64 lit. a).

4. *Direct links*

The Romanist systems especially tend to establish direct bonds between the principal and the subagent. In particular, the principal is often authorized to bring claims directly against the subagent whom the agent has substituted for himself (FRANCE, BELGIUM and LUXEMBOURG: CCs art. 1994(2); SPAIN: CC art. 1718; ITALY: CC art. 1717(4); GREECE: CC art. 716(2).

French courts have extended this rule by allowing the substituted subagent to bring her claims against the principal: Cass.com. 9 November 1987, Bull.civ. 1987 IV no. 233, and 19 March 1991, Bull.civ. 1991 IV no. 102.

Article 3:207: Ratification by Principal

(1) Where a person acting as an agent acts without authority or outside its authority, the principal may ratify the agent's acts.

(2) Upon ratification, the agent's acts are considered as having been authorised, without prejudice to the rights of other persons.

COMMENT

A. The Principle of Ratification

The first paragraph establishes the general principle that, by ratification, a principal may cure any defect in the agent's authority, including complete absence of such authority. Ratification may be made by express declaration addressed to the agent or the third party. Ratification may also be implied from acts of the principal which unambiguously demonstrate its intention to adopt the contract made by the agent.

Illustration 1: In the name of her principal P, a merchant, agent A has contracted with T, also a merchant, for the purchase of the most recent model of a computer for € 22,500 although her authority was limited to € 20,000, which T did not know. After learning what A has done, P sends instructions about delivery of the machine. This implies ratification of A's act.

B. *The Effect of Ratification*

The effect of ratification is stated by paragraph 2: The agent's acts are regarded as having bound, from the beginning, the principal and the third party. The principal takes over the benefits as well as the burdens produced by the agent's acts.

> *Illustration 2*: The facts are as in Illustration 1. The market price rose the day after P had sent its letter of confirmation. Three days later T, alleging A's lack of authority, purports to avoid the contract. That is unjustified since P had ratified the contract and T can no longer invoke the lack of authority to escape the contract.

The principal may not yet be in existence or may not yet be identifiable at the time of the agent's act (e.g. where an agent acts in the name of a company which is not yet created or of a subcontractor who has yet to be selected). In such a case, if the principal ratifies the agent's act later, the principal is bound as from the moment at which it came into existence or became identified. Special rules of the applicable company law with respect to pre-incorporation contracts take, of course, precedence.

C. *Protection of Third Person's Rights*

The question of the rights which other persons may have acquired is outside the scope of these Principles.

NOTES

1. *Ratification: the general rule*
    The principle of ratification is accepted by Member State (GERMANY: BGB § 177; AUSTRIA: ABGB § 1016; NORDIC Contracts Act § 25(1); THE NETHERLANDS: BW art. 3:69(1); FRANCE, BELGIUM and LUXEMBOURG: CCs art. 1998(2); ITALY: CC art. 1399(1); SPAIN: CC art. 1259(2); PORTUGAL: CC art. 268; GREECE: CC art. 229; ENGLAND: *Bird* v. *Brown* (1850) 4 Exch. 786, 798). The same principle is expressed in the Geneva Convention on Agency, art. 15(1), in a way similar to Article 3:207.
    Under the English common law, however, an undisclosed principal may not ratify (*Keighley Maxsted & Co.* v. *Durant* [1901] A.C. 240, H.L.). It has been held that a principal who could not have been identified at the time the agent made the purported contract with the third party is also unable to ratify, *Southern Water Authority* v. *Carey* [1985] 2 All E.R. 1077, Q.B.D., but this is doubtful, see *Treitel*, Contract 641; compare *Chitty* § 31-026.
2. *Implied ratification*
    The ratification may be express or implied (Geneva Convention on Agency art. 15(8); FRANCE, BELGIUM and LUXEMBOURG: CC art. 1998(2); GERMANY: BGH 2.11.1989, BGHZ 109, 177; GREECE: Thessaloniki 2966/1992, HellDni 1994. 636 I; IRELAND: *Bank of Ireland Finance Ltd.* v. *Rockfield Ltd* [1979] I.R. 21 at 35-36 (S.Ct.)). If the principal accepts the benefits arising from the unauthorized contract, this can be regarded as an implied ratification (AUSTRIA: ABGB § 1016). The same is true if it voluntarily performs the obligations towards the third party (cf. France, Belgium, Luxembourg: CCs art. 1338 par(2).
    An implied ratification is, however, excluded where the observation of a form is prescribed for the ratification, either the same formality as is required for the contract to be ratified (ITALY: CC art. 1399(1) or that for the grant of authority (NETHERLANDS: BW art. 3:69(2); PORTUGAL: CC art. 268(2).

3. Effect of ratification
The effect of ratification as expressed in Article 3:207(2) (corresponds to the Geneva Convention on Agency (art. 15(1) second sent.) and to the laws in the Civil Law countries (GERMANY: BGB § 184(1); THE NETHERLANDS: BW art. 3:369(1); AUSTRIA: *Rummel (-Strasser)* §§ 1016, 1017 no. 15; FRANCE, BELGIUM and LUXEMBOURG: *Malaurie & Aynès*, Special Contracts no. 584; ITALY: CC art. 1399(2); Greece: *Balis* 319; PORTUGAL: CC art. 268(2). The same rule prevails in ENGLAND (*Koenigsblatt v. Sweet* [1923] 2 Ch. 314, 325). However, the rights acquired by third persons are not affected (Portugal: CC art. 268(2); Belgium: Cass. 6 February 1953, Pas. 1953 I 436, 437). This conclusion may also follow from general rules on the effect of an approval (France, Belgium, Luxembourg: CCs art. 1338(3); Greece: CC art. 238 sent. 2).

Article 3:208: Third Party's Right with Respect to Confirmation of Authority

Where the statements or conduct of the principal gave the third party reason to believe that an act performed by the agent was authorised, but the third party is in doubt about the authorisation, it may send a written confirmation to the principal or request ratification from it. If the principal does not object or answer the request without delay, the agent's act is treated as having been authorised.

COMMENT

A. *Third Party's Right in General*
The ratification of an act of the agent which is not covered by the principal's authority, lies in the principal's discretion (cf. Article 3:207). Article 3:208, by contrast, intends to equip the third party with a means to force the principal to clarify the agent's authority.

B. *Prerequisites*
Such a burden may only be laid upon the principal for good reason. This condition consists of three elements which are set out in the first sentence.

First, the principal's statements or conduct must have given the third party reason to believe in the principal's authorisation. The third party's belief must be reasonable and bona fide.

Second, the third party must be in doubt about the authorisation. Again, this doubt must be reasonable and bona fide.

Third, the third party must send a written confirmation of the act undertaken by the agent to the principal or it must request ratification from the principal.

C. *Effects*
The receipt of the letter of confirmation, or the request for ratification in the circumstances described here, imposes upon the principal a burden. If it does not agree, it must indicate its objection to the third party without delay. If it does not do so or objects too late, its silence or delay is regarded as a confirmation of its having authorised the agent to undertake the act in question.

This rule is based on considerations similiar to those underlying Article 2:210 on the effect of letters of confirmation of professionals.

A request for ratification, under the conditions stated in Article 3:208, is treated in the same way as a confirmation since in substance both amount to the same thing and merchants would not understand it if any technical distinction were to be made between the two types of document.

NOTE

Some European codes empower the third party to request the principal's confirmation of the agent's authority (GERMANY: BGB § 177(2); ITALY: CC art. 1399(4); GREECE: CC arts. 229, 233); NETHERLANDS: BW art. 3:69(4); PORTUGAL: CC arts. 260(1), 268).

However, a rule along the lines of Article 3:208 sent. 2 which treats the principal's silence to the third party's request as a ratification of the agent's act can rarely be found. According to the aforementioned statutory provisions, if the principal does not react to the third party's request for ratification, ratification is considered to be denied (cf. the German and Italian provisions and Portuguese CC art. 268(3). Only in Portugal there is a special provision for commercial agents to the same effect as Article 3:208: if a principal has full knowledge of its agent's unauthorised contract, but does not inform the third person within five days after obtaining that knowledge about its disapproval of the contract, it is considered to have ratified it (Decree-Law no. 178/86 of 3 July 1986, amended by Decree-Law no. 118/93 of 13 April 1993, art. 22).

Article 3:209: Duration of Authority

(1) An agent's authority continues until the third party knows or ought to know that:
  (a) the agent's authority has been brought to an end by the principal, the agent, or both; or
  (b) the acts for which the authority had been granted have been completed, or the time for which it had been granted has expired; or
  (c) the agent has become insolvent or, where a natural person, has died or become incapacitated; or
  (d) the principal has become insolvent.
(2) The third party is considered to know that the agent's authority has been brought to an end under paragraph (1)(a) above if this has been communicated or publicised in the same manner in which the authority was originally communicated or publicised.
(3) However, the agent remains authorised for a reasonable time to perform those acts which are necessary to protect the interests of the principal or its successors.

COMMENTS

A. *Basic idea*

Article 3:209 deals with a predicament which may arise in two typical situations when an agent's authority ends for one reason or other. Either the third party may not know of this event (paragraphs (1)-(2)); or the ending may be so sudden that it does not allow the principal sufficient time to provide for a substitute (paragraph (3)).

In both cases, the interests of the third party and those of the principal, respectively, must be protected by providing for a (limited) continuation of the agent's authority.

B. *Grounds for Extinction of Authority*
In paragraph (1), letters (a) to (d) enumerate grounds for extinction of the agent's authority. The enumeration in letters (b) to (d) is self-explanatory. The more general formula "brought to an end" in letter (a) covers several cases: the agent's authority may have been revoked, avoided or terminated for non-performance by the principal; or the agent may have given it up; or principal and agent may have agreed to end the authority.

This chapter does not establish a special rule on the irrevocability of an agent's authority. If the principal promises a third party not to revoke an authority granted to an agent, by virtue of Article 1:107, the normal rules on formation, performance and non-performance of that promise apply.

C. *Continuation of Authority Vis-à-vis an Ignorant Third Party*
According to paragraph (1), an agent's authority, although extinguished by virtue of one of the grounds set out in litt. (a) to (d), nevertheless continues until the third party knows or ought to know of the extinction.

This rule is a reflection of the principle underlying Articles 3:102 and 3:202, that for the agent's authority to be effective vis-à-vis the third party, the third party must know or have reason to know that the agent acted as such. The same principle applies in the converse situation, so that the agent's authority must be considered as continuing until the third party obtains actual or constructive knowledge that it has come to an end. The agent's express or implied authority, although extinguished for one reason or other, remains extant vis-à-vis the third party as an apparent authority.

D. *Communicated or Publicised Revocation of Authority*
Paragraph (2) deals with a specific case of "constructive knowledge" of a revocation of authority. An authority which has been addressed to a third party can be revoked in the same manner in which it was granted. This is of particular importance if the grant of authority has been publicised, e.g. by a notice in a newspaper.

E. *Continuation of an Authority of Necessity*
In addition to the preceding ground, paragraph (3) sets out another ground of continuing an agent's authority in spite of its extinction.

Paragraph (3) extends the agent's authority after its extinction for a reasonable period, provided this is necessary for the protection of the principal's (or, in case of his death or other extinction, his successor's) interests. There is no necessity if another agent has been granted authority immediately upon extinction or if the principal himself (or his successor) is in a position to undertake all necessary and urgent acts. The extension of the agent's authority is only in time. By contrast, in substance it is restricted because it is limited to acts which are necessary for the preservation of the principal's interests.

F. *Application to Amendments of the Agent's Authority*
The rules of Article 3:209 apply *mutatis mutandis* to modifications of an agent's authority, especially to restrictions.

NOTES

1. *Authority normally depends on duration of internal relationship*
    (a)   *General*
          Even if the Codes distinguish between the internal and the external relationship (see notes to
          Article 3:101), the duration of the authority is, as a rule, made dependent upon the duration
          of the underlying internal relationship (GERMANY: BGB § 168; GREECE: CC art. 222;
          ITALY: CC art. 1396(2); PORTUGAL: CC art. 265(1). In Portugal, the reverse is also true:
          the mandate ends if the agent's authority is revoked or renounced (CC art. 1179). However,
          even though terminated the authority may well still deploy effects vis-à-vis third persons (cf.
          infra no. 2).
             In general, revocation by the principal, renunciation by the agent or contractual termina-
          tion agreed between them are considered to be grounds for the extinction of authority (Geneva
          Convention on Agency art. 17 lit. a, c; FRANCE, BELGIUM and LUXEMBOURG: CCs art.
          2003; SPAIN: CC art. 1732 no. 2, 3; THE NETHERLANDS: BW art. 3:72 lit. c, d; AUSTRIA:
          ABGB § 1020, 1021; Germany: BGB § 168, 671, 675; Greece: CC art. 222, 724, 725; Italy:
          CC art. 1722 no. 2, 3; Portugal: CC art. 265; ENGLAND: *Bowstead & Reynolds*, § 122). In
          addition, the authority may be limited in time or made dependent upon certain conditions by
          stipulation.
             The Geneva Convention on Agency refers to the applicable national law with respect to
          further grounds for termination of the agent's authority (art. 18).
    (b)   *Death or incapacity of agent*
          Under the law of almost every Member State, death or incapacity of the agent terminate his
          authority. As an exception, according to FINNISH law the agent's incapacitation does not ter-
          minate his authority (*Kivimäki & Ylöstalo* 275).
    (c)   *Death or incapacity of principal*
          In contrast, there is little agreement on the consequences of the principal's death or incapac-
          ity. Most countries provide that the agent's authority terminates if the principal dies or
          becomes incapacitated (FRANCE, BELGIUM, and LUXEMBOURG: CCs art. 2003;
          ITALY: CC art. 1722 no. 4; SPAIN: CC art. 1732 no. 3; PORTUGAL: CC arts. 265, 1174 lit.
          a; GREECE: CC art. 223; The NETHERLANDS: BW art. 3:72 lit. a; ENGLAND: *Drew* v.
          Nunn (1879) 4 QBD 661; *Yonge* v. *Toynbee* [1910] K.B. 215). The contrary rule can be found
          in GERMANY and in DENMARK, SWEDEN and FINLAND (Germany: BGB § 675, 672,
          168; Denmark, Sweden and Finland: Nordic Contracts Act § 21(1) (death), § 22 (incapacity,
          except in Finland)). In AUSTRIA, the agent's authority is extinguished by the principal's
          death (ABGB § 1022), but it continues if the principal becomes incapacitated (OGH 20 May
          1953, SZ 26 no. 132). In Italy, the agent's authority with respect to business dealings related
          to an enterprise is not terminated if the enterprise is continued (CC art. 1322 no. 4).
    (d)   *Insolvency*
          The agent's or the principal's insolvency are mostly grounds for termination of authority. In
          the COMMON LAW, insolvency may have this effect: *Chitty* § 31-144. GERMAN law
          accords with Article 3:209(1) lit. (d) in that the principal's insolvency extinguishes the agent's
          authority (Insolvency Act (KO) § 23; New Insolvency Act (InsO) § 115-117 [coming into
          force in 1999]). The insolvency of the agent, on the other hand, in general is considered not to
          terminate the authority (Germany: *Palandt (-Heinrichs)* § 168 no. 3; FINLAND: *Kivimäki &
          Ylöstalo*, p. 275). By contrast, in PORTUGAL the agent's insolvency is a ground for termina-
          tion (Insolvency Code art. 167(2), whereas the principal's insolvency does not terminate a
          contract of agency concluded also in the agent's interest (*ibid* (1), except in case of a com-
          mercial agency (Insolvency Code art. 168).
2. *Third party protected*
    Everywhere in Europe there is some protection for the third party who is unaware of the termination
    of the authority. In effect, the authority regularly is deemed to subsist until the third party knows or
    ought to know about the termination – either in the form of actual authority or as an apparent author-
    ity (Geneva Convention on Agency art. 19; GERMANY: BGB § 170-173, 674; AUSTRIA: ABGB
    § 1026; DENMARK, SWEDEN, FINLAND: Nordic Contracts Act § 12 ss.; THE NETHER-
    LANDS: BW art. 3:76(1); FRANCE, BELGIUM and LUXEMBOURG: CC arts. 2005-2006, 2008-
    2009; ITALY: CC art. 1396; SPAIN: CC art. 1738; PORTUGAL: CC art. 266; ENGLAND: *Drew* v.
    Nunn (1879) 4 Q.B.D. 661; *Pole* v. *Leask* (1862) 33 L.J. Ch. 133, 162-163; SCOTLAND: *Stair* 1,
    para. 649). As an exception, under GREEK law the principal is not bound by acts of the agent if the
    latter knew about the termination of his authority, but the principal may be liable vis-à-vis the third

party for damages if it could have easily notified the third party of the termination of the authority (CC art. 224, 225).

3. *Authority normally revocable*

The laws of all Member States agree on the principle that an agent's authority is revocable. Sometimes this principle is expressed by statute (FRANCE, BELGIUM and LUXEMBOURG: CCs art. 2004; SPAIN: CC art. 1733; ITALY: CC art. 1723; PORTUGAL: CC art. 265(2); AUSTRIA: ABGB § 1020). The Geneva Convention on Agency provides that revocation by the principal terminates the authority even if this is not consistent with the terms of the agreement between principal and agent (art. 17 lit. c). Authority is, as a rule, revocable at any time.

4. *Irrevocable authority*

Exceptionally, an authority may be granted as irrevocable. In GERMANY, ITALY and PORTUGAL, the irrevocability of the authority is a matter of agreement between agent and principal. However, such a clause has different effects: while in Germany a revocation is ineffective (BGB § 168 sent. 2), in the other two countries the principal's revocation (Italy and Geneva Convention, supra) or either party's revocation terminates the agent's authority (Italy: CC art. 1723(1); Portugal: CC art. 265(2). But in Italy the principal is liable to compensate the agent for any damage suffered, unless there was an important reason for the revocation; in Portugal, the revoking party is liable to the other party (CC art. 1172 lett. b).

In most countries the granting of an effective irrevocable authority is possible only in certain conditions. One typical condition is an authority granted in the agent's interest (The NETHER-LANDS: BW art. 3:74(1); GREECE: CC art. 218 sent. 2 and AP 187/1983, NoB 1983.1550-1551; DENMARK: *Ussing*, Aftaler 309 f.; FINLAND: *Kivimäki & Ylöstalo* 271-272; ENGLAND: *Bowstead & Reynolds*, § 10-007). In GERMANY and GREECE, irrevocability of an authority given in the agent's interest may even be implied (Germany: BGH 13 December 1990, NJW-RR 1991, 439; Greece: Thessaloniki 1236/1990, Harm 1990.214, 215 I). In ITALY and PORTUGAL an authority granted in the agent's or a third party's interest cannot, as a rule, be revoked without the consent of the person interested in its granting (Italy: CC art. 1723(2); Portugal: CC art. 265(3). FRANCE and BELGIUM have come to the same result by declaring an authority given in the common interest of principal and agent to be irrevocable (France: *Malaurie & Aynès*, Special Contracts no. 557; Belgium: Cass. 28 June 1993, Pas. 1993 I 628, 630). In AUSTRIA, an authority granted for a limit-ed period of time may be made irrevocable (*Rummel (-Strasser)* § 1020-1026 no. 4).

However, exceptionally even an irrevocable authority may be revoked for an important reason (Germany: BGH 12 May 1969, WM 1969, 1009; BGH 8 February 1985, WM 1985, 646; Austria: OGH 1 September 1954, SZ 27 no. 211; Greece: AP 1108/1984, NoB 1985.771 (772 I); Italy and Portugal: cf. provisions cited supra). In the Netherlands, an irrevocable authority may only be ter-minated by a court decision upon an important reason; the principal has to file a petition at the *recht-bank* (BW art. 3:74(4).

5. *Manner of revocation*

Provisions similar to Article 3:209(2) can be found in some European countries. Nowhere, howev-er, is this rule expressed in a comparably general manner. Commonly it is provided that the revoca-tion of authority has to take place in the same manner as that used in granting the authority (GER-MANY: BGB § 170-172; GREECE: CC arts. 219-221; DENMARK, SWEDEN and FINLAND: Nordic Contracts Act §§ 12-16). In PORTUGAL the third party has to be informed by suitable means (CC art. 266(1).

6. *Acts necessary to protect principal's interests*

The Geneva Convention on Agency art. 20 is very similar to Article 3:209(3). In the Member States there are no comparable general rules. There are, however, provisions of a more limited scope. Under the Civil Codes of FRANCE, BELGIUM and LUXEMBOURG, in case of danger the agent has to complete the tasks already begun even after the principal's death (art. 1991(2). In THE NETHER-LANDS and in ITALY, after the principal's death or incapacitation, the agent is still authorized to per-form certain acts: in the Netherlands those acts that are necessary for the management of a business enterprise or acts which cannot be put off without detriment (BW art. 3:73(1) – (2)); in Italy the agent has to continue performance of those acts which he had initiated earlier, provided delaying them would be dangerous (CC art. 1728(1)). Under the NORDIC Contracts Acts, § 24, after the principal has become bankrupt or incapacitated, the agent may on the strength of his authority perform such acts as are necessary to protect the principal or his bankrupt estate against losses, until necessary mea-sures can be taken by the person who according to law has the right to act on the principal's behalf. The PORTUGUESE law of mandate provides that mandate and authority shall be extinguished by the principal's death or incapacitation, unless the extinction would harm the principal or his heirs (CC art. 1175).

Section 3: Indirect Representation

Article 3:301: Intermediaries not acting in the name of a Principal

(1) Where an intermediary acts:
(a)   on instructions and on behalf, but not in the name, of a principal, or
(b)   on instructions from a principal but the third party does not know and has no reason to know this,
the intermediary and the third party are bound to each other.
(2) The principal and the third party are bound to each other only under the conditions set out in Articles 3:302 to 3:304.

COMMENT

A. *Indirect Representation in General*
Indirect representation, as dealt with in Section 3, is defined in Article 3:301. The situations covered by this provision are distinguished from those treated in Section 2 on direct representation by one decisive criterion: the indirect "agent" does not act in the name of his principal, either expressly or impliedly or apparently (cf. Article 3:201). In order to mark clearly the difference, the indirect "agent" is designated as "intermediary".

However, under the exceptional circumstances set out in Articles 3:302 to 3:304, indirect representation may acquire certain effects of direct representation.

B. *Undisclosed "Agency"*
In the case described in paragraph (1)(a), the third party may or may not know that the intermediary is acting on behalf of a principal. The contract concluded by the intermediary binds him personally to the third party, since the intermediary did not act in the name of the principal, as is required under Articles 3:202 and 3:201.

> *Illustration*: Customer C instructs her bank B (or a dealer in securities D) to buy 1,000 shares. B (or D), acting in their own name, purchase the shares from seller S. In the eyes of the Civil Law countries, B (or D) is a commission agent. No direct relationship between C and S arises.

Under normal circumstances, the third party must be protected from the imposition of the principal, a stranger, as a contracting party.

The situation dealt with here is comparable to the case in which the agent fails to reveal the identity of his principal, regulated in a corresponding way by Article 3:203.

In the case described in paragraph (1)(b), the third party does not even know or have reason to know that the intermediary has acted on behalf of a principal.

C. Internal Intermediary-Principal Relationship

In both subparagraphs (a) and (b) it is, as a rule, left to the internal relationship between the intermediary and his principal as to how the intermediary transfers the benefits which he was instructed to obtain to the principal, or how he is to be relieved from the obligations which he has incurred vis-à-vis the third party.

NOTES

1. *Intermediary and third party bound*
    The general rule that the agent and the third party are bound to each other in case of indirect representation is accepted everywhere in Europe. Differences exist, however, on the question of a contractual relationship between the principal and the third party.
2. *Geneva Convention on Agency*
    Although the Geneva Convention on Agency does not provide a definition of indirect representation, it describes the conditions for a contractual relationship between agent and third party similarly to Article 3:301 (art. 13(1)).
3. *Undisclosed principal: third party and principal bound*
    Under the undisclosed principal doctrine of the COMMON LAW the principal may sue the third party on a contract made by an agent on its behalf, if the agent was acting within the scope of his authority (*Siu Yin Kwan v. Eastern Insurance Co. Ltd.* [1994] 2 W.L.R. 370, 376 (P.C.)). Equally the third party may sue the undisclosed principal.
    The Common Law does not prescribe any further conditions for the direct relationship between the undisclosed principal and the third party comparable to the requirements of Articles 3:302-3:304.
4. *Indirect representation: principal and third party generally not bound*
    Comparable rules do not exist in the countries of Continental Europe. In ITALY and SPAIN the general rule is laid down that if the intermediary was acting in his own name there is no direct relationship between the third party and the principal (Italy: CC art. 1705(2) first sent.; Spain: CC art. 1717(1).
    Nevertheless, in a number of specific situations direct relations between the principal and the third party are recognized also in Continental European countries.
    Except for THE NETHERLANDS (*infra* Article 3:302, note 2), however, no country provides a full set of conditions for direct relations between principal and third party. Typically the principal's right to sue the third party, on the one hand, and the third party's right to sue the principal, on the other, are regulated differently.

Article 3:302: Intermediary's Insolvency or Fundamental Non-performance to Principal

If the intermediary becomes insolvent, or if it commits a fundamental non-performance towards the principal, or if prior to the time for performance it is clear that there will be a fundamental non-performance:

(a)   on the principal's demand, the intermediary shall communicate the name and address of the third party to the principal; and

(b)   the principal may exercise against the third party the rights acquired on the principal's behalf by the intermediary, subject to any defences which the third party may set up against the intermediary.

For Comment, see Article 3:303.

NOTES

1.   *Geneva Convention on Agency*
Generally speaking, Article 3:302 corresponds to the Geneva Convention on Agency (art. 13). Differing from Article 3:302 lit. a, under the Geneva Convention the intermediary's duty to reveal the third party's name is made dependent upon the third party's non-performance of its obligations towards the intermediary (art. 13(5)).

2.   *Principal may assume rights against third party if intermediary fails to peform*
The law of THE NETHERLANDS comes closest to Articles 3:302-3:304. According to BW art. 7:420 the principal can assume the intermediary's rights under the main contract, if the intermediary does not perform his obligations towards the principal or goes bankrupt or if the third person does not perform its obligations. The duty to reveal the third party's name comparable to Article 3:302 lit. a is laid down by para. (3).

3.   *Principal may assume rights only if intermediary insolvent*
BELGIAN and LUXEMBOURG law provide that in the case of the intermediary's bankruptcy the principal is entitled to proceed directly against the third party, but it may claim only any outstanding part of the purchase price of the goods which the intermediary had sold on the principal's behalf (Belgium: New Bankruptcy Code of 1997 art. 103(2); Luxembourg: CCom art. 567(2)).

If a DANISH or SWEDISH commission agent has acted in the course of his business (*handelskommission*), the principal may claim directly from the third party if the latter has failed to fulfil its obligations in due time or the commission agent has failed to render due accounts or has acted fraudulently against the principal or has been adjudicated bankrupt (Statute on Commission Agents § 57(2).

In ITALY and PORTUGAL the principal is generally entitled to exercise the intermediary's claims arising from the execution of his mandate against third persons (Italy: CC art. 1705(2)) sent. 2; Portugal: CC art. 1181(2)).

4.   Action oblique
In FRANCE, BELGIUM and LUXEMBOURG, the principal may sue the third party by an *action oblique* (CCs art. 1166). If the agent fails to proceed against the third party, the principal may exercise the agent's rights, but it may not acquire the results of that action for itself since such an action is for the benefit of the agent (Cass.civ. 16 June 1903, D.P. 1903.I.454; Cour Paris 12 June 1946, D. 1947.I.112).

In general, many French and Belgian legal writers are in favour of direct relations and corresponding direct actions (*action directe*) between the principal and the third party if the agent is a commission agent (*Starck* 164 ff.; *Ripert/Roblot* no. 2635, 2672; Belgium: *van Gerven* 488 ff.; *Simont* 129 ss.). The courts, however, explictly disallow such actions (France: Cass.civ. 20 July 1871, D.P. 1871.I.232; Luxembourg: Cour Supérieure de Justice 19 March 1920, Pas. 11, 84).

5.   *Undisclosed principal*
The undisclosed principal doctrine of the COMMON LAW enables the principal to sue the third party without any conditions (*supra* Article 3:301 no. 3). A similar rule applies in DENMARK and SWEDEN when a commission agent is not acting in the course of his business (i.e., in a *civilkommission*). The principal may then proceed against the third party whenever it wishes (Statute on Commission Agents § 57(1)).

Article 3:303: Intermediary's Insolvency or Fundamental Non-performance to Third Party

If the intermediary becomes insolvent, or if it commits a fundamental non-performance towards the third party, or if prior to the time for performance it is clear that there will be a fundamental non-performance:

    (a) on the third party's demand, the intermediary shall communicate the name and address of the principal to the third party; and

    (b) the third party may exercise against the principal the rights which the third party has against the intermediary, subject to any defences which the intermediary may set up against the third party and those which the principal may set up against the intermediary.

COMMENT

Comments to Articles 3:302 and 3:303:

A. *Exceptional Direct Relationship Between Principal and Third Party*
Under certain narrow conditions, a direct relationship can exceptionally be established between the principal and the third party according to Articles 3:302 to 3:303. These provisions establish two rules which "disregard" the initial separation between principal and third party which results from Article 3:301. The distinction between Article 3:302 and Article 3:303 depends upon the fact to whom a performance by the intermediary is outstanding: if vis-à-vis the principal, Article 3:302 applies; if vis-à-vis the third party, Article 3:303 applies. If performances are outstanding to both principal and third party, both provisions apply.

B. *Conditions for Direct Relationship*
The conditions on which the application of Articles 3:302 and 3:303 depends are circumscribed by the opening words which are in substance identical in the two provisions. The first alternative is that the intermediary is insolvent. Then he can no longer (fully) perform his obligations to either the principal or the third party. The second ground for establishing a direct relationship between principal and third party is a fundamental non-performance by the intermediary. An anticipated future fundamental non-performance is to be treated in the same way. The reasons are in essence the same as in case of the intermediary's insolvency.

    The intermediary's fundamental non-performance suffices; the intermediary's contracting party (be it his principal or the third party) need not take court action against the intermediary or even attempt enforcement of a judicial decision against him.

C. *Two Major Consequences*
Both Articles 3:302 and 3:303 provide for two measures. First, the intermediary must disclose to his principal or to the third party, respectively the name and address of the third party or of the principal, respectively, unless the name and address of the "economic opposite" is already known. Since the intermediary cannot and need not

know whether this name and address is already known to the principal or the third party, respectively, the latter must make a request for disclosure.

Second, the principal or the third party may exercise against the respective "economic opposite" the rights which the intermediary has acquired against that "opposite". Of course, the exercise of these rights is subject to any defences which the "opposite" may have against the intermediary, cf. comment E, below.

D. *Remedy for Non-Disclosure of Name and Address*
Which remedies are available to the principal and the third party if, in violation of subparagraphs (a) of Articles 3:302 and 3:303, the intermediary does not disclose the name and address of the "economic opposite"? Damages may be awarded but may not be recoverable from the intermediary, especially if he is insolvent. An order to disclose the name may be the only effective remedy.

E. *Preservation of Defences*
The establishment of a direct relationship between principal and third party comprises the transfer not only of the intermediary's rights vis-à-vis the third party and the principal. These latter parties must also be allowed to raise the defences which originally they had acquired, vis-á-vis the intermediary, against their economic opposite. This is provided for in subparagraphs (b) of both Articles 3:302 and 3:303.

The last phrase of Article 3:303 has no equivalent in Article 3:302. This is explained by the fact that the principal has a pre-existing underlying relationship with the intermediary, whereas the third party does not. If the intermediary has a claim against his principal, the principal may rely on defences against its intermediary. This position is to be preserved if under Article 3:303 the third party may raise claims against the principal.

NOTES

1.   *Geneva Convention on Agency*
     Under the Geneva Convention on Agency the third party's right to sue the principal is admitted under the same conditions as the corresponding right of the principal to sue the third party (art. 13(2)) lit. b, (3). Again, however, the Geneva Convention differs from Article 3.303 as to the conditions under which the third party may demand to be informed about the principal's name. Under the Convention the agent has to reveal the principal's identity only if his own non-performance is due to the principal's failure to perform (art. 13(4)).

2.   *Third party may proceed against principal if agent has not performed*
     DUTCH law is closest to Article 3:303. The third party may exercise the intermediary's rights against the principal in case of the intermediary's bankruptcy or non-performance (BW art. 7:421 (1)). Paragraph 2 corresponds to Article 3:303 lit. a.
         Under SPANISH commercial law the third party may be entitled to sue the principal in a very specific situation, namely if a factor, who according to CCom. art. 284 should act in the principal's name, did in fact act in his own name (CCom art. 287).
         A similar, but more general rule prevails in FRANCE. Indirect representation is treated as a special case of simulation (*prête-nom*, cf. CC art. 1321). If the third party acquires knowledge of the fact that the intermediary, its contracting party, was acting on behalf of a principal, it may bring a declaratory action for a judicial statement of simulation (*action en déclaration de simulation*). On the strength of such a judicial decision, the third party has the choice either to rely on the hidden contract and sue the principal or, on the other hand, sue the agent on the basis of the "simulated"

contract. The third party may not act against both the agent and the principal. By contrast, the principal may not proceed directly against the third party on the basis of the dissimulated act.

3. *Undisclosed principal*
   Under the undisclosed principal doctrine of the COMMON LAW, the third party may sue the principal without any preconditions (see Note 3 to Article 3:301 above). Therefore the third party has the choice of proceeding either against the principal or against the agent.

4. *Third party may never proceed against principal*
   In DENMARK and SWEDEN, in general the third party may not proceed against the principal.

Article 3:304: Requirement of Notice

The rights under Articles 3:302 and 3:303 may be exercised only if notice of intention to exercise them is given to the intermediary and to the third party or principal, respectively. Upon receipt of the notice, the third party or the principal is no longer entitled to render performance to the intermediary.

COMMENT

A. *Procedural Details*

Article 3:304 lays down the procedure for transferring, or delegating the exercise of, the rights which had accrued to the intermediary, and the point in time when the transfer or delegation becomes effective.

B. *Insolvency Proceedings not Prejudiced*

The provisions of Articles 3:302 to 3:304 do not prejudice the position of principal and/or third party in the intermediary's insolvency, especially the fate of assets furnished to the intermediary. This is to be decided by national law, either by the general rules on insolvency or under specific rules, for example on e.g. commission agents.

NOTE

Since only the Geneva Convention on Agency and the DUTCH BW provide for rules comparable to Articles 3:302 and 3:303, only these instruments contain rules on previous notification. Geneva Convention art. 13(3) corresponds almost literally to Articles 3:304. Also under Dutch law the principal may not proceed against the third party without having notified the latter and as well the intermediary of this intention (BW art. 7:420(1)). Also in the reverse case of the third party's action against the principal, written notification to the intermediary and to the principal is necessary (BW art. 7:421(1)).

CHAPTER 4

Validity

Article 4:101: Matters not Covered

This chapter does not deal with invalidity arising from illegality, immorality or lack of capacity.

COMMENT

For the moment, the Principles do not deal with illegal or immoral contracts. Because of the great variety among the legal systems of Member States as to which contracts are regarded as unenforceable on these grounds, and the very different consequences which follow from this categorisation, further investigation is needed to determine whether it is feasible to draft European Principles on these subjects.

Lack of capacity is not treated because it is more a matter of the law of persons than of contract proper.

Rather, Chapter 4 deals with the topics often considered under the notion of vices of consent.

NOTES

In the Civil law systems it is customary to refer to a general notion of vices of consent *(vices de consentement, Willensmängel)* under which mistake, threats and fraud are factors which prevent there being valid consent to a contract and thus give rise to a right to avoidance. This notion may be explicit in the Civil Codes: for example, ITALIAN CC arts. 1427-1440 are contained in a section headed *Dei vizi del consenso.* The FRENCH, BELGIAN and LUXEMBOURG Civil Codes simply list *erreur, violence* and *dol* as grounds on which there may be no valid consent (art. 1109) and provide common rules as to their consequences (art. 1117). See also AUSTRIAN ABGB §§ 869-877; GERMAN BGB §§ 119-124; GREEK CC arts. 140-157; PORTUGUESE CC arts. 240-257 (which cover also temporary incapacity). The French jurisprudence admits that the grounds listed are a single form of action and are to some extent fungible: *Ghestin*, Formation, No. 481. DUTCH BW art. 3:44 deals with threat, fraud and abuse of circumstances, but mistake is dealt with in Book 6 on contracts (art. 6:228).

The NORDIC laws allow relief under broadly the same circumstances but under separate provisions, mainly contained in Chapter 3 of the Nordic Contract Acts (1915-29), or in case law (see Notes to Articles 4:103 and 4:106). The courts do not employ the notion of vices of consent, but a concept of an invalid declaration of will *(ugyldige viljeerklæringer)* or of invalid legal act is used in the Contracts Acts and for pedagogic purposes (see, e.g., *Gomard,* Kontraktsret, 121 ff.)

ENGLISH and IRISH law do not recognise a unitary concept. Rather, there are several separate grounds on which a contract may be set aside because of some impropriety in the making of the contract or some problem over consent: mistake, misrepresentation, duress, undue influence and unconscionable advantage-taking. However, all but mistake are subject to apparently common rules about loss of the right to rescind, and the same is even true of certain of the rules of mistake: see further below. SCOTLAND also has no unitary concept.

In all systems, threat, fraud and (where applicable) abuse of circumstance are grounds for avoiding unilateral legal acts (including a notice to determine a contract) as well as contracts.

Some of the matters covered by this chapter are not always subsumed within the notion of vices of consent. Thus the existence of a mistake in the communications between the parties may be seen as preventing the formation of a contract at all (e.g. FRENCH *erreur obstacle*, see *Nicholas* 98-100, though the notion of *erreur obstacle* is wider than this, *Ghestin*, Formation No.495. Some English writers also explain the effect of such a mistake as resting on the absence of a valid offer and acceptance, see *Atiyah*, Essays 253-260 and the discussion in *Treitel*, Contract 286-287). See further below, note to Article 4:104.

All the legal systems now provide some relief against harsh contract terms but it is not clear to what extent there is a common conceptual basis underlying the various provisions. See further notes to Article 4:110.

Article 4:102: Initial Impossibility

A contract is not invalid merely because at the time it was concluded performance of the obligation assumed was impossible, or because a party was not entitled to dispose of the assets to which the contract relates.

COMMENT

In some legal systems a contract which, unknown to the parties, is impossible to perform, for example, because of the absence of an *objet* or because the seller has no right to dispose of the goods it is purporting to sell, may be ineffective. Under the Principles this approach is not taken. Very often such cases will be ones of fundamental mistake under which either party affected may avoid the contract, but there may be cases when a party should be treated as taking the risk of impossibility and therefore should not be entitled to avoid the contract. Specific performance of the contract will of course be impossible but the party which has taken the risk may be liable in damages for non-performance.

Illustration: A sells to B, who is a salvage contractor, the wreck of an oil tanker which A says is at a particular location. As A should have known, there never was an oil tanker at that location, but B does not discover this until his preliminary salvage expedition searches the area. The contract is not void and A is liable in damages to B.

See also Comment G to Article 4:103.

NOTE

In many of the legal systems a contract which, at the time it was made, was impossible to perform is not voidable but absolutely void: e.g., in the case of "objective" impossibility, GERMAN BGB § 306 (though for an exception see § 437); "evident" impossibility, AUSTRIAN ABGB § 878; ITALIAN CC art. 1346. FRENCH law requires *"un objet certain qui forme la matière de l'engagement"* (CC art. 1108). Thus a contract to supply a specific object which does not exist is void (*nullité absolue*), unless it is a future object (art. 1130(1)). See *Malaurie & Aynès*, Obligations No. 485-491. PORTUGUESE and SPANISH law are broadly similar, see Portuguese CC arts. 280, 399 and 401; Spanish CC arts. 1184, 1272 and 1460. French law treats the sale of an item which belongs to another in a broadly similar way, but the contract is voidable (*nullité rélative*) (CC art. 1599). German BGB § 437 differs in not treating this last case as one of impossibility, see *Larenz*, § 8 I, p.98, and so does Italian CC art. 1478. In German and Austrian law, if one party knew or ought to have known that the performance was impossible, the other may recover reliance interest damages: BGB § 307; ABGB § 878 3rd sent.. There may also be delictual liability in French law.

In other Civil law systems the same results do not necessarily follow. Thus in GREEK law initial impossibility is a ground for avoidance but does not render the contract void, CC arts. 362-364. In NORDIC law impossibility does not invalidate the contract: see *Ramberg*, Köplagen 314.

In ENGLAND and IRELAND there are traces of the traditional civil law doctrine. First, a contract to sell specific goods which without the knowledge of the seller have perished at the time the contract is made is void: Sale of Goods Act 1979, s.6. However it is now widely accepted that the common law is more flexible; a contract for non-existent goods may be void for common mistake but is not necessarily so. Thus in a case in which a seller purported to sell goods which, as the seller should have known, had never existed at all, the High Court of Australia held that the contract was not void; the seller was liable for non-delivery: *McRae v. Commonwealth Disposals Commission* (1950) 84 C.L.R. 377 (the illustration in the comment is based on this case). Secondly, the original doctrine of common mistake (the "common law" rule) resulted in the contract being void, not voidable. More recently it has been claimed that there is a separate rule in equity that a contract may be voidable for common fundamental mistake: see *Solle v. Butcher* [1950] 1 K.B. 671, C.A. The two doctrines appear to overlap and there has been some confusion about when each applies. The latest case (*Associated Japanese Bank (International) Ltd v. Crédit du Nord SA* [1989] 1 W.L.R. 255, Q.B.) accepted the existence of both common law and equitable rules but it remains unclear what are the differences between them: see *Chitty* § 5-068.

Under the Principles, initial impossibility is treated, like other mistakes, as a ground on which a contract may be avoided.

Article 4:103: Fundamental Mistake as to Facts or Law

(1) A party may avoid a contract for mistake of fact or law existing when the contract was concluded if:

    (a) (i) the mistake was caused by information given by the other party; or

            (ii) the other party knew or ought to have known of the mistake and it was contrary to good faith and fair dealing to leave the mistaken party in error; or

            (iii) the other party made the same mistake,

            and

    (b) the other party knew or ought to have known that the mistaken party, had it known the truth, would not have entered the contract or would have done so only on fundamentally different terms.

(2) However a party may not avoid the contract if:

    (a) in the circumstances its mistake was inexcusable, or

    (b) the risk of the mistake was assumed, or in the circumstances should be borne, by it.

COMMENT

A. *General*

It frequently happens that a party enters into a contract on the basis of a misapprehension about the facts or the law affecting the contract. As stated in the Survey (above, pp.xxxii-xxxiii), while the principle of freedom of contract suggests that a party should not be bound to a contract unless its consent to it was informed, the need for security of transactions suggests that the other party should in general terms be able to rely on the existence of the contract unless it:

(a)   has not acted in good faith; or
(b)   has taken deliberate advantage of the first party in circumstances in which standards of fair dealing would not permit this; or
(c)   has behaved carelessly or in some other way which was unreasonable.

Further, a party which has entered a contract under some mistake or misapprehension should not normally be entitled to avoid a contract unless the misapprehension was very serious. Thus a contract may be set aside for mistake only if the mistake is fundamental. (In less serious cases damages may be available, e.g. where one party has carelessly misled the other, see Article 4:106). The only exception is the case of fraud, where the intention to deceive is itself a sufficient ground to justify the innocent party having the power to avoid the contract (see Article 4:107).

If one of the conditions (a)-(c) above is satisfied, and, even on a correct interpretation of the contract in accordance with Chapter 5, a party has made a mistake which is to something fundamental (see D below), there may be a case for a remedy.

It may also be appropriate to allow the contract to be avoided when a mistake which both parties shared has made the contract fundamentally different to what was anticipated. Here there was usually no bad faith, advantage-taking or careless behaviour at the time the contract was made, but this is a risk that neither party anticipated and which the contract did not allocate. In such a case it may be bad faith to insist on the contract being carried through when it has turned out to be fundamentally different from what either party anticipated.

B. *Priority of Interpretation*

Before a remedy on the ground of mistake is allowed, it is frequently necessary to consult the contract and to interpret its provisions to see whether it in fact covers the situation which has now been revealed. If it does, there will be no ground for invoking mistake.

Illustration 1: A builder employed to build a house finds, when it starts to dig the foundations, that across the site runs an old sewer which is not marked on the maps and which neither it nor the employer had ever expected. This will make completion of the task very much more expensive. It must first be determined whether the contract, as properly interpreted, covers the problem. If the contract provides that in the event of "unforeseeable ground conditions" the contractor is entitled to extra time and extra payment, and a correct interpretation of "unforeseeable ground conditions" would include the sewer, there is no basis for the contractor to invoke this Article.

C. *Mistake Must Make Contract Fundamentally Different*

Security of transactions demands that parties should not be able to escape from contracts because of misapprehensions as to the nature or quality of the performance unless the mistakes are very serious. It is only in the case where the seller knows that the buyer would not enter the contract at all, or would only do so on fundamentally different terms, that the seller should be required to point out the buyer's mistake. Less important misapprehensions must be borne by the party on whom they fall. Equally only very serious shared mistakes should give rise to relief. Thus Article 4:103 confines relief for mistake to cases where the other party knew or should have known that the mistaken party, had it known the truth, would not have entered the contract or would have done so only on fundamentally different terms, see Article 4:103(1)(b).

It should be noted that the Principles require that a mistake should be as to something fundamental, not merely material. Compare the definition of "material" in Article 1:301 (5):

> *(5) A matter is "material" if it is one that a reasonable person in one party's position should have known would influence the other party in its decision as to whether to contract or as to the terms on which to contract.*

A matter may be material, for example in that it might have affected the price the mistaken party would have agreed to pay, without being fundamental. A material difference between offer and acceptance may prevent the formation of a contract (see Article 2:208); but a mistake as to something which is material but not fundamental will not give rise to a right of avoidance under Article 4:103.

D. *Mistakes Induced by Incorrect Information*

Perhaps the most likely reason for a mistake is that the mistaken party has been given incorrect information by the other party, which has thus caused the mistake. When the resulting misapprehension is fundamental, the first party should be permitted to avoid the contract. Not only was it not properly informed, but that resulted from the behaviour of the other party.

Even if the party which gave the information reasonably believed it to be true, it chose to give the information; and it cannot complain if the recipient is allowed to avoid the contract provided that the resulting misapprehension was fundamental.

> *Illustration 2*: The seller of the lease of a property which he had used for residential purposes told a prospective purchaser that the purchaser would be able to use it as a restaurant, which was the purchaser's main object. In fact the seller had forgotten that there was a prohibition on using the property other than for residential purposes without the landlord's consent and the landlord refuses consent. The purchaser of the lease may avoid the contract.

Depending on the facts of the case, the mistaken party may have a remedy under other Articles.

> (i)   If the statement amounted to a contractual promise under Article 6:101, Statements giving rise to Contractual Obligations, it will have a remedy for non-performance.
>   Even if the statement did not amount to a contractual promise,
> (ii)   if the other party was fraudulent, the mistaken party will have a remedy for fraud under Article 4:107, Fraud, or
> (iii) if the other party was not fraudulent, the mistaken party will be entitled to damages under Article 4:106, Incorrect Information, provided the mistake resulted from incorrect information which the party giving it had no reasonable grounds for believing it to be true.

In these cases the misapprehension which results from the incorrect statement need not be fundamental. But if the conditions of (i)-(iii) are not met, or if there has been no fundamental non-performance or fraud and the mistaken party wants to avoid the contract, it may only do so on the basis of fundamental mistake under this Article.

E. *Mistake Known to Other Party*

Some legal systems as a matter of general principle allow a party to take knowing advantage of even very serious mistakes by the other party; provided that the first party did not cause them it need not point them out. Increasingly, however, it is being recognised that such behaviour is unacceptable e.g., as a form of bad faith. The Principles recognise a general principle that a party should not be entitled to take advantage of a serious mistake by the other as to the relevant facts or law. The same applies when it cannot be shown that the non-mistaken knew actually knew of the mistake but the mistake should have been known to it because it was obvious.

There are situations, however, in which a party should be permitted to take advantage of another's ignorance. One is where the contract is in its nature risky and speculative, with neither party expecting the other to assist it in any way: contracts for high-risk shares are an example. Another is where one party has gone to considerable trouble to obtain the knowledge that the other does not have. If the party is not going to be allowed to use its hard-earned knowledge it will not have any incentive to invest in obtaining it in the first place and both parties will be left worse off. But there are many cases where contracts are not speculative and one party has at little or no cost acquired information that the other obviously does not have and which is crucial to the contract. In this case the non-mistaken party should not be allowed to take advantage of the other's misapprehension; it is contrary to reasonable standards of fair dealing to leave the mistaken party in error, see Article 4:103(1)(a)(ii).

> *Illustration 3*: A sells her house to B without revealing to B that A knows there is extensive rot under the floor of one room. She does not mention it because she assumes B will be aware of the risk of it from the fact that there are damp marks on the wall and will have the floor checked. B does not appreciate the risk and buys the house without having the floor checked. B may avoid the contract.

Illustration 4: Through extensive research, A discovers that demand for a particular chemical made by X Corporation is about to rise dramatically. A buys a large number of shares in X Corporation from B without revealing his knowledge, which he knows B does not share. B has no remedy.

F. *Shared Mistake*

When both parties enter into a contract under a serious misapprehension as to the facts the question is a different one. It must be asked whether the contract was intended to allocate the risk of the loss caused by the facts turning out to be different. Sometimes the parties realised that their knowledge was limited, or the contract was by its nature speculative; then it can be said that the contract was intended to apply despite the difference between what the parties assumed and reality. But sometimes it is more realistic to say that the risk of the facts turning out to be different was not allocated by the contract. If the result is that the contract would be very seriously different for one party, that party should have the right to avoid it. This usually results in the resulting losses being divided between the parties, if only in a very rough and ready way. There will normally be no right to damages in cases of shared mistake, as Article 4:117 applies only where one party knew or ought to have known of the mistake.

Illustration 5: An Englishwoman who owns a cottage in France agrees to rent it for one month to a Danish friend, although the Englishwoman does not normally rent the cottage. The lease is to start five days later. The Dane books non-refundable air tickets to fly to France. It is then discovered that the cottage had been totally destroyed by fire the night before the contract was agreed. The contract may be avoided by either party, with the result that no rent is payable and the Dane gets no compensation for the wasted air tickets.

G. *No Special Categories*

It is not necessary to lay down categories of which kind of misapprehension will give rise to a remedy for mistake and which will not. Thus Article 4:103 provides that the mistake may be about the facts surrounding the contract or the law affecting it. (This Article does not apply to cases in which one party has performed the contract or intends to do so knowing that it involves an illegal act. The effects of illegality are not covered by this Chapter, see Article 4:101.)

Mistakes which relate to the mere value of the item sold are not usually fundamental. The Principles do not have an explicit rule refusing any relief in this case.

Illustration 6: A party pays £200,000 for a antique desk made by Chippendale. She agrees to this price because she has read that such prices were commonly paid for Chippendale desks a few years ago. She does not know that subsequently the market prices for antique furniture of all types have declined dramatically and is the desk much less valuable than she supposed. The buyer may not avoid the contract.

Cases of initial impossibility and the non-existence of a thing sold are treated in the same way as other mistakes. Under the Principles the contract may be avoided for mistake but it is not void for lack of *objet*: see Article 4:102. Indeed there may be cases in which a sale of a non-existent object is valid and the seller is liable for non-performance, because the court concludes that in the circumstances the seller is the party which should bear the risk.

> *Illustration 7*: J sells K a piece of used equipment which is on a remote construction site from which K is to collect it; it is not feasible for K to inspect the equipment before agreeing to purchase. When K arrives there it finds that the equipment had been destroyed by fire some time before the contract was made. J should have known this. J is liable for non-performance and cannot avoid the contract for mistake.

See also Illustration 5 above.

Mistakes as to the person are also treated in the same way as other mistakes.

H. *Mistakes in Communication*

A frequent form of "mistake" is that one party makes some slip in communicating its intentions, e.g. by writing "£10,000" when it meant "£100,000". Such mistakes may be within Article 4:103 by virtue of Article 4:104: see the Comments to that Article.

I. *Mistake Inexcusable*

It does not seem appropriate to allow a party which itself was a major cause of the mistake to avoid the contract because of it unless the other party was at least equally to blame. That would allow it to shift the consequences of its own carelessness on to the other party. The other should not normally bear the burden of checking that the first party has not made careless mistakes. See Illustration 4 to Comment F above. On the other hand, if the second party is aware that the first has made a mistake and it would take little trouble to point it out, the fact that the first party has been careless should not prevent it from getting relief and its mistake should not be treated as inexcusable.

> *Illustration 8*: N asks for bids for a piece of construction work; the information given to tenderers indicates that the contractor will probably strike rock at one point on the site. O sends in a tender which has no item for excavating rock, only for excavating soil. N should point this out, and if it does not and the mistake is sufficiently serious, O should be able to avoid the contract.

J. *Risk*

As suggested in Comment D above, there are some contracts under which the parties are deliberately taking the risk of the unknown, or should be treated as so doing. In such a case a party should not be able to avoid the contract for mistake if the risk eventuates. One example of this is where one party is aware that it is entering the contract without full knowledge.

Illustration 9: A decides to sell the entire contents of a house he has inherited at an auction. He is conscious that he does not know the value of the items, but he deliberately decides not to bother to have them valued first. At the auction B buys a picture for a low price. B knows that it is by Constable but does not point this out. A cannot avoid the contract for mistake.

In other cases one party should be seen as taking the risk.

Illustration 10: A yacht chandler in England charters to a German amateur sailor a yacht which they believe to be moored at Marseilles. Unknown to either party, shortly beforehand the yacht had been sunk when it was rammed by another vessel. The chandler, being a professional dealing with a non-professional, and moreover being in a position to know the facts whereas the other party had no possibility of this, may not avoid the contract but is liable for non-performance.

K. *Remedies*

The normal remedy for mistake is for the party which is mistaken, or the one which wishes to escape from a contract entered under a shared mistake, to avoid the contract as a whole or in part (see Article 4:116). The mistaken party may also recover damages under Article 4.106 where the mistake was the result of incorrect information given by the other party, or under Article 4:117 where the mistake was or should have been known to the other party, or was caused by it.

NOTES

In all the systems, a contract which one or both parties have entered into as the result of a mistake may, under varying conditions, be escaped from by the mistaken party or, where the mistake is shared, by either of the parties. This includes cases in which the "mistake" involved some error in expression or communication, so that the question relates the terms of the contract; this is dealt with under Article 4:104 below. This note deals with the mistakes as to the facts or the law.

1. *Mistake, misrepresentation and other doctrines*

In the continental systems, the doctrine of mistake is available in a wide range of circumstances and is a ground on which relief is given quite frequently. In contrast, the ENGLISH and IRISH doctrines of mistake as to facts are very narrow and there are few cases. The principal reason for this is that the doctrines are limited to cases of shared (or "common") mistake. In practice, many of the cases that on the continent would fall under the doctrine of mistake will be dealt with in the common law systems under the doctrine of "innocent" misrepresentation. This is an equitable extension of the rules of fraud to cover cases in which one party has misled the other into making the contract by giving, innocently (i.e. without fraud), incorrect factual information: see *Redgrave* v. *Hurd* (1880) 20 Ch.D. 1. Thus if a seller of land has (without fraud) given the buyer incorrect information about it, on the continent the case is likely to be dealt with via mistake (e.g. in FRENCH law, *The Villa Jacqueline* case, Civ. 23.11.1931, DP 1932.1.129, n. Josserand); in the common law the mistaken party would be permitted to avoid the contract on the ground of misrepresentation. SCOTTISH law in principle allows relief on the ground of a mistake more readily than does the common law, but in practice relief is more often obtained on the ground of misrepresentation and there have been very few cases in whch mistake has been pleaded successfully (though see *Angus* v. *Bryden* 1992 SLT 884). This note must take both mistake and misrepresentation into account.

In other systems too, what in functional terms may be cases of mistake may be covered by separate rules. Thus in some systems, as an alternative to relief on the ground of mistake, relief may be given on the basis of *clausula rebus sic stantibus*: e.g. GERMAN law, where the doctrine may apply to changes which have already occurred when the contract was made if the parties were not aware of the change (*Larenz*, § 20 III, p.395); PORTUGUESE CC art. 252(1); SPANISH case law, TS 6 October 1987, 16 October 1989, 10 December 1990 and 8 July 1991. NORDIC law has a doctrine of "assumptions" or implied conditions *(Forudsætninglæren)*: see Danish Law 152-154. However, in Sweden the matter is controversial, see *Ramberg*, Avtalsrätt 214-215, and Finnish law does not accept the doctrine; it would have to give relief via interpretation or via the general clause on unfair contract terms in Contracts Act § 36.

In a French case M agreed with R (as was legally permissible) to do R's military service in R's place. Unknown to either of them, R was not liable for service. It was held that the agreement lacked both *objet* and *cause*: Req. 30 July 1873, S. 1873.1.448, D. 1873.1.330. Under the Principles this would be dealt with as a case of mistake.

A different example is that many continental systems preserve special regimes for defects in property sold, e.g. GERMAN BGB §§ 459 ff.; FRENCH CC arts. 1641-1649. There are major differences as to whether these special rules prevail over the general rules on mistake or whether a buyer who is disappointed with the qualities of the property purchased may claim on either ground, see Notes to Article 4:119.

2. *Mistake as to any matter which was fundamental to the mistaken party*
In all the systems a party who has entered a contract under a serious mistake as to the substance of the subject matter of the contract may, subject to differing conditions, avoid the contract. In the majority of systems the party seeking avoidance must show, broadly speaking, (i) that the mistake was sufficiently serious that the mistaken party would not have entered the contract on the terms it did had it known the truth, and (ii) that the other party knew or should have known that the matter was of importance to the mistaken party. Thus the systems draw a contrast with cases of fraud, where any fraud will entitle the innocent party to avoid the contract. In the Civilian systems there is a strong tradition that, to be a ground for avoidance, the mistake must relate to the subject matter of the contract, as opposed to a motive for entering the contract, but this restriction is not universal. It is discussed in Note 6(a) below.

In FRENCH, BELGIAN and LUXEMBOURG, CCs Art.1110 allow relief for *erreur* to cases of mistake as to the substance of the subject-matter of the contract. The jurisprudence has interpreted this broadly. Thus in France, provided that the error was *déterminant* for the party seeking to avoid the contract and this was known to the other party, relief may be given, see Civ. 17 November 1930, S.1932.1.17, DP 1932.1.161, Gaz.Pal 1930.2.1031, *Malaurie & Aynès,* Obligations No. 410; Civ. 23 November 1931, DP 1932.1.129, n. Josserand; Civ. 27 April 1953, D. 1953 Somm. 97; Paris 14 October 1931, D. 1934.2.128. Modern doctrine tends to base the requirement that the importance of the matter be apparent to the other party on the principle of good faith: *Ghestin*, Formation Nos. 524-525. The rules on error are interpreted similarly in Belgium: Cass. 31 October 1966, Arr. Cass. 1967, 301; Cass. 3 March 1967, Arr. Cass. 1967, 829; a party should not be able to rely on the absence of some characteristic which would not be important to the normal person unless its importance to him had been indicated to the other party, see *Storme*, Invloed No. 180 ff.; and Luxembourg, Tribunal Luxembourg 1 March 1966, Pasicrisie 20, p.142 and, on the other party's knowledge, Cour, 30 March 1993, Pasicrisie 29, p.253.

In GERMAN law the relevant article of the BGB, § 119, has two paragraphs; and the situations envisaged by Article 4:103 may fall under either. BGB § 119(1) deals with errors as to the content *(Inhalt)* of the declaration. If a party's mistake leads it to stipulate *x* when in fact it intends *y* (e.g. a pub owner offers to sell his premises "including the accessories", in the belief that "accessories" include only the furniture which is permanently fixed in the rooms, rather than its legal meaning of all the movables serving the purpose of the pub: see *Larenz*, AT § 20 II a, p.376; also Reichsgericht 11 March 1909, RGZ 70, 391 ff.) there may be a mistaken declaration under § 119(1). Other situations envisaged by Article 4:103 (except those involving error in motive, see Note 6(a)), would fall under BGB § 119(2). This covers errors relating to any characteristic *(Eigenschaften)* of the subject matter, e.g. the age of a car sold (BGH 26.10.1978, NJW 1979, 160, 161), provided the quality is essential for the contract in question and the parties concerned: BGH 22.9.1983, BGHZ 88, 240. The test under § 119(2) is whether the error concerns qualities that business regards as essential; and there has been a debate as to whether this refers to the objective perception of business in general or that of the parties concerned (*Flume* AT II, § 24 2a; *Larenz* AT § 20 II b, p.380). The BGH has ruled that a quality is essential for business if the mistaken party has based its declaration on the quality in question and that was discernable by the other party, even if it was not agreed on or made part of the mistaken party's declaration (BGH 22 September 1983, BGHZ 88, 240, 246). Under BGB § 119(1) the test is whether the person would have made the declaration he did, had he known and reasonably understood the situation. GREEK law is similar: CC arts 140, 141; AP 1109/1976, EEN 1977.311-312.

ITALIAN CC art. 1428 requires that the mistake be essential; arts. 1431 and 1429 state explicitly that the importance of the mistake must be apparent to the other party. PORTUGUESE law requires that the error as to the quality of the subject matter be as to a matter which determined the assent of the aggrieved party and that the importance of the matter was known or should have been known to the other party, CC art. 247. SPANISH CC art. 1266 provides that an error may invalidate a contract; the error must be substantial or essential and these requirements are interpreted strictly, *Ministerio de Justicia* art 1266, 462. AUSTRIAN ABGB §§ 871(1) and 872 distinguish "essential" and "non-essential" mistake; the latter does not affect the validity of the contract, though it may lead to other remedies (see Notes to Articles 4:105 and 4:106 below).

In NORDIC Contracts Acts § 33, which regulates mistakes other than errors in communication, the question is whether good faith and honesty require that the contract be annulled. The mistake must concern some fact which fundamentally influenced the contract (e.g. Finnish KKO 1972 II 84, KKO 1970 II 38) and good faith will not be contravened unless the non-mistaken party knew or must have known of the importance of the matter to the other (see *Ramberg*, Avtalsrätt 196; a more liberal test, "ought the party to have known?", may be applied under the doctrine of "failure of assumptions", Note 1 above, *Lynge Andersen* 239ff.).

In ENGLAND and IRELAND relief for mistake (which as noted earlier, must be shared mistake) only applies when the mistake is as to the existence or ownership of the subject matter of the contract, or "as to the existence of some quality which makes the thing without the quality essentially different from the thing it was supposed to be": Lord Atkin in *Bell* v. *Lever Bros.* [1932] A.C. 161, 218, H.L. This requirement seems to be interpreted very strictly. Lord Atkin said that there would be no relief if the parties mistakenly bought and sold a horse that they thought was sound when it was not, or leased a house that they thought was habitable when it was not; in neither case would the subject-matter (the horse or the house) be essentially different. IRISH law may be more liberal: see *Western Potato Co-operative* v. *Durnan* [1985] ILRM 5, CC. So are some of the English cases which have allowed relief in equity for common mistake: e.g. *Grist* v. *Bailey* [1967] Ch. 532, Ch.D.; but it is still said that the mistake must be "fundamental", see *Solle* v. *Butcher* [1951] 1 K.B. 671, C.A. As stated earlier, in English and Irish law, in cases where only one party is mistaken, any relief is given on the basis of misrepresentation. Originally, the misrepresentee could rescind as of right provided the misrepresentation was material (i.e. not so unimportant that no reasonable person would be influenced by it: see *Treitel*, Contract 312) and it had been at least one factor which had induced him to enter the contract; it did not need be of particular importance or the main reason for his decision (see *Chitty* § 6-021). However since the passing of English Misrepresentation Act 1967, s.2(2) the court has power to declare the contract subsisting, and to award damages in lieu of rescission, if that would be more equitable. The fact that the representation was relatively unimportant is one reason for refusing to permit rescission: *William Sindall* v. *Cambridge C.C.* [1994] 1 W.L.R. 1016, C.A.

SCOTTISH law also limits relief on the ground of mistake to "essential error", which must be as to something essential to both parties, Bell, *Principles*, s.11. However it also gives more liberal relief for error induced by misrepresentation: see *Smith*, Short Commentary 823-825, 828-833).

A liberal approach on the question of the other party's knowledge is that of DUTCH BW 6:228(1). This requires that the contract was entered into under the influence of error and would not have been entered had there been a correct assessment of the facts. Relief will not be given if the other party was justified in assuming that the mistake was not important to the other party. (In Dutch law relief is limited in other ways, see Note 3 below.)

Under Article 4:103 a mistake as to the facts or the law may give rise to a right to avoidance if the other party knew or should have known that the mistaken party, had he known the truth, would not have entered the contract or would have done so only on fundamentally different terms. There is the additional requirement that the other party knew or ought to have known of the mistake, or caused it or shared it (see Note 3 below).

3. *Fact of mistake known to other party or caused by him*
This note and the next consider the position of the party against whom relief is sought. One possibility is that he has made the same mistake: this is dealt with in the next note. Another is that he caused the mistake, e.g. by giving incorrect information. Even if he did not cause the mistake, it may be that he knew or should have known of it. Are any of these essential before the mistaken party can avoid the contract?

As we have seen, the more traditional civilian systems require that a party has made a serious mistake and that the non-mistaken party knew that the matter about which there was a mistake was determining; but they do not require either that the non-mistaken party knew there had been a mistake or that he had contributed to it. In GREEK law it is not necessary that the non-mistaken party knew of the mistake. Similarly, in GERMAN law, though doctrine has argued that relief should be given only when the mistake was caused by the other party or where the latter at least ought to have realised the mistake (*Münchener Kommentar (-Kramer)* I § 119 no.97ff.), the courts have not required that the other party knew of the mistake. This may seem liberal, but it should be noted that in both systems the mistaken party may be required to compensate the non-mistaken party for losses thereby caused (Greek CC art. 145; BGB § 122). The non-mistaken party's knowledge is relevant to this; under CC art 145 and BGB § 122(2) the mistaken party is not liable for damages where the other party knew or should have known of the mistake. Also in PORTUGUESE law, and in FRENCH, BELGIAN and LUXEMBOURG law, a mistaken party may get relief even though the other party did not know of the mistake (if he did, there may be *dol*) and even though he did not cause it. Again, the mistaken party might be liable if he had committed a pre-contractual fault but it is said that in practice this is not found: *Rodière*, Vices 23. However, in Belgium the tendency is to treat a mistake as excusable when it was the result of of the fault (incorrect information or failure to disclose) by the other party; but where the mistake was the consequence of one's own failure to investigate, or perhaps to check the information given, to hold that the the mistake was inexcusable and thus that there is no right to avoidance (see note 12 below). See *Kriuthof & Bocken*, TPR 1994, p.338.

Some civilian systems are less ready to grant avoidance (but they have no provision for damages to the non-mistaken party). Thus under AUSTRIAN ABGB § 871(1) a claim for avoidance on the ground of mistake may be brought only if the mistake was or should have been known to the other party, or was caused by him, or if the mistaken party notified the other of the the fact that he had made a mistake promptly. The latter is deemed satisfied if the mistake is notified before the non-mistaken party has made a disposition in reliance on the contract. ITALIAN CC arts. 1429, 1431 require that a mistake by one party be patent, i.e. one that should be apparent to the other party. DUTCH BW 6:228(1) requires that the mistake either have been caused by incorrect information given by the other party, or be one that the other party, in view of what he knew or should have known of the error, should have pointed out to the mistaken party.

We saw earlier that the NORDIC systems base relief for mistake on the principle of good faith. Thus relief will be refused unless the non-mistaken party actually knew of the mistake, see Contract Acts § 33. In some decisions this rule has been extended to situations where party "must have known" of the mistake, and FINNISH courts have extended it to situations where he "ought to have known" (e.g. KKO 1968 II 33). Relief will also be given in Nordic law if the non-mistaken party caused the mistake (see Swedish Sup. Ct. NJA 1985 p. 178, *Kalmar varv*; Ramberg, Avtalsrätt 201-205).

As stated earlier, ENGLISH and IRISH law will not allow escape from the contract on the ground of mistake unless the mistake was shared. Avoidance may be given for misrepresentation but only where one party misled the other, see above. SCOTTISH law generally requires that the error have been induced by the other party's misrepresentation (*Stewart v. Kennedy* (1890) 17 R (H.L.) 25; *Menzies v. Menzies* (1893) 20 R (H.L.) 108) and has been reluctant to recognise uninduced unilateral error (*Spook Erection (Northern) Lyd v. Kaye* 1990 SLT 676; but there may be an exception where the other party knew and took advantage of the other party's error (*Steuart's Trustees v. Hart* (1875) 3 R 192; *Angus v. Bryden* 1992 SLT 884).

Article 4.103 allows avoidance for mistake only where the mistake was caused by the other party or was known or ought to have been known to him. There is no provision for damages to the non-mistaken party.

4.   *Shared mistake*
All the systems allow avoidance by either party where the parties have entered the contract under a shared fundamental mistake; see, e.g, on ITALIAN law, *Pietrobon* 517, 527; in AUSTRIA, OGH 2 September 1980, SZ 53/108; 15 June 1983, SZ 56/96; 3 March 1988, SZ 61/53.

5.   *Relief where the other party has not yet relied on the contract*
UNIDROIT art. 3.5.1(b) adds an additional circumstace in which the mistaken party may escape: if the other has not yet relied on the contract. Of the European systems, this seems to be paralleled only in AUSTRIAN law (see above), though in certain cases the same result may follow under NORDIC Contract Acts § 39. As noted earlier, GERMAN and GREEK law require the mistaken party to compensate the other for reliance loss in some circumstances. The Principles do not allow a mistaken party to avoid the contract just because the other party has not yet relied on it.

6.   *Particular types of mistake*
   (a)   Mistaken motive
      As mentioned in Note 2, there is a strong continental tradition excluding relief when an error relates merely to motive. Thus in FRANCE, doctrine is divided but the courts have regularly refused to permit contracts to be annulled on this ground; *Ghestin*, Formation No. 509. Errors as to the facts which fall under GERMAN BGB § 119(1) (for an example, see Note 2 above) clearly relate to the subject matter of the agreement. § 119(2) deals with errors *in motivis*, but to count as a sufficient error of motive under § 119(2), the mistake must be reflected in the

contractual agreement. Thus someone who buys a wedding present may not avoid the contract if he discovers that the wedding had in fact been called off. See also AUSTRIAN ABGB § 901 (2); and PORTUGUESE CC art 252 (1). The Austrian Supreme court has applied the test whether the mistake is as to what the party wants or merely as to why he wants it: OGH 23 January 1975, EvBl 1975/205 = JBl 1976, 145. In GREEK law a mistake exclusively as to motive is not substantial (CC art. 143; see AP 268/1974, NoB 1974.1269; *Balis* No. 42), unless the motives have been discussed by the parties beforehand or good faith and business usage would require it to be taken into account: Full Bench of AP 5/1990, NoB 1990.1318 (1319 I). ITALIAN CC art.1429 seems to exclude mistakes as to motive, since it lists ways in which a mistake may be essential and mistake as to motive is not one of them; whether the mistake may relate to a circumstance extraneous to the content of the contract is disputed; see *Bianca*, II contratto 615; *P.Barcellona* 148.

In other continental systems relief may be given for errors in motive. Dutch BW 6:228 is not restricted in this way. In NORDIC Contracts Act § 33 it does not matter that the error was *in motivis*; the important question is whether good faith and honesty require that the contract be annulled (e.g. Finnish KKO 1977 II 76).

In *Bell* v. *Lever Bros.* [1932] 161, 224 Lord Atkin gives examples of mistakes which, in English law, would not invalidate a contract. Many of these involve errors of motive. But for rescission for innocent misrepresentation, it does not matter whether the misrepresentation relates directly to the subject matter or not: e.g. *Redgrave* v. *Hurd* (1880) 20 Ch.D. 1, where the misrepresentation related to a separate but linked transaction.

Under Article 4:103 a mistake as to motive can give rise to a right to avoid the contract provided the other conditions for avoidance are satisfied.

(b) *Mistake as to value*

FRENCH, BELGIAN and LUXEMBOURG law refuse relief when the mistake is simply as to the value of the subject-matter of the contract, save where there has been fraud or where a narrower ground such as *lésion* applies (CC Arts. 1118, 1674); similarly AUSTRIAN law (OGH 30 November 1966, JB1 1967, 620). However, a mistake as to the subject-matter may be grounds for avoidance even though the most obvious reason that this concerns the avoiding party is that the subject-matter is not worth what he has agreed to pay for it, or is worth more than the price at which he agreed to sell: e.g. the celebrated Poussin case in which the seller of a painting was allowed to avoid the contract when it was shown to be by that artist and not by some lesser mortal as the seller had supposed, Civ. 13 February 1983, D. 1984.340, JCP 1984.II.20186; Versailles 7 January 1987, D. 1987.485, Gaz.Pal. 1987.34. GERMAN jurisprudence is to the same effect. Error as to mere value or market price does not give rise to relief under BGB § 119(2) (BGH 18 December 1954, BGHZ 16, 54, 57), whereas an error as to the facts from which value is derived may do so; e.g. in the case of sale of a company, an error as to the possible profits from the business may be grounds for avoidance (OLG Düsseldorf, 8 November 1991, NJW-RR 1993, 377). See also *Witz* § 332. Equally GREEK law: *Georgiadis/Stathopoulos*, Art. 142 no.4; AP 268/1974, NoB 1974.1269; ITALIAN law, e.g. Cass. 24.7.1993, n. 8290 in Foro it., Rep., 1993, Contratto in genere, n. 433, and *Sacco* (- *De Nova*) 395; on lesion see CC art.1448; PORTUGUESE law, STJ 12 January 1973, BMJ 223, pp.181ff. Other systems have no specific rule on mistakes as to value but would not normally give relief for such an error. E.g. in DUTCH law a seller would not be expected to point out such a mistake under BW 6:228(1)(b). There is no specific rule in ENGLISH law but it seems that a mistake merely as to something's value would never render it "essentially different from what the parties supposed it to be", see above, 2. There could be an actionable misrepresentation as to the value of the object, provided that the statement was not merely an expression of opinion but one of fact (e.g. as to the current market price). In NORDIC law, Contract Acts § 33 could be applied to a question of value (cf. FINNISH KKO 1968 II 33).

Article 4:103 does not necessarily exclude mistakes as to value, see comment G above..

(c) *Mistake as to the identity of the other party*

The majority of systems treat a mistake as to the identity of the other party as a form of mistake as to the facts and give relief accordingly. Thus FRENCH, BELGIAN and LUXEMBOURG CCs Art. 1110 allow mistake as to the person as a ground on nullity when the "consideration of the person was the principal cause of the agreement". Attributes as well as identity may be sufficiently fundamental. Similarly AUSTRIAN ABGB § 873; GREEK law, *Georgiadis/ Stathopoulos*, Art. 140 no. 10; ITALIAN CC Art. 1429(3); SCOTS law, see *Morrisson* v. *Robertson* 1908 SC 332, *MacLoed* v. *Kerr* 1965 SC 253 and *McBryde* 202; SPANISH CC art. 1266. DUTCH law treats mistaken identity as a normal case under BW

6:228, and NORDIC law seems to accept *error in personam* as falling within Contracts Act § 32, see *Ussing*, Aftaler 179. In GERMAN law mistake as to the person is covered by BGB § 119. A mistake as to the identity of the other party is treated as a mistake in the declaration under § 119(1); while a mistake as to his attributes is explicitly dealt with by § 119(2). Portuguese CC art. 251 also treats a mistake as to identity as a mistake in declaration, so the contract may be anulled under art. 247; see *C.M.Pinto*, General Theory 517. In ENGLISH and IRISH law the case of mistaken identity does not fall under the doctrine of mistake as to the facts considered here, since in English law mistake as to the facts has no effect on the contract unless the mistake is shared. Rather it is dealt with as a mistake over the terms: the question is whether the non-mistaken party knew or should have known that the offer was open only to the individual he was supposed by the offeror to be (*Ingrams* v. *Little* [1961] 1 Q.B. 31, CA). Thus the mistake must normally be as to the identity of the other party rather than as to his attributes. The fact that a party wrongly assumed the other party to be credit-worthy is not a a sufficient ground for relief. see *Treitel*, Contract 274-279. However, an incorrect statement by one party as to one of his attributes (e.g. his qualifications) could give rise to avoidance for misrepresentation, see above.

Article 4:103 covers mistakes as to the identity or attributes of the other party.

(d)   Mistake as to law

In most systems the fact that a party's mistake is as to the legal position, rather than as to the facts, is irrelevant if the other conditions for relief are fulfilled. Thus for GERMAN law see the example of the sale of the pub and its accessories, above, note 2; but contrast the case of a pregnant worker who agrees to cancel her contract of employment without knowing that she thereby looses her legal protection (BAG 16 February 1983, AP BGB § 123 no. 22, mistake as to motive only). Under GREEK law the Supreme Court has held that a mistake of law is to be treated in the same way as a mistake of fact; similarly a mistake as to the kind of judicial act or its legal effect: AP 374/1974, NoB 1974.1364 and Full Bench of AP 3/1989, NoB 1990.606 II, 607 I). See also ITALIAN CC art. 1429(4); on FINNISH law, KKO 1960 II 47; on DANISH law, *Lynge Andersen* 251; on DUTCH law, *Asser-Hartkamp*, Verbintenissenrecht II, No.196; on PORTUGUESE law, *Ascensão* 107f.; *Fernandes* 125f. FRENCH, BELGIAN and LUXEMBOURG law allow relief for a mistake of law except where the agreement concerned is a compromise, CC arts. 2052 (2). In contrast, in ENGLISH and IRISH law have in the paste relief (either via mistake or via misrepresentation) when the mistake is purely one of law, though a mistake or misrepresentation as to "private rights" (e.g. the legal effect of a document) is different (for England, see *Chitty* §§ 5-004, 5-038 and 6-007; for Ireland, *Friel* 199). This rule is likely to change now that it has been held that a payment made under a mistake of law may be recovered: *Kleinwort Benson Ltd.* v. *Lincoln City Council* [1998] 3 W.L.R. 1095, H.L. SCOTS law seems to say that an error of law was not sufficient unless shared by both parties (*Dickson* v. *Halbert* (1854) 16 D 586; *Mercer* v. *Anstruther's Trustees* (1871) 9 M 618).

Article 4:103 applies to both mistakes as to the facts and mistakes as the law.

7.   *Cases in which one party takes the risk*

Some systems acknowledge explicitly that relief will not be given where one party has clearly undertaken the risk that the facts will not turn out to be as he hoped, or the court thinks that he should do so: e.g. the case of the bookseller who is unaware of the value of a book, when the purchaser/ collector does know it, which is discussed SCOTS law, see *Gloag* 438 and *Spook Erection (Northern) Ltd* v. *Kaye* 1990 SLT 676.

Perhaps the clearest statement of this is in DUTCH BW 6:228(2): annulment will not be given for an error for which, given the nature of the contract, common opinion or the circumstances of the case, the party in error should remain accountable. In FRENCH law relief error will not be given if the question of substantial quality was obviously aleatory: e.g if the relevant characteristic of the subject matter was explicitly stated not to be guaranteed: *Ghestin*, Formation, No. 59 et seq. It has been held that a contract for the sale of a picture "attributed to Fragonard" could not be annulled by the seller when it was later concluded by experts that the picture was indeed by that artist; the parties had both known it might or might not be genuine. Civ. 24 March 1987, D. 1987.488.

Under GERMAN law a party who bears a legal risk may not avoid the contract on account of a mistake with respect to that risk. Thus a surety may not avoid the contract of suretyship if it turns out that the debtor is in fact unable to pay, so that the surety will become liable to the creditor, even if the creditor knew of the debtor's inability: *Palandt (-Thomas)* before § 756, Rdn. 6; *Medicus* AT, Rdn. 780.

It is thought that other systems would reach similar results by other means; e.g. if one party knew or should have known that there was a risk that the subject matter would not have the quality he hoped, he has not made a mistake or the thing is not substantially different from what he expected. In

English law, the courts have also posed the question in terms of whether as a matter of construction the contract is dependant upon the facts assumed – see *Associated Japanese Bank (International) Ltd* v. *Crédit du Nord SA* [1989] 1 W.L.R. 255, Q.B. – which is rather the same question: see *Chitty* § 5-008 and *Smith,* Implied terms. In Scots law the contract will be upheld if the parties have contracted on the basis of a particular allocation of risk: *Pender-Small* v. *Kinloch's Trustees* 1917 SC 307.

In DANISH law it is said that the doctrine of implied conditions would not require the seller to point out to the buyer that the latter may not be able to resell the goods at a profit (*Gomard, Kontraktsret* 157). In NORDIC law generally it would not be contrary to good faith for one party to insist on the other respecting a contract which the latter entered knowing the risk he was taking.

Article 4.103(2)(b) is explicit that relief may not be given when one party assumed the risk of the mistake.

8. *Inexcusable error*

Relief on the ground of mistake is generally denied when the mistake was primarily the fault of the mistaken party. Thus in FRENCH, BELGIAN and LUXEMBOURG law the *erreur* must not be *inexcusable*: see for France, *Ghestin*, Formation, Nos. 522, 523; Belgium, Cass. 6 January 1944, Arr. Cass., 66; Cass. 28 June 1968, Arr. Cass., 1321; Cass. 10 April 1975, RCJB 1978, 198, note Coipel; Luxembourg, Cour 16 June 1970, Pasicrisie 21, p. 362; and see Note 7 above. In ENGLISH law it seems that relief will not be given either at common law or in equity to a party whose mistake was his own fault. In the equitable doctrine this is explicit: see *Solle* v. *Butcher* [1951] 1 K.B. 671, C.A.. At common law this is said to be also the case: see *Associated Japanese Bank (International) Ltd* v. *Crédit du Nord SA* [1989] 1 W.L.R. 255, Q.B. where Steyn J. referred to *McRae* v. *Commonwealth Disposals Commission* (1950) 84 C.L.R. 377, H. Ct. of Australia. SCOTS law also denies relief on the ground of uninduced error to a party at fault: see *Smith*, Short Commentary 820. In GREEK law rescission is permitted only if this is consonant with good faith (CC art. 144; *Balis*, No. 144); this might exclude rescission in the situation being being considered. In DUTCH law a mistake for which the party seeking relief was largely responsible would be treated as one for which he is accountable under BW art. 6:228(2), so that relief will be denied.

In NORDIC law the fault of the mistaken party is not an absolute bar to avoidance but is a factor taken into account by the court in deciding whether to grant a remedy.

In a minority of systems the fault of the mistaken party is irrelevant, e.g in AUSTRIAN law and in GERMAN law (RG 22 December 1905, RGZ 62, 201, 205). However it should be rembered that German law may require the mistaken party who avoids the contract to compensate the non-mistaken party, BGB § 122, above. In PORTUGUESE law avoidance may be permitted even if the error was inexcusable, but it has been suggested that in extreme cases avoidance might be prevented as being an abuse of right, *C.M. Pinto*, General Theory 511ff. Again, the mistaken party might incur pre-contractual responsibility, *ibid.*; *Ascensão* 110; *Fernandes* 131.

English and IRISH law also allow rescission for misrepresentation even though the party who was misled could have discovered the truth by taking reasonable steps: *Redgrave* v. *Hurd* (1880) 20 Ch.D. 1. However it has been argued that this rule may not apply to cases in which the incorrect information was given without negligence: *Treitel*, Contract 315-316.

9. *The effect on the contract*

In FRENCH, BELGIAN and LUXEMBOURG law the existence of a *vice de consentement,* or *lésion,* gives rise to relative rather than absolute nullity; i.e., only the party affected by the *vice* may invoke it. German law, BGB §§ 119-124; GREEK law, CC art. 140; ITALIAN law, CC arts. 1427, 1441; DUTCH law, BW art 3:49; and the NORDIC laws are similar in effect (except where the contract is modified under Contract Act § 36).

In ENGLISH law the situation is complicated by the fact that there are separate yet overlapping doctrines of common mistake at common law and in equity. The effect of an operative mistake at common law is that the supposed contract is void; in equity, however, a mistake merely makes the contract voidable at the option of either party. Misrepresentation also makes the contract voidable. One result is that a party who has a right to rescind on either ground may lose that right through affirmation, lapse of time and other bars to rescission (see *Treitel*, Contract 296-297, 349-356); another, in the case of mistake, that the court may impose terms on rescission (see note to Article 4:105).

10. *Damages for the mistaken party*

In many systems a party who has caused the other party's mistake by culpably (intentionally or negligently) giving incorrect information may be liable to the other party in delict: see further below, notes to Article 4:106

On mistake generally see *Kötz*, European Contract, ch. 10.

Article 4:104: Inaccuracy in Communication

An inaccuracy in the expression or transmission of a statement is to be treated as a mistake of the person which made or sent the statement and Article 4:103 applies.

COMMENT

A. *No Common Intention: Objective Interpretation Normal Rule*
It sometimes happens that because of an inaccuracy of expression in a communication, or an inaccuracy in its transmission, the communication does not express a party's true intention. For example, in an offer a party may write the price as "£10,000" in mistake for "£100,000". If the other party simply accepts this offer without noticing or pointing out the mistake, what should be the position should there later be a disagreement over the amount?

If the parties do not have a common intention (on which see Article 5:101, General Rule of Interpretation), a party is normally bound by the apparent meaning of what it says or does, because the other party will reasonably have taken the words or conduct at face value: see Article 5:101(2). So if the offeree does not know and has no reason to know that the offer contains a mistake, it may hold the mistaken party to the contract. Cf. Article 2:102, Intention.

B. *Inaccuracy in Communication May Not Prevent Parties' Having Common Intention*
If in fact the recipient of the offer knows what the offeror meant, and accepts the offer without comment because he too intended the price to be £100,000, the case is simply resolved under Article 5:101(1): the parties' common intention was that the price should be £100,000 and the contract is for that sum even if the other party later uses the inaccuracy as a pretext for avoiding the contract.

C. *Objective Rule Does Not Apply if Other Party Not Misled By Inaccuracy*
But even if the non-mistaken party did not intend to accept an offer at £100,000, if he knows that this is what was meant and simply accepts without pointing out the inaccuracy, he should not be able to take advantage of the inaccuracy. On the contrary, he should be bound to a contract at that price. Although a party is normally bound by the objective meaning of its words, the meaning that a reasonable person would give to them, this does not apply when the recipient of the words does not understand them in this sense but as they were in fact intended. By appearing to accept the offer without demur, he appears to be agreeing to what was meant and he is then bound by the apparent meaning of his conduct to the offeror. Thus a contract results on the terms actually intended by the non-mistaken party.

This is the effect of Article 5:101(2).

Illustration 1: A offers to sell B, another fur trader, hare skins at £1.00 per kg; this is a typing error for £1.00 per piece. Skins are usually sold by the piece and, as there are about six skins to the kilo, the price is absurdly low. B knows what

A meant as skins are never sold by the kilo, always by the piece, but nonetheless B purports to accept. He cannot hold A to supplying skins at £1.00 per kilo; instead there is a contract at £1.00 per piece.

D. *Party Knows of Inaccuracy but not What Was Intended*

It sometimes happens that a party knows there has been an inaccuracy but not what was meant. Nonetheless he simply accepts the offer or other communication without pointing the inaccuracy out. Then it would not be feasible to hold him to whatever the mistaken party actually meant. Nonetheless, provided the mistake is fundamental the mistaken party should be able to avoid the contract. Article 4:104 treats this a form of mistake so that the mistaken party can seek to avoid the contract in accordance with Article 4:103.

> *Illustration 2*: A and B have been negotiating for a lease of A's villa; A has been asking £1,300 per month, B has offered £800 per month. A writes to B offering to rent him the villa for £100 per month; this is a slip of the pen for £1,000. B realises that A must have made a mistake but does not know what it is. He writes back simply accepting. A may avoid the contract.

E. *Inaccuracy Should Have Been Known to Other Party*

Even if a party did not know that the other had made an inaccuracy in a communication, it should not necessarily be able to hold the mistaken party to the normal meaning of the words used.

If in the circumstances a reasonable person would not have interpreted the words in their usual meaning, but in the way in fact intended by the party making the communication, then under Article 5:101(2) the other party will be held to this interpretation.

> *Illustration 3*: As Illustration 1 above but it is not proved that B knew of the mistake. If, given the custom in the trade and the price offered, the meaning of A's communication should have been known to any reasonable person in the same circumstances, B cannot hold A to the apparent contract and is bound to buy at £1 per piece.

If it is not clear what the intended meaning was, the mistaken party may again seek to avoid the contract under Article 4:103.

F. *Mistake Caused by Other Party*

Sometimes a party makes a mistake in apparently agreeing to something which it does not intend because of the conduct of the non-mistaken party. The non-mistaken party cannot hold the mistaken party to the apparent agreement if it should have realised that the other might be agreeing to something it did not intend.

> *Illustration 4*: A books a package holiday with B Company. B offers various tours as well as the flight and hotel accommodation. A does not want these tours

as they are very expensive, but the booking form used by B is very hard to follow and by mistake A checks a box indicating that she wants all the tours. B cannot hold A to this.

G. *Fault of Mistaken Party*
Under Article 4:103, Mistakes as to facts or law, relief is denied to a party if its mistake was inexcusable. This is justified by the need for security in transactions; the
other party should not be put to the burden of investigating all the many possible misapprehensions that the other party might be labouring under; it should at least be able
to ignore any which could only arise through gross carelessness. Usually mistakes in
communication of the kind discussed above are careless, but this does not necessarily mean that they are inexcusable. In any event the concept of "inexcusable" is a relative one. When the mistake is not about the facts or law but is a problem of the accu-
racy of the communication, it is much less burdensome to ask the other party just to
check any apparent statement which it has reason to think might be a mistake, even
when the mistake was due to the mistaken party's carelessness. It has only to ask,
"You do mean what you say on page 2?", or "You are aware of clause x?" Thus the
fact that the mistaken party was seriously at fault is not necessarily a bar to relief.

H. *Seriousness*
It is necessary to restrict relief under Article 4:103 to mistakes which make the contract fundamentally different. To allow relief for lesser mistakes would undermine
the security of transactions. This applies equally to relief where there has been an
inaccuracy in communication.

I. *Mistake in Communication Treated as Mistake of Sender*
It sometimes happens that a mistake occurs in the transmission of a communication
sent via a third party, such a telegraph company, without any fault on the part of the
sender. Nonetheless the sender, having chosen that form of communication must
bear the risk. Under these Principles the situation is treated just as if the mistake had
been caused by the sender itself, except in one situation. This is where the need for
a notice has been caused by the non-performance of the recipient. Here the dispatch
principle applies, see Article 1:303(4).

NOTES

All the systems by one means or another give relief when one party has made a mistake as to the terms
of the contract he is making; but the conditions under which relief will be given differ markedly.

If the other party makes the same mistake, so that in fact they intend the same thing, or if the
other party spots the mistake and knows what was meant, it is generally accepted that the contract
stands on the terms actually intended; *falsa demonstratio non nocet*. This is discussed in the Note to
Article 5:101, and, on English and Irish law, also below. It is in the case in which the other party did
not know of the mistake that the differences between the systems appear.

In some systems, the party who has made the mistake may avoid the contract even though the
other party did not know and had no reason to know of the mistake. For example, in GERMAN law
BGB § 119(1) covers cases of mistakes in the act or declaration, so that a slip of the tongue may
entitle the mistaken party to avoid the contract. (Errors in the transmission of a declaration to the

other party are treated similarly, § 120.) There is no requirement that the other party knew or ought to have known of the mistake. Similarly, in FRENCH, BELGIAN and LUXEMBOURG law it is sometimes said that a mistake in an offer or acceptance (often referred to as *erreur matérielle*) will give rise to an *erreur obstacle* which prevents the formation of a valid contract, though this concept is not mentioned in the CC. But it usually results only in the relative nullity of the contract (e.g. French Com 15 February 1961, B.IV no.19; *Ghestin* No. 495). In practice the jurisprudence usually gives relief under the normal conditions for mistake (see e.g. Civ. 15 April 1980, D. 1981 IR 314 and cases cited in *Nicholas* 99-100). In French law the fact that a mistake has been made need not be known to the other party, but Belgian caselaw has tended to apply the principle of legitimate confidence and to refuse relief where the other party did not know and had no reason to know of the mistake (*Kruithof & Bocken,* TPR 1994, p.325 No. 108). In PORTUGUESE law the same conditions apply as to errors in general; that is the error must be determining for the mistaken party and this must have been apparent to the other party, CC arts. 247, 250(1).

In contrast, several systems, though applying the usual rules of mistake to this situation, limit mistake generally to cases in which the other party knew or should have known of the mistake (or caused it or shared it, which are not relevant here): e.g. DUTCH BW art 3:35; GREEK CC art. 146; ITALIAN CC art. 1433; NORDIC Contract Acts § 32, which simply provides that if a message, because of a misprint or other error, differs from what the sender intended, the message does not bind the sender if the recipient knew or ought to have known of the misprint or error. § 32(2) provides that if a message sent by telegram or through a third party is garbled in the transmission, the sender will not be bound by what the message appears to say if, without undue delay after discovering the distortion, he notifies the addressee. If he does not do so, the addressee may rely on what in good faith he understood the message to say. See also AUSTRIAN ABGB § 871, which also allows relief if the error is notified promptly by the mistaken party.

ENGLISH and IRISH law, by a different route again, produce a similar outcome. Mistakes as to the terms of the contract (bidding for the wrong item or expressing the price wrongly, for example) are also treated under the rubric of mistake, but a quite different type of mistake which may "negative" (prevent there being) consent – in other words, prevent there being offer and acceptance. And offers, acceptances and other declarations are interpreted objectively – that is, a party is bound by what he reasonably appears to be saying. Thus if one party made a mistake but the other had no reason to know it, no relief will be given. The only case in which relief will be given is the one where the mistake was known to the other party (e.g. *Hartog* v. *Colin & Shields* [1939] 3 All E.R. 566, Q.B.), or possibly where the other party suspected a mistake and deliberately distracted the mistaken party's attention from the matter (cf *Commission for New Towns* v. *Cooper (GB) Ltd* [1995] 2 All E.R. 929, C.A.). (It is not clear whether the contract is void or whether the non-mistaken party simply cannot hold the mistaken party to what he appeared to say, but is bound by what the mistaken party (as the non-mistaken party knew) actually meant: see *Chitty* § 5-024; *Treitel*, Contract 285-286.) SCOTTISH law appears to be broadly similar: see *McCallum* v. *Soudan* 1989 SLT 523; *Royal Bank of Scotland* v. *Purvis* 1990 SLT 262; *Angus* v. *Bryden* 1992 SLT 884.

The case where one party has made a mistake as to the terms is the only one in which the Common Law allows relief where only one party has made a mistake. A unilateral mistake which is to the facts and which was not induced by misrepresentation gives no remedy: *Smith* v. *Hughes* (1871) L.R. 6 Q.B. 597. This can produce nice distinctions as to whether the mistake was about, for example, the amount of work to be done or the total price to be charged, see *Imperial Glass Ltd.* v. *Consolidated Supplies Ltd* (1960) 22 D.L.R. (2d) 759 (C.A., British Columbia). Similar distinctions appear in other systems: thus Austrian law has special rules for so-called *Kalkulationsirrtum*. A mistake in stating the price, e.g. in a building contract, will be a mistake of expression, but a mistake in the underlying calculation will only be one of motive (OGH 6 November 1986, WBl 1987, 62; 26 January 1988, JBl 1988, 714). However if the basis of calculation has been disclosed to the other party and the latter has agreed that the contract is on this basis, relief may be given as for an error of expression. These distinctions need not be made under the Principles, since under Article 4:104 errors in expression are treated in the same way as errors as to facts or law.

Article 4:105: Adaptation of Contract

(1) If a party is entitled to avoid the contract for mistake but the other party indicates that it is willing to perform, or actually does perform, the contract as it was understood by the party entitled to avoid it, the contract is to be treated as if it had been concluded as the that party understood it. The other party must indicate its willingness to perform, or render such performance, promptly after being informed of the manner in which the party entitled to avoid it understood the contract and before that party acts in reliance on any notice of avoidance.

(2) After such indication or performance the right to avoid is lost and any earlier notice of avoidance is ineffective.

(3) Where both parties have made the same mistake, the court may at the request of either party bring the contract into accordance with what might reasonably have been agreed had the mistake not occurred.

COMMENT

A. *Mistake Which Was or Should Have Been Known to Other Party*
The most obvious application of this Article is when a party is entitled to avoid a contract because there was an error in communication and therefore a relevant mistake under Article 4:104, but the non-mistaken party did not know what the mistake was. If when it is told what the mistake was it offers to perform according to what the mistaken party actually intended, the latter's right to avoidance should be lost.

The Article may also apply to mistakes as to facts or law under Article 4:103.

Illustration 1: A flooring contractor employed to floor a large building makes a fundamental mistake over the amount of work needed. This mistake should have been known to the other party so the contractor has the right to avoid the contract. The employer offers to release the contractor from the extra work without any reduction in the payment. The contractor cannot avoid the contract.

B. *Shared Mistake*
In cases in which the contract may be avoided under Article 4:103 because both parties have made the same mistake, Article 4:105(1) applies. Thus if one party seems to stand to benefit from the mistake and the other to lose, the first may declare itself willing to perform in the way the contract was originally understood. But if it is not clear that one stands to lose more than the other, or the gaining party is not prepared to declare itself ready to perform the contract as it was originally understood, it may be more appropriate to adjust the contract than simply to avoid it. In this case Article 4:105(3) permits either party to apply to the court for the contract to be adjusted in such a way as to reflect what might have been agreed had the mistake not occurred.

Illustration 2: The facts are as in Illustration 1 except that both parties were mistaken as to the amount of work needed. The other party may declare itself ready to release the contractor from the extra work under Article 4:105(1).

Alternatively, either party may request the court to adapt the contract under Article 4:105(3). In such a case the court might apply the contract rates to the additional work, with appropriate adjustments for the volume of work involved.

Sometimes it will be clear that, but for the mistake, the parties would not have entered the contract. In this case adaptation will not be appropriate.

Illustration 3: A sells a painting, which the parties think is by a little known artist, to B for £500. It is then discovered that the painting is by a very well known artist and is worth £50,000. B could not possibly have paid £50,000. A may avoid the contract; it should not be adapted so that B has to pay A the true value of the painting.

Equally a subsequent change in one party's position may make adaptation inappropriate.

Illustration 4: The parties to a building contract were both mistaken in thinking that it would involve less work than is actually the case. Had the true quantity of work been known, the builder would have agreed to do all the work at the same unit prices as in the contract, but subsequently it has taken on other work and cannot do the extra work on this contract. Adaptation is not appropriate and the contract is avoided.

C. *Damages after Adaptation of Contract*
The adaptation of the contract by the other party or by the court under this Article does not preclude the mistaken party claiming damages under Article 4:117 if it has suffered loss which is not compensated by the adaptation of the contract.

NOTES

ITALIAN CC art. 1432 has a provision parallel to Article 4:105(1). GERMAN law would reach the same result but by invoking the principle of fair dealing: see in *Münchener Kommentar (-Kramer)* I § 119 No. 129; BGH 22 February 1995, VersR 1995, p.648. PORTUGUESE CC art. 248 is broadly similar in approach to Article 4:105 (1) and (2).

In German, Portuguese and SPANISH law a contract entered under a shared mistake may be adapted under the principle of the *clausula rebus sic stantibus* (see further above, Note 1, and Notes to Article 6:111); again, the doctrine of mistake would not be invoked.

In ENGLISH and IRISH law the court has no powers of adaptation except in one case. If a contract is held to be voidable in equity for fundamental mistake, the court may impose terms upon the party seeking rescission: *Solle v. Butcher* [1950] 1 K.B. 671, C.A.

FRENCH law does not permit adaptation of the contract in case of error; but in LUXEMBOURG, CC art. 1118 on *Lésion* has been amended (see Note to Article 4:109) and now it would be possible for the victim of a mistake which has resulted in him having *"des obligations lésionnaires"* to demand that they be reduced by the court.

Some systems go rather further than Article 4:105. DUTCH BW art 6:230(2) gives the court a general power, at the request of either party, to modify the contract instead of annulling it (see also art 3:53). GREEK doctrine has suggested that the judge may have the same power: *Balis* No. 43; *Simantiras* No. 737. In NORDIC law the court may adapt the contract on the basis of the doctrine of failed assumptions or under the general clause under Contracts Act § 36, but only at the request of the mistaken party.

AUSTRIAN ABGB § 872 allows claims for adaptation of the contract when there has been non-essential error, to bring the contract into line with what would have been agreed had the mistake not occurred.

Article 4:106: Incorrect Information

A party which has concluded a contract relying on incorrect information given it by the other party may recover damages in accordance with Article 4:117(2) and (3) even if the information does not give rise to a fundamental mistake under Article 4:103, unless the party which gave the information had reason to believe that the information was correct.

COMMENT

A. *Incorrect Information Given Without Fraud*
A party which gives information to the other during the course of negotiations may in some circumstances be treated as promising that what it says is true, see Article 6:101, Statements giving rise to Contractual Obligations. But under that Article not all statements of fact are treated as promises.

Even if there is no promise that the fact stated is true, a party should not necessarily be expected to take the risk of the information given by the other party being incorrect. If the incorrect information leads it to make a fundamental mistake, it will have a right to avoid the contract under Article 4:103 and to recover damages under Article 4:117. In cases of fraud damages could be recovered under Article 4:107. But even if the matter is not fundamental, and even where the party giving the incorrect information was not fraudulent, the party which has been misled should have a remedy by way of damages if the other party has given it incorrect information and was careless in so doing.

B. *Who Should Bear the Risk of Information Being Incorrect?*
Where there is no fraud, the incorrect information is in a sense an accident which befalls the making of the contract. In some cases there was no reason for either party to know that the information was incorrect. In those circumstances, even if one party has given the information to the other, it seems fair to leave the loss caused where it falls (unless it makes the contract fundamentally different, in which case the contract may be avoided under Article 4:103 on the basis of shared fundamental mistake). If, on the other hand, the party which has given the information cannot show that it had reasonable grounds for believing that it was true, then the party which has been misled should have a remedy. Thus Article 4:106 provides for damages where incorrect information has been given but subject to the qualification in the concluding phrase.

The remedy will apply even if the incorrect information was not the only or principal reason the party which was misled entered the contract. However the damages should compensate only for the loss which has been caused by the incorrect information.

C. *Party Could Have Discovered Truth*

Even when the party giving the information has no reasonable grounds for believing what it said, it would not be appropriate to give damages if, in the circumstances, it was unreasonable for the party given the information not to check it and the check would have revealed whether or not it was accurate.

In many cases it is perfectly reasonable for a party to accept what it is told without further enquiry. But sometimes the information is of such importance that it is unreasonable not to check it. If it fails to do so, and a check would have shown that the information was incorrect, and relatively its failure to check was as much a cause as that of the other party in giving the information, a remedy may be denied. It should bear some the risk of its unreasonable failure to safeguard its interests. The effect of this Article combined with Article 4:117 is that the party may recover damages but these will be reduced to take account of its own failure to safeguard its own interests.

> *Illustration 1*: E, an elderly lawyer who wishes to retire, invites F to buy his practice. He tells F that the income of the practice is £50,000 per year. It is normal for the buyer of such a practice to have the account books checked very carefully before deciding to purchase. E makes the books available. In fact, as an examination of the accounts would have shown, the practice has suddenly become much less valuable, though E does not know this because, due to illness, he has not been paying attention to the figures. F buys the practice without checking the accounts. It is so unreasonable to buy a practice without checking the accounts that F's damages will be reduced in accordance with Articles 4:117(3) and 9:504.

In a case where the error was predominantly caused by the party seeking damages, the damages might be reduced to nil.

D. *Information Given by the Other Party*

Article 4:106 applies only to incorrect information given by the other party to the contract. A party which has been misled by information provided by a third party cannot avoid the contract, unless the third party was acting as agent of the other party or the other party knew that the incorrect information had been given (see Article 4:111); or the other party to the contract passed on the information in a way that showed it was adopting it.

> *Illustration 2*: G leased a machine from H, relying on a statement made by J, a friend who has a similar machine, that its fuel consumption was 5 litres per hour. In fact the fuel consumption was much higher. G may not recover damages from H.

> *Illustration 3*: K sold a used car to L; K had himself bought it used from a previous owner who had told K that the car had been fitted with a re-built engine. K told L: "As the previous owner told me, the car has a re-built engine". In fact the engine had not been changed, as K should have known from its oil consumption. L may avoid the contract.

However, if the party who was given the information was dealing with a profession-al supplier and the information was given by someone earlier in the business chain (e.g. a party buys goods from a retailer relying on information from the manufac-turer), the party will have a remedy for non-performance under Article 6:101, Statements giving rise to Contractual Obligations, paragraph (3).

E. *Remedies*

The party which has been misled by incorrect information is entitled to compensa-tion for the loss which the incorrect information has caused it. As the other party did not promise that the information was correct, the injured party is not entitled to dam-ages based on the position it would have been in had the information been correct. It is only entitled to compensation for the difference between the position it is in now and the position it would have been in had it known the truth.

> *Illustration 4*: A sells B a used car, telling B that the car has done only 50,000 kms. B agrees to pay FF100,000 for the car, although the market price for that model car with 50,000 kms on the clock is FF105,000. In fact the car has done 150,000 kms and is worth only FF85,000. B may recover damages of FF15,000.

It is only the loss caused by the incorrect information for which damages may be claimed. The injured party cannot recover compensation based on the position it might have been in had it been entitled to avoid the contract for mistake.

> *Illustration 5*: The facts are as above except that she has agreed to pay FF110,000 whereas the market value of a car with 50,000 kms on it is FF95,000. The car is actually worth FF85,000 as before. B may recover only FF10,000.

Where the incorrect information causes the party which was given the information loss beyond the difference in value between what it gave and what it received (this further loss is sometimes called "consequential" loss), it may recover this also.

> *Illustration 6*: C employs D, a contractor, to lay a road across a field. C tells D that the ground all over the site has been investigated and is quite firm. In fact part of it is a quagmire. D discovers this when one of its machines sinks into it. Not only does the soft ground make the job much more expensive but D has to pay FF100,000 to have its machine recovered. It may recover the FF 100,000.

The recovery of consequential loss is subject to the normal rules on causation and to the rule on foreseeability of damages, see Article 4:117(3).

F. *Exclusion or Restriction of Remedies*

It is not uncommon to find contractual clauses purporting to exclude or restrict a party's remedies for incorrect information. Such clauses may in some circumstances be justified but can also operate unfairly, just like clauses excluding or limiting reme-dies for non-performance. Therefore Article 4:118(2) provides that such a clause will only be effective if it is not contrary to good faith and fair dealing. Compare Article 8:109, Term restricting or excluding liability, which applies to non-performance.

G. *Relation to National Law*

Under the legal systems of some Member States liability for incorrect information may be regarded as delictual rather than contractual. However, if the parties have agreed that their contract should be governed by the Principles, or if an arbitrator decides to apply the Principles to a contract stated to be "subject to general principles of contract law", it is highly desirable that all the rules which apply to the contract, even if the national system does not designate them as contractual, should be derived from the same source. The rules laid down by the European Principles should be regarded as superseding the national law which would otherwise apply on the relevant facts, so far as courts and arbitrators are permitted by their conflicts rules to achieve this result. Thus the claim on the basis of incorrect information should be governed by the Principles.

NOTE

The majority of systems will allow a party who has entered a contract on the basis of incorrect information supplied by the other party to recover damages from the other if the other was at fault, even though there was no fraud involved. For example FRENCH law grants damages on the basis of pre-contractual liability: e.g. Orléans 21 January 1931, DH 1931. 172; Civ. 29 November 1968, Gaz.Pal. 1969 January 63. In theory the liability is delictual rather than contractual. The measure of damages is the ordinary one for delictual responsibility, and is within the *pouvoir souverain* of the trial judge. AUSTRIAN law at one time allowed damages only in cases of fraud but now awards damages for *culpa in contrahendo*; the party is to be placed in the position he would have been in had the incorrect information not been given. See also GREEK CC arts 197-198 and 914; AP 1505/1988, NoB 1990.62; in ITALY, *Mengoni*, Pre-contractual responsibility and *Castronovo*, Obbligazione 147, 160ff; DUTCH BW art 6:162; SPANISH CC arts 7.1 and 1258; and SWEDEN, Sup.Ct. NJA 1989 p.156 (but in Finland *culpa in contrahendo* has little importance as the statement will normally be treated as a contractual promise, cf. article 6:101).

In GERMAN law the remedies would be based on the principle of *culpa in contrahendo*. The aggrieved party should be restored to the position he would have been in had he not made the contract. The aggrieved party may seek rescission of the contract (e.g. BGH 31 January 1962, NJW 1962, 1196; BGH 27 February 1974, NJW 1974, 849, 851; BGH 24 May 1993, NJW 1993, 2107), or claim damages to the extent of the reliance interest (e.g. BGH 28 March 1990, WM 1990, 1035; BGH 14 March 1991, BGHZ 114, 94; BGH 19 December 1997, NJW 1998, 898 (899). If the aggreived party can show that, had it not been given the incorrect information, it would have contracted with a different party, the damages may include profit that would have made on such a contract (BGH 2 March 1988, NJW 1988, 2236).

In ENGLISH and IRISH law the victim of a pure mistake cannot recover damages; but the victim of a mistake which was induced by a misrepresentation may recover damages if the person who gave the incorrect information had no reasonable grounds for believing what he said to be true: English Misrepresentation Act 1967, s.2(1), Irish Sale and Supply of Goods Act 1980, s.45(1). It may also be possible for the victim to sue on the basis of liability in tort for negligent misrepresentation, under the doctrine of *Hedley Byrne & Co Ltd* v. *Heller & Partners Ltd* [1963] A.C. 465, H.L.; and for Ireland, *Bank of Ireland* v. *Smith* [1966] I.R. 646 and, generally, *McMahon & Binchy* 150 ff.. However this requires a "special relationship" between the parties and, while there may be such a relationship between contracting parties (as *Esso Petroleum Co Ltd* v. *Mardon* [1976] Q.B. 801, C.A.) this will not always be the case: see *Howard Marine & Dredging Co Ltd* v. *A Ogden & Sons Ltd* [1978] Q.B. 574, CA. Damages cannot usually be recovered if the misrepresentor acted without negligence; but exceptionally, if an English court exercises its discretion under Misrepresentation Act 1967, s.2(2) to refuse to allow rescission on the ground of an innocent, non-negligent, misrepresentation, it may give damages instead of rescission. See also Irish Sale and Supply of Goods Act 1980, ss. 44, 45(2).

In SCOTLAND negligent misrepresentation may give rise to a delictual damages claim: Law Reform (Miscellaneous Provisions) Act 1985, s.10.

Article 4:107: Fraud

(1)   A party may avoid a contract when it has been led to conclude it by the other party's fraudulent representation, whether by words or conduct, or fraudulent non-disclosure of any information which in accordance with good faith and fair dealing it should have disclosed.

(2)   A party's representation or non-disclosure is fraudulent if it was intended to deceive.

(3)   In determining whether good faith and fair dealing required that a party disclose particular information, regard should be had to all the circumstances, including:

(a)   whether the party had special expertise;

(b)   the cost to it of acquiring the relevant information;

(c)   whether the other party could reasonably acquire the information for itself; and

(d)   the apparent importance of the information to the other party.

COMMENT

A. *Fraud*

A party which has been given incorrect information by the other party should have the right to avoid the contract if the second party was fraudulent, i.e.

(i)   it either knew that the information given was incorrect, or was reckless in that it knew that it did not know whether it was correct or not,
     and

(ii) it intended to deceive, or was reckless as to deceiving, the first party.

Under these conditions there is no reason to protect any interest the fraudulent party may have in upholding the contract; nor is the risk of being deliberately or recklessly misled one that a party should be expected to bear.

B. *Nature of Representation*

A representation is a definite statement that something is the case. It does not matter whether the fraudulent statement is as to facts or law.

The statement must be as to matters existing at the time of the contract. A statement that a party intends to do something does not become a false representation with Article 4:107 simply because the party changes its mind. For such a change of mind to give rise to a remedy, it will have to be shown that the party's statement of intention amounted to a contractual promise. However, if a party states that it holds an intention which in fact it does not hold, it is making a false representation within this Article.

Statements which are obviously mere sales talk are not representations within this Article.

Illustration 1: A leases a computer to B. A casually remarks that the computer is "the best of its size on the market". In fact a more powerful machine of similar size is available. As buyers may disagree over whether a more powerful machine is necessarily "better", B does not have a remedy.

A statement of opinion does not normally amount to a representation of fact or law. The fact that the statement is expressed as an opinion should warn the other party that it may or may not be accurate. However, a statement that a party thinks something which in fact it does not think will be a false statement of fact.

Illustration 2: C rents a country cottage to D, telling D that in C's opinion the cottage is a very quiet spot. In fact C knows that it is under the flight path of the nearest airport and at certain times is very noisy. C has made a fraudulent misrepresentation.

C. *Form of the Misrepresentation*
It does not matter whether the incorrect information is given by words or takes the form of misleading conduct.

Illustration 3: A leases a house to B. The house suffers severely from damp but just before leasing it A has had the walls repainted to conceal the damp, which B therefore does not notice. B may avoid the contract.

It is not fraud within these Principles, however, to fail to point out some fact of which the other party is ignorant if there was no intention of deception. Such conduct may fall within Articles 4:103 (Mistake as to Facts or Law).

D. *Reliance*
The party which has been given incorrect information will not have a remedy unless it has relied on the information in deciding to enter the contract.

Illustration 4: A sells a used car to B after turning back the odometer so that it shows that the car has done much less than the distance the car has been driven. However B never looks at the odometer until after she has bought the car. B has no remedy for fraud.

E. *Non-disclosure*
A party should not normally be permitted to remain silent on some point which might influence the other party's decision on whether or not to enter the contract with the deliberate intention of deceiving the other. Unless there is a good reason for allowing the party to remain silent, silence is incompatible with good faith and will entitle the other party to avoid the contract under this Article.

Often a party to whom a fundamental fact has not been disclosed will be entitled to avoid the contract for mistake under Article 4:103. It may also recover damages under Article 4:117. Otherwise there is no general duty to point out to the other party possibly disadvantageous facts, but still a party should not normally be entitled to keep quiet with the intention of deceiving the other party.

F. *Non-discosure consistent with good faith and fair dealing.*

The duty to disclose is part of a general notion of good faith and fair dealing and may not always require a party to point out facts of which it knows the other to be ignorant. For example, while a professional party will often be required by good faith and fair dealing to disclose information about the property or services it is to supply under the contract, the same may well not be true of a non-professional party (subparagraph (3) (a)).

Further, a party may fairly be expected to provide information about the performance it is undertaking, but is less likely to be required to do so about the performance the other party is to make. The latter is normally expected to know or find out relevant facts about its own performance, subparagaph (c). In particular there may not be any obligation to disclose information which concerns the other party's performance and which the informed party had to make a great investment in order to acquire: see subparagraph (b) and Comment D to Article 4:103, above.

The list in Article 4:107(3) is not intended to be exhaustive.

G. *Remedies*

Fraud gives the party which has been misled the right to avoid the contract, provided it gives notice within a reasonable time (see Article 4:113). Where the fraud relates to an individual term of the contract, the party may be able to avoid the contract partially, see Article 4:116. In addition to or instead of avoiding the contract it may recover damages, see Article 4:117. These will be limited to recovery of the amount it is out-of-pocket, since the other party did not give a contractual undertaking that what it said was true.

> *Illustration 5*: C, an art dealer, sells a picture to D stating that in his opinion, but not undertaking that, it is by Gainsborough. D pays £5,000 for the picture. D later discovers that it is not by Gainsborough but is by a lesser known artist, as C knew perfectly well. It is worth only £1,000. If it had been by Gainsborough it would have been worth £9,000. If D decides to keep the picture he may recover damages limited to £4,000.

H. *Incorrect Information Amounts to Non-performance*

In some cases the giving of incorrect information may amount to a non-performance of the contract, see Article 6:101. In this case the party misled will have the usual remedies for non-performance.

> *Illustration 6*: As in 5 but C states categorically that the picture is by Gainsborough. B may obtain remedies for non-performance which may include damages of £8,000.

H. *Remedies Cannot Be Excluded*

Fraud can never be justifiable and therefore the remedies for it cannot be excluded or restricted: see Article 4:118(1).

NOTES

1. *Fraud need not be as to an important matter*

   Fraud is a situation in which one party has been led into a mistake by the trickery of the other. Almost all the systems allow avoidance more readily than for a mere mistake. Thus in most systems it is not necessary to show that the fraud was as to an important matter. GERMAN BGB § 123 allows avoidance for every kind of fraud (see *Flume* AT II, § 29 2, p.543; *Münchener Kommentar (-Kramer)*, § 123 BGB, Rn.9, Rn.5, note 10); similarly, AUSTRIAN ABGB § 870); GREEK CC art. 147, and see AP 249/1976, NoB 1976.785; DUTCH BW art 3:44. The same rule is applied in NORDIC law under Contracts Acts § 30; and in ENGLISH and IRISH law the victim of any fraudulent statement is entitled to rescission provided it influenced in any way his decision to enter the contract (see, for England, *Chitty* § 6-019; and, for Ireland, *Friel* 226).

   The FRENCH, BELGIAN and LUXEMBOURG CC Arts.1116 refer to *manoeuvres* without which the other party would not have contracted. It is clear that a contract may be set aside when fraud has produced a mistake without having to show that the mistake went to the substance of the subject-matter. Traditionally, however, a distinction was drawn between *dol principal* (without which the victim would never have entered the contract at all) and *dol incident*, where the victim would have entered the contract but on different terms; avoidance was allowed only for *dol principal*, damages only being awarded for *dol incident*. This distinction is still applied in Belgian and ITALIAN law, but the distinction is not always followed by modern French courts; see however Com. 2 May 1984, JCP 1984.IV.218; also Com. 18 October 1994; D.95.180 note C. Atias. SPANISH CC art. 1270 provides that an incidental deception gives only a right to damages.

2. *Sales talk and opinion*

   Most systems do require that any incorrect statement be more than sales talk or *dolus bonus* (on which see *Ghestin*, Formation, No. 564); but increasingly consumer protection laws require that any factual information be correct (e.g. FRENCH Code de la Consommation, art. L. 121-1, see *Malaurie & Aynès*, Obligations § 414; BELGIAN Trade Practices and Consumer Protection Act of 14 July 1991, art. 24. In PORTUGAL it has been argued that the concept of *dolus bonus* does not apply in consumer transactions, *Almeida*, Consumer law 182; contra, *Ascensão*, 139ff.). In any event, what appears mere advertisement may constitute fraud if it contains factual elements which can be verified (e.g "a good price" that is in reality higher than other offers): see, in GERMAN law, OLG Saarbrücken, 7 October 1980, OLGZ 1981, 248; OLG Frankfurt, 12 May 1982, DAR 1982, 294; as to DANISH law, *Lynge Andersen* 212; in GREEK law, *Georgiadis/Stathopoulos*, AK 147 nos. 4, 7; as to LUXEMBOURG, see Cour 17 October 1919, Pasicrisie 11, p.190. ITALIAN law oscillates between the ideas that the statement should be one that would influence the normal person (e.g. Cass. 28 October 1993, n.10718, in Foro it., Rep., 1993, Contratto in genere, n. 428) and that it suffices that it influenced the particular plaintiff (e.g. Cass. 29 Aug. 1991, n. 9227, in Foro it., Rep., 1992, Contratto in genere, n.346); see *Bianca*, Il contratto 626ff. In ENGLISH, IRISH and SCOTS law the statement must be one of fact, rather than opinion; but it is accepted that a statement of opinion may carry the implication that the speaker knows facts to justify the opinion, and that a statement of an opinion which the speaker does not actually hold is itself a false statement of fact. See for England, *Chitty* §§ 6-004 - 6-006; and, for Ireland, *Friel* 213.

3. *Reliance*

   The systems also require that the party seeking to avoid the contract was actually influenced by the fraud. In some systems, the burden of proving reliance is on the party seeking avoidance (e.g. GERMAN and GREEK law); in others, once it is proved that an incorrect statement was made deliberately, it is presumed that the statement influenced the party to whom it was made: e.g., for ENGLISH law, *Chitty* § 6-019; for IRELAND, *Smith* v. *Lynn* [1954] 85 ILTR 737; and for NORDIC law, Contract Acts § 30(2).

4. *Dishonesty*

   It is the deliberate nature of the fraud which justifies the ready grant of avoidance, and the systems agree that the test of fraud is dishonesty, the intention to trick the other party: e.g. FRENCH Req. 27 January 1874, DP 1874.1.452; 3 January 1900, S. 1901.1.321 note Wahl; Civ.1, 12 November

1987, D.1987, IR.236; B.I no.293; NORDIC law, *Telaranta*, Sopimusoikeus 329-330); SPANISH CC art. 1269. In GERMAN law the party must have known that what he said was untrue or have turned a blind eye to the truth: BGH 16 March 1977, NJW 1977, 1055, 1056; cf BGH 21 January 1975, BGHZ 63, 382, 388. He must also have acted intentionally, that is, with the aim of influencing the other party or knowing that the trickery might influence him: BHG 28 April 1971, LM Nr. 42 zu § 123 BGB; but it is not necessary that he intended to cause loss to the other or to gain himself from the fraud: *Oertmann* § 123 B 1 b; BHG 14 July 1954, LM Nr. 9 zu § 123. AUSTRIAN law, GREEK law (see AP 249/1976), PORTUGUESE law (see *C.M. Pinto*, General Theory 520) and ITALIAN law (*Bianca*, Il contratto 626; *Sacco(-De Nova)* 443) law are similar.

5. *Non-disclosure*

A major difference between the systems is that in most of the continental systems, there can be fraud when a party deliberately does not point out some relevant fact to the other party, who is ignorant of it. In FRENCH, BELGIAN and LUXEMBOURG law *manoeuvres* may cover any kind of dishonest conduct; and, though traditionally merely acquiescing in the other party's self-deception was not fraud, it is now often held that there was a duty to disclose information and a party who deliberately keeps silent is guilty of *dol par réticence*: e.g. for France: Civ. 2 October 1974, D.1974, IR 252; Civ.1, 12 November 1987, B.I no. 293, and see *Malaurie and Aynès*, Obligations, no. 415; for Luxembourg, Tribunal Luxembourg, 24 June 1959, Pasicrisie 17, p.495; for Belgium, see Cass. 8 June 1978, RCJB 1979, 525 note J.P. Masson. The factors taken into account in deciding whether there is a duty to disclose in Belgian law are broadly simililar to those listed in Article 4:107(3): see *Kruithof & Bocken*, TPR 1994, No. 75 ff.; *Freriks*.

In GERMAN law, keeping silent may amount to fraud under BGB § 123 when there was a duty to disclose. There is no general duty, but there is one where the other party relies on the knowledge or expertise of its contracting partner or where there is already a relationship based on mutual trust and good faith (*Münchener Kommentar (-Kramer)* I § 123, nos. 15, 16.) There is a rich case law, e.g. the seller of a used car was held to be under a duty to tell the buyer that the car had been in a serious accident which had caused permanent damage to the chassis: BGH 8 January 1959, BGHZ 29, 148, 150.; an estate agent had to disclose his suspicion that a house suffered from rot (OLG Celle, 6 November 1970, MDR 1971, 392). There are similar duties to disclose in AUSTRIAN law; GREEK law, see CC art.147; ITALIAN law, CC art. 1439; DUTCH law, see BW art.3:49 and *Vranken*; PORTUGUESE law, see CC art. 253; and NORDIC law, where Contract Acts § 30 may apply when a party in bad faith fails to reveal a fact, and the Sale of Goods Act in force in Finland and Sweden may make a seller who has sold "as is" nonetheless liable for non-conformity if he failed to fulfil his duty of disclosure.

ENGLISH, IRISH and SCOTS law, in contrast, do not recognise any general duty of disclosure, even when the party knows that the other party is ignorant of a critical fact and would not contract if he knew the truth: *Smith* v. *Hughes* (1871) L.R. 6 QB 597, Q.B. There is a duty to disclose only if the contract is one of a very limited number of contracts *uberrimae fidei* (insurance contracts are the most important example); or if there is a confidential relationship between the parties: *Tate* v. *Williamson* (1866) L.R. 2 Ch.App. 55. For English law see *Chitty* §§ 6-087 - 6-098; on Irish law, *Friel* 217; on Scots law, *Gloag* 480. Thus there is fraud only if a party has made a positive representation by words or conduct. However, conduct may carry an implication of fact and, if the implication is misleading, the party must correct the impression it creates. Thus in the Irish case of *Gill* v. *McDowell* [1903] 2 I.R. 295, K.B. it was held that a seller of a hermaphrodite animal was under a duty to disclose this fact because he was selling it in a market where only cows and bulls were normally sold.

6. *Fraud by a third party*

Systems differ on the question whether a contract may be avoided because of fraud by a third party. This is dealt with below, see notes to Article 4:111.

7. *Effect of fraud*

In most systems the effect of fraud is to give the party who has been deceived the right to avoid the whole contract, even if the fraud related only to a part of it. In ENGLISH, IRISH, SCOTS and NORDIC law fraud as to any part of the contract entitles the victim to escape the whole. Provided that the fraud was the reason he entered the contract, the same is true under GREEK CC art. 181. In FRENCH, BELGIAN and LUXEMBOURG law, however, the general rules on partial invalidity apply; the question is whether the fraud relates to an essential part of the contract or overturns its whole economy. DUTCH BW art 3:44 is to the same effect, see *Asser-Hartkamp*, Verbintenissenrecht II, no. 490. In GERMAN law the part to which the fraud relates may be annulled leaving the rest of the contract standing if it is severable and this is what the parties are assumed to want: BGH 5 April 1973, LM HGB § 119 No. 10, *Münchener Kommentar (-Kramer)*, I § 143 NO.11.

On fraud generally see *Kötz*, European Contract 196-208.

Article 4:108: Threats

A party may avoid a contract when it has been led to conclude it by the other party's imminent and serious threat of an act:

    (a) which is wrongful in itself, or

    (b) which it is wrongful to use as a means to obtain the conclusion of the contract,

unless in the circumstances the first party had a reasonable alternative.

COMMENT

A. *Threats Wrongful in Themselves*

The notion of freedom of contract suggests that party should only be bound by actions which were both voluntary, in the sense that the party was aware of what it was doing, and free, in the sense that it had some choice. In practice the notion of freedom has to be tempered. On the one hand, an action which was literally forced by the other party – the person who is made to sign by the other grabbing his arm and moving it – simply does not consent and has not even appeared to agree. In such a case there would not be an agreement within the Principles, see Articles 2:101 and 2:102. On the other hand, there are frequent occasions on which the choices facing a party are constrained by his circumstances and it may feel it "has to agree" to a contract. During food shortages a hungry person may have little choice but to pay the high market price for food. The law of contract, dependent as it is on notions of the market, cannot insist that every contract should be free from such constraints.

The law can insist that a party should not be constrained by the actions of the other party when those actions are unjustifiable. First, a party should not be able to hold the other to a contract which the other agreed to as the result of a threat that some other legal wrong would be inflicted on the first party if it did not consent. Article 4:108(a) rests on this principle.

> *Illustration 1*: A and B are partners. A wishes to buy B's share of the business and, in order to induce B to sell her share, threatens to have some goods belonging to B wrongfully seized and impounded if she does not sell. B agrees to sell her share to A. B may avoid the contract.

The same would follow if A had threatened a third party, e.g. a member of B's family. It is not only threats of physical violence or damage to property which constitute wrongful threats. A threat to inflict economic loss wrongfully, e.g. by breaking a contract, can equally constitute duress.

> *Illustration 2*: X owes a large debt to Y. Knowing that Y desperately needs the money, X tells Y that he will not pay it unless Y agrees to sell X a house which Y owns at a price well below its market value. Faced with bankruptcy, Y agrees. X then pays the debt. Y may avoid the contract to sell the house.

In practice the threat of a breach of contract is often used in an attempt to secure re-negotiation of the same contract. In this case the re-negotiation agreement may be avoided.

> *Illustration 3*: C has agreed to build a ship for D at a fixed price. Because of currency fluctuations which affect various subcontracts, C will lose a great deal if the contract price is not changed and it threatens not to deliver unless D agrees to pay 10% extra. D will suffer serious harm if the contract is not performed. D pays the extra sum demanded by C. D may recover the extra sum paid.

B. *Not Every Warning of Non-performance Amounts to a Threat*

If one party genuinely cannot perform the contract unless the other party promises to pay an increased price and the first party simply informs the second of this fact, the second party cannot later avoid any promise it makes to pay a higher price. The first party's statement was merely a warning of the inevitable; there is no threat within the meaning of this Article.

> *Illustration 4*: A employs B to build a road across A's farmland at a fixed price. B finds that the land is much wetter than either party had realised and B will literally be bankrupt before it has performed the contract at the original price. B informs A of this and A agrees to pay an increased price. Although A had no real choice, it cannot avoid the agreement to pay the increased price.

C. *Threats Which It is Wrongful to Use to Obtain the Promise*

Even a threat to do something lawful may be illegitimate if it is not a proper way of obtaining the benefit sought, as in blackmail.

> *Illustration 5*: E threatens his employer F that he will reveal to F's wife F's affair with his secretary unless F increases E's wages. F complies. He may avoid the agreement to pay E the higher wages.

D. *Threat Must Have Led to the Contract*

Relief will not be given unless the threat did influence the threatened party's decision. If the primary reason for paying the amount demanded is to settle the dispute rather than to avoid the threatened action, relief will not be given.

> *Illustration 6*: E employs C to do some building work. C has underpriced the work and tells E that it will not do it unless the price is increased. E is not much affected by the threat, which it regards as a bargaining ploy, but feels that C has made a genuine mistake and deserves a better price, so it agrees to pay the extra. It cannot avoid the agreement to pay extra.

Provided the threat has some influence it need not be the only reason for the contract.

Illustration 7: A and B are partners. A wishes to buy B's share of the business and, in order to induce B to sell his share, threatens to have B murdered if he does not sell. B agrees to sell his share to A. Even if B also has good business reasons for selling to A, B may avoid the contract.

E. *No Reasonable Alternative*

Relief will not be given if a party gave in to a threat when it had a perfectly good alternative – e.g. it could have found someone else to do the work, or could have obtained an order forcing the other party to do it. If there was a reasonable alternative, that suggests that the threat was not the real reason for the threatened party agreeing to the demand. The burden of proving that the party had a reasonable alternative rests on the party which made the threat.

F. *Remedies*

The party subjected to the threat may avoid the contract, provided it gives notice within a reasonable time, see Article 4:113. It may also claim damages, see Article 4:117.

G. *No Exclusion of Remedies*

Threats are a form of wrongful behaviour and therefore the remedies cannot be excluded or restricted by contrary agreement, see Article 4:118(1).

NOTES

All the systems recognise that a contract which is procured by one party making an illegitimate threat against the other may be avoided by the latter. For example, AUSTRIAN ABGB § 870 (if illegal threat and well-founded fear); NORDIC Contract Acts §§ 28, 29; DUTCH BW art.3:44; FRENCH, BELGIAN and LUXEMBOURG CCs art.1112 (avoidance if *violence* produces in the victim a fear of present and considerable harm to his person or property); GERMAN BGB § 123(1) (party may avoid a contract into which he was induced by illicit threats); GREEK CC art. 151; ITALIAN CC art.1434; PORTUGUESE CC arts 246 and 256; SPANISH CC arts. 1267 AND 1268. For ENGLISH law ("duress") see *Chitty* §§ 7-001 - 023; for IRISH law, *Clark* 260-268; for SCOTS law ("force and fear") see McBryde 250-255. There are some variations in the conditions under which relief will be granted.

1. *Threat must have influenced the party seeking to avoid*

   In most systems the test is a subjective one: the party seeking to avoid must show that he was influenced by the threat: GERMAN law: BGH 22 January 1964, NJW 1964, 811 (though the threatening party must have acted with the intention of obtaining the other party's consent: *Larenz*, § 20 IV b, p.401); NORDIC law (*Telaranta*, Sopsimusoikeus 320); PORTUGUESE CC art. 255. In ENGLISH law the threat must have influenced the party seeking to avoid the contract; thus a payment which the threatening party had demanded and which was not due, but which was paid not because of the threat but to save trouble ("voluntarily to close the transaction"), is not recoverable: *Maskell* v. *Horner* [1915] 3 K.B. 106, C.A. However the burden of proving that the threat did not influence the threatened party is a heavy one (*Chitty* § 7-021). In cases of physical duress it suffices that the threat had some effect on the victim's consent; the threat need not be the only or even the main reason he agreed to the contract. See *Barton* v. *Armstrong* [1976] A.C. 104, P.C. It does not appear that the threat must have been one which would have influenced a reasonable person.

   Under FRENCH and LUXEMBOURG CCs art.1112 it seems that the test is not purely subjective: the threat must have been one that would influence a reasonable person of the same age, sex and condition (and see also ITALIAN CC art.1435). But it is said that the courts in France take a subjective approach (e.g. Com. 28 May 1991, D.1992.166, note P. Morvan; *Nicholas* 106, citing Req. 27 January 1919, S. 1920.1.198; Req. 17 November 1925, S. 1926.1 121.) AUSTRIAN law also seems to take a subjective approach in practice; the fear must be "well-founded" but the physical and mental state of the threatened person is taken into account as well as the gravity and probability of danger.

DUTCH law takes an objective approach in that the threat must be one that would have influenced a reasonable person BW art.3:44(1).

Article 4:108 applies whenever the threat was imminent and serious and actually led to the conclusion of the contract which the party threatened is seeking to avoid.

2.   *The threat may be of physical or financial harm*

The continental systems do not limit relief to cases of threats of physical harm, but also include threats of causing financial or moral harm provided that the threat is illicit: for example FRENCH, BELGIAN and LUXEMBOURG CCs art.1112 (*"la crainte d'exposer sa personne ou sa fortune à un mal"*); PORTUGUESE CC arts 246 (contract made under physical threat null) and 256 (if under moral threat, avoidable); in GERMAN law, BGH 25 June 1965, LM § 123, no.32 (threat not to pay bill of exchange in order to induce other party to sell real estate); GREEK CC art.151; ITALIAN CC art.1435; THE NETHERLANDS, HR 27 March 1992, NJ 1992, 377, HR 29 May 1964, NJ 1965, 104. In ENGLISH law it at one time seemed that the threat had to be one of physical violence or of wrongful siezure of property, but it is now recognised that a contract may be avoided in cases of "economic duress": that is, where the contract was made as the result of a threatened wrong, such as a breach of contract, and the party seeking relief gave in because he would suffer serious losses if the threat was carried out and he had no real alternative: e.g. he could not effectively protect himself by taking legal action. See *North Ocean Shipping Co Ltd* v. *Hyundai Construction Co Ltd, The Atlantic Baron* [1979] Q.B. 705, Q.B., which is the source of Illustration 3. Economic duress has not yet been recognised in IRISH or SCOTS law. Article 4:108 applies to all kinds of wrongful threats.

3.   *The threat must be illegitimate but need not be one of an act itself unlawful*

The threat must be illegitimate, but most systems recognise that it may be illegitimate to use a threat of something itself not unlawful to extract a payment or promise: e.g in FRENCH law, to threaten abusive use of a legal procedure such as a *saisie*: Civ.3, 17 January 1984, B.III, no.13; similarly LUXEMBOURG law, Cour, 10 May 1929, Pasicrisie 11, p.459; in BELGIAN and GERMAN law, to threaten criminal proceedings against a relative of the other party, see respectively CA Brussels, 7 February 1980, Pas. 1980, II, 55, JT 1980, 282; OLG Karlsruhe, 11 January 1991, VersR 1992, 703; PORTUGUESE CC art 255. In English law, a contract made in similar circumstances was held to be voidable (*Williams* v. *Bayley* (1866) L.R. 1 H.L. 200, H.L.). In *Universe Tankships of Monrovia Ltd* v. *ITWF* [1983] 1 A.C. 366, H.L., Lord Scarman recognised that a threat to do something itself legal for an improper purpose ("blackmail") would amount to duress, but it is doubtful whether threats of lawful action which do not amount to a crime would suffice. In *CTN Cash & Carry Ltd* v. *Gallaher Ltd* [1994] 4 All E.R. 714 the Court of Appeal has said that it will be slow to accept cases of "lawful act duress". Similarly, in AUSTRIAN law the threat must be "illegal", which may mean that the threat must amount to the crime of extortion (StGB § 144) or the misdemeanour of compulsion   (StGB § 105). Threats of lawful actions may also be illegitimate under NORDIC Contract Acts § 29.

4.   *A demand for extra payment in exchange for performing a contractual obligation will not necessarily be treated as wrongful*

Some systems recognise explicitly that a party who is faced with unforseeable expense in performing may state truthfully that he will be unable to to perform unless paid extra and that, if the other party promises the extra payment, the promise will not be avoidable on the ground of duress. See on DANISH law *Gomard*, Kontraktsret 155. Similarly in ENGLISH law it has been argued that there is no duress if the party claiming that he cannot perform is merely stating the inevitable (e.g. that he will go bankrupt if he is not paid extra) or perhaps if the threatening party acts in good faith in demanding more (see the discussion in *Burrows* 179-182). Under the Principles a truthful statement to the effect that the party will be unable to perform unless paid extra will not amount to a threat, see Comment B.

5.   *Threat made by a third party*

On this point there are considerable differences between the systems. In ENGLISH law a threat made by a third party only gives a right of avoidance if the other party had actual or constructive notice of it, or the person making the threat was his agent. AUSTRIAN ABGB § 875 and DUTCH BW art. 3:44(5) are to similar effect. In contrast, FRENCH, BELGIAN and LUXEMBOURG CCs art. 1111 explicitly covers the case of a threat made by a third party, and so do ITALIAN CC art. 1434 and PORTUGUESE CC art. 256. The latter requires that, in the case of a threat by a third person, the harm threatened be serious and the victim's fear justified, whereas these conditions do not apply to a threat made by the other party himself. GERMAN law also covers threats made by third parties and it does not matter that the other party to the contract acted in good faith (BGH 6 July 1966, NJW 1966, 2399, 2401; contrast to BGB § 123(2) which explicitly states the opposite rule for fraud). GREEK CC arts. 150 and 153 are still more liberal: the victim of a threat by a third party has an unqualified right to avoid the contract but the promisee may, at the judge's discretion, be compensated for his reliance loss if he neither knew or ought to have known of the threat (see *Maridakis* 195, 196).

NORDIC law takes an intermediate position. Under Contracts Act § 28, the promisor who was threatened with imminent violence may avoid the contract even if the threat was by a third party; other threats (§ 29) are only a defence against a promisee who knew or ought to have known of them.

The Principles adopt the rule that if a threat is made by a third person for whom a party is responsible, or if a party knew or ought to have known of a threat made to the other party by some other third person, the position will be as if the first party had made the threat itself. See notes to Article 4:111 below.

On duress generally see *Kötz*, European Contract 209-213.

Article 4:109: Excessive Benefit or Unfair Advantage

(1) A party may avoid a contract if, at the time of the conclusion of the contract:

(a) it was dependent on or had a relationship of trust with the other party, was in economic distress or had urgent needs, was improvident, ignorant, inexperienced or lacking in bargaining skill, and

(b) the other party knew or ought to have known of this and, given the circumstances and purpose of the contract, took advantage of the first party's situation in a way which was grossly unfair or took an excessive benefit.

(2) Upon the request of the party entitled to avoidance, a court may if it is appropriate adapt the contract in order to bring it into accordance with what might have been agreed had the requirements of good faith and fair dealing been followed.

(3) A court may similarly adapt the contract upon the request of a party receiving notice of avoidance for excessive benefit or unfair advantage, provided that this party informs the party which gave the notice promptly after receiving it and before that party has acted in reliance on it.

COMMENT

A. *Pacta Sunt Servanda and Unfair Advantage-taking*

Contract law does not in general insist that bargains be fair in the sense that the performances exchanged be of what others might call equal value. It is commonly held that the parties are the best judges of the relative values to be exchanged. However many systems refuse to uphold contracts which involve an obviously gross disparity in the value of the two performances when this appears to be the result of some bargaining weakness on one side and conscious advantage-taking on the other.

Article 4:109 adopts the principle that a contract which gives one party excessive advantage and which involved unfair advantage taking may be avoided or modified at the request of the disadvantaged party.

B. *Weakness or Need Essential*

It would create too much uncertainty if a party could escape from a contract, even if it is disadvantageous to him, when there is no apparent reason why he did not look after his own interests better when agreeing. Relief should only be available when the party can point to some weakness, disability or need on his part to explain what happened. This may include the fact that he had a confidential relationship with the other party and was relying on the other to advise him, if this meant that he was not exercising his own independent judgement.

C. *Knowledge of Party Obtaining Advantage*

It would also create too much uncertainty to upset contracts which are one-sided when there was no reason for the party who gains the advantage to know that the other party was in a weaker position. It is only when he should know that the other party is not in a position to safeguard his own interests that the stronger party should have to have regard to the weaker party's interests.

D. *Excessive Advantage*

The Article applies where the advantage gained by one party is demonstrably excessive in comparison to the "normal" price or other return in such contracts. The fact that a shortage of supply has led to generally high prices is not a ground for the application of this Article, even if the sudden price increase has allowed one party to make an abnormally high profit.

> *Illustration 1*: During a sudden cold snap during early summer the price of tomatoes increases dramatically. B agrees to buy tomatoes from A at the increased price. B cannot avoid the contract under this Article even though it discovers that A had bought the tomatoes at a much lower price earlier in the summer and had kept them in cold store.

Where however a party takes advantage of another's ignorance or need to make a particularly one-sided contract, this Article will apply.

> *Illustration 2*: X, an uneducated person with no business experience, is left some property. He is contacted by Y who offers to buy it for a sum much less than it is actually worth, telling X that he must sell quickly or he will lose the chance. X agrees without consulting anyone else. X may avoid the contract.

> *Illustration 3*: U and her family are on holiday abroad when they are involved in a car crash and U's husband is badly hurt. He urgently needs medical treatment which is not locally available. V agrees to take the man by ambulance to the nearest major hospital, charging approximately five times the normal amount for such a journey. U is so worried that she agrees without getting other quotations; she does not discover until later that she has been overcharged. She may obtain relief.

> *Illustration 4*: as the last Illustration. U realises that V is demanding an extortionate price but his is the only ambulance available. She may obtain relief.

E. *Grossly Unfair Advantage*

The Article may apply even if the exchange is not excessively disparate in terms of value for money, if grossly unfair advantage has been taken in other ways. For example, a contract may be unfair to a party who can ill afford it even if the price is not unreasonable.

Illustration 5: X, a widow, lives with her many children in a large but dilapidated house which Y, a neighbour, has long wanted to buy. X has come to rely on Y's advice in business matters. Y is well aware of this and manipulates it to his advantage: he persuades her to sell it to him. He offers her the market price but without pointing out to her that she will find it impossible to find anywhere else to live in the neighbourhood for that amount of money. X may avoid the contract.

F. *Risk Taking*

Relief should not be given when the apparent one-sidedness of the bargain is the result of a party gambling and losing. The contract was not unfair when it was made, even though it may have turned out badly for one party. See Illustration 9 to Article 4:103.

G. *Remedies*

It may not be appropriate simply to set aside the contract which is excessively advantageous. The disadvantaged party may wish the contract to continue but in modified form. Under paragraph (2) the court may therefore substitute fair terms.

This goes further than a right of partial avoidance under Article 4:116, since it allows the substitution of a fair term.

Conversely it may not be fair to the party which gained the advantage simply to avoid the whole contract; that could result in unfairness the other way. So the court has power to modify the contract at the request of either party, provided the request so to do is made promptly and before the party who has given a notice of avoidance has acted on it.

The court should adapt the contract only if this is an appropriate remedy in the circumstances. For example, adaptation would not be appropriate in a case like Illustration 5 above.

In addition to or instead of avoidance the disadvantaged party may recover damages under Article 4:117; these are limited to the amount by which it is worse off compared to its position before the contract was made (the "reliance interest").

H. *Remedies Cannot be Excluded*

Since it is unconscionable to take advantage of the other party to gain an excessive advantage, the remedies for excessive advantage cannot be excluded or restricted by agreement: see Article 4:118(1).

NOTES

All the systems in some circumstances permit avoidance of a contract which has been obtained by unfair means, but some allow relief simply because the substance of the contract is unfair. Most continental systems have fairly broad rules permitting avoidance where one party has deliberately taken advantage of the other party's need or circumstances to obtain a very one-sided contract (see note 1), but some do not insist on the plainitff having been in a vulnerable position (see note 2) or grant relief simply on the basis of great disproportion in value (lesion; see note 3). The common law and Scots law seem to give relief primarily in cases of abuse of a special relationship between the parties, and in the absence of such a relationship to grant it only under very limited conditions. Many systems have particular rules governing loans or consumer credit transactions.

1.   Taking advantage of a vulnerable party

Many systems give relief when one party has taken advantage of the other's particular circumstances to obtain an unfair contract. Thus FRENCH jurisprudence, although not wholly settled, treats exploitation of a party's economic necessity or other circumstances as a form of *violence*: Soc.5 July 1965, B.IV no.545; Civ.1, 24 May 1989, B.I, no.212; compare in BELGIUM, CA Brussels 7 February 1964, Pas. 1965 II 70. Otherwise relief is only given for error, threat or fraud and, in very limited circumstances, for *lésion* (see below). Belgian doctrine and case law gives relief for abuse of right when it gives rise to a disproportionate transaction, under the doctrine of qualified lesion, whereas relief for lesion without abuse of right (see Note 3 below) is rare: see *Kruithof & Bocken*, TPR 1994 p. 394 No. 149 and Cass. 21 September 1961, Pas. 1962 I 92; Cass. 25 November 1977, Arr.Cass. 1978, 343; Cass. 29 April 1993, JT 1994, 294. The new art.1118 of the LUXEMBOURG CC gives a remedy for abuse of circumstances generally. The DUTCH BW similarly allows annulment of a juridical act where there has been threat, fraud or abuse of circumstances; the latter is defined as being induced to execute a juridical act as a result of special circumstances such as state of necessity, dependency, wantoness, abnormal mental condition or inexperience (art.3:44(4)). In NORDIC law, Contracts Act § 31 applies where one party has taken advantage of the other's special circumstances to acquire a disproportionate benefit; but there is also the possibility of the setting aside or adjustment of a unfair contract under § 36 without the need for special circumstances, see below. SCOTTISH law permits "facility and circumvention" when advantage was taken a plaintiff who was "facile" – for example, elderly or unwell.

In ENGLISH and IRISH law, relief may be given under two separate rules, each involving the exploitation of a plaintiff who is particularly vulnerable. The first is the doctrine of undue influence where one party has exercised, or is in a position to exercise, a high degree of control over the other. Relief may be available if it is shown either that one party exercised such a degree of domination and control over the other that the latter's independence of mind was undermined ("actual" undue influence: see *Chitty* § 7-028), or that the parties were in a confidential relationship. In the latter situation, if the weaker party enters into a manifestly disadvantageous contract with the stronger, a presumption arises that undue influence has been used. Some relationships (e.g. doctor and patient) are treated as always giving rise to a confidential relationship; in other cases such a relationship may be proved (e.g between husband and wife, see *Barclays Bank* v. *O'Brien* [1994] 1 A.C. 180, H.L. or bank manager and client, see *Lloyd's Bank Ltd* v. *Bundy* [1975] Q.B. 326, C.A. For Ireland, see *Bank of Ireland* v. *Smyth* [1993] 2 I.R. 102, affirmed on other grounds [1996] 1 ILRM 241; Annual Review of Irish Law 1993, 194.). The doctrine of undue influence is also known in SCOTLAND but the presumption of undue influence is not used and the influence must always be proved.

Secondly, the doctrine of unconscionable bargains states that if a party takes deliberate advantage of the other party's poverty and ignorance to buy property from the poor and ignorant person at much less than its true value, the weaker party may have the contract set aside (see *Fry* v. *Lane* (1888) 40 Ch.D. 312). The doctrine is old and not much used in England, though see *Boustany* v. *Piggott* [1993] E.G.C.S. 85, P.C., and the parallel rule in a case where a party, though not completely incapable of transacting, is suffering from some mental disability, see *Hart* v. *O'Connor* [1985] A.C. 1000, P.C. In Ireland the doctrine of unconscionability is used more frequently, e.g. *Grealish* v. *Murphy* [1946] IR 35 (HC), *Lyndon* v. *Coyne* (1946) 12 Ir. Jur. Rep. 64 (H.Ct.); *JH* v. *WJH* (unrep., 20 Dec. 1979, (H.Ct.). Common law does not recognise any general doctrine of abuse of circumstances; relief in this kind of case is limited to cases of extortionate credit bargains (Consumer Credit Act 1974, ss. 137, 138) and salvage on the high seas (e.g. *The Port Caledonia and The Anna* [1903] P. 184.

Other systems seem to follow the notion of limiting relief to abuse of circumstances but give relief in more limited conditions. Thus ITALIAN law recognises that a contract made in circumstances of economic distress may be avoided but only if the performances are disproportionate in a ratio of greater than 1:2 (art.1448); or if the contract was made in a situation of danger and on iniquitous terms (art. 1447). PORTUGUESE CC arts 282 and 283 apply when the victim is inexperienced, imprudent or in a state of necessity, but it may be possible to interpret the provisions to caver all the situations referred to in Article 4:109, see *Eiró*, *Do negocio usuario* 45.

2.   Excessive advantage-taking rather than protection of particularly vulnerable plaintiffs

In contrast there are systems in which the position of the plaintiff is not so important as the disparity between the obligations. The AUSTRIAN ABGB § 879, GERMAN BGB § 138(2) and GREEK CC Arts. 178 and 179 treat contracts which involve a gross disparity as contrary to good morals and therefore voidable. The cases concentrate on the excessive disparity rather than the particular vulnerabilities of the weaker party; the most important group of cases in German law are those dealing with consumer credit and hire-purchase agreements, which are void if the overall interest rate to be paid is deemed to be excessive, e.g. if it is 100% above the average rate (BGH 24 March 1988, BGHZ 104, 102, 105; BGH 13March 1990, BGHZ 110, 336, 338.; see Palandt § 138 no.25 ff.. ABGB § 879(4) and BGB § 138(2), which refer to exploitation of the needs, inexperience, lack of judgement or weakness of will of the losing party, are consequently rarely applied. The vulnerability of the weaker party is, however, important in cases of sureties who have given guarantees without the means to meet their possible liability (e.g. BVerfG 19 October 1993, NJW 1994, 36; BGH 24 February 1994, NJW 1994, 1278). In NORDIC law a contract which is substantively unfair may be set aside or adjusted under Contracts Act § 36 without the need to show that the gaining party took advantage of the other's circumstances.

3.   *Lesion*
FRENCH and BELGIAN CCs art.1118 state that a contract for the sale of immoveables may be set aside on the ground of *lésion* only in certain situations, principally if the price paid for an immovable is less than 5/12ths of the value (arts. 1674-1685), in the case of *partage* (division between heirs, CC arts 887 and 1079) or where the contract is with a minor or someone who is incapable (art 1305). LUXEMBOURG law is the same except when undue advantage has been taken, see Note 1 above. AUSTRIAN ABGB §§ 934, 935 recognise *laesio enormis* as a ground for avoidance or adaptation of a contract where a party to a synallagmatic contract receives a counter-performance of less than 50% of the value of his own performance, judged by the relative values at the time the contract was made. The rule cannot be excluded by contrary stipulation and has become an important remedy in consumer protection..
      The Principles follow what seems to be the majority position in requiring one party to have taken advantage of the other's special weakness to obtain an unfair contract, rather than giving relief simply on the basis of a disproportion in values between the performances.

4.   *Deliberate exploitation*
Apart from the cases of lesion described in the last note, the majority of systems agree that it is only when one party has deliberately taken advantage of the other that relief will be given. Thus in ENGLISH law it has been said that relief on the grounds of mental incapacity or unconscionability can be given only where one party consciously took advantage of the other's weakness: *Hart* v. *O'Connor* [1985] A.C. 1000, P.C. But this is not required in IRISH law. DUTCH BW art.3:44 applies when the gaining party ought to have known of the other's weakness. For PORTUGUESE law see *Eiró* 51, 57. In practice courts in the various systems will infer advantage-taking from the objective facts of gross disparity: e.g. in GERMAN law BGH 14 June1984, NJW 1984, 2292; BGH 10 July 1986, BGHZ 98, 174, 178; in English law, the presumption of undue influence which arises from a manifestly disadvantageous transaction, above, and see *Crédit Lyonnais Bank Nederland NV* v. *Burch* [1997] 3 All E.R. 144, C.A.

5.   *The contract must be excessively one-sided*
In all systems the transaction must be excessively one-sided or unfair before relief will be given. In some systems it seems that the unfairness must be measured by an objective criteria such as the market price: e.g. GREEK law, AP 281/1968, NoB 1968.815; NORDIC law, Contracts Act § 31 ("obviously disproportionate", see *Telaranta* 336-337), and in ENGLISH law the transaction must be manifestly disadvantageous for the presumption of undue influence to arise, or involve a sale at undervalue for the contract to be unconscionable. But "objective unfairness" is not always required: e.g. in DUTCH law, if the old widow did not want to sell her house it is no excuse to say that she received a fair price, HR 27 March 1992, NJ 1992, 377. See also HR 29 May 1964, NJ 1965, 104; in English law in cases of actual undue influence the weaker party may set aside the transaction without showing that it was manifestly disadvantageous: *CIBC Mortgages Ltd* v. *Pitt* [1994] 1 A.C. 200, H.L.

6.   *Adaptation of the contract*
Although the traditional remedy granted is simply avoidance of the contract, some systems permit the court to adapt the contract to remove the disproportion: e.g. FRENCH CC art. 1681; LUXEMBOURG CC art.1118 (at the request of the disadvantaged party only); similarly, DUTCH BW art. 3:54; AUSTRIAN ABGB § 935 (*laesio enormis*); NORDIC Contract Acts § 36 and, at least in Denmark, § 31 (see *Lynge Andersen* 224); PORTUGUESE CC art 283 (1) and (2). BELGIAN case law applies reduction as a sanction for abuse of right, see Cass. 18 February 1988, RW 1988-89, 1226, Arr. Cass. No. 375. Additionally, many systems allow the court to reduce excessive interest rates on loans, e.g. Belgian CC art. 1907 (3); Luxembourg CC art. 1907-1; U.K. Consumer Credit Act 1974, s.139.
      The idea that a party who has received notice of avoidance may maintain the contract by offering an amendment which would remove the injustice is found in ITALIAN law (CC. art. 1450).

Article 4:110: Unfair Terms not Individually Negotiated

(1) A party may avoid a term which has not been individually negotiated if, contrary to the requirements of good faith and fair dealing, it causes a significant imbalance in the parties' rights and obligations arising under the contract to the detriment of that party, taking into account the nature of the performance to be rendered under the contract, all the other terms of the contract and the circumstances at the time the contract was concluded.

(2) This Article does not apply to:

  (a) a term which defines the main subject matter of the contract, provided the term is in plain and intelligible language; or to

  (b) the adequacy in value of one party's obligations compared to the value of the obligations of the other party.

COMMENT

A. *Scope of Application*

This provision extends the scope of application of the general clause of the EC Council Directive 93/13 on Unfair Terms in Consumer Contracts (1993) to contracts between private persons and to commercial contracts.

B. *No Black List*

Unlike the Directive, the Principles contain no list of clauses deemed to be unfair. In contracts between professionals, a listing of contract terms as being *per se* unfair, because of the diversity of commercial contracts, is generally held to be all but impossible.

The absence of a list does not prevent judges and arbitrators from finding inspiration in the list in the Annex to the EC Directive when they are applying the general clause of Article 6.110.

The Annex to the EC Directive mentions the following clauses:

"1. Terms which have the object or effect of:

  (a) excluding or limiting the legal liability of a seller or supplier in the event of the death of a consumer or personal injury to the latter resulting from an act or omission of that seller or supplier;

  (b) inappropriately excluding or limiting the legal rights of the consumer *vis-à-vis* the seller or supplier or another party in the event of total or partial non-performance or inadequate performance by the seller or supplier of any of the contractual obligations, including the option of offsetting a debt owed to the seller or supplier against any claim which the consumer may have against him;

  (c) making an agreement binding on the consumer whereas provision of services by the seller or supplier is subject to a condition whose realisation depends on his own will alone;

(d) permitting the seller or supplier to retain sums paid by the consumer where the latter decides not to conclude or perform the contract, without providing for the consumer to receive compensation of an equivalent amount from the seller or supplier where the latter is the party cancelling the contract;

(e) requiring the consumer who fails to fulfill his obligation to pay a disproportionately high sum in compensation;

(f) authorizing the seller or supplier to dissolve the contract on a discretionary basis where the same facility is not granted to the consumer, or permitting the seller or supplier to retain the sums paid for services not yet supplied by him where it is the seller or supplier himself who dissolves the contract;

(g) enabling the seller or supplier to terminate a contract of indeterminate duration without reasonable notice except where there are serious grounds for doing so;

(h) automatically extending a contract of fixed duration where the consumer does not indicate otherwise, when the deadline fixed for the consumer to express this desire not to extend the contract is unreasonably early;

(i) irrevocably binding the consumer to terms with which he had no real opportunity of becoming acquainted before the conclusion of the contract;

(j) enabling the seller or supplier to alter the terms of the contract unilaterally without a valid reason which is specified in the contract;

(k) enabling the seller or supplier to alter unilaterally without a valid reason any characteristics of the product or service to be provided;

(l) providing for the price of goods to be determined at the time of delivery or allowing a seller of goods or supplier of services to increase their price without in both cases giving the consumer the corresponding right to cancel the contract if the final price is too high in relation to the price agreed when the contract was concluded;

(m) giving the seller or supplier the right to determine whether the goods or services supplied are in conformity with the contract, or giving him the exclusive right to interpret any term of the contract;

(n) limiting the seller's or supplier's obligation to respect commitments undertaken by his agents or making his commitments subject to compliance with a particular formality;

(o) obliging the consumer to fulfil all his obligations where the seller or supplier does not perform his;

(p) giving the seller or supplier the possibility of transferring his rights and obligations under the contract, where this may serve to reduce the guarantees for the consumer, without the latter's agreement;

(q) excluding or hindering the consumer's right to take legal action or exercise any other legal remedy, particularly by requiring the consumer to take disputes exclusively to arbitration not covered by legal provisions, unduly restricting the evidence available to him or imposing on him a burden of proof which, according to the applicable law, should lie with another party to the contract.

2. Scope of subparagraphs (g), (j) and (k)
  (a) Subparagraph (g) is without hindrance to terms by which a supplier of
      financial services reserved the right to terminate unilaterally a contract of
      indeterminate duration without notice where there is a valid reason, pro-
      vided that the supplier is required to inform the other contracting party or
      parties thereof immediately.
  (b) Subparagraph (j) is without hindrance to terms under which a supplier of
      financial services reserves the right to alter the rate of interest payable by
      the consumer or due to the latter, or the amount of other charges for finan-
      cial services without notice where there is a valid reason, provided that the
      supplier is required to inform the other contracting party or parties thereof
      at the earliest opportunity and that the latter are free to dissolve the contract
      immediately.
        Subparagraph (j) is also without hindrance to terms under which a sell-
      er or supplier reserves the right to alter unilaterally the conditions of a con-
      tract of indeterminate duration, provided that he is required to inform the
      consumer with reasonable notice and that the consumer is free to dissolve
      the contract.
  (c) Subparagraphs (g), (j) and (l) do not apply to
      – transactions in transferable securities, financial instruments and other
      products or services where the price is linked to fluctuations in a stock
      exchange quotation or index or a financial market rate that the seller or sup-
      plier does not control;
      – contracts for the purchase or sale of foreign currency, traveller's
      cheques or international money orders denominated in a foreign currency.
  (d) Subparagraph (l) is without hindrance to price-indexation clauses, where
      lawful, provided that the method by which prices vary is explicitly
      described."

Courts and arbitrators may find this list useful especially when they are dealing
with commercial contracts between a small and a large business.

> *Illustration 1*: A runs a small petrol station. He obtains his oil products from a
> large oil company. In considering whether or not one or more of the contract
> terms imposed upon A by the oil company cause a significant imbalance, regard
> may be had, among others, to the list in the EC Council Directive Annex. Thus
> a set-off clause (subparagraph (b)) and a penalty clause (subparagraph (e)) in the
> contract terms may be deemed voidable.

C. *Voidability*

Since the Principles do not include a list and the general clause in itself is open, it
will usually, in the absence of precedents, not be possible to say straightaway that a
clause is unfair. In derogation of the EC Directive, the Principles therefore do not
impose the sanction that an unfair clause be not binding. Rather they impose the
sanction of voidability, which is more in line with the other provisions of this

Chapter. There is no material difference to the Directive, however, since avoidance under the Principles does not require the interference of a judge or arbitrator.

D. *Main Subject Matter*

What judges and arbitrators may not do is to judge the relation between the price and the main subject matter. Article 6.110 does not reintroduce the *iustum pretium* doctrine of canon law. The second paragraph aims to prevent this.

The second paragraph should be interpreted strictly. Terms which allow a party to raise the price are covered by the first paragraph.

> *Illustration 2*: A car dealer sells an expensive car, which is so popular that there is a six month waiting list. The dealer sells the car for the price "as listed by the manufacturer at the time of delivery". Although the term relates to the price of the car, it is to be considered a term in the sense of paragraph (1).

E. *Unfair Terms and Grossly Unfair Advantage*

Articles 4:109 and 4:110 at first sight have something in common. However, they deal with different situations. Article 4:109 deals with the case where A takes advantage of B's difficult position. The provision covers both the situation where the price or the other essentials of the contract, or the general conditions are excessive in one way or another. Article 4:110 deals only with what mainly are general conditions, and not with the price. It covers a very frequent situation, where one of the parties has drafted the contract terms in advance.

F. *Individually Negotiated*

A term has been "individually negotiated" when it has been the explicit subject of negotiations between the parties. Such negotiations may result in a draft term proposed by the other party being amended or struck out. They may also result in the term remaining unchanged.

Whether or not a term should be deemed individually negotiated will depend upon the circumstances of the case. A term in general conditions of contract which is used in a number of contracts will usually be considered not individually negotiated. A handwritten term in a unique contract will be considered to be individually negotiated. However, depending upon the circumstances this may be different in a specific case.

G. *Significant Imbalance*

A significant imbalance in the parties' rights and obligations is required for the Article to come into operation. The imbalance may be of an economic or of a legal nature. In the first case, the economic consequences are significantly abusive to the other party. In the latter case, a term may be deemed imbalanced if it confers rights upon one party and not upon the other (mirror image rule).

> *Illustration 3*: A contract between a bank and a customer allows the bank to set off any claim it wishes and the consumer none. This causes a significant imbalance between the rights of parties.

H. *Effect on Rest of Contract*

If a term is found to be unfair, the remainder of the contract may remain in force if that is possible and appropriate, but if the rest of the contract cannot survive the deletion of the unfair term, the contract as a whole will be avoided. Cf Art. 6 of the Directive and Article 4:116.

I. *Government Contracts*

In some countries government services have sought to be exempt from legislation on unfair contract terms on the ground that they are working in the public interest. However, it has often been pointed out that government services are sometimes among the worst offenders of requirements of contractual fairness. These Principles may apply to all government contracts.

J. *Other Legislation*

Legislation on unfair contract terms usually contains a number of other provisions. These Principles include several Articles on interpretation of general contract terms. Especially in consumer contracts, national legislation may lay down other rules as well. These may also affect the procedural rights of the parties concerned.

NOTES

Article 4:110 is in the same terms as Council Directive 93/13/EEC on Unfair Terms in Consumer Contracts of 5 April 1993, OJ L95/29, save that it is not limited to terms used against consumers. This reflects the law in many Member States. First, before passing any specific legislation many systems had adopted or developed judicial controls over unfair terms. These are not usually limited to consumer contracts and, for the most part, they continue to apply. Second, many member States have legislation on unfair terms which applies to unfair terms, particularly those in general conditions of contract, even when neither party is a consumer.

1. *Judicial controls developed by the courts*

   Examples of judicial controls over unfair terms, not limited to consumer contracts, are in GERMAN law, where clauses might be declared invalid under the public policy test of BGB § 138 or as contrary to good faith as required by § 242; in GREECE, under the general principle of CC arts. 281, 178 and 179 on good faith and good mores, art.371 in inequitable determination of indefinite performance or arts. 372-373 on determination of performance left to the discretion of one party; BELGIAN law, where clauses may be declared invalid under the public policy test of CC arts. 6 and 1131 or if they constitute an abuse of right, as contrary to good faith; and DUTCH law, which invalidated unfair clauses if they were contrary to the requirement of good faith or, as the BW now puts it, reasonableness and equity (art. 6: 248(2)). In other countries the judicial controls were more limited. For example, in the U.K. there were attempts by the courts to prevent the use of unfair exemption and limitation of liability clauses by holding that they could not apply when there had been a fundamental breach of contract, but the House of Lords held that there was no rule to this effect, though the courts will interpret such clauses narrowly: *Suisse Atlantique Société d'Armement Maritime SA* v. *Rotterdamsche Kolen Centrale NV* [1967] 1 A.C. 361; *Photo Production Ltd* v. *Securicor Transport Ltd* [1980] A.C. 827.

2. *Legislation applying to general conditions*

   Before the implementation of the Directive on Unfair Terms in Consumer Contracts, some countries still gave individual plaintiffs relief against unfair clauses primarily through controls which were not aimed specifically at general conditions, e.g. in the NORDIC countries, Contracts Act § 36 remains a primary basis of relief. More usually specific legislation had been adopted, particularly on terms contained in general conditions. This is sometimes limited to clauses used against consumers or "non-professionals", e.g. the system of administrative control set up in FRANCE by the *loi Scrivener* of 10 June 1978 and the subsequent cases in which courts have held that abusive clauses in consumer contracts are of no effect (e.g.Civ. 14.5.1991, D. 1991.449 note J.Ghestin; see *Malaurie & Aynès*, Obligations, § 612); LUXEMBOURG legislation of 25 August 1983 (Memorial 1983A, p.1494); BELGIAN consumer law, especially Trade Practices and Consumer Protection Act of 14 July 1991, arts. 31 ff.; but frequently the legislation applies to both consumer and non-consumer contracts. An example is the GERMAN Act on Standard Terms (AGBG) of 1976. Although the AGBG's "grey" and"black" lists of clauses, respectively presumed to be unfair until the contrary is shown (§ 10) and always deemed to be unfair (§ 11), apply directly only to consumer contracts and not to commercial contracts between persons acting in the course of their trade, the general provision (§ 9) applies to all contracts except certain categories specifically exempted from the Act by § 23(1). The black and grey lists may be applied by analogy under § 9, see *Münchener Kommentar (-Kötz)* 1, AGBG § 9 Nos. 18, 19; BGH 8 March 1984, BGHZ 90, 273, 278; BGH 3 March 1988, BGHZ 103, 316, 328; BGH 25 October 195, NJW 1996, 389. DUTCH BW arts. 6:231-247 apply to general conditions of all types but have black lists (art 6:236) and grey lists (art.6:237) in favour of consumers and small enterprises. PORTUGUESE decret-loi no. 446/85 of 25 October 1985 has two black lists and two grey; in each case one list applies to all contracts (arts. 18 and 19) and a second, more demanding, list (arts. 21 and 22) applies to consumer contracts. AUSTRIAN law has specific rules for consumer contracts in the Consumer Protection Act of 8 March 1979, BGBl 1979/140, including a blacklist; and a more general provision in ABGB § 879.

Some countries had adopted legislation which can apply to individually negotiated terms but only if they are of a particular type: e.g. Italian CC art. 1341(2) and Luxembourg CC art.1135-1 (which provide that certain clauses are valid only if specifically accepted by separate signature). U.K. Unfair Contract Terms Act 1977 and Irish Sale of Goods and Supply of Services Act 1980 apply to various types of exclusion and limitation clause irrespective of whether the clause was individually negotiated. Compare Article 8:109 of the Principles.

All Member States are now obliged to implement the Directive. In the Netherlands and Portgugal it is considered that the Directive does not require any changes to the BW or the law of 25 October 1985 respectively. A general survey of the implementation in the various Member States may be found in the *European Review of Private Law* [1997] Vol. 5, 121 ff.

3. *Significant imbalance, contrary to good faith and fair dealing*
The test used by the systems to determine whether or not a clause was valid varied in formulation: e.g. the BELGIAN Act of 14 July 1991 to "manifest disproportion"; the GERMAN AGBG § 9 to good faith and unreasonable disadvantage; the NORDIC Contract Acts to "unfair"; the U.K. Unfair Contract Terms Act 1977 to "fair and reasonable". It is not thought that the various formulations produce significantly different results to that adopted by the Directive and thus of and Article 4:110, but some recent legislation adopts the terms of the Directive explicitly, e.g. French Code de la Consommation art. L. 132-1 now refers to *"déséquilibre significative"*, and the UK Unfair Terms in Consumer Contracts Regulations 1994 to "significant imbalance", "contrary to the requirements of good faith". For a comparative account of the approach to unfairness in the Directive see *Sepe*.

4. *No review of the price*
The legislation of several Member States specifically excludes courts from reviewing the price or other main terms: e.g. DUTCH BW 6:231(a) in fine. However, under NORDIC law even the price may be reviewed under Contracts Act § 36.

5. *Applicability to contracts with Government*
In the majority of systems which apply controls to non-consumer contracts the legislation does not differentiate between contracts with the Government and other contracts. Cf. *Calais-Auloy & Steinmetz*, no.12.

On unfair terms generally, see *Kötz*, European Contract, ch.8. On the laws before the Directive see *Hondius*, Unfair Terms.

Article 4:111: Third Persons

(1) Where a third person for whose acts a party is responsible, or who with a party's assent is involved in the making of a contract:

(a) causes a mistake by giving information, or knows of or ought to have known of a mistake,

(b) gives incorrect information,

(c)   *commits fraud,*

(d)   *makes a threat, or*

(e)   *takes excessive benefit or unfair advantage,*

remedies under this Chapter will be available under the same conditions as if the behaviour or knowledge had been that of the party itself.

(2) *Where any other third person:*

(a)   *gives incorrect information,*

(b)   *commits fraud,*

(c)   *makes a threat, or*

(d)   *takes excessive benefit or unfair advantage,*

remedies under this Chapter will be available if the party knew or ought to have known of the relevant facts, or at the time of avoidance it has not acted in reliance on the contract.

COMMENT

A. *Responsibility for Agents, Employees and Others*

Under the Principles a party is generally treated as responsible for not just the actions of its employees but also of those whom it involves in the making of the contract or to whom it delegates performance: see also Article 1:305. This applies just as much to behaviour or knowledge which might invalidate a contract as to other things. The contracting party will be liable just as the third person would have been had the contract been made with him. Normally the third person will be acting on behalf of the party against whom the remedy is sought, but this need not be so if the third party was involved with the party's assent; it need not be shown that he was acting for the party.

> *Illustration1*: A supplier of goods holds an informal negotiation with a buyer; another customer is present and with the supplier's assent joins in the discussion. Out of the supplier's hearing, the other customer gives the buyer some inaccurate information. The buyer should have a remedy under Article 4.103 or 4:107 just as if the information had been given by the supplier, without having to show that the other customer was acting on the supplier's behalf.

B. *Remedies Where Fraud, etc. by a Third Person for Whom Party Is Not Responsible.*
A party cannot be fixed with the consequences of improper or careless behaviour of a third person for whom it is not responsible and who does not fall into the other categories mentioned in Comment A. But it should not be allowed to enforce a contract which it knows or should know was concluded only through such behaviour by a third person, if, had it behaved in the same way itself, the other party to the contract could have a remedy under the provisions of this chapter.

> *Illustration 2*: A bank lends money to a husband's business on the strength of a charge, signed by the wife, over the family home. The charge is very much against the wife's interest and the husband has procured the wife's signature by duress. The bank ought to know that it is most unlikely that the wife would sign

voluntarily and the bank cannot enforce the charge. It should have made enquiries to ensure that the wife was acting freely.

The party should also be liable for damages under Article 4:117 if it knows of the ground for avoidance, or if it knows that the other party has been given incorrect information by a third person but does not inform the other party that the information is incorrect.

C. *Remedy When Party Knows of Mistake*
A party may also know of a mistake which was known to or caused by a third person. There is no need for a special rule to cover this case since a party may avoid a contract entered under a fundamental mistake if the mistake was known to the other party, see Article 4:103.

D. *No Reliance on Contract by Other Party*
It also seems fair to allow a party which has entered a contract because of the fraud, etc of a third person, or because of a mistake which was or should have been known to the third person, to avoid the contract, even if the other party to the contract did not know or have reason to know of the circumstances, provided the party seeking to avoid the contract can prove that the other party has not yet acted in reliance on it, even by passing up other opportunities.

NOTES

1. *Actions by a third person for whom a party is responsible*
   All Member States adopt the principle that a contract may be avoided against a party whose employee or agent has behaved in such a way that, if the agent or employee had himself been the party to the contract, it could have been avoided on one of the grounds described in this chapter. E.g. AUSTRIAN ABGB § 1313(a); ENGLISH law, see *Chitty* § 6-014.

2. *Actions by a third person for whom the party is not responsible*
   As noted earlier, some systems allow avoidance of a contract entered as the result of a threat by a third person for whom the other party was not responsible, even if the other party did not know and had no reason to know of the threat (notes to Article 4:108 above). The majority of systems, however, hold that the contract may be avoided for duress or any other factor mentioned in this chapter only if the other party participated in the misbehaviour or knew or should have known of what was happening: e.g. AUSTRIAN AGBG § 875 (participation or actual knowledge); DUTCH BW art. 3:44(5); GREEK CC Art. 153 (duress; no rule stated for other cases). Some of the systems which do not require knowledge in the case of duress do require it in case of fraud, e.g. FRENCH and LUXEMBOURG law (CCs Art. 1111 cover only *violence* by a third person); GERMAN BGB § 123(2); ITALIAN CC art.1338 (party who knew or ought to have known that incorrect information given treated as himself guilty of pre-contractual fault); arts. 1447, 1448 (in cases of danger or need, relief only when known to party himself or to third person who was acting as agent.); NORDIC Contracts Acts §§ 29-31 (knew or ought to have known); PORTUGUESE CC art. 254(2) (fraud; not required in cases of exploitation of the weak position of a contracting party under art. 282, *Mendes* 129; *Eiró* 69). In SPAIN, the courts have interpreted CC art. 1269 as limited to cases of fraud by one of the contracting parties but this approach is criticised, e.g. by *Lasarte Álvarez*, § 3.6(c).
   In ENGLISH law it has been held that if a lender is given a guarantee or security by a party to whom the arrangement is of no advantage and who the lender should know has a relationship with the debtor (e.g. they are husband and wife) such as to make duress, misrepresentation or undue influence a likely reason for the guarantee being given, the lender must advise the surety to seek independent advice. If the lender fails to do this, it will be fixed with constructive notice of any impro-

priety which has occurred: *Barclays Bank* v. *O'Brien* [1994] 1 A.C. 180, H.L. In SCOTLAND a similar result has been reached but via the differeent route of recognising a duty of good faith by the creditor towards the surety: *Smith* v. *Bank of Scotland* 1997 S.L.T. 1061 (H.L.).

3. *Fraud etc by a third person where the party against whom avoidance is sought did not know of the fraud but has not relied on the contract*
    The question whether the party has relied on the contract may exceptionally be taken into account in NORDIC law, Contracts Acts § 39. It is not relevant in BELGIAN, DUTCH, ENGLISH, FRENCH GERMAN, GREEK or LUXEMBOURG law.

Article 4:112: Notice of Avoidance

Avoidance must be by notice to the other party.

COMMENT

Avoidance may be effected by the party entitled to avoid the contract or communication; it is not necessary to seek a court order to avoid the contract. Under Article 1:303 the receipt principle applies and the avoidance will not be effective unless the notice reaches the other party.

Conduct unequivocally indicating that a party no longer considers itself bound by the contract will amount to avoidance if it is known to the other party.

Illustration: A takes a job as manager with B's firm after B makes fraudulent statements about the commission which previous managers have made with the firm. After A discovers the truth, he takes a job with another company. The contract is avoided as soon as B reads of this in the newspaper even if A has not communicated his avoidance directly to B.

Provided the time limit for avoidance has not passed (see Article 4:113), a party may give notice of avoidance by raising the ground of avoidance as a defence when an action is brought against it by the other party.

NOTE

In some systems the effect of some of the grounds for invalidity mentioned in this chapter is that the contract is altogether void (e.g. for *erreur obstacle* in FRENCH law and mistake at common law in ENGLISH law). In such case the party need not take any step to avoid the contract, though action may be necessary to recover property, money or payment for services transferred.

Where the contract is merely voidable, in many of the legal systems of Member States, a contract may be avoided on the traditional grounds of invalidity by simple notice to the other party: e.g. GERMAN BGB § 143; DUTCH BW art. 3:49; NORDIC law (*Gomard*, Kontrakret 142); ENGLISH and IRISH law (notice dispensed with if third party has deliberately gone into hiding and party seeking to avoid has taken all reasonable steps such as notifying police: *Car & Universal Finance Co Ltd* v. *Caldwell* [1965] 1 Q.B. 625, CA.); SCOTS law (notice to police insufficient, *McLoed* v. *Kerr* 1965 SC 253). However a court action is required in in GREECE, CC art. 154; in FRANCE, BELGIUM and LUXEMBOURG (CCs art. 1117), unless the annulment is accepted by the other party; and similarly in ITALIAN law (CC art.1441) and PORTUGUESE law, *Lima/Varela*, I 264; *Ascensão* 440; *Fernandes* 393. In AUSTRIAN doctrine and court practice the opinion prevails that avoidance on the ground of error requires a court decision, and that it is not sufficient to direct an informal notice to the other party. However this is doubtful as the ABGB does not require court proceedings.

Several systems have a different regime for unfair terms, under which the term is simply of no effect and so notice of avoidance is not needed. E.g. FRENCH CCons art. L.132.1 (above, note to art. 4:110), (*reputée non écrite*); similarly BELGIAN Act of 14 July 1991; LUXEMBOURG; GERMAN AGBG. Under the Directive, Member States are to provide that unfair terms will not be binding on consumers, art. 6(1).

Article 4:113: Time Limits

(1) Notice of avoidance must be given within a reasonable time, with due regard to the circumstances, after the avoiding party knew or ought to have known of the relevant facts or became capable of acting freely.

(2) However, a party may avoid an individual term under Article 4:110 if it gives notice of avoidance within a reasonable time after the other party has invoked the term.

COMMENT

A. *Party Must Take Avoiding Action with Reasonable Speed*
The need for security in transactions requires that the party entitled to avoid a contract should do so within a reasonable time after it learns the relevant facts, or, in cases of duress or undue persuasion, it is free of the threat or influence of the other party.

B. *Knowledge of Facts*
The party should act within a reasonable time of learning the relevant facts; it is not necessary that it know that they give it a right to avoid the contract. If it is in doubt it should take legal advice. A reasonable time will include time to take advice and consider its position.

C. *Avoidance of Term*
Under Article 4:110 if a particular term is unfair the disadvantaged party may avoid just that term.

Often it will not be clear to the party that he will be disadvantaged; it may depend on whether and how the other party invokes the term. Thus it seems fair to allow the potentially disadvantaged party to "wait and see".

Illustration: A bank's general conditions for the lease of equipment to a farmer allows it, as the lessor, in the event of any default by the lessee, to seize not only the equipment concerned but also any other equipment separately leased from the lessor, even if there has been no default in paying for the other equipment. Such a "cross-default" clause results in an excessive advantage to the bank. The farmer need not protest about it, however, until a default occurs and the bank tries to seize other equipment.

A clause requiring earlier notice would itself fall within Article 4:110.

If a party who could have invoked Article 4:110 against a term enters into an agreement with the other party to settle the dispute, the first party does in effect lose the right to challenge the term. That is because he is bound by the settlement, not because of the right to challenge the original term is lost.

NOTES

1. *Avoidance for defect in consent*
    There is wide variation between the systems on the time within which avoidance must be sought. At one extreme, in ENGLISH law it has been held that the right to avoid a contract for misrepresentation may be lost within a matter of weeks, even though the misrepresentation has not been discovered (see *Leaf* v. *International Galleries* [1950] 2 K.B. 86, C.A. and *Bernstein* v. *Pamson Motors (Golders Green) Ltd* [1987] 2 All E.R. 220, Q.B.D.), or within months of the cessation of duress (*North Ocean Shipping Co Ltd* v. *Hyundai Construction Co Ltd* [[1979] Q.B. 705, Q.B.D.). In cases of fraud time will not run until the fraud has been discovered but then prompt action will be required: see *Chitty* § 6-079. At the other, BELGIAN CC art. 1304 (as am. in 1976) gives 10 years from the discovery of the fraud or error or the cessation of the threat, and even after that time the error, fraud or threat may be raised as a defence.
    The other systems take intermediate positions. FRENCH CC art. 1304 allows 5 years from cessation of threat or from discovery of fraud or error; ITALY CC art. 1442 similarly, and in other cases five years from date of contract; LUXEMBOURG, as French law but one year in cases of unfair advantage, CC art.1118; SPAIN, four years from end of threat or, in cases of fraud and error, from date of contract, CC art 1301; GERMANY: mistake, without delay (§ 121; two weeks was regarded as the upper limit by OLG Hamm 9 January 1990, NJW-RR 1990, 523); fraud or threat, one year from discovery or cessation, BGB § 124; AUSTRIA, threat or mistake, 3 years ABGB § 1487; fraud or usury, 30 years. GREECE, two years after error, fraud or threat has ceased and in any event within 20 years from the conclusion of the contract (CC art. 157); HOLLAND: 3 years from date of discovery of fraud or error or cessation of threat, BW art. 3:52; otherwise three years from when right of avoidance arises. NORDIC law: Contract Acts §§ 28(2) (physical violence) and 32(2) (message incorrectly communicated by intermediary), notice of avoidance must be given without unreasonable delay; otherwise, general limitation period. However, in Denmark the right to avoid may be lost if not claimed for a long period, see *Lynge Andersen* 169; in Finland, if the party wishing to avoid knew that the other has acted in reliance on the contract yet did not react within a reasonable time, he will be held to have lost his right: *Ämmälä*. SCOTS law has no set time limits except a general prescription period of twenty years (Prescription and Limitation (Scotland) Act 1973, s. 8.), but a right to avoid maybe lost be failure to exercise it promptly. In PORTUGAL, the contract must be avoided within a year if it has been executed but if it has not been executed there is no time limit (CC art. 287 (1) and (2)).
2. *Avoidance of an individual unfair term*
    Several systems simply apply the same general rule to avoidance of an individual unfair term e.g. GERMANY (but under AGBG simply void); HOLLAND, BW 6:235(4), which starts time running from date clause invoked by other party; ITALY, CC art. 1442(4); semble in NORDIC law. In others the clause is simply of no effect, e.g. LUXEMBOURG; PORTUGAL Law of 25 October 1985; U.K. Unfair Contract Terms Act 1977. Under the Directive, Member States are to provide that unfair terms will not be binding on consumers, art. 6(1), which seems to imply that the clause may be challenged at any time.

Article 4:114: Confirmation

*If the party which is entitled to avoid a contract confirms it, expressly or impliedly, after it knows of the ground for avoidance, or becomes capable of acting freely, avoidance of the contract is excluded.*3

COMMENT

A party cannot be allowed to avoid a contract after it has indicated that it wishes to continue with it, since the other party may act in reliance on the contract continuing. The first party's indication may be made expressly or impliedly by conduct, e.g. by continued use of goods.

In cases of mistake and fraud, this rule only applies once the party who may have been entitled to avoid knows of the relevant facts and, in cases where there has been some form of coercion, it only applies when it becomes capable of acting freely. However, if even without knowledge of the ground for avoidance, a party has given a clear indication that it intends to continue with the contract and the other party has acted on that information, the first party may be prevented from going back on its word. It will have given the appearance of having intending to confirm the contract (cf.Article 2:102, Intention) and to go back on this when the other party has acted on it would be contrary to Article 1:201, Good Faith and Fair Dealing.

Where a party has the right under Article 4:110 to avoid a particular term, the rule in Article 4:114 will not apply just because it knows it can avoid the term; it may wait to see if the other party invokes the term.

NOTE

This provision is broadly the same as FRENCH, BELGIAN and LUXEMBOURG law (CC art.1338); GERMAN law, BGB § 144 (confirmation may be implicit, e.g by continuing to use goods, BGH 28 April 1971, NJW 1971, 1795, 1800, provided that the party knew he had a right of avoidance or expected to have such a right, BGH 8 March 1961, WM 1961, 785, 787); ITALIAN CC art. 1444 (but confirmation is not recognised in cases of lesion or of iniquitous terms accepted in situations of danger); PORTUGUESE CC art. 288; SPANISH CC arts 1309ff.; DUTCH BW arts. 3:55 and 3:35 (act which reasonably appears to be a confirmation). In ENGLISH and IRISH law the right to avoid may be lost through election, which in principle requires knowledge of the right to avoid, though an act which is done without knowledge of the right to avoid but which reasonably leads the other party to believe that the contract will not be avoided may give rise to an estoppel, see *The Kachenjunga* [1990] 1 Lloyd's Rep. 391, H.L., per Lord Goff at 399). It appears that NORDIC law reaches this result also: *Ämmälä*, pp. 222-224; *Lynge Andersen* 169; *Gomard,* Kontraktsret 141. There is little clear authority on these questions in SCOTS law.

Article 4:115: Effect of Avoidance

On avoidance either party may claim restitution of whatever it has supplied under the contract, provided it makes concurrent restitution of whatever it has received. If restitution cannot be made in kind for any reason, a reasonable sum must be paid for what has been received.

COMMENT

A. *Restitution*
Avoidance involves setting aside the contract, or the part of it avoided, as if it had not been made. The mutual restoration of benefits, or where the benefits themselves can-

not be returned, their value, is a natural consequence; it would not be right that avoidance should leave either party with a benefit at the other's expense. If it is possible, restitution may be made in kind; if this is not possible, for instance because an innocent third party has acquired rights over the property, a reasonable sum should be paid instead. The right to restitution depends upon the party making concurrent restitution of benefits it itself received, compare Article 9:201, Right to Withhold Performance.

B. *Effect of Avoidance on Application of the Principles.*

A dispute about whether the contract was validly formed will still be governed by the Principles, see Article 1:104, even if the conclusion is that the contract should be avoided.

NOTES

1. *Restitution after avoidance*

    The legal systems of the Member States agree that after avoidance of a contract the parties may recover the value of performances they had rendered before avoidance by way of restitution.

    There are no particular differences between the systems in two situations. First, when money has been paid over, under all systems it must be repaid. Second, when services have been performed, the recipient must make restitution by paying their reasonable value. The Principles do not deal with the question of how the value is to be calculated.

    However there are differences in the way that the systems treat restitution of property which was purportedly transferred under the contract which has been avoided. This involves questions of the effect of avoidance and of the extent to which avoidance is permitted when restitution in kind is not possible or is not permitted.

2. *Does avoidance revest property?*

    Many legal systems of the Member States apply generally the rule that property which was transferred automatically revests in the transferor. So, in FRENCH and LUXEMBOURG law the theory of nullity holds that the parties are to be treated as if the contract had never existed, see *Malaurie & Aynès*, Obligations 579-592. ITALIAN law adopts a similar principle. In AUSTRIAN law, invalidation of the contract itself invalidates the transfer of title and the transferor remains legal owner (OGH 30 January 1980, JBl 1981, 425). Also in ENGLISH and IRISH law, if the contract is void for mistake (see note to Article 4:103, above) no property is transferred (e.g. *Ingram v. Little* [1961] 1 Q.B. 31, C.A.); if the contract is voidable and is validly avoided, the property revests in the transferor (e.g. *Car & Universal Finance Co Ltd* v. *Caldwell* [1965] 1 Q.B. 625, C.A.) In other systems, annulation of the contract is not necessarily seen as having retroactive effect on property rights which have been transferred. Thus in GERMAN law, according to BGB § 142(1), a contract which has been avoided is treated as being void from the time of conclusion of the contract; but in cases of avoidance for mistake, for example, this does not itself affect any transfer of property since German law separates the passing of property from the underlying contract.. The transferor must rely on a claim in unjust enrichment under BGB § 812(1) and, if the recipient is bankrupt, the claimant will receive only a dividend in the bankruptcy. However, a different rule is applied in cases of fraud and threat. Here, since these grounds for avoidance are strongly tainted, avoidance of the contract extends to the transfer of property also, so the avoiding party may vindicate the property itself even if the other party is bankrupt (BGB § 985). SCOTS law also treats contract and transfer of property as distinct juridical acts.

    The Principles do not deal with questions of property and take no position on whether avoidance produces an automatic re-transfer of property, with a concomitant right to restitution of any property transfered as such, or merely to a personal right to restitution. Nor do they deal with the position of third parties who may claim an interest in the property.

3. *Impossibility of restoring the property transferred*

    Under ENGLISH, IRISH and SCOTS law, if the property cannot be restored in substantially the same condition as when it was transferred, for example through being used up, the right of avoidance is lost (though the rule is applied flexibly, see *Chitty* §§ 6-070 - 072). The Principles do not follow this approach. Continental systems generally allow avoidance in such a case; they may require the party who received the property, instead of returning it, to make restitution of its value. Under Article 4:115, inability to restore property transferred is not a bar to avoidance; the party who received the property may have to make restitution of the value of the benefits received.

There are widely differing rules as to who bears the risk of accidental destruction of the property between the date of the transfer and that of avoidance, and thus whether restitution must be made in such a case: see Treitel, *Remedies* § 285. The Principles do not deal with this question.

Article 4:116: Partial Avoidance

If a ground of avoidance affects only particular terms of a contract, the effect of an avoidance is limited to those terms unless, giving due consideration to all the circumstances of the case, it is unreasonable to uphold the remaining contract.

COMMENT

A. *Party Wishes to Avoid Only Part of the Contract*
The ground of avoidance may relate only to a particular term which the avoiding party wishes to avoid without affecting the remainder of the contract. The party should be permitted to do this.

> *Illustration 1*: C takes a ball room gown to be cleaned. She is asked to sign a contract limiting the cleaner's liability for any damage to the dress. She asks why she has to agree to this and is told that it is just to protect the cleaners if any of the sequins on the dress come off in the cleaning. She signs. The dress comes back with a large stain on it and the cleaners try to rely on the clause. C may avoid the clause without avoiding the whole contract.

If a party is entitled to avoid a term because it is unfair under Article 4:110 this may be done without reference to Article 4:116.

B. *Appropriate to Limit Avoidance to Part of Contract*
An incorrect statement or a mistake in communication may relate to a minor term of the contract. In such a case it may not be necessary or desirable to permit the party affected to avoid the whole contract if it feasible to allow it to avoid just the term involved and this would not result in the contract being unbalanced in its favour.

> *Illustration 2*: B, a builder, submits a bid for a major project. The total of its tender is made up of a number of items shown in the bid. There is clearly a mistake in one of these items, though it is not clear what the correct figure should be. The employer accepts the bid without pointing out the mistake. B may not avoid the whole contract but it can avoid the price stated for the item in question. It will be paid a reasonable sum for the item.

> *Illustration 3*: D buys a household insurance policy. Because the clauses of the contract are confusingly written he does not realise that the policy has an exclu-

sion of any loss caused by theft which does not involve forcible entry. Such clauses are common in insurance policies of the type he is sold, given that he lives in a high crime area; insurance against theft without forcible entry is much more expensive. D may avoid the whole contract and recover his premium but he cannot avoid just this exception, since the effect would be to give him "expensive" cover at a low price.

In some cases a mistake as to a single term may make it reasonable to avoid the whole contract. The burden of proving that it would be unreasonable to uphold the remainder of the contract shall be on the party which argues that it should be avoided as a whole.

One of the circumstances which is relevant is the behaviour of the party against whom avoidance is sought. In cases of fraud or duress, it may well be appropriate to allow the other party to avoid the whole contract if it so wishes.

NOTES

In some systems, when there is a ground of avoidance affecting only part of the contract, and the clause is not essential to the rest of the contract, the contract may be upheld without the offending clause. This is the case with unfair clauses, both under the Directive on Unfair Terms in Consumer Contracts and many national laws; but it is in some systems true for other grounds of invalidity, e.g. in FRENCH, BELGIAN and LUXEMBOURG law (see *Malaurie & Aynès*, Obligations §§ 580-584); in GERMAN law, if the clause is severable within BGB § 139; similarly in DUTCH law, BW art. 3:41. Other systems allow avoidance of the whole contract if the avoiding party can prove that he would not have entered the contract at all without the offending part: e.g. GREEK CC art.181; ITALIAN CC 1419 (cases of nullity); PORTUGUESE CC art. 292. This is the result reached by BELGIAN case law.

In NORDIC law the remedy is in principle avoidance of the whole contract but in practice there have been cases in Finland in which partial avoidance has been used (KKO 1961 II 100 and 1962 II 80) and in all Nordic countries the aggrieved party may ask for adjustment of the contract under Contracts Act § 36. In ENGLISH, IRISH and SCOTTISH law the remedy is usually thought of as avoidance of the whole contract, and in a recent case of misrepresentation as to the content of a contract, the court refused to enforce the contract in the form that the misrepresentee had been led to expect (*TSB Bank plc* v. *Camfield* [1995] 1 W.L.R. 430, C.A.). But where a party misrepresented the effect of an exclusion clause in a contract the court simply enforced the rest of the contract without the clause, *Curtis* v. *Chemical Cleaning Co Ltd* [1951] 1 K.B. 805, C.A.

Article 4:117: Damages

(1)   A party which avoids a contract under this Chapter may recover from the other party damages so as to put the avoiding party as nearly as possible into the same position as if it had not concluded the contract, provided that the other party knew or ought to have known of the mistake, fraud, threat or taking of excessive benefit or unfair advantage.

(2)   If a party has the right to avoid a contract under this Chapter, but does not exercise its right or has lost its right under the provisions of Articles 4:113 or 4:114, it may recover, subject to paragraph (1), damages limited to the loss caused to it by the mistake, fraud, threat or taking of excessive benefit or unfair advantage.

The same measure of damages shall apply when the party was misled by incorrect information in the sense of Article 4:106.

(3) In other respects, the damages shall be in accordance with the relevant provisions of Chapter 9, Section 5, with appropriate adaptations.

COMMENT

A. *Liability in Damages*

It is not sufficient that the party which has entered a contract because of mistake which the other party did not share, fraud, threats or excessive or unfair advantage should only have a right to avoid the contract or part of it. First, it may not wish to exercise its right of avoidance. In such a case should it be without any remedy? At the very least it should be entitled to recover any gain that the other party made at its expense as a result of the conduct giving rise to the right of avoidance.

However, the recovery of this "restitutionary" interest may not suffice. It may have suffered some further loss which it would not have done had the wrong not been done to it. It should be entitled to recover the amount of its injury. Article 4:117 permits this.

Illustration 1: L tells the prospective tenant of a house that the drains are in good order. Relying on this the tenant signs the lease. They are not and the tenant becomes ill as a result. Whether L was fraudulent or merely careless, he should have to compensate the tenant.

Illustration 2: O employs P to build a house for it on a particular site. O knows that under the site there is an old sewer which is in danger of collapsing. It is obvious that P does not know this but O says nothing. One of P's lorries gets stuck when the sewer gives way under its weight and P has to pay a large sum to have it pulled out. O is liable for this cost.

Note that in many legal systems liability in these cases would be regarded as delictual. Nonetheless, if the contract is subject to the Principles, so should be any claim under this Article. See Comment G to Article 4:106, above.

It may be that on some facts the tenant in Illustration 1 would have a claim for non-performance, e.g. under Article 6:101, Statements giving rise to Contractual Obligations. In this case the damages would include any higher cost involved in finding another house with drains which are in good order, see next Comment.

B. *Measure of Damages*

Damages for non-performance aim to put the aggrieved party into the position it would have been in had the contract been performed, see Article 9:502. In cases within Chapter 4 there has not been a non-performance, or at least not necessarily so: even in cases of fraud or incorrect information, the person making the statement is not necessarily giving a contractual undertaking that it is true, see Comments to Article 6:101, Statements giving rise to Contractual Obligation. If there was no promise that what was stated was true, the untrue statement should not have caused any "loss of expectation" and the damages should not include an element for this. The aim should be to put the party back into the position it would have been in had it not entered the contract (see also Comment to Article 4:106(2)).

> *Illustration 3*: L lets a flat to T, telling T that the occupier of the flat has the right to use a garden in the square opposite the apartment building. L should have known that this is not true. T agrees to pay £400 per month; the normal rent for such a flat would be £350 a month. Some similar flats in the building do have the use of the garden; the "going rent" for these is £500 a month. T may recover damages of £50 a month, not of £150 a month.

Sometimes a statement which is made fraudulently, or which is incorrect, does also amount to a contractual promise within Article 6:101. In this case the aggrieved party may choose between remedies under this chapter or remedies for non-performance, see Article 4:119.

If the contract has been avoided and the aggrieved party suffered no consequential loss, there may be no further loss which is compensable under this Article.

> *Illustration 4*: A leases a used car to B, fraudulently telling B that is has only done 20,000 km when in fact the odometer has been "clocked" and it has done 70,000 km. Because the car has covered such a great distance, a fair rental would be much less than B agreed to pay. Soon after he has taken delivery of the car, B discovers the truth and avoids the contract. His money is refunded. He has not suffered any further loss for which damages can be compensable under this Article, even if it costs him more to lease a car from another company.

Damages under Article 4:117 may include compensation for opportunities which the party passed over in reliance on the contract.

> *Illustration 5*: E accepts an offer of employment from F after F fraudulently tells him that the job carries an index-linked pension. E finds that the job does not have such a pension scheme and he resigns. To take the job he had passed up another job offer at a much better salary than he can now get elsewhere. E may recover as damages the difference between what he would have earned in the other job and the salary he can now get.

C. *Measure of Damages Where the Contract is Not Avoided.*
A party which has the right to avoid the contract but does not do so, for instance because it fails to act quickly enough to avoid the contract, should, as we have said, be able to recover damages. However, it should not necessarily be put into the same position as if it had not entered the contract. To allow this might permit it to throw other losses, such as a decline in the value of the property, on to the other party, when that item of loss was in no way related to the ground for avoidance. The same applies particularly to case of incorrect information under Article 4:106.

Illustration 6: A, a developer, buys a plot of land for £5 million, relying inter alia on a statement by the seller that the land is not subject to any rights in favour of third parties. Later A finds that there is a right of way running across part of the site. This is not serious enough to constitute a mistake within Article 4:103 but it will cost £10,000 to divert the path. A has a claim under Article 4:106. Meanwhile, because of a slump in property prices, the value of the site has fallen from £5 million to £2.5 million. A's damages are limited to £10,000.

D. *Cases Where No Fault*
In cases of mistake as to the nature or circumstances of the obligation where the mistake was shared, there is not the same reason to make either party liable, except where one of them was at fault.

E. *Contributed to Own Loss*
Sometimes the victim of a fraud or mistake failed to look after its own interests and thus contributed to its loss. In such a case the damages may be reduced: cf. Article 9:504, Loss Attributable to Aggrieved Party, and Article 9:505, Reduction of Loss.

F. *Damages after Adaptation of Contract*
The adaptation of the contract by the other party or by the court under Article 4:105 does not preclude the mistaken party claiming damages under this Article if it has suffered loss which is not compensated by the adaptation of the contract.

G. *Exclusion or Restriction of Liability in Damages*
On exclusion or restriction of liability in damages, see Article 4:118.

NOTES

1. *Availability of damages*
   It is widely recognised that damages are available where the ground for avoidance of the contract was the result of the fault of one of the parties. This may be based on general principles of delictual responsibility (as in FRENCH and LUXEMBOURG law, CCs art.1382; in BELGIAN law, *culpa in contrahendo* is seen as an application of general tort principles); or on "contractual" *culpa in contrahendo* (as in ITALIAN law, see *Sacco(-De Nova)*, Il contratto, II p.575 ff.); or on either ground. Thus in GERMAN law, in a case of excessive advantage taking, the victim may recover damages if the requirements of BGB § 826 or those of *culpa in contrahendo* are fulfilled, BGH 12 November 1986, BGHZ 99, 101, 106. PORTUGUESE law is similar: STJ, 13 January 1993; O Direito 125, I-II, pp.145 ff.; *Cordeiro* 157ff.; *Prata* n.17, 45, 53, 58; *Prata*, n.16, 167ff.. NORDIC law probably also allows claims on either basis, though there is little authority; in Danish law it is accepted that the aggrieved party may recover his reliance losses if the other party has acted negligently or in bad faith, *Gomard*, Kontraktsret 140. See also *Ramberg*, Pre-contractual liability and *Kleineman*. In some systems general principles may be supplemented by special provisions on particular topics, as in AUSTRIAN law, where ABGB § 874 covers fraud and coercion, but error is dealt with by *culpa in contrahendo*; GREEK law, where a provision on error (CC art. 145) supplements the general delictual provisions (CC arts. 149, 152).
   ENGLISH, IRISH and SCOTS law do not have rules applicable generally to cases covered by this Chapter of the Principles. Damages may be recovered for fraud and for negligent misrepresentation (e.g. English Misrepresentation Act 1967, s.2(1); Irish Sale of Goods and Supply of Services Act 1980), s.45; Law Reform (Miscellaneous Provisions) (Scotland) Act 1985, s.10.) Duress may in certain circumstances amount to a tort: see *Carty and Evans*. Even in the rare cases in which English

law recognises a duty of disclosure, non-disclosure is normally only a ground for avoidance of the contract and not for damages, unless the non-disclosing party has assumed responsibility towards the other within the doctrine of *Hedley Byrne & Co Ltd* v. *Heller & Partners Ltd* [1964] A.C. 465, H.L.: see *Banque Financière de la Cité SA* v. *Westgate Insurance Co Ltd* [1989] 2 All E.R. 952, C.A., at p.1007. It does not appear that damages can be given in other cases of mistake not involving misrepresentation , nor in cases of undue influence. Equally SPANISH law has rules on specific situations, e.g. CC art. 1270(2) on fraud.

2.   *Measure of damages*
In those systems in which the measure of damages is discussed, it is generally accepted that in cases of *culpa in contrahendo* and delictual claims only the plaintiff's negative interest, or reliance loss, will be compensated: GERMAN law; NORDIC law (see on Finnish law *Taxell*, Avtal ach rättsskydd 391); ENGLISH law (fraud: *East* v. *Maurer* [1991] 1 W.L.R. 461, C.A.; negligent misrepresentation, *Royscot Trust Ltd* v. *Rogerson* [1991] 2 Q.B. 297, C.A.). It has been argued that in DUTCH law a mistaken party may be able to claim his expectation interest: *Asser-Hartkamp*, Verbintenissenrecht II nr. 487. In PORTUGUESE law, some writers accept that negative interest damages are sufficient, e.g. *Costa*, Responsibilidade n. 3712, 206ff.; others argue that sometimes the positive interest should be protected, *Lima/Varela* I 216; *Prata*, n. 17, 98.

Illustration 6 is modelled on the English case of *Sindall (William) plc* v. *Cambridgeshire County Council* [1994] 1 W.L.R. 1015, C.A., and the Article produces a similar result to that which the court indicated it would have reached if there had been a misrepresentation. On the facts, no misrepresentation had been made.

Article 4:118: Exclusion or Restriction of Remedies

(1) Remedies for fraud, threats and excessive benefit or unfair advantage-taking, and the right to avoid an unfair term which has not been individually negotiated, cannot be excluded or restricted.

(2) Remedies for mistake and incorrect information may be excluded or restricted unless the exclusion or restriction is contrary to good faith and fair dealing.

COMMENT

Fraud, threats and excessive or unfair advantage taking are of such seriousness that a party should not be able to exclude or restrict its liability; they are all forms of bad faith, cf Article 1.201. There is a close parallel here to clauses which purport to exclude or limit liability for intentional non-performance and which are invalid under Article 8:109.

Mistake and the giving of incorrect information do not involve bad faith and it is permissible to exclude or restrict remedies for them provided that the clause is consistent with good faith and fair dealing and not for instance, one which was hidden in small print or over which the party relying on it refused to negotiate. Compare the Comment to Article 4:110.

The burden of proving that the clause is contrary to good faith and fair dealing should rest on the party seeking to avoid its effect.

See Comments to Articles 4:106, 4:107, 4:108 and 4:109.

This Article does not prevent a party agreeing to a settlement of a claim which in effect involves surrendering rights under this Chapter. See Comment to Article 4:114 Confirmation, above.

NOTE

Those legal systems in which this question has been discussed have generally held that remedies for grounds of invalidity involving immoral behaviour cannot be excluded, but that remedies for others may be. Thus in FRENCH law the parties may exclude remedies for mistake. In GERMAN law, remedies for mistake may be excluded by an individually negotiated term, though generally not in general conditions, BGH 28 April 1983, NJW 1983, 1671; exclusion is not possible if an agreement is *contra bonos mores* within BGB § 138. SPANISH CC art. 1102 prevents exclusion of liability for fraud. PORTUGUESE law would appear to prevent exclusion of liability for what is contrary to good morals, CC art. 280(2). In AUSTRIAN law, remedies for mistake caused by simple negligence may be excluded, OGH 20 March 1968, SZ 41/33; 7 March 1978, RZ 1979/14, but remedies for fraud cannot be and the same is probably true for gross negligence, OGH 19 December 1991, SZ 64/190. In NORDIC law the rules on avoidance in Contracts Act §§ 28-36 are mandatory; but liability for misrepresentation by simple negligence may sometimes be excluded (see e.g. Swedish Supreme Court NJA 1987 s.692, 703; the clause may have to be reasonable, *Gomard,* Kontraktsret 187). In ENGLISH law, remedies for fraud cannot be excluded (*Pearson* v. *Dublin Corp.* [1907] A.C. 351, H.L.); a clause excluding or restricting remedies for any other type of misrepresentation will only be valid if it is fair and reasonable, Misrepresentation Act 1967, s.3 (as amended by Unfair Contract Terms Act 1977, s.8). Unfair Terms in Consumer Contract Regulations 1994, SI 1994 no. 3159 may also apply. For IRELAND, see Sale of Goods and Supply of Services Act 1980 and EC Unfair Terms in Consumer Contract Regulations, SI 27 of 1995.

Article 4:119: Remedies for Non-performance

A party which is entitled to a remedy under this Chapter in circumstances which afford that party a remedy for non-performance may pursue either remedy.

COMMENT

In some situations the same facts may be analysed either as a case of mistake or incorrect information, or as one in which there is a non-performance. For example there may be a remedy for non-performance under Article 6:108 Quality of Performance, because the performance of one party is not of average quality; or one party may have given a contractual undertaking that a particular fact relating to the performance is true, see Article 6:101, Statements giving rise to Contractual Obligations.

In such cases there seems no good reason to prevent the aggrieved party from choosing which set of remedies to pursue. Normally the remedies for non-performance will give a fuller measure of recovery, but the aggrieved party may find it simpler to exercise its rights under this Chapter, e.g. just to give notice of avoidance on the ground of mistake.

Needless to say, the aggrieved party will still have to choose remedies which are compatible. It cannot, for example, both avoid the contract and claim damages for non-performance. Cf. Article 8:102 below.

NOTE

In GERMAN law, when the case falls within the special rules on defective goods, the buyer's only remedy is under those provisions. Other systems accept that there may be overlaps between the various sets of rules and allow the aggrieved party to choose which remedy to apply. Thus in FRENCH law a plaintiff will often seek annulment of the contract for error when he could have *recours en garantie*; the jurisprudence allows the victim to choose, Civ.3, 18 May 1988, B.III, No. 96. See *Ghestin*, Formation, nos.544-548. The boundary between the *garantie* and *erreur* is rather unclear, see *Malaurie & Aynès*, Contrats spéciaux no.284. Equally an aggrieved party may claim damages under CC art. 1382 in place of an action for nullity: Com. 14 March 1972, D. 1972.653, note Ghestin; Com.18 October 1994, D.1995.180 note C.Atias. See generally *Tallon*, Hamel. BELGIAN law is in practice similar, as is LUXEMBOURG law, Cour 30 June 1993, Pasicrisie 29, page 253; Cour, 16 March 1900, Pasicrisie 5, 245. A choice of remedies is also permitted in AUSTRIA, GREECE, ITALY, THE NETHERLANDS and the NORDIC countries. In ENGLISH, IRISH and SCOTTISH law the principal overlap is between remedies for misrepresentation and for non-performance; here English Misrepresentation Act 1967, s.1, confirms that the aggrieved party may choose. In PORTUGAL it appears that the party may choose between remedies for non-performance and for error, but that the same short limits laid down by CC arts. 916 and 917 and CCom. 471 will be applied whichever remedy is chosen, *Martinez*, 413.

See generally *Kötz*, European Contract 175-178.

CHAPTER 5

Interpretation

Article 5:101: General Rules of Interpretation

(1) A contract is to be interpreted according to the common intention of the parties even if this differs from the literal meaning of the words.

(2) If it is established that one party intended the contract to have a particular meaning, and at the time of the conclusion of the contract the other party could not have been unaware of the first party's intention, the contract is to be interpreted in the way intended by the first party.

(3) If an intention cannot be established according to (1) or (2), the contract is to be interpreted according to the meaning that reasonable persons of the same kind as the parties would give to it in the same circumstances.

COMMENT

A. *General*

Contracts are interpreted in order to determine their contents. This is particularly the case when the contract contains a clause which is ambiguous, obscure or vague; that is, when one cannot immediately see the exact meaning. But interpretation will also be necessary if clauses which seem clear enough in themselves contradict each other, or cease to be clear when the general setting of the contract is taken into account.

When a contract contains lacunae which need to be filled, the process is sometimes referred to as completive interpretation *(ergänzande Auslegung)*. In this situation the Principles resort to implied obligations, for example those referred to in Article 6:102 below.

Determining the exact meaning of the contract may be necessary before it can be determined whether the contract is valid or whether there has been a non-performance. For example, it may be necessary to decide whether the debtor's obligation was one to produce a particular result *(obligation de résultat)* or only one to use reasonable care and skill *(obligation de moyens)*.

Any kind of contract may need interpretation, even a formal contract such as one made in the presence of a notary. Similarly, the rules of interpretation apply to contracts made on general conditions or standard forms. In fact some of the rules apply particularly to these types of contract (Articles 5:103 and 5:104). Interpretation may be needed for the whole or part of a contract.

Moreover, the provisions of this Chapter may be applied, with appropriate adjustments, to agreements sometimes classified as other than contracts, such as agreements to change the terms of an existing contract, and to unilateral declarations of will (Articles 5:103 and 5:104).

B. *The Search for Common Intention (First paragraph)*

Following the majority of laws of EU Member States, the general rules on interpretation combine the subjective method, according to which pre-eminence is given to the common intention of the parties, and the objective method which takes an external view by reference to objective criteria such as reasonableness, good faith etc. The judge is thus encouraged to start by looking to see what was the parties' common intention at the time the contract was made. This is normal because the contract is primarily the creation of the parties and the judge should respect their intentions, expressed or implicit, even if their will was expressed obscurely or ambiguously.

In seeking this common intention the judge should pay particular attention to the relevant circumstances as set out in Article 5:102.

It should be noted that there may be a common intention of the parties even in the case of a contract of adhesion, in so far as the party who was not responsible for drafting the contract had a sufficient knowledge of the clauses and adhered to them.

The search for common intention is compatible with rules which forbid the proof of matters in addition or contrary to a writing, for example if the parties have negotiated a merger clause to the effect that writing contains all the terms of the contract (see) Article 2:105: Merger Clause), as it refers to external elements only to clarify the meaning of a clause, not to contradict it.

Article 5:101 states another important point: the judge should give effect to the common intention of the parties over the letter of the contract. This means that in case of conflict between the words written and the common intention, it is the latter which must prevail. Thus if a document is described as a loan but its content indicates that it is really a lease, the judge should not attach importance to the description in the document.

> *Illustration 1*: The owner of a large building employs a painting firm to repaint the "Exterior window frames". The painters repaint the outside of the frames of the exterior windows and claim that they have finished the job; the owner claims that the inside surfaces of the frames to exterior windows should also have been painted. It is proved by the preliminary documents that the representatives of the owner and of the painting firm who negotiated the contract had clearly contemplated both surfaces being done. Although the normal interpretation might suggest that only the outside surfaces were within the contract, since exterior and interior decoration are usually done separately, the parties' common intention should prevail.

All the same, the judge must not, under the guise of interpretation, modify the clear and precise meaning of the contract. This would be to ignore the principle of the binding force of contract. In the case of unforeseen supervening circumstances, Article 6:111 provides a way of adjusting the contract overtly without the need to resort to tortured interpretation.

C. *Party Knows the Real Intention of the Other Party (Second paragraph)*
If one party's words do not accurately express its intention, for instance because it expresses its intention wrongly or uses the wrong words, the other party can normally rely on the reasonable meaning of the first party's words. But this is not the case if the second party knew or could not have been unaware of the first party's actual intention. If it makes the contract without pointing out the problem it should be bound by the first party's intended interpretation. The point may be made by repeating an illustration given in the Comments to Article 4:104: Inaccuracy in Communications above:

> *Illustration 2*: A, a fur trader, offers to sell B, another fur trader, hare skins at £1.00 a kilo; this is a typing error for £1.00 a piece. In the trade skins are usually sold by the piece and, as there are about six skins to the kilo, the stated price is absurdly low. B nonetheless purports to accept. There is a contract at £1.00 per piece as A intended.

One may see in this rule also a consequence of the rule that the intention of the parties prevails over the letter of the contract.

D. *Objective Method*
The judge should not try to discover the intentions of the parties at any price and end up deciding what they were in an arbitrary way. When a common intention cannot be discerned, the judge should apply Article 5:101(3). This refers not to fictitious intentions but to the meaning that reasonable persons placed in the same circumstances as the parties would have given to the contract.

> *Illustration 3*: A clause in an insurance contract provides that the policy covers the theft of jewellery only if there has been "clandestine entry" into the place where the jewellery was. An individual, A, pretends to be a telephone repairman and presents himself at Madame B's home to repair her telephone. A distracts B with some pretext and takes the opportunity to steal her jewels. The insurance company refuses to pay up, on the basis that there has been no "clandestine entry". On a reasonable interpretation entry gained by fraud is a form of "clandestine entry".

But equally this use of objective interpretation does not empower the judge to overturn the contract under the guise of interpretation and to go against the unequivocal will of the parties.

Notes

1. *General*
Some legal systems have detailed legislative provisions on interpretation: FRENCH, BELGIAN and LUXEMBOURG CCs. arts. 1156-1164 (see *Terré, Lequette & Simler*, Obligations, nos. 418-436); SPANISH CC arts. 1258 and 1281-1289, and see *Ministerio de Justicia* II, 509 ff.; ITALIAN CC arts 1362-1371 (see *Sacco(-De Nova)* II 357 ff. and *Bianca*, Il contratto 384 ff.; also UNIDROIT arts. 4.1-4.8.

Others content themselves with statements of general principle: e.g. GERMAN BGB § 133 and 157 (see *Larenz/Wolf* AT § 28; *Münchener Kommentar (Mayer-Maly)* § 133, Rn 19, 20; *Witz* I nos. 194-199: AUSTRIAN ABGB §§ 914, 915; GREEK CC arts 173 and 200; PORTUGUESE CC arts. 236-238 (see *Fernandes* II, 343 ff.) ; CISG art. 8.

The DUTCH BW deliberately omits rules of interpretation as being too general and too well-known. They are to be found in the case law (*Asser-Hartkamp*, Verbintenissenrecht II, nos. 279 ff.). Similarly, in the NORDIC countries rules of interpretation are to be found in case law and doctrine. See for Denmark, *Lynge Andersen, Madsen & Nørgaard*, 344 ff. and *Gomard*, Kontraktsret 245 ff.; for Finland, *Hemmo*, Sopimusoikeus II, 12 ff. and *Wilhelmsson*, Standardavtal, *passim*; for Sweden, *Adlercreutz* II 31 ff. and *Ramberg*, Avtalsrätt 129 ff.

ENGLISH, SCOTTISH and IRISH rules of interpretation are case law and are not clearly distinct from rules of evidence and rules about mistake (for England, see *McKendrick* 149-150; Scotland, *McBryde*, Contract 420-439; see also Scottish Law Commission, Report on Interpretation, which proposes a systematisation of the rules on Interpretation, drawing on the Unidroit Principles and a draft version of these Principles.).

In FRANCE and LUXEMBOURG the rules of interpretation are sometimes considered to be mere guidelines which do not have to be followed (see for France, Cass. Req. 24 February 1868, DP 1868.1.308). The BELGIAN case law has abandoned this position (Cass. 22 March 1979, Arr. Cass 860; Cass. 27 April 1979, Arr. Cass. 1023), as has the ITALIAN doctrine and case law (see *Scognamiglio* 179 and, e.g., Cass. 30 January 1995, n. 1092; Cass. 17 April 1996, n. 3623).

In France, interpretation is a question of fact which is not reviewed by the *Cour de cassation*, unless clear and unambiguous clauses of the agreement have been "denatured" (since Cass. civ. 15 April 1872, DP 1872.1.176). The position is similar in Italy (*Bianca*, Il contratto 383ff.), and generally also in Germany, see *Larenz/Wolff* § 28 Rdn. 124 ff.. In England, on the other hand, interpretation is a question of law,as it is in Greece (AP 1176/1997, NoB 1977.709) and Portugal (STJ 8 May 1991, BMJ 407, 487 ff).

See generally *Zweigert & Kötz* 400-409; *Kötz*, European Contract ch. 7.

2. *Principle of common intention*
The most generally accepted principle, which flows from the will theory of contract (on the doctrine, see *Ghestin, Jamin & Billiau*, Nos. 6 ff.), is that of interpretation according to the common intention of the parties, complemented sometimes by the warning that "one should not simply take the words in their literal meaning" (FRENCH, BELGIAN and LUXEMBOURG CCs art. 1156). See also GERMAN BGB § 133; AUSTRIAN ABGB § 914; ITALIAN CC art. 1362; GREEK CC arts. 173 and 220; DUTCH BW art. 3:33 (by implication) and the case law, e.g. the *Haviltex* case, HR 13 March 1981, NJ 1981, 635; SPANISH law, CC art. 1281. The NORDIC laws are to the same effect, *Gomard*, Kontraktsret 249. See also UNIDROIT art. 4.1(1) and CISG art. 8.1.

In contrast, ENGLISH and IRISH law traditionally did not permit a search for the intentions of the parties outside the document which contains their agreement (*Lovell & Christmas Ltd* v. *Wall* (1911) 104 L.T. 85, C.A. However, if the meaning of the words is not clear, one must take into account commercial certainty and the factual matrix of the contract (*Prenn* v. *Simmonds* [1971] 1 W.L.R. 1381, H.L.) The contract must be interpreted in a way that will make commercial sense, even if that means disregarding the literal meaning of the words used; *Investors Compensation Scheme Ltd* v. *West Bromwich Building Society* [1998] 1 W. L. R. 896 (H.L.)

In SCOTS law the contract is to be interpreted according to the common intention of the parties as expressed in the contract; *McBryde*, Contract 420. A Report of the Scottish Law Commission, No.160, proposes reforms which would bring Scots law closer to the Principles.

3. *One party aware of the other party's real intention (paragraph (2))*
This rule is to be found in ENGLISH and IRISH law: *Centrovincial Estates plc* v. *Merchant Investors Assurance Ltd* [1983] Com. L.R. 158, C.A. (illustration 2 is derived from *Hartog* v. *Colin & Shields* [1939] 3 All E.R. 566, Q.B.D.; though in that case it was said that the contract was void for mistake, it is thought that the mistaken party (the seller) could have held the non-mistaken party (the buyer) to a contract on the terms the seller intended: see *Chitty* § 5-024, and it seems that the

contract document can be rectified accordingly, cf. *Commission for New Towns* v. *Cooper* [1995] 2 W.L.R. 677, C.A. The rule in the form stated is not known in SCOTS law, however: *McBryde*, Contracts 434-435.

A nearly similar rule is to be found in CISG art. 8(1) and see also SPANISH CC art. 1258. It is also to be found in the DUTCH and AUSTRIAN jurisprudence (see respectively the *Haviltex* case, above, and OGH 11 July 1985, JBl 1986 176. It is generally accepted in NORDIC law, based on Contract Acts § 32(1), see *Gomard*, Kontraktsret 169; *Ramberg*, Avtalsrätt129. GERMAN law is to the same effect: RGZ 8 June 1920, RGZ 99, 147; *Münchener Kommentar (-Kramer)* § 119, Rn 48.

In FRENCH, BELGIAN and LUXEMBOURG law, the rule in paragraph (2) does not appear openly in the jurisprudence, nor is it discussed in doctrine. These laws rely on general rules on interpretation (e.g. the common intention will prevail over the letter of the contract), good faith and error. It is the same in ITALIAN law.

4.   *Principle of objective interpretation (paragraph (3))*
Interpretation according to the meaning which would be given to the words by a reasonable person in the same situation is the basic rule in some systems: PORTUGUESE CC art. 236(1) (theory of the "impression gained by the recipient"); ENGLISH law which applies the normal meaning of the words in the context in which they were used (see Lord Wilberforce's judgments in *Prenn* v. *Simmonds* [1971] 1 W.L.R. 1381, H.L. and in *Reardon Smith Line Ltd.* v. *Yngvar Hansen-Tangen* [1976] 1 W.L.R. 898, H.L., especially at 995-996), unless it is clearly established that the parties shared a different intention (see *The Karen Oltmann* [1976] 2 Lloyd's Rep. 708, Q.B.D.). The rule is expressly stated to apply when it is not possible to discover any common intention of the parties by CISG art. 8(2) and Unidroit art. 4.1(2); see also Austrian ABGB § 914 and NORDIC law (*Gomard*, Kontraktsret 251). More frequently, the principle of reasonable interpretation is not formulated explicitly but is applied in the guise of good faith: this is the case in GERMAN law, FRENCH and BELGIAN law, DUTCH law (see *Haviltex*, supra), ITALIAN law (see CC art.1366 and also arts. 1367-1371), SPANISH law (on the latter see CC art. 1258) and GREEK law (*Balis* § 90).

Article 5:102: Relevant Circumstances

In interpreting the contract, regard shall be had, in particular, to:

(a)   *the circumstances in which it was concluded, including the preliminary negotiations;*

(b)   *the conduct of the parties, even subsequent to the conclusion of the contract;*

(c)   *the nature and purpose of the contract;*

(d)   *the interpretation which has already been given to similar clauses by the parties and the practices they have established between themselves;*

(e)   *the meaning commonly given to terms and expressions in the branch of activity concerned and the interpretation similar clauses may already have received ;*

(f)   *usages; and*

(g)   *good faith and fair dealing.*

COMMENT

Article 5:102 give the judge a non-exhaustive list of matters which may be relevant in determining either the common intention of the parties (Article 5:101(1)) or the reasonable meaning of the contract (Article 5:101(3)).

Thus the judge may consider the preliminary negotiations between the parties (letter (a)): for example, one of the parties may have defined a term in a letter and the other not have contested this interpretation when an opportunity arose. He may do this even where the parties have agreed that the written document embodies the entirety of their contract (merger clause), unless in an individually negotiated clause the parties have agreed that anterior negotiations may not be used even for purpose of interpretation (Article 2:106).

This sort of clause may be very useful when long and complicated negotiations were necessary for the contract.

The conduct of the parties, even after the making of the contract, may also provide indications as to the meaning of the contract (letter (b)).

Illustration 1: A German manufacturer of office supplies has engaged B to represent A in the north of France. The contract is for six years but it may be terminated without notice if B commits a serious non-performance of its obligations. One of these obligations is to visit each of the 20 universities in the area "every month". Assuming that this obligation applies only to the months, in the country concerned, when the universities are open and not to the vacations, B only visits each one 11 times a year, and A knows this from the accounts which are submitted to it by B. After 4 years A purports to terminate the contract for serious non-performance. Its behaviour during the four years since the conclusion of the contract leads to the interpretation that the phrase "every month" must be interpreted as applying only to the months when universities are active.

The nature and the purpose of the contract may also be considered (letter (c)).

Illustration 2: The manager of a large real estate development makes a fixed price contract with a gardening company for the maintenance of the "green spaces". The manager later complains that A has not repaired the boundary wall. The contract cannot be interpreted as covering this as it is a contract for gardening.

The practices established between the parties (letter (d)) are often decisive.

Illustration 3: A has made a franchise contract with B. A clause provides that B shall pay for goods that he receives from A within 10 days. For a three month period B pays within 10 working days. Then A demands payment within ten days including holidays. The practice adopted by the parties indicates that this is not a correct interpretation.

The reference to interpretation which the clause may already have received is primarily to standard clauses which may have been the object of a *jurisprudence*. This obviously may inform the judge's decision (letter (e) in fine).

The meaning generally given to terms and expressions in a particular sector may also be useful when one is dealing with terms which have a technical meaning different to their ordinary meaning, for example the "dozen" which is understood to mean thirteen (the "baker's dozen", which is thirteen).

Furthermore, it is normal to refer to usages as defined in Article 1:105 whether the parties may be considered to have contracted with reference to them or whether these usages form the basis of a reasonable interpretation used to resolve an uncertainty in the meaning of the contract. They may also play a role in interpretation which is filling gaps in the contract (Article 6:102).

The Article refers in principle to usages which are current at the place the contract is made, although there may be difficulty in establishing this place.

Illustration 4: A wine merchant from Hamburg buys 2,000 barrels of Beaujolais Villages from a co-operative cellar B. In Beaujolais a barrel contains 216 litres, whereas a Burgundian barrel contains more. A cannot claim that the barrels referred to in the contract are Burgundian barrels.

Illustration 5: A film producer A and a distributor B make a distribution contract in which there is a clause providing for payment of a certain sum if the number of exclusive screenings (i.e. screenings only in a single cinema or chain of cinemas) is less than 300,000. A meant exclusive for the whole of France, B only for the Paris region. According to usages of the French film industry, exclusivity means exclusivity only in the Paris region. It is this meaning which applies.

Finally, good faith and fair dealing will often determine the intepretation of the contract, see Comments to Article 1;201, illustration 1.

NOTES

The circumstances which are to be taken into account in discovering the common intention of the parties are indicated in some of the laws of the EU Member States. They may be found either in legislative texts or in the case law. E.g.: ITALIAN CC arts. 1362(2) (behaviour), 1368 (usage), 1369 (nature and purpose of the contract); FRENCH CC art. 1159 (usage; see *Terré, Lequette & Simler* no. 425 and refs. there; SPANISH CC arts. 1282 (behaviour), 1258 (nature of contract); GERMAN BGB § 157 (usage; see *Larenz*, AT § 19 II b); AUSTRIAN HGB § 345 (usages between merchants). PORTUGUESE doctrine and the jurisprudence look at the same indicators , see *Fernandes* 349 ff.; GREEK case law is to the same effect, as is DANISH law (*Gomard*, Kontraktsret 251 ff.); FINNISH law (*Commission Report* 17 ff.); and SWEDISH law, *Ramberg*, Avtalsrätt 90 ff. UNIDROIT art 4.3 refers to six factors; CISG art 8.3 to four (the negotiations, practices between the parties, usages and subsequent conduct of the parties).

ENGLISH and IRISH law are different in that they show a marked reluctance to rely on the pre-contractual negotiations as being an unreliable guide (see *Prenn v. Simmonds* [1971] 1 W.L.R. 1381, H.L.); and the subsequent conduct of the parties is not taken into account; *James Miller & Partners* v. *Whitworth Street Estates (Manchester) Ltd* [1970] A.C. 583, H.L. However, the circumstances in which the contract was made and its aim and purpose are considered (see references in Note 4 to Article 5:101 above and *Chitty* §§ 12-104 - 12-105). The elements listed under (e) (meaning given to the provision previously) and (f) (usages) are also accepted by English law, and even a usage may not be accepted if it is not consistent with the written agreement (*Palgrave Brown & Sons* v. *SS Turid* [1922] 1 A.C. 397, H.L.. In contrast, SCOTTISH law uses the factors listed in Article 5:102 except for (b) (subsequent conduct).

Article 5:103: Contra Proferentem Rule

Where there is doubt about the meaning of a contract term not individually negotiated, an interpretation of the term against the party which supplied it is to be preferred.

COMMENT

This rule, which is expressed by the ancient formula *verba cartarum fortius accipiuntur contra proferentem* (Bacon's Maxims 3), is widely recognised both in legislation and above all in case law in the different national and international laws. It rests on the idea that the party who has drafted a clause, or the whole contract, unilaterally should normally bear the risk of any defect in the drafting. The rule applies not only against the author but also against anyone who uses pre-drafted clauses. This will be the case when the clauses have been prepared by a third party, for example the professional association to which the party employing the clauses belongs.

It applies in particular to general conditions of contract drawn up unilaterally by one party, but it may also apply to a contract of adhesion which has been drawn up for the particular occasion but which is non-negotiable.

Illustration: An insurance contract contains a clause excluding losses caused by "floods". The insurance company which drafted the contract cannot maintain that this exclusion applies to damage caused by water escaping from a burst pipe, since it has not made this clear.

It should be noted that the Article states only that the interpretation against the party who supplied the term "is to be preferred". A judge could, in appropriate circumstances, interpret a clause which has not been individually negotiated in favour of the party who proposed it.

NOTES

The *contra proferentem* rule is very widely recognised, either explicitly or implicitly; it appears frequently in texts on consumer protection, particularly in those which consider the Directive 93/13 of 5 April 1993 on Unfair Terms in Consumer Contracts, art.5 and the legislation which implements it. See for GERMANY: AGBG § 5, following earlier case law, which continues to apply to non-consumer contracts; AUSTRIA, ABGB § 915, applying to all pre-formulated contracts; ENGLAND: *Hollier* v. *Rambler Motors (AMC) Ltd* [1972] 2 Q.B. 71, C.A. (English law has sometimes applied the rule in an exaggerated way to restrict the effect of clauses limiting liability); DENMARK: Contracts Act § 38(b) and *Gomard,* Kontraktsret 257; FINLAND: Consumer Protection Act, chapter 4, § 3 and for other applications see *Wilhelmsson,* Standardavtal 91; SWEDEN: see *Ramberg,* Avtalsrätt 173-177; SPAIN: CC art. 1288 and Law 26/1984 of 19 July 1984 on Consumer Protection, art. 10-2; FRANCE, case law applying CC arts. 1162 (interpretation against the *stipulant*) and 1602 (interpretation against the seller) and Code de Consommation art. L.133-2 (Law of 1 February 1995); BELGIUM: caselaw which applies the rule if the other rules do not give a result; ITALY: CC art. 1370, which the caselaw applies only to "mass contracts" (see also CC art. 1469(4), 2nd co.); THE NETHERLANDS: the rule, which has not yet been adopted legislatively, is viewed by the recent decisions of the Hoge Raad as "one point of view", see HR 12 January 1996, NJ 1996, 683). In GREECE the rule is recognised directly only for consumer contracts, Law 2251/1994, arts. 2.6 and 2.7. In PORTUGAL the rule applies only to general conditions (D.L. 12446/85 of 25 October 1985, art. 11(2); in other cases the judge may, if in doubt, choose the meaning which will give better balance to the contract. See also UNIDROIT art. 4.6.

Article 5:104: Preference to Negotiated Terms

Terms which have been individually negotiated take preference over those which have not.

COMMENTS

If in an otherwise non-negotiable contract (standard form or otherwise) there is, exceptionally, a clause which has been negotiated, it is reasonable to suppose that this clause will represent the common intention of the parties, other indications apart. This rule complements Article 5:103.

The preference given to negotiated clauses applies also to modifications made to a printed contract, whether by hand or in any other way (e.g. typed or stamped on). One may in effect assume that these modifications were negotiated. However, it is a rebuttable presumption.

Illustration: A printed form is used for the conclusion of an option to purchase land. One of the clauses provides that the eventual buyer will deposit a cheque for 10% of the price with an intermediary until the option is either taken up or is refused. The parties agree to replace the requirement for a cheque with a bank guarantee. The intermediary writes this change on the margin of the document but omits to cross out the printed clause. The contradiction between the two clauses is to be resolved in favour of the hand-written clause.

The rule applies even if the modification was oral.

This rule must be distinguished from that in Article 2:209 Conflicting General Conditions, which, by definition, concerns contracts which were not individually negotiated.

NOTES

This rule is sometimes formulated only in legislation on consumer protection or on particular contracts, for example on insurance contracts. See for AUSTRIA: Law on Protection of Consumers of 8 March 1979, § 6; SPAIN: Law 26/84 on Protection of Consumers, art. 10.2.2; PORTUGAL: Law 446/85 of 25 October 1985, art.10. In other laws the rule applies generally; see for GERMANY AGBG § 4; on NORDIC law see for Denmark, *Gomard*, Kontraktsret 254; Sweden, *Ramberg*, Avtalsrätt 178 and NSA 1993, 436; Finland, *Hoppu* 46. ENGLISH and SCOTTISH law are to the same effect, *Glynn* v. *Margetson* [1893] A.C. 351, H.L. In FRENCH and BELGIAN case law (for France see Cass.com. 7 January 1969, JCP 1969.II.16121) the same result is reached by application of the common intention test; similarly the DUTCH case law, see *Asser-Hartkamp*, Verbintenissenrecht II, no. 287. In ITALY the rule is formulated in CC art. 1342 in a section on "Agreement of the parties"; this is an imperative rule and not a presumption left to the appreciation of the judge (Cass. 5 April 1990, no. 2863, Foro it. Rep., Contratto in genere, no. 240).

Article 5:105: Reference to Contract as a Whole

Terms are to be interpreted in the light of the whole contract in which they appear.

COMMENT

It is reasonable to assume that the parties meant to express themselves coherently. It is thus necessary to interpret the contract as a whole and not to isolate clauses from each other and read them out of context. It must be presumed that the terminology will be coherent; in principle, the same term should not be understood to have different meanings in different parts of the same contract. The contract must be interpreted in a way that gives it basic coherence, so that the clauses do not contradict each other.

There is normally no particular hierarchy between the elements of a contract, save under special circumstances: for example, particular emphasis should be given to any definition of terms or to a preamble which could have been introduced into the contract.

Article 5:105 may also be applied to groups of contracts. For example one can treat a frame-work (master) contract and the various contracts made under it as a whole. By the "whole contract" must be understood the "whole group of contracts".

Illustration: Miss A, an inexperienced singer, is taken on for six months by B, the manager of a cabaret on the Champs-Elysées. The contract contains a clause authorising the manager to end the contract in the first three days of the singer starting work. Another clause allows either party to determine the contract on payment of a significant sum of money as a penalty. Miss A is fired after one day and claims payment of the sum. Her claim should fail because the penalty clause is to be read in the light of the clause allowing determination within three days, which is a trial period.

NOTES

This rule is stated in a number of texts: ITALIAN CC art. 1363; FRENCH, BELGIAN and LUXEMBOURG CCs art. 1161; SPANISH CC art. 1285; UNIDROIT art. 4.4. In PORTUGAL it is found in Law 446/1985 of 15 October 1985 and has been extended to all contracts. It is also found in NORDIC law: Swedish Supreme Court, NJA 1990, 24; for Denmark, see *Lynge Andersen* 357 ff. The rule is also found in English law, see *Chitty* §§12-053 - 2-059 and refs. there, SCOTTISH, GERMAN, AUSTRIAN and GREEK law.

The illustration is inspired by French Cass. soc. 7 March 1973, B 73 V no.145.

Article 5:106: Terms to Be Given Effect

An interpretation which renders the terms of the contract lawful, or effective, is to be preferred to one which would not.

COMMENT

The parties must be treated as sensible persons who intended that their contract should be fully effective (*magis ut res valeat quam pereat*). Thus if a clause is ambiguous and could be interpreted in one way which would make it invalid or another which would make it valid, the latter interpretation should prevail (*favor negotii*).

Illustration 1: Architect A assigns his practice to architect B and undertakes not to exercise his profession for five years "in the region". If region is interpreted to mean the administrative region which contains several departments, the clause would be invalid as too wide. If region is interpreted in a less technical and more reasonable sense (a reasonable area) the clause will be valid and fully effective.

For identical reasons, if one of two possible interpretations would lead to an absurd result the other must be taken.

Illustration 2: A grants B a licence to produce pipes by a patented method. B must pay a royalty of 500 BF per 100 metres if annual production is less than 500,000 metres and 300 BF if it is over 500,000 metres. To calculate the royalties on 600,000 metres, one can interpret the clause as fixing the price at 500 BF/m for the first 500,000 m and 300 BF/m for the remainder, or the rate of 300 BF/m could be applied to the whole quantity. The latter interpretation is not valid because it leads to an absurd result: the royalty for a production of 600,000 m. would be less than that for 400,000 m.

NOTES

The rule in favour of full effect is to be found in several codes: FRENCH, BELGIAN and LUXEMBOURG CCs art. 1157; ITALIAN CC art. 1367; SPANISH CC art. 1284. See also indirectly PORTUGUESE CC art. 237. It is adopted by UNIDROIT art. 4.5. It is recognised by case law in GERMANY, BGH 3 March 1971, NJW 1971, 1035; AUSTRIA, OGH 4 December 1985, JBl 1987, 378; ENGLAND, e.g. *NV Handel Smits* v. *English Exporters Ltd* [1955] 2 Lloyd's Rep. 317, C.A.; *Chitty* § 12-064. IRISH and SCOTS law are similar. For DANISH law see *Lynge Andersen* 377 ff.; for FINLAND, *Hoppu* 47; for SWEDEN, *Ramberg*, Avtalsrätt 178.

It should be noted that for the purposes of Article 7(2), collective action, of the Directive on Unfair Terms in Consumer Contracts of 5 April 1993 (93/13/EEC), the interpretation in favour of full effect is not applied because in this case the article intends to strike down abusive clauses.

Illustration 2 is taken from Restatement of Contracts 2d, § 206, comment (c).

Article 5:107: Linguistic Discrepancies

Where a contract is drawn up in two or more language versions none of which is stated to be authoritative, there is, in case of discrepancy between the versions, a preference for the interpretation according to the version in which the contract was originally drawn up.

COMMENT

International contracts are sometimes drafted in more than one language and there may be divergences between the different linguistic versions. The parties may provide a solution by stating that one version is to be authoritative, in which case that version will prevail. If nothing is provided and it is not possible to eliminate the divergences by other means (e.g. by correcting obvious errors of translation in one version), Article 5:107 gives a reasonable solution by providing that the original version shall be treated as the authoritative one, since it is likely to express best the common intention of the parties.

> *Illustration*: A French business and a German business make a contract in French and in German. The contract contains an arbitration clause. The French text provides that the arbitrator "*s'inspire*" from the rules of the ICC, i.e. he may follow them. The German version provides "*er folgt*", i.e. the arbitrator must follow the ICC rules. The French version was the original and this is the one which should prevail.

If the contract provides that the different versions shall be equally authoritative, the will of the parties must be respected by observing this and resorting to the general rules of interpretation. It is not possible simply to give precedence to one version. It must be decided which version corresponds better to the common intention of the parties or, if this cannot be established, what reasonable persons would understand.

It is important to read this provision with the *contra proferentem* rule of Article 5:103 if the original version was drafted by one of the parties.

NOTES

The nearest provision to Article 5:107 is UNIDROIT art. 4.7, which deals only with discrepancies between versions which are stated to be equally authoritative. The national laws do not appear to contain any rules on the points covered by the Article applying specifically to contracts.

CHAPTER 6

Contents and Effects

Article 6:101: Statements giving rise to Contractual Obligations

(1) A statement made by one party before or when the contract is concluded is to be treated as giving rise to a contractual obligation if that is how the other party reasonably understood it in the circumstances, taking into account:

(a) the apparent importance of the statement to the other party;

(b) whether the party was making the statement in the course of business; and

(c) the relative expertise of the parties.

(2) If one of the parties is a professional supplier which gives information about the quality or use of services or goods or other property when marketing or advertising them or otherwise before the contract for them is concluded, the statement is to be treated as giving rise to a contractual obligation unless it is shown that the other party knew or could not have been unaware that the statement was incorrect.

(3) Such information and other undertakings given by a person advertising or marketing services, goods or other property for the professional supplier, or by a person in earlier links of the business chain, are to be treated as giving rise to a contractual obligation on the part of the professional supplier unless it did not know and had no reason to know of the information or undertaking.

COMMENT

A. *Statements*

Paragraph (1) reiterates the rule that statements may become part of the contract. Whether or not this is the case is dependent upon how this is perceived by the parties to the contract. The paragraph enumerates some elements which may make it easier to ascertain the parties' perception.

B. *Supplier*

The rules in paragraphs (2) and (3) relate only to information and promises on quality or use given by a supplier of services goods or other property. Goods are tangible movables. Other property includes immovables and intangibles such as industrial property. The Commission takes no definite stand as to whether the rules could apply by way of analogy to other information.

C. *Remedies for Incorrect Information or Broken Promises*
Under the rule in paragraph (2) information given and promises made by a supplier become part of the contract. If the information is incorrect or if the promise (undertaking) is broken, the other party may resort to the remedies for non-performance of the contract provided in chapters 7, 8 and 9. Thus, it can make the supplier perform the contract as promised, and hold it liable in damages irrespective of fault, unless the non-performance is excused. Even if the non-performance is excused the aggrieved party may terminate the contract if the non-performance is substantial.

D. *Statement must have Influenced Decision*
In order for the aggrieved party to invoke the rule, the information or the undertaking must have influenced its decision to conclude the contract. Statements or promises which are mere sales talk are not covered by the rule. This means that statements of opinion such as "these goods will make your customers happy" are not to be considered as information. Information and undertakings which are gross overstatements such as "we will give you a royal treatment" are not to be taken literally (see also Illustration 1 to Article 4:107). Nor can information or promises which the other party considered irrelevant become part of the contract. A seller of a horse will not be held liable for telling the buyerthat the horse has belonged to the Queen if the buyer is a horse butcher buying the horse for its flesh.

E. *Mistake may Also be Invoked*
A misrepresentation by a party may also give rise to the right to avoidance on the grounds of a mistake under Chapter 4, Article 4:103; or to a right to damages for Incorrect Information under Article 4:106. However, if before the conclusion of the contract a supplier, or another for whom the supplier is liable (see para. (3)), gives incorrect information on quality or use, this information will always be treated as forming part of the contract. The other party may choose between remedies, see Article 4:119.

F. *Liability for Others*
The rule in paragraph (3) extends the liability of a supplier to information or promises given by persons acting for the suppliers or by persons in earlier links of the business chain who promote the sale of the services or property.

Persons acting for the supplier are its agents and independent persons whom it has hired, such as advertising agencies. It is the same category of persons as those covered by Article 1:305. Information and undertakings made by persons in earlier links of the business chain are such as is supplied in advertisements, in the press or in advertising matters distributed by manufacturers or wholesale dealers. The rule does not apply to information etc. supplied by persons marketing the same goods or services in competition with the supplier, even though the supplier has profited by their information.

On the other hand, the rule applies even though the supplier has not invoked the information, etc. or referred to it when marketing its goods or services or when making the contract.

In most cases the rule in paragraph (3) will come into operation in case of supplies to end users, be they consumers or business enterprises. However, it may also apply to supplies to middlemen.

Illustration 1: In an advertisement published all over Europe a Swedish manufacturer announces that its new tiles for outdoor use are absolutely frost-proof. Some tiles are bought by a German importer and re-sold to a Belgian dealer. The dealer may hold the importer liable when the tiles delivered are damaged by frost.

G. *The Innocent Supplier*
Paragraph (3) does not apply if the supplier did not know or ought not to have known of the information or undertaking.

Illustration 2: Before buying type Z fibreboard from S, B asks the manufacturer M whether the fibreboard, which B intends to use in the construction of a building, is fireproof. M by an error transmits the information on fibreboard T which is fireproof. S, who knows nothing of the information given to B, is not responsible for the error.

Nor will the rules in paragraph (2) or (3) apply when the supplier, those for whom it is responsible, or others have corrected the information and made the correction clear and accessible to the buyer before it made the contract.

NOTES

1. *Statements become part of the contract*
   The rule in paragraph (1) is part of the common core of the legal systems of the Union, see for example for GERMANY, Larenz/Wolf 481f, and for FRANCE Ghestin, Formation no 388. It is also in accordance with DANISH law, see *Lynge Andersen* 189 ff.. The legislation of the last decades imposing penal sanctions for misleading marketing has made civil liability for marketing information more stringent; statements made by a party as marketing information will now more often than before become contractual undertakings – see *Gomard*, Kontraktsret 117 and the decision of the Supreme Court in *Ugeskrift for Retsvaesen* 1984, 384.
   In ENGLISH law, a statement made by one party, if it is a statement of fact, may amount to a representation. If it is not correct, there will then be a remedy for misrepresentation (avoidance and damages if there was fault – see Notes to Article 4:103 and 4.106). However, a statement may also amount to a contractual undertaking that what is stated is true. The question is one of the intention of the parties (*Heilbut Symons & Co v. Buckleton* [1913] A.C. 30, H.L.), but this is judged objectively, as the other party should reasonably understand the statement. In practice, the courts look at whether the statement was particularly important (e.g. *Bannerman v. White* (1861) 10 CBns 844); whether the person speaking was expert in relation to the other party or vice versa (see *Oscar Chess Ltd v. Williams* [1975] 1 W.L.R. 370, C.A. and *Dick Bentley Productions Ltd v. Harold Smith Motors Ltd* [1965] 2 All E.R. 65, C.A.; and similar factors, see *Treitel*, Contracts 326-330; *Chitty* § 41-043. SCOTS law is broadly similar, see *Stair*, vol. 15 §§ 698-701.
   PORTUGUESE law also looks to the intention of the parties to determine the existence and content of contractual declarations, *P.M.Pinto*, Declaracào tacita 188 ff.; these are judged by reasonable understanding of the recipient, *Almeida* 177 ff.

2.   *Advertising by manufacturers and producers*

A rule similar to paragraph (2) covering warranties by the seller is found in the U.S., UCC Article 2-313. FINNISH and SWEDISH Sale of Goods Acts, § 18 provide

(1)   Goods are to be considered defective if they do not conform with information about their quality or use which the seller has supplied before the conclusion of the contract and which must be presumed to have influenced the buyer when making his purchase.

(2)   Goods are to be considered defective if they do not conform with information about their quality or use supplied by other persons than the seller in earlier links of the sales chain or on account of the seller when marketing the goods, and which must be presumed to have influenced the buyer when making his purchase. There is, however, no defect if the seller did not know or ought not to have known of the said information.

(3)   The rules in paragraph (1) and (2) do not apply if the information has been corrected in time and in clear terms.

This provision is found in the chapter on consumer sales, as is the similar DANISH Sale of Goods Act § 76(2), but *Gomard*, Kontraktsret 118 assumes that the rule also applies to contracts, whether they are sale of goods or supply of services, as between merchants.

A rule similar to para (3) is found in DUTCH BW, art. 7:18, where it only applies to protect the consumer (and only in the case of sale of goods); and in the PORTUGUESE law 24/94 of 31 July 1996, art. 7, No.6.

Under art. 24 (3) of the BELGIAN Trade Practices and Consumer Protection Act of 14 July 1991, contracts may be interpreted in the light of the factual elements contained in advertisements (including the qualities and use of the products offered).

Other laws, such as AUSTRIAN law, do not have similar provisions; but in some, doctrine has developed a similar approach, particularly as a way of protecting consumers against misleading advertising, treating what was said in the advertisment as part of the contract. See for SPAIN, *Lasarte*, RPD (1980) 50 ff.; *Font Galán*, CDC (1988) 7 ff. In ENGLISH law there is no direct equivalent to Article 6:101(2) but, as stated earlier (see note 1), a statement by a party who is relatively expert (e.g. a professional supplier) is likely to be treated as a term of the contract. English law does not recognise the rule in paragraph (3); the seller or supplier will not be liable for the statement made in advertising by another party unless the seller or supplier expressly or implictly adopted the statement.

See generally: *Regeringens Proposition* 87-90; *McGregor*, Contract Code § 103; *Asser-Hijma* Nr. 341.

Article 6:102: Implied Terms

In addition to the express terms, a contract may contain implied terms which stem from

(a)   the intention of the parties,

(b)   the nature and purpose of the contract, and

(c)   good faith and fair dealing.

COMMENT

A. *Lacunae in the Contract Terms Agreed by the Parties*

To determine the content of a contract, it is not sufficient to resolve any ambiguities in what the parties had expressly agreed; it may also be necessary to complete it where the parties have not provided some clause which is necessary for the working of the contract, in other words where the contract has a lacuna. This may occur whether or not the parties have discussed the possibility of including such a clause. Article 2:103, Sufficient Agreement, defines the degree of agreement sufficient for a contract to be created and then refers to other supplementary Articles, contained in this Chapter, under which other terms can be determined. Some of these deal with specific issues: e.g. the price (Article 6:104), the quality of performance (Article 6:108) and what is to happen if an agreed mechanism for determining the price or some other term fails (Articles 6:105-6:107). It is also important to refer to Article 1:105, Usages and Practices.

When these specific supplementary Articles do not apply, Article 6:102 allows the court or arbitrator to fill the lacuna in an appropriate way.

B. *Implied Terms*

The Article achieves this by stating that a contract may contain implied terms. Most legal systems will consider this self-evident, but some do not.

C. *Factors to be Taken into Account*

The provision also gives an indication as to where an implied term may arise from. The first indicator refers to the presumed intention of the parties; the court should consider what parties, acting in accordance with good faith and fair dealing, would reasonably have agreed if they had discussed the question.

> *Illustration 1*: Madame A enters a retirement home, paying a premium of £5000. The contract provides for a six-months trial period; if, at the end of the trial period, she decides not to remain in the home, her premium will be returned. She dies after three months. The contract does not provide for this eventuality but during the negotiations the parties clearly regarded the whole arrangement as provisional for the trial period. The £5000 must be repaid to her estate.

The second indicator, the nature and purpose of the contract, allows the court to consider how the contract can best be carried out. Considerable guidance may be obtained by looking at terms usually contained in similar contracts, or laid down in International Conventions dealing with analogous contracts.

The final indicator, good faith and fair dealing, requires the court to look in an objective fashion at what good faith and fair dealing would require. If the contract would be very risky for one party unless a term is implied to give that party some protection, a suitable term should be implied.

> *Illustration 2*: A shipowner contracts to unload the ship alongside a wharf in the Thames, where at low tide the ship will rest on the river-bed. The state of the river-bed is unknown to the shipowner, and in fact there is a ridge of rock across it which damages the ship. The wharfinger is under an implied obligation to warn the shipowner of any such danger.

D. Obligation de résultat *and* obligation de moyens

It is frequently necessary to determine whether a contract to do something is one which imposes a duty to achieve a specific result, or one which requires the party to use reasonable efforts to achieve it. Some jurisdictions refer to this as the distinction between an *obligation de résultat* and an *obligation de moyens*. The latter only obliges the debtor to "use reasonable efforts"; the former requires a certain result to be arrived at.

In determining which is required by the contract, regard may sometimes be had to, among others things,
- (a)   the way in which the obligation is expressed in the contract;
- (b)   the contractual price and the other terms of the contract;
- (c)   the degree of risk normally involved in achieving the expected result;
- (d)   the ability of the other party (the creditor) to influence the performance of the obligation.

The distinction should not serve as a boundary between contracts for the sale of goods and construction contracts on the one hand and contracts for the supply of services on the other. Either contract may contain either type of term.

Illustration 3: A surgeon is employed to carry out a sterilisation operation on a man. The surgeon uses all reasonable care and skill but the operation reverses itself naturally and the man's wife becomes pregnant. As medical operations are well known to carry an element of risk, and patients seldom expect a guaranteed cure, the surgeon is not treated as guaranteeing that the man will be rendered sterile, though he might be liable if he failed to warn the man of the risk of spontaneous reversal.

Illustration 4: A building contractor instructs a roofing sub-contractor to use a particular type of roofing tile, which the subcontractor has to buy from the manufacturer. The manufacturer is reputable and there is nothing to suggest to the subcontractor that the tiles are not of proper quality, but in fact they have not been made properly and they crack in the frost. The roofing subcontractor will be liable even though it had used all reasonable care and skill, as the aim of the contract is to provide a useable roof. Also, if the subcontractor were not liable, the building contractor might not have any remedy, as in many jurisdictions (and under these Principles) it will have no direct claim against the manufacturer.

Rather one may often distinguish within a specific contracts various obligations of the former and of the latter type.

Illustration 5: A company employs a firm of tax advisers to prepare the company's tax return which, by law, must be completed by a certain date. The advisers are under an obligation to use reasonable care and skill in the preparation of the return and will not be liable if, for instance, they adopt a practice which is widely used by competent firms of advisers even if at a later date the tax courts hold that the practice was incorrect. However, the tax advisers are under a strict obligation to have the return completed by the deadline, so that the serious illness of the partner responsible does not constitute a defence.

NOTES

1. *Implied terms*

   The phrase "implied terms" derives from the COMMON LAW, and refers to the process by which the ENGLISH and IRISH courts supply terms to fill lacunae in the contract. The approach of Article 6:102 is in accordance with the English law except that (1) the latter does not normally refer to good faith and fair dealing; and (2) the English courts are reluctant to imply terms into a contract. This is particularly the case when the term is an unusual one (a term to be "implied in fact") which would not be applicable to the general run of contracts of that type. Then the term will be implied only if it is necessary to give the contract business efficacy or is so obvious that it goes without saying. In the case of a more general nature (terms to be "implied in law") it has sometimes been said that the test is again one of necessity (e.g. Lord Wilberforce in *Liverpool CC* v. *Irwin* [1977] AC 229, H.L.; other judges have taken a less restrictive approach, e.g. Lord Denning M.R. in *Shell UK Ltd* v. *Lostock Garage Ltd* [1976] 1 W.L.R. 1187, C.A. See *Treitel*, Contract 193-194; *Chitty* § 13-003 - 13-004. SCOTS law also recognises implied terms, *Stair* vol.15 711-717.

   AUSTRIAN ABGB § 863 (1) expressly recognises implied terms: a party's "intention is manifest not expressly by words and generally adopted signs but also tacitly by acts which in regard to their circumstances reveal an intention beyond substantial doubt". Whether an implied or "conclusive" term forms part of an agreement must be scrutinized by taking "[t]he custom and usage prevailing in honest transactions" into consideration. Again, there is hesitation to imply a term and a term will be implied only if there is no substantial doubt about the significance of the relevant act or omission: OGH 11 May 1986, Juristische Blätter 1986, 97. The rule is in accordance with SWEDISH law, see *Adlercreutz* II, 32 ff..

   The GERMAN courts use the term "constructive interpretation" (*ergänzende Vertragsauslegung*). "Where the parties have omitted to say something", the judge must "discover and take into account what, in the light of the whole purpose of the contract, they would have said if they had regulated the point in question, acting pursuant to the requirements of good faith and sound business practice", see BGH 18 December 1954, BGHZ 16, 71, 76. Also the FRENCH and BELGIAN CCs arts. 1135 provide that "the obligations under contract extend not only to what is expressly stipulated, but also to everything which by law, equity or custom must follow from the nature of the particular contract". See on French law *Malaurie & Aynès*, Obligations no. 632 ff.

   Some legal systems do not refer to implied terms: for example, PORTUGUESE law. All the same, a result similar to that of the Principles is arrived at under the application of the general principles on tacit declarations, interpretation and the filling of contractual gaps, and the execution of obligations in good faith (*Pinto,* Declaraçâo tácita 138). In SPANISH law, CC art. 1258 provides that contractual duties can also arise even if they have not been agreed expressly; so long as they are in accordance with usage and practice, the law and good faith. Even in England it is recognised that "[t]erms implied by law are, in truth, simply duties prima facie arsing out of certain types of contracts, or, as it has been put, "legal incidents of those kinds of contractual relationship"" (*Treitel*, Contracts 190, quoting *Mears* v. *Safecar Securities Ltd* [1983] Q.B. 54, 78, C.A.).

2. *Obligation de résultat and obligation de moyens*

   The distinction between *obligation de résultat* and *obligation de moyens* is well known in some European jurisdictions, such as BELGIUM, FRANCE, ITALY and the NETHERLANDS: e.g. for France see *Terré, Simler & Lequette* Nos. 552 ff; for Italy, *Mengoni*, Riv. dir. comm 1954, I, 185. It is not used in others, such as DENMARK, FINLAND and GERMANY.

   However, the distinction coincides with the criterion generally accepted in Germany to distinguish a contract for services, under which the services themselves are owed but the result is not guararanteed, from a contract for work in which the specific result must be achieved, cf. BGB §§ 631, 652(1) sent. 1, HGB § 425.

   The COMMON LAW and SCOTS law do not use the distinction, but it is clear that some obligations are strict, in the sense that there is liability without fault (e.g. the seller's obligations quality under Sale of Goods Act 1979, ss.13 and 14 to supply goods which correspond to the description and, if the sale is in the course of a business, which are of satisfactory quality), while others, particularly under contracts for services, are only obligations to use reasonable care and skill (Supply of Goods and Services Act 1982, s.13)

   Illustration 2 is based on *The Moorcock* (1889) 14 P.D. 64; Illustration 3 on *Thake* v. *Maurice* [1986] Q.B. 644, C.A.; and Illustration 4 on *Young & Marten Ltd* v. *McManus Childs Ltd* [1969] 1 A.C. 454, H.L..

   See generally *Kötz*, European Contact 117-120.

Article 6:103: Simulation

When the parties have concluded an apparent contract which was not intended to reflect their true agreement, as between the parties the true agreement prevails.

COMMENTS

A. *Definition and Types of Simulation*

Simulation is the situation in which the parties, with the aim of concealing their real intentions, have made two agreements: an overt one (the sham transaction) and another which is intended to remain secret. This covert agreement is sometimes described as a counter-letter (*contre-lettre*). It is thus different to the case where there is a single agreement which is merely ambiguous or vague, so that its meaning falls to be discovered by interpretation under the rules of Chapter 5.

The simulation may have the aim of making it appear that there is an agreement which in fact the parties have no intention of entering: for example if a debtor who is threatened with distraint of his goods by creditors enters a fictitious sale of his goods, or an entrepreneur creates a fictitious company to limit his liability. It may also relate to the nature of the transaction (thus a fictitious sale with a secret agreement that the price shall not be paid is a disguised gift) or to the content of the agreement (e.g. the price).

Finally, the simulation may relate to the true beneficiary of the contract: a sale is concluded with one person for whom another will really be substituted, the true buyer. In this case the secret agreement is one of agency, which reveals that the person who has ostensibly made the agreement is in reality an agent and, at the demand of the seller, may be treated as such (*prête-nom*, or man of straw). This operation, bringing in the undisclosed principal, imports the rules on the authority of agents, see Article 3:301.

B. *Effect as between the Parties.*

As between the parties, it is the secret agreement which prevails so long as the proper conditions exist for that agreement to be valid. Thus simulation is not in itself a cause of invalidity when it does not have a fraudulent purpose (in which case the agreement may be illegal; the question of illegality is not yet within the scope of these Principles, see Article 4:101). It is the covert act which expresses the real intentions of the parties and it follows from the principle of freedom of contract that it should govern.

> *Illustration*: A, a wine merchant, is in urgent need of cash. As it does not want to drive down market prices and as it cannot find a buyer quickly at the current price in a dull market, it sells part of its stock to B, apparently at the current market price but with a counter-letter to the effect that the real price will be 30% lower than the market price. A cannot recover the full market price from B, only the price fixed in the counter-letter.

For the same reason one party cannot, as against the other, use the apparent agreement as a defence.

C. *Effects as against Third Parties*

The Principles do not regulate the consequences of simulation as against third parties (in particular, holders of negotiable instruments) as the national solutions are too divergent. The matter must therefore be referred to the applicable national law.

NOTES

The rule stated in the Article is recognised in all Member States. In contrast, the rules in relation to third parties differ.

The COMMON LAW does not have a general theory of simulation; the problems are dealt with by way of proof of the true contents of the contract, of illegality and of estoppel (*Nicholas* 195; *Goode*, Commercial Law 692). SCOTS law is similar. However, note the particular provision of the U.K. Sale of Goods Act 1979, s. 62(4) (security disguised as a sale).

Some other laws content themselves with stating that the apparent act is invalid, even in relation to third parties. Only the hidden act is valid. See for GERMANY, BGB § 117 (*Larenz* AT § 20; *Witz* I nos. 224-233; the rule may apply even in cases of good faith, though this is discussed in the doctrine); for AUSTRIA: ABGB § 916(2) (which protects the third party who acted in good faith); for GREECE: CC arts 138 and 139 (the third party who acted in good faith may always invoke the apparent act, *Georgiadis & Stathopolous* art 138, no. 8, or demand annulation of the contract: AP 475/1991, HellDni 1993.564); for PORTUGAL, CC arts. 240-242.

Other laws have a more subtle theory which allows the third party or chirographic creditors a choice. Thus in FRANCE, CC art. 1321 and the jurisprudence allow the third party to invoke the apparent act and, if there is a conflict between third parties, preference is given to the one who relied on the apparent act, *Malaurie & Aynès*, Obligations nos. 623-629. Some other systems produce similar results: ITALIAN CC arts. 1414-1417; SPANISH CC arts. 1275, 1300, 1301-1302; BELGIAN law; and DUTCH law, see *Hartkamp-Tillema* no.74. In NORDIC law the secret act is valid as between the parties but the third party who acquires in good faith is protected, particularly as a result of Contracts Acts § 34 (for DENMARK, see *Gomard*, Kontraktsret 136; for SWEDEN, *Ramberg*, Avtalsrätt 129.

Article 6:104: Determination of Price

Where the contract does not fix the price or the method of determining it, the parties are to be treated as having agreed on a reasonable price.

COMMENT

A. *Introduction to Articles 6:104-6:107*

Article 6:104 and the articles which follow it are intended to govern cases in which there is no doubt that the parties intended to be bound by the contract, but some element of it is not determined sufficiently precisely for it to be performed. The Articles create rules which can be used to "save" the contract in those cases in which it seems reasonable to do so because it is probable that the parties meant there to be a binding contract.

The commonest case is where the price, that is, a counter-performance to be paid in money, is not fixed, and it is this which is covered by Article 6:104. Other terms may also be missing; these may be supplied under Article 6:102 above.

The approach taken by the Principles abandons the traditional, rigorous attitude of some legal systems, under which the absence or insufficient determination of the object necessarily means that the contract is void or is discharged. Rather than take such a dogmatic attitude it seems better to empower the court to save the contract.

As far as quality is concerned, Article 6:108 of the Principles provides that, if the quality of a performance to be rendered is not defined by the contract, it must be of at least average quality. The provisions are clearly not intended to exclude the possibility of the court resorting to the implication of terms in other circumstances.

B. *The presumption in Article 6:104*

Article 6:104 assumes that, on the one hand, the parties intended to conclude a contract and, on the other, that they did not agree on a price. It may have been an emergency.

> *Illustration 1*: A helicopter carrying urgently needed medical supplies has to land after having engine trouble. The carrier telephones the helicopter manufacturer and asks for a repairman to be sent as soon as possible. Nothing is said about the price. The contract is valid nonetheless and is considered to be one for a reasonable price.

In some other contracts it is not the custom to ask the price in advance; or the debtor leaves it to the creditor to fix the price (e.g. when an opinion is sought from a professional person).

To avoid all dispute about the validity of a contract which does not contain a price, the Article creates a presumption that the parties intended the normal price. Thus there will nearly always be some price, through either express or implicit agreement of the parties or according to the presumption. The presumption will cease to apply if the parties have tried to fix a price but did so in such an uncertain manner that the price is neither determined nor determinable. In such a case there will be no contract.

C. *Conditions of application*

It is important to note the precise conditions under which this Article will apply.

Firstly, the provisions cannot apply unless the parties themselves have not fixed the price, directly or indirectly, explicitly or implicitly. Usages and any practices established between the parties must be taken into account. Thus if it is customary for a contract with an architect to be at the scale fee established by the architects' professional association, the price is already determinable.

Secondly, Article 6:104 may not be used to allow the court to intervene when the parties had failed to agree; if, for instance, during the negotiations the parties have been unable to come to any agreement over the price. Similarly, if the parties left the question open for future negotiation and when this took place they were unable to reach an accord, the court may not intervene to fix a reasonable price. However, the subsequent behaviour of the parties may show that they did intend to enter contractual relations. In this case, the rule created by Article 6:104 can be applied to fill the gap.

> *Illustration 2*: Construction Company A normally hires the cranes it uses for its works from Company B. The latter informs A that it is increasing its prices "to a figure to be agreed by the parties". Before any agreement on the price has been reached A orders a further crane. The crane is delivered and put into use. The contract may be considered as concluded at a reasonable price.

On what constitutes a reasonable price, see Article 1:302.

NOTES

1. *Agreement on subject matter*

    Parties who wish to make a contract must determine its subject matter; they must agree on what is to be performed. All the laws agree on that. Several of the legal systems call this subject matter the "object" (*objet*) of the contract and insist that the object must be possible and lawful. See Note to Article 2:103.

2. *Price as a requirement*

    Systems also differ as to whether the price must be determined by the parties, or be determinable, in order for the contract to be valid. In some of the systems this question is linked to the object.

    The laws of the countries which do not apply the concept of object do not require the parties to have agreed on the price of a party's performance. The law will decide which price is to be paid, see below. Even some of the systems which require an object will make exceptions as far as the price is concerned, see ITALIAN CC art.1474(1) for the sale of goods, art.1657 for supply of work and materials, art.1709 for mandate, art.1733 on factorage and art.2233 for professional services; POR-TUGUESE CC art.883 for sale of goods and art.1211 for work and materials; and SPANISH CC art. 1447 for sale of goods, arts. 1543 and 1547 for *locatio conductio rei*, art. 1589 for work contracts and art. 1711 for mandate.

    The FRENCH courts have been strict in their requirement on the agreement on the price, notably in sales contracts, see for instance Cass.com. 1 October 1978, D 1979 135, note *Houin*. The *"Alcatel"* case (Ass. Plén. 1 December 1995, J.C.P. 1995.II.22.565, note *J. Ghestin*) has changed the position of French Law by deciding first that CC art. 1129 (on the determination of the object) does not apply to the price and secondly that when an agreement provides for the conclusion of further contracts (framework contract), the non-determination of the price in the initial agreement does not affect its validity, the abusive fixation of the price opening only the right to terminate or to obtain damages. The exact significance of this case has yet to be clarified. BELGIAN case law has also been ready to infer a reference to the current price, though sometimes the absence of an agreed price has been taken to mean that one party may determine it unilaterally: *M.E.Storme*, TPR 1988, 1259, no. 29ff.. The LUXEMBOURG courts have been exacting in exclusive supply agreements which have been held void for lack of determination (Cass. 27 Sept. 1989, No.10470) but have been less severe as regards contracts for exclusive dealership, which were held valid (Cass. 26 Oct. 1988, No.9804) and other framework contracts, which need not fix the terms of the contracts to be made under them (Cour d'appel (commercial), 2 October 1996, Pasicrisie 30, p. 145). SPANISH courts favour a flexible approach under CC arts. 1539 and 1711: the court may fix the price according to the market price, uses or, preferably, the specific circumstances of the contract (See TS 21 May 1983, 12 June 1984, 16 January 1985 and 21 October 1985).

3. *What price?*

    Those States which do not require an object and those which make exceptions as far as the price is concerned have often provided in their laws that if the parties have not agreed upon the price it is the one which is usually charged: see for AUSTRIA, ABGB § 1152 on labour contracts; for GER-MANY BGB § 612(2) on labour relationships, § 632(2) on supply of work and materials and § 653(2) on agents' commissions; for PORTUGAL and ITALY see the provisions cited above; and for the NETHERLANDS see BW art. 7:4 on sales, 7:405(2) on mandate and 7:601(2) on deposit. Under Dutch sales law, where the price has not been determined a reasonable price may be charged. In deciding what is reasonable regard shall be had to the seller's customary charges. In mandate and deposit the rule is reversed: the customary price may be charged unless it is unreasonable.

    Under several provisions the parties are taken to have agreed upon a price which is fair and reasonable, and this seems to have been accepted as a general principle: see GERMAN BGB § 315 and GREEK CC art.371, which applies to specific contracts as well. Under the DANISH Sale of Goods Act § 5 the price is the one charged by the seller unless it is unreasonable, and this rule applies to other contracts as well. § 45 of the FINNISH and SWEDISH Sale of Goods Acts provides that if the price is not determinable from the contract, the buyer shall pay what is reasonable with regard to the nature and condition of the goods, the current price at the time of the conclusion of the con-tract and other circumstances; § 47 treats the buyer as accepting the price stated on the seller's invoice if it is not unfair and he does not object to it within a reasonable time. In AUSTRIAN law the parties are taken to have agreed a reasonable price only if there is some indication that this was what they intended: *Rummel (-Aicher)* ABGB § 1054 NO. 10.

Under the COMMON LAW the price to be charged in the absence of an agreement is the reasonable price, see U.K. Sale of Goods Act 1979, s.8 and *British Bank for Foreign Trade Ltd.* v. *Novinex Ltd.* [1949] 1 K.B. 623; SCOTS Law, *Avintair Ltd* v. *Ryder Airline Services Ltd* 1994 SLT 613; IRISH Sale of Goods Act 1893, s.8; U.S. UCC § 2-305 and Restatement 2d § 204.

4.   *International instruments*

A rule similar to the one stated in Article 6:104 is to be found in Art.6 of the EC Directive on the Co-ordination of the Laws of Member States Relating to the Self-employed Agent of 18 Dec. 1986 (OJEC No. L 382/17). CISG art.14 makes a fixed or determinable price a necessary element of the offer. Where a contract is nonetheless concluded without such a price, Art.55 makes reference to the price generally charged for similar goods, see *Honnold*, §§ 137.4-137.8 and 324-325. Under the *Unidroit* Principles art 5.7(1) the parties are considered to have made reference to the price generally charged for such performance in comparable circumstances in the trade concerned, and if no such price is available, to a reasonable price.

See generally *Zweigert & Kötz* 383-386; *Tallon* chap.1; *Nicholas* 49-50.

Article 6:105: Unilateral Determination by a Party

Where the price or any other contractual term is to be determined by one party and that party's determination is grossly unreasonable, then notwithstanding any provision to the contrary, a reasonable price or other term shall be substituted.

COMMENT

The text first of all recognises that the parties may leave the price to be determined unilaterally by one of them. This determination must be made in a reasonable manner. If it is not, the court may intervene to protect the debtor against the creditor fixing the price abusively. Thus if a broker were to fix its commission at a grossly unreasonable level, the court could reduce it to a reasonable level.

The rule may work the other way round if it is the debtor who is to fix the price. The court could then increase an unreasonably low price.

The operation of this Article cannot be excluded by contrary agreement; any clause (which might be a standard clause) which purported to exclude the jurisdiction of the court to review a price fixed unilaterally will be void.

It should be noted that, to prevent abuse of this section, the section stipulates that the price or other term fixed must be grossly unreasonable.

As to what is reasonable, see Article 1:302.

NOTES

1.   *Unilateral determination allowed*

Most of the Member Sates allow agreements whereby a party may unilaterally determine a contractual term, and therefore also the price: see GERMAN BGB § 315; GREEK CC arts.371 and 372; PORTUGUESE CC art.400; DANISH Sale of Goods Act, § 5; FINNISH AND SWEDISH Sale of Goods Acts, § 45; and *Gomard*, Obligationsret I, 34. The term must be reasonable and is subject to the court's control. The latter rule also applies to those countries where in principle a unilateral determination is not allowed (see below) but where exceptions are made, e.g. on excessive charges by agents (*mandataires*) in FRANCE, Cass.req. 29 Jan. 1897, DP 1897 1 153. AUSTRIAN ABGB

§ 1056 provides expressly only for determination of the price by a third party, but unilateral determination is permitted provided the price fixed is reasonable: See OGH 10 July 1997 JBI 1980, 151; 10 July 1991 SZ 64/92, *F. Bydlinski,* JBI 1975, 245; *Krejci,* ZAS 1983, 204; *Bürge,* JBI 1989, 687. In the DUTCH BW there are no provisions which expressly allow unilateral determination, but one will be set aside by the courts only if it is unreasonable and unfair, BW art. 6:248(2). The same is true for BELGIAN law: *M.E.Storme,* TPR 1988, 1259; FINNISH law, see *Wilhelmsson,* Standardavtal 147; SWEDISH law, *Ramberg,* Köplagen 485. See also *Unidroit* art. 5.7(2).

In ENGLAND *May & Butcher Ltd* v. *R.* (1929) [1934] 2 K.B. 17n. contains a dictum to the effect that the price may be left to the determination of one party. However there is no authority to the effect that the determination must be reasonable, nor does any such rule exist in SCOTTISH law or IRISH law, see *Tradax (Ireland)* v. *Irish Grain Board* [1984] I.R. 1.

2. *Unilateral determination allowed in certain cases*
Some legal systems only admit the validity of a contract which allows the price to be fixed by one party alone only in certain circumstances. Thus SPANISH CC art. 1449 forbids unilateral determination in the sale of goods context, but the rule has been construed narrowly in order to perserve the general principle stated in art. 1256: unilateral determination is allowed if accepted *ex post* by the other party or if related to objective circumstances such as prices in reasonably competitive markets (arts. 1447 and 1448). FRENCH sales law did not even permit a reference to published tarriffs; BELGIAN law applies the same rule but with greater flexibility, but French law has now changed with the *Alcatel* Case, above notes to Article 6:104. LUXEMBOURG law does not permit one party to fix prices in a sales contract, CC art.1590, but does in a service contract. French, Belgian and Luxembourg law have long accepted judicial reduction of excessive charges by *mandataires,* see note 1 above.

3. *Unilateral determination not allowed*
In ITALY CC arts. 1349 and 1473 allow determination by a third person; the implication is that determination by a party is not permitted. See *Sacco* 553ff.

See generally *Tallon* § 2.2.1.15.

Article 6:106: Determination by a Third Person

(1) Where the price or any other contractual term is to be determined by a third person, and it cannot or will not do so, the parties are presumed to have empowered the court to appoint another person to determine it.

(2) If a price or other term fixed by a third person is grossly unreasonable, a reasonable price or term shall be substituted.

COMMENT

A. *Term to be fixed by court*

Using a variety of forms and types of clause, it is common practice in international contracts for the price or part of it to be fixed by a third person chosen by the parties.

It may be that the price for a work of art is to be fixed by an "expert opinion". The whole or a fraction of the price may be left to be determined either as at the date of the contract or later. For example in the FIDIC Conditions for Engineering Work it is provided that the engineer will fix the price for, among other things, additional work. If he does not do so, or does not do it properly, the contract is not void: the contractor is entitled to a reasonable sum.

Frequently the third person is in a contractual relationship with one of the parties. He still acts as a third person if he is to act independently (for example, the consulting engineer under the FIDIC conditions).

The purpose of the Article is to save the contract in the case where the third person chosen cannot carry out his task (for example because he has died) or refuses to do it. Of course, the parties may agree on a replacement, but it can happen that one refuses to do so in order to escape a contract which has turned out to be disadvantageous to it.

One solution would be to hold that the contract disappears (French CC art. 1592(1); UK Sale of Goods Act 1979, Section 9). It seems better to treat the parties as having given the court power to replace the third person.

It is, however, only a rebuttable presumption. The parties may expressly or implicitly agree that the third person shall be irreplaceable, for instance when an expert is chosen *intuitu personae*. In this case, if the third person does not act, there is no contract.

B. *Term fixed by third person unreasonable*

If the price or other term fixed by the third person is grossly unreasonable, it seems coherent, particulary in the light of Article 6:105 which allows for the revision of a price fixed unilaterally by one party, to give the court power to avoid an unreasonable valuation. However, taking into account that the parties in choosing valuation by a third person have taken the risk of errors, judicial intervention is only permitted under this Article when the error is manifestly unreasonable, such as a clear mistake of arithmetic or a grossly wrong valuation.

NOTES

1. *Determination by third person*
    All the legal systems permit the parties to appoint a third person to determine the price or any other contract term. However, they differ as to what will happen if the third person fails to fix the price or the term.
    (a) *Third person replaced*
        The solution adopted by Article 6:106, leaving it to the court to appoint another person to determine the price or the term in all cases where the third party fails to do so or fixes an unreasonable price or term, is in accordance with DUTCH law, see BW arts. 6:2 and 6:248, and BELGIAN law: there the judge will appoint another third person to act unless the parties agree that the court should act for him (*M.L. and M.E.Storme* TPR 1985, 732 Nos. 15 and 16). It is probably not found in the other Member States.
    (b) *Court determination*
        In GERMANY, BGB § 317(1), GREECE, CC art.371, ITALY, CC art. 1349(1) and PORTUGAL, CC art.400, there is a presumption that the third person was appointed to fix a reasonable price. If he fails to act the court will act for him and fix a reasonable price (see, for GREECE, Full Bench of Areios Pagos 678/1977, NOB 26 (1978) 360-361). In ENGLAND, where the agreement is generally avoided if the third party fails to fix the price, see below, the court will nevertheless fix the price or the term provided that the third party provision is subsidiary and inessential, and only made to provide a machinery for fixing a reasonable price or term, see *Chitty*, § 2-094 and *Sudbrook Trading Estate Ltd v. Eggleton* [1983] A.C. 444 (H.L.); similarly for IRELAND, see *Cotter v. Minister for Agriculture* (High Court, 15 Oct. 1991, unrep.).
        Under *Unidroit* art. 5.7.(3) where the price is to be fixed by a third person, and that person cannot or will not do so, the price shall be a reasonable price. This means that in cases where the parties cannot agree on what is a reasonable price the court may have to decide it.
    (c) *Contract void*
        Several legal systems treat the contract as void if the third person fails to determine the price: FRANCE and LUXEMBOURG CC arts.1592; AUSTRIA, ABGB §§ 1056, 1057; ENG-

LAND and SCOTLAND, Sale of Goods Act 1979, s.9(1) (but see above); SPANISH CC art. 1447(2) for sale of goods, though the rule has been construed strictly in order to preserve the contract if possible. See further *Tallon* § 3.3.2.01 ff. The same rule applies in GERMANY under BGB § 319(2), GREECE under CC art.373 and ITALY, CC art.1349(2), and BELGIUM in cases where the third person has a free discretion as to how to determine the price or term.

2. *Determination by third person unreasonable*

If the price or term fixed by the third person is unreasonable the court will fix a reasonable price or term in GERMANY, GREECE, ITALY and PORTUGAL, see note 1(b) above. In ITALY a revision by the court is also possible if a third person who has unfettered discretion acts in a way which is contrary to good faith, and in GERMANY, if the third party's determination is contrary to law or good morals; but GREEK case law does not permit judicial intervention in such cases: AP 217/1974, NoB 22 (1974) 1164. In DENMARK, FINLAND and SWEDEN the general fairness clause in Contract Act § 36 would apply in this situation.

FRENCH and LUXEMBOURG law do not permit the court to fix a reasonable price or term in case the one fixed by the third person is unreasonable. "Having left the decision to fix the price to a third person in accordance with Art.1592 of the Civil code the parties have given his decision the force of law. The judge may not by modifying this decision impose upon the parties a contract different from their agreement": FRENCH Cour de Cassation, Civ. 2, 6 June 1950, Bull. II no.205, p.141. (The rule may differ in respect of service contracts.) ENGLISH law takes a similar attitude, see *Collier* v. *Mason* (1858) 25 Beav. 200.

See generally *Tallon* § 3.3.2.01 ff.

Article 6:107: Reference to a Non-Existent Factor

Where the price or any other contractual term is to be determined by reference to a factor which does not exist or has ceased to exist or to be accessible, the nearest equivalent factor shall be substituted.

COMMENT

In periods of inflation it becomes common practice to use price fluctuation clauses. But it can happen that the index of prices selected as the basis of the clause ceases to be available, perhaps because the organisation which published it stops doing so or because the components of the index are changed so that it no longer complies with the clause. It is not easy to determine the consequences of the disappearance of the index and thus of the indexation. Does the contract continue at a price fixed in accordance with the last price published in the index? Or does it cease to be enforceable? It seems preferable in this situation to use the nearest equivalent index, which if necessary can be determined by the court, so that the contract can continue more or less as intended by the parties.

Illustration 1: In a long-term lease the rent is indexed by reference to the index of construction costs published by the Academy of Architects. The latter discontinues publications of the index. The index of construction costs published by the National Statistical Institute may be substituted.

The rule can apply to factors necessary to determine other terms than price.

Illustration 2: An employment contract provides for holidays in accordance with the nationally agreed terms of employment of a certain category of employees.

When this category of employees ceases to exist, there is no longer such an agreement. The nationally agreed terms on holidays for the nearest equivalent category of employees may be substituted.

NOTES

1. *Modification of the contract*

    When the price or another term is to be determined by reference to a factor and this factor proves not to exist or disappears, some of the legal systems provide for a modification of the contract. Thus in DENMARK the situation has been considered a "failure of assumptions" (see note to Article 4:103), in GERMANY a *Wegfall der Geschäftsgrundlage*, see BGB § 242, and in the NETHERLANDS an unforeseen contingency under BW art. 6:258. In these countries the contract is modified and the missing factor is replaced by the nearest equivalent one, see eg DENMARK, Supreme Court 15 June 1977, UfR 1977 641 and *Gomard*, Kontraktsret 79. See also *Unidroit* art. 5.7(4). In contrast, in ITALY CC art. 1467 allows the plaintiff to obtain termination unless the defendant offers a fair modification.

2. *Interpretation*

    The disappearance of a factor is in FRANCE and LUXEMBOURG considered to put an end to the contract because the *objet* (price) has dissappeared. Some FRENCH decisions have followed this rule and have not allowed a modification. Other more recent decisions have, however, used the rules on interpretation. Relying on the presumed intention of the parties they have modified the contract, see eg. Cass. Civ.2, 18 July 1985, Bull. II no.113 p.84. The BELGIAN courts have taken the same attitude, see Cour de Bruxelles 29 Oct. 1962, JT 1963 102. Similar methods are used in PORTUGAL, GREECE and SPAIN where the courts may resort to the presumed intention of the parties and the good faith principle, see Portuguese CC art.239; Greek CC art. 200; Spanish CC art. 1158. A similar approach may be taken by the AUSTRIAN courts on the basis of ABGB § 194. In ENGLAND it is thought that the court would hold the contract to have become of no effect unless it is decided that the reference to the factor was merely a way of fixing a reasonable term or price, in which case the court would presumably either substitute an equivalent index or fix the reasonable price or term itself, see Note 1(b) to Article 6:106. SCOTTISH law seems to be to this effect. In *Wight Civil Engineering* v. *Parker* (O.H.), 1994 S.L.T. 140 the contract referred to interest fixed in accordance with the Minimum Lending Rate published by the Bank of England. When this ceased to be published the Average Base Lending Rate of four leading banks was substituted.

    See generally *Rodière & Tallon* § 3.1.2.01 and *Tallon* 191f.

Article 6:108: Quality of Performance

If the contract does not specify the quality, a party must tender performance of at least average quality.

COMMENT

It may be helpful to provide a rule to supplement the parties' agreement on the quality of the performance due. In the absence of a contrary indication, the debtor is bound to tender a performance of at least average quality. In many countries this rule applies contracts to sell generic goods. Article 6:108 applies not only to goods sold or hired but also to the performance of services.

Thus a car hire firm must provide customers with vehicles which are in roadworthy condition, but they need not be capable of high performance. Equally one cannot expect a general practitioner to diagnose very rare or exotic illnesses, but, if she is in doubt, she must refer her patient to a specialist.

Where the debtor is one to take care, the standard required is one of reasonable care.

In determining the degrees of quality required, the various factors mentioned in the Article on reasonableness (Article 1:302) should be taken into account. Thus whether or not the debtor is acting in the course of a business, and the amount (if any) charged for the performance compared to the normal price for the same performance, are relevant to fixing the standard required. Equally, reference should be made to usages which may show what is normally expected in the trade or contract in question, and which may have made precise definition in the contract unnecessary.

NOTES

Under *Unidroit* art. 5.6. where the quality of performance is neither fixed by, nor determinable from, the contract a party is bound to render a performance of a quality that is reasonable and not less than average quality. No Member State has a statutory provision of this general nature. As for the delivery of goods the statutes either focus on the quality of the goods or the purpose for which they are meant. For services the requirements concern the care and skill with which the services are to be performed.

1. *Average quality of goods*
   The GERMAN BGB § 243 lays down that the performance of a generic obligation must be of average kind and quality, and GREEK CC art.289(2) contains a similar provision. In AUSTRIA the same rule is laid down in the Commercial Code HGB § 360, but is applied generally by way of analogy. Under art.1246(3) of the FRENCH, BELGIAN and LUXEMBOURG Civil Codes he who delivers generic goods need not deliver the best but may not deliver the worst quality. In the NETHERLANDS and ITALY he may not deliver goods which are below average good quality: Italian CC art.1178, Dutch BW art. 6:28. The COMMON LAW rule was that goods delivered must be of merchantable quality, IRISH SGA 1893, s.14(2) as amended by Sale of Goods and Supply of Services Act 1980, s.10; and U.S. UCC § 2-314. Cf.UK SGA 1979, s.14(2)-(2c) as amended by Sale and Supply of Goods Act 1994, s.1 ("satisfactory quality").
   In assessing whether goods delivered meet the requirements as to quality under PORTUGUESE law one has to take into account the purpose for which the goods are meant, CC art.913(2); CISG art. 35(2)(a) and the NORDIC Sale of Goods Act, § 17 (in force in FINLAND and SWEDEN) provides that the goods must be fit for the purposes for which goods of the same description would ordinarily be used.
   In some systems (e.g. the Common Law) the same rules apply to specific goods. In other systems (e.g. FRANCE, BELGIUM and LUXEMBOURG) quality requirements for specific goods may be determined by statutory provisions (e.g. CC arts. 1693, 1694 and 1792 (durability)).

2. *The good paterfamilias and services*
   If the obligation of a party is to provide services, the debtor must act as a *bon père de famille*: see for services in general ITALIAN CC art.1176, under which the standard must be appropriate to the nature of the activity (*Cendon -(Castronovo)* art.1176 no.6); on deposits FRENCH, BELGIAN and LUXEMBOURG Civil Codes art.1137(1); and Dutch BW art. 7:602. DANISH case law requires that a professional party render a professionally satisfactory performance, see *Gomard*, Obligationsret I 179, and GERMAN law seems to have the same requirement, see BGB § 276 and *Palandt* § 276 Comment 4 B. The ENGLISH Supply of Goods and Services Act 1982, s.13 provides that services must be carried out with reasonable care and skill; similarly IRISH Sale of Goods and Supply of Services Act 1980, s.39(b); SCOTTISH common law is to the same effect.
   See on sales generally *Honnold* no.233 ff; *Bianca & Bonell (-Bianca)* 268 ff.

Article 6:109: Contract for an Indefinite Period

A contract for an indefinite period may be ended by either party by giving notice of reasonable length.

COMMENT

A. *Two Principles expressed*

Article 6:109 applies both to contracts which purport to be everlasting (e.g. "at all times hereafter") and to contracts which are for an indeterminate period. It expresses two principles:

(1) even a contract which purports to be everlasting may be ended. No party is bound to another for an indefinite period of time.

(2) to end such a contract, or one which is for an indeterminate period, either party must give reasonable notice.

B. *Scope*

The principle is applicable to contracts which are made for an indefinite period. This is often the case for agency and distributorship contracts, for franchising, partnerships and joint ventures, for contracts for the supply of services, goods and electricity and for leasing. Such contracts often do not contain any provision for their termination.

The principle does not cover contracts for which statutory provisions of notice apply.

The principle also applies to contracts which were originally made for a definite period which has expired, but upon which the parties have continued to act although they have not expressly agreed to renew them.

C. *Reasonable time*

The party which wishes to end the contract must give notice of a reasonable length of time. If the notice given is unreasonably short the contract continues until a reasonable period has expired.

What is reasonable depends, *inter alia*, upon the period the contract has lasted, the efforts and investments which the other party has made in performance of the contract, and the time it may take the other party to obtain another contract with somebody else. The length of notice will often be governed by usages. See on the concept of reasonableness Article 1:302.

D. *Receipt principle governs notice*

Following the principle laid down in Article 1:303, the notice which purports to end the contract will not be effective unless and until it reaches the person to whom it is sent, see Article 1:303(3).

NOTES

1. *Eternal engagements prohibited*
That nobody can be contractually bound to another eternally is a generally accepted principle. Art. 4(1) of the European Convention of Human Rights prohibits slavery and bondage. Therefore, a servant cannot be bound to work for his employer indefinitely. The GERMAN BGB § 624 provides that an employment contract for the lifetime of the employee or employer or for more than five years can always be ended by a six months notice after five years. FRENCH and LUXEMBOURG law prohibit "eternal engagements" (*Malaurie & Aynès* Obligations nos. 321 and 747). SPANISH law is the same, CC art 1583. Under BELGIAN, ITALIAN and PORTUGUESE law contracts entered into for an indefinite period may be ended, see respectively Belgian Cass. 22 Nov. 1973, Arr. Cass. 327; *Bianca*, II contratto 704ff. and, for employment contracts, Italian CC art. 2118; *Jorge* 212. Under AUSTRIAN law there is a general principle based on a number of provisions of the ABGB (§§ 1117, 1118, 1162, 1210) that obligations for a indefinite period of time may be terminated by notice for serious reasons.
ENGLISH law does not in principle refuse to admit an everlasting contract but a contract term creating an obligation to supply water at a fixed price "at all times hereafter" has been construed to mean that the contract may be ended by giving notice, see *Staffordshire Area Health Authority* v. *South Staffordshire Waterworks Co* [1978] 1 W.L.R. 1387 (C.A.). In SCOTTISH law the position is not clear (*McBryde* Chapters 15-17). In SWEDISH law the question whether an everlasting contract should be upheld depends upon the circumstances, NJA 1994 p. 359.

2. *Contracts for indefinite period determinable on reasonable notice*
A general principle by which a contract for an indefinite period of time may be ended after a reasonable period of notice is found in DANISH law (*Gomard*, Obligationsret I, 26); ENGLISH law (see the *Staffordshire* case above, note 1); SCOTS law, see *McBryde* para. 6.21); FRENCH, BELGIAN and LUXEMBOURG law, where it is founded on the doctrine of abuse of rights (*Malaurie & Aynès, loc.cit.*); ITALIAN law (*Bianca, loc.cit.*) and PORTUGUESE law (*Jorge, loc.cit.*). In SPANISH law contracts for an indefinite period may be terminated at will (mandate, CC art. 1732), or according to the uses (loan for use, CC art. 1750) or after a reasonable period if the circumstances so require and, always, according to the good faith principle (CC art. 1705), depending on the terms considered, to fix the rent (CC art. 1581: land leases).
Many, if not all the laws provide for special periods of notice for specific contracts (e.g. SWEDISH Partnership Act § 2:24; FRENCH and BELGIAN CC arts. 1869, 1870). GERMAN law does not provide a general principle of reasonable notice, but the BGB lays down special rules on notice for leases (§ 565), services (§§ 620(2), 622 and 624), cf. also mandate (§ 671) and civil companies (§ 723). The same holds true of other laws such as DUTCH, FINNISH and GREEK law which do not provide a general principle.

3. *Determination at short notice in special cases*
In some laws shorter periods of notice (or no notice) may apply in case of hardship (see also Article 6:111 below). This is the case in GERMANY (BGB § 242); ITALY (CC art. 1467) and in the NETHERLANDS (BW art. 6:258). Furthermore, on the basis of rules in the BGB on premature ending of some "continuous" contracts "for an important reason", German case law has developed a general rule by which continuous contracts may be ended without notice or with a shorter notice if "evidence is brought showing that, taking into consideration all the circumstances of the case and weighing the interests of both parties, you cannot reasonably expect the person giving notice to continue the relationship until it ends or may be ended under the contract". See also on employment contracts, BGB § 626(1); on mandate, § 671(2); and on partnership, § 723(1) and (2). However, most cases covered by the rule on "important reason" are cases of a substantial non-performance by the person to whom notice is given, and therefore under these Principles would be covered by the rules of non-performance.

Article 6:110: Stipulation in Favour of a Third Party

(1) A third party may require performance of a contractual obligation when its right to do so has been expressly agreed upon between the promisor and the promisee, or when such agreement is to be inferred from the purpose of the contract or the circumstances of the case. The third party need not be identified at the time the agreement is concluded.

(2) *If the third party renounces the right to performance the right is treated as never having accrued to it.*

(3) *The promisee may by notice to the promisor deprive the third party of the right to performance unless:*

    (a) *the third party has received notice from the promisee that the right has been made irrevocable, or*

    (b) *the promisor or the promisee has received notice from the third party that the latter accepts the right.*

COMMENT

A. *Scope and purpose*

Article 6:110 lays down the rule that a third party beneficiary may require performance of an obligation if this has been agreed upon by the promisor and the promisee.

There are various reasons why such an agreement may be made. One may be that the promisee wishes to furnish support or in other ways give the third party the benefit of the performance, another that the promisee owes something to the third party and wishes to discharge that obligation.

The purpose of the promise in favour of the third party beneficiary is often to avoid an additional transaction. If this way of performing an obligation was not possible, the promisor would have first to perform to the promisee which would then perform to the beneficiary; or the promisee, having obtained a promise from the promisor to perform the obligation to itself, would then have to assign the claim to the third party beneficiary.

B. *Agency and trusts not covered*

Article 6:110 does not cover cases where the person who receives the promise acts as an agent of the third person since in that case the third person is in fact the promisee.

In collective investment agreements, trustees or representatives of the bondholders may be appointed by the issuers of the bonds. The relationships between issuers, bonds - and securityholders and the trustees, representatives and depositaries are to be regarded as agency or fiduciary relationships (trusts) which are not agreements in favour of third parties and therefore not covered by Article 6:110.

C. *"Legal beneficiaries" not covered*

Nor does the Article deal with situations where the promisor did not intend to give third parties any rights under the contract but where the law extends its obligation vis-a-vis the promisee to cover other persons as well. Under the laws of some countries the seller's warranty to the buyer extends to members of the buyer's household. If a breach of the warranty causes personal injury to them, they have a direct claim in contract against the seller.

D. *The beneficiary need not be known*

The beneficiary need not be known when the promise is made. An insurance company may promise the policy-holder to pay the insurance proceeds to any future owner of the goods insured. A bank may promise a customer to pay the purchase price to any seller which delivers a certain piece of equipment to the customer.

E. *The promisee may require performance*

It goes without saying that the promisee may require performance to the beneficiary. The promisee may require performance also when the beneficiary may claim performance.

There will be due performance of the contract when the promisor makes performance to the beneficiary.

F. *When may the beneficiary claim performance*

In many situations the promisor and the promisee do not intend to confer any right on the third person. This is most often the case where the promisor has undertaken to pay the promisee's debt to the third person.

In other situations the parties may have intended that the third party beneficiary will have the right to claim performance from the promisor. In such cases the beneficiary can claim performance.

> *Illustration 1*: P opens a bank account in his own name and pays regularly € 800 per month to the account. The bank promises to pay this sum to P's son B on B's demand. B may claim performance.

It may be agreed between the promisor and promisee that the former's promise to perform an obligation to a third person creates a duty in the promisor which the third party beneficiary has an independent right to enforce. Thus it may follow from a transport insurance contract that a promise from the insurance company to the policy holder to pay the amount insured to any owner of the insured goods will create a duty in the company to pay the owner which the latter may enforce when the goods are damaged or lost.

In some other cases it follows from the agreement between the promisor and the promisee that the beneficiary shall make the claim because it will be the one which knows when to make it and how much it should claim:

> *Illustration 2*: The landlord L gives P permission to erect high voltage lines over a quarry which is worked by T, his tenant. P has promised L to pay an indemnity for damage done to T's property. T has a direct claim against P when damage is done.

> *Illustration 3*: When taking a lease P, which intends to carry on production of inflammables, promises the landlord L that it will compensate the other tenants for any increase of their household insurance premiums which is caused by P's dangerous activity. The tenants who are informed by L about P's promise have a direct claim against P to have the increase of their premiums reimbursed.

G. *The beneficiary may refuse the right*

If the beneficiary by giving notice to the promisor refuses to accept the right to performance, the right is considered never to have accrued to the beneficiary. The provision in paragraph (2) only regards the relationship between promisor, promisee and beneficiary. It does not treat the question whether third parties, such as the creditors of the beneficiary, may challenge the refusal.

H. *May the beneficiary's right be revoked?*

If the promisee has not notified the beneficiary that the parties have agreed that it may claim performance from the promisor, the beneficiary cannot do so. It is for the promisee to enforce the promise; it may change its mind and claim performance for itself or waive it.

> *Illustration 4*: The purchaser B has promised the seller V that B will pay the price to F which has financed V's acquisition of the goods. Later B and V agree that B should pay the price to V. F cannot claim the purchase price.

Even if under Article 6:110(1) the beneficiary has acquired a right to claim performance, the promisor and the promisee may nevertheless agree that its rights is to be modified or revoked.

> *Illustration 5*: P has made B his beneficiary of a life insurance which he has taken out with C. P may agree with C that C shall surrender the insurance to P and thereby annull B's right.

> *Illustration 6*: The facts are the same as in Illustration 1 except that after having in May transferred 800 Euros to the account, P gives the bank order to withdraw 500 Euros and transfer them back to his other account. B may then only claim the remaining 300 Euros.

If, however, having learned of the right from one of the parties the beneficiary has given notice to the promisor or the promisee that it accepts performance, the promisee cannot modify or revoke its right, and the promisor has to make performance to the beneficiary.

> *Illustration 7*: The facts are the same as in Illustration 6 except that, before the bank received notice of withdrawal from P, his son B has claimed the 800 Euros. P's order of withdrawal is then inoperative and the bank must pay the money to B.

In general the beneficiary can only accept a performance which it has learned about from the promisor or the promisee. In the case mentioned in Illustration 4 the beneficiary F which has heard about the agreement between B and V only by chance cannot demand payment of the purchase price.

The beneficiary's acceptance need not be express. It is sufficient that having learned about the right from one of the parties it has acted in reliance on it, and makes that fact known to the promisor or the promisee.

Illustration 8: B buys goods from S and S promises that it will deliver the goods to C, to whom B has sold goods of that quantity and description. Having learned from B that it will get the goods from S, C resells the goods to D and asks S to deliver them to D. C has thereby accepted a right in the goods of which neither S nor B can deprive it.

Furthermore, a promise by the promisee to the beneficiary not to modify or revoke its right is binding upon the promisee. A message from it to the beneficiary that the promisor has undertaken to perform to the beneficiary, or that the beneficiary may now claim the performance which the promisee owes it from the promisor, usually amounts to a promise not to revoke or modify the beneficiary's right.

The contract may permit the promisee to deprive the third party of the promised benefit either at any time or before certain events have taken place.

Illustration 9: P has made B a beneficiary of a life insurance policy P has taken out with C, on terms that P may change the intended beneficiaries. P may alter the beneficiary from B to D, but after P's death his executors cannot do so.

Third parties' rights often accrue in contracts for the carriage of goods. A carrier (the promisor) promises the consignor (the promisee) to deliver the goods to the consignee (the beneficiary).

The conditions under which the consignee may claim delivery of the goods are provided for in international conventions. They vary depending upon the special procedures followed for each means of transport. As a rule, however, the consignee acquires a right to have the goods delivered to him when they have arrived at the place of destination, see Article 13 of the Warsaw Convention on the International Carriage by Air, Article 16(4) of the Uniform Rules Concerning the Contract for the International Carriage of Goods by Rail (CIM) and Article 13 of the Convention on International Carriage of Goods by Road (CMR).

However, under most of the transport conventions the consignor has a right to dispose of the goods in transit. The carrier acting as agent of the consignor must follow his instructions, see Article 20 of CIM and Article 12 of CMR. This right to dispose of the goods ceases when the consignee claims the goods after they have arrived at the place of destination. It also ceases to exist when the carrier has handed over the transport document to the consignee, see e.g. Article 21(4) of CIM and Article 12(2) of CMR. This may seem to be at variance with the rule in Article 2.115(3)(a) under which a promise from the consignor to grant the consignee an irrevocable right is required. However, in handing over the transport document, and thereby making the consignee's right to the goods irrevocable, the carrier acts as the agent of the consignor.

NOTES

1. *The beneficiary's claim for performance*
    A stipulation in favour of a third party beneficiary is recognized as valid in the CIVIL LAW systems; the stipulation gives the third party a claim under the circumstances laid down in Article 6:110(1). See for AUSTRIA, ABGB § 881(1); DENMARK, *Lynge Andersen* 151. FINLAND: *Kivimäki & Ylöstalo* 204 and *Telaranta* 446; FRANCE, BELGIUM and LUXEMBOURG, CC art. 1121 as interpreted (and extended) by the courts, see for France *Malaurie & Aynès*, Obligations no. 669ff. and for Belgium *Dirix*, Obligatoire no.115, and Belgian Insurance Contract Act of 25 June 1992, art.22; GERMANY, BGB § 328; GREECE, CC arts. 410 and 411 (see AP 1017/1990, Hell.Dni. 33(1992) 74-75); ITALY, CC art. 1411; NETHERLANDS, BW art. 6:253; PORTUGAL, CC art. 443; SPAIN, CC art. 1257(2) (see *Diez Picazo* I, 398; *Lacruz(-Rams)* II, 1, 549); SWEDEN, *Rodhe*, Obligationsrätt 609H. The same holds true of SCOTLAND, see *McBryde*, Contract 412-419. However, the rule in Article 6:110 is subject to several exceptions both in the statutes and in the case law of the Member States.
    In ENGLISH law the doctrine of privity of contract (and of consideration) is held to prevent stipulations in favour of third parties. In order to confer an enforceable right upon the third party it would be necessary for the promisor to execute a deed in the third party's favour, or for the promisee to make a declaration in trust in his favour, or (provided that the third party was furnishing some consideration) for the promisee to act as an agent of the third party. However, statute has created exceptions to the doctrine of privity, for instance in the field of insurance: see *Treitel*, Contract 582-588. The position in IRELAND is the same, see *Clark* 383-394. In England reform of the doctrine of privity has often been advocated, for example by Lord Scarman in *Woodar Investment Development Ltd.* v. *Wimpey Construction (U.K.) Ltd.* [1980] 1 W.L.R. 277 (H.L.), by Steyn L.J. in *Darlington BC* v. *Wiltshier Northern* [1995] 1 W.L.R. 68 (C.A.) and by the *Law Commission*, Report on Privity; in 1998 the Contracts (Rights of Third Parties) Bill was introduced in Parliament to give effect to this Report.

2. *May the promisee revoke the beneficiary's right?*
    The conditions under which the third party beneficiary's right becomes irrevocable are treated differently in the legal systems.
    Rules which agree with or which come close to the rules in Article 6:110(3) are found in AUSTRIA, ABGB § 881(2); BELGIUM, see *Dirix*, Obligatoire no.123; DENMARK, see *Lynge Andersen 156*; GERMANY, see BGB §§ 328(2), 331 and 332; NETHERLANDS, BW art. 6:253(2)-(4); PORTUGAL, CC art. 448; SCOTLAND, *McBryde* 416-419;
    Some of the laws seem to make the third party's right irrevocable only when he has accepted it: FRANCE, see *Malaurie & Aynes, loc.cit.*; GREECE, CC art. 412; ITALY, CC art. 1411(3), but see the exception in art. 1412(1); SPAIN, CC art. 1257(2) (see *Diez Picazo* I, 398).

3. *Life insurance*
    In the case of life insurance contracts the beneficiary acquires an irrevocable right at least upon the death of the promisee. This is provided in BELGIUM, Insurance Contract Act of 25 June 1992, art. 112; DENMARK, Insurance Contract Act 1930, § 102; ENGLAND, Married Women's Property Act 1882, s.11 (only in favour of spouses or children); FINLAND, Insurance Contract Act § 47; GERMANY, Insurance Contract Law, § 166(2); ITALY, CC art. 1921; SCOTLAND, Married Women's Policies of Assurance (Scotland) Act 1880, s.2; SWEDEN, Insurance Contract Act, § 102; SPAIN, Insurance Act 1980, ART. 87; compare FRENCH Insurance Code (*Code des assurances*) art. L.132.9.;
    See generally *Zweigert & Kötz* 456ff., *Kötz*, IECL s.II.; *Kötz*, European Contract ch. 13.

Article 6:111: Change of Circumstances

(1) A party is bound to fulfil its obligations even if performance has become more onerous, whether because the cost of performance has increased or because the value of the performance it receives has diminished.

(2) If, however, performance of the contract becomes excessively onerous because of a change of circumstances, the parties are bound to enter into negotiations with a view to adapting the contract or ending it, provided that:

(a) the change of circumstances occurred after the time of conclusion of the contract,

(b) the possibility of a change of circumstances was not one which could reasonably have been taken into account at the time of conclusion of the contract, and

(c) the risk of the change of circumstances is not one which, according to the contract, the party affected should be required to bear.

(3) If the parties fail to reach agreement within a reasonable period, the court may:

(a) end the contract at a date and on terms to be determined by the court; or

(b) adapt the contract in order to distribute between the parties in a just and equitable manner the losses and gains resulting from the change of circumstances.

In either case, the court may award damages for the loss suffered through a party refusing to negotiate or breaking off negotiations contrary to good faith and fair dealing.

COMMENT

A. *General*

The majority of countries in the European Community have introduced into their law some mechanism intended to correct any injustice which results from an imbalance in the contract caused by supervening events which the parties could not reasonably have foreseen when they made the contract. In practice contracting parties adopt the same idea, supplementing the general rules of law with a variety of clauses, such as "hardship" clauses.

The Principles adopt such a mechanism, taking a broad and flexible approach, as befits the pursuit of contractual justice which runs through them: they prevent the cost caused by some unforeseen event from falling wholly on one of the parties. The same idea may be expressed in different terms: the risk of a change of circumstances which was unforeseen may not have been allocated by the original contract and the parties or, if they cannot agree, the court must now decide how the cost should be borne. The mechanism reflects the modern trend towards giving the court some power to moderate the rigours of freedom and sanctity of contract.

Admittedly, it can be argued that if sanctity of contract were applied strictly, and the idea that relief might be given when circumstances change unforeseeably were rejected, parties would be given a stronger incentive to introduce appropriate clauses into their contracts. But experience suggests that frequently the parties are not sufficiently sophisticated, or are too careless of their own interests, to do this; or they insert clauses which do not cover every eventuality. It can also happen that the operation of the clause itself runs into some unforeseen difficulty. For instance, a price fluctuation clause which operates by reference to the price of oil may have been drafted with only moderate rises in that price in mind and may give distorted results during an oil crisis.

It is therefore impractical to leave such questions to be expressly agreed. But it should always be borne in mind that the rules adopted by the Principles are not mandatory. The parties can adopt whatever they want in the way of adjustment or renegotiation, and they are perfectly free to agree that a particular change in circumstances shall not affect the terms of the contract – for instance, they may exclude any change on the grounds of a fall in the value of money.

In any case, it will only be in exceptional circumstances that the rules permitting renegotiation will operate. They must not provide a means for a party which has entered a contract which has simply turned out badly to revise it. The first paragraph restates the principle of sanctity of contract in unambiguous terms, and the exceptional nature of the intervention is reinforced by the word "However" which introduces the rule on renegotiation in paragraph (2). The mere fact that a contract has become more onerous than expected is not enough: to adopt the phrase used by the Italian Civil Code, art. 1467, the contract must have become "excessively" burdensome. This point is developed in paragraph (2).

On the other hand, this concept of "*imprévision*" (it is convenient to borrow this term from French administrative case law) is distinct from "impossibility", which is covered by Article 8:108. Although in either case an unforeseen event has occurred, impossibility presupposes that the event has caused an insurmountable obstacle to performance, whereas in "*imprévision*" performance may still be possible for the debtor but will be ruinous for it. Of course there is sometimes a very fine line between a performance which is only possible by totally unreasonable efforts, and a performance which is only very difficult even if it may drive the debtor into bankruptcy. It is up to the court to decide which situation is before it (see also the comment to Article 8:108).

"*Imprévision*" is also differentiated from impossibility by its consequences. The latter, if it is total, can only lead to the end of the contract (see Article 9:301 and comment). "*Imprévision*" gives the court the choice of declaring the contract terminated or revising its terms.

However, the court's decision to terminate or to modify the contract is very much a last resort. The whole procedure is devised to encourage the parties to reach an amicable settlement: hence the obligation to enter negotiations. The court may also remit the matter to the parties for a last effort of negotiation. In the absence of an agreement, it is up to the court to decide. The victim who withholds its performance on the grounds that it is excessively onerous (for instance during renegotiation) does so at its own risk.

The procedure adopted does not impinge on rules allowing the contract to be brought to an end in other circumstances, for example the right to terminate a contract of indefinite duration by giving notice.

B. *Conditions for the procedure to apply*
Strict conditions must be fulfilled for the renegotiation mechanism to be triggered: these are set out in Article 6:111(2)).

(i) *Performance Excessively Onerous*
The first condition follows directly from the first subsection: the change in circumstances must have brought about a major imbalance in the contract. Any contract, especially one of a long duration, is made in a particular economic context which

may not last – it is this notion which underlies the ancient *"clausula rebus sic stantibus"*. A subsequent change in the economic context is not enough to give rise to the right to have the contract revised. The *"imprévision"* mechanism only comes into play if the contract is completely overturned by events, so that although it still can be performed, this will involve completely exorbitant costs for one of the parties. The terms of the paragraph show clearly that the court should not interfere merely because of some disequilibrium.

The "excessive onerosity" may be the direct result of increased cost in performance – for example, the increased cost of transport if the Suez Canal is closed and ships have to be sent round the Cape of Good Hope. Or, as the paragraph states, it may be the result of the expected counter-performance becoming valueless; for example if the cost of building work which has already been executed is to be determined by reference to some index of a price which collapses in a quite unforeseeable way. In neither situation is it possible to give precise rules to cover the diversity of situations which may arise.

> *Illustration 1*: A canning business buys the whole of a producer's future crop of tomatoes at 10 pence per kilo. It cannot demand renegotiation when by harvest time the market price has fallen to 5 pence per kilo because of an unexpected flood of imported tomatoes.

> *Illustration 2*: A contract is made to supply for irrigation for fifty years at a fixed price but the price becomes derisory through inflation. The supplier may be able to demand renegotiation.

(ii) *Time Factor*
The second condition is that the change of circumstances must have occurred after the contract was made. If unknown to either party circumstances which make the contract excessively onerous for one of them already existed at that date, the rules on mistake will apply, see Articles 4:103 and 4:105.

(iii) *Circumstances could not have been taken into Account*
Thirdly, the change of circumstances should not have reasonably been taken into account by the parties. This condition is parallel to that applicable to impossibility of performance and should be interpreted in the same way. Hardship cannot be invoked if the matter would have been foreseen and taken into account by a reasonable man in the same situation, by a person who is neither unduly optimistic or pessimistic, nor careless of his own interests.

> *Illustration 3*: During a period when the traffic in a particular region is periodically interrupted by lorry driver's blockades, the reasonable man would not choose a route through that region in the hope that on the day in question the road will be clear; he would choose another route.

(iv) *Risk*

Lastly it must be decided whether the party affected by a change in circumstances should be required to bear the risk of the change, either because it expressly undertook to do so (for instance by taking the risk of a shift in exchange rates) or because the contract is a speculative one (for instance a sale on the futures market). If so, the party cannot make use of this section.

C. *The obligation to renegotiate*

Like many expressly agreed clauses, Article 6:111 envisages at the outset a process of negotiation to reach an amicable agreement varying the contract. Under the general duty of good faith, the party which will suffer the hardship must initiate the negotiation within a reasonable time, specifying the effect the changed circumstances have had upon the contract. The other party, if it is concerned about maintaining the contractual relationship, may also seek to open negotiations. The negotiations must be conducted in good faith, that is to say, they must not be either protracted or broken off abusively. There will be bad faith if one party continues to negotiate after it has already entered another, incompatible contract with a third party. Normally the principle of good faith will require that every point of dispute between the parties should be brought up in the negotiations.

The obligation to renegotiate is independent and carries its own sanction in paragraph (3)(c). The compensation provided by (3)(c) will normally consist of damages for the harm caused by a refusal to negotiate or a breaking off of negotiations in bad faith (for instance, the expenses of bringing the action insofar as these have not been recouped by an award of costs). It may be awarded against either party.

D. *The court's powers*

If the parties' negotiations do not succeed, either of the parties may bring the matter before the court.

The court will intervene only in the last resort, but it is given wide powers. The court may, in effect, either terminate the contract or modify its terms. In accordance with the purpose of the provision, its first aim should be to preserve the contract. The court could even require the parties to make a last effort at renegotiation if it believes that there is still a chance of saving the contract. It may employ any means that are permitted under its national law, such as appointing a mediator to assist the parties. If the negotiations are unsuccessful it will have to make a decision on the merits in accordance with paragraph (3).

The modification of the clauses of the contract must be aimed at re-establishing the balance within the contract by ensuring that the extra cost imposed by the unforeseen circumstances are borne equitably by the parties. They may not be placed solely on one of them.

> *Illustration 4*: A town council has arranged for the supply of electricity by a private company at a fixed tariff. If the price of the coal used to produce the electricity increases dramatically because of shortages, the additional payment which the town should be required to make should not cover the whole of the additional cost of the coal. Part of the extra cost should fall on the company.

Unlike the risks which result from total impossibility, the risks of unforeseen events are to be shared.

The court may intervene in a variety of ways. According to the text, the proposed solutions are only options. First, the court may reject the application. It will do so if, in its opinion, the remedy would be worse than the harm: if, for instance, the remedy were to create a new hardship on the other party's side. Second, it may extend the period for performance, increase or reduce the price or the contract quantity or order a compensatory payment (compare the case where the means of fixing the price becomes impossible under Article 6:107, above). Much will depend on the procedural rules of the forum, but these will often permit similar results to be reached e.g. by granting a *délai de grâce* or by reducing the counter-performance to be rendered.

There is, however, a limit to this power: the court can modify clauses of the contract but it cannot rewrite the entire contract. The modifications made to the contract must not amount to imposing a new contract on the parties. For example, in illustration 4 the court could not impose requirements which would in effect force the electricity producer to change its plant to burn oil instead of coal.

In such a case, the only option open to the court would be to declare the contract ended. It is obvious that if the parties fail to agree on a change to the contract, the resulting difficulties will usually be such that the court will end up declaring the contract ended. And the court will fix the date for the contract to end in such a way as to ensure that the aggrieved party is not unfairly prejudiced by the other party's failure to agree on ending the contract or to negotiate for adaptation of the contract.

It is in effect the court which declares the contract ended, in contrast to what happens when the non-performance is imputable to one of the parties or when performance becomes impossible. It may be that, after fruitless negotiations, one of the parties will take the initiative and announce unilaterally the end of the contract. If the other challenges this, the court must decide whether the party was justified in taking this attitude. In addition the court will have to fix the date as from which the contract is ended, taking into account how much of it has been performed. It is this date which will determine the extent of restitution which will become due. The Article also empowers the court to end the contract upon terms, for instance provided that an indemnity is given. It may also order the payment of an addition to the price or of compensation for a limited period and the termination of the contract at the end of the period.

So the mechanism adopted by Article 6:111 gives the court wide powers. These must be used in moderation, to avoid any reduction in the vital stability of contractual relations. This moderation is shown by the experience of countries which have already a similar rule.

NOTES

Unidroit arts. 6.2.1-6.23 are similar to Article 6.111. The various national laws solve in very different ways the problem of changes of circumstances which make the obligations of one party much more onerous but which do not amount to *force majeure* (on *force majeure* see notes to Article 8:108 below). Some accept it as a basis for modifying the contract, others do not.

1. *Change of circumstances accepted as basis for modifying contract*
    A famous example, though applying only to administrative contracts, is the FRENCH doctrine of *imprévision*. Under this doctrine change of circumstances may lead to the ending of the contract or its modification by the court granting a monetary compensation, see the *Gaz de Bordeaux* case, Conseil d'Etat 30 March 1916, D.P. 1916 3:25; *Ghestin, Billiau & Jamin* No.283.
    Several laws, whether by statute or case law, admit as a general principle that the contract may be ended or modified, when as expressed in a GERMAN case, "to maintain the original contract would produce intolerable results incompatible with law and justice". See BGH 25 May 1977, NJW 1977, 2262, 2263; BGH 13 Nov. 1975, NJW 1976, 565, 566; *Staudinger & Schmidt*, s. 242 no. 838 and references there. According to another German case, RG 3 Feb. 1922, RGZ 103, 328, 33, the normal consequence is that the contract will not be terminated unless it is impossible to adapt it. The German case law is based on the good faith principle in BGB § 242. Also the DUTCH BW art.6:258 applies the good faith principle to provide for an ending or modification of the contract in the case of changed circumstances. This provision was "applied" by the Dutch courts under the former Code's good faith rule before the new provision came into force in 1992.
    Art. 1467 of the ITALIAN CC provides that if contracts for continued or periodic performance or for deferred performance are made excessively onerous for the debtor by extraordinary and unforeseeable events, he may demand that the contract be ended. The other party may avoid this by an equitable offer to modify the terms of the contract, though revision of the contract not provided for in art.1467 (but see Art. 1664 (Construction Contracts). SPANISH caselaw permits the court to end the contract if a less radical way of preseving it cannot be found (*Diez Picazo*, II 873: *"rebus sic stantibus"* clause, TS 23 December 1963, 12 November 1990, 23 April 1991, 8 July 1991, 10 February 1997); but the principle is applied only exceptionally (*"pacta sunt servanda"*: see *Albaladejo* II, 1, § 78).
    Art. 388 of the GREEK Civil Code gives the judge wide powers to adapt the contract to new circumstances or to end it altogether. The same solution appears in PORTUGUESE law (CC art. 437).
    In AUSTRIAN ABGB §§ 936, 1052, 1170a form, by way of analogy, the statutory foundation for the recognition of the rule that a fundamental change of circumstances may, under certain rather restrictive conditions, affect the validity of a contract. The change must have been unforeseenable for both parties at the time of the conclusion of the contract and relate to characteristic features of the type of the relevant agreement.
    In a few decisions SCANDINAVIAN courts, which generally do not accept change of circumstances as a ground for the revision of a contract, have modified the terms of long-lasting continuing contracts, at first by invoking an "implied condition" (see note to Article 4:103) but lately by applying § 36 of the Contract Act on unconscionable clauses, see for DENMARK, *Gomard*, Kontraktsret 179ff.; for FINLAND, *Wilhelmsson*, Standardavtal 130ff.; for SWEDEN, *Hellner*, Speciell avtalsrätt II; 2, 59ff.. In the U.S. change of circumstance has made a hesitant appearance, see e.g. *Aluminum Co. of America* v. *Essex Group* 499 F.Supp 53 (W.D.Pa. 1980); U.C.C. § 2-615 and Restatement 2d of Contracts, § 261 comment (a).

2. *Change of circumstances not accepted as basis for modification*
    Some legal systems do not give any relief. This is the case for FRENCH, BELGIAN and LUXEMBOURG law except for administrative contracts, see note 1 above, though in Belgium relief may be given on the basis of other doctrines, see generally *Philippe*. ENGLISH law seems to reject any notion of relief for changed circumstances not amounting to impossibility: *Davis Contractors Ltd.* v. *Fareham U.D.C.* [1956] A.C. 696 (H.L.) The only possible exception, frustration of the venture, may follow from the isolated decision in *Krell* v. *Henry* [1903] 2 K.B. 740 (C.A.) where a change of circumstances rendered the contract pointless. SCOTTISH law seems to be the same as English law, as is the law of IRELAND, see *Clark* 422-438. CISG art. 79 appears to be limited to cases of impossibility though there is disagreement among the various commentators.
    See generally *Zweigert & Kötz* 516-536; *Abas; Philippe; Rodière & Tallon; Chambre de Commerce Internationale*: Force majeure et imprévision; on CISG art.79 see *Bianca & Bonell (-Tallon)* 572; *Honnold* § 423ff; *von Caemmerer & Schlechtriem* 675ff.

CHAPTER 7

Performance

Article 7:101: Place of Performance

(1) If the place of performance of a contractual obligation is not fixed by or determinable from the contract it shall be:

    (a) in the case of an obligation to pay money, the creditor's place of business at the time of the conclusion of the contract;

    (b) in the case of an obligation other than to pay money, the debtor's place of business at the time of conclusion of the contract.

(2) If a party has more than one place of business, the place of business for the purpose of the preceding paragraph is that which has the closest relationship to the contract, having regard to the circumstances known to or contemplated by the parties at the time of conclusion of the contract.

(3) If a party does not have a place of business its habitual residence is to be treated as its place of business.

COMMENT

A. *Significance*

The place of performance is significant in several respects. A party who is to perform services will have to bear the inconvenience and the costs of presenting himself at the place and tendering performance there. For an debtor to tender or offer performance at a wrong place will often constitute a non-performance. In a contract for the delivery of goods the party who is to perform will in general have to bear the costs and carry the risk of the goods until they have been put at the disposal of the creditor at the place of performance. An creditor who is unable to receive performance in due time because it mistook the place of performance may also fail to perform the contract or bear the risk of a non-performance by the other party see, Article 8:103(3).

B. *Place determinable from the contract*

Very often the place of performance is fixed in the agreement or determinable from the agreement. An employee will have to work at the employer's premises or at another place at the employer's instruction. A catering company will bring the food and cater for the party at the address given to the enterprise by the host. If a seller has undertaken to dispatch the goods to the buyer it will in general perform its duties by handing over the goods to the carrier, see CISG Article 31(a).

C. *Money obligations*
If the place of performance is not fixed or determinable from the contract the place of performance of a money obligation is the creditor's place of business. "The debtor must seek the creditor". This rule will leave the debtor with a free choice of how it will send or transfer the money to the creditor, which, when the debtor carries the risk of transmission, will have no right to interfere with the mode of transportation or transfer used.

D. *Other obligations*
As far as obligations other than money obligations are concerned the place of performance is the debtor's place of business. This is in conformity with the general principle that in cases of doubt the debtor is implied to have undertaken the least burdensome obligation.

E. *The term "Place of business"*
It is difficult to give an exact definition of the term "place of business". In most cases it is a party's permanent and regular place for the transaction of general business and not a temporary place of sojourn during sales negotiations.

> *Illustration 1*: Seller A wants to make a sales drive in country B and hires salesrooms in a hotel in the capital of B for a week. From these rooms it solicits orders from buyers. Thereafter the salesrooms are closed down. A has not had a place of business in the capital of B.

F. *Several places of business*
If the party at whose place of business performance is to be made has more than one place of business, the place of performance is that which has the closest connection with the contract and its performance having regard to the circumstances known to or contemplated by the parties at the conclusion of the contract.

> *Illustration 2*: Company A which has its headquarters with accounts department and a shipbuilding yard in Hamburg runs a shipbuilding yard in Bremerhaven as well. By a telex to A in Hamburg B, who is a shipowner in London, orders a repair of his ship which, known to both parties, is on its way to Bremerhaven. The repair of the ship is to be done in Bremerhaven, and the payment for the repair to be made to Hamburg.

G. *Habitual residence*
If the party with whom performance is to be made has no place of business, performance is to be effected at his habitual residence. This is a "factual" not a "legal" concept. A person has his habitual residence at the place where he actually lives, regard-

less of whether he has a permit to live in the country, and whether he sometimes goes to another place to stay for some time, provided that he normally returns to the first place, see Resolution 72 of the Council of Europe of 18 January 1972.

H. *Impact of usages*

Usages and practices may fix a different place of performance, see Article 1:105. It is probably a universal usage that a customer of a bank who wishes to draw his money will have to come to the bank. However, if the bank agrees to send the money to a customer the money will travel at the bank's risk.

I. *Change of the place of performance*

The place of performance is the party's place of business (or his habitual residence) at the time of the conclusion of the contract. If after that time the party moves to another place the first place remains the place of performance. However, if the party chooses to move the place of performance to its new place, good faith requires that it should be permitted to do so unless it will cause an unreasonable inconvenience for the other party or the party which moves does not notify the other party in due time, see Article 1:201.

If as a result of a change of the place of performance there is any increase in the expense of performance, this increase must be born by the party which has changed the place of performance. If as a result of the change of the place of performance the risk of transportation is perceptibly increased the party whose change of place of performance increases the risk of transportation will have to carry that risk.

NOTES

1. Money obligations

In many systems the place of performance, if it has not been agreed expressly, is the creditor's residence or place of business, see for the NORDIC countries Instrument of Debts Acts (1938) § 3(1); GREECE CC art. 321(1); ENGLAND, SCOTLAND and IRELAND, *Chitty* § 21-043 and *Bank of Scotland* v. *Seitz* 1990 S.L.T. 584, I.H.; ITALY CC art. 1182(3); NETHERLANDS BW 6:115 - 6:118, especially 6:116; PORTUGAL CC art. 774.

In ENGLISH, IRISH and SCOTTISH law the place is the creditor's place of business at the time the contract is made: *Chitty* § 21-043. In AUSTRIAN, GREEK, ITALIAN, DUTCH, NORDIC and PORTUGUESE law the place of payment is the creditor's place of business at the time of payment. These laws, however, have provisions protecting the interests of the debtor in case the place of payment is different from the place at the time of the conclusion of the contract, see AUSTRIAN ABGB § 902(2); NORDIC Instruments of Debts Acts, § 3(1), second sentence; GERMANY BGB § 270(3); GREECE CC art. 322; ITALY CC art. 1182(3); NETHERLANDS BW art 6:117; PORTUGAL CC arts. 772(2) and 775. CISG art. 57 is similar; see also ULIS art.59 and *Unidroit* art. 6.1.6(1)(a)

In some of the laws the debtor's residence or place of business is the place of performance of a money obligation, see SPANISH CC art. 1171(3); FRENCH, BELGIAN and LUXEMBOURG Civil Codes art. 1247(3), except that if the price for goods is payable on delivery it is payable at the place of delivery, art.1609 and 1651. The debtor who sends money to the creditor bears the risk of loss or delay, see for Belgian law Cass. 6 Jan. 1972, Arr. Cass., 441; Cass. 23 Sept. 1982, Pas. I, 118; similarly Luxembourg District Court 31 Jan. 1874, 1, 128.

In GERMAN law it is the debtor's place of business which for the purposes of jurisdiction and venue is the place of performance, see BGB §§ 269 and 270(4). However, the debtor is responsible for transferring the money to the creditor and bears both the expense and the risk of loss in transfer, BGB § 270. But if he sends it in time the creditor must suffer the loss of a delay in transit, see on BGB § 270 *von Caemmerer & Schlechtriem (-Hager)*, Art. 57 No. 5.

2.   *Other than money obligations*
It seems to be generally accepted that for obligations other than money obligations the place of performance is, unless otherwise agreed, the debtor's residence or place of business.

However, some laws provide that the place of performance of an obligation relating to specific goods is the *situs* of the goods: FRANCE, BELGIUM and LUXEMBOURG, Civil Codes art. 1247(1); ENGLAND and SCOTLAND, for sale of goods, see Sale of Goods Act s.29(2); IRELAND, Sale of Goods Act 1893, s.29(1); ITALY, CC art. 1182(2); NETHERLANDS, BW art 6:41 (a); POR-TUGAL, CC art. 773; SPAIN, CC art. 1171 (1) and (2); FINLAND and SWEDEN, Sale of Goods Act § 6. See also CISG art.31, ULIS art. 23(2) and *Unidroit* art. 6.1.6(1)(b). Paragraphs (2) and (3) of Article 7:101 are based on CISG art.10.

Article 7:102: Time of Performance

A party has to effect its performance:
(1) if a time is fixed by or determinable from the contract, at that time;
(2) if a period of time is fixed by or determinable from the contract, at any time within that period unless the circumstances of the case indicate that the other party is to choose the time;
(3) in any other case, within a reasonable time after the conclusion of the contract.

COMMENT

A. *Significance*
The time for performance has significance in several connections. An early performance by a party may be and a late performance is almost always a non-performance of the contract, see Article 8:101. If the party which is to receive performance which is duly tendered at the time for performance does not do so at that time it will often bear the risk for performance not being effected.

B. *Concurrent performance of the parties' obligations*
It is the general rule that the two performances have to be rendered simultaneously, so that each party can withhold its performance until the other performs (*Pflicht zur Leistung Zug um Zug*, as it is put in German). These issues are treated in Article 9:201, Right to Withhold Performance.

C. *Time determinable from the contract*
If a time is fixed by or determinable from the contract, performance must be made at that time. This may be a date which at the conclusion of the contract is fixed by the calendar, for instance "delivery on October 15", or it may be otherwise determined.

> *Illustration 1:* A and B have agreed that B shall begin to harvest A's crop one week after A has called upon it. The time is determinable from the contract.

D. *Performance within a period of time*
It may also occur that the time of performance is to be set within a period of time or by a certain time; and in that case Article 7:102(2) comes into operation.

If the contract or the circumstances do not indicate that the receiving party is to choose the time of performance, it is for the party which has to make the performance to choose the time.

An example of where the time for performance is to be determined by the party which is to receive the performance is the f.o.b. sale where delivery is to be made during a period of time. Here it is for the buyer to provide the vessel (see INCOTERMS 1990 f.o.b. under B7) and thus decide the date he will receive the goods on board the ship.

It may follow from the circumstances of the case that the period of the time fixed for the performance begins as soon as the contract is made and as soon as the creditor – or in an appropriate case the debtor – requires performance.

Illustration 2: A makes an agreement with bank B for a cash-credit in favour of A up to €100,000. The agreement does not mention anything about when A can begin to draw money under the credit, but it follows from the circumstances that he can start drawing at once.

E. *Performance within reasonable time*

If no time is fixed or determinable from the contract, performance is to be made within a reasonable time after the conclusion of the contract. What is reasonable time is a question of fact depending upon the nature of the goods or services to be performed and the circumstances, see Article 1:302.

NOTES

1. *Time of performance agreed*
   The rule in Article 7:102(1) appears to be in accordance with the laws of the Member States. It follows from the parties' freedom of contract and is only, as in CISG art.33(a), provided for the sake of clarity.
2. *Performance within a period of time*
   The rule in Article 7:102(2) seems to be widely accepted, see GERMAN BGB § 271(2), ITALIAN CC art.1184 and PORTUGUESE CC art. 779. The same rule probably applies in FRANCE, compare CC art. 1187 and *Malaurie & Aynès* no. 1100; in DENMARK, see Sale of Goods Act § 13, which applies to other kinds of contract also; and FINLAND and SWEDEN, Sale of Goods Act § 9(2). See also CISG art.33(b) and *Unidroit* art. 6.1.1.(b).
3. *No time for performance agreed*
   The rule in Article 7:102(3) is in accordance with the COMMON LAW rule, see U.K. Sale of Goods Act 1979, s.29(3); IRISH Sale of Goods Act 1893, s.29 and *Macauley* v. *Horgan* [1925] I.R. 1; FINNISH and SWEDISH Sale of Goods Act § 9(1). It has also been adopted by CISG art.33(c) and *Unidroit* art. 6.1.1.(c).
   Most of the other laws provide rules which are different but which will often bring about the same or very similar results as the rule on performance within a reasonable time laid down in Article 7:102(3). They generally provide that the creditor may demand performance at once. See for FRANCE CC art. 1901 and *Ponsard & Blondel* nos 136 and 137; AUSTRIA, ABGB § 904; DENMARK, Sale of Goods Act § 12; GERMANY, BGB § 271(1); GREECE, CC art. 323; ITALY, CC art. 1183; NETHERLANDS, BW art. 6:38; PORTUGAL CC art. 777(1). However usage, the nature of the contract or other circumstances will often prevent the creditor from demanding immediate performance: ITALIAN CC art. 1183; PORTUGUESE CC art. 777(2); and SPAIN, CC art. 1128, under which the court may fix the time for performance. In GERMANY the rule on immediate performance is tempered by the principle of good faith, BGB § 242 and the same applies in DENMARK (semble), Court of Appeal (East) 31 March 1987 , U.f.R. 1987, 738; GREECE, CC art. 288; and the NETHERLANDS, BW art. 6:2.

Article 7:103: Early Performance

(1) A party may decline a tender of performance made before it is due except where acceptance of the tender would not unreasonably prejudice its interests.

(2) A party's acceptance of early performance does not affect the time fixed for the performance of its own obligation.

COMMENT

A. *Declining an early tender*

Though some codes maintain the presumption that the debtor may perform its obligation early, this rule does not meet the needs of modern contractual relations. Usually the performance is scheduled in accordance with the creditor's activities and availability and an earlier performance may cause it extra expense or inconvenience.

> *Illustration 1*: A sells to B 10 tons of perishable goods. The date of delivery provided in the contract is October 1. Since the ship on which the goods were loaded arrives at the place of destination earlier than expected, A asks B to take delivery of the goods on September 20. B is entitled to refuse the earlier performance.

B. *Good faith*

On the other hand, good faith may be invoked to avoid abusive refusals when the creditor will not suffer any inconvenience through early performance.

> *Illustration 2*: The facts are the same as in Illustration No. 1, except that B has storage room available and A is ready to cover the expenses and to carry the risk for the storage of the goods during the period from September 20 to October 1. B must accept the earlier performance, since a refusal on its part would be contrary to good faith.

C. *Money obligations*

The principle according to which the creditor has the right to refuse an earlier performance is unjustified in relation to monetary obligations, where the creditor faces no prejudice in receiving the money before the expected time, provided that an earlier payment does not affect the interest due.

> *Illustration 3*: The date for the payment of the price fixed in the contract is July, 1. In order to avoid late payment, the debtor instructs its bank to transfer the funds on the creditor's account well in advance. The price is credited on the creditor's account on June 20. The creditor may not refuse the payment.

D. *Creditor's duty not affected*

A party's acceptance of an earlier performance does not affect the time fixed for the performance of its own obligation, even if the other party's right to withhold its performance is lost.

Illustration 4: The facts are the same as in Illustration 2 with the addition that payment is to be made at the time agreed for delivery on October 1 when the goods are to be handed over to B. B is not obliged to pay the price when he receives the goods on September 20. A cannot withhold the goods because it is not paid on September 20.

NOTES

1. *Early tender may be refused*
    As in Article 7:103(1), an early tender may be refused in SPAIN (CC art. 1127: time of performance is presumed to have been fixed for the benefit of both the parties) and PORTUGAL (*Jorge* 309 f.) unless the time for performance has been fixed exclusively in favour of the debtor. Similarly the creditor cannot be compelled to accept early performance under AUSTRIAN law: ABGB § 1413.
    In the UNITED KINGDOM a buyer of goods may refuse an early tender, see *Benjamin* § 8-039, and in DENMARK the buyer may do so if an early delivery of the goods will amount to a substantial breach of contract: *Nørager-Nielsen & Theilgaard* 293. In ITALY the creditor may refuse early performance but not if the time was fixed in the interests only of the debtor (see *di Majo* 167-168). CISG art. 52(1) provides that the buyer may take delivery or refuse to take delivery but this rule is probably subject to the good faith principle provided in art. 7(1), see *Bianca & Bonell (-Will)* 380.
2. *Early tender must be accepted*
    In some laws there is a presumption that the time for performance is fixed in favour of the debtor, and that, therefore, the creditor must accept an early performance, see on BELGIAN, FRENCH and LUXEMBOURG law CC art. 1187; GREEK CC art. 324. The same presumption is found in GERMAN law (BGB § 271 (2), DUTCH law (BW art. 6:39) and, for money debts, NORDIC law, see Instrument of Debts Act § 5 (note that in FINNISH law it is said that a creditor need not accept early performance of an interest-bearing money obligation if he is not compensated for loss of the interest he would receive according to the contract: *Hakulinen*, Velkakirjelaki 61). The presumption is rebutted when this follows from the agreement or from the circumstances of the case. Thus in FRANCE, BELGIUM, LUXEMBOURG, GERMANY and DENMARK money debts carrying interest cannot be repaid in advance, and a person who has agreed to provide services at a certain time cannot choose to perform earlier.
3. *No duty for the creditor to perform earlier*
    The rule in Article 7:103(2), under which an earlier performance does not affect the time for performance of the receiving party's obligation, seems to be accepted by those systems which have addressed the issue, see e.g. for DANISH law, *Nørager-Nielsen & Theilgaard* 293 and for SWEDISH LAW, *Ramberg*, Köplagen *263*.
    Unidroit art. 6.1.5.(1) and (2) are similar to Article 7.103.

Article 7:104: Order of Performance

To the extent that the performances of the parties can be rendered simultaneously, the parties are bound to render them simultaneously unless the circumstances indicate otherwise.

COMMENT

In any synallagmatic contract it must be determined whether the parties are to perform simultaneously or whether one is to perform before the other. Article 7:104 provides that in general performances should be rendered simultaneously. This is because, if one party is to perform first, it will necessarily have to extend credit (in one form or another) to the other party, thereby incurring a risk that the other will default when the time for its performance comes. This additional risk is avoided if the performances are made simultaneously. Thus it is the general rule in sales contracts that, unless otherwise agreed, delivery and payment are to be simultaneous.

However, simultaneous performance is often impracticable. An employer cannot realistically be expected to pay a builder brick by brick. Either the employer must pay in advance or, as is more usual, the builder must complete some or all of the work before payment.

The Article does not provide a presumption as to which party should perform first if simultaneous performance is not appropriate. The variety of circumstances is too great for this to be practical. In most cases the matter is settled by usages (cf. Article 1:105), and almost every general rule seems to have many exceptions. Thus in contracts for services it is common to find the custom, "work first, payment later", which may reflect the fact that the employer is a better credit risk than the service provider or may simply be a reflection of market power or social standing; but there are situations in which payment is expected in advance.

> *Illustration 1*: A employs B to spend three afternoons a week tending the garden of A's villa. The time for payment is not discussed when the contract is made. B demands payment in advance. A can refuse to pay in advance.

> *Illustration 2*: C books theatre tickets in advance over the phone and comes to collect them from the box office. The theatre may demand payment before C is admitted to the show.

The question will have to be decided by references to such usages or, if there are none, by the factors listed in Article 6:102, Implied terms – (a) the intention of the parties, (b) the nature and purpose of the contract and (c) good faith and fair dealing.

> *Illustration 3*: Hamlet engages a troupe of players to perform at his country house. Whether the players may demand payment in advance will depend on usages in the country or previous practices between the parties. If there are none, the question will depend on other factors such as whether the play to be performed had to be specially written and rehearsed.

Even where simultaneous performance is feasible, the contract or the circumstances may lead to a different result. Thus it is possible for food in a restaurant to be handed over in exchange for an immediate cash payment, as happens in some cheaper restaurants and bars; but in others the customer is obliged to pay only after the meal has been finished.

NOTE

This provision is in line with the law in most jurisdictions in Europe, such as AUSTRIA, ABGB § 904; FRANCE (case law as set out by *Terré, Simler & Lequette* no. 616) and ENGLAND (see *Beale*, 28-34 and *Treitel*, Contract. 677-685) -and with *Unidroit* art. 6.1.4. In other European jurisdictions, the rule is the same although there is no express provision. This is the case in ITALY, where it follows from CC art. 1460 on *exceptio non adimpleti contractus*, unless something different is provided by the contract or results from the nature of the contract, and PORTUGAL.

In all systems, the rule that performances are due simultaneously is only a presumption which will not apply if the parties have agreed otherwise, for example when credit is given by one party to the other, or if the circumstanecs make it inappropriate, e.g. when the performance by one party is necessary before the other party can perform (see e.g. in BELGIUM, Cass. 5 May 1971, Arr. 871, *Rechtskundig Weekblad* 1971-72, 147, *Journal des Tribunaux* 1972, 85).

Some jurisdictions provide a further rule for the case where performance by one of the parties requires some time. The other party will then only have to perform his side after the performance of the former party has been rendered. Thus in BELGIAN law, when the obligation of one party concerns a continuous performance, and the other one not, the former party normally has to perform first. Similarly *Unidroit* art. 6.1.4(2) provides that to the extent that the performance of only one party requires a period of time, that party is bound to render its performance first, unless the circumstances indicate otherwise. But in all systems there are customary exceptions: for example, it is customary for theatre-goers to have to pay in advance of seeing the performance. See also notes to Article 9:201.

Article 7:105: Alternative Performance

(1) Where an obligation may be discharged by one of alternative performances, the choice belongs to the party which is to perform, unless the circumstances indicate otherwise.

(2) If the party which is to make the choice fails to do so by the time required by the contract, then:

    (a) if the delay in choosing is fundamental, the right to choose passes to the other party;

    (b) if the delay is not fundamental, the other party may give a notice fixing an additional period of reasonable length in which the party to choose must do so. If the latter fails to do so, the right to choose passes to the other party.

COMMENT

This provision lays down some rules for the not infrequent situation, where an obligation may be performed by any one of two or more alternatives. The basic rule is that the party who is to perform, may then choose which alternative to perform. However, this is subject to a number of conditions. The contract may indicate that it is the other party, who is to make the choice. Or it may be the Principles which make the choice, see e.g. Articles 7:108(3) and 7:109. Finally, usages may also determine who is to make the choice among the alternatives.

Whoever has the right to choose should exercise this power within a reasonable time, especially after having been asked to do so by the other party. The sanction is that otherwise the right to choose may pass to the other party. The point at which the right to choose will pass depends on whether the time for the exercise of the choice was fundamental or, if it was not, whether it has been made fundamental by the other party serving a notice, see Article 8:106(3).

NOTE

Paragraph (1) of the Article is in line with European Civil Codes – see for instance DUTCH BW art. 6:19, FRENCH CC arts. 1189-1196; GERMAN BGB § 263; GREEK CC art. 306, ITALIAN CC art. 1286(1), PORTUGUESE CC arts. 543(2) and 548. As for DENMARK see *Gomard*, Obligationsret I, 37 and *Ussing*, Alm del 24. However, the law in ENGLAND is less certain – see *Treitel*, Contract 671. Rules equivalent to the second paragraph are less common but are found in some countries, e.g. Dutch BW art. 6:19.

Article 7:106: Performance by a Third Person

(1) Except where the contract requires personal performance the creditor cannot refuse performance by a third person if:
- *(a) the third person acts with the assent of the debtor; or*
- *(b) the third person has a legitimate interest in performance and the debtor has failed to perform or it is clear that it will not perform at the time performance is due.*

(2) Performance by the third person in accordance with paragraph (1) discharges the debtor.

COMMENT

A. *Scope*
Article 7:106 treats the questions, under what conditions does performance by a third person constitute due performance in relation to the creditor who cannot then refuse performance, and under what conditions does the performance by a third person discharge the debtor vis-à-vis the creditor. It does not address the question whether a third person who has made a performance acquires the rights of the creditor vis-à-vis the debtor by way of assignment or subrogation.

B. *When will a tender constitute performance?*
The third person making the performance is often acting with the assent of the debtor or on its directions. An agent or a sub-contractor of the debtor may have been entrusted to perform the contract. In these cases the creditor cannot refuse performance, unless the contract requires personal performance, see Article 7:106(1)(a).

However, performance by a third person may also be made without the volition of the debtor. The third person may have a legitimate interest in doing so. A surety pays a debt in order to avoid costly proceedings against the debtor which eventually the surety will have to pay. A tenant pays the mortgage in order to avoid a forced sale of the property. In the interests of the family, a wife pays the debt of her husband for which she is not liable. A parent company pays the debt of its subsidiary to save the latter's credit rating. In these cases the creditor cannot refuse performance by the third person provided that the debtor has failed to perform when performance fell due or it is clear that it will not perform at the time when it falls due, see Article 7:106(1)(b).

C. *Is the debtor discharged?*

Due performance by the third person who is entitled to perform discharges the debtor, see Article 7:106(2).

It follows from Article 8:107 that the debtor remains responsible if a third person who has promised to perform and who has got the debtor's assent to performance fails to perform or makes a defective tender. Where performance has been undertaken or carried out by a third person who has a legitimate interest in performance the debtor will also remain responsible, if the third person fails to tender performance when it is due, or if his tender is refused because it is defective. The debtor will not be excused under Article 8:108 for a failure to perform by a third person unless the third person's non-performance was due to an impediment which would also have excused the debtor. Whether the debtor is responsible for a defective performance by the third party which has caused a greater loss to the creditor than the expected non-performance by the debtor is to be decided by the applicable law.

An creditor who refuses to accept a performance by a third person made in pursuance of Article 7:106(1) will normally have failed to perform the contract and cannot exercise any of the remedies for non-performance set out in chapter 9. Article 7:110 or 7:111 may also apply.

D. *When may a tender be refused?*

There are, however, situations where the creditor is entitled to refuse performance by a third party. Such performance may be excluded by the terms of the contract. The terms which exclude third party performance may be express or they may be inferred from the language of the contract. There are also situations where it follows from the nature or purpose of the contractual obligation that it cannot be performed vicariously.

Where in contracts for the performance of personal services it can be inferred that the debtor has been selected to perform because of his skill, competence or other personal qualifications, the creditor may refuse performance by a third person. However, if it is usual in the type of contract to allow delegation of the performance of some or all of the services, or if this can be done satisfactorily by third persons, the creditor must accept such performance.

Where the third person cannot show any assent by the debtor or any legitimate interest the creditor is entitled to refuse his tender of performance. Thus it can refuse payment from a person who attempts to collect claims against the debtor. If the debtor has not assented to the performance the creditor may also refuse performance by a friend of the debtor whose motive is unselfish. Article 7:106 does not treat which consequences it has for the debtor if in these cases the creditor accepts performance by the third person.

NOTES

1.   *Debtor assents to vicarious performance*
     The legal systems all seem to agree that performance by a third person which is agreed to by the debtor before or after it is made (vicarious performance) is, in principle, admitted. However, it may not be permitted if it is against the interests of the creditor. This idea is expressed differently in the legal systems.

GREEK and PORTUGUESE law will not permit vicarious performance when it is prejudicial to the interests of the creditor, see Greek CC art. 317 *in fine* and PORTUGUESE CC art. 767(2). Under DUTCH law a third party may perform an obligation "unless this is contrary to its content or necessary implication", see BW art. 6:30.

Most of the laws exclude vicarious performance of obligations which have a personal character: DENMARK, see *Ussing*, Alm. Del. 58; FRANCE and BELGIUM, CC art. 1237, see *Malaurie & Aynès*, Obligations no. 962 and for Belgium Cass. 28 Sept. 1973, R.W. 1973-74, 1158, R.C.J.B. 1974, 238 obs. *van Damme*; ENGLAND, *Treitel*, Contract 672-673; AUSTRIA, a generally-acknowledged principle based on provisions for specific contracts: ABGB § 1153 (labour contract), § 1171 (work contract), etc.; GERMANY, see BGB § 267(1); ITALY, CC art. 1180; GREECE: *Zepos* in Ermak II/1 art.317 no.13 (1949); NETHERLANDS, BW art. 6:30(1); SCOTLAND, *McBryde* 378-382; SPAIN, CC arts.1158, 1161 and see *Diez-Picazo* II, 481; SWEDEN, see *Rodhe, Obligationsrätt* 158.

2.   *Performance without the consent of the debtor*

(a)   *The civil law*

Provided the performance by the third party is not excluded as being against the interests of the creditor under the rules discussed in note 1 above, the other civil law systems seem to allow it on varying conditions. Under AUSTRIAN law, the debtor's consent is not necessary, if the creditor accepts performance by the third party (see ABGB § 1423). In GERMANY, BGB § 267(2) and ITALY, CC art. 1180 the creditor must accept performance but may refuse if the debtor objects to it. If he objects the creditor has a choice whether or not to accept. This rule also applies in DENMARK, see *Ussing*, Alm.Del. 307; the NETHERLANDS, BW art 6:30(2); PORTUGAL, CC arts. 592(1) and 768(2); and SWEDEN, *Rodhe*, Obligationsrätt 66. In FRANCE the debtor can oppose performance if he can show that he will be prejudiced by it, see *Malaurie & Aynès*, Obligations, no.962. In BELGIUM the debtor cannot oppose performance, but the third party will not acquire the rights of the creditor by subrogation unless the third party acted with the debtor's consent or had a legitimate interest in performance, CC art.1236.

Under BW art. 6:73 the creditor may refuse performance, but if the third party has a legitimate interest in performance the rules on creditor *mora creditoris* will apply.

Under SPANISH law the creditor must accept performance by a third party even if the debtor opposes it, but the third party will then not have a right of subrogation but only a claim for enrichment (CC arts. 1158(3) and 1159; *Diez-Picazo* II, 484; *Albaladejo* II, 1 § 24.3; TS 26 June 1925, 16 June 1969, 30 September 1987 and 12 November 1987).

In GREECE the creditor may not accept performance if the debtor opposes it, see CC art.318.

(b)   *England, Ireland and Scotland*

In ENGLISH law a performance made without the permission of the debtor is not admitted. This holds true when the effect would be a subrogation in favour of the third party: "a man cannot make himself the creditor of another without his knowledge or consent". The same seems even to hold true when there is no subrogation, see *Chitty* § 29-093. It is probably now settled that payment by a third party will only discharge the debtor if he authorized or subsequently ratified the payment, see *Goff and Jones* 17. There are, however, specific provisions allowing a sub-tenant of a lease to intervene to prevent forfeiture of the head lease, see Law of Property Act 1925, s.146. The IRISH and SCOTTISH laws are probably the same as the English.

Article 7:107: Form of Payment

(1)   Payment of money due may be made in any form used in the ordinary course of business.

(2)   A creditor which, pursuant to the contract or voluntarily, accepts a cheque or other order to pay or a promise to pay is presumed to do so only on condition that it will be honoured. The creditor may not enforce the original obligation to pay unless the order or promise is not honoured.

COMMENTS

A. *General remarks*

Payment is not only made by legal tender but also by bank transfer, handing over of a cheque and in many other ways. The development of new techniques for payment must not be prevented by a detailed enumeration of possible manners of payment. It is in the general interest of business to allow payment to be made in any manner which is currently being used and is easy, quick and reliable. Without special permission the debtor can pay in such manner, e.g. by cheque, and the creditor is bound to accept it (see on this specific way also paragraph (2)).

B. *Manner of payment*

Many national laws provide that payment must be made by legal tender and that the creditor is not entitled to demand any other method of payment except where the contract so provides. However, the debtor may prefer another manner of payment, provided this is in conformity with the ordinary course of business. The creditor must be protected against a surprising, unusual or burdensome manner of payment.

> *Illustration 1*: A owes B 5000 DM. As A wants to annoy B, A takes 500,000 pieces of one Pfennig and sends them to B. Since it is not in the ordinary course of business to pay such a large sum by such a small unit, even though it is legal tender, A is not allowed to make payment in this manner.

What manner is usual depends on the nature of the transaction involved and on the usages prevailing at the place of performance for the payment (see Article 7:101). The creditor does not have the right unilaterally to demand or refuse any particular manner.

C. *Acceptance of promise of alternative performance conditional only*

It often occurs that the creditor, in order to accommodate the debtor, accepts in lieu of cash a cheque, a bill of exchange, a claim for the payment of money (transferred by way of assignment) or even an instruction (written, oral or in any other form) to a third person to pay. In all these cases the creditor generally does not wish to run the risk that the cheque or other claim for payment will not be honoured. Therefore paragraph (2) sent. 1 makes it clear that the original claim subsists until satisfaction of the substituted performance has in fact been achieved. If this is not done the creditor may enforce the underlying claim. But it cannot proceed with the latter until the substituted performance becomes due and remains unperformed (paragraph (2) sent. 2).

> *Illustration 2*: A owes B £3000. A accepts B's request to give it a promissory note payable two months later. B's remedies on the original contract are suspended until the promissory note is due but revive if the note is dishonoured (see Comment D).

Paragraph (2) sent. 1 applies only to an assignment as payment and not to an ordinary assignment of debt.

As paragraph (2) sent. 1 establishes a rebuttable presumption, parties may expressly or impliedly stipulate otherwise.

D. *Consequences of dishonouring the substituted performance*
If the claim created or assigned in substitution of the original claim is not honoured the creditor may proceed with the underlying claim for payment as if no substituted performance had been accepted. If interest was due on the debt, it is recoverable. But where the creditor took a promissory note or another negotiable instrument in substitution for the original promise of payment, it will usually find it more efficient to ignore this promise and sue on the instrument.

However, if the creditor fails to take any steps necessary to enforce the claim received by it as a substitute, it cannot then revert to the original remedies for non-performance except to enforce the payment due itself.

Illustration 3: B owes A £5000 from a contract of sale. A has declared that it will accept the £5000 no later than August 1, otherwise it wants to terminate the contract. On this day B gives A a cheque which A accepts. The cheque is not presented to B's bank until several months later and is not honoured by the bank because of the expiry of the period of presentation. A cannot declare the contract terminated since it has not presented the cheque in the ordinary way.

NOTES

1. *Ordinary method of payment*
    In many countries the ordinary method of paying a monetary obligation is by transfer of legal tender. This rule is expressly fixed in ITALY (CC art. 1277 (1)) PORTUGAL (CC art. 550) and SPAIN CC art. 1170), but it is valid also in several other countries, especially in those of the French-inspired legal orbit (e.g. FRANCE, BELGIUM and LUXEMBOURG); in GREECE, see *Stathopolous* 191-192; in ENGLAND and SCOTLAND, see *Chitty* § 21-044 and *Wilson*, Debt paras. 1.2, 12.1; and in IRE-LAND, see *Forde* § 1.086. In AUSTRIA ABGB § 1054 requires in respect of sales that payment of the price be "in cash"; this provision is liberally interpreted, however. Special legislation in these countries often authorizes or even obliges a debtor to make payment of substantial sums of money in cash-less form, e.g. by bank transfer or cheque. DUTCH BW art. 6:112 allows payment in "current" form and art. 6:114 authorizes a bank transfer if the creditor has a bank account in the country of the place of performance, unless the creditor has validly objected. In BELGIUM a Royal Decree of 10 Nov. 1967 makes it obligatory to accept a bank transfer or cheque for payments of more than 10,000 BF in commercial transactions; similarly in FRANCE for payment of over 5,000 FF (L. 22 October 1940).
    Other countries allow payments to be made in any form that is current and acceptable for present-day business (DENMARK: *Gomard*, Obligationsret I 121; SWEDEN: *Rodhe*, Obligationsrätt 33; but in FINLAND a creditor is usually not obliged to accept payment by cheque, *Aurejërin* 13). This rule is expressly laid down in the UNITED STATES, although the creditor may refuse to accept a payment other than by legal tender provided he gives a reasonable extension of time for the debtor to procure it (UCC § 2-511(2)).

2. *Substituted payment*
    The disadvantage of most forms of substituted payment is that they do not immediately transfer a monetary value to the creditor. Therefore in most countries the handing over of a cheque or the production of a credit card or any transfer of a similar form of substituted payment is considered to be a conditional performance of the monetary obligation, the condition being that the substituted obligation will be honoured. This general principle is quite elaborately laid down in the US: UCC § 3-802(1) (a) and (b) and § 2-511(3); Restatement of Contracts 2d, § 249). A more general regulation is given by GERMAN BGB § 364(2), and see DUTCH BW art. 6:46.

In FRANCE it is held on the basis of CC art. 1243 and special texts that the collection, not the handing over a cheque is a performance of, the monetary obligation (Cass. Req. 21 March 1932, D.P.33.1.65). However it is sometimes said that so called *"paiement par chèque"* – even in cases required by law, see note 1 above – is a conditional performance (*Issa-Sa-yegh*, J. Cl. civ. art. 1235 à 1248 Fasc. II no. 117-118). A presumption to this effect has been established in ENGLAND *(D&C Builders Ltd.* v. *Rees* [1966] 2 Q.B. 617 (C.A.); *Chitty* §§ 21-061-062), SCOTLAND (*Leggat Bros.* v. *Gray* 1908 S.C. 67, I.H.) and IRELAND (*Forde* § 1.087, though it can be rebutted: *P.M.P.S.* v. *Moore* [1988] I.L.R.M. 526). According to SPANISH CC art. 1170 (2) and (3) the transfer of a negotiable instrument or similar commercial instrument has the effect of payment only after the instrument has been honoured. In PORTUGAL it is assumed that acceptance of those instruments normally is a *datio pro solvendo* and therefore does not constitute payment until the instrument is actually honoured (*Varela* II 173). This latter rule is expressly laid down in ITALY (CC art. 1197(1) sent. 2), where the creditor may refuse payment in such form unless it has been accepted on a previous occasion (Cass. 13 June 1980, no.3771, Giur. it. 1981 I, I 1984). The rule is also confirmed by case law in GREECE (AP 1209/1963, NoB 11 (1963) 1050). For FINLAND see *Wilhelmsson, Sevón* 150.

In some countries, commercial practice and case law turn the condition precedent of factual honouring into a condition subsequent: payment is regarded as effected by handing over the substituted form of payment, unless it later turns out that the instrument is not in fact honoured (FRENCH Cass.Civ.I, 2 Dec. 1968, JCP 1969.II.15775; banking practice in GERMANY and AUSTRIA). *Unidroit* art. 6.1.7 is similar to Article 7:107.

Article 7:108: Currency of Payment

(1) The parties may agree that payment shall be made only in a specified currency.

(2) In the absence of such agreement, a sum of money expressed in a currency other than that of the place where payment is due may be paid in the currency of that place according to the rate of exchange prevailing there at the time when payment is due.

(3) If, in a case falling within the preceding paragraph, the debtor has not paid at the time when payment is due, the creditor may require payment in the currency of the place where payment is due according to the rate of exchange prevailing there either at the time when payment is due or at the time of actual payment.

COMMENTS

A. Definitions

Three different currencies may be involved in an international contract.

The currency of account indicates in which currency the primary payment obligation, i.e. typically the price, is measured. The parties or the circumstances usually clearly indicate this currency. Doubts may, however, arise, as to the currency of account of damages; this problem is addressed by Article 9:510.

The agreed currency of payment may and often does, on grounds of convenience, differ from the currency of account. It is one agreed upon by the parties (paragraph (1)). Absent such an agreement, the currency of account will normally be the currency of payment.

The currency of the due place of payment may differ from the agreed currency of payment and become relevant under certain circumstances (paragraphs (2)-(3)).

Illustration 1: A merchant in Colombia sells a quantity of coffee for 100,000 US$ (currency of account) to a trader in London. It is agreed that payment of the purchase price be made in French francs (agreed currency of payment) to the seller's account at a bank in Geneva (Swiss francs being the currency of the due place of payment).

B. *Payment in the agreed currency of payment*

The rule of Article 7:108 starts from the assumption that in the first place the creditor may require and the debtor must make payment in the agreed currency of payment, i.e. the currency in which the obligation to pay is expressed. This is but a consequence of the creditor's right to require performance, as laid down in Article 9:101(1). Whether the courts at the place of payment or elsewhere are willing to give judgment in a currency which is foreign to them, is a matter of procedure; it is not affected by these Principles. This provision also does not state how the money of payment has to be ascertained, if this is doubtful.

Illustration 2: A Canadian manufacturer sells machines to a foreign buyer for a purchase price of "$" 540,000: Canadian or U.S.$? This is a question of interpretation which has to be solved according to rules of interpretation.

C. *Payment in the currency of the due place of payment*

If a monetary obligation is expresed in another currency than that of the due place of payment, the debtor may wish to make payment in the local currency; usually this is also in the creditor's interest. The rule of Article 7:108(2) presupposes that the agreed currency of payment and the currency of the due place of payment differ.

Illustration 3: As in Illustration 2, but it is provided that the purchase price of $ 540,000 is to be paid in London.

Two basic issues arise: First, does either party have the right to effect such a conversion, or does only one have such a right or even a duty to effect the conversion? Second, if so, which rate of exchange is to apply? The latter question is of special interest if the debtor delays payment and the currency of account, the agreed currency of payment or the currency of the due place of payment has depreciated in the meantime.

D. *Right of conversion*

The Principles adopt the widely accepted rule that the debtor has the option of effecting payment in the currency of the due place of payment rather than in the currency of payment (see Comment A). This is usually practical for both parties.

If the creditor wants to avoid this result, it must stipulate that payment be made only in the currency of the money of account (or in the agreed currency of payment). This right of the parties to agree on a different solution is stated expressly in paragraph (1).

E. *Rate of exchange*

The debtor's right of conversion must not be allowed to diminish the extent of its monetary obligation. Consequently, the rate of exchange for the conversion into the currency of payment must be that prevailing at the due place of payment at the date of maturity (paragraph (2)).

This rule also covers the case where payment is made before the date of maturity (cf. Article 7:103).

Difficulties arise where the debtor pays after the date of maturity and in the meantime either the currency of account, the agreed currency of payment or the currency at the due place of payment has depreciated. Should the date of maturity or the date of actual payment determine the rate of exchange? Neither solution is fully satisfactory. If after maturity the currency of account has depreciated, the creditor would be disadvantaged if the rate of exchange on the date of payment were selected. If, on the other hand, after maturity the agreed currency of payment or the currency of the due place of payment has depreciated, the creditor would be injured if the debtor were to be allowed to convert at the rate of exchange of the date of maturity, because this exchange rate places the risk of depreciation of the local currency on the creditor.

The guiding principle for an equitable solution ought to be that the defaulting debtor, and not the creditor, must bear the risk if a currency depreciates after the date of maturity of a monetary obligaton. If the creditor had been paid in time, it would bear both the chances and the risks of a depreciation; it could have avoided any foreseeable currency risk by converting the money received in a weak currency into money of a strong currency. It is thus the debtor which, actually or in effect, is speculating by delaying payment. Two solutions may be envisaged.

One would be to select the rate of exchange of the date of maturity and to grant, in addition, a claim for those damages that have been occasioned through currency depreciation during the debtor's delay. However, this route relies on two separate remedies and may entail a duplication of proceedings.

It is therefore preferable to allow a choice of the dates for the rate of conversion, and this choice must be the creditor's. It may choose between the date of maturity and the date of actual payment. This rule is laid down in paragraph (3).

Of course, the parties may agree on a fixed rate of conversion, and such an agreement takes precedence.

F. *Exchange restrictions*

The rules of Article 7:108 may not operate if and insofar as exchange restrictions affect the payment of foreign money obligations. The question as to which country's exchange restrictions must be taken into account is not addressed.

NOTES

1. *Uniform laws*
   Article 7:108 has been modelled upon two widely adopted uniform laws: (Geneva) Uniform Law on Bills of Exchange of 1930, art. 41 and (Geneva) Uniform Law on Cheques of 1931, art. 36. Both

laws are in force in more than 30 continental European countries. (See also *Unidroit* art 6.1.9.) A closely related, more elaborate model is the European Convention on Foreign Money Liabilities of 1967 (not yet in force).

The national laws are more diversified.

2.   *Currency clause*

Almost all national laws recognize a currency clause, i.e. a stipulation that the debtor must make payment in an agreed currency. While some countries have express provisions (NORDIC Instruments of Debt Act 1938 § 7(1); ITALIAN CC arts. 1270 and 1278; SPANISH CC art. 1170), other laws recognize a currency clause only implicitly (BELGIUM: Cass. 4 Sept. 1975, Pas. I 16 R.W. 1975-76, 1561); GERMAN BGB § 244(1); GREEK CC art. 291; LUXEMBOURG CC art. 1153-1 (1); NETHERLANDS BW art. 6:121(2); PORTUGUESE CC art. 558).

Only in FRANCE is such a clause void insofar as payment is to be made in FRANCE (Civ.I, 11 Oct. 1989, J.C.P. 1990 II 21393).

3.   *Payment in local currency*

In the absence of a currency clause, payment in the local currency of the due place of payment, irrespective of the currency of account, is permitted almost everywhere. This rule is based either upon statutory provisions of NORDIC Instruments of Debt Act 1938 § 7(1); GERMAN BGB § 244(1); GREEK CC art. 291; ITALIAN CC art. 1278; NETHERLANDS BW art. 6:121(1) AUSTRIAN law: 4th Introductory Regulation of the Commercial Code (4.EVHGB) Art 8 No 8(1) which also applies in matters of civil law; and SPANISH CC art. 1170(1), the meaning of which is debated by scholars, see *Diez Picazo* II, 278) or upon case law (ENGLAND: *Barclays International Ltd.* v. *Levin Brothers* [1977] Q.B. 270, 277 (Q.B.); FRANCE: Cass.req. 17 Feb. 1937, S. 1938.1.140; BELGIUM: Cass. 4 May 1922, Bull. Institut Belge Droit Comparé 1923, 299).

4.   *Exchange rate*

The exchange rate is controversial. If payment is made at maturity, so that the dates of payment and of maturity coincide, the exchange rate of this day applies.

Difficulties appear to exist on late payment. Under one approach, the rate of exchange is that of the day of payment (NORDIC laws: Instrument of Debts Act § 7(1); ENGLAND: *Miliangos* v. *George Frank (Textiles) Ltd.* [1976] A.C. 443 (H.L.); AUSTRIAN law, 4. EVHGB Art. 8 No 8(2); GERMAN BGB § 244(2); GREEK CC art. 291; NETHERLANDS BW art. 6:124). Under another approach, the rate of exchange is that at the date of maturity (FRANCE: case law, Cass. req. 17 Feb.1937, S. 1938 I 140; ITALY: CC art. 1278; also BELGIUM, LUXEMBOURG and PORTUGAL).

The two conflicting approaches are, however, mitigated by supplemental rules. Where the exchange rate is that of the date of maturity and the currency of account has been devalued between that date and the time of payment, several countries grant damages to the creditor for delayed payment. These damages are based either on the general rules on late performance (BELGIUM: case law, e.g. Cass. 4 Sept. 1975, Pas. 1976.I.16 (impliedly); Cour d'appel Bruxelles 15 Jan., 5 Feb. 1965, Pas. 1965.II.310 – damages after debtor's default; NETHERLANDS BW art. 6:125; PORTUGAL: *Varela* I 896; *Costa* 641); or they comprise the difference between the rates of exchange at maturity and at payment (ITALY: Cass. 12 March 1953 no. 580, Giust.civ. 1953, I 830; LUXEMBOURG: CC art. 1153-1, as inserted by Law of 12 July 1980, with qualifications in favour of the debtor which are in accordance with the general rules as to liability for non-performance).

Conversely, in those countries which use the exchange rate at the date of payment, the debtor has to pay the difference between the exchange rates at the date of payment and a higher rate either at default (AUSTRIA: OGH 10 January 1989, ÖBA 1989, 735; GERMANY: RG 13 May 1935, RGZ 147, 377, 381; GREECE: Athens 3030/1969, Hazm 24 (1970) 409; 1905/1978, NoB 27 (1979) 221, 222, under a theory of damages) or even at the date of maturity (NORDIC countries: Instrument of Debts Act § 7(2); ENGLAND: *Ozalid Group (Export) Ltd.* v. *African Continental Bank Ltd.* [1979] 2 Lloyd's Rep. 231, 233 (Q.B.)).

An alternative remedy allows the creditor to elect between the exchange rates of the date of payment and of maturity (FRANCE: *semble* Civ. 2, 29 May 1991, B.II, no.165, p.89: creditor allowed to elect the date of *mise en demeure;* Similarly SPAIN, Law of Exchange art. 1, see *Diez Picazo* II, 279). This solution corresponds to Article 7:108(3) of the Principles.

Article 7:109: Appropriation of Performance

(1) Where a party has to perform several obligations of the same nature and the performance tendered does not suffice to discharge all of the obligations, then subject to paragraph (4) the party may at the time of its performance declare to which obligation the performance is to be appropriated.

(2) If the performing party does not make such a declaration, the other party may within a reasonable time appropriate the performance to such obligation as it chooses. It shall inform the performing party of the choice. However, any such appropriation to an obligation which:

(a)   is not yet due, or

(b)   is illegal, or

(c)   is disputed,

is invalid.

(3) In the absence of an appropriation by either party, and subject to paragraph (4), the performance is appropriated to that obligation which satisfies one of the following criteria in the sequence indicated:

(a)   the obligation which is due or is the first to fall due;

(b)   the obligation for which the creditor has the least security;

(c)   the obligation which is the most burdensome for the debtor;

(d)   the obligation which has arisen first.

If none of the preceding criteria applies, the performance is appropriated proportionately to all obligations.

(4) In the case of a monetary obligation, a payment by the debtor is to be appropriated, first, to expenses, secondly, to interest, and thirdly, to principal, unless the creditor makes a different appropriation.

COMMENTS

A. *The problem*

Sometimes a party is obliged under a single contract or separate contracts to accomplish two or more performances of the same nature – in particular, to pay money. If the performance tendered does not suffice to discharge all these obligations, the question arises which obligation has been discharged by such performance, i.e. to which obligation such performance is to be appropriated. The question may become relevant if different securities have been created for the different obligations, or if they bear interest at different rates, or if the periods of limitation expire at different dates.

B. *Performing party's right to appropriate its performance*

The generally accepted principle is that the debtor may at the time of payment expressly or impliedly declare which obligation shall be discharged.

Illustration 1: Bank B grants to A a loan of € 2000 for buying a Peugeot car and some months later a loan of € 2500 for buying another car, a Ford. Security interests are created in both cars for B. When later paying € 2000 to B, A may declare that his payment concerns the loan for the Peugeot. B cannot object and the security interest in the Peugeot lapses.

A debtor may distribute a payment among various outstanding obligations, thus liquidating them partially. However, the effects of such partial performance are subject to the general rules on non-performance.

The performing party's appropriation must, in general, be declared to the other party. Otherwise the latter would not know to which of the several obligations the other party wishes to appropriate the performance. Usually, such a declaration must be express. An implied appropriation may, however, be inferred from the fact that the debtor paid the exact amount of one of the debts or that the other debts are barred by limitation.

The debtor's right of appropriation is limited in two ways. First, where the contract already provides for a mode or sequence of appropriation, such agreement prevails.

> *Illustration 2*: A and B, to whom A owes different sums, including interest, agree on a scheme for discharge of A's debts. The payments then made by A are appropriated according to the scheme for discharge and not according to declarations which A may make on payment.

This limitation of the debtor's right of appropriation need not be made explicit because agreement prevails over the Principles.

Second, the debtor of a sum of money is in certain cases prevented from appropriating its payment according to its will or interest. Paragraph (4) prescribes that the sequence of appropriation is: expenses – interest – principal; the term "interest" covers both contractual and statutory interest. Such sequence even applies if the creditor has accepted a tender of performance in which the debtor has declared to appropriate differently, unless the creditor has clearly consented to such declaration.

> *Illustration 3*: A owes B 50,000 DM. B starts enforcement proceedings and obtains a judicial mortage of 50,000 DM on A's land; the costs of these proceedings are 10,000 DM. A then pays to B 50,000 DM. B accepts this payment but refuses to sign a receipt stating that payment is made on the principal and not the costs. According to paragraph (4) the costs and 40/50 of the principal are discharged. Consequently, the remaining 10,000 DM are still secured by the mortgage.

C. *Receiving party's subsidiary right to appropriate*

Where the contract does not provide a rule of appropriation and the performing party fails to appropriate its performance the law must supply a solution. Basically, there are two different approaches: either the right of appropriation is granted to the receiving party; or objective criteria are fixed for the appropriation. Paragraphs (2) and (3) combine those two approaches but give a preference to the first. According to paragraph (2) the right to appropriate devolves upon the receiving party if the performing party does not appropriate its performance. But the receiving party must exercise this right within a reasonable time after receiving the performance; if it fails to do so, the performance is appropriated according to paragraphs (3) and (4).

Appropriation by the receiving party, which must be within a reasonable time, is the decisive act. However, the performing party must know where it stands. Consequently, the receiving party is obliged by the general requirement of good faith to inform the performing party of the appropriation. That notice, however, is merely declaratory. The appropriation is, therefore, not invalidated if the receiving party fails to give notice; but such failure may give rise to a claim for damages.

In order to protect the performing party from being impaired by the receiving party's appropriation the latter's choice is restricted by paragraph (2) sentence 2 sub-paragraphs (a) to (c). Thus, the receiving party cannot appropriate the performance to an obligation which is not yet due (sub-paragraph (a)), which is illegal (sub-para-graph (b)) or which – on whatever grounds – is disputed (sub-paragraph (c)). It is true that the meaning of the term "illegal" differs in the various national legal systems; however, it is not feasible to deal with these variations.

The receiving party is not restricted from appropriation of a performance to an obligation which is already barred by a statute of limitation. This follows from the general rule that the statute of limitation only operates if invoked by the party required to perform; it also avoids uncertainties about the applicable period of limitation.

D. *Appropriation by law*
Where neither the performing party (under paragraph (1)) nor the receiving party (under paragraph (2)) have validly appropriated the performance, the law determines to which obligation a performance is appropriated.

Under paragraph (3) the performance is appropriated to that obligation which according to the sequence of the criteria is the first to correspond to one of the following criteria:
(a) earlier date of falling due;
(b) less security – this criterion must be interpreted in accordance with its economic bearing: also a debt for which a third person is liable *in solidum* or for which enforcement proceedings can already be started offers more security;
(c) more burdensome character – e.g. producing interest at a higher rate, a penalty (Article 9:509),
(d) earlier date of creation.

Illustration 4: B grants a loan of 240,000 F to A, which is guaranteed by C. Later, B grants another loan of 220,000 F to A. A pays back to B only 220,000 F. B may sue C for 240,000 F because according to paragraph (3) (b) the payment of 220,000 F is appropriated to the unsecured second loan.

This sequence of criteria is considered to correspond to the interests of both parties. If none of the four criteria leads to appropriation of the performance, it is appropriated proportionally.

E. *Appropriation to part of single obligation*

Article 7:109 presupposes that there are several distinct obligations (cf. paragraph (1)). Some rules of Article 7:109 may, however, be extended to cases where partial payment of a single debt needs to be appropriated to a proportion of the debt.

Illustration 5: B grants a loan of 240,000 F to A which is guaranteed by C up to 150,000 F. If A repays 50,000 F, this amount is appropriated to the unsecured part of B's loan if neither A nor B makes an appropriation.

Whether Article 7:109 applies directly if payment is made on a current account being in debit depends on the nature of the current account, which must be determined under the applicable law. The rule applies directly and fully if the (negative) current account is not regarded as an integration (novation) for the individual obligations constituting the account; in this case, the current account in law still consists of the original number of several obligations towards the creditor. If, by contrast, the negative balance of the current account is regarded as constituting an integrated single obligation, Article 7:109 does not apply.

NOTES

1. *Performing party's choice*
   The principle expressed in Art. 7:109(1) is generally accepted (cf. BELGIUM, FRANCE and LUX-EMBOURG: CC art. 1253; DENMARK: *Ussing*, Alm.Del. 25 and 309), but there are certain restrictions: of FRANCE, cf. *Couturier*, J.Cl.civil art. 1253-1255, fasc. 84-85 nos. 21-30; BELGIUM: *De Page* III no.488; ENGLAND: *Chitty* § 21-046 et seq.; FINLAND: Commercial Code of 1793 Chapter. 9 § 5 and Consumer Protection Act Chapter. 7 § 15; GERMANY: BGB § 366(1); GREECE: CC art. 422 sent. 1; ITALY: CC art. 1193 (1); NETHERLANDS: BW art. 6:43 (1); PORTUGAL: CC arts. 783-785; SCOTLAND: *Walker* no. 31.36; SPAIN: CC art. 1172 (1); SWEDEN: *Rodhe*, Obligationsrätt 162; USA: Restatement of Contracts 2d s. 258(1), but with a restriction for cases where the debtor is obliged to a third party to devote the performance to the discharge of another obligation, cf. § 258(2). In AUSTRIA, ABGB § 1415 requires the creditor's consent to debtor's choice.
   Illustration 1 is based on French Cour de cassation Civ. I, 4 Nov. 1968, Bull.civ. I no. 261 p. 199.
2. *Express provision in contract*
   It is probable that a contractual stipulation prevails (cf. FRANCE: *Couturier*, J.Cl. civil art. 1253-1255, fasc. 84-85 no. 15; GERMANY: Reichsgericht 25 April 1907, RGZ 66, 54, 57-59, but see *Enneccerus & Lehmann* s. 62 I pr. with note 1).
3. *Debtor has not appropriated payment*
   If the debtor has not declared any appropriation, the laws show two different approaches:
   (a) *Receiving party's choice*
       Like Article 7:109(1) sent. 1, the COMMON LAW, SCOTTISH, BELGIAN, DANISH and SWEDISH law devolve the right to appropriate to the creditor if the debtor has not made an appropriation (ENGLAND: *Chitty* § 21-046, but s.81 of the Consumer Credit Act 1974 deviates from the general rule; USA: Restatement of Contracts 2d § 259; SCOTLAND: *Walker* no. 31.36; BELGIUM and FRANCE: CC art.1255 (in effect: see note 4 below); DENMARK: *Ussing*, Alm.Del. 310; SWEDEN, *Rodhe*, Obligationsrätt and Handelsbalken; but cf. also the *ius commune*, *Windscheid & Kipp* § 343). But there are restrictions to the accepting party's right to appropriate: he may not appropriate a performance to an obligation which is not yet due if there are debts which are already due (USA: 15 *Williston* § 1797 with note 8, Restatement of Contracts 2d § 259 comment a); to an obligation which is illegal (ENGLAND: *Chitty* § 21-049; SCOTLAND: *Walker* no. 31. 36; USA: 15 *Williston* para. 1797 with note 7, cf. also Restatement of Contracts 2d § 259(2) lit. c); or to an obligation which is disputed (Scotland: *Walker* no. 31. 36; USA: Restatement of Contracts 2d § 259(2) lit. c, 15 *Williston*

§ 1797 with note 6). Restatement of Contracts 2d § 259(2) lit. b contains a special rule precluding the accepting party from appropriating a performance to another obligation if failure to appropriate it to a specific debt would cause a forfeiture. However, the fact that an obligation is barred by the statute of limitation does not hinder appropriation to such obligation by the accepting party (England: *Chitty* § 21-050; USA: 15 *Williston* § 1797 with note 7, Restatement of Contracts 2d § 259 comment a; to the contrary: SCOTLAND: *Walker* no. 31. 36). In BELGIUM the accepting party may not make an appropriation in which he has no legitimate interest, *De Page* III p.494; *van Ommeslaghe*, R.C.J.B. 1988, p.110 no.203.

(b) *Objective criteria*

By contrast, most Continental legal systems lay down objective criteria (cf. AUSTRIA: ABGB § 1416; GERMANY: BGB § 366(2); GREECE: CC art. 422 sent. 2; ITALY: CC art. 1193(2); NETHERLANDS: BW art. 6:43(2); PORTUGAL: CC art. 784; SPAIN: CC art. 1174). Even systems following the first approach are forced to fall back on objective criteria if the accepting party also fails to appropriate (cf. SCOTLAND: *Walker* 31. 36; for FRANCE and LUXEMBOURG cf. CC art. 1256, which – as Illustration 4 shows – is somewhat different; USA: Restatement of Contracts 2d § 260; for the *ius commune* of Germany before 1900 cf. *Windscheid & Kipp* § 343; BELGIUM CC art.1256). Article 7:109(3) is the consequence thereof.

Illustration 4 is modelled upon French Cour de cassation Civ. I, 29 Oct. 1963, D. 1964.39 (which, however, reached the contrary result).

4. *Receipt accepted*

Some codes contain express provisions on the effect of the acceptance of a receipt which indicates the appropriation (cf. FRANCE, BELGIUM and LUXEMBOURG: CC art. 1255; ITALY: CC art. 1195; SPAIN: CC art. 1172 (2); in the NETHERLANDS such a provision, previously contained in the old BW art. 1434, was considered to be superfluous for the NBW, cf. Parlementaire Geschiedenis Boek 6, 180 note 1). In France and Belgium it is controversial whether this means that the creditor has the right to appropriate where the debtor has failed to exercise his option (in this sense *De Page* III no. 489) or whether the rule concerns appropriation by agreement of both parties (*Couturier*, J.Cl. civil, art. 1253-1255, fasc. 84-85, no. 56; *Planiol & Ripert (-Esmein/Radouant/Gabolde)* VII no. 1204).

5. *Money debts*

The rule of Article 7:109(4) is, as far as general private law is concerned, common to Continental legal systems (cf. BELGIUM, FRANCE and LUXEMBOURG: CC art. 1254; AUSTRIA: ABGB § 1416 (interest); FINLAND, Commercial Code chap. 9 § 5 (interest); GERMANY: BGB § 367; GREECE: CC art. 423; ITALY: CC art. 1194; NETHERLANDS: BW art. 6:49; PORTUGAL: CC art. 785; SPAIN: CC art. 1173 (for interest)).

However, in consumer credit legislation special provisions deviating from this rule exist (GERMANY: § 11 (3) Verbraucherkreditgesetz) because the indebted consumer is to be encouraged in his efforts to repay (see reasons for § 11 Verbraucherkreditgesetz, (Deutscher Bundestag, 11. Wahlperiode, Drucksache 11/5462, p. 27 left column); see also DANISH Credit Act § 28 and SWEDISH Consumer Credit Act, § 19. Further, the rules on imputation are subject to a different appropriation declared by the debtor, if the creditor has accepted the performance (FRANCE: *Couturier*, J.Cl. civil art. 1253-1255, fasc. 84-85 no. 36; GERMANY: *Staudinger (-Kaduk)* § 367 nos. 7, 8; NETHERLANDS: Parlementaire Geschiedenis Boek 6, 182; GREECE AP 702/1976, NoB 25 (1977) 51).

Illustration 3 is modelled upon Oberlandesgericht Düsseldorf 27 May 1975, RPfleger 1975, 355 (which, however, reached the opposite result).

6. *Debt partially secured*

Whether the principle of Article 7:109(1) can be applied to partial payment on a debt which is only partially secured is disputed (cf. *contra* for FRANCE: *Couturier*, J.Cl. civil art. 1253-1255 nos. 28, 29 with ref.; *pro* for GERMANY: Bundesgerichtshof 13 July 1973, NJW 1973, 1689). In LUXEMBOURG it has been decided that where the debt is unsecured and another is secured by a guarantee from a third party, partial payment is appropriated to the latter debt: 11 November 1987, Pasicrisie XXVII, p. 319.

7. *Current accounts*

The rules on appropriation of performance usually are not applied to payments made on a current account (cf. for BELGIUM: Cass. 26 Feb. 1886, Pas. 1886 I 90; ENGLAND: *Clayton's case* (1816) 1 Mer. 572, 608; 35 E.R. 781, 793; FRANCE: *Chavanne & Ponsard* no. 46; GERMANY: Reichsgericht 7 Jan. 1916, RGZ 87, 434, 438, Bundesgerichtshof 11 June 1980, BGHZ 77, 256, 261; *contra*: HGB-RGRK (-Canaris) § 355 nos. 74, 75, 83 and § 356 no. 9; SCOTLAND: *Royal Bank v. Christie* (1841) 2 Rob. 118 (H.L.)).

Article 7:110: Property Not Accepted

(1) A party which is left in possession of tangible property other than money because of the other party's failure to accept or retake the property must take reasonable steps to protect and preserve the property.

(2) The party left in possession may discharge its duty to deliver or return:

   (a) by depositing the property on reasonable terms with a third person to be held to the order of the other party, and notifying the other party of this; or

   (b) by selling the property on reasonable terms after notice to the other party, and paying the net proceeds to that party.

(3) Where, however, the property is liable to rapid deterioration or its preservation is unreasonably expensive, the party must take reasonable steps to dispose of it. It may discharge its duty to deliver or return by paying the net proceeds to the other party.

(4) The party left in possession is entitled to be reimbursed or to retain out of the proceeds of sale any expenses reasonably incurred.

COMMENTS

A. *Scope of the rule*

This Article deals with a specific form of prevention of performance, namely the creditor's failure to take delivery or to retake tangible property, other than money, tendered by the debtor. The effect of failure to accept a tender of money is covered by Article 7:111.

The scope of the provision is fixed in paragraph (1) and comprises three different situations. In the first a party which is by a contract obliged to deliver tangible property (e.g. under a contract of sale) has made a tender conforming to the contract but the other party refuses to take delivery. In the second situation the party to whom delivery was to be made has received the property but has lawfully rejected it, and the other party fails to retake it.

The third situation occurs where a contract has been lawfully terminated. According to Article 9:308 a party which had received property has then to return it to the other party. If the other party refuses to accept it, Article 7:110 applies.

For the application of Article 7:110 it is irrelevant whether or not the refusal to accept property is a non-performance (cf. Article 1:301(4)).

B. *Protection and preservation of the property*

Where this provision applies, the party which is unwillingly left in possession of property is not on that account entitled to abandon the goods or wantonly to leave them exposed to loss, damage or theft. It must take reasonable steps for their protection, e.g. by taking them back into its own custody or depositing them in a store or warehouse (paragraph (2)).

C. *Perishables and goods expensive to preserve*

In the case of perishables, the duty to protect encompasses sale of the perishables where they are in danger of deteriorating. The same applies if the expenses of preserving the goods are unreasonably high, i.e. disproportionate to the value of the goods; this covers also the case where the goods take much space which is urgently needed by the debtor. In both cases the party must take reasonable steps for disposition, depending on the value of the goods on the one hand and the trouble and expense of finding a favourable opportunity for sale on the other hand (paragraph (3)).

D. *Legal consequences*
Article 7:110(1) imposes a duty to protect and preserve the goods. However, the party which is left in possession of them is not relieved from its duty to deliver or return them.

If the party left in possession wishes to discharge its duty to deliver (or to return) it must make the property or its substitute available to the other party. The steps it can take to achieve this purpose are prescribed in paragraph (2) for property in general and in paragraph (3) sentence 2 for perishables and equivalent goods.

E. *Discharge of party left in possession*
In paragraph (2) two ways are set out by which the party which was left in possession of property (the debtor) may discharge its duty to deliver or to return the property.
(a) The debtor may deposit the property on reasonable terms with a third party to be held to the order of the creditor. The debtor can recover under paragraph (4) all storage charges reasonably incurred. In most cases, the deposit is likely to be a prelude to the debtor's exercise of its power of sale under sub-paragraph (b), for the debtor will itself be responsible to the depositary for the latter's charges and may find it impossible to recover these from the creditor.
(b) Alternatively, the debtor may sell or otherwise dispose of the object on reasonable terms. The interests of the creditor are protected by requiring that the debtor normally act only after reasonable notice; in the case of perishables this notice may be very short or no notice may be needed at all. The debtor must then account to the creditor for the net proceeds of the disposal. The debtor may be entitled under the applicable law to set off a claim against the creditor's entitlement to the net proceeds (e.g. for damages for breach of contract).

If the debtor had already sold the goods according to paragraph (2) sent. 1, it may discharge its duty by paying the net proceeds (see paragraph (4)) of the sale to the creditor.

F. *Other remedies unaffected*
If by not taking delivery the creditor fails to perform a contractual duty, the debtor is entitled to exercise any of the remedies available for non-performance, including damages and termination of the contract. If the creditor initially refuses to receive the goods but later is willing to take them, but meanwhile the debtor has incurred expenses in preserving them, the debtor may withhold the goods until the creditor is willing to reimburse the debtor. This right of withholding follows from the idea underlying Article 9:201.

NOTES

In combining in one rule several factual situations where a party has not accepted property, Article 7:110 uses a new and original approach.

1. *Duty of preservation*

Some European laws expressly provide that if the buyer without justification fails to take delivery of the goods, the seller must take reasonable care of them (U.K. Sale of Goods Act 1979, s.20(3); DANISH Sale of Goods Act § 33; FINNISH and SWEDISH Sale of Goods Acts, §§ 72-78; see also CISG art. 85). In other European laws, there is no special duty of protection which would exceed what is required by good faith and fair dealing (for PORTUGAL *Soares & Ramos* 243 and 245). By contrast, for the case of *mora creditoris* it is expressly provided that the debtor is responsible only for deliberate or reckless acts or omissions (GERMAN BGB § 300(1); GREEK CC art. 355; POR-TUGUESE CC art. 814(1); this is acknowledged by AUSTRIAN courts also as a result of the general rule laid down in ABGB § 1419); compare BELGIAN Court of Appeals Antwerpen 29 Oct. 1980, R.W. 1981-82, 1563, and see *Pothier*, Vente no.55. See also NETHERLANDS BW art. 6:90 which includes both non-performance and *mora creditoris*. In SPANISH law there is a duty of preservation as a result of CC arts. 1167 ff., 1185, 1452(3), 1505, 1589 and 1590.

The other factual situation covered by Article 2.113(1), i.e. that of the party left in possession of non-conforming goods, is in the NETHERLANDS governed by a general rule in BW art. 7:29, in FINLAND and SWEDEN by Sale of Goods Act § 73; and in CISG by art. 86. In GERMANY and AUSTRIA a corresponding rule applies to commercial transactions and where delivery is made from one place to another (HGB § 379 – *Distanzkauf;* see *Heymann (-Emmerich)* § 379 HGB nos. 3 and 4). In non-commercial cases, good faith and fair dealing may require the party not to let the goods perish, but he may send them back (*Schlegelberger (-Hefermehl)* § 379 HGB no. 1).

Some countries have specific provisions placing the cost of preserving goods on a party who has failed to accept them (e.g. a buyer who has failed to accept delivery, UK Sale of Goods Act 1979 s. 37, CISG art. 85 sent 2; a seller who has failed to take back goods properly rejected by the buyer, CISG art. 86(1) sen 2; or generally, DANISH Sale of Goods Act § 36, FINNISH and SWEDISH Sale of Goods Act § 75). Other laws deal with the issue in the context of *mora creditoris*, and therefore impose the costs on the creditor (GERMAN BGB § 304; GREEK CC art. 358 and AP 115/1970, NoB 18 (1970) 811, 812; PORTUGUESE CC art. 816).

2. *Depositing goods*

A party left with goods after a failure to take them by the other (*mora creditoris*) is expressly given a right of deposit by CISG art. 87 as well as in FRANCE, BELGIUM and LUXEMBOURG (CC arts. 1264 and 1961(3): judicial permission is required; *M.E.Storme*, Invloed no.451); AUSTRIA (ABGB § 1525); NETHERLANDS (BW art. 6:66); FINNISH and AND SWEDISH Sale of Goods Act § 74; and in ITALY (CC art. 1210 – see also arts. 1514-1515, 1686 and 1690), but rigid procedural rules must be complied with (cf. Italian CC art. 1212). The situation is similar SPAIN (CC art. 1176, Commercial Code art. 332 and Civil Procedure Code art. 2.127); and in PORTUGAL, where deposit discharges the obligation (see CC arts. 841 ff.) but a court procedure is necessary (CC Proc. art. 1.024 ff., see *Varela* II 184, *Cordeiro* II 217). In GERMANY, discharge by deposit is provided for in BGB § 378 only for money and valuables.

In FRANCE, the party left in possession has an effective alternative to the complicated method of depositing: he may ask for a court injunction against the creditor to take away or accept the goods, combined with an *astreinte* (judicial penalty) in case of disobedience (*Malaurie and Aynès*, Obligations no. 1019).

By contrast, in GERMANY deposit in a case of *mora creditoris* between merchants does not discharge the debtor under HGB § 373(1) *Heymann (-Emmerich)* § 373, 374 HGB no. 9, *Schlegelberger (-Hefermehl)*, § 373 no. 16). Nor is there a direct equivalent to Article 7:110(2)(a) in ENGLAND. If a buyer refuses to take the goods and the property has not yet passed, the seller's only remedy will be to terminate the contract and claim damages from the buyer (see e.g. *Stein, Forbes & Co. Ltd. v. County Tailoring Co. Ltd.* (1916) 86 L.J.K.B. 448 (K.B.)).

3. *Resale*

Resale as a means of self-help in Article 7:110(2)(b) is known in AUSTRIA and GERMANY in HGB § 373(2)-(5) in cases of *mora creditoris* between merchants; similarly PORTUGUESE Comm. C. art. 474; FINNISH and SWEDISH Sale of Goods Acts, § 76. Except in the Scandinavian laws, however, generally only sale by auction is permitted. Only when the goods have a market price is a sale through officially licensed brokers or auctioneers for the current price admitted. Place and time of such sale are not expressly regulated, but are subject to the seller's diligent determination (*Heymann (-Emmerich)* §§ 373, 374 HGB nos. 21 and 22). In DENMARK (Sale of Goods Act § 34),

FINLAND and SWEDEN (Sale of Goods Act § 76(3)), AUSTRIA and GERMANY (HGB § 373(2)) prior notice of the sale must be given; it must be so timely and sufficiently clear as to give the buyer the opportunity to take proper steps to protect his interests (ROHG 11.1.1876, ROHGE 19, 293 (293 f.); *Heymann (-Emmerich)* §§ 373, 374 HGB no. 12). The notice is dispensed with for emergency sales and when it is not reasonably feasible (§ 373 (2) sent. 3 and 4). According to § 373(3) resale which is justified as self-help takes place for the account of the defaulting buyer; the latter remains liable for that part of the purchase price which is not covered by the proceeds of the resale.

Also GREEK law allows the debtor, during the creditor's default and after notice to the latter, to dispose of the object at public auction and to pay the proceeds to a public entity ("Deposits and Loans Fund") for the creditor's account; notice may be dispensed with if the object is liable to perish or if notice is particularly difficult (CC art. 428). An auction can be dispensed with by leave of the judge, if the object has a market price or small value (art. 429). On sale by auction or "in a similar reasonable way", see also DANISH Sale of Goods Act § 34. In ITALY, resale on merely "reasonable terms" is allowed only in the special case of deposit of goods in a public warehouse (CC art. 1789). Under SPANISH law, resale is permitted after termination of the contract (CC art. 1258, Commercial Code art. 57; see *Vicent Chuliá* II 108).

BELGIAN law has different provisions for different contracts: sales, see CC art.1657; carriage, see Transport Contract Act art.8; on contracts for custody, cleaning, repair, etc of goods, see Act of 21 Feb. 1983.

In ENGLAND, by contrast, resale according to Sale of Goods Act 1979, s.48 has the effect of terminating the original contract. The resale is on the seller's own account and the buyer is liable in damages for the seller's net loss (*R. V. Ward Ltd.* v. *Bignall* [1967] 1 Q.B. 534 (C.A.). SCOTTISH law is the same.

4. *Rapid deterioration*

In sales, the party's duty to effect a resale in case of rapid deterioration or unreasonably expensive preservation (Article 7:110(3)) is recognised in AUSTRIA and GERMANY (HGB § 379(2)), DENMARK (Sale of Goods Act § 35), FINLAND and SWEDEN (Sale of Goods Act § 76 (2)) and in the NETHERLANDS (BW arts. 6:66 and 7:30). BELGIAN case law reaches the same result: Court of Appeals Brussels 3 July 1931, J.P.A./R.H.A. 418; see *M.E. Storme,* Invloed N 393; *Demogue* VI, no.s 26 and 45. In ITALY, CC art. 1211 on *mora creditoris* is similar, but it requires judicial approval and merely authorizes the debtor to resell but does not oblige him to do so (*Cattaneo* 217). CISG art. 88 also allows resale as a form of self-help; similarly SPANISH law, *Vicent Chuliá* II 108..

Article 7:111: Money not Accepted

Where a party fails to accept money properly tendered by the other party, that party may after notice to the first party discharge its obligation to pay by depositing the money to the order of the first party in accordance with the law of the place where payment is due.

COMMENTS

A. *Explanation*

This provision authorises the debtor, after notice, to discharge its obligation to pay by depositing the money in any manner authorised by the law of the contractual place for payment, e.g. by paying it into court. The deposit must be to the order of the creditor so that it obtains the right to dispose of the money deposited (cf. Article 7:110 paragraph (2) sub-paragraph (a)). The notice to the creditor must be reasonable (cf. Article 1:201) both with respect to the method of transmission and with respect to the time given to the first party to reply.

B. *Scope of application*

This provision applies to two different situations. First, it applies where a debtor attempts to perform a primary duty to pay under a contract, e.g. to pay the price for goods, services or work; in this case the rejected tender must have conformed to the contract. Secondly, it applies to secondary obligations to pay, e.g. after termination of the contract to repay money received (Article 9:307) or to pay damages according to Chapter 9 section 5.

For the application of Article 7:111 it is irrelevant whether or not the refusal to accept money is a non-performance (cf. Article 1:301 sub-paragraph (d)).

C. *Payment by a third person*

According to Article 7:106 an obligation which does not require personal performance can be performed by a third person. The payment of money will not usually require personal performance. Consequently, the term "tendered by the other party" must be read broadly so as to encompass a third person which makes payment in conformity with Article 7:106.

NOTES

1.   Depositing money

European continental laws generally have detailed rules on deposit of money for cases of *mora creditoris* (DENMARK: Law on Depositing 1932 § 1; FINLAND: Act on Depositing, 1931; FRANCE BELGIUM and LUXEMBOURG: CC arts. 1257-1264; GERMANY: BGB §§ 372 ff.; GREECE: CC art. 427; ITALY: CC art. 1206 ff., PORTUGAL: CC art. 841(1)(b); SPAIN: CC art. 1176). In SWEDEN, depositing is permitted only in certain cases, particularly when the debtor has difficulty in discovering whom he should pay: *Rodhe, Obligationsrätt* 130. In contrast, ENGLAND and SCOTLAND have no equivalent rule. In IRELAND payment may be made into court, *Clark* 403.

Deposit is to be made either with a court (AUSTRIA: ABGB § 1425; GERMANY: Regulation on Deposits, § 1(2); SPAIN: CC art. 1178) or with a special Deposits and Loans Fund (BELGIUM: Royal Decree of 18 March 1935, though there is some flexibility in judical practice; FRANCE: Law of 28 July 1875, D. 15 Dec. 1875; GREECE: CC art. 430 and Presidential Decree of 30 December 1926/3 January 1927) or the enforcement authority or a financial institution (DENMARK: Law on Depositing § 6; FINLAND and SWEDEN, Laws on Depositing, § 1) or a person whose business it is to take custody of sums of money (NETHERLANDS: BW art. 6:67, 6:68).

A deposit often has the effect of discharging the monetary obligation (for BELGIUM, FRANCE, the NORDIC countries and PORTUGAL see above, para. 1; the same applies in GERMANY, provided the depositor waives the right of reclaiming the money, see BGB § 378), and in ITALY and SPAIN when the deposit is accepted by the creditor or approved by the court, Italian CC art. 1210(2), Spanish CC art. 1180.

In DENMARK and GERMANY if the depositor does not waive his right to reclaim the money, and generally in SPAIN, deposit does not discharge the obligation. In Germany, the debtor has merely the right to refer the creditor to the deposited asset; the debtor no longer bears the risk and need no longer pay interest or compensation for fruits reaped (German BGB § 379).

2.   Notice to creditor

A prior notice to the creditor is, in contrast to Article 7:111, not required in GREECE (*Capodistrias* in ErmAK II/2 art. 427 no. 11 (1954)) and GERMANY, where a subsequent notice given without undue delay suffices (BGB § 374(2) sent. 1; see also FINNISH Act on Depositing, § 2(2)); a notice may sometimes even be dispensed with (Greek CC art. 430; BGB § 374(2) sent. 2). In Germany, Greece and DENMARK, if notice is omitted, the deposit is nevertheless valid (*Palandt (-Heinrichs)* § 374 no. 1), but it may give rise to a claim for damages (Germany: BGB § 374(2) sent. 1; Greece: AP 161/1977, NoB 25 (1977) 1156, 1157; Danish Law on Depositing, § 1(3)). Other countries require a judicial or other procedure (FRANCE: CC art. 1258(7); ITALY: CC art. 1212; PORTUGAL: CC Proc. arts. 1024 ff.; SPAIN: CC art 1178, Royal Decree 34/1988, Code of Civil Procedure art. 2127 (third parties who are interested must be given prior notice, CC art. 1177)).

3. *Costs of deposit*
   The costs of deposit are imposed upon the creditor who failed to accept the money (FRANCE: CC art. 1260; GERMAN BGB § 381, ITALIAN CC art. 1215; SPANISH CC art. 1179).

Article 7:112: Costs of Performance

Each party shall bear the costs of performance of its obligations.

COMMENT

The performance of commercial obligations usually entails costs. Transportation, money transfers, government licences, risk insurance, etc. will all have to be paid for. This provision lays down that such costs are to be borne by the performing party.

Illustration: A orders a book from Publishers B, located in another country, after B has stated a price for the book knowing that A resides in another country. The Publishers may not invoice A extra for the costs of mailing the book to him, unless this was agreed. Likewise, A has to bear the costs of paying for the book through an international money order or other means of payment.

NOTES

This provision is in line with the law in most jurisdictions in Europe. See for instance FRENCH and BELGIAN CCs art. 1248, DUTCH BW art. 6:47, GERMAN BGB § 364 and ITALIAN CC art. 1198. The rule is considered self-evident under AUSTRIAN law. The same applies to English law: there is no explicit statement of a general rule but the principle is illustrated by Sale of Goods Act 1979, s. 29 (6), under which the seller must bear the expenses of putting goods into a deliverable state: see *Chitty* § 41-195. The rule also applies in PORTUGAL (*Telles*, p. 287), although the present Civil Code has dropped the express provision to this point contained in art. 746 of the old Code of 1867. *Unidroit* art. 6.1.11 is to the same effect as Article 7:112.

CHAPTER 8

Non-Performance and Remedies in General

Article 8:101: Remedies Available

(1) Whenever a party does not perform an obligation under the contract and the non-performance is not excused under Article 8:108, the aggrieved party may resort to any of the remedies set out in Chapter 9.

(2) Where a party's non-performance is excused under Article 8:108, the aggrieved party may resort to any of the remedies set out in Chapter 9 except claiming performance and damages.

(3) A party may not resort to any of the remedies set out in Chapter 9 to the extent that its own act caused the other party's non-performance.

COMMENT

A. *Non-performance*

Under the system adopted by the Principles there is non-performance whenever a party does not perform any obligation under the contract. The non-performance may consist in a defective performance or in a failure to perform at the time performance is due, be it a performance which is effected too early, too late or never. It includes a violation of an accessory duty such as the duty of a party not to disclose the other party's trade secrets. Where a party has a duty to receive or accept the other party's performance a failure to do so will also constitute a non-performance.

B. *Remedies available*

The remedies available for non-performance depend upon whether the non-performance is not excused, is excused due to an impediment under Article 8:108 or results from behaviour of the other party.

(i) *Non-performance which is not excused*

A non-performance which is not excused may give the aggrieved party the right to claim performance – recovery of money due or specific performance – to claim damages, to withhold its own performance, to terminate the contract and to reduce its own performance, see chapter 9. If a party violates a duty to receive or accept performance the other party may – apart from exercising the rights under Articles 7:110 and 7:111 – also make use of the remedies just mentioned.

(ii) *Non-performance which is excused*

A non-performance which is excused due to an impediment does not give the aggrieved party the right to claim specific performance or to claim damages, see Article 8:108. However, the other remedies set out in chapter 9 may be available to the aggrieved party.

> *Illustration 1*: A has let his land to B for ten years and B has undertaken to grow vines on the land. B plants vines but the vines die from phylloxera which invades the region. Although B's failure to grow vines is excused, and B therefore is not liable in damages, B has not performed his obligations under the contract and A can terminate it before it expires.

> *Illustration 2*: A in Torino has undertaken to lease a motor lorry to B in Grenoble from December 1 and to deliver it on that day in Grenoble. The lorry is held up at the frontier due to a road block unexpectedly effected by French farmers, and arrives in Grenoble on December 15. Although A is not liable for the delay, B can withhold payment until delivery is made of the lorry, and may then deduct 15 days rent from the sum to be paid.

(iii) *Non-performance wholly or partially caused by the creditor*

The fact that the non-performance is caused by the creditor's act – or omission, see Article 1:301 – has an effect on the remedies open to the creditor. This is expressed by the third paragraph of the text. It would be contrary to good faith and fairness for the creditor to have a remedy when it is responsible for the non-performance.

The most obvious situation is the so-called *mora creditoris*, where the creditor directly prevents performance (e.g.: access refused to a building site). But there are other cases where the creditor's behaviour has an influence on the breach and its consequences. For example, when there is a duty to give information to the other party, and the information given is wrong or incomplete, the contract is imperfectly performed.

> *Illustration 3*: A has contracted to design schools to be built by B in the Tripolis area, and is expecting instructions from B as to the exact location of the schools. Due to dissensions in its staff, B fails to give the instructions within the stipulated period of time, which prevents A from designing the schools. The non-performance on A's side does not give B the right to exercise any remedy, but A will have a remedy against B.

> *Illustration 4*: The facts are the same as in Illustration 3 except that B's failure to give instructions is due to the fact that B's staff has been killed in an air crash on the way to Libya. Although B is not liable for its failure to instruct A, the non-performance on A's side does not give B any remedies either.

In other cases where there is also a non-performance by the debtor, the creditor may exercise the remedies for non-performance to a limited extent.

When the loss is caused both by the debtor – which has not performed – and the creditor – which has partially caused the breach by its own behaviour – the creditor should not have the whole range of remedies.

The creditor's contribution to the non-performance has an effect on the remedy "to the extent that (the other party's) failure to perform (is) caused by its own act or omission". This effect may be total, that is to say that the creditor cannot exercise any remedy, or partial.

Illustration 5: A agrees to carry B's glassware from Copenhagen to Paris but subjects the packages to rough handling. This would have broken some of the glass which is fragile but not some heavy pieces of thick glass. B, however, has not packed any of the glass properly and all is ruined. B can refuse to pay the carriage charges and recover damages in respect of the fragile glass, but not in respect of the heavy glass.

The exact consequence of the creditor's behaviour will be examined with each remedy, see chapter 9.

NOTES

1. *Non-performance as a unitary concept*

Non-performance as used in the Principles covers failure to perform an obligation under the contract in any way, whether by a complete failure to do anything, late performance or defective performance. Furthermore, it covers both excused and non-excused non-performance. This unitary concept of non-performance is found in some but not all of the legal systems.

Breach of contract in ENGLISH law covers the non-performance of any contractual obligation, and so does the FRENCH *"inexécution du contrat"*. This corresponds to the concept of *"tekortko-ming"* in DUTCH law, see BW arts. 6:74 and 6:265, and in BELGIAN law; non-performance in ITALIAN law, see CC arts. 1218 and 1453 ff; and *"kontraktsbrott"* or *"misligholdelse"* in NORDIC law, see *Ussing,* Alm. Del. 20, 50 (In FINNISH law, *"kontraktsbrott"* or *"sopismusrikkomus"*, see *Taxell,* Avtal och rättsskydd 171). See also on "breach" in CISG arts.45-52, 61-65 and 75-80 and on "non-performance" *Unidroit* art. 7.1.1.

In GERMAN law non-performance *("Vertragsverletzung")* only covers cases of impossibility, delay in performance, and what is called "positive breach of contract" *("positive Vertragsverletzung")* which includes, *inter alia,* breach of a contractual duty of care in the performance, and to which the rules on delay are applied by analogy , see *Zweigert & Kötz* 494 ff. Delivery of defective goods is not considered to be a non-performance; the buyer's remedies are governed by specific provisions with respect to warranty *(Gewährleistung),* cf. BGB § 459 ff.

2. *Remedies covered – the excused non-performance*

Several legal systems use the concept of non-performance both for the excused and the non-excused non-performance. This is true of *kontraktsbrott* and *misligholdelse* in NORDIC (or *sopimusrikkomus* in FINNISH law, of *tekortkoming* in DUTCH and BELGIAN law and of breach under CISG, see art.45. Remedies such as termination and price reduction are available to the creditor in both situations. Thus a performance prevented by *force majeure* is treated as a non-performance.

Some laws follow another system. In the COMMON LAW breach of contract only occurs when the aggrieved party has a right to damages for non-performance, i.e. in the case of a non-excused non-performance. Under the Common Law, however, contract liability is strict liability, and will occur in most cases of non-performance. In the rarer case where the failure to perform is excused, the aggrieved party's remedies will be circumscribed. The most obvious case is if the contract has been discharged by frustration, when the remedies will be of a generally restitutionary nature (see Law Reform (Frustrated Contracts) Act 1943, but this Act does not apply in IRELAND; there the common law still applies, see note 8 to Article 9:309). In SCOTLAND, the remedies for frustrated contracts depend upon the general law of unjustified enrichment, see *Cantiere San Rocco* v. *Clyde Shipbuilding & Engineeering Co.* 1923 S.C. (H.L.) 105. However, under the Common Law a party may be excused from a particular obligation without invalidating the rest of the contract. It appears that the outcome is that the aggrieved party may not claim damages in respect of the portion which is impossible though he may enforce the remainder, *H & R Sainsbury Ltd.* v. *Street* [1972] 1 W.L.R. 834 (Q.B.). If the failure to perform deprives him of the substance of what he was contracting for he may terminate the contract (*Poussard* v. *Spiers & Pond* (1876) 1 Q.B.D. 410 (C.A.)). It will be seen that the outcome is similar to Article 8:101(2).

In GERMAN law *"Vertragsverletzung"* presupposes that the debtor's non-performance was attributable to his fault, and the remedies for non-performance are available only in case of a non-excused failure to perform those obligations which are covered by the rules on *Vertragsverletzung*, see BGB § 276. This, however, is not true in the case of warranty (*Gewährleistung*) or of a failure to deliver generic goods, where the debtor's liability is strict, see BGB § 279. In all other cases the debtor's fault is presumed and the burden of disproving fault will be on him. In case of an impossibility which existed at the time of the conclusion of the contract the contract is void. (In contrast GREEK CC art. 362 provides for damages, implying that the contract is valid.) In case of a subsequent impossibility which is excused the creditor has no remedies. If the impossibility is permanent both parties are freed from their obligation; if it is temporary the performance cannot be claimed so long as the impossibility persists. In the case of a subsequent impossibility which is not excused the rules on delay apply. If defective goods are delivered the purchaser may terminate the contract or claim reduction in the price even if the defect is excused. AUSTRIAN law is basically similar, see AGBG §§ 918 ff.; damages may be awarded only if the non-performing party was at fault.

For certain obligations some CIVIL LAW systems will grant remedies for non-performance only if the non-performance was "imputable" to the obligor, and this frequently requires that he has committed a fault. Thus in BELGIAN, DUTCH, FRENCH, AND LUXEMBOURG law there is non-performance of an *"inspanningsverbinteris"* or *"obligation de moyens"* only if there has been fault. The creditor must prove that the debtor did not act with the care which he had undertaken to exercise. However, in case of an *"resultaatsverbinteris"* or *"obligation de résultat"*, the creditor must only prove that the result which the debtor undertook to provide has not been achieved. In either case the debtor is excused by *force majeure* which extinguishes the obligation. SPANISH law has developed on similar lines, see *Diez Picazo* II 575; *Lacruz-Sancho, Delgado, Rivero* II, 1, 25, 194. See also Note 2 to Article 6:102.

3. *Non-performance caused by the creditor*
    There is agreement among the legal systems that a non-performance which is due solely to the other party's wrongful prevention does not give the latter any remedy. In most of the systems the party who has prevented performance will himself be the non-performing party against whom the remedies may be exercised. However, in BELGIAN, DUTCH, GERMAN, GREEK and NORDIC law it is not generally considered to be a *tekortkoming, Vertragsverletzung* or *Kontraktsbrott* to prevent performance by the other party. It will depend upon whether the acceptance of the performance is a main obligation *(Hauptpflicht)* of the creditor.

    See generally *Mengoni*, Contractual responsibility 1072; *Zweigert & Kötz*, Chapter 36; *Treitel*, Remedies *passim.*

Article 8:102: Cumulation of Remedies

Remedies which are not incompatible may be cumulated. In particular, a party is not deprived of its right to damages by exercising its right to any other remedy.

COMMENT

A. *Cumulation of remedies*

Remedies which are not incompatible are cumulative. A party which is entitled to withhold its performance and to terminate the contract may first withhold and then terminate. A party which pursues a remedy other than damages is not precluded from claiming damages. A party which terminates the contract may, for instance, also claim damages.

B. *Incompatible remedies*

It is a truism that a party cannot at the same time pursue two or more remedies which are incompatible with each other. Thus it cannot at the same time claim specific performance of the contract and terminate it. If it has received a non-conforming tender, it cannot exercise its right to reduce its own performance and at the same time terminate the contract. A non-performance which causes the aggrieved party to suffer a loss may give it a right to be compensated for that loss, but it cannot be awarded more than the *"réparation intégrale"*. Thus, if it has accepted a non-conforming tender, the value of which is less than that of a conforming tender, and if it has claimed or obtained a reduction of the price under Article 9:401 corresponding to the decrease in value, it cannot also claim compensation for that same decrease in value as damages.

When two remedies are incompatible with each other, the aggrieved party will often have to choose between them, see comment C below.

C. *Change of remedy*

However, Article 8:102 does not preclude an aggrieved party which has elected one remedy from shifting to another later, even though the later remedy is incompatible with the first elected. If, after having claimed specific performance, it learns that the defaulting party has not performed or is not likely to do so within a reasonable time, the aggrieved party may terminate the contract. On the other hand, an election of a remedy is often definite and will preclude later elections of incompatible remedies. A party which has terminated the contract cannot later claim specific performance, because by giving notice of termination the aggrieved party may have caused the other party to act in reliance of the termination. If a defaulting party has adapted itself to a claim for specific performance and taken measures to perform within a reasonable time, the aggrieved party cannot change its position and terminate the contract. This applies when the defaulting party has received a notice fixing an additional time for performance under Article 8:106. The rule is in accordance with the widely accepted principle that when a party has made a declaration of intention which has caused the other party to act in reliance of the declaration the party making it will not be permitted to act inconsistently with it. This follows from the general principle of fair dealing provided in Article 1:201.

NOTE

The rule in Article 8:102 is in accordance with CISG art. 45 (2) and with the laws of the Member States except, perhaps, GERMANY. The BGB §§ 325 and 326 give the aggrieved party the choice between damages and "termination" *(Rücktritt)*, and thus it is often said that the aggrieved party cannot both "terminate" and claim damages for non-performance: *Rücktritt* means that the creditor "abandons the contract" and thus it precludes the creditor who has "terminated" the contract from claiming damages under the contract (expectation interest). "Termination" is here being used in the sense of both refusing to perform in the future and reclaiming restitution of performances already made (see Notes to Articles (9:305-9:309). This is not the sense in which it is used in the Principles, see Article 9:305, under which termination does not necessarily affect accrued rights and liabilities. The same articles of the BGB state that the aggrieved party who has no interest in further performance by the other is not bound to seek *Rücktritt* and may instead claim damages for non-performance. This seems to amount to the same thing as "termination" in the sense in which it is used in the Principles. In AUSTRIAN law, however, termination of the contract does not prevent a claim for damages for non-performance against a party at fault, see ABGB § 921. Under GREEK CC art. 387 the creditor who has terminated a synallagmatic contract may ask for equitable damages (AP 33/1980, NoB 28 (1980) 1145-1146.

See generally *Treitel*, Remedies § 288.

Article 8:103: Fundamental Non-Performance

A non-performance of an obligation is fundamental to the contract if:
(a) strict compliance with the obligation is of the essence of the contract; or
(b) the non-performance substantially deprives the aggrieved party of what it was entitled to expect under the contract, unless the other party did not foresee and could not reasonably have foreseen that result; or
(c) the non-performance is intentional and gives the aggrieved party reason to believe that it cannot rely on the other party's future performance.

COMMENT

A. *Significance of a non-performance being fundamental*
If a non-performance or prospective non-performance is fundamental the aggrieved party has a substantially wider range of rights than for other kinds of non-performance. In particular, it can:
– decline a late tender of performance (Article 8:104)
– demand adequate assurance of due performance (Article 8:105)
– terminate the contract (Articles 9:301, 9:302, 9:304).

B. *Strict compliance with contractual obligations*
Under Article 8:103(a) the relevant factor is not the actual gravity of the breach but the agreement between the parties that strict adherence to the contract is essential and that any deviation from the obligation goes to the root of the contract so as to entitle the other party to be discharged from its obligations under the contract. This agreement may derive either from express or from implied terms of the contract. Thus, the contract may provide in terms that in the event of any breach by a party the other party may terminate the contract. The effect of such a provision is that every failure in performance is to be regarded as fundamental. Even without such an express provision the law may imply that the obligation is to be strictly performed. For example, it is a rule in many systems of law that in a commercial sale the time of delivery of goods or of presentation of documents is of the essence of the contract. The duty of strict compliance may also be inferred from the language of the contract, its nature or the surrounding circumstances, and from custom or usage or a course of dealing between the parties.

C. *Gravity of the consequences of non-performance*

Article 8:103(b) looks not at the strictness of the duty to perform but at the gravity of the consequences of non-performance. Where the effect of non-performance is substantially to deprive the aggrieved party of the benefit of its bargain, so that it loses its interest in performing the contract, then in general the non-performance is fundamental. This is not the case, however, where the non-performing party did not foresee and could not reasonably have foreseen those consequences. For this purpose the test is whether a person in the same situation as the non-performing party and using reasonable skill and diligence would have known or foreseen the consequences at the time of conclusion of the contract. The other party may properly expect more skill and knowledge from a highly paid specialist than from an unskilled, modestly paid employee.

> *Illustration 1*: A, a contractor, promises to erect five garages and to build and pave the road leading to them for B's lorries, all the work to be finished before October 1st, when B opens its warehouse. On October 1st the garages have been erected; the road has been built but not paved, which prevents B from using the garages. A's non-performance is fundamental.

> *Illustration 2*: The facts are as in Illustration 1 except that the unpaved road is sufficiently smooth that the garages may be used by B's lorries in spite of the fact that the road is not yet paved, and A paves the road soon after October 1st. A's non-performance is not fundamental.

> *Illustration 3*: A agrees to instal a temperature control system in B's wine cellar which will ensure that his fine wines are not adversely affected by substantial temperature fluctuations. Owing to a defect in the installation the control system proves ineffective, with the result that B's stock of fine wines is made undrinkable. A's non-performance is fundamental, since it was aware of the likely consequences of an inadequate system.

> *Illustration 4*: A agrees to instal central heating in B's house with a temperature control system which will enable the temperature to be maintained at a constant temperature of 20 degrees centigrade. Unknown to A one room is required to develop and preserve certain rare species of plant which are extremely sensitive to changes in temperature and which have taken several years' intensive work to breed. As a result of a defect in one of the heating pipes in the room the temperature falls by two degrees centigrade and all the plants die, rendering abortive years of work. A's non-performance is not fundamental, as it could not reasonably have foreseen that such grave consequences would ensue from a slight temperature fluctuation in the room of a private house.

D. *Intentional non-performance*

Even where the contractual term broken is minor and the consequences of the non-performance do not substantially deprive the aggrieved party of the benefit of the bargain it may treat the non-performance as fundamental if it was intentional and gave it reason to believe that it could not rely on the other party's future performance (see Article 8:103(c)).

> *Illustration 5*: A, who has contracted to sell B's goods as B's sole distributor and has undertaken not to sell goods in competition with those goods, nevertheless contracts with C to sell C's competing goods. Although A's efforts to sell C's goods are entirely unsuccessful and do not affect his sales of B's goods, B may treat A's conduct as a fundamental non-performance.

> *Illustration 6*: P's agent, A, who is entitled to reimbursement for his expenses, submits false vouchers to P. Although the amounts claimed are insignificant P may treat A's behaviour as a fundamental non-performance and terminate his agency.

But where no future performance is due from the non-performing party, other than the remedying of the non-performance itself, or where there is no reason to suppose that it will not properly perform its future obligations, the aggrieved party cannot invoke paragraph (c) of this Article.

> *Illustration 7*: A contracts to build a supermarket for B for € 150,000. A completes performance except that, angered by a dispute over an unrelated transaction, it refuses to build a cover over a compressor. B can have the cover built by another contractor for € 300. A's non-performance is not fundamental.

> *Illustration 8*: A contracts to build a supermarket for B; the specification calls for the building to be faced with an expensive type of brick. A's supervisor orders that a cheaper type of brick to be used to face a wall which is not easily visible but, as soon as B points out the discrepancy, A agrees to remove the cheaper bricks and to use the proper sort in future. A's non-performance does not give B reason to believe that it cannot rely on A's performance in future.

NOTES

1.   Common law and Unidroit

The concept of fundamental non-performance as set out in Article 8:103 corresponds very closely to ENGLISH law. In particular there is a direct correspondence to the three following cases: (i) where the term broken was a condition (e.g. *Bunge Corp. v. Tradax S.A.* [1981] 1 W.L.R. 711, H.L.); (ii) where the effect of the breach was to deprive the aggrieved party of the substance of what he was contracting for (see *Hong Kong Fir Shipping Co Ltd. v. Kawasaki Kisen Kaisha Ltd.* [1962] 2 Q.B. 26, C.A.) and (iii) where the breach evinces an intention not to perform the remainder of the contract (e.g. Sale of Goods Act 1979, s.31(2)). The only substantial difference between Art 8:103 and English law seems to be that Art. 8.103(3) is confined to intentional breaches, whereas it is established in English law that even an unintentional breach may give rise to an anticipatory repudiation of the rest of the contract (cf. *Universal Cargo Carriers Corp. v. Citati* [1957] 2 Q.B. 401, 438, Q.B.). IRISH law is similar and so is SCOTTISH law, though the latter uses the phrase "material breach" and does not use the concept of "condition".

Note that "fundamental non-performance" is not equivalent to the notion of "fundamental breach" in English law. The doctrine of "fundamental breach" was developed to declare certain exclusion clauses void. It has been overruled in *Suisse Atlantique Societe d'Armement Maritime S.A.*

v. *N.V. Rotterdamsche Kolen Centrale* [1967] 1 A.C. 361, H.L. In IRELAND caselaw still accepts the doctrine, *Clayton Love* v. *B. & I. Line* (1970) 104 I.L.T.R. 157, but writers favour the *Suisse Atlantique* approach, *Clark* 150.

Unidroit art. 7.3.1. also provides for termination for fundamental non-performance. Art. 7.3.1(2) provides a list of factors relevant to deciding whether the non performance was fundamental, including the situations mentioned in Article 8:103.

2. *Nordic laws and CISG*

In the laws of the NORDIC countries the aggrieved party can terminate the contract or claim that a defective performance be replaced by a conforming tender only if the non-conforming performance is substantial. This rule is provided in the DANISH Sale of Goods Act §§ 21, 28, 42 and 43 and is applied to other contracts as well. The same rules are laid down in CISG arts. 45, 49 and 64. The corresponding sections of the Sale of Goods Acts in FINLAND and SWEDEN (§§ 25, 39, 54 and 55) are to similar effect as Article 8:103(1) and (2). CISG art. 25 provides that a "breach ... is fundamental if it results in such detriment to the other party as substantially to deprive it of what he is entitled to expect under the contract, unless the party in breach did not foresee and a reasonable person of the same kind in the same circumstances would not have foreseen such a result." CISG has no provision on intentional non-performance like the one provided in Article 8:101(3). Nor do the Nordic Acts, but it is generally held that the aggrieved party can terminate the contract if the defaulting party has committed fraud either when making or performing the contract , see DANISH Sale of Goods Act §§ 42 and 43. It is the prevailing view that in sales governed by CISG the remedies for fraud are to be found in national law, see e.g. *Honnold*, no.65.

3. *Other legal systems*

Most of the other legal systems do not apply the doctrine of fundamental non-performance but approach it in various ways:

(a) *Austrian, German, Greek and Portuguese law*

Those systems which like AUSTRIAN, GERMAN, GREEK and PORTUGUESE law have no unitary concept of non-performance have different rules for the various kinds of non-performance. For delay and impossibility German and Greek law make a distinction between non-performance of the "main" obligation and of a "subordinate" obligation; only the non-performance of the main obligation permits the aggrieved party to terminate the contract. Under these laws termination is possible in certain cases of "qualified delay", such as when the contract has provided for performance at a definite time which has not been met, or if the aggrieved party has lost any interest in performance, see AUSTRIAN, HGB § 376 and ABGB § 919; GERMAN HGB §§ 376 and 326(2); GREEK CC arts. 401 and 385(2); PORTUGUESE CC art. 808. On termination after a *Nachfrist* see notes to Article 8:106.

In a case of defects in goods sold, GERMAN law permits the buyer to reduce the price or to terminate unless the defect is trifling, see BGB §§ 459 and 462, or the termination would be contrary to good faith. See also GREEK CC arts. 534, 540. AUSTRIAN law is similar to GERMAN law but provides in addition a right to demand repair, ABGB § 932(1). POR-TUGUESE law permits the buyer to terminate if repair is impossible or if the goods delivered are so different from the goods contracted for that the buyer cannot be fully satisfied (*Telles* 330; *Varela* II 127).

Under GERMAN law, if a positive breach of contract (see note 1 to Article 8:101) imperils the purpose of the contract and takes away the aggrieved party's trust in due performance in the future, he may terminate the contract.

(b) *Dutch law*

DUTCH law does not apply the concept of fundamental non-performance. In principle any non-performance will entitle the aggrieved party to terminate the contract. However the law requires that, unless the contract provides for performance at a definite time, the aggrieved party must give the the non-performing party a *Nachfrist* in case of delay, and provides that a non-performance of minor importance for the aggrieved party will not justify termination, see Dutch BW art. 6:82-83 and 6:265.

(c) *Italian law*

Under ITALIAN law the contract cannot be terminated when the non-performance has little importance for the other party, CC art. 1455.

(d) *Spanish law*

In SPANISH law, termination is permitted if the non-performance is material even if it is less than total. The traditional view that only an intentional non-performance will justify termination has been rejected by recent case law, see *Diez Picazo* II, 716; *Lacruz-Delgado* II, 1 § 26, 200; *Albaladejo* II, 1, § 20.2.

(e)   French, Belgian and Luxembourg law
In FRENCH, BELGIAN and LUXEMBOURG law the question of termination is in principle left to the discretion of the trial judge. However it appears that the gravity of the non-performance is an important factor to be taken into account: see, e.g., Belgian Cass.8 Dec. 1960,Pas 1, 382; Cass. 12 Nov. 1976, Arr. Cass. 1977, 293; Cass. 13 March 1981, R.W. 1982-83, 1049. Termination has also been granted when the non-performance in itself is slight if there is an indication of bad faith, on French law see *Terré*, No. 630; *Nicholas* 242ff. The French Cour de Cassation has held that a buyer could not avail himself of a clause in a sales contract whereby he could terminate the contract without previous notice and without the court's intervention unless the time for delivery of the goods was a *"condition essentielle et déterminante"* (Cass.Com 13 Apr. 1964, Bull. 3 no.180, p.153).

See generally *Treitel*, Remedies § 253ff.; *Honnold* no. 181ff.; *Bianca & Bonell (-Will)* 205; *v. Caemmerer & Schlechtriem* 207ff.; *Flessner*.

Article 8:104: Cure by Non-Performing Party

A party whose tender of performance is not accepted by the other party because it does not conform to the contract may make a new and conforming tender where the time for performance has not yet arrived or the delay would not be such as to constitute a fundamental non-performance.

COMMENT

This section states the right to cure a non-conforming tender by making a new and conforming tender if there is still time to do so. For this purpose the party making the non-conforming tender will still be in time to cure the defect if he makes a new tender either before the due date for performance or where the delay is not such as to constitute a fundamental non-performance. This will depend on whether time is of the essence or has become of the essence, e.g. by the giving and expiry of a notice under Article 8:106. In either of these cases there is no right to cure under this Article.

Illustration 1: In May S, a commodity dealer, contracts to sell a quantity of cocoa to B and to ship this by 1st September. In mid-July S ships the cocoa to B but upon arrival the cocoa is lawfully rejected by B as not in accordance with the contract description. S has until 1st September to ship a fresh quantity of cocoa which conforms with the contract.

Illustration 2: The facts are as in Illustration 1 except that the cocoa does not reach B until 2nd September, on which date he rejects it. Assuming (as is usually the case upon a commercial sale of a commodity) that time of delivery is of the essence, it is too late for S to make a new and conforming tender.

Illustration 3: A agrees to build a house for B by 1 March. By 1 March some important items of work remain incomplete. Since time for completion is not normally of the essence in a building contract, A may complete the work at any time before the delay has become a fundamental non-performance, e.g. through the giving and expiry of a notice under Article 8:106.

NOTES

1. *Common law*
   Most national laws recognise in some form a defaulting party's right to cure a non-performance. However, except for the U.S. UCC § 2.508 on the seller's right to cure, no statutes have expressed the rule in the same general terms as Article 8:104. However the article seems to correspond to ENGLISH and SCOTTISH law: for England see *Borrowman Phillips & Co.* v. *Free & Hollis* (1878) 4 Q.B.D. 500 (C.A.) and *Goode*, Commercial Law 298-301; for SCOTLAND, *McBryde* 328-329 and *Strathclyde Regional Council* v. *Border Engineering Contractors* 1997 S.C.L.R. 100.

2. *CISG and ULIS*
   CISG art. 48 and ULIS art. 37 provide a general right for the seller to cure even after the date for delivery, as long as the buyer has not terminated the contract. However the seller cannot cure in cases where this would lead to unreasonable inconvenience or uncertainty of reimbursement for the aggrieved party.

3. *Nordic law*
   The DANISH Sale of Goods Act, § 49 gives the seller a right to cure if he can do it before the buyer becomes entitled to terminate the contract because of late performance, and it is apparent that the buyer will not be put to expense or inconvenience thereby. In contracts other than sale of goods and related contracts (such as leasing), the right for the defaulting party to cure is wider. He may cure unless the aggrieved party will suffer serious inconvenience thereby. The aggrieved party will not be permitted to terminate the contract unless his request for cure has proved in vain, see *Gomard*, Obligationsret II 67f. The FINNISH and SWEDISH Sale of Goods Acts allow the seller a right to cure in the same manner as CISG, see § 34 and *Ramberg*, Köplagen, 402 H.

4. *Dutch law*
   DUTCH law has introduced the right to cure a non-performance. The aggrieved party may refuse performance by the party in default if the latter does not offer payment of due damages and costs at the same time (cf. BW art.6:86). This right to cure ends at the moment the aggrieved party notifies the defaulting party that he claims damages instead of performance (BW art.6:87) or sets the contract aside (BW art. 6:25).

5. *German law*
   Under GERMAN law a seller can only exceptionally cure a non-conforming tender after the non-performance has occurred. In contracts for work and materials the contractor may cure before the owner can terminate or claim price reduction or damages, see BGB §§ 634 and 635 and v. *Caemmerer & Schlechtriem(-Huber)* § 48 n.10.

6. *Italian law*
   The only provision in the ITALIAN Civil Code which provides the right to cure a non-performing tender is art.1192 which gives the seller who has performed by delivering goods of which he had no right to dispose the right to tender goods which he does have the right to dispose of. However case law and legal writers agree in general that, whenever the aggrieved party does not accept a tender of performance because it does not conform to the contract, the defaulting party may make a new and conforming tender as long as the other party has not brought an action for termination (*Giorgianni* 80; Cass. 31 July 1987 no.6643, in Foro It., 1988, I, c.138). CC art. 1512 allows the court to give the debtor extra time to repair or replace defective goods if the contract on usages provide a warranty that the goods will operate correctly for a period of time, see *Castronovo, Contract and Tore* 281ff..

7. *Spanish law*
   In SPANISH law the defaulting debtor may cure his default at any time before the creditor has given him notice of default (CC arts. 1100 and 66) or, according to some writers, before the creditor has terminated the contract (*Diez Picazo* II, 622; *Lacruz-Delgado*, II, 1, § 23, 184; contra, *Albaladejo*, II, 1, § 32.4). The cases take a pragmatic approach, requiring the creditor to accept the performance if refusal would be contrary to good faith. In the Law on Real Estate Sales late payment must be accepted before the seller has specifically demanded termination, CC art. 1504.

8. *Greek law*
   In GREEK law the question appears to be unsettled. In the absence of a stipulation in the contract, it is doubtful whether a result similar to Article 8:104 can be reached on the basis of CC art.188 requiring performance in accordance with good faith and business usage (cf. *Spiliopoulos* in Erm.AK III/I, Intro. to arts. 534-562, nos. 46-47, 1972).

9. *Portuguese law*
   In PORTUGUESE law a result similar to that provided in Article 8:104 may be reached in that before the time for performance has expired, or even after that time but before a *Nachfrist* has expired, the defaulting party may offer a conforming tender. Since the aggrieved party will still have an interest in performance he cannot refuse the tender (*Telles* 301).

10. *French Belgian and Luxembourg law*

In FRENCH BELGIAN and LUXEMBOURG law an offer to cure made by the defendant in an action for *résolution* will sometimes prevent this being granted. The court's decision on this matter cannot be reviewed by the Cour de Cassation, (Cass.Civ 1, 15 Feb. 1967, B.I No.68, p.50). In other cases when the offer has been made slightly late the court has held that the delay did not amount to a sufficiently serious non-performance to justify termination, see Cass.Civ. 24 Feb. 1970, B.I No 67 p.54.

11. *Austrian law*

In AUSTRIAN law there is no express provision that would correspond to Article 8:104. However a supplier of a defective good may prevent termination by replacing it by a conforming one.

Generally see *Treitel*, Remedies § 276.

Article 8:105: Assurance of Performance

(1) A party which reasonably believes that there will be a fundamental non-performance by the other party may demand adequate assurance of due performance and meanwhile may withhold performance of its own obligations so long as such reasonable belief continues.

(2) Where this assurance is not provided within a reasonable time, the party demanding it may terminate the contract if it still reasonably believes that there will be a fundamental non-performance by the other party and gives notice of termination without delay.

COMMENT

A. *Purpose of rule*

This Article is intended to protect the interests of a party which believes on reasonable grounds that the other party will be unable or unwilling to perform the contract at the due date but which may be reluctant to invoke Article 9:304 in case it transpires that the other party would after all have performed. In the absence of a rule along the lines of this Article the potentially aggrieved party will be in a dilemma. If it waits until the due date for performance and performance does not take place it may incur heavy losses. If on the other hand it terminates the contract under Article 9:304 but it is later found that it was not clear that the other party would commit a fundamental non-performance, it itself will have failed to perform the contract, with a consequent liability for damages. Article 8:105 enables it to obtain an assurance of performance, in default of which it can terminate the contract, with the result that the other party will be considered guilty of a fundamental non-performance.

B. *Right to withhold performance*

So long as the aggrieved party's reasonable belief in future non-performance by the other party continues it may withhold its own performance, until it has received adequate assurance of performance.

C. *Effect of non-receipt of adequate assurance*

If the aggrieved party does not receive adequate assurance of performance and still believes on reasonable grounds that performance will not be forthcoming, it may terminate the contract. The other party's failure to give the assurance requested is itself treated as a fundamental non-performance, giving the aggrieved party the right to terminate the contract and also a right to damages where the deemed non-performance is not excused under Article 8:108.

Illustration 1: A, a caterer, contracts with B to cater for the reception at the wedding of B's daughter in three months' time. A month before the wedding B telephones A to discuss some outstanding details of the arrangements and is then told by A: "I am having some staff problems and there is a slight risk that I will not be able to organize the reception. But do not worry too much, everything should turn out all right." B is entitled to demand an adequate assurance that the reception will be provided. If this is given, as by A informing B that its staff difficulties have now been resolved, both parties remain bound by the contract and there is no breach by A. If the assurance is not given, B is not expected to court disaster on the occasion of his daughter's wedding. He is entitled to terminate the contract, engage another caterer and recover from A any additional expense involved.

Illustration 2: A, a boatbuilder, agrees to build a yacht for B, to be delivered in three months' time. B stipulates that time of delivery is to be of the essence of the contract. Soon after the making of the contract B learns that S's boatyard has been seriously damaged by fire. B is entitled to ask for an adequate assurance from A that the yacht will be delivered on time. A might give this assurance by showing that it has rented facilities to build the yacht at another yard.

D. *What constitutes an adequate assurance*
This will depend on the circumstances, including the standing and integrity of the debtor, its previous conduct in relation to the contract and the nature of the event that creates uncertainty as to its ability and willingness to perform. In some cases the debtor's declaration of intention to perform will suffice. In other cases it may be reasonable for the creditor to demand evidence of the debtor's ability to perform.

Illustration 3: B enters into three successive contracts for the purchase of goods from S. Subsequently B defaults in payment of the price under each of the first two contracts. S is entitled to demand a bank guarantee of the purchase price under the third contract or other reasonable assurance that payment will be made and is not obliged to rely solely on B's promise of payment.

NOTES

1. *Likelihood of non-performance*
   Several European systems have rules which entitle a party to terminate when it is clear that the other party will not perform, see notes to Article 9:304. Further, many systems allow a party to suspend his performance where there is a real and manifest danger that the other party will not perform his obligation when it falls due. Most of the laws deal with the situation where the other party becomes insolvent, see note 2 below. However, except for the UNITED STATES UCC § 2-609 no statutory provision is known which provides a general rule equivalent to Article 8:105. The provision which comes

closest is CISG art.71 which is more detailed and which entitles a party to withhold his performance when, after the conclusion of the contract, it becomes apparent that the other party will not perform a substantial part of his obligations. The first party must give notice of the suspension to the other party, and must continue with his performance if the other party provides adequate assurance of his performance. CISG art.71 includes, but is not limited to, cases of insolvency. The FINNISH and SWEDISH Sale of Goods Acts. § 61 are similar to CISG; see *Ramberg*, Köplagen 586 ff. In IRELAND, where the non-performance is by an employee who is on strike, the contract of employment is treated as suspended if notice of the strike has been given: *Becton Dickinson* v. *Lee* [1973] I.R. 1.

The Dutch BW art. 6:263 provides that the party who is obliged to perform first is entitled to suspend his performance if circumstances come to his attention after the conclusion of the contract which gave him good reason to fear that the other party will not perform his correlative obligations. The contract may be terminated if the conditions of art. 6:80 are met; see also note 2 to Article 9:304.

2.   *Insolvency*

The other laws deal primarily with the situation where one party has become insolvent.

In general there must be a serious deterioration in the other party's financial situation (AUSTRIAN ABGB § 1052, second sent.; GERMAN BGB § 321; GREEK CC art.377; ITALIAN CC art.1461; PORTUGUESE CC art.780(2); DANISH Bankruptcy Act §§ 54 and 57; SPANISH CC arts. 1129, 1467, 1502 and 1503). The first party may then suspend his performance.

Some laws provide similar rules on the seller's right to withhold or stop delivery in case of the buyer's insolvency or bankruptcy, see SPANISH CC art.1467 and FRENCH and BELGIAN CC arts.1613 (seller may withhold his performance if he is in imminent danger of losing his price).

The U.K. Sale of Goods Act 1979, s.39(1)(b) gives the unpaid seller a right to withhold or stop goods when the buyer becomes insolvent and s.41(1) gives him a lien in the goods. For IRELAND see Sale of Goods Act 1893, ss.39 and 41. A right to withhold and to stop goods already sent is provided also in the DANISH SGA § 39 and in other legal systems as well.

The right to withhold performance generally persists until the other party provides adequate security, or performs his obligation: e.g. AUSTRIAN ABGB § 1052 second sent.; FINNISH and SWEDISH Sale of Goods Acts. § 61(4); GERMAN BGB § 321; SPANISH cc art. 1467(2). If security is not provided the DANISH SGA § 39 gives the seller the right to terminate the contract when the time for delivery of the goods has come. In GERMAN law not to provide security is considered to be a "positive breach of contract" which may give the creditor a right to terminate the contract (BGH 8 Oct. 1990, BGHZ 112, 279, 287). Similarly under GREEK law see *Michaelides-Nouaros* in Erm.AK II/1 art. 377 nos. 8, 11 (1949). Under ITALIAN cc art. 1461 the creditor can withhold his performance, but cannot terminate the contract. However under CC art 1186, if a debtor is insolvent the creditor can demand immediate performance and, if this is not forthcoming or security provided, the creditor may terminate.

In those laws in which only insolvency is a ground for suspension of performance or for demanding an assurance, to demand an assurance of performance in other circumstances may be wrongful. Thus in SCOTLAND a party who threatened to terminate unless assurance of performance was given was held to be in material breach: *GL Group plc* v. *Ash Gupta Advertising Ltd* 1987 S.C.L.R. 149.

See generally *Treitel*, Remedies 405ff.

Article 8:106: Notice Fixing Additional Period for Performance

(1)   In any case of non-performance the aggrieved party may by notice to the other party allow an additional period of time for performance.

(2)   During the additional period the aggrieved party may withhold performance of its own reciprocal obligations and may claim damages, but it may not resort to any other remedy. If it receives notice from the other party that the latter will not perform within that period, or if upon expiry of that period due performance has not been made, the aggrieved party may resort to any of the remedies that may be available under chapter 9.

(3)   If in a case of delay in performance which is not fundamental the aggrieved party has given a notice fixing an additional period of time of reasonable length,

it may terminate the contract at the end of the period of notice. The aggrieved party may in its notice provide that if the other party does not perform within the period fixed by the notice the contract shall terminate automatically. If the period stated is too short, the aggrieved party may terminate, or, as the case may be, the contract shall terminate automatically, only after a reasonable period from the time of the notice.

COMMENT

A. *General*

Article 8:106 in effect contains two rules:

(1) Even where the aggrieved party has an immediate right to terminate because of the other's non-performance, if the aggrieved party has indicated that it is still prepared to accept performance, it may not change its mind without warning.

(2) Where there has been a delay in performance but the delay is not fundamental (because time was not of the essence and the delay has not yet had serious consequences for the aggrieved party) the aggrieved party may terminate the contract after having given the non-performing party reasonable notice.

Two preliminary points need to be borne in mind:

(1) Under the Principles there is no need for the aggrieved party to serve a notice on the non-performing party in order to put the latter into breach (cf *Mahnung, Mise en demeure*: see notes to Article 8:101 above).

(2) Under the Principles termination is an act of the aggrieved party, not an act of a court or arbitrator. Provided there has been a fundamental non-performance or the other conditions for termination are met (see Articles 8:103 and 8:105) the aggrieved party may terminate by giving notice of termination to the non-performing party (see Article 9:303 below).

When there has been a non-performance by one party (the debtor), the other (the aggrieved party) may always fix an additional period of time for performance. During the period fixed the aggrieved party may not take further action against the debtor; it may withhold its own performance and it may claim damages for the delay in performance or other losses caused by the non-performance, but it may not seek specific performance or terminate the contract during the period of notice.

Illustration 1: A company leases a new car to B for 2 years, and B collects it from the company's premises. The car breaks down and B has to have it towed back to the company's premises. The defect in the car amounts to a fundamental non-performance but B tells the company that he will accept the car if it is fixed within 3 days. B may refuse to pay the rental and may claim damages for any inconvenience in not having the car while it is repaired and for the cost of the tow, but he may not demand delivery of another car or terminate unless the car is not repaired and redelivered within the 3 days.

B. *Setting a time-limit for performance in cases of non-fundamental delay*
Not every delay in performance will constitute a fundamental non-performance within Article 8:103 and thus the aggrieved party will not necessarily have the right to terminate immediately merely because the date for performance has passed. It will only have this right if time was "of the essence". In cases of non-fundamental delay, however, Article 8:106(3) allows the creditor to fix an additional period of time of reasonable length for performance by the debtor. If upon expiry of that period of time performance has not been made, the aggrieved party may terminate the contract, see Article 9:301(2). This case is probably the one in which the notice procedure will be used most frequently.

> *Illustration 2*: C employs D to build a wall in C's garden. The work is to be completed by April 1st but prompt completion is not fundamental. By that date D has not completed the work and appears to be working very slowly. Less than a week's work is necessary to complete the wall. C may give D a further week in which to complete the wall and, if D does not do so, C may terminate the contract.

The notice procedure can also be used when it is the aggrieved party who is to perform a service but the other party has refused to accept or to allow performance.

> *Illustration 3*: E employs F to decorate the interior of an empty apartment owned by E but E fails to give F a key to the apartment by the date on which it was agreed that F should start work. F may give E a reasonable time in which to arrange access for F and, if E fails to do so, F may terminate the contract.

It should be noted that Article 8:106(3) applies even if the non-performance is excused because of a temporary impediment under Article 8:108(2).

C. *Fixing an additional period for performance in other cases.*
In other cases the notice procedure does not give the aggrieved party any additional rights but is nonetheless useful. Even where the delay or other non-performance is fundamental, and thus the aggrieved party has the right to terminate immediately, it may not wish to do so: it may be prepared to accept a proper performance by the debtor provided it is rendered within a certain period. The procedure set out in Article 8:106 permits it to give the debtor a final chance to perform (or to correct a defective performance), without the aggrieved party losing the right to seek specific performance or to terminate if by the end of the period of notice the debtor has still not performed in accordance with the contract. At the same time, however, the rule that the aggrieved party may not seek specific performance or terminate during the period of notice protects the debtor from a sudden change of mind by the aggrieved party. The debtor may have relied on having the period set in the notice in which to perform.

The notice procedure may also be used when a performance is prompt but defective in a way which is not fundamental. In such a case the aggrieved party will not have the right to terminate and serving a notice fixing an additional time for performance will not give it that right, because Article 8:106(3) applies only to delayed performance, not to defective performance.

> *Illustration 4*: A finance company has leased to B a photocopy machine which it warranted could make 100 copies of a page a minute. B's tests reveal that it makes 98 copies a minute. If the defect is not a fundamental one under Article 8:103, B cannot apply the notice procedure to terminate the contract.

Nonetheless, serving a notice may still perform the useful functions of informing the debtor that the aggrieved party still wants proper performance and of giving the debtor a last chance before the aggrieved party seeks specific performance. In these respects the notice serves the same function as a *mise en demeure* in French law or *Mahnung* in German law, though under these Principles the aggrieved party is not required to serve a notice before exercising a remedy except in the case of termination for non-fundamental delay (see comment B) above).

D. *When the notice must be for a definite reasonable period*
When a notice fixing an additional period for performance is served after a non-fundamental delay, it will only give the aggrieved party the right to terminate if, first, it is for a fixed period of time, and secondly, if the period is a reasonable one.

If the notice is not for a fixed period of time it may give the defaulting party the impression that it is free to postpone performance indefinitely. It will not suffice to ask for performance "as soon as possible". It must be a request for performance "within a week" or "not later than July 1". The request must not be couched in ambiguous terms; it is not sufficient to say that "we hope very much that performance can be made by July 1".

Because in cases of non-fundamental delay the notice procedure is conferring an additional right on the aggrieved party, the period of notice must be reasonable. If the aggrieved party serves a notice of less than a reasonable period it need not serve a second notice; it may terminate after a reasonable time has elapsed from the date of the notice. (On what is a reasonable time see comment E below).

In cases other than non-fundamental delay the aggrieved party is granting a concession to the debtor. Here the aggrieved party can give the debtor as long or as short a period as it chooses, though having done so it will not be able to resort to termination or specific performance within that period. It may serve a notice which fixes an ambiguous deadline for example, "Please perform as soon as possible". In this case it may not terminate or seek specific performance unless the non-performance has continued for long enough that it would be consistent with good faith for the aggrieved party to terminate despite its earlier notice.

E. *What period of time is reasonable?*
The determination of which period of time is reasonable must ultimately be left to the court. Regard should be had to several factors such as the period of time originally set for performance. If the period is short, the additional period of time may also be short;

- the need of the aggrieved party for quick performance, provided that this is apparent to the defaulting party;
- the nature of the goods, services or rights to be performed on conveyed. A complicated performance may require a longer period of time than a simple one;
- the event which caused the delay. A party which has been prevented from performance by bad weather should be granted a longer respite than a party which merely forgot its duties.

F. *The aggrieved party may provide for automatic termination.*

When upon expiry of the period of time fixed for performance the defaulting party has not performed, or when it has declared before that time that it will not perform, the aggrieved party may declare the contract terminated. However, the aggrieved party may provide for automatic termination. It may say in its notice that the contract shall terminate without further notice if the defaulting party fails to perform within the period of the notice.

If the defaulting party in fact tenders performance after the date set in the notice, the aggrieved party may simply refuse to accept it. However, if the aggrieved party actually knows that the defaulter is still attempting to perform after the date, good faith requires it to warn the defaulter that the performance will not be accepted. If the defaulting party asks the aggrieved party whether it will accept performance after the date set, good faith requires the aggrieved party to give an answer within a reasonable time (see Article 1:201).

NOTES

1. *The aggrieved party who gives extra time but changes his mind*
    The first situation covered by Article 8:106, the case of the aggrieved party who indicates that he will still accept tender of performance or the cure of a defective performance but then changes his mind, gives rise to little problem in systems such as the FRENCH or SPANISH where a court order is needed for termination (French CC art.1184(3); Spanish CC art. 1124(3)): instead of terminating the contract at once the court can simply grant a further delay for performance (see *Treitel*, Remedies § 247).
    Systems such as the COMMON LAW which allow termination by simple notice without prior warning have often developed rules to prevent a sudden change of mind by the aggrieved party; eg the Common law rule that if the aggrieved party has "waived" his right to terminate for the time being he can only withdraw the waiver by giving reasonable notice: *Charles Rickards Ltd* v. *Oppenhaim* [1950] 1 K.B. 616 (C.A.).
    CIVIL LAW systems also recognise that the aggrieved party should not be allowed to terminate during the period in which he indicated that he would still accept performance: e.g. AUSTRIAN law, e.g. OGH 21. December 1987, SZ 60/287; 12.3.1991 JBI 1992, 318; FINNISH and SWEDISH Sale of Goods Acts, §§ 25(3), 54(3) and 55(3); GREEK law (*Michaelides Nouaros* Erm.AK vol.II/1 art.383 nos.17-18 (1949). The aggrieved party may also be barred from seeking performance *in natura*, as, for example, in ITALIAN law (cc art. 1454(3)). It is often recognised that the aggrieved party may resort to termination immediately, however, if the other party indicates that he will not perform within the time allowed (GREEK law, *ibid.*, no.18; GERMAN law *Zweigert & Kötz* 493-494).
    A rule preventing the aggrieved party suddenly changing his mind may be inferred from ULIS art. 44(2); it is explicit in CISG arts. 47(2) and 63(2).
2. *Termination for delay in performance*
    Several systems provide that even if the aggrieved party has no immediate right of termination for delay (because for instance in Germany there was no *Fixgeschäft* or in England time "was not of the essence"), the right to terminate may be acquired by giving the other party a reasonable time in which to perform, provided that the obligation which remains unperformed at the end of the period of notice is sufficiently serious to warrant termination.

The best known device, and the one which has inspired Article 8:106, is the GERMAN *Nachfrist*. This applies to all kinds of delay in performance except impossibility, *Fixgeschäft* or where the non-performing party has repudiated; nor does it apply to *positive Vertragsverletzung*. The *Nachfrist* is primarily aimed at protection of the debtor (see *Treitel*, Remedies § 245) but the practical effect is the same as that of Article 8:106 of the Principles. Like Article 8:106, the German rule will in general apply if the defaulting party is in delay in performing a major obligation (*Hauptflicht*); the aggrieved party may then withdraw from the contract or claim damages for non-performance. If the defaulting party does not comply with a minor obligation, the aggrieved party can only avail himself of the *Nachfrist* procedure if the breach of that obligation imperils the purpose of the whole transaction (*Staudinger-Otto* § 326 no.185). In requiring that the *Nachfrist* make clear to the non-performing party that the aggrieved party will refuse to accept performance at the end of the period, German law may appear to be stricter than the Principles, but under the Principles an aggrieved party would not be allowed to rely on a notice which was not clear (Article 1:201 Good Faith and Fair Dealing).

Some other systems, eg AUSTRIAN and PORTUGUESE law, follow the German model closely, but very different systems also produce close parallels. The FINNISH and SWEDISH Sale of Goods Acts. § 25(2), 54(2) and 55(2) give a right to terminate after expiry of a *Nachfrist*. In COMMON LAW the aggrieved party may sometimes be able to "make time of the essence" once the date for performance has passed by serving on the non-performing party a notice to perform within a reasonable time; if the non-performance continues the aggrieved party may terminate at the end of the period. There is some doubt as to the scope of the rule: the traditional view is that it applies only to certain categories such as sale of land and sale of goods (see *Treitel*, Remedies § 249) but the House of Lords has on two recent occasions approved a passage from *Halsbury* 9 § 481 which states as a general rule that a party may make time of the essence by serving a reasonable notice on the defaulting party, just as Article 8:106(3) envisages (*United Scientific Holdings Ltd* v. *Burnley Borough Council* [1978] A.C. 904; *Bunge Corp.* v. *Tradax SA* [1981] 1 W.L.R. 771; for Scotland see *Rodger (Builders)* v. *Fawdry* 1950 S.C. 483 (I.H.)). Under the DANISH Sale of Goods Act the aggrieved party can always terminate the contract in case of a fundamental non-performance, and may do so without having given the non-performing party a *Nachfrist*. In other contracts a notice of a reasonable length may sometimes make time of the essence, see *Gomard*, Obligationsret II 103ff.

The idea that the aggrieved party may terminate for non-fundamental delay after giving reasonable notice is not accepted by all systems: for instance it is unknown to FRENCH law, though remedies for non-performance, as a rule, can only be administered if the defaulting party has received a notice demanding performance (*mise en demeure*, art. 1146 and 1139 C.civ.). In SPANISH law delay justifies termination only if it is fundamental or frustrates the purpose of the contract, according to case-law (Supreme Court 5 January 1935; see *Diez Picazo* II, 714.) In such cases prior warning to the debtor is not required (*Lacruz-Delgado*, II, 1 § 36, 201). However many Civil law systems have accepted rules permitting termination after notice (eg GREEK CC art.383 sent. 1; ITALIAN CC art.1454(1), (3)).

In BELGIUM doctrine and case law now accepts that sometimes termination may be effected by the aggrieved party; whether notice has been given to the other party is a relevant factor, though it is not necessary if the non-performing party has indicated that it will not perform. See *De Page* II, no.891; Cass. 24 March 1972, Arr. Cass., 707; Cass 17 Jan. 1992, TBH/RDC 1993, 239.

The rule contained in Article 8:106 of the Principles is also adopted by ULIS (arts. 27(2), 44(2), 62(2) and 66(2)) and by CISG (arts. 47, 49(1)(b) 63 and 64(1)(b)).

There are differences in detail between the various national rules. For instance in GERMAN law at the end of the notice period the aggrieved party loses his right to seek performance *in natura* unless previously he has extended the *Nachfrist*, whereas in COMMON LAW the aggrieved party can probably simply set a fresh period of time. In German law a notice which was too short will automatically be extended, so that the aggrieved party may still terminate after a reasonable time, unless the period set was so short that it indicated a lack of good faith (see *Treitel*, Remedies § 245); in Common law a fresh notice may have to be served, as a notice which is too short seems to be treated as having no effect (eg. *Behzadi* v. *Shaftesbury Hotels Ltd.* [1992] Ch. 1, C.A.

See generally *Zweigert & Kötz* 492-494; *Treitel*, Remedies §§ 252.

Article 8:107 Performance Entrusted to Another

A party which entrusts performance of the contract to another person remains responsible for performance.

COMMENTS

A. *General*

Under modern conditions, most contracts are not performed in fact by the contracting parties personally. This provision deals with one aspect of this modern division of labour, namely the contracting party's responsibility for non-performance. Two other aspects, namely the imputation of actual or constructive knowledge as well as of certain states of mind of persons assisting in the performance of the contract, are dealt with by Article 1:305.

B. *Purpose*

The basic principle is that if a party does not perform a contract personally but entrusts performance to a third person, it remains nevertheless responsible for the proper performance of the contract vis-à-vis the other party. The internal relationship between the party and the third person is irrelevant in this context. The third person may be subject to instructions of the party, such as an employee or an agent; or he may be an independent subcontractor.

C. *Impediment in the third person*

On the conditions under which an impediment that arises in the other person excuses the contracting party, see Article 8:108, Comment C.

NOTE

In several countries there are code provisions which are either close equivalents to Article 8:107 (see DUTCH BW art.6.76; ITALIAN CC art. 1228 and PORTUGUESE CC art. 800(1)) or which in other terms lay down the same principle, see AUSTRIAN ABGB § 1313a; in DENMARK Danske lov 1683 art.3.19.2; GERMAN BGB § 278; GREEK CC arts.317 and 477. Under SPANISH law the debtor may entrust performance to another unless the contract requires personal performance, CC art. 1161; but unless the creditor accepts the substitution, the debtor remains responsible, *Ministero de Justicia*, II, art. 1721.

In other countries, the principle is not provided by legislation but is recognized by the courts or writers. This is the case in FINLAND, see *Hoppu* 130; FRANCE see *Viney*, la Responsabilité no.813-847; BELGIUM, Cass. 5 Oct. 1990, Arr. Cass., 125 no.58; *De Page* II, no.592; *van Oevelen*, R.W. 1987-88, (1168) 1187ff.; *Dirix*, Aansprakelijkheid 341ff; ENGLAND: *Treitel*, Remedies § 15; SCOTLAND: *McBryde* ch.17-48, 17-50; SWEDEN; *Ramberg*, Köplagen 358 ff..

Article 8:108: Excuse Due to an Impediment

(1) A party's non-performance is excused if it proves that it is due to an impediment beyond its control and that it could not reasonably have been expected to take the impediment into account at the time of the conclusion of the contract, or to have avoided or overcome the impediment or its consequences.

(2) Where the impediment is only temporary the excuse provided by this Article has effect for the period during which the impediment exists. However, if the delay amounts to a fundamental non-performance, the creditor may treat it as such.

(3) The non-performing party must ensure that notice of the impediment and of its effect on its ability to perform is received by the other party within a reasonable time after the non-performing party knew or ought to have known of these circumstances. The other party is entitled to damages for any loss resulting from the non-receipt of such notice.

COMMENT

A. *General*

Article 8:108 governs the consequences when an event which is not the fault or responsibility of a party prevents it from performing. The Principles also contain a provision for revision of the contract if unforeseen circumstances supervene and makes performance excessively onerous (Article 6:111). Thus, unlike the equivalent article of CISG (see Notes below), Article 8:108 has to apply only in cases where an impediment prevents performance.

The rules in Article 8:108 are not mandatory. The parties may modify the allocation of the risk of impossibility of performance, either in general or in relation to a particular impediment; usages (especially in carriage by sea) may have the same effect.

B. *Scope*

The excuse may apply to any obligation arising out of the contract, including obligations to pay money. While insolvency would not normally be an impediment within the meaning of the text, as it is not "beyond the control" of the debtor, a government ban on transferring the sum due might be.

The term "impediment" covers every sort of event (natural occurrences, restraints of princes, acts of third parties).

It is conceivable that an impediment at the time the contract was made existed without the parties knowing it. For example, the parties might sign a charter of a ship which, unknown to them, has just sunk. This situation is not covered by Article 8:108 but the contract might be avoidable under Article 4:103, Mistake as to Facts or Law.

C. *The circumstances of the impediment*

The conditions laid down for the operation of the Article are analogous to the conditions traditionally required for *force majeure*. They are necessarily in general terms, given the great variety of fact situations to which they must apply. It is for the party which invokes it to show that the conditions are fulfilled.

(i) *outside the debtor's control*

First, the obstacle must be something outside the debtor's sphere of control. The risk of its own activities it must bear itself. Thus the breakdown of a machine, even if unforeseeable and unpreventable, cannot be an impediment within the Article and this avoids investigation of whether the breakdown was really unforeseeable and the consequences unpreventable. The same is true of the actions of persons for whom the debtor is responsible, and particularly the acts of the people it puts in charge of the performance. The debtor cannot invoke the default of a subcontractor unless it was outside its control – for instance because there was no other subcontractor which could have been employed to do the work; and the impediment must also be outside the subcontractor's sphere of control.

> *Illustration 1*: In consequence of an unexpected strike in the nationalized company which distributes natural gas, a chinaware manufacturer which heats its furnaces only with gas is obliged to interrupt its production. The manufacturer is not liable toward its own clients, if the other conditions of excuse are fulfilled. The cause of non-performance is external.

> *Illustration 2*: The employees of a company unforeseeably go on strike in order to force the management to buy foreign machines which will improve the working conditions. For the time being it is actually not possible to obtain these machines. The company cannot claim as against its customers that the strike is an excuse, as the event is not beyond its control.

The *force majeure* must have come about without the fault of either party. There will be no excuse if an unforeseeable event impedes performance of the contract when the event would not have affected the contract if the party had not been late in performing.

> *Illustration 3*: A French bank, A, is instructed by company B to transfer a sum of money to a bank in country X by 15 July. It has not carried out the instruction by 18 July when all transfers of money between France and X are suspended. Bank A cannot claim to be excused from its obligation to B; the transfer could have been made if it had been done in the time allowed under the contract.

(ii) *could not have been taken into account*

Secondly, the impediment must be one that could not have been taken into account at the time the contract was made. If it could have been, one may say either that the party affected took the risk or that it was at fault in not having foreseen it. This condition also applies, in the same way, to the operation of Article 6:111.

However, it may be relevant whether the parties could have taken into consideration not just the event itself but the date or period of its occurrence. A price control for some period may be foreseeable, but it could be an excuse if the period for which it is kept in force was not foreseeable by the parties. Equally it is stated that the test is "reasonable" foreseeability: that is to say, whether a normal person, placed in the same situation, could have foreseen it without either undue optimism or undue pessimism. Thus in a particular area cyclones may be foreseeable at certain times of year, but not a cyclone at a time of year when they do not normally occur – that would not be reasonably foreseeable by the parties.

On the question of to whom the event should have been foreseeable, see Article 1:305 (knowledge and behaviour of persons for whom a party is responsible).

(iii) *insurmountable impediment*
Reasonableness also qualifies the condition that the impediment must be insurmountable or irresistible. It must be emphasised that both conditions – that the party could not have avoided it and could not have overcome it – must be fulfilled before an excuse can operate. The Article states that the party to be excused must prove that it could not have done either.

Whether an event could have been avoided or its consequences overcome depends on the facts. In an earthquake zone the effects of earthquakes can be overcome by special construction techniques, though it would be different in the case of a quake of much greater force than usual.

One cannot expect the debtor to take precautions out of proportion to the risk (e. g. the building of a virtual fortress) nor to adopt illegal means (e. g. the smuggling of funds to avoid a ban on their transfer) in order to avoid the risk.

D. *Effects*
An impediment to performance which fulfils the conditions just set out relieves the party which has not performed from liability. But again it is necessary to define just what is meant by this rather general expression, which may be ambiguous. Here the approach is a pragmatic one: one must start with the remedies that are available to the aggrieved party (as does Article 8:101, which in paragraph (2) sets out the remedies which do not apply when a non-performance is excused, namely specific performance and damages).

First, any form of specific performance (Article 9:101 and 9:102) is by definition impossible. Nor do damages of any kind, including "liquidated damages" and penalties, apply unless the parties have agreed otherwise.

The question of the ending of the contract, on the other hand, is more complex. For the sake of simplicity, the Principles have retained in this case the same general system as applies in the case of non-performance of contract: the aggrieved party may put an end to the contract by a unilateral declaration provided the non-performance is fundamental. It follows that in principle it will be for the creditor to exercise this right by giving notice of termination to the debtor under Article 9:303. However, as it would be pointless to give the aggrieved party the right to keep in force a contract which has become totally and permanently impossible to perform, it follows that in such a case it is unnecessary to require a declaration of termination. Hence Article 9:303 (4) (see the comment to Article 9:301). The result is the same as in those legal systems under which force majeure brings automatic termination of the contract.

It is primarily in the case of a partial impediment, when a divisible part of the main obligation or a secondary obligation becomes impossible, that the creditor has a real choice; it must be permitted to decide whether or not to maintain the contract according to whether partial performance will be of any value to it. This option is governed by the general rules, that is to say the right to terminate depends on whether or not the non-performance is fundamental.

If the aggrieved party does not elect to terminate the contract, it may demand performance of that part of the contract which still can be performed. In this case its own obligation will be reduced proportionately under Article 9:401 (Reduction of Price).

> *Illustration 4*: If A has leased a warehouse to B and subsequently it is partially destroyed by fire, causing a temporary impediment, B may terminate the contract if occupation of the whole of the premises was an essential part of the contract. If, on the other hand, it does not give notice of termination, B cannot obtain damages for loss of occupation but the rent will be reduced proportionately.

E. *Temporary impediment*

It is commonly agreed that a temporary impediment, in principle results in only a temporary excuse. This is what is provided by paragraph (2)).

Temporary impediment means not only the circumstances which cause the obstacle but also the consequences which follow; these may last longer than the circumstances themselves. The excuse covers the whole period during which the debtor is unable to perform.

> *Illustration 5*: The warehouse containing a pharmaceutical manufacturer's raw materials is unforeseeably flooded and the raw materials are rendered unuseable. The delays in delivering to clients which will be excused include not only the period of the flood itself but also the time necessary for the manufacturer to obtain new supplies.

It may be, however, that late performance will be of no use to the aggrieved party. Therefore it is given the right to terminate the contract provided that the delay is itself fundamental (see Article 8:103).

> *Illustration 6*: An impresario in Hamburg has engaged a famous English tenor to sing at the Hamburg Opera from 1 to 31 October. The singer catches asian flu and has to retire to bed (this would constitute an impediment within paragraph (1); he tells the impresario that he will be unable to come to Hamburg before 10 October. Assuming that the tenor's presence for the whole month is an essential part of the contract, the impresario may terminate. If he chooses not to do so, the contract remains in force for the remaining period but the tenor's fees will be reduced proportionately.

Equally in the case of a temporary excuse, the aggrieved party can use the procedure laid down in Article 8:106 (2) to serve a notice making time of the essence.

F. *Notice*

Paragraph (3) of Article 8:108 is an application of the obligation of good faith which governs the whole of the Principles. The non-performing party must in effect warn the other party, within a reasonable time, of the occurrence of the obstacle and of its consequences for the contracts. The notice must, in effect, allow the other party the chance to take steps to avoid the consequences of non-performance. It is also necessary in order for it to be able to exercise any right it may have to terminate when performance is partial or late.

> *Illustration 7*: In the example given in illustration 5, the manufacturer must notify its customers of the loss of the raw materials and also of the time it will take to replace them and the probable date for resumption of deliveries.

The reasonable time may be a short one: circumstances may even require immediate notification. The time starts to run as soon as the impediment and its consequences for the contract become known (see above); or from when the non-performing party should have known. Good faith may even require two successive notices, if for example the non-performing party cannot immediately tell what the consequences of the impediment will be.

The risk of the notice not getting through is placed on the non-performing party, see Article 1:303.

The sanction for failing to give this notice is liability for the extra loss suffered by the aggrieved party as the result of not being informed; normally the aggrieved party will recover damages.

> *Illustration 8*: In the example given in Illustration 6, if the tenor does not warn the impresario immediately of his unavailability, the latter may recover compensation for being deprived of the chance to obtain a replacement, so reducing his loss.

NOTES

1. *Force majeure and impossibility*

   Article 8:108(1) is modelled on CISG art. 79(1), which has been followed in the FINNISH and SWEDISH Sale of Goods Acts, §§ 27 and 40. See also *Unidroit* art. 7.1.7.

   (a) *Civil law systems*

   Even if all legal systems now admit that impossibility of performance should be excused, the way the excuse is given effect varies considerably.

   The Romanistic legal systems rest on the theory of *force majeure* laid down in arts. 1147 and 1148 of the FRENCH, BELGIAN and LUXEMBOURG Civil Codes, on which has developed detailed caselaw on the conditions under which the debtor will be excused.

   In FRANCE these conditions are strict. Performance must be impossible and this must be due to circumstances which were unforeseeable at the time when the contract was made and which are outside the control of the debtor *(cause étrangère)*. SPANISH CC art.1105 has a similar rule.

A related doctrine of impossibility is found in AUSTRIAN, GERMAN, ITALIAN and PORTUGUESE law, see ABGB § 1447, BGB § 275, Italian CC Arts. 1218 and 1256 and Portuguese CC art.790.

Some laws take a more flexible approach. CISG art. 79, the FINNISH and SWEDISH Sale of Goods Acts §§ 27 and 40 and DANISH Sale of Goods Act § 24, which is held to embody a general principle of contract law, include impediments which must be equated with impossibility: see *von Caemmerer & Schlectriem* 694 f.; *Honnold* 542; *Ramberg*, Köplagen 346 f.; and *Gomard*, Obligationsret II 172. DUTCH and GREEK law will also excuse the debtor in cases other than absolute impossibility, see respectively BW arts. 6:74 and 6:75; Greek CC arts. 336 and 380. Traces of a more flexible attitude are also to be found in recent BELGIAN case law, which comes close to Article 3.108(1) see Trib. Comm. de Bruxelles 9 March 1981, JCB/BRH 1982 I 182; compare.Cass. 13 April 1956, Arr. Cass. 670, R.C.J.B., 1957, 85, obs. *Heenen*. See *Kruithof*, Hommage Dekkers 281.

Several legal systems, and notably the AUSTRIAN, DUTCH, GERMAN, GREEK, ITALIAN, PORTUGUESE and SPANISH have, in addition to the rules on impossibility or *force majeure*, accepted that changed circumstances may excuse the debtor, see notes to Article 6:111 above.

(b)   Common Law

ENGLISH and IRISH law take a different route. A party is normally obliged to fulfil his promise and will be liable in damages for failure to perform. However, he is sometimes excused where performance has become impossible without his fault, e.g. because the subject matter of the contract has been destroyed. If the impossibility occurred after the contract was made, and it is impossible to perform the contract as a whole, the non-performing party may be excused under the doctrine of frustration, see *Taylor* v. *Caldwell* (1863) 3 B. & S. 828, Q.B.. The results of frustration are similar to those under Article 8:108, in that both parties are discharged automatically. SCOTTISH law broadly follows the Common law.

2.   *Temporary impediment*

CISG art.79(3) is equivalent to the first sentence of Article 8:108(2). CISG does not address the question of termination but writers support the rule laid down in the second sentence of 8:108(2), see *v. Caemmerer & Schlechtriem* 670. It is probably the rule in all legal systems that the excuse has effect as long as the impediment lasts. The rule is expressed in ITALIAN CC art.1256(2) and POR-TUGUESE CC art.792, and is accepted in GREEK law, see *Gasis* in Erm.AK II/1, intro. to arts. 335-348 no. 42, art. 336 no.7 (1949).

Under several legal systems the creditor may terminate the contract if the delay has lasted so long that he would be entitled to terminate under the rules on non-performance. This holds true of ITALIAN and PORTUGUESE law, see the provisions cited above, of AUSTRIAN law, see ABGB § 918; of DUTCH law, see BW art. 6:74(2); and of BELGIAN law (*Kruithof*, TPR 1983, 629 no.119, see also Cass. 13 June 1956, Arr. Cass., 367). GREEK and DANISH case law support the same rule: Greece, Athens 3384/1976, NoB 25 (1977) 389 II. It is unlikely that this rule would follow from ENGLISH and IRISH law but a long delay may frustrate the contract. In SPANISH law a temporary impediment may justify termination if it frustrates the purpose of the contract (*Diez Picazo*, II 660; *Lacruz-Delgado* II, 1, § 25. 193).

3.   *The duty to give notice*

Article 8:108(3) is similar to CISG art.79(4), and see the FINNISH and SWEDISH Sale of Goods Acts, §§ 28, 40 and 58. The duty of the defaulting party to give notice of the impediment has been stated in DANISH, GREEK and GERMAN case law: see respectively *Ussing*, Alm.Del.141; 4271/1956 EEN 25(1958) 226, 227 II; and OLG Hamburg 13 May 1901, OLGE 3 no. 4 p.8. In ITALY writers have expressed the view that the duty follows from the principle of good faith and CC art.1780 imposes a duty on the depository to notify loss of goods in custody. In other civil law countries the duty to give notice may also follow from good faith or from the debtors' duty to warn of risks which may affect the performance due, e.g. SPANISH CC art. 1559.

Under ENGLISH, IRISH and SCOTTISH law there is no such principle.

See generally *Zweigert & Kötz* Chapters 36 and 37; *Rodière & Tallon*; *Mengoni* Riv. Dir.Comm. 1954, I, 185; *Honnold* no. 423ff., *v. Caemmerer & Schlechtriem* 679-704; *Bianca & Bonell-(Tallon)* 572-595; *Force majeure and hardship; Treitel*, Frustration.

Article 8:109: Clause Excluding or Restricting Remedies

Remedies for non-performance may be excluded or restricted unless it would be contrary to good faith and fair dealing to invoke the exclusion or restriction.

COMMENTS

A. *General*

Just as the parties are free to determine the content of their obligations, so they can in the contract agree on the consequences of non-performance. In particular they may limit or exclude altogether the remedies which would otherwise be available.

In any event it is sometimes difficult to distinguish between the parties' agreement on the obligations to be imposed by the contract and clauses excluding liability. The parties may agree that one of them shall not be under a particular obligation (so long as it is not a fundamental one, in which case there would be no contract at all); if however the contract imposes a contractual obligation but excludes or limits liability for its non-performance, the situation is theoretically different. Determining what obligations have been imposed is a matter of interpretation of the contract. The present article applies only where there is a contractual obligation but liability is limited or excluded in case of non-performance.

The practice of relying on limitation and exclusion clauses is widely recognised by national laws and used by business practice.

Exclusion clauses cannot always be given full effect. In the extreme case they would allow a debtor to undertake to perform and at the same time exclude all sanctions for failure to perform. Even in less extreme cases the other party may not really have consented to the full implications of the clause because he may not have understood them. This is why national systems have developed specific controls over clauses outside the field of consumer protection and, often applying rules relating to the reality or quality of consent, even before the advent of legislation.

Article 8:109 prevents the clause applying if it would be contrary to good faith and fair dealing to invoke it.

B. *The clauses covered*

The formulation is in very general terms and covers all clauses which in practice prevent the aggrieved party from obtaining the normal remedy. No distinction is drawn between clauses which limit responsibility and those which exclude it altogether. It is difficult to distinguish them anyway since a derisory limit on recovery is effectively an exclusion, and there is no good reason for imposing different controls in the two cases.

The limitation of liability may be fixed directly as a figure or by a formula relating to some element of the contract (e.g. so may times the contract price).

Liquidated damages and penalty clauses, such as envisaged by Article 9:508, operate so as to limit the recovery of the innocent party. In this case the latter can demand full compensation if it can prove that the conditions of Article 8:109 are met.

Illustration 1: The contract for the construction of a factory contains a penalty clause imposing liability for 10,000 francs per week for late completion. The work is completed late because the contractor has deliberately neglected the job in favour of another, more profitable one. If the loss suffered by the employer amounts to 20,000 francs per week, the latter may recover this amount despite the clause, as for the contractor to invoke it when it has deliberately disregarded the contract would be contrary to good faith and fair dealing (see further below).

Exclusion or limitation clauses most frequently concern liability for damages. However, nothing in the text prevents its application to clauses limiting or excluding other remedies for non-performance (termination, reduction of the price, etc...).

C. *Contrary to Good Faith to Invoke the Clause*

The criterion applied by Article 8:109 is whether it would be contrary to good faith and fair dealing to invoke the clause. This is related to the criterion used in Article 4:110, Unfair terms not individually negotiated, but there are differences between the two.

Article 4:110 applies to any type of clause which may be unfair, but only if the clause was not individually negotiated. Like the EC Directive on Unfair Terms in Consumer Contracts from which it is derived, Article 4:110 is aimed at clauses which may not have been fully understood or agreed to by the party affected; and, like the Directive, it employs the test of whether, in the circumstances in which the contract was made, the clause causes a significant imbalance in the rights and obligations to the detriment of that party, contrary to the requirements of good faith and fair dealing. In other words, the test is whether it was contrary to good faith and fair dealing to include the clause in the contract, at least without further steps to warn the party affected.

Article 8:109 is more limited in that it applies only to clauses which would exclude or restrict one party's remedies, but it may apply even to a clause which has been individually negotiated. The fact that the clause has been negotiated will often mean that it is not contrary to good faith and fair dealing to include it. Nonetheless, it may still be contrary to good faith and fair dealing for the other party to invoke the clause, particularly if it does so in circumstances which the first party would not have contemplated, such as a deliberate decision by the party invoking the clause to perform the contract in a quite different way not in accordance with its other terms.

Illustration 2: A security firm agrees to send men to check on a customer's premises once an hour during the hours of darkness. It limits its responsibility to the customer. It deliberately decides to send men only every three hours. It would be contrary to good faith and fair dealing to invoke the limitation of responsibility clause.

An intentional disregard of the other terms of the contract may make it contrary to good faith to invoke the clause even if there was no intention to harm the other party. It should suffice that the non-performance was committed knowingly.

Illustration 3: A carrier which has undertaken to provide a lorry capable of carrying a refrigerated load at -10°C, but which does not have one, provides a lorry capable of refrigeration only to -5°C. The carrier thinks that for the short journey involved this will not matter. The goods are damaged. It cannot rely on a clause limiting its liability for damage caused by inadequate refrigeration.

One must remember that according to Article 1:301(c) an intentional act includes an act done recklessly. But some breaches, though intentional, may be within the contemplation of the parties as a decision one of them may have to make. Such intentional breaches would not mean that it is contrary to good faith to invoke the clause.

Illustration 4: A voyage charter allows a certain number of "lay days" for the charterer to have the ship loaded and unloaded; if the lay days are exceeded, the charterer must pay damages for demurrage, but the amount is limited to £1,000 per day. As both parties are aware, the loading port is subject to congestion, and the charterer deliberately delays having the ship loaded until after another of its vessels has been loaded. Loading of the chartered vessel is not completed within the lay days. The loss to the owner exceeds the limit set in the demurrage clause. Even though the delay by the charterer was deliberate, it is not contrary to good faith for it to invoke the £1,000 per day limit.

It should be noted that the test in Article 8:109 is less severe than that in Article 4:110. It may be contrary to good faith and fair dealing to include a very broad limitation of liability clause when the clause has not been negotiated, and the clause will be invalid under Article 4:110, even though under the criteria used in Article 8:109 it would not be unfair to limit liability in the actual circumstances which have subsequently arisen.

Illustration 5: A contract for the carriage of goods in a refrigerated lorry limits the carriers' liability, in the event of inadequate refrigeration however arising, to FF100 per box of food. The food is damaged because the refrigeration machinery, despite proper maintenance, breaks down. If the clause were not individually negotiated, it might be invalid under Article 4:110 as it is capable of limiting liability even when the carrier had been reckless or grossly negligent. If it has been individually negotiated and is therefore outside Article 4:110, it does not seem contrary to good faith and fair dealing for the carrier to invoke it on the actual facts, so the clause will not be invalid under Article 8:109.

Compare also Article 4:118, Exclusion or Restriction of Remedies, whch covers the exclusion or restriction of remedies for mistake and incorrect information.

D. *Negotiated clause which is still contrary to good faith*.
Even though there has been some negotiation over a clause, so that it is outside Article 4:110, in an extreme case it might still be contrary to good faith to invoke it. If the party in whose favour the clause operated had refused to make more than mar-

ginal concessions and the other party had no real choice but to accept, the court may decide under this Article that the clause cannot be invoked.

> *Illustration 6*: A seed company offers seed to a farmer on terms that its liability if the seed is defective is limited to returning the contract price. The farmer protests at this but the seed company refuses to amend the clause except by adding that, in the event of seed failure, the farmer will be entitled to a 10% discount on the next purchase of similar seed. Other seed companies all take a similar attitude. The seed companies could cover liability in defective seed by insurance; the farmer cannot easily insure against crop failure due to defective seed. The seed supplied is of completely the wrong type and the farmers' crop fails. It is contrary to good faith and fair dealing for the seed company to invoke the clause.

In practice the mandatory national laws on consumer protection will often supersede the rule in Article 8:109.

It should not be possible to set aside by agreement the restrictions on the validity of clauses within Article 8:109; this exclusion would be contrary to the duty of good faith and fair dealing (Article 1:201).

E. *The consequences*
If to invoke the clause is found to be contrary to good faith and fair dealing, the exemption clause will not operate (whether it is treated as null, void or unenforceable). Whilst Article 9:508 allows the court to reduce the amount of a stipulated payment for non-performance where this is grossly excessive, the converse is not true of limitations of liability under Article 8:109, which does not give the court a discretion simply to increase the liability but leaves it to be assessed in accordance with the rules in chapter 9, as there is no valid limitation of liability.

NOTES

In principle clauses excluding or limiting a party's liability are valid in all the Member States. There are, however, restrictions on the validity of such clauses. The techniques of these restrictions differ. Some systems refer to a test of good faith or a very close equivalent; some employ a test of reasonableness; and some have rules about intentional or grossly negligent non-performance.
1.   *Good faith*
     A test of good faith was employed by GERMAN courts, applying BGB § 242 (e.g. BGH 29 October 1956, BGHZ 22, 90; see *Kötz*, European Contract 141-142). The AGBG of 1976 uses the same test, as does Council Directive 93/13/EEC of 5 April 1993 on Unfair Terms in Consumer Contracts (OJ L 95/29). All Member States were required to implement this by 31 December 1994. However, the German rules, both of case law and legislation, and the Directive, apply only to clauses which were pre-formulated or not individually negotiated. See Notes to Article 4:110 above.
2.   *Unreasonable clauses*
     Exclusion and limitation clauses are covered by the general principles in DUTCH BW art 6:248(2) and of NORDIC Contract Acts § 36 under which unreasonable contract clauses are invalid. The ENGLISH Unfair Contract Terms Act 1977 applies rules dealing with contracts between businessmen and with consumer contracts. Exemption and limitation clauses may either be invalid *per se* or valid only if they are reasonable. The Unfair Contract Terms Act 1977 is in force also in SCOTLAND. These rules are not restricted to clauses which were not individually negotiated: e.g. the Unfair Contract Terms Acts invalidates certain types of clause (such as restrictions on liability for

death or personal injury caused by negligence in the course of a business, s.2(1)), and holds other valid only if they are reasonable (such as restrictions on a seller's liablity if the goods are not of satisfactory quality, s.6(3)), even if the clauses were negotiated. In matters not covered by the Act, such as most international contracts, the House of Lords after some judicial hesitation has laid down a rule of interpretation that an exclusion clause will normally not apply when there has been a breach of a fundamental term, a fundamental breach or simply a serious breach, see *Photo Production Ltd* v. *Securicor Transport Ltd* [1980] A.C. 827 (H.L.). But the courts have frequently used such rules of construction to prevent a party relying on a clause when the circumstances of the case seem outside what could have been contemplated by the parties. See *Treitel*, Contract 201-22; *Kötz*, European Contract 141.

In IRELAND, some unreasonable exclusion clauses are regulated by the Sales of Goods and Supply of Services Act 1980. Beyond that, case law favours the rule that an exclusion clause cannot excuse a fundamental breach of contract (*Clayton Love* v. *B. & I. Line* (1970) I.L.T.R. 157) while doctrine favours the position reached under the English cases, see *Clark* 150.

3. *Intentional and grossly negligent non-performance*
Art.1229 of the ITALIAN CC and arts.1102, 1256 and 1476 of the SPANISH CC also invalidate clauses which exonerate the debtor from liability or limit his liability for fraud, malice or gross negligence; in Spain it is thought that clauses excluding or limiting liability for simple negligence are valid, *Diez-Picazo* 730-731. Rules on specific contracts are found in the Italian CC in arts. 1490(2), 1579, 1580 and 1838(5). This latter provision also covers clauses which exclude or limit a bank's liability for ordinary negligence. AUSTRIAN case law has established a clear and undisputed rule that liability for intentional wrongdoing can neither be excluded nor restricted by party agreement (OGH 24 April 1958, SZ 31/67; 22 October 1968, SZ 41/139; 19 November 1968, Jbl 1970, 201).

FRENCH case law also invalidate clauses excluding or limiting liability for intentional and grossly negligent non-performance, see Cass. Req. 24 Oct. 1932, S.1933.1.289 and Cass. Civ, 4 Feb. 1969, D.69.601. The "Chronopost" case (Com. 22 October 1996, D.1997, 121, note *A.Sériaux*) has specified that a limitation clause cannot be enforced in the case of non-performance of an "essential obligation". In PORTUGAL, according to the prevailing opinion, only vicarious liability may be excluded, CC arts. 809 and 800; clauses limiting liability are valid except for intentional or grossly negligent non-performance. Under the Law of 25 Oct. 1985 general conditions of contract exempting the defaulting party from liability for intentional and grossly negligent non-performance are invalid. Under BELGIAN case law, exclusion or limitation of liability for intentional non-performance is not permitted, but exclusion for grossly negligent non-performance is, see Cass. 22 March 1979, RCJB 1981, 196, unless it goes to the essence of the obligation, see Cass. 25 Sept. 1959, Arr.Cass. 1960, 86. However use of an unreasonable clause may be an abuse of rights.

In other systems it is frequently accepted that liability for intentional acts cannot be excluded. In FINLAND clauses limiting liability for intentional non-performance as well as gross negligence have usually not been accepted as valid, *Taxell*, Avtal och rättsskydd 457-457 and Supreme Court 1983 II 91. Liability for intentional and grossly negligent non-performance cannot be excluded or limited in GERMANY, see BGB § 276(2). However such limitation clauses are valid as regards the acts of persons to whom the debtor has entrusted performance, and for whose acts he is responsible, see BGB § 278. This latter rule does not apply to clauses in consumer contracts under § 11 no 7 of the General Conditions of Business Act 1976, which will probably also apply to business contracts, see *Palandt(-Heinrichs)* AGBG § 11 no. 7. A rule similar to the GERMAN BGB § 276(2) is found in GREEK CC art.332. GREEK law permits exclusion clauses covering persons entrusted with performance, as does BGB § 278, and even in cases of deliberate or reckless non-performance: AP 57/1966, NoB 14 (1966) 793. However, liability towards persons in the service of the debtor and liability arising out of a licensed business cannot be excluded or limited even in cases of ordinary negligence, see art. 332(2). In the NETHERLANDS, the Hoge Raad has stated that a clause may not be invoked to limit liability for damage caused by intentional or grossly negligent conduct by the debtor or a person with whom the debtor charged direction of his business: e.g. HR 31 December 1993, NJ 1995, 389; 5 September 1997, RvdW 1997, 161.

In English law there is no special rule about intentional breaches, either at common law, see *Photo Production Ltd* v. *Securicor Transport Ltd* [1980] A.C. 827 (H.L.), or under the Unfair Contract Terms Act 1977. But clauses are less likely to be interpreted as applying such breaches than to mere negligence, and the fact that a clause may exclude liability for intentional breaches may be a factor in holding it to be unreasonable, see *Thomas Witter Ltd* v. *TBP Industries Ltd* [1976] 2 All E.R. 573.

4. *Consumer Contracts*
Special rules against the use of exclusion clauses in consumer contracts have been found for some years in several Member States, see AUSTRIAN Consumer Protection Act (Ksch 9) § 6(1) No.9; art.

32 (11) and (12) of the BELGIAN Law on Trade Practice and Information and Protection of Consumers of 14 July 1991; DANISH Sale of Goods Act § 80(1); FRANCE: Code Coms. art L. 132-1; GERMAN General Conditions of Business Act § 11 no 7 (see note 1 above); GREEK law on Consumers' Protection No. 2251/1994 arts. 2(7) nos. 12, 13, 6(12) and 8(6); LUXEMBOURG Consumer Protection Acts 1984 and 1987, CC art. 1135(1); DUTCH BW art. 6:237(f); POR-TUGUESE Decree Law of 25 Oct. 1985 arts. 18(c) and 20; and SPANISH Consumer Protection Law of 19 July 1984 art. 10, especially 10.1(c) (6). (see *Bercovitz*, Consumers: total exclusion of liability would be contrary to good faith). In FINLAND and SWEDEN general consumer protection legislation invalidates exclusion clauses. The DUTCH rule may, as in GERMANY, have repercussions on the validity of exclusion clauses in contracts between businessmen. The IRISH legislation referred to in note 2 is designed to protect consumers.See further Notes to Article 4:110 above.

5.   *Stipulated payment*

In some Member countries the courts will treat a penalty or liquidated damages clause as a clause limiting liability if the stipulated sum is below the damages which the aggrieved party could recover. Thus, the reasonableness test dealt with in note 2 can apply to increase an unreasonably low payment, especially if the purpose of the clause is to limit liability. For BELGIAN law see *Kruithof* TPR 1986 no.6. In FRENCH law a stipulated payment can be increased if it is *"manifestement dérisoire"*, see CC art. 1152 (2) and *Malaurie & Aynès*, Obligations nos. 864-869. See further notes to Article 9:509.

   See generally *Ghestin* (ed), Les Clauses limitatives; *Hondius; Kötz*, European Contract 137-153.

CHAPTER 9

Particular Remedies for Non-Performance

Section 1: Right to Performance

Article 9:101: Monetary Obligations

(1) The creditor is entitled to recover money which is due.

(2) Where the creditor has not yet performed its obligation and it is clear that the debtor will be unwilling to receive performance, the creditor may nonetheless proceed with its performance and may recover any sum due under the contract unless:

(a) it could have made a reasonable substitute transaction without significant effort or expense; or

(b) performance would be unreasonable in the circumstances.

COMMENTS

A. *The principle*
As a rule it is always possible to enforce monetary obligations.

This is the basis of the rule in paragraph (1). A monetary obligation for the purposes of this rule is every obligation to make a payment of money, regardless of the form of payment or the currency. This includes even a secondary obligation, such as the payment of interest or of a fixed sum of money as damages. But in each case, the monetary obligation must have been earned by the creditor, i.e. it must be due.

B. *Money not yet due*
The principle that monetary obligations always can be enforced is not quite so certain where the monetary obligation has not yet been earned by the creditor's own performance and it is clear that the debtor will refuse to receive the creditor's future performance. This is the situation regulated by paragraph (2).

(i) *Basic approach*
The basic approach underlying the rules of paragraph (2) is obvious. Under the principle of *pacta sunt servanda* the creditor is entitled to make its performance and thereby to earn the price for it. The debtor's unwillingness to receive the creditor's performance is therefore, as a rule, irrelevant.

However, according to sub-paragraphs (a) and (b) there are two situations where the above principle does not apply.

(ii) (a) *Cover transaction*

A creditor which can make a reasonable cover transaction without involving itself in significant trouble or expense is not entitled to continue with performance against the debtor's wishes and cannot demand payment of the price for it (paragraph (2) sub-paragraph (a)). The creditor should terminate the contract and either make a cover transaction, thus becoming entitled to invoke Article 9:506, or simply claim damages without making any cover transaction (see Article 9:507 and Comment thereon). The debtor cannot invoke sub-paragraph (a) of paragraph (2) unless two conditions are satisfied. The first is that the creditor can make a cover transaction on reasonable terms because there is a market for its performance or some other way of arranging a substitute transaction. The second is that the cover transaction does not substantially burden the creditor with effort or expense.

> *Illustration 1*: A sells 10,000 ball bearings to B for DM 50,000, payment to be made in advance. If B indicates that it will not accept delivery, A cannot sue for the price if there is a ready market for ball bearings or if A can easily find a new customer. In contrast, if A would have to make considerable efforts in finding a new customer and would have to shoulder the costs of transportation to another continent, A would not be obliged to make a cover transaction. It could sue for the price under the contract and, if B maintains its refusal to accept the goods, could proceed under Article 7:110.

In certain situations the creditor may even be bound by commercial usage to effect a cover transaction. Whenever the creditor makes, or would have been obliged to make, a cover transaction, the creditor may claim from the debtor the difference between the contract price and the cover price as damages under Article 9:506.

(iii) (b) *Unreasonable performance*

A very different situation is dealt with in paragraph 2 sub-paragraph (b): Here performance by the creditor would be unreasonable. A typical example is where, before performance has begun, the debtor makes it clear that it no longer wants it. This situation can arise, for example, in construction contracts, other contracts for work and especially long term contracts.

> *Illustration 2*: H has hired for a period of three years advertising space on litter bins supplied to local councils by C. Before commencement of that period and before preparation of the advertisement plates by C, H purports to cancel the contract. Even though paragraph 2 sub-paragraph (a) does not apply because there is abundance of advertising space available, C may not proceed to perform the contract and then claim the hire charges, for it is unreasonable for it to undertake performance of a contract in which C no longer has an interest.

The non-performance may be actual (i.e. the date for performance has passed) or anticipatory.

An instance which would not involve unreasonable expenditure is where the creditor must continue to employ its workforce.

(iv) *Common features*

The feature common to the two cases dealt with in paragraph (2) is that the debtor is at risk of having forced upon it a performance which it no longer wants.

The burden of proving that the existence of one of the exceptions applies is on the debtor.

However, none of the two exceptions laid down in paragraph (2) affects the right of a beneficiary under a letter of credit to claim payment from the bank. This is because letters of credit are treated as independent of the underlying contract.

(v) *Legal consequences of exceptions*

One of the consequences that arise if either one of the exceptions applies, is spelt out in paragraph (2): the creditor may not demand the money owed under the contract for the counterperformance, in particular the price (*supra* Comment A). However, damages for non-performance may be claimed, see Article 9:103.

NOTES

1. *Money due generally recoverable*
   In accordance with the general principle of *pacta sunt servanda*, continental law allows a creditor to require performance of a contractual obligation to pay money (cf. *Dölle – v. Caemmerer* § 1 KG no. 9; see for DENMARK *Gomard*, Obligationsret II 33). Also according to COMMON LAW an action for an agreed sum is often available, although it is limited in certain respects: it may be brought only when the price has been "earned" by performance, e.g. the performance of a service or the passing of property in the goods (e.g. U.K. Sale of Goods Act 1979, s.49(1), IRISH Sale of Goods Act 1893, s.49(1)).

2. *Resale possible without unreasonable effort or expense*
   The restriction in Article 9:101(2)(a) has a precursor in ULIS art. 61. ULIS art. 61(2) restricts the seller's right to require payment of the price where a resale was in conformity with usage and reasonably possible. CISG art. 62 has dropped this restriction. The seller is bound to the contract; it is therefore obliged to tender performance to the buyer even if the latter is unwilling to receive performance, and may claim the purchase price. This approach expresses the general rule which seems to prevail in most continental European countries.

3. *Performance would be unreasonable*
   Article 9:101(2)(b) is based on considerations to be found in experience gained from ENGLISH, IRISH and SCOTTISH practice. Once an action for the price was available there was no requirement that it must be reasonable to pursue it rather than to enter a cover transaction. This gave rise to difficulties when a party had announced in advance that it no longer required a service but the other performed it nonetheless and then sued for the price: see *White & Carter (Councils) Ltd. v. McGregor* [1962] A.C. 413 (H.L.) (see Illustration 2 of the Comment). The rule in contracts other than sale of goods now appears to be that if at the date of the repudiation the innocent party has not yet performed his part of the contract, he may complete his performance and claim the price only if he has a legitimate interest in doing so: see *Attica Sea Carriers Corp. v. Ferrostaal Poseidon Bulk Reederei GmbH* [1976] 1 Lloyds' Rep. 250 (C.A.). If he has no legitimate interest in performing he is confined to an action for damages, and his recovery will be limited by the principle of mitigation. SCOTTISH law is the same – *White & Carter* (above) is a Scottish case. The guilty party has the onus to show that the innocent party has no legitimate interest in performing (Scotland: *Salaried Staff London Loan Co. Ltd. v. Swears & Wells Ltd.* 1985 S.L.T. 326, I.H.).

Continental European legal systems do not know the general restriction upon a claim for payment provided for in Article 9:101(2)(b). However in BELGIAN law there are a number of situations in which the creditor is obliged to terminate the contract and claim damages, e.g. in a construction contract, CC art. 1794, or more generally in all obligations to be rendered in exchange for work or services. The creditor must also terminate when to insist on performance would be contrary to good faith or an abuse of right, see Cass. 16 Jan. 1986, Arr.Cass. no.317, R.W. 1987-88, 1470 obs. *van Oevelen*, R.G.D.C./T.B.B.R. 1987, 130. The FINNISH and SWEDISH Sale of Goods Acts, § 52 provide that, in the case of goods which the seller must procure or produce specifically for the buyer, if the buyer cancels the contract the seller may not procure or produce the goods and claim the price. The seller may only claim damages, including any loss of profit. However, this does not apply if the cancellation would result in substantial inconvenenience for the the seller or if he would be at risk of not being reimbursed for his losses resulting from the cancellation. See *Ramberg*, Köplagen 512 ff.

Article 9:102: Non-monetary Obligations

(1) The aggrieved party is entitled to specific performance of an obligation other than one to pay money, including the remedying of a defective performance.

(2) Specific performance cannot, however, be obtained where:

(a) performance would be unlawful or impossible; or

(b) performance would cause the debtor unreasonable effort or expense; or

(c) the performance consists in the provision of services or work of a personal character or depends upon a personal relationship, or

(d) · *the aggrieved party may reasonably obtain performance from another source.*

(3) The aggrieved party will lose the right to specific performance if it fails to seek it within a reasonable time after it has or ought to have become aware of the non-performance.

COMMENTS

A. *General*

This Article allows the aggrieved party to require performance of a contractual obligation other than one to pay money by the non-performing party. Due to lack of a better, generally understood term, the common law phrase "specific performance" is used. The aggrieved party has not only a substantive right to demand the other party's performance as spelt out in the contract. The aggrieved party has also a remedy to enforce this right, e.g. by applying for an order or decision of the court.

Article 9:102 covers all obligations which are not covered by Article 9:101, e.g. to do or not to do an act, to make a declaration or to deliver something. In some cases a court order itself will act as a substitute for performance by the non-performing party.

Illustration 1: A who had first rented his immovable to B and later on agreed to sell it to him, refuses to transfer ownership to B. Unless paragraph (2) applies, B is entitled to a court order directing A to transfer ownership to B or, in some countries, the court order itself takes the place of a document of transfer executed by A.

Rules on the means and the procedure of enforcement of a judgment for performance must be left to the national legal systems.

The right to require performance of a non-monetary obligation applies to three situations: first, if no performance at all is tendered by the non-performing party; second, where tender of a non-conforming performance has been made but has been validly rejected by the aggrieved party; third, where the performance is defective but has not been rejected (see Comment C below).

However, the right to performance is subject to four exceptions (paragraph (2), sub-paragraphs (a)-(d)) and a special time limit (paragraph (3)).

B. *The principle and exceptions*
Whether an aggrieved party should be entitled to require performance of a non-monetary obligation, is very controversial. The common law treats specific performance as an exceptional remedy whilst the civil law regards it as an ordinary remedy. These Principles have sought a compromise: a claim for performance is admitted in general (paragraph 1) but excluded in several special situations (paragraphs (2) and (3)).

A general right to performance has several advantages. Firstly, through specific relief the creditor obtains as far as possible what is due to it under the contract; secondly, difficulties in assessing damages are avoided; thirdly, the binding force of contractual obligations is stressed. A right to performance is particularly useful in cases of unique objects and in times of scarcity.

On the other hand, comparative research of the laws and especially commercial practices demonstrate that even in the Civil Law countries the principle of performance must be limited. The limitations are variously based upon natural, legal and commercial considerations and are set out in paragraphs (2)-(3). In all these cases other remedies, especially damages and, in appropriate cases, termination, are more adequate remedies for the aggrieved party.

C. *Right to require remedying of defective performance*
If the non-performing party performs, but its performance does not conform to the contract, the aggrieved party may choose to insist upon a conforming performance. This may be advantageous for both parties. The aggrieved party obtains what it has originally contracted for and the non-performing party eventually obtains the full price.

A conforming performance may be achieved in a variety of ways: for example, repair; delivery of missing parts; or delivery of a replacement.

The right to require a conforming performance is, of course, subject to the same exceptions as the general right to performance (laid down in paragraphs (2)-(3), see D-J). Thus a non-performing party cannot be forced by court order to accomplish a performance conforming to the contract if the aggrieved party has failed to demand performance within a reasonable time (paragraph (3)) or if the latter may reasonably be expected to make someone else effect repair of the performance (paragraph (2) sub-paragraph (d)).

Illustration 2: A sells and delivers to B a television set. On delivery B discovers that the colour adjustment of the set is defective. The defect can easily be cured by fitting a spare part. If B can easily get someone else to fit the part she cannot require A to fit it.

D. *Exceptions, but no judicial discretion*
Under these Principles the aggrieved party has a substantive right to demand and to enforce performance of a non-monetary obligation. Granting an order for performance thus is not in the discretion of the court; the court is bound to grant the remedy, unless the exceptions of paragraphs (2) or (3) apply. National courts should grant performance even in cases where they are not accustomed to do so under their national law.

E. *Impossibility and illegality*
For obvious reasons, there is no right to require performance if it is impossible (paragraph (2) sub-paragraph (a)). This is particularly true in case of factual impossibility, i.e. if some act in fact cannot be done. The same is true if an act is prohibited by law. Even if this prohibition does not nullify the contract, its performance may be illegal. Similarly, specific performance is not available where a third person has acquired priority over the plaintiff to the subject matter of the contract.

If an impossibility is only temporary, enforcement of performance is excluded during that time.

Whether or not the impossibility makes the non-performing party liable in damages is irrelevant in this context.

F. *Unreasonable effort or expense*
Performance cannot be required if it would involve the non-performing party in unreasonable effort or expense (paragraph (2) sub-paragraph (b)). No precise rule can be stated on when effort or expense is unreasonable. However, considerations as to the reasonableness of the transaction or of the appropriateness of the counterperformance are irrelevant in this context. Nor is paragraph (2) sub-paragraph (b) limited to the kind of supervening event cases covered by Article 6:111. These Articles, as the more specific rule, prevails over the present section.

> *Illustration 3*: A, who has sold his yacht "Eliza" to B, promised to deliver it at B's domicile. On the way "Eliza" is hit by a ship and is sunk in 200 metres of water. The costs of raising her would amount to forty times her value. The cost of forcing A to perform would be unreasonable.

Performance may have become useless for the aggrieved party. In such cases it may then be vexatious to force the non-performing party to stick to its promise, cf. Article 1:201.

> *Illustration 4*: A leased his farm for five years to mining company B for strip mining. In addition to paying rent, B promised to restore the land after completing the mining operation. In the meantime, A decides to lease the land after its return from B to the army for use as a training area for tank crews. If B would have to spend $29,000 in order to restore the land and its value would thereby increase by only $300, the restoration would be unreasonable.

G. *Provision of services or work of a personal character*

Paragraph (2) sub-paragraph (c) covers two different situations: (1) it excludes a right to require performance of services or work of a personal character. This rule is based on three considerations: firstly, a judgment ordering performance of personal services or work would be a severe interference with the non-performing party's personal liberty; secondly, services or work which are rendered under pressure will often not be satisfactory for the aggrieved party; and thirdly, it is difficult for a court to control the proper enforcement of its order.

The term "services or work of a personal character" does not cover services or work which may be delegated. A provision in the contract that work may not be delegated does not necessarily make the work of a personal character. If the contract does not need the personal attention of the contracting party but could be performed by its employees, the clause prohibiting delegation may be interpreted as preventing only delegation to another enterprise, e.g. a sub-contractor.

Services requiring individual scholars of an artistic or scientific nature and services to be rendered in the scope of a confidential and personal relationship are personal services.

Illustration 5: A, a famous artist, contracts with B, a wealthy merchant, to paint a picture for him. If A does not comply with her promise B cannot require performance, because performance of A's obligation requires individual scholars of an artistic nature and thus consists in work of a personal nature.

The signing of a document would not usually constitute service or work within the meaning of this provision. Such an obligation can mostly be enforced since the non-performing party's declaration can be replaced by a court decree (See Comment A).

Similarly, Paragraph (2) sub-paragraph (c) excludes specific performance where the parties would be forced to enter or to continue a personal relationship.

In case of agreements to enter into a partnership, paragraph 2 sub-paragraph (c) second alternative applies if and insofar as the partnership presupposes a close personal contact. But as in case of a contract to form a public company, the specific personal element is sometimes lacking; in this case this rule does not prevent the promise being enforced.

Illustration 6: The six heirs of a factory-owner conclude a contract in due form to establish a limited company in order to continue the inherited business. Later A, one of the heirs, who was not to assume any management functions in the company, refuses to co-operate in the creation of the company. The other heirs may require performance of the preliminary agreement. The result would be different if the agreement were one to create a partnership in which all the partners were to play an active role.

Paragraph (2) sub-paragraph (c) speaks only of positive acts ("provision, performance"). It is possible to require performance of a negative obligation, e.g. to forebear from rendering services for someone else or from entering into a partnership with someone else. If, however, enforcement of a negative obligation concerning services, work or a personal relationship would result in indirect enforcement of a positive act to provide or maintain the same, paragraph (2) sub-paragraph (c) applies.

> *Illustration 7*: A, a specialist in marketing by mail order, has been employed by B on terms that for two years A will not work as a marketing specialist for any other firm. A ceases advising B without notice because C, B's competitor, has offered A a much higher fee. B cannot obtain an injunction to restrain A from working for C or anyone else because A's obligation to provide services for B would be enforced indirectly.

H. *Cover transaction*

Paragraph (2) sub-paragraph (d), like Article 9:101(2) lit. (a), excludes a right to require performance if the aggrieved party can more easily obtain performance from other sources. Paragraph (2) sub-paragraph (d) does not introduce any kind of a test of adequacy of damages in the sense that performance could only be required if damages were an inadequate remedy. Rather, this rule should encourage the aggrieved party to choose from among the remedies which would fully compensate it the one which can most simply be obtained. According to practical experience, termination and damages will often satisfy its requirements faster and more easily than enforcement of performance.

If the aggrieved party chooses to require performance, this will generally create a presumption that this remedy optimally satisfies its needs. Consequently, the non-performing party will have to prove that the aggrieved party can obtain performance from other sources without any prejudice and that therefore it may reasonably be expected to make a cover transaction.

> *Illustration 8*: A sells to B a certain set of chairs which are of an ordinary kind and without special value. A refuses to deliver. A proves that B may without suffering a prejudice obtain chairs of the kind sold from other sources. B cannot require performance by A.

If, in contrast, the chairs are unique antiques, B may require performance.

An aggrieved party may reasonably be expected to obtain performance from other sources, even if the cost is higher than the contract price, but only if the defaulting party is in a position to pay the damages for the difference. If this is not so, paragraph (2) sub-paragraph (d) does not exclude a request for performance.

I. *Reasonable time*

A request for performance of a non-monetary obligation must be made within a reasonable time, paragraph (3). This provision is supplementary to provisions on limitation and is intended to protect the non-performing party from hardship that could arise in consequence of a delayed request for performance by the aggrieved party. The latter party's interests are not seriously affected by this limitation because it may still choose another remedy.

The length of the reasonable period of time is to be determined in view of the rule's purpose. In certain cases, it may be very short, e.g. if delivery can be made out of the non-performing party's stock in trade, in other cases it may be longer.

It is the non-performing party which has to show that the delay in requesting performance was unreasonably long.

A corresponding rule for termination is embodied in Article 9:303(2).

J. *Legal consequences of exceptions*

One of the consequences that arise from the exceptions provided for in paragraph (2) and (3) is expressly set out in these rules: performance cannot be demanded by the aggrieved party. The aggrieved party may still claim damages, see Article 9:103.

NOTES

1. General Approaches

With respect to non-monetary obligations, traditionally there are important differences between the common law and civil law, at least in theory.

In the common law specific performance is a discretionary remedy that will only be granted if damages are inadequate (cf. ENGLAND: *Chitty* § 27-003; IRELAND, *Keane*, §§ 16.01 ff; USA: Restatement of Contracts 2d §§ 345(b), 357-369). There is also some doubt as to whether specific performance will be given of a continuing obligation, see e.g. *Co-operative Insurance Society Ltd.* v. *Argyll Stores (Holdings) Ltd* [1997] 3 All E.R. 297 (H.L.). In SCOTLAND specific implement is usually said to be a remedy available as of right but in fact it is granted only in the court's discretion and it is not granted in the cases set forth in Article 9:102(2) (*McBryde* Chap. 21), though in Scotland continuing obligations may be enforced more readily than in England, see, *Retail Parks Investments Ltd* v.*Royal Bank of Scotland plc* 1996 S.L.T. 669. However, in England injunctions for enforcement of express negative stipulations are sometimes said to be granted as a matter of course (*Chitty* § 27-040).

In the civil law countries the aggrieved party's right to performance is generally recognized. In the German legal family this is "axiomatic" (*Zweigert & Kötz* 472). The AUSTRIAN ABGB §§ 918, 919, ITALIAN Civil Code (art. 1453 (1)) and the DUTCH BW (art. 3:296(1)) expressly so provide. So do the DANISH Sale of Goods Act, § 21 which is expressive of a general principle of contract law, see *Gomard*, Obligationsret II 33; and the FINNISH and SWEDISH Sale of Goods Acts, § 23.

The principle of enforced performance *in natura* is particularly emphasised in FRENCH law. It follows from CC art. 1184 (2) and from the contemporary interpretation of CC art. 1142 (see *Jeandidier* Rev.trim.dr.civ. 1976, 700-724). CC art. 1143 empowers the aggrieved party to demand destruction of anything that has been produced contrary to an agreement. And recently, art. 1 of the Law of 9 July 1991 on the reform of civil enforcement proceedings has established the principle that every aggrieved party may force the non-performing party, in accordance with legal provisions, to perform his obligations. Performance *in natura* is facilitated by the liberal use of judicial penalties (*astreinte*) (*Malaurie and Aynès*, Obligations no. 1017-1023). Whether enforced performance *in natura* is available as a matter of right for the aggrieved party (and therefore the judge must grant it if it is asked for) is, however, unsure. According to traditional case law, the judge holds a sovereign power to choose the mode of reparation that appears to him the most appropriate, and in particular he can reject enforced performance *in natura* asked for by the aggrieved party, based on art. 1142 (see Cass.Civ. 1, 30 June 1965, B. I no. 437, p. 327, Gaz.Pal. 1965.2.329). But there is a new *"courant"* to grant specific performance, based on the literal wording of CC art. 1184(2) (Cass.com. 3 December 1985, B. IV No. 286 p. 244; 28 Feb. 1969, motifs, B. III No. 182 p. 139).

In BELGIAN law the preeminence of specific performance is acknowledged (Cass. 30 Jan. 1965, Pas. I 58; Cass. 5 Jan. 1968, Pas. I 567) (though subject to the fact that the demand must not be an abuse of right) and the same is true for PORTUGAL (CC art. 817) and SPAIN (CC arts. 1096, 1098; *Diez Picazo*, II 679; *Lacruz-Delgado*, § 21, 170; *Ministerio de Justicia*, II art. 1096.

ULIS and CISG give the buyer generally a right to performance (ULIS arts. 24, 26, 30, 42; CISG art. 46). However, courts are not bound to decree performance if they would not do so according to their national law (ULIS art. 16 and art. VII of the convention relating to ULIS; CISG art. 28).

2. *Practical Convergence*

The basic differences between common law and civil law are of theoretical rather than practical importance. Even in civil law countries an aggrieved party will pursue an action for performance, in general, only if he has a special interest in performance which would not be satisfied by damages (cf. *Zweigert & Kötz* 484).

3. *Exceptions to Specific Performance*

(a) *Judicial discretion and exceptions*

In common law countries specific performance is a discretionary remedy. Nevertheless, this discretion will be exercised in accordance with settled principles (cf. *Hanbury & Maudsley* 651 with refs.), some of which have been followed in drafting the exceptions in Article 9:102(2) litt. (a) to (d) and (3). Also in FRANCE it had been said that in principle the judge was free to grant damages even though performance *in natura* has been demanded (*Derrida*, Obligations no. 127 with ref.). However the cases where this has in fact been done seem to fall under Article 9:102(2) litt. (b) (unreasonable effort or expense) or (d) (other sources of supply available). In SPANISH law the courts may refuse specific performance if it would not be reasonable in the circumstances to grant it: *Diez Picazo* II, 696; *Ministerio de Justicia*, art. 1124; *Lacruz-Delgado* II, 1, § 26, 204; *Albaladejo*, II, 1, § 33.1.B. For BELGIAN law see note 2 to Article 9:101 above.) In GERMAN law the right to performance and its enforcement do not depend upon the judge's discretion (cf. *Dawson* 57 Mich.L.Rev. 495, 530 (1959)); the same is true of AUSTRIAN law.

Under CISG art. 28 and under ULIS art. 16 in connection with art. VII of the covering convention, restrictions under national laws are preserved even under the uniform sales laws.

(b) *Performance impossible*

Article 9:102(2)(a) expresses the rule *"impossibilium nulla est obligatio"*. If restricted to the right to performance as such (as distinct from subsidiary remedies), the rule seems to be common to the laws of Europe (cf. ENGLAND: *Forrer* v. *Cash* (1865) 35 Beav. 167, 171; 55 E.R. 858, 860; IRELAND, *Keane* § 16.10; FRANCE and BELGIUM: CC art. 1184(2) sent. 2, 1234, 1302; GERMANY: BGB § 275; AUSTRIA, ABGB § 1447; GREECE: CC art. 336; ITALY: CC arts. 1256, 1463; PORTUGAL: CC art. 828; SPAIN: CC arts. 1182, 1184; NETHERLANDS: BW art. 3:236; DENMARK: *Gomard*, Obligationsret II 45): FINLAND: *Taxell*, Avtal och rättsskydd 196 and SGA § 23; SWEDEN: *Rodhe*, Obligationsträtt 348 ff.. CISG art. 79 (5) appears to be to the contrary, but this is controversial (cf. *Schlechtriem* 51, 96-97 with references; *Audit* nos. 185-186).

(c) *Performance unreasonable*

Article 9:102(2)(b) corresponds to a view which is widely accepted in NORDIC case law and literature (cf. *Ussing*, Alm. Del 68, *Gomard, op.cit.* 57 *Taxell*, op.cit. 197; *Ramberg*, Köplagen 313 ff.; FINNISH and SWEDISH SGA § 23 and is being discussed in GERMANY (cf. *Medicus* no. 158) and ITALY (*Mengoni*, Contractual responsibility 1089-1090). It is a clear rule under AUSTRIAN law, that specific performance is not available if it would be unreasonable: see e.g OGH 20 March 1963 SZ 36/44. In PORTUGAL, such a rule is expressly provided for in the case of an obligation to demolish a building erected in violation of a duty not to do so (CC art. 829 no. 2). IRISH law achieves this position, *Keane* § 16.12. GREEK courts have refused a claim for performance *in natura* where that would burden the non-performing party with excessive and disproportionate sacrifices (AP 93/1967, NoB 15 (1967) 791; cf. ATHENS 5917/1976, NoB 25 (1977) 401). In FRANCE, the cases which recognize the judge's sovereign power to refuse performance *in natura* (see above, note 1) are sometimes based on the excessive cost of the operation (see e.g. Cass. req. 23 March 1909, S. 1909.1.552; Cass. civ.1, 8 June 1964, B. I, No. 297, p. 232). However, the recent *"courant"* which orders works of reparation (or payment for reparation) is not limited by its cost (e.g. Cass. civ.3, 9 December 1975, B. III, No. 363, p. 275). In BELGIAN law the restrictions mentioned in note 3 to Article 9:101 apply also to the choice between specific performance and damages: Cass. 10 Sept. 1971, Pas. 1972, I, 28 note *Ganshof*, R.C.J.B. 1976, note *van Ommeslaghe*. Specific performance will not be ordered if the performance would be quite different to the original obligation, e.g. a lessee which has carelessly burned down the leased premises will not be ordered to re-build them.

Illustration 4 is modelled upon *Peevyhouse* v. *Garland Coal & Mining Co.* 382 P. 2d 109, 116 (Okl. 1962).

(d) *Performance of a personal character*

Article 9:102(2)(c) first alternative is based on considerations common to the laws of Europe (see *Remien*, (1989) RabelZ 53, 165 ff..).

Thus, in ENGLAND, IRELAND, SCOTLAND and the UNITED STATES specific performance is not available for contracts involving personal services (cf. *Treitel*, Contract 927; *Keane* § 16.05; Restatement of Contracts 2d § 367 with § 318; cf. *ibid.* § 367 comment b). Similarly in FRENCH law under CC art. 1142 there is no right to enforcement of certain personal obligations to do or not to do (Cass. civ. 20 Jan. 1953, JCP 1953, 7677 note *Esmein*). In BELGIUM the rule is also applied though only where specific performance would involve physical coercion, (Cass. 23 Dec. 1977, Arr. Cass. & Pas 505) and agency cases (CC art. 2007). In SPAIN it is admitted that there is no right to specific performance of obligations consisting in the provision of services or work of a personal nature (Civ. Proc. Code arts. 924 and 925; CC arts, 1098 and 1911; *Diez-Picazo*, II 124 and 680). In NORDIC law a claim for performance in kind is excluded for employment contracts and in some other cases (DENMARK *Lyngsø* 125; and generally when performance consists of work of a personal character, *Gomard, op.cit.* 6; FINLAND: *Taxell*, op.cit. 192; SWEDEN: *Ramberg*, Avtalsrätt52). While GERMAN law allows a claim for personal services, CCProc. § 888 (2) excludes the enforcement of judgments for non-delegable personal services. GREEK CCProc. art. 946 (2) takes a similar position.

ITALIAN law, however, does not have a rule about specific peformance of contracts involving personal services and difficulties have arisen: *Mazzamuto*.

The idea underlying the second alternative of Article 9:102(2)(c) is common to many laws, although often differently expressed. In ENGLAND and SCOTLAND specific performance of an agreement for partnership will be granted only in some special situations (*Lindley* on Partnership 536). FRENCH law, too, excludes a right to performance *in natura* of a promise to form a *"société"* (*Perrot*, J.Cl. Sociétés Fasc. 7bis, nos. 23 and 37). GERMAN law, however, allows the enforcement of preliminary contracts to form a limited liability company (*Schlosser (-Emmerich) § 2 No. 81* with references).

Illustration 5 is modelled upon *Barrow* v. *Chappell & Co. Ltd.* [1959] Ch.14. Illustration 6 is based on Reichsgericht 8 May 1907, RGZ 66, 116.

(e) *Performance from another source*
Article 9:102(2)(d) is a compromise between different basic attitudes of the common law and the civil law. It does not directly copy any national legal order. But it links up with ULIS arts. 25, 42(1) (c) (cf. note 1 above) which trace back to considerations of *Rabel* (I 378).

Under the common law the possibility of a cover transaction is an important consideration for denying specific performance (cf. Restatement of Contracts 2d §§ 360 (b), 359; *Treitel*, Contract 919). In European continental laws, cover is merely an option for the buyer, but he is not obliged to use it, unless there is a usage to that effect. Some BELGIAN authors have suggested a rule similar to Article 9:102(2)(d) in certain, mainly commercial, contexts, *Fredericq*, III no.1432, *van Ryn & Heenen* III no.688.

Illustration 9 is based on *Cohen* v. *Roche* [1927] 1 K.B. 169 (K.B.).

4. *Delay*
Article 9:102(3) takes up the COMMON LAW view that an aggrieved party who delays unreasonably in requiring performance *in natura* may lose his claim (c.f. *Hanbury & Maudsley* 677; *Keane* § 3.10). A similar rule is found in the FINNISH and SWEDISH Sale of Goods Acts, § 23. In DENMARK Sale of Goods Act § 26 provides that the aggrieved party must give a notice to the non-performing party within a reasonable time that he will continue the contract; otherwise the aggrieved party will lose his right to claim specific performance (see *Ussing*, Alm. Del. 70). This idea can be found in CISG, too, but it is limited to cases where the buyer claims delivery of substitute goods and repair of non-conforming goods (art. 46 (2) and (3)). No equivalent rule exists in FRANCE, PORTUGAL or SPAIN but in BELGIAN law a similar rule has been accepted: Cass. 5 Dec. 1946, Arr.Cass., 428, Cass. 29 Nov. 1962, Pas. 405; see *M.E.Storme*, Invloed nos. 394 and 389-391.

5. *Defective Performance*
The rules on performance *in natura* after a non-conforming ("defective") tender has been made differ very much.

The uniform laws on international sales grant a right to performance *in natura* in case of "non-conforming" goods (cf. ULIS art. 42, 52; CISG art. 41, 46). However, the right to require delivery of substitute goods in CISG art. 46(2) is limited to cases of fundamental "breach of contract".

Recent European codifications tend to grant a right to demand cure of non-conformities. The DUTCH BW provides for such a right in case of lack of full title (art. 7:20) and in case of "non-conforming" goods (art. 7:21 litt. b) and c)). In DENMARK the Sale of Goods Act, which formerly provided only for a right to delivery of substitute goods in case of sale of generic goods (art. 43(1)), has been amended by the addition of a new § 78 which provides for consumer sales in general a right to demand cure of defects. The New Nordic Sale of Goods Act § 34 which is now in force in FINLAND

and SWEDEN provides a right (with certain limitations) to demand cure of defects in commercial sales in general. In PORTUGAL a right to have a defective performance corrected or to receive a new delivery is expressly provided for contracts of sale and for work (CC art. 914, 1221); it can be considered as an application of a general principle relating to defective performances (*Jorge* 479).

AUSTRIAN law provides in respect of all contracts for consideration a general right to have a defective performance cured: see ABGB § 932 (1) granting the aggrieved party the right either to demand reduction of the price, or the repair of the defect or the addition of missing parts of the performance by the party in breach: the exchange or repair of the defective piece may be seen as a type of performance.

In GERMANY a general right to have defects cured already exists for cases of third party claims (BGB §§ 434, 440, and also §§ 515, 523; cf. *Larenz* II/1, 27 ff..), for lack of quality in contracts for work (§ 633) and – limited to a right to delivery of substitute goods – in case of sales of generic goods (BGB § 480). And it has been proposed that a rule should be introduced for all sales providing for a right to demand cure of defects consisting of lack of quality or quantity (*Huber* 765, 874 ff.. who proposes a new § 461 a). GREEK, ITALIAN and SWISS law (for cases of lack of quality) are similar to the present state of German law (cf. Greek CC arts. 559 and 688; Italian CC art. 1482(2), 1512(2), 1668(1); Swiss CO art. 689, 206, 368(2)). In Greece it is acknowledged that there is, as a rule, no general right of the buyer to demand the remedying of defects (see *Spiliopoulos* in the Commentary to the Civil Code (Erm. AK) vol. III/1, Introductory remarks to arts. 534-562 no. 46 (1972); *Aigaiou* 41/1967, NoB 16 (1968) 195, 196 I). In SPANISH law, both writers and the courts accept that a buyer may demand cure in the form of replacement of defective goods (cf. CC arts. 1166, 1484ff., 1553 and 1591; see *Diez Picazo* II, 670; *Albaladejo* II, 1 §§ 23.5 and 31.3; Supreme Court 3 March 1979, 14 March 1981 and 28 June 1982.

In FRANCE and BELGIUM it is uncertain whether the non-performing party can be constrained to cure himself or to provide cure of a defective performance (generally, no distinction is made between cases where it is for the debtor or the creditor to have the cure made). Formerly, in such cases the Cour de cassation appeared to deny a duty of performance *in natura* (Cass.civ. 4 June 1924, S. 1925.1.97 with note *Hugueney*, D.P. 1927.1.136 with note *Josserand*; Cass.civ. 15 March 1948, D. 1948.346, S. 1948.1.100) but presently the courts are more flexible (cf. *Viney*, La responsabilité II nos. 14-36 with references).

In ENGLAND, IRELAND and SCOTLAND there seems to be no right to have non-conformities cured.

Article 9:103: Damages Not Precluded

The fact that a right to performance is excluded under this Section does not preclude a claim for damages.

COMMENTS

A. *The basic situation*

In the exceptional cases set out in Article 9:101 (2) and Article 9:102 (2) and (3), an aggrieved party cannot require performance. Article 9:103 makes it clear that even in these cases the aggrieved party may recover damages. Damages are always available according to the rules of Section 9 unless the non-performance is excused under Article 8:108.

B. *Other consequences*

The provision does not take a stand on the more general issue whether in the cases in which a claim to performance is excluded the contract is terminated. At least in the case of a permanent impossibility or illegality (Article 9:102 (2) sub-paragraph (a)) the contract is terminated automatically, see Article 9:303 (4).

The same may be true in those cases in which the aggrieved party is required to conclude a cover transaction and has in fact done so (see Article 9:101 (2) sub-paragraph (a) and Article 9:102 (2) sub-paragraph (d)). The non-performing party would therefore no longer be entitled to tender performance.

NOTE

The rule in Article 9:103 is in accordance with NORDIC, ENGLISH, FRENCH BELGIAN, LUXEMBOURG, ITALIAN, PORTUGUESE and SPANISH law, see e.g. French CC art.1184(2). Generally speaking it also corresponds to GERMAN law and AUSTRIAN law (see ABGB § 921). See also the note to Article 8:102.

Section 2

Withholding Performance

Article 9:201: Right to Withhold Performance

(1) A party which is to perform simultaneously with or after the other party may withhold performance until the other has tendered performance or has performed. The first party may withhold the whole of its performance or a part of it as may be reasonable in the circumstances.

(2) A party may similarly withhold performance for as long as it is clear that there will be a non-performance by the other party when the other party's performance becomes due.

COMMENT

A.*General*

Where under a synallagmatic (that is, a bilateral or multilateral) contract one party is to perform first but has not yet done so, or is to perform simultaneously with the other but is not able or willing to do so (on the order of performance see Article 7:104), it is both just and commercially convenient for the other party to have the right to withhold or suspend its own performance. This both protects the withholding party from having to advance credit to the non-performer and gives the latter an incentive to perform, since until it does so it will not receive the counterperformance. The well-known *exceptio non adimpleti contractus* is an expression of this idea. Performance of one obligation may be withheld so long as the other is not fully performed.

> *Illustration 1*: A employs B to build a house for him; the contract provides that within two days of the contract being signed, A will make an advance payment of £10,000 to B. B need not start work until the payment has been made.

A party whose own conduct causes the other party's non-performance may not invoke this Article to withhold its own performance. See Article 8:101(3).

> *Illustration 2*: The owner of a house enters a contract with a municipal organisation for communal steam heating. The account is to be sent out by the 15th of

one month and to be paid by the 15th of the next month. Because of a computer breakdown the organisation does not send out the account for 15 January until 10 February, and the house-owner has not paid by 15 February. The municipality cannot suspend the supply of steam.

The text envisages that the obligation which has not been performed and the obligation of which performance is to be withheld are parts of the same contract. The text takes no view on whether performance may be withheld because of the non-performance of another contract between the same parties.

B. *Non-performance need not be fundamental*

Where the obligations of the two parties are to be performed simultaneously a party's non-performance need not be fundamental in order to entitle the other party to withhold its own performance. But it is not necessarily appropriate for a party to be entitled to withhold the whole of its performance if the obligations not performed by the other party are not fundamental. In the common law countries the right to withhold performance is restricted to cases where the contract expressly or impliedly makes the obligations conditional upon one another and to cases of fundamental non-performance; in other cases the aggrieved party must perform its obligations in full (though if the non-performance is a breach it may have a claim for damages). Other systems are more flexible, permitting withholding of performance as a way of coercing the non-performing party even where the non-performance is minor, provided that the amount withheld is not wholly disproportionate and the withholding party acts in good faith. It is this approach which is adopted by this Article, which must be read together with Article 1:201 (Good Faith and Fair Dealing).

> *Illustration 3*: A agrees to buy a new car from B, a dealer. When A comes to collect the car he finds it has a scratch on the bodywork. He may refuse to accept the car or pay any part of the price until the car is repaired.

> *Illustration 4*: The same except that the car is to be shipped to A's home in another country, where B has no facilities. Since it would be unrealistic to expect B to repair the scratch, it would be contrary to good faith for A to withhold more than the cost of having the car repaired locally.

In some cases the aggrieved party cannot practicably withhold part of its performance – for instance, many obligations to perform a service must realistically be performed in full or suspended in full. The aggrieved party may only withhold its performance in full if in the circumstances that is not unreasonable. However, it may be expressly provided in the contract that a performance is made reciprocal to the other performance.

C. *Order of performance*

It is obvious that a party which is obliged to tender performance first is not entitled to withhold performance merely because the other is not willing to perform its part at that stage.

Illustration 5: A contracts with B to have a wall built in A's garden for £500 payable on completion. B cannot require an advance payment as a condition of starting work.

If the order of performance is not stated in the contract, it will have to be determined. Whether the parties to a contract are to perform simultaneously, or one before the other, is to be determined in accordance with Article 7:104, Order of Performance. However, even it is clear that one is to perform before the other, it will have to decided whether the party to perform first must perform the whole of its obligation, or only part of it, before the other need perform. Thus in Illustration 5, if the contract had not stated that payment was due on completion the court would have first to decide whether payment was due only then or whether some or all was due at an earlier stage. Thus if it is determined that, as a matter of construction of the contract, payment is due as the work progresses, the employer will not normally be entitled to withhold payment for the work that has already been completed.

However, a party which is to perform first should have the right to suspend its performance if it is clear that there will be a fundamental non-performance by the other when the other's performance is due, and paragraph (2) so provides. In such case the first party has the right to terminate for anticipatory non-performance under Article 9:304, but it may prefer to hold the contract open for performance.

Illustration 6: In January B agrees to build a house for O and to start work on 1st May. O undertakes to make an advance payment of £20,000 as part of the price by not later than 1st June, time of payment being of the essence of the contract. During May O tells B that because of recent heavy expenditure he has incurred he will not be able to pay the £20,000 until the beginning of July. Instead of terminating the contract under Article 9:304, B may keep the contract open for performance by O and may meanwhile suspend the building works.

If it is not clear that O will not perform but B has reasonable grounds for believing that it will not, B may demand an assurance of performance under Article 8:105.

Notes

1. *Presumption on concurrent performances*
   (a) *Civil law*
      The GERMAN BGB § 320 provides that, unless he has to perform first, the debtor of a reciprocal obligation may withhold his performance until the counter-performance has been tendered. A similar presumption on concurrent obligations has been established in GREECE, see CC arts. 374, 375 and 378: ITALY, see CC art. 1460 (1); the NETHERLANDS, see BW art. 6:262; and AUSTRIA (for barter and sale: see ABGB §§ 1052, 1062).
      The FRENCH, BELGIAN, LUXEMBOURG and SPANISH codes and the NORDIC statutes do not have general provisions but only fragmentary rules to the same effect as the BGB, see on sales French, Belgian and Luxembourg CC arts. 1651, Spanish CC art. 1100, 1466, 1467, 1500, and 1502, Danish Sale of Goods Act § 14 and FINNISH and SWEDISH Sale of Goods Acts, §§ 10, 49. However, in these countries the courts have established a general

principle similar to the one just mentioned: see on France, *Huet* J.Cl.Civ. art. 1184; on Belgium, *de Bersaques* R.C.J.B. 1949, 125, no.8, and *M.E. Storme* De Exceptio, R.W. 1989-90, 317 no.12 who stresses that it is a question of interpretation; on Spain, *Diez-Picazo* II 692; *Albladejo* II, 1, § 20.1; on Denmark, *Gomard*, Obligationsret II 71ff.; on SWEDEN, *Ramberg*, Köplagen 202 ff. For sale of goods CISG art. 58 (1) also provides for concurrent performances.

It may however follow from the parties' agreement or from the circumstances of the case that one party has to perform or to begin performance first. This is the case when concurrent performance is impossible such as in contracts for lease and services. See Article 7:104

(b)   *United Kingdom and Ireland*

Section 28 of the UNITED KINGDOM Sale of Goods Act 1979 provides that unless otherwise agreed, delivery of goods and payment of the price are concurrent conditions, that is to say, the seller must be ready and willing to give possession of the goods to the buyer in exchange for the price and the buyer must be ready and willing to pay the price in exchange for possession of the goods. IRISH Sale of Goods Act 1893, s.28 is to the same effect. Also in other contracts than sales there is a tendency to treat the parties' promises as concurrent conditions, see *Treitel*, Remedies § 214; but as in the civil law it may follow from the circumstances that one of the parties will have to perform first, such as where simultaneous performances are not possible.

2.   *Withholding performance of a reciprocal obligation*
(a)   *The civil law countries*
  (i)   *In general*

The rule laid down in Article 9:201(1), first sentence, seems to be widely accepted in the civil law countries where a party may withhold his performance until the other party performs, both in cases of concurrent obligations and where the other party has to perform first. See on contracts in general GERMAN BGB § 320; GREEK CC art. 374; ITALIAN CC art. 1460(1); DUTCH BW art. 6:52; and PORTUGUESE CC art. 428. In FRANCE, BELGIUM, LUXEMBOURG, AUSTRIA, SPAIN and DENMARK the courts have established this rule as a general principle based on specific provisions and the spirit of the law: see on sales French, Belgian and Luxembourg CC arts. 1653, 1707 and (semble) 1612 and 1613; on recognition as a general principle in Belgian case law, Cass. 26 April 1945, Pas. I; 24 April 1947, R.C.J.B. 1949, 125; 12 Sept. 1973, Arr.Cass. 1974, 36. For AUSTRIA see ABGB §§ 1052, 1062 and *Jabornegg*; in SPAIN, CC art. 1466, and the literature cited above, para 1(a). For Denmark see *Ussing*, Alm.Del. 79. For FINLAND and SWEDEN see SGA §§ 10 and 42 and respectively *Taxell*, Avtal och rättssky-dd 237 and *Rodhe*, Obligationsrätt 391 ff. CISG art. 58 gives each party a similar right to withhold his performance. See also *Unidroit* art. 7.1.3.

  (ii)   *Proportionality (reasonableness test)*

Provisions to the same effect as Article 9:201(1), second sentence, under which a party may withhold the whole of his performance or part of it as may be reasonable in the circumstances are found in some of the civil law systems. Thus the DUTCH BW art. 6:262(2) provides that in the event of partial or defective performance, withholding of the aggrieved party's own performance is allowed only to the extent justified by the non-performance. GREEK law (CC art. 376) and ITALIAN law (CC art. 1460(2)) prevent the aggrieved party from withholding his own performance when this would be contrary to good faith. Greek case law holds that part performance by one party may only entitle him to a corresponding counter-performance from the other: AP 574/1990, EEN 58 (1991) 166-167. Italian writers have argued in favour of a partial withholding when the non-performance by the defaulting party does not justify a withholding of the entire performance, see *Persico* 145. Similarly GERMAN BGB § 320 (2) provides that after partial performance the aggrieved party may not withhold its own performance in as much as this would be contrary to good faith. Under AUSTRIAN law the right to withold performance is limited by the provision of ABGB § 1295 (2) prohibiting the vexatious abuse of legal right: such abuse of the right to withhold performance may be found in a flagrant disproportion in the interests of the parties, see e.g. OGH 31 October 1989 JBl 1990, 248. The PORTUGESE Civil Code does not have an explicit provision. However, Portuguese writers have invoked the rule on the aggrieved party's right to reduce his own performance (see Article 9:401 of these Principles) to reach the same result as under Article 9:201 (1) second sentence; see Varela II 364. Also SPANISH, FRENCH and LUXEMBOURG courts have adopted the proportionality test, the exercise of which in France is left to the free and final appreciation of the trial judge. For SPAIN see Supreme

Court 27 March 1991 (*Diez Picazo* II 693) and 11 July 1991 (*Lacruz-Delgado* § 26, 199) On BELGIAN law see *M.E.Storme*, De Exceptio, R.W. 1989-90, 319-321.

(b)   Common law

In COMMON LAW a party may only withhold his performance because the other has not performed if:

(a)   the first party's obligation to perform is expressly or by implication made dependant on the performance by the second party, or

(b)   the court construes the second party's obligation as being a condition of the contract, or

(c)   the second party's non-performance will have the effect of depriving the first party of the substance of what he was contracting for.

In other words the test for withholding performance is the same as for termination save that termination also requires the time for performance to have expired, see *Beale* chapters 2 and 3.

In SCOTTISH law, the principle of mutuality of contract enables a party to withold performance in response to the other party's breach, so long as there is a link between the breach and the performance witheld: *Bank of East Asia v. Scottish Enterprise*, 18 January 1996 (H.L.) (unrep.).

3.   *Anticipatory non-performance (Article 9:201(2))*

CISG art. 71(1) provides that a party may suspend the performance of his obligations if, after the conclusion of the contract, it becomes apparent that the other party will not perform a substantial part of his obligations as a result of:

(a)   a serious deficiency in his ability to perform or his creditworthiness; or

(b)   his conduct in preparing to perform or in performing the contract.

A very similar rule is adopted by the FINNISH and SWEDISH Sale of Goods Acts, § 61, see *Ramberg*, Köplagen 586 ff.

GERMAN BGB § 321 provides that a party who is to perform first may withhold performance if, due to an essential deterioration of the other party's financial position after the conclusion of the contract, the first party's claim for the counter performance is endangered. AUSTRIAN ABGB § 1052 second sent. is to similar effect. GREEK CC art. 377 is wider: it covers cases of pre-existing financial difficulties of which the first party did not and had no reason to know, *Michaelides-Nouaros* in Erm. AK II/1, art.377 no.4 (1949). See also DUTCH BW arts. 6:80 and 6:263; ITALIAN CC art.1461 DANISH Bankruptcy Act § 54.

Provisions which provide a right to withhold the goods in case of the buyer's insolvency or bankruptcy are found in the DANISH SGA § 39; FRENCH, BELGIAN and LUXEMBOURG CC art. 1613; SPANISH CC arts. 1467 and 1502; PORTUGUESE CC art. 429; and UK Sale of Goods Act 1979, s.41(1). Furthermore, the French and Belgian CC art. 1653 and the Spanish CC art. 1502 permit the buyer to suspend payment of the price if he has reason to fear that a third party's claim to the goods will disturb him in his possession of them. In Belgian law the existence of a more general principle is disputed: see *van Ommeslaghe* R.C.J.B. 1975, 615, no.68; *M.E.Storme,* Invloed, nos.299ff; *Vanwijck-Alexandre.*

See generally *Treitel,* Remedies, Chapter VIII; *Rabel* I 135.

Section 3

Termination of the Contract

Article 9:301: Right to Terminate the Contract

(1) A party may terminate the contract if the other party's non-performance is fundamental.

(2) In the case of delay the aggrieved party may also terminate the contract under Article 8:106(3).

COMMENT

A. *The underlying considerations*
Whether the aggrieved party should have the right to terminate the contract in the case of a non-performance by the other party depends upon a weighing of conflicting considerations.

On the one hand, the aggrieved party may desire wide rights of termination. It will have good reasons for terminating the contract if the performance is so different from that for which it bargained that it cannot use it for its intended purpose, or if it is performed so late that its interest in it is lost. In some situations termination will be the only remedy which will properly safeguard its interests, for instance when the defaulting party is insolvent and cannot perform its obligations or pay damages. The aggrieved party may also wish to be able to terminate in less serious cases. A party which fears that the other party may not perform its obligations may wish to able to take advantage of the fact that the threat of termination is a powerful incentive to the other to perform to ensure that the other performs every obligation in complete compliance with the contract.

For the defaulting party, on the other hand, termination usually involves a serious detriment. In attempting to perform it may have incurred expenses which are now wasted. Thus it may lose all or most of its performance when there is no market for it elsewhere. When other remedies such as damages or price reduction are available these remedies will often safeguard the interests of the aggrieved party sufficiently so that termination should be avoided.

For these reasons it is a prerequisite for termination that the non-performance is fundamental in the sense defined in Article 8:103.

Illustrations have been supplied in the comments to in Article 8:103.

B. *Action in court not required; No period of grace*

As a rule termination is effective only if notice thereof is given by the aggrieved party to the defaulting party, see Article 9:303 and Article 8:106. For exceptions to this rule, see Article 8:106(3) and Article 9:303(4). Termination may be effected by the act of the aggrieved party alone; it does not have to bring an action in court in order to have the contract terminated.

If the requirements of Article 9:301 are satisfied the Principles do not provide for any period of grace to be granted to the defaulting party by a court or an arbitral tribunal.

C. *The "notice" procedure.*

Under Article 8:106(3), when a delay in performance does not amount to a fundamental non-performance the aggrieved party may fix an additional period of time of reasonable length for performance. If by the time the period expires the defaulting party has still not performed, the aggrieved party may treat the contract as terminated. The same applies if the defaulting party has declared that it will not perform within the period so fixed.

D. *Non-performance partly due to aggrieved party's own act*

One factor which should be taken into account is the extent to which the detriment to the aggrieved party is the result of its own conduct. If the detriment was substantially due to its own conduct it might be inappropriate to say that the non-performance was fundamental.

> *Illustration 1*: A manufacturer undertakes to install a machine for supplying molten material in a factory. After it is installed, the machine is left on to warm up ready for testing; the factory owner undertakes to provide a watchman. A slight defect causes a fire which, because the owner failed to provide a watchman, spreads and causes substantial damage to the factory. The manufacturer's non-performance was not fundamental and the factory owner cannot terminate the contract.

In other cases it may be appropriate to permit termination but to hold that the aggrieved party's conduct amounted to a non-performance itself for which the other party may claim damages.

> *Illustration 2*: An exclusive dealership contract between a manufacturer and a dealer is terminated because the dealer has contravened the exclusive purchase clause. However the dealer can show that it was led to purchase elsewhere by the financial demands of the manufacturer which, contrary to the terms of the agreement, had demanded payment in cash. The court should investigate the effect of each party's behaviour and, if it concludes that the manufacturer's actions led to the dealer's default, may award damages to the dealer.

NOTES

1. *Termination when non-performance is fundamental*

    The Principles determine the circumstances in which an aggrieved party may terminate the contract by reference to whether the non-performance is "fundamental". Not all systems allow the aggrieved party to terminate by giving notice. FRENCH, BELGIAN and LUXEMBOURG CCs art. 1184 requires that *résolution* be by judicial pronouncement, and the court must decide whether the non-performance is sufficiently important to justify ending the contract; but clauses allowing automatic termination (*clauses résolutoire de plein droit*) are permitted (*Malaurie & Aynès*, Obligations, nos. 735-759). However, as seen earlier (see the notes to Article 8:103) similar results are reached in most systems, even those which rely on judicial discretion to decide when a contract should be terminated.

2. *Excused and non-excused non-performance treated alike*

    The Principles use the same rules for termination whether or not the non-performance was excused; the aggrieved party may give notice of termination. DUTCH BW arts. 6:74 and 6:265, NORDIC law (see *Taxell*, Avtal och rättsskydd 225), ULIS (for excused non-performance see art.74), CISG (see art.79) and *Unidroit* (see art. 7.3.1) take a similar approach. This is a contrast to many systems in which the case of termination of a contract which has become impossible is treated separately from the case of termination because of a breach of contract. Thus in FRENCH and BELGIAN law in the case of impossibility the contract will be determined according to the theory of risks, CC arts. 1302 and 1624 (c.f. *Treitel*, Remedies § 254); in SPANISH law see CC arts. 1182 ff. and 1124. In GERMAN law a separate paragraph of the BGB, § 323, applies to impossibility due to circumstances for which neither party is responsible (see *Treitel*, Remedies § 255), and a similar approach is taken by AUSTRIAN ABGB § 1147 and by GREEK CC art.380; in ITALIAN law there is a separate regime for impossibility, CC arts.1463-1466; and in COMMON LAW the doctrine of frustration will apply. See the notes to Article 8:108 above.

3. *No additional time once right to terminate has arisen*

    It should be noted that the Principles do not permit the non-performing party to be given extra time once the non-performance is fundamental; compare the FRENCH and BELGIAN *délai de grâce* (CC art.1184; similarly, SPANISH CC art. 1124 (3)) or relief against forfeiture in the COMMON LAW systems (in which, for instance, a tenant may be able to obtain relief against forfeiture of a lease by the landlord for non-payment of rent: see *Treitel*, Remedies § 247).

    On Article 9:301(2) see note to Article 8:106 above.

Article 9:302: Contract to be Performed in Parts

If the contract is to be performed in separate parts and in relation to a part to which a counter-performance can be apportioned, there is a fundamental non-performance, the aggrieved party may exercise its right to terminate under this Section in relation to the part concerned. It may terminate the contract as a whole only if the non-performance is fundamental to the contract as a whole.

COMMENT

A. *General principle*

Where the contract calls for a series of performances by one party, each with a matching counter-performance (typically, a separate price for each performance), the contract may be seen as divisible into a series of units. If one party fails to perform one unit, the other may want to put an end to its obligation to accept performance of that unit: for instance, in a contract for services it may want to arrange for someone else to do the work. However, it may not be appropriate for the aggrieved party to have the right to terminate the whole contract because the failure may not be fundamental in relation to the whole. The unit not performed may not affect the rest of the contract significantly, and the non-performance may not be likely to be repeated. In these circumstances, it is appropriate to allow the aggrieved party to terminate in relation to the part not performed, leaving the rest of the contract untouched. Only if the non-performance is fundamental to the whole contract should the aggrieved party be entitled to terminate the whole.

> *Illustration 1*: An office cleaning company agrees to clean a law firm's office on Saturday of each week for fifty weeks at a price of £500 per week. One Saturday the cleaning company's employees hold a one day strike. The law firm may terminate in relation to that part of the contract and bring in another cleaning firm to clean the office for that week. They may not terminate the contract as a whole unless it is clear that that the strike will be repeated and that therefore there will be a fundamental non-performance, so that there is an anticipatory non-performance within Article 9:304.

> *Illustration 2*: The contract is as in Illustration 1. The cleaning work done in the first week is completely inadequate. It is clear that the cleaning company is trying to do the work using too few employees to cover an office of that size. The cleaning company refuses to use more employees. The law firm may terminate the whole contract.

See also the comment to Article 9:306, Illustrations 1 and 2.

B. *Terminology*
"Termination in relation to a part" of the contract is a slightly awkward phrase, as the contract is not terminated, but it has the advantage that the general rules on termination (such as the need to give notice under Article 9:303) applies. CISG Article 73 takes the same approach.
  Termination "of the contract as a whole" normally means only termination of all the future obligations on each side. See Article 9:305.

C. *Performances which are divisible though not to be paid for separately*
Sometimes one party's obligation to perform consists of distinct parts, and the non-performance affects only one of those parts, but the payment to be made for them is not split up into equivalent sums. If nonetheless the first party's performance is really divisible and the payment can be properly apportioned, Article.9:302 applies and termination is allowed in respect of the part affected.

> *Illustration 3*: as Illustration 1 but the price is £25,000 for the fifty week period. This price was initially calculated by the cleaning company simply by multiplying the weekly charge by 50. The aggrieved party may again terminate in respect of the week missed.

NOTE

Where a contract is to be performed in instalments or separate parts, most systems recognise that the aggrieved party should have the right to refuse to accept, and to refuse to render its promised counter-performance for the defective instalment or part, without necessarily having the right to refuse to accept further performance of the remaining performance under the contract; but it may be entitled to refuse to accept any further performance when the non-performance affects the whole contract. This is provided, for instance by DANISH Sale of Goods Act §§ 22, 29 and 46; FINNISH and SWEDISH Sale of Goods Act, § 43, 44 (see *Ramberg*, Köplagen 462); IRISH Sale of Goods Act 1893, s.31(2); UK Sale of Goods Act 1979, s.31(2) (and in the case law similar results are reached for other contracts; see *Treitel*, Remedies § 278); GREEK CC art.386 (under which the aggrieved party may choose between damages and termination even with respect to parts already performed: *Michaelides-Nouaros* Erm. AK vol.II/1 art.386 nos.7-14). GERMAN law does not recognise a single principle but reaches similar results. Thus in the case of a contract for delivery in instalments (*Sukzessivlieferungsvertrag* or *Ratenlieferungsvertrag*) the aggrieved party can terminate the contract with respect to the improper instalment or with respect to all future instalments. In the latter case it is often required that the aggrieved party's interest in the performance has fallen away (cf *Palandt(-Heinrichs)* Intro. to § 305, nos.31-33, distinguishing the different kinds of non-performance). Virtually the same rule applies in AUSTRIAN law, see ABGB §§ 918(2) and § 920 second sent. Similar results are reached in BELGIUM, see *Lefebve* Rev. de Notariat Belge (1988) 266ff; *Fontaine* R.C.J.B. 1990, 382ff.; *M.E.Storme* T.B.B.R/R.G.D.C 1991, 112, no.12ff; Cass. 29 May 1980, Arr.Cass. no.310, R.W. 1980-81, 1196; and in FRANCE, where according to its *pouvoir souverain*, the court may partially terminate the contract for a partial non-performance (*Malaurie et Aynès* nos.742-744); it will take into account the divisibility of the performance. In SPANISH law termination is not necessarily retrospective *(Diez-Picazo*, II 724; contra; *Albaladejo*, II, 1 § 20.4.5. ITALIAN CC art.1564 provides that in contracts for the periodical supply of goods the whole contract may be terminated if the non-performance is of major importance and leads to loss of confidence in future performance, but according to CC art.1458(1) termination does not extend to performances already executed; on the question of partial termination see *Corrado* 363ff. PORTUGUESE CC art.434(2) provides for termination of the whole of a contract for performance by instalments or over a period of time when the ground for termination relates to the unperformed instalments. DUTCH BW art 6:265 allows the creditor in all cases to choose between termination in part or of the whole, but subject to the general principle that the failure must justify the type of termination chosen.

ULIS arts. 45 and 75 and CISG art. 73 are similar to Article 9:302.

Article 9:303: Notice of Termination

(1) A party's right to terminate the contract is to be exercised by notice to the other party.

(2) The aggrieved party loses its right to terminate the contract unless it gives notice within a reasonable time after it has or ought to have become aware of the non-performance.

(3) (a) When performance has not been tendered by the time it was due, the aggrieved party need not give notice of termination before a tender has been made. If a tender is later made it loses its right to terminate if it does not give such notice within a reasonable time after it has or ought to have become aware of the tender.

(b) If, however, the aggrieved party knows or has reason to know that the other party still intends to tender within a reasonable time, and the aggrieved party unreasonably fails to notify the other party that it will not accept performance, it loses its right to terminate if the other party in fact tenders within a reasonable time.

(4) If a party is excused under Article 8:108 through an impediment which is total and permanent, the contract is terminated automatically and without notice at the time the impediment arises.

COMMENT

A. *The requirement of notice*

Fair dealing requires that an aggrieved party which wishes to terminate a contract normally give notice to the defaulting party. The defaulting party must be able to make the necessary arrangements regarding goods, services and money at its disposal. Uncertainty as to whether the aggrieved party will accept performance or not may often cause a loss to the defaulting party which is disproportionate to the inconvenience which the aggrieved party will suffer by giving a notice. When performance has been made, passiveness on the side of the party which was to receive performance may cause the performing party to believe that the former has accepted the performance even if it was too late or defective. If, therefore, the aggrieved party wishes to terminate the contract it must notify the other party within reasonable time. The need to notify the other party within a reasonable time does not apply to cases of anticipatory repudiation (see Article 9:304).

Notice may be given either by expressly declaring the contract terminated or by rejecting the tender of performance.

B. *When performance has already been tendered but it was late or is defective*

Article 9:303 (2) states the general rule that will apply both when the aggrieved party has received a late tender of performance and when it has received a tender which was defective. In either case, once it knows or should know of the tender, it should have a reasonable time to check it for defects and to decide what to do; but if it waits for more than a reasonable time without notifying the other party that it is terminating the contract it loses the right to terminate. If it is prepared to accept the tender, it need not give any notice.

What is a reasonable time will depend upon the circumstances. For instance the aggrieved party must be allowed long enough for it to know whether or not the performance will still be useable by it. If delay in making a decision is likely to prejudice the defaulting party, for instance because it may lose the chance to prevent a total waste of its efforts by entering another contract, the reasonable time will be shorter than if this is not the case. If the defaulting party has tried to conceal the defects, a longer time may be allowed to the aggrieved party.

C. *When performance is overdue*

When a tender of performance is due but has not been made, the courses of action open to the aggrieved party will depend on the circumstances.

(1) It does not know whether the other party intends to perform or not but it wants performance. In that case it should seek specific performance, and under Article 9:102 (3) it must seek it within a reasonable time after it has or ought to have become aware of the non-performance.

(2) It does not know whether the other party intends to perform and either it does not want the performance or is undecided. In this case it may wait to see whether performance will ultimately be tendered and under Article 9:303 it may make up its mind if and when this happens. If the defaulting party wishes it may ask the aggrieved party whether it still wishes to receive performance, in which case the latter must answer without delay, see Article 1:201.

(3) It has reason to know that the defaulting party is still intending to perform within a reasonable time, but it no longer wishes to receive the performance. In this case it would be contrary to good faith for it to allow the defaulter to incur further effort in preparing to perform and then to terminate when performance is tendered. Therefore Article 9:303 (3)(b) requires it in this situation to notify the other party that it will not accept the performance, on pain of losing its right to terminate if the other party does in fact perform within a reasonable time.

D. *Exceptions to requirement of notice*
There are two exceptions to the rule that notice of termination must be given. The first is under Article 8:106 (3), according to which a notice setting a reasonable period during which the defaulting party must perform may provide that at the end of the period the contract shall terminate automatically if performance has still not been made.

The second is under Article 9:304 (4), which provides that where a party's non-performance is excused because it was due to a total and permanent impediment, the contract terminates automatically. Some legal systems regard the contract as destroyed by such an event.

Illustration: A famous tenor is engaged to sing at the opening ceremony of the World Cup. The tenor falls seriously ill and has not recovered by the date of the opening ceremony. Notice of termination need not be given.

In cases of only partial or temporary impediment, the defaulting party may still tender performance, and a notice of termination by the aggrieved party will be needed. Note that in cases of excused non-performance, the non-performing party has a duty under Article 8:103(3) to give notice of the impediment.

NOTES

Legal systems differ in their approach to the question of how termination is to be effected and how quickly the aggrieved party must act if he is not to lose the right. See *Treitel*, Remedies §§ 243-252.
1.   *Termination by notice to non-performing party*
    The Principles merely require notice to the non-performing party in order to terminate the contract. This accords with the COMMON LAW; DANISH Sale of Goods Act §§ 27, 32, and 52; FINNISH and SWEDISH Sale of Goods Acts, §§ 29, 39, 59. PORTUGUESE CC art. 436(1); and the DUTCH BW 6:267 allows rescission by notice. In SCOTTISH law, even notice is not always required: *McBryde* 324-325.
        Article 9:303 of the Principles is markedly different to systems such as the FRENCH, BELGIAN, ITALIAN or SPANISH which at least in general principle require court proceedings to effect termination: see FRENCH , BELGIAN and LUXEMBOURG CC art. 1184(2), ITALIAN CC art. 1453 and SPANISH CC art. 1124 (though in SPAIN a notice of termination may be effective if it is

accepted by the defaulting party: *Diez-Picazo*, II, 722; *Lacruz-Delgado* II, 1, § 26, 204; and *Ministerio de Justicia*, art. 1124). The time limit on the court's power to order termination is the general period of limitation (see French CC art.2262 and CCom. art. 189 bis; Italian CC art. 1453(1) and (2); Spanish CC art.1124); but in the case of defective goods the buyer, if he elects for *résolution*, must do so *dans un bref délai*, French and BELGIAN CC art. 1648. ITALIAN CC arts. 1454, 1456 and 1457, and Belgian caselaw, recognise exceptions to the rule that the creditor needs a court order to terminate: see *Dirix and van Oevelen*, R.W.1992-93, 1236; *van Ommeslaghe* R.C.J.B. 1986, nos.98-100; *M.E.Storme* T.B.B.R./R.G.D.C. 1991, 110-11, no.12. Article 9:303 also differs from rules such as the GERMAN and AUSTRIAN *Nachfrist* procedure noted earlier (see note to Article 8:106) which may require that the debtor be given reasonable notice before the contract is terminated even in cases other than simple delay.

CISG arts. 49 and 64 and *Unidroit* art. 7.3.2 adopt an approach similar to that of the Principles.

2.   *Notice of termination must be given within reasonable time*
The notice must generally be within a reasonable time of the non-performance. This corresponds broadly to many systems: eg DANISH Sale of Goods Act §§ 27, 32 ("promptly" or "within a short time"); FINNISH and SWEDISH Sale of Goods Acts, §§ 29, 32, 39, 59 ("reasonable time"); DUTCH BW art. 6:89 ("promptly"); FRENCH, BELGIAN and LUXEMBOURG CC art.1648 for *garantie des vices cachés ("dans un bref délai")* and, in Belgium, in some other cases on the basis of good faith, see Cass. 18 May 1987, Arr. Cass. 546 and Cass. 8 Apr. 1988, Arr.Cass., no.482; IRELAND "promptly and decisively", *Clark* 420; UK Sale of Goods Act 1979, ss.34 and 35 (and see *Treitel*, Contract 711); PORTUGUESE CC art.436(2); or the same result may be reached by application of the doctrine of good faith, eg in SPAIN and in GERMANY, see *Staudinger (-Otto)* § 325 no.96. AUSTRIAN and GERMAN law have special time limits for claims to terminate in cases of defects, e.g. ABGB §§ 932, 933, HGB § 377.

Some systems offer protection to the debtor by requiring that he be given reasonable notice before the contract is terminated: for example the German *Nachfrist* procedure noted earlier (see note to Article 8:106), under which the aggrieved party cannot demand performance after the notice period has expired, so that the non-performing party will know that after that date he no longer has to perform his obligations. Where a commercial contract containing a *Fixgeschäft* is not performed on time no *Nachfrist* is required, but the aggrieved party must notify the non-performing party promptly if he does not want to terminate, HGB § 376 (1) sentence 2. In other cases where no *Nachfrist* is required the aggrieved party may lose his right to terminate if he does not exercise it promptly (eg in the case of a non-commercial *Fixgeschäft: Palandt (-Heinrichs)* § 361 No. 3). DUTCH law also requires notice of default, unless the contract provides for a fixed time for performance, or the creditor must conclude from a communication by the debtor that the latter will fail to perform (BW § 6:82 and 6:83).

German law is not alone in allowing the non-performing party to set a reasonable time within which the aggrieved party must decide whether or not he wants to terminate (§§ 327, 355 BGB); see GREEK CC arts. 546, 395, 387(2): see *Michaelides-Nouaros* ErmAK II/1 art.382 no.15, art.383 no.22 (1949); PORTUGUESE CC art.436(2)).

3.   *The aggrieved party which knows the other still intends to perform*
There is no direct equivalent in any of the legal systems studied to Article 9:303(3)(b) but the same results might be reached by application of the doctrine of good faith or, in COMMON LAW, by promissory estoppel, at least where the aggrieved party had given some positive indication that he was still willing to accept performance; mere silence or inactivity would not create an estoppel, however, see *The Leonidas D* [1985] 1 W.L.R. 925, 937, C.A.

4.   *Automatic termination in cases of impossibility*
Several systems recognise that a contract comes to an end automatically if performance becomes impossible: e.g. ITALIAN CC art.1463. See further notes to Article 8:108 above.

Article 9:304: Anticipatory Non-Performance

Where prior to the time for performance by a party it is clear that there will be a fundamental non-performance by it, the other party may terminate the contract.

COMMENT

A. *Anticipatory non-performance equated with actual non-performance*

This Article entitles the aggrieved party to terminate the contract for "anticipatory non-performance", by which is meant an obvious unwillingness or inability to perform where the failure in performance would be fundamental within Article 8:103. The right to terminate for anticipatory non-performance rests on the notion that a party to a contract cannot reasonably be expected to continue to be bound by it once it has become clear that the other party cannot or will not perform at the due date. The effect of this Article is that for the purpose of the remedy of termination an anticipatory fundamental non-performance is equated with a fundamental non-performance after performance has become due.

> *Illustration 1*: In January B agrees to build a house for O and to start work on 1st May. In April B tells O that owing to labour troubles he will not be able to carry out the contract. O may immediately terminate the contract.

B. *Threatened non-performance must be fundamental*

Termination under this Article is permitted only where the obligation of which non-performance is threatened is of such kind that its breach would entitle the aggrieved party to terminate the contract. This applies also to a threatened delay in performance. If a party indicates that it will perform but that its performance will be late this does not constitute an anticipatory non-performance within this Article except where time of performance is of the essence of the contract or the threatened delay is so serious as to constitute a fundamental non-performance within Article 8:103.

> *Illustration 2*: B has agreed to build a house to O's design. B informs O that the double glazing specified by O is no longer available but that it can install double glazing from a different supplier which is almost identical. The failure to provide the double glazing originally specified would not, in these circumstances, be a fundamental non-performance, and O therefore cannot treat B's statement as indicating an anticipatory non-performance within this Article.

> *Illustration 3*: In January S contracts to sell goods to B for delivery on 1st March. In February S tells B that delivery will be a few days late. B can treat this as an anticipatory non-performance if time of delivery is of the essence, but not otherwise.

C. *Inability or unwillingness to perform must be manifest*

In order for this Article to apply it must be clear that a party is not willing or able to perform at the due date. If its behaviour merely engenders doubt as to its willingness or ability to perform the other party's remedy is to demand an assurance of performance under Article 8:105. See Illustration 1 of that Article.

D. *Remedies consequent on termination*

It is implicit in this Article that a party which exercises a right to terminate the contract for anticipatory non-performance has the same rights as on termination for actual non-performance and is therefore entitled to exercise any of the remedies available under this Chapter, including damages, except that damages are not recoverable where the non-performance at the due date would be excused under Article 3.108. See Article 8:101(2).

E. *Time for notification of termination*

The party faced with an anticipatory non-performance may terminate the contract at any time while it remains clear that there will be a fundamental non-performance by the other party.

NOTES

1.   *Anticipatory repudiation a recognised doctrine*
The root of this provision lies in COMMON LAW (cf. *Hochster* v. *de La Tour* (1853) E. & B. 678, Q.B.; *Universal Cargo Carriers Corp* v. *Citati* [1957] 2 Q.B. 401, Q.B.; *Clark* 414) and corresponds to SCOTTISH law. *Unidroit* art. 7.3.3, art. 72(1) CISG and art. 76 ULIS also adopt the notion of anticipatory repudiation. The FINNISH and SWEDISH Sale of Goods Acts, §§ 61 and 62 adopt the CISG rule: see *Ramberg,* Köplagen, 583 ff.

2.   *Some equivalent rule recognised*
The GERMAN BGB does not contain an express provision. However, there is unanimity that an umambiguous and definite refusal to perform is a non-performance, by analogy to BGB §§ 280, 286, 325, 326; cf. *Staudinger(-Otto)*, BGB § 326 nos. 135 FF.. Similarly in AUSTRIA, see *Rumell (-Reischauer)* ABGB § 918 no. 14.

Under DANISH Law the right of a party to terminate the contract in case of anticipatory non-performance is, in general, limited to cases where there is certainty, or probability amounting almost to certainty, that there will be a fundamental non-performance by the other party. This rule, however, is qualified: (1) when a buyer goes bankrupt or becomes insolvent and the time for delivery has come, the seller may terminate the contract unless security is provided (cf. § 39 Sale of Goods Act; § 57 Bankruptcy Act); (2) where the buyer of goods has been declared bankrupt and the administrator of the estate does not confirm the take-over of the contract within a reasonable time, the seller may terminate the contract (cf. § 40 Sale of Goods Act); (3) in a sale where the goods are to be delivered in instalments and where the delay or defect in respect of one instalment or payment for one instalment amounts to a fundamental non-performance (cf. Sale of Goods Act § 29: "unless there is no reason to expect a future delay"; see also §§ 22 and 46).

In DUTCH law, BW art. 6:80 provides that the consequences of non-performance operate although the obligation is not yet due (a) if performance is not possible without breach; (b) if from a communication of the debtor the creditor cannot but conclude that there will be a breach of performance; (c) if the creditor has good reasons to fear a breach of performance by the debtor, and has not received adequate assurance of the debtor's willingness to perform.

Under GREEK law, genuine anticipatory breach exists where the debtor before the date for performance expressly declares (AP 339/1982, NoB 30 (1982) 1459 at 1460) or by conduct necessarily implies (Athens 2671/1957, EEN 25 (1958) 538-539), that he will not perform. In such situations, CC art. 385(1) equally relieves the creditor from setting an additional period of performance, and allows him the remedies for damages and termination even prior to the date of performance (*Gasis* Erm. AK II/1 Introd. remarks to arts. 335-348 no. 62 (1949); *Georgiadis & Stathopoulos* II Introd. remarks to arts. 335-348 no.6 (1979); also cf. CC art. 686; in any case, the notice of termination, in terms of time and otherwise, may not result in an abuse of right (CC art. 281)).

In ITALIAN law CC art.1219 provides an automatic *mora debitoris* if the debtor declares in writing his unwillingness to perform. The way is then open for termination. On insolvency of the debtor, see CC art.1461.

3. No equivalent doctrine
In contrast, there is no general rule as to termination for anticipatory non-performance in FRENCH law, SPANISH law and PORTUGUESE law. This problem has hardly been subject to academic discussion nor regulated in the Codes. In general, the law is reluctant to support the aggrieved party prior to the time of performance (cf.SPAIN: *Lacruz-Delgado* II, 1, § 26, 200; *Albaladejo* II. 1, § 20.4 K and M; but termination for anticipatory non-performance is possible if the defaulting party's behaviour makes it clear that performance will not tke place: CC arts. 1129 and 1183). In Portuguese law, some of the results of anticipatory non-performance are reached in other ways: *Soares-Ramos* 195 ff.; STJ 15 March 1983, BMJ 325, 561; STJ 19 March 1985, BMJ 345, 400; STJ 19 February 1990, Act. jur., 1990. 2. 10. The same is true for BELGIUM: Cass. 5 June 1981, R.W. 1981-82, 245, R.C.J.B. 1983, 199; Cass. 15 May 1986, R.C.J.B. 1990, 106, Arr.Cass. no.565; *Vanwijck-Alexandre* Nos.177 and 199ff; *M.E.Storme,* Invloed no.299ff.

Article 9:305: Effects of Termination in General

(1) Termination of the contract releases both parties from their obligation to effect and to receive future performance, but, subject to Articles 9:306 to 9:308, does not affect the rights and liabilities that have accrued up to the time of termination.

(2) Termination does not affect any provision of the contract for the settlement of disputes or any other provision which is to operate even after termination.

COMMENT

A. *Meaning of termination*
Articles 9:305-9:309 govern the nature and effect of termination under the Principles.

"Termination" may have several distinct consequences (see *Treitel*, Remedies for Breach of Contract, ch. 9):

(1) The aggrieved party may wish to refuse to perform its own obligations. It may do this on a temporary basis without terminating the contract by withholding its performance under Article 9:201, but if it wishes to ensure that it will never be called upon to perform it will have to terminate the contract permanently.
(2) The aggrieved party may wish to refuse future performance (including cure of any defective performance already made) from the other party. This will also necessitate termination of the contract.
   Termination may involve nothing more than (1) and (2) where nothing has been done by either party, or where any performance made has already properly been rejected, or where the contract is to be performed in successive parts and the parts already performed are not affected. But either party may be left with property transferred by the other, or with a payment made by the other. If this is the case, then a third situation arises:
(3) Either party may wish to rid itself of a performance already received, to recover money transferred to the other party and/or to recover property, or its value, transferred to the other party; in other words, in some sense to "undo" what has taken place before the date of termination.

B. *Termination should not have retroactive effect*

Termination of the contract releases both parties from their duty to effect and to receive performance. It would be very inconvenient, however, to treat a contract which has been terminated as cancelled in the sense of never having been made. First, if the contract had never been made the aggrieved party might be precluded from claiming damages for loss of its expectations, which would not seem an appropriate outcome. Article 8:102 states that a party does not lose its right to damages by exercising another remedy. Secondly, if the contract were cancelled in the sense of never having been made, this might prevent the application of dispute settlement clauses or other clauses which were clearly intended to apply even if the contract were terminated. Therefore this article states that termination is not retroactive and specifically states the position on the clauses just mentioned.

> *Illustration 1*: The holder of a patent licences a firm in another country to make its product but forbids it to sell it under anything but the patent holder's trade mark. The licensee receives confidential information about production methods which it undertakes not to divulge so long as it is not publicly known. The contract contains a clause referring all disputes to arbitration. The licensee, in breach of the licence, markets the patented product under its own brand name, and the patent holder justifiably terminates the contract. Termination does not release the licensee from its obligation to keep the production information confidential, nor does it prevent the patent holder from seeking damages for non-performance of the contract, and the dispute must be referred to arbitration.

It would also be inconvenient to treat a contract which has been terminated as being retrospectively cancelled in the sense that performances received must be returned or restitution made of their value. This is not appropriate where the contract was to be performed over a period of time when there can be termination for the future without undoing what has been achieved already.

> *Illustration 2*: A cleaning company is employed to clean a law firm's office for 50 weeks at £500 per week. In the 25th week the cleaning company ceases trading and the law firm justifiably terminates the contract. The first 24 weeks' work have already been paid for; the payments are not affected by the termination.

C. *When performances received can be or should be returned*

Even though termination is forward looking in the way just explained, there are situations in which it is appropriate to "undo" what has taken place before termination. Thus the aggrieved party may need the right to reject a performance already received if termination means that it is of no value to it; either party may need to recover money already paid to the other party if nothing has been received in return; and either may need to be able to recover other property which has been transferred. These points are dealt with in Articles 9:306, 9:307 and 9:308 respectively.

NOTE

See Notes following Article 9:309.

Article 9:306: Property Reduced in Value

A party which terminates the contract may reject property previously received from the other party if its value to the first party has been fundamentally reduced as a result of the other party's non-performance.

COMMENT

Under many different types of contract there is a possibility that the aggrieved party may have received from the other some property which is of no value to it because of the other party's non-performance itself or because it has terminated the contract and will therefore not receive the rest of the performance. In such cases it should have the right to reject the useless property and this Article so provides.

Illustration 1: A firm of accountants agrees to lease a computerised accounts system, which requires a particular kind of computer. The lessor supplies the hardware but completely fails to supply the software. The accountants have no use for the hardware alone and may reject it.

This Article may also apply where the contract is to be performed in distinct instalments, if failure to deliver a later instalment makes the earlier instalments useless.

Illustration 2: A complete computer system is to be installed and paid for one component at a time so that it can be fitted into a new office as the building is being built. An essential item is not delivered and the buyer terminates. The buyer may reject the components already received.

In all the cases suggested the aggrieved party could in the alternative claim damages under Article 9:502 or reduction in price under Article 9:401 for the reduced value that the property received now has to it. However it will often be more convenient for it simply to return the unwanted property than to have to dispose of it some other way and, since it is by definition the aggrieved party, it seems appropriate to give it the right to reject. There will be a considerable advantage in rejecting the property if it has not yet paid for it, as it can thus avoid having to pay even a reduced price.

NOTE

See Notes following Article 9:309.

Article 9:307: Recovery of Money Paid

On termination of the contract a party may recover money paid for a performance which it did not receive or which it properly rejected.

COMMENT

A. *The general approach to restitution*
Article 9:305 states the general rule that termination of a contract has no retroactive effect. It does not follow from the fact that the contract has been terminated that the party which has performed can get restitution of what it has supplied.

In many contracts a literal restoration is not possible. This applies to work and labour, services, the hiring out of goods, the letting of premises, and the carriage and custody of goods. A party which has received a performance of this kind cannot give it back. In contracts for sale or barter restoration may become impossible when the goods have perished or have been consumed or resold. In all these situations the party which has received a performance which it cannot return might restore the value of it and various legal systems provide for such a restitution.

In contrast the Principles only give a restitutionary remedy after termination, where one party has conferred a benefit on the other party but has not received the promised counter-performance in exchange. The benefit may consist of money paid (Article 9:307), other property which can be returned (Article 9:308) or some benefit which cannot be returned, e.g. services or property which has been used up (Article 9:309).

B. *Restitution of money paid*
Under Article 9:307 a party may claim back money which it has paid for a performance which it did not receive. This rule has general application where a party which has prepaid money rightfully rejects performance by the other party or where the latter fails to effect any performance, Article 9:301. It applies equally to contracts of sale, contracts for work and labour and contracts of lease.

C. *Application to contracts to be performed in parts*
Where a contract is to be performed over a period of time, or in instalments, and the performance is divisible, the rule applies to payments made in respect of so much of the performance as was not made or has been rejected.

> *Illustration*: A has given B advance payment for the construction of 12 houses. B only builds 3 houses, and A terminates the contract. A can claim back the advance payment for the 9 houses which were not built.

If the aggrieved party is entitled to terminate under Article 9:302 in respect of a part of a contract, it may recover a payment made in respect of that part.

D. *Interest*
The party claiming restitution for money paid may also claim interest, Article 9:508.

NOTE

See Notes following Article 9:309.

Article 9:308: Recovery of Property

On termination of the contract a party which has supplied property which can be returned and for which it has not received payment or other counter-performance may recover the property.

COMMENT

A. *Restitution of property other than money*
Article 9:308 provides restitution after termination where a party has supplied a performance other than money without receiving the counterperformance, and the performance can be restored. If the contract is terminated it may claim back what it has supplied under the contract.

> *Illustration 1*: The contract called for A to deliver goods to be paid for by B upon their receipt. B did not pay for the goods when it received them. A may terminate the contract and claim back the goods from B.

B. *Third-party rights are not affected*
Like other Principles Article 9:308 deals exclusively with the relationship between the parties and not with the effect which the contract may have on the property in goods sold or bartered. Whether a creditor of the buyer, the buyer's receivers in bankruptcy, or a bona fide purchaser may oppose the restitution of goods sold is to be determined by the applicable national law.

C. *Claims by defaulting party*
The defaulting party may have transferred property to the aggrieved party before termination. If the aggrieved party can restore the property but does not do so, the court may order it to restore it or its value under Article 9:308.

D. *Contracts to be performed in parts*
The rule applies to contracts which are to be performed in parts. If the aggrieved party is entitled to terminate in respect of a part under Article 9:302, it may recover property transferred under that part of the contract.

E. *Negotiable instruments, securities and shares*
A contract for the sale or assignment of stocks, shares, investment securities, negotiable instruments and debts is often performed by delivering the warrant certificate or other instrument which gives evidence of the right. If the contract is terminated the seller or assignor should be entitled to recover the paper irrespective of whether

this paper is a negotiable instrument or not, subject to third party rights, see Comment B above.

F. *Industrial and intellectual property*

If a contract for the assignment of a product of the mind is terminated literal restoration of the intangible is sometimes not possible.

However, the assignment of patents, trade marks, and other legally protected intangible rights may be called off by a formal declaration or other act of the assignee and thereby returned to the assignor.

Furthermore, restoration is possible of things which attach to the intangible. Know-how and literary works are written on paper, paintings are made on canvas, sculptures cast in bronze. Tangible things which in this way materialize the product of the mind may be restored when the contract is terminated. These things often have a value.

Illustration 2: A famous artist contracts with B to make illustrations for a new edition of Homer's Odyssey to be published by B; the copyright is to rest in B. When B receives the drawings he does not pay for them. The artist may terminate the contract and claim the illustrations back; the copyright must also be revested in him.

G. *Restitution in case of bad bargains*

Restitution may be claimed when the aggrieved party has performed all its obligations under the contract and only the other party's obligation to pay the price remains outstanding. It does not matter that the property is worth more than was to be paid for it so that by obtaining restitution the aggrieved party escapes a bad bargain.

Illustration 3: A has sold a Renoir painting to B for US$200,000; the true value of the painting is over US$250,000. When the picture is delivered to B, he does not pay for it. A is entitled to claim back the painting.

H. *Restitution is impossible or too onerous*

The rules in Chapter 4 Section 1 on right to performance apply *mutatis mutandis* to the claim for restitution. The aggrieved party cannot claim back the goods or other tangibles when it has become impossible or would involve the defaulting party in an unreasonable effort or expense.

Illustration 4: A has painted a fresco which has been mounted on a wall in B's house and for which B has not paid A. Although it would be physically possible to dismantle the fresco the costs would be disproportionately high. A cannot claim back the fresco. Its remedy is under Article 9:309.

NOTES

See Notes following Article 9:309.

Article 9:309: Recovery for Performance that Cannot be Returned

On termination of the contract a party which has rendered a performance which cannot be returned and for which it has not received payment or other counter-performance may recover a reasonable amount for the value of the performance to the other party.

COMMENT

A. *General*

It frequently happens that after a contract has been terminated one party is left with a benefit which cannot be returned – either because the benefit is the result of work which cannot be returned, or because property which has been transferred has been used up or destroyed – but for which it has not paid. The other party may have a claim for the price, but this will depend upon the agreed payment terms and the price may not yet be payable. It may have a claim for damages, but the party which has received the benefit may be the aggrieved party, or, though it is the one which has failed to perform, it may not be liable for damages because its non-performance was excused under Article 8:108. It would be unjust to allow it to retain this benefit without paying for it, and Article 9:309 requires it to pay.

Illustration 1: A contract to build a garage onto a house provides that the builder is to be paid only upon completion of the work. After doing two-thirds of the work, the builder becomes insolvent and stops work. The employer gets another builder to finish the garage. The amount the employer has to pay the second builder plus compensation for the employer's inconvenience is less than the original contract price and the employer receives a net benefit. Under Article 9:309 it must pay the first builder a reasonable sum for the work done: in this case the reasonable sum would be the net benefit the employer received from the first builder's work.

Illustration 2: A farmer employs a contractor to lay drain pipes in her field for a lump sum of £10,000. The contractor lays some of the pipes which drain part of the field. Then exceptionally bad weather causes the remaining parts of the field to become waterlogged and, because the contractor's machinery will churn up the field and damage it, the farmer tells the contractor to stop work temporarily. After serving a notice under Article 8:106, the contractor terminates. Although the farmer is not liable in damages because her non-performance was excused under Article 8:108, the contractor may recover for the pipes already laid under Article 9:309.

B. *Calculating the benefit*

The party which has received the benefit should not be required to pay the cost to the other of having provided it, if the net benefit to it is less, since it is only enriched by the latter amount.

Illustration 3: as Illustration 2, but the contractor has not yet installed enough pipe to carry off a significant amount of water and it has used its own special type of pipe so that the drainage system cannot be completed by another contractor. The net benefit to the farmer is nil and she should not have to pay anything under Article 9:309.

Occasionally it may happen that the net benefit to the recipient is greater than the cost of providing it. Then the recipient should not be liable under this article for more than an appropriate part of the contract price.

Illustration 4: The holder of an oil concession in a foreign country employs an exploration company to make a geological survey of the concession for £250,000. After the exploration company has worked for only a short time it is prevented from completing the survey by the government of the foreign country nationalising the concession, but in that time it has found oil and because of this the owner is paid millions in compensation by the government. The exploration company should recover only a proportionate part of the exploration fee, not a proportion of the compensation.

Notes

Notes to 9:305-9:309
These notes covers Articles 9:305-9:309, which together govern the effects of termination.
The various legal systems exhibit great differences in concepts and terminology in this area. The differences in the practical results obtained are not so great but are still significant.
The most apparent difference is between systems such as the FRENCH which treats *résolution* as essentially retrospective and those such as the COMMON LAW which sees termination (or "rescission for breach") as essentially prospective (see *Treitel*, Remedies §§ 282-283). However, as the differences are sometimes more apparent than real it may be helpful to consider the effect of "termination" in the various systems in a number of factual situations:
1. *Effect on claims by either party which arose before the date of termination*
    In "prospective" systems such as the COMMON LAW these claims are largely unproblematic: they are not affected by subsequent termination, except that if money due but as yet unpaid would in any event have to be repaid after termination, it will for obvious reasons cease to be payable (see *Treitel*, Contract 911). It seems likely that other systems would reach the same result even if in theory termination was retrospective; for instance, in FRENCH law for a contract *à exécution successive* only *résiliation* for the future might be ordered (see note 4 below).
    In GERMAN law it used to be said that *Rücktritt* had a retrospective effect but this view is no longer accepted. Contractual claims for damages which arose before termination are now treated as surviving termination which is said only to end the primary duty to perform and the right to damages for loss of expectation (see, *Larenz* I 404; *Treitel*, Remedies § 282 and refs. there).
    In DUTCH law termination does not have a retroactive effect: BW art. 6:269. In SPANISH law some writers favour prospective termination (*Diez-Picazo*, II, 724), others maintain the traditional, retrospective approach (*Lacruz-Delgado*, II, 1, § 26.206 and *Albadejo* II, 1, § 24.45) The Supreme Court, 28 June 1977, has adopted prospective termination when past performances were unaffected. See also *Unidroit* art. 7.3.6(2).
2. *Damages for the non-performance itself*
    The conceptual difficulties felt in some systems in awarding full damages for breach of a contract which has been terminated are discussed above, see note to Article 8:102. Most systems now allow full damages despite termination.
3. *Effect on contract clauses intended to apply even after termination*
    All systems now accept that termination will not affect the application of clauses such as arbitration

clauses which were intended to apply despite termination. Eg COMMON LAW: *Heyman* v. *Darwins* [1942] A.C. 356, H.L.; FINLAND: *Aurejärvi* 106; FRANCE: *clause compromissoire* (NCPC art. 1466) and penalty clause (*Malaurie & Aynès,* Obligations no.543); GERMANY, see *Stein-Jonas* (*-Schlosser*) § 1025 No. 00; GREEK law, see *Kerameus* 171-173, with further refs, and *Papanicolaou* in *Georgiadis & Stathopoulos* II art.389 no.14 (1979); ITALIAN law: no specific text but see *Satta* 852; Cass. 5 Aug.1968 n.2803, in Foro It., 1969, I c.445 and Cass. 27.May.1981 n.3474, in Foro It., 1982, I c.199; NETHERLANDS BW art.6:271; PORTUGUESE CC art. 434(1); SPANISH Arbitration Act 1988 (see *Bercovitz*, Arbitraje, art. 1, 17 ff.); and *Unidroit* art. 7.3.5.(3).

4. *Effect on previously performed parts of a contract for successive performances*
All systems now accept that where a contract for performance in successive parts or instalments is terminated after some parts of it have been performed, it may be terminated for the future without the need to undo the completed parts (see *Treitel*, Remedies § 283). In FRENCH, BELGIAN and LUXEMBOURG law, *résolution* is only retroactive when the contract is to be performed at one time: for a contract *à exécution successive* the contract is treated as disappearing only from the date at which the debtor ceased performing or was given notice of termination by the aggrieved party. In this context the process is often termed *résiliation* (*Malaurie & Aynès*, Obligations nos. 743 and 744). In ITALIAN law termination is in principle retrospective but for contracts involving continuous or periodic performance see CC art.1458. In PORTUGUESE law termination does not affect performances already rendered unless they are affected by the non-performance, CC art. 434(2). In SPANISH law termination is not necessarily retroactive and does not affect past performance if this is not rendered useless by the non-performance, see note 1 above.

5. *Property already received and reduced in value by the subsequent non-performance*
Most systems also recognise the rule embodied in Article 9:306 that the aggrieved party may reject property which has already been delivered to him, and which was itself in conformity to the contract, if the subsequent non-performance has rendered it of no use or interest to him. For instance, in GERMAN law, if the performances are inter-related either party can demand return of the earlier -delivered part. In ENGLISH and IRISH law, where a part of the goods to be delivered are defective, the buyer may reject the whole (U.K. Sale of Goods Act 1979, s.30; for Ireland, see *Forde* § 1.192), and this will apply even if the goods are to be delivered in instalments provided that the instalments are similarly inter-connected and thus the contract is not severable (see *Gill & Dufus SA* v. *Berger & Co Inc* [1983] 1 Lloyd's Rep. 622, reversed without reference to this point [1984] A.C. 382, H.L.; *Atiyah* 452). The position with severable contracts is less clear but probably there is a right to reject instalments already received if they are rendered useless by the later breach (*Atiyah* 455; *Forde* § 1.198). The DANISH Sale of Goods Act, § 46, and the FINNISH and SWEDISH Sale of Goods Acts §§ 43 and 44 (see *Ramberg*, Köplagen 462), provide that a buyer who has received a defective instalment can reject instalments received earlier if the instalments are so inter-connected that it would be detrimental to the buyer to have to keep the earlier ones. In ITALIAN law there is no general provision but under CC art.1672 when a construction contract is terminated the purchaser has only to pay for work done so far as it is of value to him.

6. *Inability to restore property may be a bar to termination*
Under some systems a party who has received property may not be permitted to terminate either the contract as a whole, where it was for a single performance, or, where it was by instalments, in relation to the part already received, if he cannot return what he has received, for instance because he has consumed or resold it. Generally this rule applies where the inability to restore is attributable to the acts of the party who received the goods: DANISH Sale of Goods Act, §§ 57 and 58; FINNISH and SWEDISH Sale of Goods Acts, § 66 (see *Ramberg*, Köplagen 637 f.); BELGIAN case law, e.g. C.A. Gent 22 Oct. 1970, R.W. 1970-71, 893; C.A. Liège 10 Nov. 1982, J.L. 1983, 153; GERMAN law, BGB § 351; GREEK CC arts. 391-394. It does not apply when the defect constitutes a non-performance: FRENCH CC art. 1647(1); GERMAN law, BGB § 351 and *Enneccerus & Lehmann* 169, 445-446; ENGLISH law, *Rowland* v. *Divall* [1923] 2 K.B. 500, C.A.. When the inability is due to accidental destruction, solutions differ: see the discussion in *Treitel*, Remedies § 285.

With services, in contrast, the usual rule seems to be that the fact that there is nothing to be returned does not prevent termination (*ibid.*). Systems differ as to whether the aggrieved party must make restitution of the value of what he received (see below).

The Principles, like AUSTRIAN and FRENCH law (see Malaurie & Aynès § 762) and the DUTCH BW, do not follow this distinction. In neither case is inability to restore a bar to termination; the aggrieved party will however be expected to pay for benefits received, see below. In this the Principles differ from CISG art.82.

7. *Action for price may be the only remedy*
In some systems, eg the COMMON LAW, there is a rule that if the claiming party has completed its

performance, or a severable part of it, the only remedy is an action for the agreed price. Thus a seller of goods who has delivered them to the buyer but has not been paid cannot terminate the contract and recover the goods but can only bring an action for the price. The only exception is if the property in the goods has not passed to the buyer, for instance because the contract provided that property would not pass until the goods were paid for (see *Aluminium Industrie* v. *Romalpa Aluminium* [1976] 1 W.L.R. 676, C.A.). DANISH Sale of Goods Act § 28(2), FINNISH and SWEDISH Sale of Goods Acts, § 54(4) and GREEK CC art.531 provide the same rule and so does GERMAN BGB § 454 where the seller has allowed time for payment of the purchase price. The AUSTRIAN Commercial Code is to the same effect, 4.EVHGB Art. 8 No.21.

The Principles do not adopt this rule, but they do not deal with the rights of creditors and other third parties to oppose restoration of property delivered, see below.

8.   *Effect of termination on performances already received*

Assuming that the right to terminate exists, what effect will termination have on performances made already? Most systems require that each party returns benefits received from the other or makes restitution of their value. However the situation is complex and the remainder of this note is devoted to it.

The position is simpler under systems which regard termination as retroactive, for then restitution of benefits appears as a natural concomitant of termination: eg FRENCH, BELGIAN and LUXEMBOURG CC arts. 1379 and 1380 read with art.1184; GREEK CC art.389(2); AP 661/1974, NoB 23 (1975) 275, 276 I; AP 696/1982, NoB 31 (1983) 659-660; PORTUGUESE CC arts. 434(1) and 289; SPANISH law, see note 1 above.

Other systems under which termination is not retrospective nonetheless recognise a general duty to make restitution: DUTCH BW art. 6:271. For SCOTTISH law, under which there may be restitution of unreciprocated performances, see *MacQueen* 1997 Acta Juridica 176. In GERMAN law it is now held that *Rücktritt* does not retrospectively do away with the contract but it creates general obligations of restitution, BGB § 346. In AUSTRIA ABGB § 921 provides that as a result of a notice of termination because of late performance or non-performance, any consideration previously given must be returned or refunded in such a manner that neither party profits from any losses the other may suffer.

In contrast, the COMMON LAW allows only partial restitutionary remedies.

It may be helpful to consider each of the three situations covered by Articles 9:307 to 9:309 in turn.

(a)   *Money paid*

If money has been paid before the date of termination, and assuming that it was not paid as a deposit or on terms that it would be forfeited if the contract was not performed, systems in which termination is seen as retroactive will normally allow the money to be recovered. It does not matter whether the party seeking to recover the money is the aggrieved party or the non-performing party: FRENCH law, *Malaurie & Aynès*, Obligations no.376 and FRENCH and BELGIAN CC arts. 1376-1377; ITALIAN CC arts. 1458, 2033 and, for sales, arts. 1479(2) and 1493(1). For GERMAN, GREEK, PORTUGUESE and SPANISH law see above; DANISH law see Sale of Goods Act § 57 and *Ussing, Køb* 164-165; FINNISH and SWEDISH law see Sale of Goods Acts, § 64 and *Ramberg,* Köplagen 614ff.

The COMMON LAW is more restrictive. Except in cases of frustration (now governed by Law Reform (Frustrated Contracts) Act 1943, s.1(2)), it allows recovery by the aggrieved party only where there has been "a total failure of consideration" and by the non-performing party only where the party who had received the money can be restored to his original position (see *Treitel*, Remedies § 284; *Treitel*, Contract 822-824, 906-907, and 911).

ULIS art. 78(2) and CISG art.81(2) take the same broad approach to restitution as the Principles.

(b)   *Property transferred*

If the property remains in the possession of the party to whom it was transferred, and is not claimed by a third party, the "retroactive" systems allow the transferor to recover it: eg FRENCH law, *Malaurie & Aynès*, Obligations no.376 and FRENCH and BELGIAN CC art. 1379; ITALIAN CC arts. 1458(2) and 1493(2) (sales); FINNISH and SWEDISH Sale of Goods Act § 64(2).

Systems differ where a third party such as a creditor of the recipient claims the property. In GERMAN law the right to the return of the property is only a "contractual" one and third parties' interests will not be affected. See also AUSTRIAN ABGB § 921, second sentence; SPANISH law (*Albaladejo*, II, 1, § 20.4.U: Supreme Court 1 October 1986); GREEK CC art.393. The result is the opposite in FRENCH law, where the effect is in principle (but subject to important restrictions) "proprietary" (see *Malaurie et Aynès*, Obligations, No.743; *Nicholas*, 245-246; *Treitel*, Remedies § 282). The Principles follow ULIS and CISG in leaving the question of whether the right to restitution enables the claiming party actually to recover the goods in the face of competing claims by third parties to the law applicable to the issue.

(c)   *Restitution for services.*

"Retroactive" systems again have little difficulty in allowing either party upon termination to recover the value of services rendered under the principle of unjust enrichment. On FRENCH law, see *Ghestin, Jamin & Billiau* § 482ff.; BELGIAN law, Cass. 27 March 1972, Arr. Cass. 707; ITALIAN law, where there is no provision as to contracts in general (but see CC art.1672 and Cass. 5 Aug. 1988 no.4849, in Mass. Foro It., 1988; Cass. 23 June 1982 no.3827, in Mass. Foro It., 1982; Cass. 13.1.1972 n.106 in Rassegna Avvocatura Stato, part I, 1972, 161); POR-TUGUESE CC arts. 434(1) and, when the performance cannot be returned, 289(1); for SCOT-TISH law, see *Graham* v. *United Turkey Red Co.* 1922 S.C. 583.

For this case GERMAN law has a special rule that where the counter-performance has been fixed in money this amount shall be paid: BGB § 346 sent.2 (see further Treitel, *Remedies* § 284). GREEK law reaches the same result: *Gasis* in Erm.AK II/1, art.389 no. 11 (1949). In DANISH law the party who has rendered a performance which cannot be returned is not entitled to its value or the enrichment which the other party has received if he can claim the counter-performance or damages, *Ussing*, Alm.Del. 98. Under DUTCH BW art. 6:272 the party who has rendered performance is entitled to its value.

In SCOTLAND if a contract is frustrated the obligations of the parties under the contract cease but there may be an equitable adjustment of the rights of the parties under the principles of unjust enrichment (*Cantiere San Rocco* v. *Clyde Shipbuilding and Engineering Co* 1923 S.C. (H.L.) 105).

The COMMON LAW provides, as already mentioned, that if the claiming party has completed its performance, or a severable part of it, the only remedy is an action for the agreed price. In the situation of partial performance it distinguishes between cases of frustration (impossibility) and cases of breach. Where the contract has been frustrated, the court has discretion under Law Reform (Frustrated Contracts) Act 1943, s.1(3) to award what are basically restitutionary awards (see the judgment of Robert Goff J in *BP Exploration Co (Libya) Ltd* v. *Hunt* [1979] 1 W.L.R. 783, though see also Lawton LJ in [1981] 1 W.L.R. 232, C.A.). Where the contract is terminated for breach, the aggrieved party may recover a reasonable sum; the defaulting party may recover nothing (see *Treitel*, Contract 696-699, 592).

Again the Principles follow ULIS, CISG and *Unidroit* art. 7.3.6(1) in taking a broad flexible approach.

Thus the Principles are broadly in accordance with those systems which take a liberal approach to restitution after termination and thus enable the court or arbitrator to order full restitution of benefits received. This normally achieves a just settlement on the facts.

Section 4

Price Reduction

Article 9:401: Right to Reduce Price

(1) A party which accepts a tender of performance not conforming to the contract may reduce the price. This reduction shall be proportionate to the decrease in the value of the performance at the time this was tendered compared to the value which a conforming tender would have had at that time.

(2) A party which is entitled to reduce the price under the preceding paragraph and which has already paid a sum exceeding the reduced price may recover the excess from the other party.

(3) A party which reduces the price cannot also recover damages for reduction in the value of the performance but remains entitled to damages for any further loss it has suffered so far as these are recoverable under Section 5 of this Chapter.

COMMENT

A. *The principle of price reduction*
This Article generalises the remedy provided by the *actio quanti minoris*. In the conditions laid down in paragraph (1) the aggrieved party is entitled to a reduction in the contract price where the other party's performance is incomplete or otherwise fails to conform to the contract. The remedy is given whether the non-conformity relates to quantity, quality, time of delivery or otherwise. The remedy is designed both as an alternative to damages (see Illustration 2 below) and for cases where the non-performing party is excused from liability for damages (see comment B below). The Article applies only where the aggrieved party accepts the non-conforming tender. If it does not, its remedy is either to pursue a restitutionary claim under Article 9:307 or to claim damages under Section 5.

The amount of the price reduction is proportional to the reduction in the value of the promised performance. In some cases the value of the performance will be directly related to the proportion of the contract performed and the contract price may simply be reduced accordingly.

Illustration 1: S contracts to sell 50 tonnes of coffee to B at a price of £2,400 a tonne. S tenders only 30 tonnes. B may accept the short tender and reduce the price under this Article from £120,000 to £72,000 (see Illustration 3). Alternatively B can reject the short tender, in which case it can either claim recovery of the price under Article 9:307 or claim damages under Section 5, but it cannot invoke the present Article.

In other cases the value of the performance may be reduced by a greater (or less) proportion.

Illustration 2: B agrees to build a house for O for £150,000. If the work had been properly executed the house would have been worth £100,000 when completed, but because of B's defective workmanship it is worth only £80,000. As an alternative to claiming damages of £20,000, O may withhold or recover one-fifth of the price, i.e. £30,000.

B. *Price reduction available even where non-performance excused*
The fact that a shortfall in performance is excused under Article 8:108 does not affect the aggrieved party's right to a price reduction under this Article, for under Article 8:101(2) the only remedies which are excluded in the case of an excused non-performance are specific performance and damages.

Illustration 3: S in Marseilles contracts to sell 20 hospital scanning machines to B in London. As the result of the introduction of a quota system governing the export of scanning machines S is only able to supply B with 15 machines. S's non-performance is excused under Article 8:108 but if B decides to accept the 15 machines it is entitled to a price reduction of 25 per cent.

C. *Price reduction may be obtained before or after payment*
The aggrieved party may obtain a price reduction under this Article either by withholding payment, if it has not already paid the price, or by recovering the amount of the price reduction if the price has already been paid.

D. *Price reduction is alternative to damages for reduction in value*
Where the aggrieved party reduces the price under this Article it cannot also claim damages for reduction in the value of the performance as tendered compared with the value of a conforming tender (see Illustration 1). The two remedies are incompatible so that there is no right to cumulate them under Article 8:102. However, other loss remains recoverable within the limits laid down by Section 5.

Illustration 4: The facts are as in Illustration 2. O cannot live in the house until the defects in it have been put right and he incurs a loss of £500 in renting an apartment to live in meanwhile. The £500 remains recoverable whichever of the above remedies he pursues.

NOTES

1. *Civil law*
   (a) *The actio quanti minoris*
   The right to reduce the price, as provided in Article 9:401, is found in the civil law countries and in CISG art. 50. It is primarily applied when goods sold are defective, see AUSTRIAN ABGB § 932(1); DANISH Sale of Goods Act § 42 and 43; FINNISH and SWEDISH Sale of Goods Acts, §§ 37, 38; FRENCH, BELGIAN and LUXEMBOURG CC art. 1644; GERMAN BGB § 462; GREEK CC arts. 534, 535, 540; ITALIAN CC art. 1492(1); and PORTUGUESE CC arts. 911 and 913. However, in many countries the rule also applies to other contracts, see DANISH Lease Act §§ 11 (2)15 and 16 (2) and on construction contracts, *Gomard*, Obligationsret II 129 ff.; FINLAND, Sale of real property and service contracts, see *Sisula-Tulokas* 18-36; GERMAN BGB §§ 515 (barter), 537 (lease), 634(1) and (4) (work, but not services) and 651(d) (travel); GREEK CC arts. 573 (barter), 576 (lease) and 688 and 689 (work); ITALIAN CC art. 1668 (construction contracts); PORTUGUESE CC art. 1222 (work); and SPAIN CC art. 1486 (sales). In FRANCE, outside cases of defects, price reduction *(réfaction)* is limited to commercial cases, as a consequence of usages: *Terré*, No 630, in fine; but there is a tendency to generalise it to other contracts: Civ.3, 15 December 1993, D.1994.462, note Storck (lease).

   The DUTCH BW treats price reduction as partial termination which in principle is available in all contracts, see BW arts. 6:265 and 6:270.

   In the civil law the *actio quanti minoris* applies also where the non-performance is excused.
   (b) *Calculation of the reduction*
   As in Article 9:401, CISG art. 50 provides that the buyer may reduce the price in the same proportion as the value that the goods actually delivered had at the time of delivery bears to the value that conforming goods would have had at that time, and the same rule applies in most civil law countries, see e.g. GERMAN BGB § 472 (value at the time of contracting).
   (c) *Recovery of the excess paid*
   The rule stated in Article 9:401(2) under which a party which has paid the full price may recover the excess is probably accepted in all countries.
   (d) *Damages not excluded*
   It is in the nature of things that a party which reduces the price cannot also claim a sum equal to the reduction in value as damages. However, most laws allow the aggrieved party to recover damages for further loss. See e.g. AUSTRIAN ABGB § 932(1) last sentence stating, that "in all cases, the transferor is liable for damages caused by his fault". See also CISG art. 45(2) and notes to Article 8:102, above. In GERMANY, however, damages and reduction of price exclude each other, see BGB §§ 463, 480(2); *Münchener Kommentar (-Westermann)* § 472 no. 3. This is also true in GREECE, but further loss may be recovered: *Deliyannis & Kornlakis* I 243-244. Under SPANISH law the aggrieved party can recover damages if the other party acted in bad faith (CC art. 1486(2)).

2. *Common Law*
   The *actio quanti minoris* of the civil law is unknown in the COMMON LAW, but when the non-performance is not excused Common law reaches very similar results.
   (a) *Cases of breach*
   Where goods are defective the *prima facie* rule is that the buyer can recover as damages the difference between the value of the goods actually delivered and the value which the goods would have had if they had been in accordance with the contract, see *Treitel*, Remedies § 100. Further,
   (i) where the performance is incomplete and the price can easily be apportioned, the buyer may treat the contract as apportionable and pay only for the units delivered (e.g. *Dawood Ltd.* v. *Heath Ltd.* [1961] 2 Lloyd's Rep 512, Q.B.);
   (ii) The UK Sale of Goods Act 1979, s.53(1) allows the buyer in case of defects to set up certain claims "in diminution or extinction of the price"; and
   (iii) The aggrieved party may also – and this applies to all contracts – set off claims arising out of the same transaction against sums he would otherwise have to pay.
   On (ii) and (iii) see *Beale*, Remedies 50-52 and *Goode*, Commercial Law 671. As in most civil law countries, further loss may be claimed as damages.
   (b) *Non-performance excused*
   In cases of frustration the position of English law differs from that of the civil law. The Law Reform (Frustrated Contracts) Act 1943 s. 1 (3) will normally apply. As a measure, sometimes

described as essentially restitutionary (see Robert Goff J. in *B.P. Exploration Co.(Libya) Ltd. v. Hunt (No.2)* [1979] 1 W.L.R. 783, though see also Lawton LJ in the C.A. [1981] 1 W.L.R. 232), the court may order the return of money paid and payment for benefits (other than money) received before the time of discharge of the obligation, subject to deductions for expenses incurred, see *Treitel*, Contracts 825-829.

In the unusual case where the contract is not frustrated but non-performance of part of the obligation is excused, whether the price may be reduced will probably depend on whether the performance can easily be apportioned, see (a)(i) above.

In SCOTLAND if a contract is frustrated the obligations of the parties under the contract cease but there may be an equitable adjustment of the rights of the parties under the principles of unjust enrichment (*Cantiere San Rocco* v. *Clyde Shipbuilding and Engineering Co* 1923 S.C. (H.L.) 105).

See generally on the common law *Treitel*, Remedies § 100; *Beale*, Remedies 50-52.

Section 5

Damages and Interest

Article 9:501: Right to Damages

(1) The aggrieved party is entitled to damages for loss caused by the other party's non-performance which is not excused under Article 8:108.

(2) The loss for which damages are recoverable includes:

    (a) non-pecuniary loss; and

    (b) future loss which is reasonably likely to occur.

COMMENT

A. *No damages without loss*

This Article enables the aggrieved party to recover damages whenever it suffers loss from the other party's unjustified failure to perform. The section does not provide for nominal damages for a breach which has caused the aggrieved party no loss.

B. *No fault necessary*

Where a party's obligation is to produce a given result, its failure to do so entitles the aggrieved party to damages whether or not there has been fault by the non-performing party, except where performance is excused (see Article 8:108 and Comment). Where a party's obligation is not to produce a result but merely to use reasonable care and skill it is liable only if it has failed to fulfill its obligation, that is to say if it has not exercised the care and skill it has promised. In the absence of a clause specifying the required degree of care and skill, this is equivalent to the commission of a fault.

Illustration 1: A contracts to supply and install in B's house a central heating system that will provide a temperature of up to 22 degrees C when the outside temperature is no greater than 0 degrees C. A installs the sytem but despite the exercise of all reasonable care and skill on its part the maximum temperature it can achieve is 18 degrees C. A is liable for damages.

Illustration 2: A, a surgeon undertakes to carry out a major operation on B. Despite all reasonable care and skill on A's part, the operation is unsuccessful. A is not liable, for her undertaking was merely to act carefully, not to guarantee a successful outcome.

C. *All forms of failure in performance covered*

This Article applies to all forms of failure in performance: see Article 1:301(a). There is no requirement that the aggrieved party serve a notice to perform before it can recover damages for delay.

Illustration 3: S agrees to build a boat for B for £ 100,000. No time for completion is fixed by the contract but a reasonable time would be six months. S takes nine months to complete the boat and make it available to B. S is liable for damages for the delay, whether or not B has given notice requiring the boat to be finished within a given period.

D. *Loss that would not have occurred without the failure in performance*

The aggrieved party may not recover damages for loss not caused by the failure to perform. However, not every intervening event, even if unforeseeable, which exacerbates the loss falls within this principle. The question in each case is whether that event would have had an impact on the contract if the failure in performance had not occurred. Only if this question is answered in the affirmative will the event in question be treated as breaking the chain of causation.

Illustration 4: S agrees to sell to B machinery which S knows is required by B to manufacture goods in its factory. The machinery is due to be delivered on 1st June but S fails to make delivery. B is losing profit at the rate of £1,000 for each week's delay. This is a normal level of profit for a business of this kind. On 29th June a fire breaks out in B's factory, which is burnt to the ground. On 16th July S delivers the machinery. B, which would not have been able to put the machinery to use elsewhere during this period, can recover £4,000 damages for the loss of profit up to 29th June but nothing for loss suffered beyond that date.

Illustration 5: In June S in London agrees to sell a quantity of machine guns to a weapons dealer, B, in Serbia for £50,000, the guns to be shipped by 30th September against payment. In July S decides that he does not wish to support B's arms business and informs B that he does not intend to ship the guns. In August the British government places an embargo on the exportation of arms to the former Yugoslavian Republics and this is still in force when B's claim for damages is heard 18 months later. B is not entitled to damages.

Illustration 6: In June S in Paris contracts so sell a Seurat painting to B in Hamburg for FF. 1 million, the painting to be shipped to B in Hamburg by the end of August. Because of the delays on the part of its staff S is unable to arrange shipment earlier than 1st October. On 5th September the French governement impose a ban on the exportation of works of art without a licence, and despite using its best endeavors S is unable to obtain a licence to export the Seurat painting. The value of the painting at the end of August is considered by experts to be FF. 2 millions. B is entitled to damages of FF. 1 million, the difference between the value of the painting and its price, since but for S's delay in shipping the painting its export would not have been affected by the ban.

E. *Non-pecuniary loss*

Recoverable loss is not confined to pecuniary loss but may cover, for example, pain and suffering, inconvenience and mental distress resulting from the failure to perform.

> *Illustration 7*: A books a package holiday from B, a travel organisation. The package includes a week in what is described as spacious accommodation in a luxury hotel with excellent cuisine. In fact, the bedroom is cramped and dirty and the food is appalling. A is entitled to recover damages for the inconvenience and loss of enjoyment he has suffered.

F. *Future loss*

The loss recoverable by the aggrieved party includes future loss, that is, loss expected to be incurred after the time damages are assessed. This requires the court to evaluate two uncertainties, namely the likelihood that future loss will occur and its amount. As in the case of accrued loss before judgment (see Article 9:502) this covers both prospective expenditure which would have been avoided but for the breach and gains which the aggrieved party could reasonably have been expected to make if the breach had not occurred. Future loss often takes the form of the loss of a chance.

> *Illustration 8*: E is appointed sales manager of F's business under a three-year service contract. She is to be paid a salary and a commission on sales. After 12 months E is wrongfully dismissed, and despite reasonable efforts to find an alternative post she is still out of work when her action for wrongful dismissal is heard six months later. E is entitled to damages not only for her accrued loss of six months salary but also for the remaining 18 months of her contract, due allowance being made for her prospects of finding another job meanwhile. She is also entitled to damages for loss of the commission she would probably have earned.

NOTES

1. *Loss*

    It is a common feature of the legal systems in the European Communities that damages are awarded only if and to the extent the aggrieved party has suffered a loss as a consequence of the non-performance of the contract. This applies both to pecuniary and to non-pecuniary loss, see on the latter note 4 below. The only exception may be the COMMON LAW where even if the aggrieved party has suffered no loss, nominal damages are allowed in case of breach of contract. In SCOTLAND, while what are described as nominal damages have been awarded, it would appear that in the cases concerned there has been loss in the form of inconvenience, see *McBryde* § 20-87.

    The legal systems seem to agree that damages are not awarded if there has been a gain for the defaulting party but no loss to the aggrieved party. Nor are punitive damages awarded.

2. *Strict liability or fault liability*
    Some laws impose strict liability on the defaulting party, others require fault, and others again have a mixed system, where the defaulting party is strictly liable in some cases and where it is liable only for fault in other cases. See on this issue the notes to Article 8:101, above.

3. *Notice*

    (a) *Notice of non-performance not required*
         As in the Principles, notice of the non-performance is not a condition for claiming damages in the COMMON LAW. Performance is due without demand even when no time for performance has been set. The same rule is followed in CISG as far as delay of performance is concerned, see *Treitel*, Remedies § 115; on defects see (b) below.

    (b) *Notice of non-performance necessary*
         Unlike the Principles, several laws require that the aggrieved party gives notice of the non-performance. However, the effects of the notice varies.
         In sale of goods between merchants, GERMAN and AUSTRIAN HGB §§ 377 and 378 require notice of defects to be given without delay, or the buyer will lose all remedies, including his claim for damages. The same rule applies for all sales in DENMARK, see Sale of Goods Act § 52, and in CISG, see art. 39. See also DUTCH BW 7:23. (Indeed, FRENCH, BELGIAN and LUXEMBOURG CC art. 1648. AUSTRIAN ABGB § 933 and GERMAN BGB § 477 deprive the buyer of his right to damages for defects if he does not sue the seller within certain time limits, i.e. *"dans un bref delai"* and within 6 months respectively. In Belgian law this is considered to be an application of a more general rule based on good faith: Cass. 8 April 1988, Arr.Cass. no.482; *Foriers* 261 no.4; *M.E.Storme* Invloed no.461ff. See also GREEK CC arts. 554-558; ITALIAN CC art.1495.) See also FINNISH and SWEDISH Sale of Goods Acts, §§29 and 59, see *Ramberg* Köplagen 573 f.
         Most other rules requiring notice do not deprive the aggrieved party who has not given notice, or sued the other party within certain time limits, of all his rights. However, whether notice has been given has other effects. Damages may not be recovered unless notice has been given. Notice may also increase the defaulting party's liability: damages for delay will start to run, and some losses will be recoverable, only if they occur after notice has been given. On notice, see FRENCH, BELGIAN and LUXEMBOURG CC arts. 1139 and 1146; SPANISH CC art. 1100; ITALIAN CC art. 1219; AUSTRIAN ABGB § 904; DUTCH BW art. 6:82; GERMAN BGB § 284; and GREEK CC art. 340. See also *Treitel*, Remedies §§ 111-114.

4. *Non-pecuniary loss*
    Non-pecuniary loss may be pain and inconvenience following from physical harm or from disappointment or vexation, and may be due to attacks on a person's personality, reputation or honour or to the death of a spouse or other closely related person. The legal systems differ not only in the extent to which they award damages but also as to which harm they will compensate.

    (a) *Préjudice moral*
         Important developments have occurred in FRANCE and BELGIUM. Non-pecuniary damages were formerly seldom awarded, but today damages are allowed for *"préjudice moral"* which includes damages for attacks on a person's honour or reputation, loss of a closely related person, certain kinds of physical harm which do not entail economic loss (loss of sense of smell, disfiguring scar) and disappointment. See *Viney*, Conditions nos.253ff. and *Treitel*, Remedies § 156.
         PORTUGUESE law also provides rules on damages for non-pecuniary loss, see *Telles* 383, *Jorge* 597 and *Costa*, Obrigações 505 ff.. So does SPANISH law, Supreme Court 9 May 1984, 13 December 1984, 16 December 1986, 3 June 1991 (*Lacruz-Delgado*, II, 1, § 27, 211-212; *Diez-Picazo* II, 688.

    (b) *Pain and suffering and disappointment distinguished*
         In ENGLISH law damages for non-pecuniary loss such as pain and suffering or physical inconvenience may be recovered for breach of contract: e.g. *Godley* v. *Perry* [1960] 1 W.L.R. 9, Q.B.; *Hobbs* v. *L.S.W.R.* (1875) LR 10 Q.B. 111, C.A. However, damages are not awarded for vexation or disappointment unless the contract was specifically meant to provide enjoyment (e.g. a package holiday contract: *Jarvis* v. *Swan Tours Ltd.* [1973] Q.B. 233, C.A.) or to give peace of mind (*Heywood* v. *Wellers* [1976] Q.B. 446, C.A.): see *Bliss* v. *SETRHA* [1985] I.C.R. 700, C.A. These authorities have been followed in IRELAND, see *Clark* 461. SCOTTISH law seems to be similar to English law, see e.g. *Diesen* v. *Samson* 1971 S.L.T. (Sh.Ct.) 49. In AUSTRIAN law, damages for pain and suffering may be recovered in contract as well as in tort (ABGB § 1325; see also § 1331). General recovery of non-pecuniary losses is unrestricted, see (c) below.

    (c) *Limited recovery for non-pecuniary loss*

ITALIAN, GERMAN, DANISH, FINNISH, GREEK and DUTCH law will only allow damages for non-pecuniary loss if this is provided for by statute; see, e.g. GERMAN BGB § 253; *Treitel*, Remedies § 157. ITALIAN CC art. 2059 limits recovery in tort to cases where the defendant's conduct amount to a criminal offence, which excludes non-pecuniary damages for non-performance of contracts, see *Cian & Trabucchi* arts. 1223 and 2059. In GERMANY the tort rule in BGB § 847 on non-pecuniary damages for bodily harm and false imprisonment has been applied in cases giving rise to liability both in tort and contract, but not where the claim was based on contract only. However, BGB § 651 f entitles a customer to a reasonable compensation for wasted holiday where a supplier of travel facilities through breaking the contract has prevented or seriously prejudiced the customer's journey, see on BGB § 253 etc. *Treitel*, Remedies § 157. In AUSTRIA, an influential writer has argued that all types of non-pecuniary loss may be recovered if there has been gross negligence: *Bydlinski* Jbl 1965, 173, 237. In DENMARK and the NETHERLANDS non-pecuniary damages are mostly available in tort but the rules such as BW art. 6:106 and §§ 3 and 26 of the Danish Damages Act 1984 may in certain cases also apply to contracts, see on DUTCH law BW art. 6:95 and 6:106, and on DANISH law, *Vinding Kruse* 345 ff.; similarly SWEDISH law, see *Hellner*, Skadeståndsrätt 357 ff and FINNISH law, see *Taxell*, Skadestånd 183. On GREEK law, see CC art. 299 (only for tort cases where personality rights have been infringed) and *Ligeropoulos*, Erm.AK art. vol II/1 299 nos. 2-4, 8 (1994), who criticizes the existing rule.

5.   *Future loss*

All the legal systems will allow damages for loss which will occur after the day damages are assessed provided the loss is not too remote, see notes to Article 9:503 below. Such loss may follow from the death of a breadwinner (spouse or parent) or personal disablement, where recoverable as contract damages, and from loss of future profit. See for instance CISG art. 74 and, on the indemnity which the commercial agent whose contract with the principal has been ended may claim for future commissions, art. 17 of the Council Directive of 18 Dec. 1986 (86/653 EC). In some legal systems damages are awarded even if the loss is to some extent speculative, see on FRENCH and ENGLISH law the notes to Article 9:503. Under AUSTRIAN law, recoverability of loss of future profits is, according to ABGB §§ 1324, 1325 and 1331, dependent on the degree of fault: lost profits may only be recovered if the injury is attributable to the defaulting party's intentional or grossly negligent act. However, the dependants of a person who has been killed may claim compensation for loss of support from the person who caused the death irrespective of the degree of fault.

See generally *Treitel*, Remedies Chapter IV.

Article 9:502: General Measure of Damages

The general measure of damages is such sum as will put the aggrieved party as nearly as possible into the position in which it would have been if the contract had been duly performed. Such damages cover the loss which the aggrieved party has suffered and the gain of which it has been deprived.

COMMENT

A. *Nature of interest protected*

This Article combines the widely accepted "expectation interest" basis of damages and the traditional rule of *"damnum emergens"* and *"lucrum cessans"* of Roman law, namely that the aggrieved party is entitled to compensation of such amount as will give it the value of the defeated contractual expectation. In a contract for the sale of goods or supply of services this is usually measured by the difference between the contract price and the market or current price; but where the aggrieved party has made a cover transaction then in the conditions set out in Article 9:506 it can elect to claim the difference between the contract price and the cover price. The sums recoverable as general damages embrace both expenditure incurred and gains not made. Damages under this Article are not intended to provide restitution (i.e. restoration of the parties of the status quo ante by mutual surrender of benefits received); this remedy is available in the circumstances described in Article 9:307.

Illustration 1: S sells a Renault car to B for £5,000, warranting it to be a 1990 model. In fact it is a 1988 model, the market value of which is £1,500 less than that of a 1990 model. The contract price is not as such relevant to the computation of damages. S is entitled to damages of £1,500, the difference between the value of the car as warranted and its value as delivered.

B. *Other loss*
In addition to its primary claim for loss of bargain (that is, the loss which any aggrieved party would be likely to suffer from the non-performance) the aggrieved party can recover for loss resulting from its particular circumstances, so far as foreseeable within Article 9:503. In Anglo-American usage such loss is sometimes termed "consequential loss".

Illustration 2: B buys a washing machine in a sale at a special price of £200. The normal cost is £300. Because of a serious defect in the machine garments put into it for washing, worth £50, are ruined. On rejecting the machine B is entitled to recover not only the price paid and £100 for loss of bargain but also the sum of £50 for consequential loss.

The damages recoverable may include interest upon the amount of the loss from the date at which the loss was incurred to the date of payment.

C. *Computation of losses and gains*
The aggrieved party must bring into account in reduction of damages any compensating gains which offset its loss; only the balance, the net loss, is recoverable. Similarly, in computing gains of which the aggrieved party has been deprived, the cost it would have incurred in making those gains is a compensating saving which must be deducted to produce a net gain. Compensating gains typically arise as the result of a cover transaction concluded by the aggrieved party. But it is for the non-performing party to show that the transaction generating the gains was indeed a substitute transaction, as opposed to a transaction concluded independently of the default. A compensating saving occurs where the future performance from which the aggrieved party has been discharged as the result of the non-performance would have involved the aggrieved party in expenditure.

Illustration 3: O, a construction company which owns a piece of equipment for which it has no immediate need, enters into an agreement to lease the equipment to H for a year at a rental of DM 1000 a month. After three months, O terminates the agreement and repossesses the equipment because of H's default in payment of the rent. Two months later, O succeeds in re-letting the equipment for seven months at a rent of DM 1200 a month. O is entitled to the rent due and unpaid at the time it terminated the original agreement and to damages for loss of future rental income, but its claim for the two months' loss of rent after termination of the agreement, i.e. DM 2000, is reduced by DM 1400, the additional rental it will receive over the remaining 7 months of the original agreement.

Illustration 4: S, a commodity dealer, contracts to sell to B 50 tonnes of soyabean meal at a price of 300,000 lire a tonne for delivery on 1st August. On that date, when the price of soyabean meal has fallen to 250,000 lire a tonne, B fails to take up and pay for the meal. A week later S sells 50 tonnes of soyabean meal to C at 375,000 lire a tonne. Even if the market price rule (that is to say the rule that, in the case of goods of a kind available on a market, the normal measure of damages is taken to be the difference between contract price and market price) did not apply, S would not have to bring into account in its claim against B the extra profit on its sale to C, in the absence of evidence that its transaction was a substitute for the contract with B.

Notes

1. *Expectation interest*
   The legal systems seem to agree that the general measure of damages should be such as to put the aggrieved party into the position in which he would have been if the contract had been duly performed. In the COMMON LAW this measure of damages has come to be called the expectation interest (see *Fuller & Perdue* (1936) 46 Yale L.J. 52), in GERMANY and AUSTRIA *"positives Interesse"* or *"Erfüllungsinteresse"*. It is contrasted with the reliance interest which aims at putting the aggrieved party into the position in which he would have been if the contract had not been concluded (German *"Vertrauensinteresse"*). On this distinction see in DENMARK, *Gomard*, Obligationsret II 153 ff.; ENGLAND, *Treitel*, Remedies § 82, and on the expectation interest *Robinson* v. *Harman* (1848) 1 Ex. 850, 855; FINLAND, *Aurejärvi* 132-136; GERMANY, *Palandt (-Heinrichs)* nos.16-18; AUSTRIA, *Kozoil*, I 34; ITALY, *Visintini* 196; SWEDEN, *Ramberg.*, Köplagen 112, 649 f. In FRENCH law writers are generally unfamiliar with the distinction, see *Treitel*, Remedies § 89; But in SPAIN, it is increasingly accepted (*Diez Picazo* II, 683; *Pantaléon*, 1019 ff.).

2. *Loss and gain*
   That damages generally may cover both loss which the aggrieved party has suffered and gain of which he had been deprived is expressly provided in FRENCH, BELGIAN and LUXEMBOURG CC art. 1149, GREEK CC art. 298, GERMAN BGB § 252 cfr. § 249, ITALIAN CC 1223, the DUTCH BW 6:96, PORTUGUESE CC art. 564(1) and SPANISH CC art. 1106; see also CISG art. 74.

3. *Consequential loss*
   Damages for loss due to personal injury and damage to property (other than the thing contracted for) are allowed in most of the legal systems, see for ENGLAND, *McGregor*, Damages §57 ff.. In GERMANY these damages are awarded for positive breach of contract (*"positive Vertragsverletzung"*), see notes to Article 8:101, above. Under AUSTRIAN law recovery of "loss of profits" in addition to "positive damage" (loss suffered) is, according to ABGB §§ 1323, 1324, provided only if the party responsible therefor is to blame for gross negligence.

4. *"Compensatio lucri cum damno"*
   It seems to be universally accepted that loss should be offset by the gains which the aggrieved party has made due to the non-performance, see on ENGLISH and GERMAN law *Treitel*, Remedies §§ 149-50; FINNISH law, *Sevon-Wilhelmsson & Koskelo*, 87; FRENCH law, Cass.req. 1 Jan. 1927, D.H.27.65; ITALIAN law, Cass. 5 April 1990 no. 2802 in Mass. Foro It. 1990; GREEK law, *Georgiadis & Stathopoulos* II arts. 297-298 nos. 87-111; PORTUGUESE law, *Telles* 390 and *Costa*, Obrigações 688 f; BELGIAN law, *Ronse* nos. 519ff.; DUTCH BW art. 6:100; and SPANISH law, Supreme Court 17 February 1925, 19 November 1928, 20 June 1953, 13 May 1965 (*Alabaladejo*. II, 1, § 33.3).

5.   *Reliance interest*
     Some laws allow the aggrieved party to claim reliance interest instead of expectation interest. This is possible under DANISH law where the aggrieved party can claim it, even though he would thereby be put into a better position than he would have been had the contract been performed, see *Gomard*, Obligationsret II 202. In GERMANY reliance interest may be claimed if the aggrieved party terminates the contract and thereby is excluded from getting expectation interest, see *Palandt (-Heinrichs)* § 325 no.25. GREECE has a specific provision permitting equitable damages (see notes to Article 8:102 above). The position in SWEDISH law is unresolved, see *Ramberg*, Avtalsrätt 56 f.
     ENGLISH law allows recovery of the reliance interest but this cannot put the aggrieved party in a better position than he would have been if the contract had been performed, see *Treitel*, Remedies § 94. Thus expenditures which are wasted can be recovered as reliance interest, but if these expenditures would not have been recouped if the contract had been performed they cannot be recovered, for this would put the aggrieved party into a better position than he would have been in: *C&P Haulage Ltd. v. Middleton* [1983] 1 W.L.R. 1461 (C.A.). For SCOTTISH law see *Macgregor*.
     See generally *Treitel*, Remedies §§ 75-107.

Article 9:503: Foreseeability

The non-performing party is liable only for loss which it foresaw or could reasonably have foreseen at the time of conclusion of the contract as a likely result of its non-performance, unless the non-performance was intentional or grossly negligent.

COMMENT

A. *Foreseeable consequences of failure to perform*

This Article sets out the principle adopted in many jurisdictions by which the non-performing party's liability is limited to what it foresaw or ought to have foreseen at the time of the contract as the likely consequence of its failure to perform. However, the last part of this Article provides a special rule in the case of intentional breach or gross negligence.

Illustration 1: B, a stamp dealer, contracts to buy from S for £10,000 his set of stamps, to be delivered to B on 1st June. S fails to deliver the stamps, which on 1st June have a market value of £12,000. Because of S's breach, B is unable to fulfil a contract to resell the collection to T for £25,000. S, though aware that B required the stamps for resale, was not aware that B would resell the stamps as a collection. B is entitled to recover as damages the sum the £2,000, being the difference between the market value of the stamps on 1st June and the sale price. S is not liable for the remaining £13,000 of B's loss, which S could not reasonably have foreseen at the time he contracted to sell the stamps to B.

Illustration 2: S sells an animal food compound to B for feeding to pigs. B does not tell A for what breed of pigs the food is required. The compound contains a mild toxin which is known to cause discomfort to pigs but no serious harm. B's pigs are, however, of a unusual breed which is peculiarly sensitive to the toxin and after being fed with the compound many of the pigs die. S is not liable for the loss since it could not reasonably have foreseen it.

B. *Exception in case of intentional breach or gross negligence*

Although in general the non-performing party is liable only for loss which it foresaw or ought to have foreseen at the time of the contract, the last part of this Article lays down a special rule in cases of intentional failure in performance or gross negligence. In this case the damages for which the non-performing party is liable are not limited by the foreseeability rule and the full damage has to be compensated, even if unforeseeable.

Illustration 3: A contracts with B to construct and erect stands for a major exhibition at which leading electronic firms will display their equipment, hiring the stands from B. A week before the exhibition is due to open A demands a substantial increase in the contract sum. B refuses to pay, pointing out that A's failure to complete the remaining stands will not only cost B revenue but expose it to heavy liability to an exhibitor, C, which intended to use the exhibition to launch a major new product. A nevertheless withdraws its workforce, with the result that C's stand is not ready in time and it claims substantial compensation from B.

A's breach being intentional and with knowledge of the likely consequences, the court has to award B an indemnity in respect of its liability of C, even though A could not reasonably have foreseen the magnitude of such liability at the time it made its contract with B. The same may be done even if A was not aware of the serious consequences for B of the intentional breach.

NOTES

The presentation in the following covers mainly ENGLISH, FRENCH, GERMAN and DUTCH law.

IRISH, SCOTTISH and DANISH laws seem to follow English law, see on Danish law, *Gomard*, Obligationsret II 188 ff.; on Irish law *Clark* 543ff.; and on SCOTTISH law, MacQueen 295-303.

BELGIAN, LUXEMBOURG, SPANISH and ITALIAN laws are similar to French law, see Spanish CC art. 1107 and on Italian CC art. 1223 and 1225, *Visintini* 209.

GREEK and *(semble)* PORTUGUESE laws seem to follow German law. See on Greek law *Ligeropoulos*, Introd. remarks to arts. 297-300 nos. 44-46 a, 49-50, 53 and *Stathopoulos* in *Georgiadis & Stathopoulos* II arts. 297-298 nos. 51-56; on Portuguese law, *Varela* I 866.

1.   Foreseeability

As in Article 9:503, ENGLISH law limits liability to foreseeable losses. The rule was stated in *Hadley v. Baxendale* (1854) 9 Ex. 431 (Court of Exchequer). The defaulting party is liable for loss which he foresaw or which a reasonable person in his position ought to have foreseen when the contract was made having regard to the facts he knew or ought to have known. If a seller of machinery wrongfully delays delivery with the result that the buyer is unable to reap the profits from using the machinery, the buyer may recover the profits which in the normal course of things he would have made on the machinery. However, he cannot recover the profit which he could have earned on some exceptionally lucrative contracts he had made of which the seller knew nothing, see *Victoria Laundry (Windsor) Ltd. v. Newman Industries Ltd.* [1949] 2 K.B. 528, C.A. See on English law, *Treitel*, Contracts 870-879. This limitation to the foreseeable loss, which has been adopted in CISG art. 74, must be seen in light of the strict contract liability in English law and in CISG. On CISG see v. *Caemmerer & Schlechtriem (-Stoll)* § 623 ff. See also *Unidroit* art. 7.4.4.

This foreseeability test is also provided in FRENCH, BELGIAN and LUXEMBOURG law, see CC art. 1150. In Belgium and France the test is applied broadly: only the possibility of the particular kind of damage needs to have been foreseeable, see respectively Cass., 23 Feb. 1928, Pas. 85 and Cass.com. 1965, D. 1965.449.

2. *"Immediate and direct" consequences*

In addition to the foreseeability test of art.1150, FRENCH, BELGIAN and LUXEMBOURG CC art. 1151 provides that liability for damages is limited to losses which are the "immediate and direct" consequences of the non-performance. It has been questioned whether this additional test adds anything to the foreseeability test, see *Treitel*, Remedies §§ 140 and 141. In FRENCH law, however, it is considered that a loss may be direct yet unforeseeable, see *Malaurie and Aynès*, Obligations no. 839-842. In Belgium it is held to add nothing, Cass. 24 June 1977, Pas. 1087. On ITALIAN law see *Realmonte*.

3. *The principle of "adequate causation"*

GERMAN law has rejected the foreseeability test and applies instead the theory of "adequate causation". The loss must have been caused by the non-performance and only such kind of loss which occurs in the ordinary course of things are recoverable. However, if there is causation the principle will make the defaulting party liable if the default appreciably increased the possibility of the loss that in fact occurred. In determining whether this was the case the court will apply the standard of an experienced observer at the time of the non-performance.

The rule puts the plaintiff in a better position than under the foreseeability test, as the experienced observer may foresee more than a reasonable person would have at the time the contract was made. The German rule must be seen in the light of the fault principle governing German contract law, see notes to Article 8:101. On German law, see *Treitel*, Remedies §§ 137-138, *Dölle (-Weitnauer)*, Introd. to arts. 82-89, 525 ff., particularly 534-535.

AUSTRIAN law (see *Kozoil*, 140) and SWEDISH law (see *Rodhe*, Obligationsrätt 121) resemble GERMAN law. FINNISH law also uses "adequate causation" but in practice elements of forseeability appear, see *Taxell*, Skadeständ 178 and *Hemmo*.

4. *"Imputability"*

DUTCH law applies an imputability test, see BW art. 6:98. Damages can only be recovered for loss which is related to the event which made the debtor liable in such a way that the loss, having regard to its kind and that of the liability, can be imputed to the debtor as a consequence of the event.

5. *Intentional non-performance*

In FRENCH and ITALIAN law the foreseeability requirement – but not the "directness" requirement – is excluded in case of intentional non-performance (*dol*), see French CC art. 1150 and 1151 and Italian CC art. 1225. However, in French law gross negligence is regarded as *dol*. SPANISH CC art. 1107(2) is similar to French CC art. 1150 (see *Pantaléon*, (1991) 1019-1091 and (1993) 1719-1745).

Under AUSTRIAN law the degree of fault affects the extent of damage to be recovered, since loss of profit is only compensated in the case of gross negligence and intentional wrongdoing, as well as the method of computation (whether based on objective or on subjective criteria).

The degree of the defaulting party's fault is not taken into account as a general rule for the purpose of awarding damages in the COMMON LAW systems, in SCOTLAND or in GERMAN law, see *Treitel*, Remedies §§ 123-126.

6. *Certainty*

The systems generally require a sufficient degree of "certainty" of loss in order to award damages, but this is not to be taken literally. In FRANCE, BELGIUM, GERMANY, ENGLAND and SCOTLAND the courts have awarded damages for loss of future profit, which is not always "certain", see notes to Article 9:501, and damages for the loss of a chance, e.g. to win a beauty contest, have also been awarded, see the English case of *Chaplin* v. *Hicks* [1911] 2 K.B. 786, C.A. and, on SCOTTISH law, *Hogg*. GREEK CC art. 298 sent.2 provides for the recovery of lost profit which probably could have been made in the ordinary course of events or according to the special circumstances.

See generally *Treitel*, Remedies, Chapter IV; *Dölle (-Weitnauer)* Introd. to arts. 82-89, 525 ff.., esp. 531-549.

Article 9:504: Loss Attributable to Aggrieved Party

The non-performing party is not liable for loss suffered by the aggrieved party to the extent that the aggrieved party contributed to the non-performance or its effects.

COMMENT

A. *Loss caused by unreasonable action or inaction*
This Article embodies the principle that an aggrieved party should not recover damages to the extent that its loss is caused by its own unreasonable behaviour. It embraces two distinct situations. The first is where the aggrieved party's conduct was a partial cause of the non-performance; the second, where the aggrieved party, though not in any way responsible for the non-performance itself, exacerbated its loss-producing effects by its behaviour. A third situation, where the loss resulting from the non-performance could have been reduced or extinguished by appropriate steps in mitigation, is covered by Article 9:505.

The reason for the division between this and the next Article is that some legal systems distinguish these situations, at least in some degree. Thus in English law the first two situations fall within the concept "contributory negligence" and the third involves a "failure to mitigate". Most continental European legal systems do not distinguish the two concepts, though they reach similar results by using concepts such as causation.

B. *Conduct contributing to the non-performance*
To the extent that the aggrieved party contributed to the non-performance by its own act or omission he cannot recover the resulting loss. This may be regarded as a particular application of the general rule set out in Article 8:101 (3).

> *Illustration 1*: B orders a computer system from S which is to be specially designed to allow B to send to prospective property buyers details of houses coming on to the market which appear to meet their requirements. The computer system fails to operate properly, due partly to a design defect and partly to the fact that B's instructions to S were incomplete. B's loss is irrecoverable to the extent that it results from its own inadequate instructions.

C. *Conduct contributing to the loss-producing effects of non-performance*
Where the aggrieved party, though not in any way responsible for the non-performance, exacerbates its adverse effects he cannot recover damages for the additional loss which results.

> *Illustration 2*: A leases a computer which under the terms of the contract is to be ready for use in England where the voltage is 240v. The computer supplied is capable of operating on various voltages and, in breach of contract, is actually set for 110v. A prominent sign pasted on the screen warns the user to check the voltage setting before use. A ignores this and switches on without checking. The computer is extensively damaged and repairs will cost A £1,500. The court may take the view that the loss was at least half A's fault and award only £750 damages.

NOTES

See Notes to Article 9:505.

Article 9:505: Reduction of Loss

(1) The non-performing party is not liable for loss suffered by the aggrieved party to the extent that the aggrieved party could have reduced the loss by taking reasonable steps.

(2) The aggrieved party is entitled to recover any expenses reasonably incurred in attempting to reduce the loss.

A. *Failure to mitigate loss*

Even where the aggrieved party has not contributed either to the non-performance or to its effects, it cannot recover for loss it would have avoided if it had taken reasonable steps to do so. The failure to mitigate loss may arise either because the aggrieved party incurs unnecessary or unreasonable expenditure or because it fails to take reasonable steps which would result in reduction of loss or in offsetting gains.

> *Illustration 1*: B buys an old car from S for £750. S warrants that the car is in good running order. B discovers that it will cost £1,500 to put the car into good running order, and he has this work done although similar cars in good condition are available for £800. B's damages will be limited to £800; the extra amount represents an expenditure which was quite disproportionate to the value of the car as repaired (The result might be different if there were some good reason for B to have repairs done, e.g., the car was unique in that it had once belonged to General de Gaulle).

> *Illustration 2*: C hires a camper van to take his holiday in Portugal. When he comes to collect the camper van, the car hire company tells C that it has made a mistake in bookings and no van is available from it, but it has managed to find for him another company which has a van available at a higher price. Even if C unreasonably ignores this and abandons his holiday, his damages should be limited to the loss he would have suffered if he had acted reasonably in taking the substitute van, namely the difference in cost between the vans and compensation for inconvenience in having to collect his replacement.

The aggrieved party will not necessarily be expected to take steps to mitigate its loss immediately it learns of the breach; it will depend on whether its actions are reasonable in the circumstances.

> *Illustration 3*: O engages B, a builder, to come within 24 hours to repair the roof of O's house, which is leaking and causing damage to the decorations. B does not come within the 24 hours but assures O that it will come the next day. It is

reasonable for O to wait until the day after before calling in another builder, and O may claim damages resulting from this period of delay; but it may not be reasonable to wait any longer and if O does so it may not recover damages for the resulting additional loss.

The aggrieved party is only expected to take action which is reasonable, or to refrain from action which is unreasonable, in the circumstances. Thus it need not act in any way that will damage its commercial reputation just to reduce the non-performing party's liability.

Illustration 4: D buys goods from E in order to resell them to F. The goods supplied by E are not of proper quality. Although under the terms of its contract with F, D could require F to take the goods without a price reduction, this would be unreasonable in the light of their long-standing business relationship and D gives F a reduction of price. D may recover the amount by which it reduced the price as damages from E.

The principle applies also when one party is guilty of anticipatory non-performance within Article 9:304, e.g., by announcing that it will not perform the contract when the time comes. The aggrieved party should not incur further expenditure needlessly and should take steps to reduce its loss.

Illustration 5: K contracts to build a yacht to L's special design. L repudiates the contract. If K has done little work on the yacht and it would not be able to find a ready buyer for such a unique design of boat, it is reasonable to expect it to stop work; it may recover the cost of the work done to date and the loss of anticipated profit. If, on the other hand, it has done most of the work and can find another buyer at a reasonable price, then even where it has terminated the contract under Article 9:304 it may be expected to complete the boat and resell it. It will be entitled to damages of the difference between the original contract price and the resale price (Article 9:506), plus the incidental costs of arranging the resale.

C. *Expenses incurred in mitigating loss*
Frequently the aggrieved party will have to incur some further expenditure in order to mitigate its loss. This incidental expenditure is also recoverable provided it is reasonable.

Illustration 6: X agrees to buy Y's chalet, which Y had advertised widely. Later X repudiates the contract. Y decides to make a cover transaction. In order to resell the house he has to advertise it again. He is entitled to the reasonable cost of the further advertising as well as to the difference between the prixe X had agreed to pay and the price for which the chalet was ultimately sold.

D. *Reasonable attempts to mitigate which in fact increase the loss*
Sometimes a party may take what at the time appears to be a reasonable step to reduce its loss but in fact increases it. The full loss suffered is recoverable.

Illustration 10: G enters a long term supply contract to buy oil from H; deliveries are to commence in six months' time. Three months later oil prices rise rapidly because of a threatened war in the Gulf and H repudiates the contract. G quickly terminates the contract and enters a substitute contract with J at the price then being quoted for delivery three months later. By the time the date for delivery comes the threat of war has receded and G could have bought the oil for the original contract price. It acted reasonably in entering the substitute contract and is entitled to damages based on the difference between the original contract price and the price it had to pay to J.

E. *Loss reduced by steps going beyond what could reasonably be expected*

Sometimes a party will take a step which reduces its loss and which goes beyond what it might reasonably have been expected to do. The reduction in loss will still be taken into account, as it is entitled only to damages for actual loss: see Article 9:501.

NOTES

Notes to Articles 9:504 and 9:505

1. *Loss caused by aggrieved party (Articles 9:504 and 9:505(1))*
   (a) *Different treatment of loss caused by aggrieved party and "mitigation"*
       Some legal systems treat the aggrieved party's contributory negligence and his "duty" to mitigate his loss differently. FRENCH cases, which mostly have dealt with tort liability, have admitted that in contracts also contributory negligence by the aggrieved party may reduce his claim for damages. The creditor's act will constitute a cause of exoneration even if it doe not constitute *force majeure*: Civ.1, 31 January 1973, D.1973.149, note Schmelk; see *Malaurie & Aynès*, Obligations no. 833. French law does not know mitigation as such, but some similar results may be obtained by the application of the general rule about fault. See Cass. civ. 1, 29 April 1981, JCP 1982, 19730 where damages were reduced, as it was a "fault" of the creditor not to avoid loss due to the negligent non-performance of the debtor, and Paris, 7 Jan. 1924 DP 24.1.143 where the court would not permit the creditor to let the loss grow without notifying the debtor so that he could stop the supply of defective goods. See also on leases CC art. 1760. However, French law is reluctant to impose duties on the aggrieved party: Com. 28 June 1994, B.IV. no 248 (warranty against *vices cachées*). On SPANISH law, Supreme Court 1960, 15 November 1994 (see *Bercovitz*, CCJC 550; Angel 13 ff.; and *Diez Picazo*, II, § 89). On DANISH law see *Gomard*, Obligationsret II, 186 (duty to mitigate) and 187 (contributory negligence).
       In ENGLISH law "contributory negligence" will generally either be no defence to a claim in contract or, on the theory that the loss was not caused by the breach, will lead to no compensation at all. However, a reduction of damages may be allowed in certain cases where the debtor was under a concurrent duty of care in tort and the plaintiff also failed to act carefully, see *Treitel*, Contract 886-891. The aggrieved party's failure to mitigate may lead to a reduction of the damages: *ibid.*, 881-886. SCOTTISH law is to the same effect, *McBryde*, Contract, 454-462. The same rule is laid down in art. 77 of CISG. Furthermore, CISG art. 80 provides that a party may not rely on the failure of the other party to perform, to the extent that such failure was caused by the first party's act or omission. It has been convincingly argued that this rule may be extended by way of the interpretation by analogy rule provided in art. 7(2) so as to allow reduction of damages in case of the aggrieved party's "contribution" to the non-performance, see *Bianca & Bonell (-Tallon)* Art. 80 note 2.5 p. 598, but see v. *Caemmerer & Schlechtriem (-Stoll)* 677. For *Unidroit* see arts. 7.4.7 and 7.4.8.
       In IRELAND there is a duty to mitigate the loss, as in England, thereby matching Article 9:505(1). Furthermore, ss.2 and 34(1) of the Civil Liability Act 1961 allow the court to reduce the damages by reason of the defendant's contributory negligence, thereby matching Article 9:504.
   (b) *Contributory negligence and "duty" to mitigate loss treated alike.*
       Several of the Civil Law systems treat the aggrieved party's contributory negligence and his "duty" to mitigate his loss on an equal footing. Contributory negligence and failure to miti-

gate may lead the court to reduce or to disallow the claim for damages. This is the position in GERMANY, see BGB § 254(1) dealing with contributory negligence and § 254(2) with the failure to mitigate the loss. The ITALIAN CC has similar provisions in art. 1227(1) treating contributory negligence and in art. 1227(2) dealing with avoidance of loss, see *Gorla*, which in recent decisions has been extended to cover mitigation of loss: see e.g. Cass. 3 March 1983, no. 1594 in Giust. civ., 1984 I c. 3156. See also AUSTRIAN ABGB § 1304 and GREEK CC art. 300, covering both contribution to the damage and mitigation of damage, and DUTCH BW art. 6:101; *Asser-Hartkamp*, Verbintenissenrecht nos. 448 ff., 453. Contributory negligence is treated in the PORTUGUESE CC art. 570 and the "duty" to mitigate may be imposed upon the aggrieved party by way of an analogy of art. 570, or under the rule of abuse of right. In BELGIAN law mitigation is treated as a sub-species of contributory negligence, Cass. 14 May 1992; *Ronse* no.460ff.; *Kruithof*, R.C.J.B 1989, 12ff. It is mentioned as a separate duty only in Insurance Contracts Act of 25 June 1992, art.20. SPANISH law seems similar: there is no express provision in the CC on the topic and doctrine seems to consider mitigation as a sub-species of contributory negligence or *mora creditoris*, Diez-Picazo 733 ff..In FINLAND Sale of Goods Act § 70 provides an express duty to mitigate the loss. This is seen as connected to the general principle of contributory negligence, *Sevón, Wilhelmsson & Koskelo* 87.

2.   *Expenses incurred (Article 9:505(2))*
Like Article 9:505(2), the legal systems will allow the aggrieved party to recover expenses reasonably incurred in attempts to avoid or mitigate the loss. Expenses are to be reimbursed even if they increased the total loss, provided they were reasonable. This is the law in AUSTRIA, see e.g. *Ehrenzweig (-Mayrhofer)*, 309; BELGIUM, see esp. Insurance Contracts Act of 25 June 1992, art. 52; DENMARK, see *Nørager-Nielsen* 410; ITALY, Cass. 28 April 1988 no. 3209, Archivio civile 1988, 1054, *Cian & Trabucchi* art. 1227, 964; GERMANY, BGH 22 Jan. 1959, NJW 1959, 933, 934; ENGLAND, *McGregor*, Damages §§ 333-334; the NETHERLANDS, BW 6:96(2)(a); SWEDEN, see *Ramberg*, Köplagen 649 ff. In GREECE the rule is based upon the rule on adequate causation in CC art. 300, or on the *"negotiorum gestio"* rule in CC art. 736, and in PORTUGAL on the rule in CC 566(2) on full compensation , see notes to Article 9:502, above. The right to recover expenses incurred is implicit in CISG art. 77, see also art. 74.
See generally *Treitel*, Remedies, § 145 ff..

Article 9:506: Substitute Transaction

Where the aggrieved party has terminated the contract and has made a substitute transaction within a reasonable time and in a reasonable manner, it may recover the difference between the contract price and the price of the substitute transaction as well as damages for any further loss so far as these are recoverable under this Section.

COMMENT

A. *Cover transactions*
It is often appropriate to measure the aggrieved party's loss by the cost of procuring a substitute performance. Where the aggrieved party has in fact made a reasonable cover transaction, Article 9:506 provides that the difference between the contract price and the cover price is recoverable. The non-performing party may also be liable for any further loss which the aggrieved party proves it has suffered, e.g. the cost of arranging a cover transaction.

Illustration 1: O agrees to allow H the use of its art gallery for an exhibition at a fee of £1,000. Shortly before the exhibition is to take place O informs H that the gallery will not after all be available. H succeeds in obtaining the use of a nearby gallery of similar size and quality for a fee of £1,500. She is entitled to damages of £500 representing the amount by which the cost of the cover transaction exceeds the contract price, as well as damages for any reasonable expenses (e.g. changing the address on leaflets and posters).

B. *Alternative transaction must be a reasonable substitute*
The aggrieved party cannot recover the difference between the contract price and the price of an alternative transaction which is so different from the original contract in value or kind as not to be a reasonable substitute.

Illustration 2: O supplies a Renault 9 on hire to H for three weeks at a rent of FF1000 a week. The car breaks down at the end of the first week while H is on holiday, and as no other Renault 9 is available he hires a Rolls Royce Silver Cloud for the remaining two weeks at a rent of FF5000 a week. H's damages for extra rental charges will be restricted to the additional cost, if any, of hiring the nearest available equivalent of the Renault 9 in size and value.

NOTES

The assessment of damages on the basis of a cover transaction, as provided in Article 9:506, is possible in all the legal systems; however, in some of them it is subject to restrictions.

A general rule on cover transactions is found in the FRENCH, BELGIAN and LUXEMBOURG Civil Codes art. 1144 on the creditor's *faculté de remplacement*. This in principle must be ordered by the court but French usages have allowed the aggrieved party to do it by himself in commercial transactions. Belgian case law has accepted the same even in non-commercial cases provided the non-performance was sufficiently fundamental (*van Ommeslaghe* R.C.J.B. 1986, nos.98-100). In the other legal systems, where the cover transaction is a "self help" remedy, the rules are found in provisions on sales, see DANISH Sale of Goods Act §§ 25, 30(2) and 45; FINNISH and SWEDISH Sale of Goods Acts, § 68; GERMAN and AUSTRIAN HGB § 376(3) (applicable to commercial sales but extended in practice); the DUTCH BW art. 7:37; and ITALIAN CC arts. 1515 and 1516. CISG art. 75 and Unidroit art. 7.4.5. are similar to Article 9:506; so are GREEK and SPANISH case law: see respectively AP 1137/1990, EEN 58 (1991) 444-445 and *Vicent Chuliá*, II, 107.

The DUTCH BW, BELGIAN caselaw the FINNISH and SWEDISH Sale of Goods Acts and CISG require that the transaction is a reasonable one. The DANISH, GERMAN and ITALIAN provisions contain procedural rules; in Italy these have restricted the use of the cover transactions, see Cass., 14 July 1956, no. 2670 and 18 June 1957, no. 2313 in Mass.Foro.It. 1956 and 1957.

ENGLISH law does not specifically adopt the "cover price" as means of measuring the damages. However, where there is no market for the performance, and a current price cannot be established, see notes to Article 9:507, English courts will treat the cover price as a strong evidence of the amount of loss, see *Beale*, Remedies 196-197. SCOTTISH law is similar.

See generally, *Treitel*, Remedies §§ 102 ff..; *Honnold* §§ 409-415.

Article 9:507: Current Price

Where the aggrieved party has terminated the contract and has not made a substitute transaction but there is a current price for the performance contracted for, it may recover the difference between the contract price and the price current at the time the contract is terminated as well as damages for any further loss so far as these are recoverable under this Section.

COMMENT

Damages measured by current price

Insofar as the cost of substitute performance fairly measures the shortfall in the value of the non-performing party's performance, it is recoverable as such whether or not the aggrieved party actually incurs the expenditure.

Illustration 1: S agrees to sell 50 tons of coffee to B at £1,800 a ton for delivery on 1st July. S fails to deliver the coffee. The market price on 1st July is £2,000 a ton. B is entitled to damages of £10,000 (i.e. 50 x £200 = £10,000) even if he does not make a substitute purchase on the market.

Illustration 2: S sells a car to B promising that it is in good condition. In fact it has engine defects which would cost £500 to rectify. Assuming that it would not be uneconomic to repair the car at this cost, B is entitled to £500 damages even though he decides not to have the repairs carried out.

Notes

1.   *Current price as a measure of loss*

As in Article 9:507 this "abstract" way of assessing the amount of loss is used in all the legal systems. The relevant provisions are mostly found in the provisions on sales, see DANISH SGA §§ 25, 30(1) and 45; DUTCH BW art. 7:36; FINNISH and SWEDISH Sale of Goods Acts, § 69; GERMAN and AUSTRIAN HGB § 376(2); ITALIAN CC art. 1518; U.K. Sale of Goods Act 1979, §§ 50(3) and 51(3); and in IRELAND see *Forde* § 1.207. A provision similar to Article 9:507 is found in CISG art. 76.

Though not provided in the legislation, the assessment of damages on the basis of the current price is admitted in FRANCE, BELGIUM and in the NETHERLANDS, where it is covered by the general clause in BW art 6:97 under which the court evaluates the damages in the manner best corresponding to its nature. The assessment is also admitted in SPAIN (TS 27 March 1974, 30 January 1976, 31 March 1977, 14 November 1977, 28 February 1978; see (*Vicent Chuliá*, II, 106; see also *Diez Picazo*, II, 683-684 and *Carrasco* 670) and in GREECE with respect to commercial transactions, *Ligeropoulos* in Erm.AK II/1, art. 298 nos. 23-29, 83-86 (1949).

2.   *Time of assessment*

As in Article 9:507, in CISG art. 76, *Unidroit* art. 7.4.6 and the FINNISH and SWEDISH SGA, the current price is generally that at the time of termination. In several other laws it is, however, the price at the time when performance was due, see UNITED KINGDOM SGA s.51(3); IRELAND, see *Forde* § 1.206; ITALIAN CC art. 1518; GERMAN and AUSTRIA HGB § 376(2); DANISH SGA § 25; and SPANISH Commercial Code arts. 329, 363 and 371 (see *Vicent Chuliá*, II, 106).

Literature: see notes to Article 9:506 above.

Article 9:508: Delay in Payment of Money

(1)   If payment of a sum of money is delayed, the aggrieved party is entitled to interest on that sum from the time when payment is due to the time of payment at the average commercial bank short-term lending rate to prime borrowers prevailing for the contractual currency of payment at the place where payment is due.

(2)   The aggrieved party may in addition recover damages for any further loss so far as these are recoverable under this Section.

COMMENTS

A. *Purposes*

This Article provides for interest and damages on failure to pay money by the date at which payment is due, see Article 7:102.

B. *Interest*

Paragraph (1) confers a general right to interest on primary contractual obligations to pay; the provision does not cover interest on secondary monetary obligations, such as damages or interest.

Interest is not a species of ordinary damages. Therefore the general rules on damages do not apply. Interest is owed whether or not non-payment is excused under Article 8:108. Also, the aggrieved party is entitled to it without regard to any question whether it has taken reasonable steps to mitigate its loss.

The rate of interest is fixed by reference to the average commercial bank short-term lending rate. This rate applies also in the case of a long delay in payment since the creditor at the due date cannot know how long the debtor will delay payment. Since interest rates differ, the lending rate for the currency of payment (Article 7:108) at the due place of payment (Article 7:101) has been selected because this is the best yardstick for assessing the creditor's loss. Unless otherwise agreed, interest is to be paid in the same currency (cf. Article 9:510 Comment D) and at the same place as the principal sum. The parties are free to exclude or modify paragraph (1) e.g. by fixing the rate of default interest and/or its currency in their contract.

C. *Additional damages*

Paragraph (2) makes it clear that the aggrieved party's remedy for non-payment or delay in payment is not limited to interest. It extends to additional and other loss recoverable within the limits laid down by the general provisions on damages, in particular Article 9:503 and Article 9:505. This might include, for example, loss of profit on a transaction which the aggrieved party would have concluded with a third party had the money been paid when due; a fall in the internal value of the money, through inflation, between the due date and the actual date of payment, so far as this fall is not compensated by interest under paragraph (1); and, where the money of payment is not the money of account, loss on exchange. However, in this last case the aggrieved party has the option of proceeding instead under Article 7:108(3).

Illustration 1: A agrees to pay B £50,000 if B will vacate A's property and find alternative accommodation. B moves out of the property but A fails to pay the agreed sum. In consequence B, who as A knew intended to use the payment to buy a house from C, has to negotiate with C to leave part of the purchase price outstanding on mortgage at interest. B is entitled to sue A for the interest and legal costs reasonably incurred.

Illustration 2: C agrees to lend £200,000 to D to enable D to purchase a business at a price equal to that sum from E. Under the contract of sale, the terms of which are known to C, time of payment is of the essence. At the last moment C refuses to advance the money and D is unable to obtain alternative funds in time. E terminates the contract and sells his business to F for £300,000, its true value. D is entitled to damages from C for the loss of the contract.

Illustration 3: S in London agrees to sell goods to B in Hamburg at a price of US$ 100,000 payable in London 28 days after shipment. The goods are duly shipped to B, who is three months late in paying the price. During this period the value of the US dollar in relation to the pound sterling (the currency in which S normally conducts his business) depreciates by 20 per cent. Assuming that these consequences of delay in payment could reasonably have been foreseen by B at the time of the contract, S is entitled to recover US$ 20,000 damages from B, in addition to interest, for the loss on exchange.

NOTES

1. *Duty to pay interest*
    A statutory duty to pay interest exists under several international conventions and in all continental European countries; for references see note 2 below. CISG also recognizes this obligation (arts. 78, 84(1)). Contrary to all other conventions and statutes, CISG does not, however, fix a rate of interest because it proved impossible to agree upon a standard: the discount rate was thought to be inappropriate for measuring credit costs; nor could agreement be reached on whether the credit costs in the seller's or the buyer's country were to be selected. See however *Unidroit* art. 7.4.9.
    ENGLISH law did not impose, in general, a statutory or common law obligation to pay interest upon default (*President of India v. La Pintada Cia. Navegacion SA* [1985] A.C. 104 (H.L.)). This rule was, however, much criticised; before the *President of India* case the English *Law Commission* had proposed the introduction of statutory interest on contractual obligations to pay money (Report on Interest, No.88, Cmnd 7229, 1978). The rule has recently been changed for commercial debts by Late Payment of Commercial Debts (Interest) Act 1998. In any case, if proceedings have been commenced the court has discretion to award interest: Administration of Justice Act 1982, amending the Supreme Court Act 1981, s.35A. SCOTTISH law is the same.
    In IRELAND, although a court can order a contractual debtor to pay interest from the date of judgment, and a creditor who has served notice claiming interest on a defaulting debtor can have interest from the date of demand (Debtors (Ireland) Act 1840, s.53), there is equally no general duty on a defaulting debtor to pay interest on the unpaid sum for the period of delay: see *Clark* 467.
2. *Normal rates*
    The rates of statutory interest and the methods of computing them vary considerably.
    (a) *Fixed rate*
        The traditional method is to fix a statutory rate; it varies between 10 and 4 percent.
        4%: GERMAN BGB § 288 (1).
        5%: GERMAN HGB § 352 (1);
        5%: ITALIAN CC art. 1224 (1), 1284 (as amended in 1996);
        6%: the Geneva Conventions on Bills of Exchange of 1930, art. 48(2) and on Cheques of 1931, art. 45(1);
    (b) *Flexible rates*
        In recent years many countries have introduced flexible interest rates. The methods of determining the rate vary considerably.
        DENMARK adds a percentage, to be fixed biennually by the Minister of Justice, to the respective official discount rate (Law on Interests of 1 September 1986, § 5); interest is due from the time a payment which is fixed in advance becomes due (§ 3). In FINLAND the Act on interest, as amended 3 March 1995, prescribes different rates: if there is an agreed rate of interest on the debit, the interest for delay is 4% above the agreed interest rate, in other cases the interest for delay is 7% (in certain cases 4%) above an official reference rate determined by the Bank of Finland. SWEDEN adds 8% to the official discount rate and, when time for

payment has not been fixed in advance, allows a grace period of 30 days after notice that interest will be charged. In FRANCE the rate is the arithmetic average of the last twelve monthly figures of the official discount rate (Law of 11 July 1975, art. 1, as am. by Law of 23 June 1989); two months after a judicial condemnation to pay, that rate is increased by 5% (Law of 11 July 1985 art.3). The GERMAN Consumer Credit Law of 17 December 1990 (BGBL I 2840) § 11(1) fixes a rate of 5% above the respective official discount rate. GREECE adds 4% to the rate of interest charged by the central bank for financing of credit institutions against state funds given as a pledge (Act of the Council of Ministers 261/1996), which at the time of writing (July 1997) gives an interest rate for arrears of 23%. In BELGIUM an Act of 30 June 1970, as amended in 1986, now allows rate to be fixed by Royal Decree;

In other countries, the interest rate is fixed (and amended) annually by the government (GREEK CC art. 345; LUXEMBOURG: Law 22 Feb. 1984; the NETHERLANDS: BW art. 6:120; PORTUGAL: CC art. 559(1), Comm. C art. 102(2); SPAIN: CC art. 1108 and Law of 29 June 1984, arts. 1 and 2.)

3. *Higher contractual rates*
In some countries if there is a contractual interest rate that is higher than the statutory rate, the higher rate is applied to the time after default (DANISH law, see note 2(b) above, § 6; ITALIAN CC art. 1224(1) sent. 2; the NETHERLANDS: BW art. 6:119(3); PORTUGUESE CC art. 806(2)); GREEK Introductory law to the Civil Code art. 109(1) 3. SPANISH CC art. 1108; also see Civil Procedure Code art. 921 establishing higher, punitive rate; SWEDISH Interest Act, § 1. In GERMANY, in contrast, the Federal Supreme Court has expressly refused to apply such a rule because it might give a windfall profit to the creditor if the market rate is much lower at the time of default. A bank is merely entitled to the average market rate for its various types of credits and, if the bank cannot establish this, to the market rate for its cheapest type of credit (BGH 8 Oct. 1991, BGHZ 115, 268, 269f., 271f.).

4. *Loss in addition to interest*
Loss in addition to interest may be claimed in most countries by virtue of the general rules on damages but lost profits and loss through inflation cannot always be recovered. See DENMARK (*Gomard*, Obligationsret II 197); FINLAND (*Wilhelmsson & Sevón* 156); FRENCH CC art. 1153(4); GERMAN BGB §§ 288(2); GREEK CC art. 345 sent.2; ITALIAN CC art. 1224 (2), except if the parties had fixed the rate of interest for default in the contract; SWEDEN (*Ramberg*, Köplagen 568); SPANISH law, TS 28 November 1983, 6 May 1988, (*Albaladejo* II, 1, § 33.3). The possibility is not recognised in BELGIUM, see CC art. 1153, except for losses caused by devaluation of foreign currency.

Further loss may be recovered in ENGLAND (*Wadsworth* v. *Lydall* [1981] 1 W.L.R. 598, C.A., confirmed by the *President of India* case, supra note 1) and in FRANCE (Civ. 1, 21 June 1989, Bull, I. No 251); and the position is thought to be the same in IRELAND.

In contrast, additional damages may not be claimed in the NETHERLANDS (except in the special case mentioned in note 4 on Article 7:108, above); in PORTUGAL; and in SCOTLAND, *McBryde* ch. 20-78.

See generally *Treitel*, Remedies §§ 159-162.

Article 9:509: Agreed Payment for Non-performance

(1) Where the contract provides that a party which fails to perform is to pay a specified sum to the aggrieved party for such non-performance, the aggrieved party shall be awarded that sum irrespective of its actual loss.

(2) However, despite any agreement to the contrary the specified sum may be reduced to a reasonable amount where it is grossly excessive in relation to the loss resulting from the non-performance and the other circumstances.

COMMENT

A. *Stipulation as to agreed payment binding*

It is common for the parties to a contract to specify a sum to be paid for non-performance, with a view to avoiding the difficulty, delay and expense involved in proving the amount of loss in a claim for unliquidated damages. Such a clause may also prompt the debtor to perform voluntarily, when the penalty is heavy. To perform is then cheaper than paying the penalty. Paragraph (1) gives effect to such a provision, so that except as provided by paragraph (2) the court must disregard the loss actually suffered by the aggrieved party and must award it neither more nor less than the sum fixed by the contract. It follows that the aggrieved party is under no obligation to prove that it has suffered any loss.

Illustration 1: B agrees to build a house for A and to complete it by April 1st. The contract provides that for every week's delay in completion B is to pay A the sum of £200. B completes the house on April 29th. A is entitled to £800 as agreed damages, whether his actual loss (e.g., the cost of renting alternative accommodation during the four week period of delay) is greater or less than that sum.

Illustration 2: A agrees to sell his house to B, from whom he obtains a deposit of 20 per cent of the price to secure B's performance of the contract. B refuses to complete the transaction. A may forfeit the deposit.

Where, however, the contract specifies merely the minimum sum payable by the non-performing party, the aggrieved party may recover a higher figure if it can prove that its loss exceeds the minimum sum. In this case the aggrieved party may elect to sue for damages at large instead of invoking the provision for agreed damages.

B. *Court's power to reduce grossly excessive stipulations*

To allow the parties complete freedom to fix the sum payable for non-performance may lead to abuse. If there is a gross disparity between the specified sum and the actual loss suffered by the aggrieved party the court may reduce the sum even if at the time of the contract it seemed reasonable. Since the purpose is to control only those stipulations which are abusive in their effect, the court's reducing power is exercisable only where it is clear that the stipulated sum substantially exceeds the actual loss. This power of the court has a limit: it should respect the intention of the parties to deter default and therefore should not reduce the award to the actual loss. The court has to fix an intermediate figure.

Illustration 3: A supplies equipment to B on lease for five years at a rent of £50,000 a year. The agreement provides that if the lease is terminated because of default by B in performing its obligations B shall pay A by way of agreed damages a sum equal to 80% of the future rentals. In the light of circumstances existing at the time of the contract this stipulation is not unreasonable. After a year the agreement is terminated because of B's default in payment. As the result of an unexpected increase in the demand for the type of equipment in question A, having secured the return of the equipment, is able to re-let it at twice the rent payable under the original lease. The court may reduce the agreed damages payable so as to take account of this fact.

C. *"Excessive" sum*

In deciding whether the stipulated sum is excessive the court should have regard to the relationship between that sum and the loss actually suffered by the aggrieved party, as opposed to the loss legally recoverable within the foreseeability principle embodied in Article 9:503. On the other hand, the computation of actual loss should take into account that element of the loss which has been caused by the unreasonable behaviour of the aggrieved party itself, e.g. in failing to take reasonable steps in mitigation of loss.

D. *Genuine options not covered*

Article 9:509 does not apply to a genuine option to pay a sum of money instead of performing, since Article 9:509 (1) deals with non-performance, not with alternative performance (forfait clause, *"clause de dédit"*). On Alternative Performance see Article 7:105.

NOTES

1. *Stipulated payment clause valid*
   As is provided in Article 9:509, the laws of the CIVIL LAW countries will enforce a stipulation in a contract under which the debtor undertakes to pay a fixed sum of money in the event of his non-performance. The stipulated payment clause will be enforced whether its purpose was to coerce the debtor to perform his principal obligation (penalty clause) or to serve as a pre-estimate of the loss suffered by the creditor in case of non-performance (liquidated damages clause). See also *Unidroit* art. 7.4.13. As we shall see in note 4 below the COMMON LAW countries will not enforce a penalty clause.
   The civil law codes confirm the validity of stipulated payment clauses either expressly or impliedly, see AUSTRIAN ABGB § 1336(1); BELGIAN CC art. 1152 and 1229; FRENCH CC arts. 1152 (as amended in 1975 and 1985) and 1229; LUXEMBOURG CC arts. 1152 and 1226 ff. (as amended in 1987); GERMAN BGB §§ 339-345; GREEK CC art. 405(2); ITALIAN CC art. 1382-1384; NETHERLANDS BW art 6:91-6:94; PORTUGUESE CC art. 810(1); and SPANISH CC art. 1152. The same holds true of DANISH law, see *Gomard*, Obligationsret II 239 ff..; FINNISH law (see *Taxell*, Avtal och rättsskydd 441); and SWEDISH law (see *Ramberg, Avtalsrätt* 309).
   Unless otherwise agreed the stipulated payment is not payable if the non-performance is excused, see expressly DUTCH BW art.6: 92(3); GREEK CC art. 405(1); and by implication LUXEMBOURG CC arts. 1152 and 1226 ff. (as amended in 1987); GERMAN BGB § 339. On the other hand, and subject to the rules on reduction, see note 3 below, the stipulated payment is due irrespective of whether the aggrieved party suffered any loss, and irrespective of how great the loss was.
2. *Stipulated payment replaces damages*
   In most of the Civil law systems the stipulated payment replaces the damages for non-performance which the aggrieved party would have recovered. This means that the defaulting party cannot claim damages instead of the stipulated payment. Nor can the aggrieved party claim damages in addition to the stipulated payment, unless, as provided in the ITALIAN CC art. 1382(1), PORTUGUESE CC art. 811(2) and (3) and SPANISH CC art. 1153, the parties have agreed on such payment. In AUSTRIAN law, damages over and above the stipulated sum may be claimed in respect of commercial transactions (4. EVHGB Art. 8 No. 3). By contrast, under GERMAN law the aggrieved party may claim damages for non-performance or improper performance in addition to stipulated payment (BGB §§ 340(2), 341(2)). If payment is stipulated for a failure to perform properly (as opposed to a

performance which is not tendered), the aggrieved party is entitled to claim both performance and the agreed payment (BGB § 341(1)). These latter rules also apply in GREECE, see CC arts. 406(2) and 407 sent.2. In ITALY a payment stipulated for delay in performance may be recovered together with a claim for performance, CC art.1383. On DENMARK, see *Gomard,* Obligationsrett II, 239 f. In FINNISH law the solution depends on the intrepretation of the term, *Aurejärvi 151.*

3.   *Reduction*

Under several Civil law systems the court may reduce the stipulated payment if it is manifestly excessive, see AUSTRIAN ABGB § 1336(2); DANISH, FINNISH and SWEDISH Contract Acts § 36; DUTCH BW 6:94; ITALIAN CC art. 1384; FRENCH and LUXEMBOURG CC art. 1152(2); GREEK CC art. 409, even if the parties have agreed otherwise; and GERMAN BGB § 343. However in Germany and Austria a payment stipulated in contracts between merchants cannot be reduced, see HGB § 348. At first sight the same rule appears to apply in BELGIUM, see CC art. 1152, which is not restricted to merchants. In GERMANY, however, the payment may be set aside or modified if it would be unconscionable to enforce it, see BGB § 242 and *Baumbach & Duden & Hopt* HGB § 348 note B. And in BELGIUM the Supreme court has held that if a stipulated payment is so excessive in relation to the loss which was foreseeable at the time the contract was made that it loses its function as a pre-estimate of the loss suffered and becomes a mere private penalty, it should be set aside as violating public policy, see Cass 24 Nov. 1972, R.C.J.B. 1973 302. Even if this is not the case, the stipulated payment may still be reduced if it is manifestly unreasonable at the moment of non-performance, see Law of 23 November 1998, in effect confirming Cass. 18 Feb. 1988, Arr. Cass. 1987-88, 790 no.375; T.B.H./R.D.C. 1988, 636 note *Dirix.* Under the SPANISH CC art. 1154 the court may reduce payment to an equitable amount if the principal obligation has been performed partly or irregularly. In PORTUGAL reduction is also possible; however, in a decision of the Supreme Court it has been held that the payment may only be reduced if it was stipulated as a pre-estimate of the loss suffered and not if it was made to coerce the defaulting party to perform his principal obligation, see on STJ 3 Nov. 1983, *Pinto Monteiro* 474 ff.. See also *Unidroit* art. 7.4.13(2).

4.   *Penalty clauses in the Common law*

In the COMMON LAW stipulated payment clauses are divided into penalty and liquidated damages clauses. The former are invalid, the latter are valid. Penalty clauses are clauses stipulated *"in terrorem"* in order to coerce the debtor to perform the principal obligation. Liquidated damages clauses are clauses by which an attempt is made to pre-estimate the loss suffered by a breach of contract. The latter clauses cannot be modified. A clause will be regarded as a penalty clause if it is extravagant and unconscionable in amount in comparison with the greatest loss that could be proved to follow from such a breach, see *Dunlop Pneumatic Tyre Co. Ltd* v. *New Garage and Motor Co. Ltd.* [1915] A.C. 79, 87 (H.L.). A stipulation is a liquidated damages clause if the circumstances were such that an accurate or precise pre-estimate of the loss was impossible and the stipulated payment was a genuine attempt to make a pre-estimate of the loss, *ibid.* SCOTTISH law is the same; a clause has been upheld when precise assessment of damages was not possible: *Clydebank Engineering & Shipbuilding Co. Ltd.* v. *Castaneda* (1904) 7 F 77 (H.L.).

5.   *Clauses setting a sum less than the likely loss*

On clauses which though drafted as penalty or liquidated damages clauses in effect limit the liability of the non-performing party, see note 4 to Article 8:109, above.

   See generally ICC Guide to Penalty and Liquidated Damages Clauses no. 478; *Fontaine,* Contrats 127-170; *Treitel,* Remedies §§ 164-181.

Article 9:510: Currency by which Damages to be Measured

Damages are to be measured by the currency which most appropriately reflects the aggrieved party's loss.

COMMENTS

A. *General remarks*

1. *Economic context*
Exchange rates between individual currencies are subject to more or less heavy fluctuations. Consequently, the question in which currency damages have to be measured is relevant. Over or under-compensation must be avoided by fixing damages measured by reference to the correct currency.

2. *Legal context*
This provision fixes the currency in which contractual damages are to be measured. Technically speaking, the currency of account for damages is laid down.

By contrast, Article 7:108 deals in a general way with the currency of payment. If damages (or interest) have arisen in a currency other than the local currency of the place of payment, any conversion into the latter currency is governed by Article 7:108.

B. *Purpose*
Since damages have the purpose of putting the aggrieved party into the same position in which it would have been upon performance (Article 9:502) they have to be expressed in the currency which is most appropriate to achieve that result. Damages therefore should not automatically be measured in the local currency of the court; in most countries judgments in foreign currency are allowed. Even if they are not allowed, but the damages had arisen in a foreign currency and are measured in that currency, the conversion into the local currency at current exchange rates will lead to an appropriate result.

C. *Explanation*
In view of the vast variety of the facts of international commercial intercourse, the currency of the damages which is most appropriate to compensate the aggrieved party cannot generally be determined with precision. In many cases it will be the contractual currency of account. But where this is not the currency which the aggrieved party had to utilize in order to make good its loss, e.g. by making a cover transaction, the latter currency may be more appropriate, especially if the creditor utilizes the currency of its home country for this purpose. Generally this will be the currency in which it makes its business deals.

Illustration 1: Austrian machine manufacturer C has made a contract for delivery of certain machinery with Norwegian importer F. F wrongfully cancels the contract. C's damages have arisen in Austrian Schilling.

However, the factors may be different.

Illustration 2: As in Illustration 1, but C is an internationally active company stipulating that payments for its export sales are to be made on a US-Dollar bank account in New York. C's lost profits are to be calculated in US dollars.

It is also possible for loss to arise in several currencies.

D. *Derived claims*

Where a party is entitled to interest, such interest is usually measured and payable in the same currency as the principal. This is so in particular where the interest is expressed as a percentage of the principal sum.

The same is true if the amount of damages is fixed in the contract as a percentage of the price.

Illustration 3: In a construction contract, the parties have agreed on a penalty of 1% of the price for every week of default in completion of the construction, the price being expressed in Deutsche Mark. The penalty will be due in DM as well.

E. *Autonomy of the parties*

Of course, the parties are free to fix the currency of damages or interest by reference to any currency they like.

NOTES

1.   *Case law*

Article 9:510 follows the modern ENGLISH and SCOTTISH rule on the currency of damages, which has been developed in *The Despina R. & the Folias* [1979] A.C. 685 (H.L.) (see also *Goode*, Commercial Law 1133; *Goode*, Payment Obligations 136 ff..). Also in some GERMAN and ITALIAN cases it has been accepted by the courts that a foreign currency may reflect the aggrieved party's loss more appropriately (Germany: especially OLG Hamburg 7 Dec. 1978, Versicherungsrecht 1979, 833; Italy: Cass. 6 June 1981 n. 3656, Mass. Foro It. 1981; see also Trib. Udine 24 Dec. 1987, Foro It. 1989, I p. 1618). However, in Germany the Bundesgerichtshof still accepts that damages may be awarded in DM provided that the debtor does not object (BGH 9 Feb. 1977, WM 1977, 478 (479); BGH 10 July 1954, BGHZ 14, 212 (217)). In FRANCE, judgment is mostly given in French francs, but as the tendency is to use the rate of exchange of the date of payment for the conversion (see Réponse Ministerielle No. 949, JCP 1982, IV, 166; *Derrida* no. 919 ff..; *Chartier* no. 442) the result is practically the same as in case of a proper foreign currency judgment. In SPAIN a decision of the Tribunal Supremo (TS 26 Nov. 1987) has calculated damages in foreign currency but converted in pesetas according to the official rate of exchange of the day of the definitive judgment. The same holds true in GREECE under CC art. 291 which, however, focusses on the official rate of exchange at the date of payment. Claims for damages in foreign currency are accepted by the courts in AUSTRIA; the relevant time for converting is the time when the obligation is due (see e.g. *Ehrenzweig (Mayrhofer)* Schuldrecht AT, 49-53). Under DUTCH BW art. 6:121 when, pursuant to an obligation, payment must be made in a currency other than that of the country where the payment must be made, the debtor is entitled to pay in the currency of the place of payment.

2.   *Legal writers*

The position of legal writers in Europe appears not to be uniform. Whereas in ITALY judgments awarding damages in foreign currency have been criticized (*Ascarelli* 416, *Campeis & De Pauli* 412 ff..), there is support for awarding damages in foreign currency not only in ENGLAND and in BELGIUM (*Fallon*, Annal. dr. Liège 33 (1988) 77-89; *Niyonzima* 206 ff.. no. 233, 214 no. 239), but the same is true also for GERMANY, where some authors advocate a more careful analysis of the currency of the loss and propose following either the very wide English formula (*Alberts*, NJW 1989,

609-615 (612); *idem*, Währungsschwankungen 48 f., 135, 137, 166) or, more precisely, recommend the creditor's currency (*von Hoffmann* 125-141) or the currency of the assets of the creditor (*Remien*, RabelsZ 53 (1989) 245-292). See also in GREECE *Kallimopoulos* 130-138, 350-375. In SPAIN, traditional doctrinal analysis and case law (TS 7 November 1957, 6 April 1963) favoured payment in the national currency but more recent scholarship would allow the debtor the choice: *Paz-Ares*.

3. *Currency of the contract*

It is sometimes thought that damages for breach of contract should be measured in the currency of [account of] the contract (*Staudinger (-K. Schmidt)* § 244 no. 17), but such a rule is not accepted in ENGLISH practice (see *The Despina R and the Folias, ibid.* 700-701) and also disputed in GERMANY (see *Remien*, RabelsZ 53 (1989) 245, 276-280: only where contractual claims for damages take the place of a contractual claim for the price). See also *Unidroit* art. 7.4.12.

Bibliography

Books, articles and similar sources referred to in the Notes are listed both in the General List and in the National Bibliographies.

In the Notes, books, etc. are indicated by the author's name, volume number (if applicable) and page or paragraph number. Where more than one work by an author is cited, an identifying word is used following the author's name, e.g. Treitel, Contract. The identifying word is shown in square brackets after the entry in the bibliography, e.g.;

Treitel, Law of Contract, 9th ed. (1995) [Contract]

Titles by Greek authors have been translated into English.

References to periodical articles in the Notes are distinguished by giving the author's name and a brief reference. A full reference will be found in the Bibliography.

GENERAL LIST

Abas, Rebus sic stantibus, 2nd. ed. (1993)
Adlercreutz, Avtalsrätt I, 10th ed. (1995) [*Adlercreutz* I]
Adlercreutz, Avtalsrätt II, 4th ed. (1996) [*Adlercreutz* II]
Albaladejo, Comentarios al Código Civil y Compilaciones Forales (1978, 2nd. ed. 1982)
Albaladejo, Derecho Civil, 2, Derecho de Obligaciones, 9th ed., (1994)
Alberts, "Der Einfluß von Währungsschwankungen auf Zahlungsansprüche nach deutschem und englischem Recht" (1986)
Alberts, "Schadensersatz und Fremdwährungsrisiko" (1989), NJW 1989, 609-615
Alfaro, Las condiciones generales de la contratación (1991)
Almeida, Os direitos dos consumidores (1982) [Consumer law]
Almeida, Texto e enunciado na teoria do negocio juridico (1992) [Negocio juridico]
Ämmälä, Sopimuksen pätemättömyyden korjaantumisesta (1993)
Ángel, Tratado de responsibilidad civil, 3rd ed., (1993), Annual Review of Irish Law 1993
Ascarelli, Saggi di diritto commerciale (1955) [Diritto commerciale]
Ascarelli, Studi in tema di contratti (1952) [Contratti]
Ascensão, Teoria geral do direito civil, III, Actos e factos jurídicos (1992)
Asser-Hartkamp, 4 -II, Algemene leer der overeenkomsten (10th ed., 1997) [Algemene leer]
Asser-Hartkamp, Verbintenissenrecht, 3 vols., (1996-98) [Verbintenissenrecht]
Asser-Hijma, Bijzondere overeenkomsten, I. Koop en ruil (1994)
Atiyah, Essays on Contract (1986) [Essays]

Atiyah, The Sale of Goods, 9th ed. (ed. *Adams*) (1995)
Audit, La vente internationale de marchandises (1990)
Aurejärvi, Velvoiteoikenden oppikirja (1988)
Balis, General Principles of Civil Law (8th ed. 1961)
Baumbach - Duden - Hopt, Handelsgesetzbuch mit Nebengesetzen, 29th ed. (1995)
Beale, Bishop and Furmston, Contract cases and materials, 3rd ed. (1995)
Beale, Remedies for Breach of Contract (1980)
Becker, Gegenopfer und Opferverwehrung (1958)
Bell, Principles of the Law of Scotland, 10th ed. (1899)
Benjamin, Benjamin's Sale of Goods, 4th ed. by *Guest* (1992)
Bercovitz, R., CCJC 38 (Cuadernos Civitas de Jurisprudencia Civil), no. 1019, 550.
Bercovitz, Comentarios a la Ley General para la Defensa de Consumidores y Usuarios (1992) [Consumers]
Bercovitz, R., Comentarios a le Ley de Arbitraje (1991) [Arbitrage]
Berdejo-Rebudilla-Echevarria-Hernandez, Derecho de Obligaciones Vol.1 (2nd ed., 1985-87)
Bernitz, Standardavtalsrätt (6 ed., 1993)
Betti, Teoria generale delle obbligazioni, Vol. I (1953)
Bianca & Bonell, Commentary on the International Sales Law, the 1980 Vienna Sales Convention (1987)
Bianca, Dell'inadempimento delle obbligazioni, in *Scialoja & Branca*, Commentario al Codice civile (1979) [Commentario]
Bianca, Diritto Civile, Vol. IV, L'obbligazione (1990) [Obbligazione]
Bianca, Diritto Civile, Vol.3, Il contratto (1987) [Il contratto]
Bianca, La vendita e la permuta in *Vassalli*, Trattato di diritto civile italiano, Vol. 7 (1972) [Vendita]
Boele Woelki, "Principles and and Private International Law", [1996] Uniform Law Review 652.
Boergen; Die Effektivität von Schriftformklauseln, Der Betriebs-Berater 1971, 202
Bonell, "Contratti internazionali". in Enciclopedia guiridica Treccani [ed.?] (1988), vol IX [Enciclopedia guiridica Treccani]
Bonell, An International Restatement of Contract Law (2nd ed., 1997) [International Restatement]
Bowstead & Reynolds, Agency, 16th ed. (1996)
Breccia, Le obbligazioni (1991)
Bürge, "Preisbestimmung durch einen Vertragspartner und die Tagespreisklausel", JBl 1989, 687
Burrows, Contractual Cooperation and the Implied Term (1968) 31 Modern L.R. 390
Burrows, Law of Restitution (1993)
Bydlinski, F. "Der Ersatz idellen Schadens als sachliches und methodisches Problem", JBl 1965, 173, 237
Bydlinski, F. "Die Baukostenabrechnung als Bestimmung der Leistung des einen Vertragsteils durch den anderen", JBl 1975, 245
Caemmerer, von & Schlechtriem, Kommentar zum einheitlichen UN-Kaufrecht, 2nd ed., (1995)
Calais-Auloy & Steinmetz, Droit de la consommation, 4th ed. (1996)
Campeis & De Pauli, La responsabilità civile dello straniero (1982)
Capodistrias, in Erm. AK, Vol.II/2 (1954)
Carresi, "Il contratto" in Trattato di diritto civile e commerciale, ed. *Cicu-Messineo*, II (1987)
Carrasco, art.1106, Comentarios Albaladejo, XV, 1 (1989)
Carty and Evans, "Economic Duress", [1983] Journal of Business law 218.
Castan Tobeñas, Dereco Civil Español Comun Y Foral, Vol.3 (1978)
Castronovo, "Contract and the idea of codification in the principles of European contract law", in Festskrift til Ole Lando 109-124 (1997) [Lando]
Castronovo, "L'obbligazione senza prestazione ai confini tra contratto e torto", in Le ragioni del diritto, Scritti in honore di L. Mengoni (1995) [Obbligazione]
Castronovo, "Liability between Contract and Tort", in *Wilhelmsson* (ed): Perspectives of critical contract law (1993) 273ff [Contract and Tort]
Castronovo, Obblighi di Protezione, Enciclopedia giuridica, XXI (1990) [Protezione]
Cattaneo, La cooperazione del creditore all'adempimento (1964)
Cendon, Commentario al codice civile (1991)
Chartier, La réparation du préjudice dans la responsabilité civile (1983)
Chavanne & Ponsard in Rep.Droit Civ. 2nd ed. (Compte no.46)
Cheshire, Fifoot and Furmston's Law of Contracts, 13th ed. (1996)
Chitty, Chitty on Contracts, Vol.1, General Principles, 27th ed. by *Guest* (1994)
Cian & Trabucchi, Commentario breve al codice civile (1988)
Clark, Contract Law in Ireland, 3rd ed. (1992)
Collaço. "L'Arbitrage international dans la recente loi portuguaise sur l'arbitrage volontaire ". in Droit international et droit communautaire, Actes du colloque 5-6 April 1990 (1991), 55.

Commission Report, Oikeustoimilakitoimikunnan mietintö (Report of the Commission for reform of the Contracts Act), Komiteanmietintö 1990:20 (1990)

Coote, "The effect of discharge by breach on exception clauses" (1970) Cambridge L.J. 221

Cordeiro, Teoria geral do direito civil (1989) [General Theory]

Cornelis, "Het aanbod bij het tot stand komen van overeenkomsten", TBH, 1983, 6 ff.

Corrado, La somministrazione, in *Vassalli*, Trattato di diritto civile, Vol.VII,2 (1963)

Costa, Direito das obrigações, 6th ed. (1994) [Obrigações]

Costa, Responsibilidade civil por ruptura das negociações preparatórias de um contrato, RLJ, 1983-84, n. 3708ff. [Responsibilidade]

Couturier, J.Cl.Civil. Art.1253-1255

Dahl, Melchior, Rehof & Tanm (eds.), Danish Law in a European Perspective (1996) [*Dahl*]

Damme, van, "Aspects juridiques d'un paiement par un tiers", R.C.J.B. 1974, 238

Dawson, "Specific Performance in France and Germany" (1959) 57 Mich.L.Rev. 495

de Page & Dekkers, Traité élémentaire de droit civil belge, 10 vols, 3rd ed. (1962-1972)

Delebecque, Jurisc.Resp.Civ. Fasc.110

Delebecque, Les clauses allégeant les obligations dans les contrats, Thèse Aix (1981) [Clauses allégeant]

Deliyannis & Kornilakis, Special Law of Obligations, vol.I (1992)

Demogue, Traité des Obligations en général (1924-28)

Department of Trade and Industry, Consultative paper on an Arbitration Bill, July 1995 [Consultative paper]

Derrida, Rep.Dr.Civ. 2nd ed., (Obligations) [Obligations]

Derrida, Rep.Dr.Civ. 2nd.ed., (Dommages-Intérêts) [Dommages-Intérêts]

di Majo, L'adempimento dell'obbligazione (1993)

Dicey & Morris, The Conflict of Laws (12 ed., 1993)

Diez-Picazo, Fundamentos de Derecho Civil Patrimonial I and II, 4th.ed. (1993)

Dirix & van Oevelen, "Kroniek van het verbintenissenrecht 1985-1992", R.W., 1992-1993, 1209

Dirix, "Over de beperkende werking van de goude trouw", T.B.H./R.D.C., 1988, 660

Dirix, Obligatoire verhoudingen tussen contractanten en derden, diss. Antwerpen (1984) [Obligatoire]

Dirix, Obligatoire verhoudingen tussen contractanten en derden, diss. Antwerpen (1984) [Obligatoire]

Dirix,"Aansprakelijkheid van en voor hulppersonen", in Recht halen uit aansprakelijkheid, (1993), 341 [Aansprakelijkheid]

Dölle, Kommentar zum einheitlichen Kaufrecht (1976)

Drafts and Reports for a new Code of Civil Procedure in Greece, Vol.V (1957), vol.VI (1961)

Durany, "Sobre la necesidad", A.D.C., 1992, 1011

Ehrenzweig-Mayrhofer, Schuldrecht Allgemeiner Teil (1986)

Eiró, Do negócio usuário (1990)

Enneccerus & Lehmann, Schuldrecht (1958)

Erm. AK, Commentary to the Civil Code, vols. II/1 (1949), II/2 (1954), III/1 (1972)

Erman (-Hefermehl), Handkommentar zum Burgerlichen Gesetzbuch, 9th ed. (1993)

European Review of Private Law [1997] Vol.5, 121 ff.

Fagnart, "L'exécution de bonne foi des conventions: un principe en expansion", note to Cass. (B) 19 Sept 1983, R.C.J.B., 1986, 285

Fallon, "la monnaie du jugement en matière de contrats", Annal.Dr.Liege 33 (1988) 77-89

Farnsworth, Farnsworth on Contracts (1990)

Fernandes, Teoria geral do direito civil, II, 2nd ed. (1996)

Flessner, "Befreiung vom Vertrag wegen Nicht-Erfüllung", Zeitschrift für Europäisches Privatrecht (1997), 255-320

Flume, Allgemeiner Teil des bürgerlichen Rechts, Vol. 2, 3rd. ed. (1979) [AT]

Font Galán, "La integración publicitaria del contrato: un instrumento de derecho privado contra la publicidad engañosa", Cuaternos de Derecho y Comercio No. 4 (1988), 7

Fontaine, "La rétroactivité de la résolution des contrats pour inexécution fautive", R.C.J.B., 1990, 382 ff.

Fontaine, Droit des Contrats Internationaux (1989) [Contrats]

Force majeure and Hardship, International Chamber of Commerce, Publication No.421 (1985)

Forde, Commercial Law in Ireland (1990)

Foriers, "La responsibilité de l'entrepreneur après réception. Réflexions à propos de l'arrêt de la Cour de cassation du 25 octobre 1985", Entreprise et droit /Tijdschrift Aannemingsrecht 1988, 261

Fredericq, Handboek van Belgisch Handelsrecht (1976-1981)

Freriks, "Onderzoeks- en mededelingsverplichtingen in het contractenrecht" TPR 1992, p.1187

Friel, Law of Contract (1995)

Fuller & Perdue, "Reliance interest in contract damages" (1936) 46 Yale L.J. 52

Galgano-Visintini in *Scialoja-Branca* (ed.), Commentario al codice civile (1993)

464 *Bibliography*

Garrigues, Tratado de Derecho Mercantil Vol.III,1 (1963)
Gasis, in Erm. AK. Vol.II/1 (1949)
Georgiadis & Stathopoulos, eds., Civil Code Commentary, vol.II (1979).
Gerven, van & Dewaele, "Goede trouw en getrouw beeld", in Liber Amicorum Jan Ronse (1986) 103
Gerven, van, Beginselen van Belgisch privaatrecht, Algemeen deel (1973)
Gerven, van, Beginselen van Belgisch privaatrecht, Algemeen deel (1973)
Ghestin (Ed.), Les Clauses limitatives ou exonératoires de responsabilité en Europe (1990) [Clauses limitatives]
Ghestin, Goubeaux & Fabre-Magnan, Traité de droit civil sous la direction de *Ghestin*, Introduction generale, 4th ed. (1994)
Ghestin, Jamin & Billiau, Droit Civil, Les Obligations, Les Effets (2nd ed., 1994)
Ghestin, Traité de droit civil, La formation du contrat, 3rd ed. (1993) [Formation]
Giorgianni, L'inadempimento (1974)
Gloag, Law of Contract, 2nd ed. (1985)
Goff & Jones, The Law of Restitution, 5th.ed. (1998)
Gomard & Rechnagel, International Købelov (1990)
Gomard, Almindelig kontraktsret, 2nd ed., (1995) [kontraktsret]
Gomard, Obligationsret Vol.1, 2nd ed. (1989); Vol.2, 2nd ed., (1995); Vol. 3 (1993) [Obligationsret I; Obligationsret II; Obligationsret III]
Goode, "Abstract payment undertakings", in *Cane and Stapleton* (eds), Essays for Patrick Atiyah (1991) [Abstract payment undertakings]
Goode, Commercial Law, 2nd ed., (1995) [Commercial Law]
Goode, Payment Obligations in Commercial and Financial Transactions (1983) [Payment Obligations]
Göransson, Kolliderande standardavtal (1988)
Gorla, "Sulla cosiddetta causalità giuridica, Riv. dir. comm. 1951, I, 405
Gorla, Il contratto, Problema fondamentali trattati con il metodo comparativo e casistico I & II (1954)
Grönfors, Avtalslagen, 2ne ed. (1989) [Avtalslagen]
Grönfors, Ställningsfullmakt och bulvanskap (1961) [Ställningsfullmakt]
Guide to Penalties and Liquidated Damages Clauses, International Chamber of Commerce, Publication No.478 (1990)
Hakulinen, Velkakirjalaki, 2nd ed., (1965)
Halsbury, Halsbury's Laws of England, 4th ed. (1974)
Hanbury & Maudsley, Modern Equity, 13th ed (1989)
Hartkamp, "Interplay between Judges, Legislators and Academics, the Case of the New Civil Code of the Netherlands" in *Markesinis* (ed.), Law Making, Law Finding and Law Shaping (1997), p. 91 [Interplay]
Hartkamp, "The Use of the UNIDROIT Principles of International Commercial Contracts by National and Supranational Courts", in UNIDROIT Principles for International Commercial Contracts: A New Lex Mercatoria", ICC/ Dossier of the Institute of International Business Law and Practice (1995), 253 [Unidroit]
Hartkamp, "Civil Code Revision in the Netherlands", in Nieuw Nederlands Burgerlijk Wetboek, Het Vermogensrecht (1990) [Civil Code]
Hellner, Kommersiell avtalsrätt (4 ed., 1993) [Kommersiell avtalsrätt]
Hellner, Skadeståndsrätt (1995)
Hellner, Speciell avtalsrätt II:2 (1996) [Speciell avtalsrätt]
Hemmo, Sopimusoikeus I (1997)
Hemmo, Vahingonkorvauksen määräytymisestä sopimussuhteissa (1994)
Hertzen, von, Sopimusneuvottelut (1983)
Heymann, Handelsgesetzbuch, Kommentar, 1st ed., (1989-90); 2nd ed., (1995 ff.)
Hoffmann, "Deliktischer Schadensersatz im internationalen Währungsrecht", in: Festschrift für Karl Firsching zum 70. Geburtstag (ed. by *Henrich & Hoffmann*) (1985), p.125-141
Hogg, "Lost chances in contract and delict", 1997 Scots Law Times 71-76
Hondius, "De "entire agreement" clausule: Amerikaanse contractsbedingen in het Nederlandse recht", in *ten Berge, van Hoof, Jaspers & Swart* (eds.), Recht als norm en asperatie (1986) 24-34 [Entire Agreement Clauses]
Hondius, Pre-contractual Liability, Reports to the XIIth Congress of the International Academy of Comparative Law (1991) [Pre-contractual Liability]
Hondius, Unfair Terms in Consumer Contracts (1987) [Unfair terms]
Honnold, Uniform Law for International Sales, 2nd ed. (1991)
Hoppu, Handels-och förmögenhetsrätten i huvuddrag, 2nd ed., (1995)

Hörster, A parte geral do código civil português (1992)
Huber, "Empfiehlt sich die Einführung eines Leistungsstörungsrechts nach dem Vorbild des Einheitlichen Kaufgesetzes? Welche Änderungen im Gesetzestext und welche praktischen Auswirkungen im Schuldrecht würden sich dabei ergeben?" in: Gutachten und Vorschläge zur Überarbeitung des Schuldrechts, Vol.1 (1981), p.647-909.
Hudson, Building and Engineering Contracts, 11th ed. by *Duncan Wallace* (1995)
Huet, "Exception d'inéxecution ou 'exceptio non adimpleti contractus'" J.Cl.Civ.App. Art.1184
Incoterms 1990, International Chamber of Commerce Publication No. 460 (1990)
Issa-Sayegh, J.Cl.civ. Art.1235 A 1248 Fasc.II.
Jarbornegg, Zurückbehaltungsrecht und Einrede des nicht erfüllten Vertrages (1982)
Jeandidier, "L'exécution forcée des obligations contractuelles de faire", Rev.trim.dr.civ. (1976) 700-724.
Jhering, von, "Culpa in contrahendo oder Schadensersatz bei nichtigen oder nicht zur Perfektion gelangten Verträgen", *Jherings Jahrbücher* IV (1861), pp. 1-113
Jordano Frago, La responsabilidad contractual (1987)
Jorge, Direito das obrigações (1975-76)
Kaisto, Tiesi tai olisi pitänyt tietää (1997)
Kallimopoulos, Law of Money (1993)
Keane, Equity and Law of Trusts in the Republic of Ireland (1988)
Kerameus, Harmenopoulos (Journal of Thessaloniki Bar) 31 (1977) 169
Kerameus-Kozyris (eds), Introduction to Greek Law, 2nd ed. (1993)
Kivimäki & Ylöstalo, Lärobok i Finlands civilrätt (1960)
Kleineman, Ren förmögenhetskada, 1987
Kötz, "Rechtsvereinheitlichung und Rechtsdogmatik", RabelsZ 54 (1990), 203
Kötz, "Rights of Third Parties", in International Encyclopedia of Comparative Law, VII, chap.13 (1992) [IECL]
Kötz, European Contract Law I (1997) [European Contract]
Kozoil-Welser, Grundriß des bürgerlichen Rechts I, 10th ed., (1995)
Krejci, ZAS 1983, 204
Kropholler, Internationales Privatrecht (3rd ed., 1997)
Kruithof, "Schuld, risico, imprevisie en overmacht bij niet-nakoming van contractuele verbintenissen" in Hommage/ Hulde René Dekkers (1982) [Hommage Dekkers]
Kruithof, "Schuld, risico, imprevisie en overmacht bij niet-nakoming van contractuele verbintenissen" in Hommage/ Hulde René Dekkers (1982) [Hommage Dekkers]
Kruithof, "Contractuele aansprakelijkheidsregelingen", TPR 1984, 233
Kruithof, "L'obligation de la partie lésée de restreindre le dommage", note to Cass,. (B) 22 March 1985, R.C.J.B., 1989, 12
Kruithof, "L'obligation de la partie lésée de restreindre le dommage", note to Cass,. (B) 22 March 1985, R.C.J.B., 1989, 12
Kruithof, "Overzicht van rechtspraak 1974-1980 Verbintenissen", TPR 1983, 495
Kruithof-Bocken, "Overszicht van rechtspraak Verbintenissen 1981 - 1992", Tijdschrift voor Privaatrecht 1994
Lacruz, Elementos de Derecho Civil II, 1 and 2, Derecho de Obligaciones, 3rd ed., (1995)
Lando, "Contracts", in International Encyclopedia of Comparative Law, III, Private International Law, chap. 24, (1976) [IECL]
Lando, "Some Issues Relating to the Law Applicable to Contractual Obligations", (1996-97) 7 *King's College Law Journal* 55 [Applicable Law]
Lando, Kampen om formularen, Ugeskrift for retsvæsen 1988, 1 [Kampen]
Lando, Lex mercatoria 1985-96, *Festskrift for Stig Strömholm* (1997) 567 [Lex mercatoria].
Larenz, Allgemeiner Teil des deutschen Bürgerlichen Rechts, 7th ed. (1988) [AT]
Larenz, Schuldrecht, Vol.1, 14th ed. (1987); Vol. II/1, 13th ed., (1986)
Larenz/Wolf, Allgemeiner Teil des Bürgerlichen Rechts (8th ed., 1997)
Lasarte Álvarez, Principios de derecho civil, III, §3.6(c) (3rd ed., 1995)
Lasarte, "Sobre la integración del contrato: la buena fe en la contratación", Revista de Derecho Privado (1980) 50
Law Commission, Report No. 154, Law of Contract: The Parol Evidence Rule, Cmnd 9700 (1986) [Report on Parol Evidence Rule]
Law Commission, Report No. 242, Privity of Contract: Contracts for the Benefit of Third Parties, Cm 3329 (1996) [Report on Privity]
Law Commission, Report No.88, Interest, Cmnd.7229 (1978). [Report on Interest]
Lefebve, "Les effets de la résolution judiciaire des contrats successifs", *Revue du notariat belge*, 1988, 226

Ligeropoulos, in Erm. AK Vol. II/1 art. 299 Nos. 2,4,8 (1949)
Lima & Varela, Codigo civil annotado. 3rd ed. (1986-87)
Lima/Varela: Lima, Varela & Mesquita, Código Civil annotado, I, 4th ed. (1987)
Lindenmaier- Möhring, Nachschlagswerk des BGH's (1969)
Lindley, Lindley and Banks on Partnerships, 6th ed. (1990)
Ly, de & Burggraaf, 'Battle of forms en internationale contracten', in: *Wessels and van Wechem* (eds.), Contracten in de internationale praktijk (1994)
Lynge Andersen & Nørgaard, Aftaleloven 2nd ed. (1993)
Lynge Andersen, Madsen & Nørgaard, Aftaler og mellemmænd, 2nd ed. (1991) [*Lynge Andersen*]
Lyngsø, Afbestillingsret (1971)
McBryde, "The Intention to Create Legal Relations", 1992 Juridical Review 274
McBryde, Law of Contract in Scotland (1987)
McGregor, Contract Code Drawn up on behalf of the English Law Commission (1993) [Contract Code]
McGregor, Damages, 16th ed. (1997) [Damages]
Macgregor, "The expectation, reliance and restitution interests in contract damages", 1996 Juridical Review 227-249
McKendrick, Contract Law, 3rd ed. (1997) [Contract]
McMahon & Binchy, The Irish Law of Torts 2nd ed. (1990)
MacQueen, "Remedies for breach of contract: the future development of Scots law in its international and European context", (1997) 1 Edinburgh Law Review 200-226
MacQueen, "Remoteness and breach of contract" 1996 Juridical Review 295-302
MacQueen, "Contract, unjustified enrichment and concurrent liability: a Scots perspective", [1997] Acta Juridica 176
Mahé, "Conflit de conditions générales: quelle tactique adopter?", in: F.W. Grosheide, K. Boele-Woelki (Eds.), Europees privaatrecht 1997 (1997), 85-138
Mahé, "Conflit de conditions générale: quelle tactique adopter?", in *Grosheide, & Boele- Woelki* (eds), Europees privaatrecht (1997)
Malaurie & Aynès, Contrats spéciaux, 8th ed. (1994) [Contrats spéciaux]
Malaurie & Aynès, Droit civil, Les Obligations, 9th. ed. (1998) [Obligations]
Marchandise, "La libre négociation. Droits et obligations des négociateurs", Journal des Tribunaux 1987, 621-622
Maridakis, Report to the draft of the Civil Code, General Principles [Athens 1936]
Marini, Clausola penale, in Enciclopedia giuridica Vol.6 (1988)
Martinez, Cuprimento defeituoso, em special na compra e venda e na empreitada (1994)
Marty & Raynaud, Droit Civil, Introduction générale à l'étude du droit, 2nd ed. (1972) [Introduction]
Marty & Raynaud, Droit Civil, Les Obligations, Vol.1, Les Sources, 2nd ed. (1988) [Obligations]
Mazzamuto, L'attuazione degli obblighi di fare (1978)
Medicus, Allgemeiner Teil des BGB, 6th ed. (1994) [AT]
Medicus, Bürgerliches Recht, 17th ed., (1996)
Mehren, von, "Formation of contracts", in International Encyclopedia of Comparative Law, VII, chap.9 (1992)
Mendes, Teoria geral do direito civil, II (1979)
Mengoni, Obbligazioni "di risultato" e obbligazioni "di mezzi", Riv.dir.comm.1954, I, 185
Mengoni, Responsibilità contrattuale, Enc.dir. XXXIX (1988) 1072 [Contractual responsibility]
Mengoni, Sulla natura della responsabilità precontrattuale, Riv.Dir Comm. 1956 II p. 360ff [Pre-contractual responsibility]
Michaelides-Nouaros, in Erm. AK Vol.II/1 (1949)
Ministerio de Justicia, Commentario del Código Civil, 2nd ed., (1993)
Münchener Kommentar, Münchener Kommentar zum Bürgerlichen Gesetzbuch, 2nd ed., (1984-90); 3rd ed., (1992 ff.)
Neumayer, "Das Wiener Kaufrechtübereinkommen und die sogenannte "Battle of Forms"", in Festschrift Hans Giger (1989) 501-526
Nicholas, French Law of Contract, 2nd ed. (1992)
Niyonzima, La clause de monnaie étrangère (1970)
Nørager-Nielsen & Theilgaard, Køøbeloven med kommentarer, 2nd ed. (1993)
Oertmann, Recht des Bürgerlicher Gesetzbuches, 3rd. ed (1927)
Oevelen, van. " De civielrechtelijke aansprakelijkheid van de werknemer en van de werkgever voor de onrechtmatige daden de werknemer in het raam van de uitvoering van de arbeidsovereenkomst", R.W., 1987-88, 1168

Ommeslaghe, van, "L'engagement par volonté unilatérale en droit belge" J.T. 1982, 144
Ommeslaghe, van, "L'exécution de bonne foi, principe général de droit?", T.B.B.R./R.G.D.C., 1987, 101
Ommeslaghe, van, "Examen de jurisprudence, Les obligations 1968-1973", R.C.J.B., 1975, 423 en 597
Ommeslaghe, van, "Examen de jurisprudence. Les obligations 1974-1982", R.C.J.B., 1986, 32 en 1988, 33
Palandt, Bürgerliches Gesetzbuch und Nebengesetze, 56th ed., (1997)
Pantaleón, El sistema de responsibilidad contractual, (1991-III) 1019-1091
Pantaleón, Las nueras bases de la responsibilidad contractual, ADC (1993-IV), 1719-1745
Papantoniou, General Principles of Civil Law, 3rd. ed. (1983)
Paz-Ares, see *Ministerio de Justicia*
Perrot, J.Cl. Societes Fasc. 7 bis
Persico, L'eccezione di inadempimento (1955)*Realmonte,* Il Problema del Rapporto di Causalitá nel Risarcimento del Damno (1967)
Philippe, Changement de circonstances et bouleversement de l'économie contractuelle (1986)
Picod, L'obligation de cooperation dans l'éxecution du contrat JCP 1988, I-3318
Pinto Monteiro, Cláusula Penal e Indemnizaçào (1990)
Pinto, C.M, Cessão da posição contratual (1970) [Cessão]
Pinto, C.M., Teoria geral do direito civil, 3rd ed. (1985) [General theory]
Pinto, P.M., Aparência de poderes de representação e tutela de terceiros, 1993 [Aparência]
Pinto, P.M., Declaração tacita e comportamento concludente no negócio juridico (1995) [Declaração tacita]
Planiol & Ripert, Traité pratique de droit civil, Vol.10 by *Hamel* 2nd ed. (1956)
Ponsard & Blondel, Rep. Droit Civil, 2nd ed., V Paiement
Pothier, Traité des Obligations [Obligations]
Pothier, Traité de la Vente [Vente]
Pothos, note (1961) 28 EEN (Journal of Greek Jurists) 220
Prata, Notas sobre responsabilidade précontratual, Revista da Banca, n.16, 1990, 75 ff.; n.17, 1991, 43 ff.
Rabel, Das Recht des Warenkaufs, Vol.1 (1936, reprint 1957) [Warenkauf]
Rabel, Das Recht des Warenkaufs, Vol.1 (1936, reprint 1957) [Warenkauf]
Ramberg, Allmän avtalsrätt (1996) [Avtalsrätt]
Ramberg, Köplagen (1995) [Köplagen]
Realmonte, Il problema del rapporto di causalità nel risarcimento del danno (1967)
Reed, Digital Information Law (1996)
Regeringens Proposition 1988/89: 76, Ny Köplag (1988/89)
Remien, "Die Währung von Schaden und Schadensersatz" (1989) RabelsZ 53, 245-292
Rescigno, Manuale di diritto privato, 4th ed. (1984)
Restatement, Restatement of the Law Second, Contracts 2d. (1981). [Restatement of Contracts]
RGRK, Das Bürgerliche Gesetzbuch, Kommentar, 12th ed. (1974-1981)
Ripert/Roblot, Traité de droit commercial II (11th ed. 1989)
Rodhe, Obligationsrätt (reprint, 1994)
Rodière & Tallon (eds.), Harmonisation du droit des pays du marché commun du contrat, Les modifications du contrat en cours d'éxecution en raison de circonstances nouvelles (1985)
Rodière, (ed.), Harmonisation du droit des pays du marché commun du contrat, La formation du contrat (1976) [Formation]
Rodière, Les vices du consentement dans le contrat (1977) [Vices]
Routamo, Kaupan lait (1996)
Rubino, La compravendita, in *Cicu Messineo,* Trattato di diritto civile e commerciale, Vol.23 (1971)
Rummel (ed.), ABGB-Kommentar, 2nd ed., (1997)
Ryn, van & Heenen, Principes de droit commercial belge, 2nd ed. 1976-, Vol. 1 (1976), Vol. 3 (1981), Vol. 4 (1987)
Sacco (- de Nova), "Il contratto"in *Sacco* (ed.), Trattato di Diritto Civile, vols I & II (1993)
Sacco, I rimedi sinallagmatici, in *Rescigno,* Trattato di Diritto privato, Vol.10 (1982)
Sancho, Elementos del Derecho Civil, II, 2nd ed. (1985)
Sanders & van den Berg, International Handbook on Commercial Arbitration, 4 vols., sub UNCITRAL (1984)
Sanders, P., "Unity and Diversity in Adoption of the Model Law", (1995) 11 *Arbitration International* 1
Santos Briz, La Responsabilidad Civil, 3rd ed. (1981)
Santos, dos, "Nota sobre a nova lei portuguesa relativa à arbitragem voluntária", [1987] Revista de la Corte Española de Arbitrage 15
Satta, Commentario al codice di procedura civile (1971)
Schaick, van, Contractsvrijheid en nietigheid (1994)
Schlechtriem, Einhertliches UN-Kaufrecht (1981)

Schlegelberger, Handelsgestzbuch, 5th ed. (1973ff.)

Schlesinger, (ed.), Formation of contracts, a study of the common core of legal sysytems, I & II (1968)

Schmitthoff, International Trade Usages (1987)

Scholz, Kommentar zum GmbH-Gesetz, 8th ed. (1993)

Schwimann, (ed.), ABGB-Praxiskommentar IV/1 (1988)

Scognamiglio, "Dei contratti in generale", in Commentario del codice civile, ed. *Scialoja* (1970)

Scottish Law Commission Memorandum No.42 on Defective Consent and Consequential Matters

Scottish Law Commission, Report No. 144 on Formation of Contract (1993)

Scottish Law Commission, Report No.160 on Interpretation in Private Law (1997)

Sepe, "National Models of European Contract Law: a Comparative Approach to the Concept of Unfairness in Directive 93/13", [1997] Consumer LJ 115-122

Sevón, Wilhelmsson & Koskelo, Huvudpunkter i köplagen (1987)

Simantiras, General Principles of Civil Law, 4th ed. (1988)

Simont, Le problème de la représentation dans le contrat de commission sur marchandises, Jurisprudence commerciale de Bruxelles 1956

Sisula-Tulokas, Felpåföljden prisavdrag (1990)

Smith, "Contracts - Mistake, Frustration and Implied Terms" (1994) 110 L.Q.R. 400 [Implied terms]

Smith, Short Commentary on the Law of Scotland (1962) [Short Commentary]

Smits, Het vertrouwensbeginsel in de contractuele gebondenheid (1995)

Soares & Ramos, Contratos internacionais (1989)

Soergel, Bürgerliches Gestzbuch mit Einführungsgetz und Nebengesetzen, Kommentar, 12th ed. (1987-92)

Spiliopoulos, in Commentary to the Civil Code, Erm. AK Vol.III/1 (1972)

Stair: Laws of Scotland: Stair Memorial Encyclopedia, Vol. 15, Obligations (1996) [Stair]

Starck in: Hamel (ed.), Le contrat de commission (1949)

Stathopoulos, Law of Contracts, Vol.A/1, General Part , 3rd ed., (1997) [Contract]

Staudinger, Kommentar zum Bürgerlichen Gesetzbuch, 12th ed. (1978ff.); 13th ed., (1993 ff.)

Stein & Jonas, Kommentar zur Zivilprozeßordnung, 21st ed.

Stewart, ""Of Purpose to Oblige": a Note on Stair I, x, 13", 1991 Juridical Review 216

Stewart, "Stair I, x, 13: a Rejoinder", 1993 Juridical Review 83

Storme, M.E, "De bepaling van het voorwerp van een verbintenis bij partijbeslissing", TPR 1988, 1259

Storme, M.E, "De exceptio non adimpleti contractus, als uitlegvraag. Uitwerking van enkele aspekten in de verhouding tussen partijen, meer bepaald evenredigheid en volgorde van de prestaties", R.W. 1989-90, 313-324 [De exceptio]

Storme, M.E, "Het ingaan en de terugwerkende kracht van de ontbinding van wederkerige overeenkomsten", T.B.B.R. / R.G.D.C., 1991, p. 101-119

Storme, M.E, "Bewijs - en verbintenisrechtelijke beschouwingen omtrent het stilzitten van de aangesprokene bij een faktuur en bij andere vormen van aansprakbevestiging" TBH 1991, 463 ff.

Storme, M.E., "Het misverstand: de vertrouwensleer geldt ook tussen partijen", Tijdschrift voor belgisch burgerlijk recht (1993), 336 ff.

Storme, M.E., De invloed van de goede trouw op de kontraktuele schuldvorderingen (1990) [Invloed]

Storme, M.E., De invloed van de goede trouw op de kontraktuele schuldvorderingen (1990) [Invloed]

Storme, M.L. and M.E., "De bindende derdenbeslissing naar belgisch recht", TPR 1985, 713-748

t'Kint, "Negociation et conclusion du contrat", in *Dieux, Fontaine, Forriers, t'Kint, Parmentiers & van Ommeslaghe*, Les Obligations Contractuelles (1984)

Tallon (ed.), La détermination du prix dans les contrats, étude de droit compare (1989)

Tallon, "Erreur sur la substance et garantie des vices cachés dans la vente mobilière, étude comparé des droits français et anglais" in Mélanges Hamel (1961) [Hamel]

Taxell, Avtal och rättsskydd (1972) [Avtal och rättsskydd]

Taxell, Avtalsrättens normer (1987) [Avtalsrättens normer]

Taxell, Skadestånd vid avtalsbrott (1993) [Skadestånd]

Telaranta, Sopimusoikeus (1990)

Telles, Direito das obrigações, 6th ed. (1989)

Terré, Simler, Lequette, Droit Civil, Les Obligations, 6th ed., (1996)

Terré, Simler, Lequette, Introduction au droit (1991)

Timonen, (ed.), Inledning till Finlands rättsordning (1996)

Torrente Schlesinger, Manuale di diritto privato, 14th ed., (1995)

Treitel, Frustration and Force Majeure (1994) [Frustration]

Treitel, Law of Contract, 9th ed. (1995) [Contract]

Treitel, Remedies for Breach of Contract (1988)

Tsirintanis, in Erm. AK Vol.II/1 (1949)

Unidroit, Principles of International Commercial Contracts (1994)

Ussing, Aftaler, 3rd ed. (1950) [Aftaler]

Ussing, Køb, 4th ed. by Vinding Kruse (1962) [Køb]

Ussing, Obligationsretten, Almindelig Del, 4th ed. by Vinding Kruse (1961) [Alm. Del.]

Vanwijck-Alexandre, Aspects nouveaux de la protection du créancier à terme; les droits belge et français face à l'"anticipatory breach" de la common law, diss. Univ. Liège 1982

Varela, Das obrigações em geral, Vol.1, 9th ed. (1996); Vol.2, 6th ed. (1995)

Vaz Serra, Perfeição da declaração de vontade, BMJ 103, 1961, 5

Verougstraete, "Wil en vertrouwen bij de totstandkoming van verbintenissen", Tijdschrift voor Privaatrecht (1990) 1163 ff.

Vicent Chuliá, Compendio crítico de Derecho Mercantil, 3rd ed., (1990)

Vinding Kruse, Erstatningsretten, 5th ed. (1989)

Viney, Traité de droit civil sous la direction de *Ghestin*, Les Obligations: La responsabilité: conditions (1982) [Conditions]

Viney, Traité de droit civil sous la direction de *Ghestin*, Les Obligations: La responsabilité: effets (1988) [Effets]

Visintini, L'inadempimento delle obbligazioni, in *Rescigno*, Trattato di diritto privato, Vol.9/1 (1984)

Vranken, Mededelings-informatie- en Onderzoeksplichten in het verbintenissenrecht (1989)

Walker, The Law of contract and related obligations in Scotland, 3rd ed. (1995)

Wilhelmsson & Sevón, Räntelag och dröjsålsränta (1983)

Wilhelmsson (ed.), Perspectives of Critical Contract Law (1993) [Perspectives]

Wilhelmsson, Standardavtal, 2nd ed., (1995) [Standardavtal]

Williston, Contracts, 3rd ed. (1953)

Wilson, Scottish Law of Debt, 2nd ed., (1991)

Windscheid & Kipp, Lehrbuch des Pandektenrechts, 9th ed. (1906)

Witz, Droit privé allemand, I: Actes juridiques, droits subjectifs (1992)

Zeben & du Pon (eds.), Parlementaire Geschiedenis van het Nieuwe Burgerlijk Wetboek, Boek 6, Algemeen gedeelte van het verbintenissensrecht (1981)

Zepos in Erm. AK Vol. II/1 art.317 no.13 (1949)

Zimmermann, "Civil Code and Civil Law", 1 Columbia Journal of European Law (1994/95), 63 [Civil Code and Civil Law]

Zimmermann, The Law of Obligations, Roman Foundations of the Civilian Tradition (1990) [Obligations]

Zweigert & Kötz, An Introduction to Comparative law, 3rd ed. (trans. Weir), (1998)

National Bibliographies

English, Irish and United States materials are listed under COMMON LAW. Compartive and General Works are listed at the end.

AUSTRIA

Bürge, "Preisbestimmung durch einen Vertragspartner und die Tagespreisklausel", JBl 1989, 687
Bydlinski, F., "Der Ersatz idellen Schadens als sachliches und methodisches Problem", JBl 1965, 173, 237
Bydlinski, F., "Die Baukostenabrechnung als Bestimmung der Leistung des einen Vertragsteils durch den anderen", JBl 1975, 245
Ehrenzweig-Mayrhofer, Schuldrecht Allgemeiner Teil (1986)
Jarbornegg, Zurückbehaltungsrecht und Einrede des nicht erfüllten Vertrages (1982)
Krejci, ZAS 1983, 204
Kozoil-Welser, Grundriß des bürgerlichen Rechts I, 10th ed., (1995)
Rummel (ed.), ABGB-Kommentar, 2nd ed., (1997)
Schwimann, (ed.), ABGB-Praxiskommentar IV/1 (1988)

COMMON LAW (ENGLAND, IRELAND, UNITED STATES)

Annual Review of Irish Law 1993
Atiyah, Essays on Contract (1986) [Essays]
Atiyah, The Sale of Goods, 9th ed. (ed. *Adams*) (1995)
Beale, Remedies for Breach of Contract (1980)
Beale, Bishop and Furmston, Contract cases and materials, 3rd ed. (1995)
Benjamin, Benjamin's Sale of Goods, 4th ed. by *Guest* (1992)
Bowstead & Reynolds, Agency, 16th ed. (1996)
Burrows, Law of Restitution (1993)
Burrows, Contractual Cooperation and the Implied Term (1968) 31 Modern L.R. 390
Carty and Evans, "Economic Duress", [1983] Journal of Business law 218
Cheshire, Fifoot and Furmston's Law of Contracts, 13th ed. (1996)
Chitty, Chitty on Contracts, Vol.1, General Principles, 27th ed. by *Guest* (1994)
Clark, Contract Law in Ireland, 3rd ed. (1992)
Coote, "The effect of discharge by breach on exception clauses" (1970) Cambridge L.J. 221
Department of Trade and Industry, Consultative paper on an Arbitration Bill, July 1995 [Consultative paper]
Dicey & Morris, The Conflict of Laws (12 ed., 1993)
Farnsworth, Farnsworth on Contracts (1990)
Forde, Commercial Law in Ireland (1990)
Friel, Law of Contract (1995)

Fuller & Perdue, "Reliance interest in contract damages" (1936) 46 Yale L.J. 52
Goff & Jones, The Law of Restitution, 5th.ed. (1998)
Goode, "Abstract payment undertakings", in *Cane and Stapleton* (eds), Essays for Patrick Atiyah (1991)
    [Abstract payment undertakings] ·
Goode, Payment Obligations in Commercial and Financial Transactions (1983) [Payment Obligations]
Goode, Commercial Law, 2nd ed., (1995) [Commercial Law]
Halsbury, Halsbury's Laws of England, 4th ed. (1974)
Hanbury & Maudsley, Modern Equity, 13th ed (1989)
Hudson, Building and Engineering Contracts, 11th ed. by *Duncan Wallace* (1995)
Keane, Equity and Law of Trusts in the Republic of Ireland (1988)
Law Commission, Report No.88, Interest, Cmnd.7229 (1978). [Report on Interest]
Law Commission, Report No. 154, Law of Contract: The Parol Evidence Rule, Cmnd 9700 (1986)
    [Report on Parol Evidence Rule]
Law Commission, Report No. 242, Privity of Contract: Contracts for the Benefit of Third Parties, Cm
    3329 (1996) [Report on Privity]
Lindley, Lindley and Banks on Partnerships, 6th ed. (1990)
McGregor, Damages, 16th ed. (1997) [Damages]
McGregor, Contract Code Drawn up on behalf of the English Law Commission (1993) [Contract Code]
McKendrick, Contract Law, 3rd ed. (1997) [Contract]
McMahon & Binchy, The Irish Law of Torts 2nd ed. (1990)
Reed, Digital Information Law. (1996)
Restatement, Restatement of the Law Second, Contracts 2d. (1981). [Restatement of Contracts]
Smith, "Contracts - Mistake, Frustration and Implied Terms" (1994) 110 Law Q.R. 400 [Implied terms]
Treitel, Frustration and Force Majeure (1994) [Frustration]
Treitel, Law of Contract, 9th ed. (1995) [Contract]
Williston, Contracts, 3rd ed. (1953)

DENMARK

Dahl, Melchior, Rehof & Tanm (eds.), Danish Law in a European Perspective (1996) [*Dahl*]
Gomard, Almindelig kontraktsret, 2nd ed., (1995) [kontraktsret]
Gomard, Obligationsret Vol.1, 2nd ed. (1989); Vol.2, 2nd ed., (1995); Vol. 3 (1993) [Obligationsret I;
    Obligationsret II; Obligationsret III]
Gomard & Rechnagel, International Købelov (1990)
Lando, Kampen om formularen, Ugeskrift for retsvæsen 1988, 1 [Kampen]
Lando, Lex mercatoria 1985-96, *Festskrift for Stig Strömholm* (1997) 567 [Lex mercatoria].
Lynge Andersen & Nørgaard, Aftaleloven 2nd ed. (1993)
Lynge Andersen, Madsen & Nørgaard, Aftaler og mellemmænd, 2nd ed. (1991) [*Lynge Andersen*]
Lyngsø, Afbestillingsret (1971)
Nørager-Nielsen & Theilgaard, Købeloven med kommentarer, 2nd ed. (1993)
Ussing, Obligationsretten, Almindelig Del, 4th ed. by Vinding Kruse (1961) [Alm. Del.]
Ussing, Køb, 4th ed. by Vinding Kruse (1962) [Køb]
Ussing, Aftaler, 3rd ed. (1950) [Aftaler]
Vinding Kruse, Erstatningsretten, 5th ed. (1989)

FINLAND

Ämmälä, Sopimuksen pätemättömyyden korjaantumisesta (1993)
Aurejärvi, Velvoiteoikenden oppikirja (1988)
Commission Report, Oikenstoimilakitoimikunnan mietintö (Report of the Commission for reform of the
    Contractes Act), Komiteenmietintö 1990: 20 (1990).
Hakulinen, Velkakirjalaki, 2nd ed., (1965)
Hemmo, Sopimusoikeus I (1997)
Hemmo, Vahingonkorvauksen määräytymisestä sopimussuhteissa (1994)
Hertzen, von, Sopimusneuvottelut (1983)
Hoppu, Handels-och förmögenhetsrätten i huvuddrag, 2nd ed., (1995)

Kaisto, Tiesi tai olisi pitänyt tietää (1997)
Kivimäki & Ylöstalo, Lärobok i Finlands civilrätt (1960)
Routamo, Kaupan lait (1996)
Sevón, Wilhelmsson & Koskelo, Huvudpunkter i köplagen (1987)
Sisula-Tulokas, Felpåföljden prisavdrag (1990)
Taxell, Avtal och rättsskydd (1972) [Avtal och rättsskydd]
Taxell, Avtalsrättens normer (1987) [Avtalsrättens normer]
Taxell, Skadestånd vid avtalsbrott (1993) [Skadestånd]
Telaranta, Sopimusoikeus (1990)
Timonen, (ed.), Inledning till Finlands rättsordning (1996)
Wilhelmsson, Standardavtal, 2nd ed., (1995) [Standardavtal]
Wilhelmsson (ed.), Perspectives of Critical Contract Law (1993) [Perspectives]
Wilhelmsson & Sevón, Räntelag och dröjsålsränta (1983)

FRANCE, BELGIUM, LUXEMBOURG

Audit, La vente internationale de marchandises (1990)
Calais-Auloy & Steinmetz, Droit de la consommation, 4th ed. (1996)
Chartier, La réparation du préjudice dans la responsabilité civile (1983)
Chavanne & Ponsard in Rep.Droit Civ. 2nd ed. (Compte no.46)
Cornelis, "Het aanbod bij het tot stand komen van overeenkomsten", TBH, 1983, 6 ff
Damme, van, "Aspects juridiques d'un paiement par un tiers", R.C.J.B. 1974, 238
Couturier, J.Cl.Civil. Art.1253-1255
Delebecque, Les clauses allégeant les obligations dans les contrats, Thèse Aix (1981) [Clauses allégeant]
Delebecque, Jurisc.Resp.Civ. Fasc.110
Demogue, Traité des Obligations en général (1924-28)
Derrida, Rep.Dr.Civ. 2nd.ed., (Dommages-Intérêts) [Dommages-Intérêts]
Derrida, Rep.Dr.Civ. 2nd ed., (Obligations) [Obligations]
Dirix, Obligatoire verhoudingen tussen contractanten en derden, diss. Antwerpen (1984) [Obligatoire]
Dirix, "Over de beperkende werking van de goude trouw", T.B.H./R.D.C., 1988, 660
Dirix, "Aansprakelijkheid van en voor hulppersonen", in Recht halen uit aansprakelijkheid, (1993), 341 [Aansprakelijkheid]
Dirix & van Oevelen, "Kroniek van het verbintenissenrecht 1985-1992", R.W., 1992-1993, 1209
Fagnart, "L'exécution de bonne foi des conventions: un principe en expansion", note to Cass. (B) 19 Sept 1983, R.C.J.B., 1986, 285
Fallon, "la monnaie du jugement en matière de contrats", Annal.Dr.Liege 33 (1988) 77-89
Fontaine, "La rétroactivité de la résolution des contrats pour inexécution fautive", R.C.J.B., 1990, 382 ff.
Foriers, "La responsibilité de l'entrepreneur après réception. Réflexions à propos de l'arrêt de la Cour de cassation du 25 octobre 1985", Entreprise et droit /Tijdschrift Aannemingsrecht 1988, 261
Fredericq, Handboek van Belgisch Handelsrecht (1976-1981)
Freriks, "Onderzoeks- en mededelingsverplichtingen in het contractenrecht" TPR 1992, p. 1187
Gerven, van, Beginselen van Belgisch privaatrecht, Algemeen deel (1973).
Gerven, van & Dewaele, "Goede trouw en getrouw beeld", in Liber Amicorum Jan Ronse (1986) 103
Ghestin, Traité de droit civil, La formation du contrat, 3rd ed. (1993) [Formation]
Ghestin, Goubeaux & Fabre-Magnan, Traité de droit civil sous la direction de *Ghestin*, Introduction generale, 4th ed. (1994)
Ghestin, Jamin & Billiau, Droit Civil, Les Obligations, Les Effets (2nd ed., 1994)
Huet, "Exception d'inéxecution ou 'exceptio non adimpleti contractus'" J.Cl.Civ.App. Art.1184
Issa-Sayegh, J.Cl.civ. Art.1235 A 1248 Fasc.II
Jeandidier, "L'exécution forcée des obligations contractuelles de faire", Rev.trim.dr.civ. (1976) 700-724
t'Kint, "Negociation et conclusion du contrat", in *Dieux, Fontaine, Forriers, t'Kint, Parmentier & van Ommeslaghe*, Les Obligations Contractuelles (1984)
Kruithof, "Overzicht van rechtspraak 1974-1980 Verbintenissen", TPR 1983, 495
Kruithof, "L'obligation de la partie lésée de restreindre le dommage", note to Cass,. (B) 22 March 1985, R.C.J.B., 1989, 12
Kruithof, "Contractuele aansprakelijkheidsregelingen", TPR 1984, 233
Kruithof, "Schuld, risico, imprevisie en overmacht bij niet-nakoming van contractuele verbintenissen" in Hommage/ Hulde René Dekkers (1982) [Hommage Dekkers]

Kruithof-Bocken, "Overszicht van rechtspraak Verbintenissen 1981 - 1992", Tijdschrift voor Privaatrecht 1994

Lefebve, "Les effets de la résolution judiciaire des contrats successifs", *Revue du notariat belge*, 1988, 226

Mahé, "Conflit de conditions générales: quelle tactique adopter?", in: F.W. Grosheide, K. Boele-Woelki (Eds.), Europees privaatrecht 1997 (1997), 85-138

Malaurie & Aynès, Droit civil, Les Obligations, 9th. ed. (1998) [Obligations]

Malaurie & Aynès, Contrats spéciaux, 8th ed. (1994) [Contrats spéciaux]

Marchandise, "La libre négociation. Droits et obligations des négociateurs", Journal des Tribunaux 1987, 621-622

Marty & Raynaud, Droit Civil, Introduction générale à l'étude du droit, 2nd ed. (1972) [Introduction]

Marty & Raynaud, Droit Civil, Les Obligations, Vol.1, Les Sources, 2nd ed. (1988) [Obligations]

Nicholas, French Law of Contract, 2nd ed. (1992)

Oevelen, van, "De civielrechtelijke aansprakelijkheid van de werknemer en van de werkgever voor de onrechtmatige daden die werknemer in het raam van de uitvoering van de arbeidsovereenkomst", R.W., 1987-88, 1168

Ommeslaghe, van, "Examen de jurisprudence, Les obligations 1968-1973", R.C.J.B., 1975, 423 en 597

Ommeslaghe, van, "Examen de jurisprudence. Les obligations 1974-1982", R.C.J.B., 1986, 32 en 1988, 33

Ommeslaghe, van, "L'engagement par volonté unilatérale en droit belge" J.T. 1982, 144

Ommeslaghe, van, "L'exécution de bonne foi, principe général de droit?", T.B.B.R./ R.G.D.C., 1987, 101

de Page & Dekkers, Traité élémentaire de droit civil belge, 10 vols, 3rd ed. (1962-1972)

Perrot, J.Cl. Societes Fasc. 7 bis

Picod, L'obligation de cooperation dans l'éxecution du contrat JCP 1988, I-3318

Planiol & Ripert, Traité pratique de droit civil, Vol.10 by *Hamel* 2nd ed. (1956)

Ponsard & Blondel, Rep. Droit Civil, 2nd ed., V Paiement

Pothier, Traité des Obligations [Obligations]

Pothier, Traité de la Vente [Vente]

Ripert/Roblot, Traité de droit commercial II (11th ed. 1989)

Ryn, van & Heenen, Principes de droit commercial belge, 2nd ed. 1976-, Vol. 1 (1976), Vol. 3 (1981), Vol. 4 (1987)

Simont, Le problème de la représentation dans le contrat de commission sur marchandises, Jurisprudence commerciale de Bruxelles 1956

Starck in: Hamel (ed.), Le contrat de commission (1949)

Storme, M.E, "De invloed van de goede trouw op de kontraktuele schuldvorderingen", (1990) [Invloed]

Storme, M.E, "De bepaling van het voorwerp van een verbintenis bij partijbeslissing", TPR 1988, 1259

Storme, M.E, "De exceptio non adimpleti contractus, als uitlegvraag. Uitwerking van enkele aspekten in de verhouding tussen partijen, meer bepaald evenredigheid en volgorde van de prestaties", R.W. 1989-90, 313-324 [De exceptio]

Storme, M.E, "Het ingaan en de terugwerkende kracht van de ontbinding van wederkerige overeenkomsten", T.B.B.R. / R.G.D.C., 1991, p. 101-119

Storme, M.E. "Bewijs - en verbintenisrechtelijke beschouwingen omtrent het stilzitten van de aangesprokene bij een faktuur en bij andere vormen van aanspraakbevestiging", TBH 1991, 463 ff

Storme, M.E., "Het misverstand: de vertrouwensleer geldt ook tussen partijen", Tijdschrift voor belgisch burgerlijk recht (1993), 336 ff

Storme, M.L. and M.E., "De bindende derdenbeslissing naar belgisch recht", TPR 1985, 713-748

Tallon, "Erreur sur la substance et garantie des vices cachés dans la vente mobilière, étude comparé des droits français et anglais" in Mélanges Hamel (1961) [Hamel]

Terré, Simler, Lequette, Introduction au droit (1991)

Terré, Simler, Lequette, Droit Civil, Les Obligations, 6th ed., (1996)

Vanwijck-Alexandre, Aspects nouveaux de la protection du créancier à terme; les droits belge et français face à l'"anticipatory breach" de la common law, diss. Univ. Liège 1982

Verougstraete, "Wil en vertrouwen bij de totstandkoming van verbintenissen", Tijdschrift voor Privaatrecht (1990) 1163 ff

Viney, Traité de droit civil sous la direction de *Ghestin*, Les Obligations: La responsabilité: conditions (1982) [Conditions]

Viney, Traité de droit civil sous la direction de *Ghestin*, Les Obligations: La responsabilité: effets (1988) [Effets]

GERMANY

Alberts, "Schadensersatz und Fremdwährungsrisiko" (1989), NJW 1989, 609-615

Alberts, "Der Einfluß von Währungsschwankungen auf Zahlungsansprüche nach deutschem und englischem Recht" (1986)

Baumbach - Duden - Hopt, Handelsgesetzbuch mit Nebengesetzen, 29th ed. (1995)

Boergen; Die Effektivität von Schriftformklauseln, Der Betriebs-Berater 1971, 202

Dölle, Kommentar zum einheitlichen Kaufrecht (1976)

Enneccerus & Lehmann, Schuldrecht (1958)

Erman (-Hefermehl), Handkommentar zum Burgerlichen Gesetzbuch, 9th ed. (1993)

Flume, Allgemeiner Teil des bürgerlichen Rechts, Vol.2, 3rd ed. (1979) [AT]

Heymann, Handelsgesetzbuch, Kommentar, 1st ed., (1989-90); 2nd ed., (1995 ff.)

Hoffmann, "Deliktischer Schadensersatz im internationalen Währungsrecht", in: Festschrift für Karl Firsching zum 70. Geburtstag (ed. by *Henrich & Hoffmann*) (1985), p.125-141

Huber, "Empfiehlt sich die Einführung eines Leistungsstörungsrechts nach dem Vorbild des Einheitlichen Kaufgesetzes? Welche Änderungen im Gesetzestext und welche praktischen Auswirkungen im Schuldrecht würden sich dabei ergeben?" in: Gutachten und Vorschläge zur Überarbeitung des Schuldrechts, Vol.1 (1981), p.647-909

Jhering, von "Culpa in contrahendo oder Schadensersatz bei nichtigen oder nicht zur Perfektion gelangten Verträgen", *Jherings Jahrbücher* IV (1861), pp. 1-113

Kropholler, Internationales Privatrecht (3rd ed., 1997)

Larenz, Allgemeiner Teil des deutschen Bürgerlichen Rechts, 7th ed. (1988) [AT]

Larenz, Schuldrecht, Vol.1, 14th ed. (1987); Vol. II/1, 13th ed., (1986).

Larenz/Wolf, Allgemeiner Teil des Bürgerlichen Rechts (8th ed., 1997)

Lindenmaier- Möhring, Nachschlagswerk des BGH's (1969)

Medicus, Allgemeiner Teil des BGB, 6th ed. (1994) [AT]

Medicus, Bürgerliches Recht, 17th ed., (1996)

Münchener Kommentar, Münchener Kommentar zum Bürgerlichen Gesetzbuch, 2nd ed., (1984-90); 3rd ed., (1992 ff.)

Oertmann, Recht des Bürgerlicher Gesetzbuches, 3rd. ed (1927)

Palandt, Bürgerliches Gesetzbuch und Nebengesetze, 56th ed., (1997)

Rabel, Das Recht des Warenkaufs, Vol.1 (1936, reprint 1957) [Warenkauf]

Remien, "Die Währung von Schaden und Schadensersatz" (1989) RabelsZ 53, 245-292

RGRK, Das Bürgerliche Gesetzbuch, Kommentar, 12th ed. (1974-1981)

Schlegelberger, Handelsgestzbuch, 5th ed. (1973ff.)

Scholz, Kommentar zum GmbH-Gesetz, 8th ed. (1993)

Soergel, Bürgerliches Gestzbuch mit Einführungsgetz und Nebengesetzen, Kommentar, 12th ed. (1987-92)

Staudinger, Kommentar zum Bürgerlichen Gesetzbuch, 12th ed. (1978ff.); 13th ed., (1993 ff.)

Stein & Jonas, Kommentar zur Zivilprozeßordnung, 21st ed.

Windscheid & Kipp, Lehrbuch des Pandektenrechts, 9th ed. (1906)

Witz, Droit privé allemand, I: Actes juridiques, droits subjectifs (1992)

GREECE

Balis, General Principles of Civil Law (8th ed. 1961)

Capodistrias, in Erm. AK, Vol.II/2 (1954)

Deliyannis & Kornilakis, Special Law of Obligations, vol.I (1992)

Drafts and Reports for a new Code of Civil Procedure in Greece, Vol.V (1957), vol.VI (1961)

Erm. AK, Commentary to the Civil Code, vols. II/1 (1949), II/2 (1954), III/1 (1972)

Gasis, in Erm. AK. Vol.II/1 (1949)

Georgiadis & Stathopoulos, eds., Civil Code Commentary, vol.II (1979)

Kallimopoulos, Law of Money (1993)

Kerameus, Harmenopoulos (Journal of Thessaloniki Bar) 31 (1977) 169

Kerameus-Kozyris (eds), Introduction to Greek Law, 2nd ed. (1993)

Ligeropoulos, in Erm. AK Vol. II/1 art. 299 Nos. 2,4,8 (1949)

Maridakis, Report to the draft of the Civil Code, General Principles [Athens 1936]

Michaelides-Nouaros, in Erm. AK Vol.II/1 (1949)

Papantoniou, General Principles of Civil Law, 3rd ed., (1983)

Pothos, note (1961) 28 EEN (Journal of Greek Jurists) 220
Simantiras, General Principles of Civil Law, 4th ed. (1988)
Spiliopoulos, in Commentary to the Civil Code, Erm. AK Vol.III/1 (1972)
Stathopoulos, Law of Contracts, Vol.A/1, General Part , 3rd ed. (1997) [Contract]
Tsirintanis, in Erm. AK Vol.II/1 (1949)
Zepos in Erm. AK Vol. II/1 art.317 no.13 (1949)

ITALY

Ascarelli, Saggi di diritto commerciale (1955) [Diritto commerciale]
Ascarelli, Studi in tema di contratti (1952) [Contratti]
Betti, Teoria generale delle obbligazioni, Vol. I (1953)
Bianca, Dell'inadempimento delle obbligazioni, in *Scialoja & Branca*, Commentario al Codice civile (1979) [Commentario]
Bianca, Diritto Civile, Vol.3, Il contratto (1987) [Il contratto]
Bianca, Diritto Civile, Vol. IV, L'obbligazione (1990) [Obbligazione]
Bianca, La vendita e la permuta in *Vassalli*, Trattato di diritto civile italiano, Vol. 7 (1972) [Vendita]
Breccia, Le obbligazioni (1991)
Campeis & De Pauli, La responsabilità civile dello straniero (1982)
Carresi, "Il contratto" in Trattato di diritto civile e commerciale, ed. *Cicu-Messineo*, II (1987)
Castronovo, "Contract and the idea of codification in the principles of European contract law", in Festkrift til Ole Lando 109-124 (1197) [Lando]
Castronovo, "Liability between Contract and Tort", in *Wilhelmsson* (ed): Perspectives of critical contract Law (1993) 273ff [Contract and Tort]
Castronovo, "L'obbligazione senza prestazione ai confini tra contratto e torto", in Le ragioni del diritto, Scritti in honore di L. Mengoni (1995) [Obligazione]
Castronovo, Obblighi di Protezione, Enciclopedia giuridica, XXI (1990) [Protezione]
Cattaneo, La cooperazione del creditore all'adempimento (1964)
Cendon, Commentario al codice civile (1991)
Cian & Trabucchi, Commentario breve al codice civile (1988).
Corrado, La somministrazione, in *Vassalli*, Trattato di diritto civile, Vol.VII,2 (1963)
di Majo, L'adempimento dell'obbligazione (1993)
Galgano-Visintini in *Scialoja-Branca* (ed.), Commentario al codice civile (1993)
Giorgianni, L'inadempimento (1974)
Gorla, Il contratto, Problema fondamentali trattati con il metodo comparativo e casistico I & II (1954)
Gorla, "Sulla cosiddetta causalità giuridica, Riv. dir. comm. 1951, I, 405
Marini, Clausola penale, in Enciclopedia giuridica Vol.6 (1988)
Mazzamuto, L'attuazione degli obblighi di fare (1978)
Mengoni, Obbligazioni "di risultato" e obbligazioni "di mezzi", Riv.dir.comm.1954, I, 185
Mengoni, Responsabilità contrattuale, Enc.dir. XXXIX (1988) 1072 [Contractual responsibility]
Mengoni, Sulla natura della responsibilità precontrattuale, Riv.Dir Comm. 1956 II p. 360ff [Pre-contractual responsibility]
Persico, L'eccezione di inadempimento (1955)*Realmonte*, Il Problema del Rapporto di Causalitá nel Risarcimento del Damno (1967)
Realmonte, Il problema del rapporto di causalità nel risarcimento del danno (1967)
Rescigno, Manuale di diritto privato, 4th ed. (1984)
Rubino, La compravendita, in *Cicu Messineo*, Trattato di diritto civile e commerciale, Vol.23 (1971)
Sacco, I rimedi sinallagmatici, in *Rescigno*, Trattato di Diritto privato, Vol.10 (1982)
Sacco (- de Nova), "Il contratto" in *Sacco* (ed.), Trattato di Diritto Civile, vols I & II (1993)
Satta, Commentario al codice di procedura civile (1971)
Scognamiglio, "Dei contratti in generale", in Commentario del codice civile, ed. *Scialoja* (1970)
Torrente Schlesinger, Manuale di diritto privato, 14th ed., (1995)
Visintini, L'inadempimento delle obbligazioni, in *Rescigno*, Trattato di diritto privato, Vol.9/1 (1984)

THE NETHERLANDS

Asser-Hartkamp, 4 -II, Algemene leer der overeenkomsten (10th ed., 1997) [Algemene leer]
Asser-Hartkamp, Verbintenissenrecht, 3 vols., (1996-98) [Verbintenissenrecht]
Asser-Hijma, Bijzondere overeenkomsten, I. Koop en ruil (1994)

Becker, Gegenopfer und Opferverwehrung (1958)
Hartkamp, "Civil Code Revision in the Netherlands", in Nieuw Nederlands Burgerlijk Wetboek, Het Vermogensrecht (1990) [Civil Code]
Hartkamp, "Interplay between Judges, Legislators and Academics the Case of the New Civil Code of the Netherlands" in *Markesinis* (ed.), Law Making, Law Finding and Law Shaping (1997). p. 91 [Interplay]
Hondius, "De "entire agreement" clausule: Amerikaanse contractsbedingen in het Nederlandse recht ", in *ten Berge, van Hoof, Jaspers & Swart* (eds.), Recht als norm en asperatie (1986) 24-34 [Entire Agreement Clauses]
Schaick, van, Contractsvrijheid en nietigheid (1994)
Smits, Het vertrouwensbeginsel in de contractuele gebondenheid (1995)
Vranken, Mededelings-informatie- en Onderzoeksplichten in het verbintenissenrecht (1989)
Zeben & du Pon (eds.), Parlementaire Geschiedenis van het Nieuwe Burgerlijk Wetboek, Boek 6, Algemeen gedeelte van het verbintenissensrecht (1981)

PORTUGAL

Almeida, Os direitos dos consumidores (1982) [Consumer law]
Almeida, Texto e enunciado na teoria do negocio juridico (1992) [Negocio juridico]
Ascensão, Teoria geral do direito civil, III, Actos e factos jurídicos (1992)
Collaço, "L'Arbitrage international dans la recente loi portuguaise sur l'arbitrage volontaire ", in Droit international et droit communautaire, Actes du colloque 5-6 April 1990 (1991), 55
Cordeiro, Teoria geral do direito civil (1989) [General Theory]
Costa, Direito das obrigações, 6th ed. (1994) [Obrigações]
Costa, Responsibilidade civil por ruptura das negociações preparatórias de um contrato, RLJ, 1983-84, n. 3708ff. [Responsibilidade]
Eiró, Do negócio usuário (1990)
Fernandes, Teoria geral do direito civil, II, 2nd ed. (1996)
Hörster, A parte geral do código civil português (1992)
Jorge, Direito das obrigações (1975-76)
Lima/Varela: Lima, Varela & Mesquita, Código Civil anotado, I, 4th ed. (1987)
Martinez, Cuprimento defeituoso, em special na compra e venda e na empreitada (1994)
Mendes, Teoria geral do direito civil, II (1979)
Pinto, C.M, Cessão da posição contraçtual (1970) [Cessão]
Pinto, C.M., Teoria geral do direito civil, 3rd ed. (1985) [General theory]
Pinto, P.M., Aparência de poderes de representação e tutela de terceiros, 1993 [Aparência]
Pinto, P.M., Declaração tácita e comportamento concludente no negócio juridico (1995) [Declaração tácita]
Pinto Monteiro, Cláusula Penal e Indemnizaçào (1990)
Prata, Notas sobre responsabilidade précontratual, Revista da Banca, n.16, 1990, 75 ff.; n.17, 1991, 43 ff
Santos, dos, "Nota sobre a nova lei portuguesa relativa à arbitragem voluntária", [l987] Revista de la Corte Española de Arbitrage 15
Soares & Ramos, Contratos internacionais (1989)
Telles, Direito das obrigações, 6th ed. (1989)
Varela, Das obrigações em geral, Vol.1, 9th ed. (1996); Vol.2, 6th ed. (1995)
Vaz Serra, Perfeição da declaração de vontade, BMJ 103, 1961, 5

SCOTLAND

Bell, Principles of the Law of Scotland, 10th ed. (1899)
Gloag, Law of Contract, 2nd ed. (1985)
Hogg, "Lost chances in contract and delict", 1997 Scots Law Times 71-76
McBryde, Law of Contract in Scotland (1987)
McBryde, "The Intention to Create Legal Relations", 1992 Juridical Review 274
Macgregor, "The expectation, reliance and restitution interests in contract damages", 1996 Juridical Review 227-249
MacQueen, "Remoteness and breach of contract" 1996 Juridical Review 295-302
MacQueen, "Remedies for breach of contract: the future development of Scots law in its international and European context", (1997) 1 Edinburgh Law Review 200-226

MacQueen, "Contract, unjustified enrichment and concurrent liabilty: a Scots perspective", [1997] Acta Juridice 176
Scottish Law Commission Memorandum No.42 on Defective Consent and Consequential Matters
Scottish Law Commission, Report No. 144 on Formation of Contract (1993)
Scottish Law Commission, Report No.160 on Interpretation in Private Law (1997)
Smith, Short Commentary on the Law of Scotland (1962) [Short Commentary]
Stair: Laws of Scotland: Stair Memorial Encyclopedia, Vol. 15, Obligations (1996) [Stair]
Stewart, "'Of Purpose to Oblige': a Note on Stair I, x, 13", 1991 Juridical Review 216
Stewart, "Stair I, x, 13: a Rejoinder", 1993 Juridical Review 83
Walker, The Law of contract and related obligations in Scotland, 3rd ed. (1995)
Wilson, Scottish Law of Debt, 2nd ed., (1991)

Spain

Albaladejo, Derecho Civil, 2, Derecho de Obligaciones, 9th ed., (1994)
Albaladejo, Comentarios al Código Civil y Compilaciones Forales (1978, 2nd. ed. 1982)
Alfaro, Las condiciones generales de la contratación (1991)
Ángel, Tratado de responsibilidad civil, 3rd ed., (1993)
Bercovitz, R., Comentarios a le Ley de Arbitraje (1991) [Arbitraje]
Bercovitz, A. & R., Comentarios a la Ley General para la Defensa de Consumidores y Usuarios (1992) [Consumers]
Bercovitz, R., CCJC 38 (Cuadernos Civitas de Jurisprudencia Civil), no. 1019, 550
Berdejo-Rebudilla-Echevarria-Hernandez, Derecho de Obligaciones Vol.1 (2nd ed., 1985-87)
Carrasco, art.1106, Comentarios Albaladejo, XV, 1 (1989)
Castan Tobeñas, Dereco Civil Español Comun Y Foral, Vol.3 (1978)
Diez-Picazo, Fundamentos de Derecho Civil Patrimonial I and II, 4th.ed. (1993)
Durany, "Sobre la necesidad", A.D.C., 1992, 1011
Font Galán, "La integración publicitaria del contrato: un instrumento de derecho privado contra la publicidad enganõsa", Cuaternos de Derecho y Comercio No. 4 (1988), 7
Garrigues, Tratado de Derecho Mercantil Vol.III,1 (1963)
Jordano Frago, La responsabilidad contractual (1987)
Lacruz, Elementos de Derecho Civil II, 1 and 2, Derecho de Obligaciones, 3rd ed., (1995)
Lasarte, "Sobre la integración del contrato: la buena fe en la contratación", Revista de Derecho Privado (1980) 50
Lasarte Álvarez, Principios de derecho civil, III, §3.6(c) (3rd ed., 1995)
Lima & Varela, Codigo civil annotado. 3rd ed. (1986-87)
Ministerio de Justicia, Commentario del Código Civil, 2nd ed., (1993)
Pantaleón, El sistema de responsibilidad contractual, ADC (1991-III) 1019-1091
Pantaleón, Las Nuevas bases de la resonsibilidad contractual, ADC (1993-IV) 1719-1745
Paz-Ares, see *Ministerio de Justicia*
Sancho, Elementos del Derecho Civil, II, 2nd ed. (1985)
Santos Briz, La Responsabilidad Civil, 3rd ed. (1981)
Vicent Chuliá, Compendio crítico de Derecho Mercantil, 3rd ed., (1990)

Sweden

Adlercreutz, Avtalsrätt I, 10th ed. (1995) [*Adlercreutz* I]
Adlercreutz, Avtalsrätt II, 4th ed. (1996) [*Adlercreutz* II]
Bernitz, Standardavtalsrätt (6 ed., 1993)
Göransson, Kolliderande standardavtal (1988)
Grönfors, Avtalslagen, 2ne ed. (1989) [Avtalslagen]
Grönfors, Ställningsfullmakt och bulvanskap (1961) [Ställningsfullmakt]
Hellner, Kommersiell avtalsrätt (4 ed., 1993) [Kommersiell avtalsrätt]
Hellner, Speciell avtalsrätt II:2 (1996) [Speciell avtalsrätt]
Hellner, Skadeståndsrätt (1995)
Kleineman, Ren förmögenhetskada, 1987
Ramberg, Köplagen (1995) [Köplagen]
Ramberg, Allmän avtalsrätt (1996) [Avtalsrätt]
Regeringens Proposition 1988/89: 76, Ny Köplag (1988/89)
Rodhe, Obligationsrätt (reprint, 1994)

COMPARATIVE AND GENERAL WORKS

Abas, Rebus sic stantibus, 2nd ed. (1993)
Bianca & Bonell, Commentary on the International Sales Law, the 1980 Vienna Sales Convention (1987)
Boele Woelki, "Principles and and Private International Law", [1996] Uniform Law Review 652.
Bonell, "Contratti internazionali". in Enciclopedia guiridica Treccani [ed.?] (1988), vol IX [Enciclopedia guiridica Treccani]
Bonell, An International Restatement of Contract Law (2nd ed., 1997) [International Restatement]
Castronovo, "Contract and the idea of codification in the principles of European contract law", in Festskrift til Ole Lando 109-124 (1997) [Lando]
Castronovo, "Liability beteen Contract and Tort", in *Wilhelmsson* (ed): Perspectives of critical contract law (1993) 273ff
Caemmerer, von & Schlechtriem, Kommentar zum einheitlichen UN-Kaufrecht, 2nd ed., (1995)
Dawson, "Specific Performance in France and Germany" (1959) 57 Mich.L.Rev. 495
Demogue (-Rousseau), Traité des Obligations en général (1924-28)
Dirix, Obligatoire verhoudingen tussen contractanten en derden, diss. Antwerpen (1984) [Obligatoire]
European Review of Private Law [1997] Vol.5, 121 ff
Flessner, "Befreiung vom Vertrag wegen Nicht-Erfüllung", Zeitschrift für Europäisches Privatrecht (1997), 255-320
Fontaine, Droit des Contrats Internationaux (1989) [Contrats]
Force majeure and Hardship, International Chamber of Commerce, Publication No.421 (1985)
Gerven, van, Beginselen van Belgisch privaatrecht, Algemeen deel (1973)
Ghestin (Ed.), Les Clauses limitatives ou exonératoires de responsabilité en Europe (1990) [Clauses limitatives]
Gorla, Il contratto, Problema fondamentali trattati con il metodo comparativo e casistico I & II (1954)
Guide to Penalties and Liquidated Damages Clauses, International Chamber of Commerce, Publication No.478 (1990)
Hartkamp, "The Use of the UNIDROIT Principles of International Commercial Contracts by National and Supranational Courts", in UNIDROIT Principles for International Commercial Contracts: A New Lex Mercatoria", ICC/ Dossier of the Institute of International Business Law and Practice (1995), 253 [Unidroit]
Hondius, Pre-contractual Liability, Reports to the XIIth Congress of the International Academy of Comparative Law (1991) [Pre-contractual Liability]
Hondius, Unfair Terms in Consumer Contracts (1987) [Unfair terms]
Honnold, Uniform Law for International Sales, 2nd ed. (1991)
Incoterms 1990, International Chamber of Commerce Publication No. 460 (1990)
Kötz, European Contract Law I (1997) [European Contract]
Kötz, "Rechtsvereinheitlichung und Rechtsdogmatik", RabelsZ 54 (1990), 203
Kötz, "Rights of Third Parties", in International Encyclopedia of Comparative Law, VII, chap.13 (1992) [IECL]
Kruithof, "L'obligation de la partie lésée de restreindre le dommage", note to Cass, (B) 22 March 1985, R.C.J.B., 1989, 12
Kruithof, "Schuld, risico, imprevisie en overmacht bij niet-nakoming van contractuele verbintenissen" in Hommage/ Hulde René Dekkers (1982) [Hommage Dekkers]
Lando, "Contracts", in International Encyclopedia of Comparative Law, III, Private International Law, chap. 24, (1976) [IECL]
Lando, "Some Issues Relating to the Law Applicable to Contractual Obligations", (1996-97) 7 *King's College Law Journal* 55 [Applicable Law]
Ly, de & Burggraaf, "Battle of forms en internationale contracten", in: *Wessels and van Wechem* (eds.), Contracten in de internationale praktijk (1994)
Mahé, "Conflit de conditions générale: quelle tactique adopter?", in *Grosheide, & Boele- Woelki* (eds), Europees privaatrecht (1997)
Mehren, von, "Formation of contracts", in International Encyclopedia of Comparative Law, VII, chap.9 (1992)
Niyonzima, La clause de monnaie étrangère (1970)
Neumayer, "Das Wiener Kaufrechtübereinkommen und die sogenannte "Battle of Forms"", in Festschrift Hans Giger (1989) 501-526
Philippe, Changement de circonstances et bouleversement de l'économie contractuelle (1986)
Rabel, Das Recht des Warenkaufs, Vol.1 (1936, reprint 1957) [Warenkauf]

Rodière, (ed.), Harmonisation du droit des pays du marché commun du contrat, La formation du contrat (1976) [Formation]

Rodière, Les vices du consentement dans le contrat (1977) [Vices]

Rodière & Tallon (eds.), Harmonisation du droit des pays du marché commun du contrat, Les modifications du contrat en cours d'éxecution en raison de circonstances nouvelles (1985)

Sanders, P., "Unity and Diversity in Adoption of the Model Law", (1995) 11 *Arbitration International* 1

Sanders & van den Berg, International Handbook on Commercial Arbitration, 4 vols., sub UNCITRAL (1984)

Schlechtriem, Einhertliches UN-Kaufrecht (1981)

Schlesinger, (ed.), Formation of contracts, a study of the common core of legal sysytems, I & II (1968)

Schmitthoff, International Trade Usages (1987)

Sepe, "National Models of European Contract Law: a Comparative Approach to the Concept of Unfairness in Directive 93/13", [1997] Consumer LJ 115-122

Storme, M.E., De invloed van de goede trouw op de kontraktuele schuldvorderingen (1990) [Invloed]

Tallon (ed.), La détermination du prix dans les contrats, étude de droit compare (1989)

Treitel, Remedies for Breach of Contract (1988)

Unidroit, Principles of International Commercial Contracts (1994)

Zweigert & Kötz, An Introduction to Comparative law, 3rd ed. (trans. Weir), (1998)

Zimmermann, "Civil Code and Civil Law", 1 Columbia Journal of European Law (1994/95), 63 [Civil Code and Civil Law]

Zimmermann, The Law of Obligations, Roman Foundations of the Civilian Tradition (1990) [Obligations]

Table of Cases

BELGIUM

DENMARK

ENGLAND, AUSTRALIA AND CANADA

Civ. 24 March 1987, D. 1987.488......240
Civ.1, 12 November 1987, B.I no. 293......255,256
Civ.3, 18 May 1988, B.III, no. 96......285
Cass. 29 November 1988, Bull.civ. 1988 I no. 341......211
Cass.civ.1, 24 May 1989, B.I, no. 212......263
Cass.civ. 1, 21 June 1989, Bull, I. No 251......453
Cass.civ.1, 11 October 1989, J.C.P.1990 II, 21393......346
Cass.civ.2, 19 May 1991, B.II no. 165, p.89......346
Cass.com. 4 Feb 1992, B.IV. no. 64, p.48......102
Cass.civ.3, 15 December 1993, D.1994.462......432
Cass.com.18 October 1994, D.1995.180......255,286
Ass. PlJn. 1 December 1995, J.C.P. 1995.II.22.565......309, 311
Cass.com. 22 October 1996, D.1997, 121......119, 389

ROHG 11 January 1876 ROHGE 19, 293......354
OLG Hamburg 13 May 1901 OLGE 3 (no. 4), 8......384
RG 22 December 1905, RGZ 62, 201......241
RG 25 April 1907 RGZ 66, 54......350
RG 8 May 1907 RGZ 66, 116......401
RG 11 March 1909, RGZ 70, 391 ff......236
RG 31 March 1909 RGZ 70, 239......125
RG 7 January 1916 RGZ 87, 434......351
RGZ 8 June 1920, RGZ 99, 147......291
RG 3 February 1922 RGZ 103, 328......328
RG 10 January 1925 RGZ 110, 47......106
RG 2 March 1933, RGZ 140, 335......200
RG I3 May 1935 RGZ 147, 377......346
BGH 18 October 1952 BGHZ 7, 311......125
BGH 10 July 1954 BGHZ 14, 212......458
BGH 18 December 1954, BGHZ 16, 54......239,305
BGH 18 December 1954, BGHZ 16, 71......239,305
BGH 22 June 1956, BGHZ 21, 102......145
BGH 8 January 1959, BGHZ 29, 148, 150......256
BGH 22 January 1959 N.J.W. 1959, 933......448
BGH 31 January 1962, NJW 1962, 1196......251
BGH 14 October 1964 W.M. 1964, 1247......259
BGH 6 July 1966, NJW 1966, 2399, 2401......260
BGH 6 February 1969......192
BGH 12 May 1969, WM 1969, 1009......219
OLG Celle, 6 November 1970, MDR 1971, 392......256
BGH 3 March 1971, NJW 1971, 1035......297
BHG 28 April 1971, LM Nr. 42 zu ' 123 BGB......255

GREECE

IRELAND

THE NETHERLANDS

PORTUGAL

SCOTLAND

SPAIN

SWEDEN

UNITED STATES OF AMERICA

Table of Code Provisions and Legislation

StGB:
  §105......260
  §144......260

Legislation

1871   Law on Compulsory Notarial Acts......143

1979   Consumer Protection Act (8 March 1979)......152,154,271,295,389

Belgium

Civil Code articles:
  6......270
  887......265
  931......143
  1101......139
  1103......139
  1104......139
  1108......139,141,148
  1109......227
  1110......236,239
  1111......260
  1112......259
  1117......227,274
  1118......239,264
  1121......322
  1126-1130......148
  1131......141,270
  1133......141
  1134......118
  1135......119
  1137(1)......315
  1139......437
  1144......449
  1146......437
  1147......383
  1148......383
  1149......440
  1150......443
  1151......443
  1152......455,456
  1153......453
  1156......290

Denmark

Finland

France

Germany

Greece

Civil Code articles:

Netherlands

European and international conventions and legislation

Legislation and restatements of other national systems

Index

QM LIBRARY
(MILE END)

CIM LIBRARY

(WHITE GMO)

WITHDRAWN
FROM STOCK
QMUL LIBRARY